STRUCTURED COBOL PROGRAMMING

STRUCTURED COBOL PROGRAMMING

GARY B. SHELLY
THOMAS J. CASHMAN
ROY O. FOREMAN

boyd & fraser publishing company

An International Thomson Publishing Company

Danvers • Albany • Bonn • Boston • Cincinnati • Detroit • London • Madrid • Melbourne
Mexico City • New York • Paris • San Francisco • Singapore • Tokyo • Toronto • Washington

SHELLY
CASHMAN
SERIES®

Special thanks go to the following reviewers of this book:

Deborah Fansler, Purdue University Calumet; **James Hightower**, California State University, Fullerton; **James Horn**, Vincennes University; **Robert Landrum**, Jones County Junior College; **Gerald Marquis**, Texas Tech University; **Marilyn Markowicz**, Educational Consultant; **Michael Walton**, Miami-Dade Community College North Campus; and **Kay Weimer**, Southwestern Michigan College.

Contents

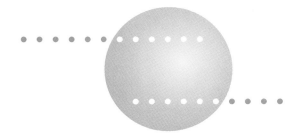

Preface

Structured COBOL Programming emphasizes a practical approach to learning how to design and write COBOL programs that will be error free, reliable, and easy to modify and maintain. Toward this end, this textbook teaches students, from the very beginning, the proper methods of top-down design and structured COBOL programming.

The book is written so the student begins writing COBOL programs almost immediately in the course. The first program illustrated in Chapter 2 serves as a guideline for all subsequent programs the student will write, both in the classroom and as a COBOL programmer in industry. In the chapters that follow, the programs become more complex, building upon the knowledge and skills attained from previous chapters and programs. In every case, a disciplined style of programming is adhered to and the COBOL coding is carefully explained. Beginning with the very first program, the student studies top-down design and structured programming as well as the COBOL language itself.

OBJECTIVES OF THIS BOOK

This book was developed specifically for a first course in structured COBOL programming. After completing this book, students should have a firm foundation in the concepts and techniques of structured program design and structured COBOL programming and should be able to solve a wide variety of business-related application problems using COBOL. The objectives of this book are to:

* Acquaint the reader with the proper and correct way to design and write high-quality COBOL programs.
* Teach the fundamental organization of a COBOL program.
* Teach good problem-solving techniques that can be used with any programming language.
* Teach both batch and interactive programming techniques available in the COBOL language.
* Use practical applications to illustrate the use of the COBOL language.
* Encourage reading and understanding of the key language elements of COBOL.
* Accelerate the learning of COBOL programming using the assignments and programming exercises at the end of each chapter.
* Teach basic logic constructs that will serve as models for future program development.

LEVEL OF INSTRUCTION

This book is designed to be used in a one-quarter or one-semester course on structured COBOL programming. It is assumed that the student has successfully taken at least one programming course; but with some supplemental materials, this book easily could be adopted for a first course in programming. No mathematics beyond the high school level is required. This book was written specifically for the student with average ability, for whom continuity, simplicity, and practicality were considered essential.

DISTINGUISHING FEATURES

Top-Down (Modular) Approach and Structured Programming

From the very first sample program, the students are shown the advantages of using top-down design and top-down programming to break complex problems into smaller problems and solve each one independently. Structured programming techniques are emphasized throughout the text and used in all examples. Thus, in this book, the student sees only proper programs—one entry point, one exit point, no unreachable code, and no infinite loops. Using the early programs as models, students are lead into more complicated logic and program organization one step at a time.

Programming Design Aids

The authors recognize hierarchy charts and flowcharting as excellent pedagogical aids and as the tools of an analyst or programmer. Hence, all of the sample programs are preceded by both hierarchy charts and program flowcharts to demonstrate programming style, high-level design, and documentation.

Emphasis on Style

Heavy emphasis is placed on producing well-written and readable COBOL programs. Students are urged to choose clarity over efficiency in their code. A disciplined style is used consistently in all sample programs. Thorough documentation and indentation standards illustrate the implementation programs that are easy to read, and therefore, easy to maintain.

Unique Pedagogy

Structured COBOL Programming uses a unique pedagogy, whereby each chapter presents a complete sample program, which is then broken into pieces and discussed in detail over the remainder of the chapter. The sample program is preceded by a top-down chart and program flowcharts. Students can experiment with the sample programs by loading them from the Student Diskette.

Student Assignments

A set of pencil-paper exercises, identified as Student Assignments, appears at the end of each chapter. These short-answer exercises are included for practice. Through the use of these exercises, the student can master the concepts presented, and instructors are afforded a valuable diagnostic tool. Answers to these exercises can be found in Appendix B.

COBOL Laboratory Exercises

More than thirty challenging, field-tested COBOL Laboratory Exercises are included at the end of the chapters. Each of these exercises includes a statement of purpose, a problem definition, sample input data, and a description of the output results. The required data files are on the Student Diskette that accompanies this book.

Student Diskette

The Student Diskette that accompanies this book includes all the sample programs presented. It also includes all the data files needed as input to the sample programs and the data files needed as input to the programming exercises. Using a personal computer, students can upload the programs to a larger computer system, if available, or use a personal computer-based COBOL compiler, such as that produced by Micro Focus and available with this book. See the post card at the back of the book.

COBOL Reference Guide

A COBOL Reference Guide, found in the sleeve on the inside back cover of this book, contains a list of the COBOL reserved words and a summary of the COBOL statements. Students can use this reference guide to assist with the syntax of statements when writing COBOL programs or for quizzes and examinations, if the instructor approves.

Micro Focus Personal COBOL

The most popular personal computer COBOL compiler, Micro Focus Personal COBOL, can be bundled with this book or purchased separately using the post card at the back of the book, so each student has a personal copy for use on his or her own computer. Micro Focus Personal COBOL is a powerful way to learn COBOL programming on personal computers. Features of this compiler include:

- An integrated editor-compiler-debugger package offers fast testing cycles.
- ANSI 85 standards allows students to upload programs to minicomputers and mainframes with no code changes.
- The best COBOL debugger, Micro Focus Animator®, gives students the tools to quickly fix their programs.
- Support for indexed, variable-length, sequential, and relative file formats gives users mainframe capabilities.
- The online help system allows students to answer their own questions quickly and efficiently.
- A 500-page manual accompanies the software to support the student in gaining a better understanding of the software.
- More than 60 sample programs, utilities, and tutorials assist the student in learning how to program in COBOL.

Instructors can obtain review copies of Micro Focus Personal COBOL by calling Micro Focus Publishing at 1-800-551-5269.

Appendix F introduces students to Micro Focus Personal COBOL. All the programs on the Student Diskette can be compiled and executed successfully using Micro Focus Personal COBOL. Appendix G provides a brief introduction to Micro Focus COBOL Workbench in a Windows environment. All the COBOL Laboratory Exercises presented at the end of the chapters can be completed successfully using Micro Focus Workbench.

ANCILLARY MATERIALS

Instructor's Manual

The Instructor's Manual provides:

* Lecture outlines for each chapter
* Hard copy solutions, as well as electronic solutions on diskette, to the more than thirty COBOL Laboratory Exercises found at the end of the chapters
* A test bank of nearly 1,000 true/false, multiple choice, and fill in the blank questions
* Transparency masters of all figures and tables in the book
* An Instructor's Diskette, which includes all sample programs and data files presented in the book and the solutions to all COBOL Laboratory Exercises

ACKNOWLEDGMENTS

Structured COBOL Programming would not be the quality textbook it is without the contributions of many people. We want to express our appreciation to the following individuals who worked diligently to assure an excellent publication: Becky Herrington, director of production; Peter Schiller, production manager; Dennis Tani, cover design; Rebecca Evans, interior design and composition; Greg Herrington, illustrator; Ginny Harvey, copy editor; Nancy Lamm, proofreader; Tracy Murphy, series coordinator; and Jim Quasney, series editor.

Special thanks to Tom Walker, president and CEO of boyd & fraser publishing company, for his vision and support of this project.

Gary B. Shelly
Thomas J. Cashman
Roy O. Foreman

Visit Shelly Cashman Online at
http://www.bf.com/scseries.html

NOTES TO THE STUDENT

Structured COBOL Programming introduces you to COBOL (**CO**mmon **B**usiness **O**riented **L**anguage), the most popular computer programming language ever developed. COBOL's applications are numerous and varied. COBOL continues to be the number one programming language, and thus one about which you should learn as much as possible. Analysts claim that millions of COBOL programs are in use today in business, government, and industry, with more than 70 billion lines of code. The authors hope that this book will make your study of COBOL smooth, easy, and pleasurable.

A few things to help you get going:

1. The first occurrence of a COBOL or programming key term in this book is printed in **bold**. Its definition can be found in the same sentence.

2. Beginning with Chapter 2, each chapter begins with a complete sample program, including a top-down chart and flowcharts. The sample program then is divided into smaller pieces, and each piece of the program is discussed in detail.

3. The figures in each chapter are used to help illustrate and explain the concepts presented. Through the use of bubbles and arrows, a significant amount of documentation has been included on the figures to assist you in learning the concepts presented.

4. Each chapter ends with an important and useful chapter summary, which is followed by a list of the key terms presented within the chapter. Use the summary and key terms to prepare for quizzes and examinations.

5. The answers to all Student Assignments can be found in Appendix B. The Student Assignments are designed to test your knowledge of the chapter and to better assist you in understanding COBOL. It is to your advantage to work out each assignment and then compare your answer to that presented in Appendix B.

6. Every sample program in the text is stored on the Student Diskette, which can be found in the back of this book. All the input data files needed for the sample programs, as well as for the COBOL Laboratory Exercises, are also included on the Student Diskette. Use the sample program on the Student Diskette that corresponds to your assignment to begin your program. Many of the exercises suggest the specific sample program to open. Few COBOL programmers ever begin to write a program with an empty screen. Most open a previously written COBOL program to begin a new one. This is the approach we hope you will take with the sample programs on the Student Diskette.

7. The Micro Focus Personal COBOL compiler is an option your instructor may have selected. If the Micro Focus Personal COBOL compiler is bundled with this book, then you should be aware of the following:

   a. The Micro Focus Personal COBOL diskettes must be installed on the hard drive of your personal computer system.
   b. The Personal COBOL compiler is designed to run on IBM PC or compatible systems using MS-DOS version 3.3 or greater.
   c. Micro Focus Personal COBOL requires 640K of main memory and at least 8 megabytes of free space on your hard drive.
   d. Appendix F provides you with an introduction to using Micro Focus Personal COBOL.

   Personal COBOL will be valuable to those of you who find working on your own computer system more convenient than working in the school's computer laboratory. If your instructor did not include the Micro Focus Personal COBOL compiler as part of this book, you may purchase it. See the post card at the back of this book.

8. Appendices C and D are reprinted in the COBOL Reference Guide, which can be found in the sleeve on the inside of the back cover of this book. This guide includes a complete list of the COBOL reserved words and the basic formats of the COBOL statements.

SHELLY CASHMAN SERIES—TRADITIONALLY BOUND TEXTBOOKS

The Shelly Cashman Series presents computer textbooks across the entire spectrum including both Windows- and DOS-based personal computer applications in a variety of traditionally bound textbooks, as shown in the table below. For more information, see your CTCG representative or call 1-800-648-7450.

COMPUTERS	
Computers	Using Computers: A Gateway to Information Using Computers: A Gateway to Information, Brief Edition Using Computers: Record of Discovery
Computers and Windows Applications	Using Computers: A Gateway to Information and Microsoft Office (also available in spiral bound) Using Computers: A Gateway to Information and Microsoft Works 3.0 (also available in spiral bound)
Computers and Programming	Using Computers: A Gateway to Information and Programming in QBasic

WINDOWS APPLICATIONS	
Integrated Packages	Microsoft Office: Introductory Concepts and Techniques (also available in spiral bound) Microsoft Office: Advanced Concepts and Techniques (also available in spiral bound) Microsoft Works 3.0 (also available in spiral bound)* Microsoft Works 3.0—Short Course Microsoft Works 2.0 (also available in spiral bound)
Windows	Microsoft Windows 95 Microsoft Windows 3.1 Introductory Concepts and Techniques Microsoft Windows 3.1 Complete Concepts and Techniques
Windows Applications	Microsoft Word 2.0, Microsoft Excel 4, and Paradox 1.0 (also available in spiral bound)
Word Processing	Microsoft Word 6* • Microsoft Word 2.0 WordPerfect 6.1* • WordPerfect 6* • WordPerfect 5.2
Spreadsheets	Microsoft Excel 5* • Microsoft Excel 4 Lotus 1-2-3 Release 5* • Lotus 1-2-3 Release 4* Quattro Pro 6 • Quattro Pro 5
Database Management	Paradox 5 • Paradox 4.5 • Paradox 1.0 Microsoft Access 2* Visual dBASE 5/5.5
Presentation Graphics	Microsoft PowerPoint 4*

DOS APPLICATIONS	
Operating Systems	DOS 6 Introductory Concepts and Techniques DOS 6 and Microsoft Windows 3.1 Introductory Concepts and Techniques
Integrated Package	Microsoft Works 3.0 (also available in spiral bound)
DOS Applications	WordPerfect 5.1, Lotus 1-2-3 Release 2.2, and dBASE IV Version 1.1 (also available in spiral bound) WordPerfect 5.1, Lotus 1-2-3 Release 2.2, and dBASE III PLUS (also available in spiral bound)
Word Processing	WordPerfect 6.1 WordPerfect 6.0 WordPerfect 5.1 Step-by-Step Function Key Edition WordPerfect 5.1 Function Key Edition Microsoft Word 5.0
Spreadsheets	Lotus 1-2-3 Release 4 • Lotus 1-2-3 Release 2.4 • Lotus 1-2-3 Release 2.3 Lotus 1-2-3 Release 2.2 • Lotus 1-2-3 Release 2.01 Quattro Pro 3.0 Quattro with 1-2-3 Menus (with Educational Software)
Database Management	dBASE 5 dBASE IV Version 1.1 dBASE III PLUS (with Educational Software) Paradox 4.5 Paradox 3.5 (with Educational Software)

PROGRAMMING AND NETWORKING	
Programming	Microsoft Visual Basic 3.0 for Windows* Microsoft BASIC QBasic QBasic: An Introduction to Programming Structured COBOL Programming
Networking	Novell NetWare for Users Business Data Communications: Introductory Concepts and Techniques
Internet	The Internet: Introductory Concepts and Techniques (UNIX) Netscape Navigator 2.0 Netscape Navigator: An Introduction

SYSTEMS ANALYSIS	
Systems Analysis	Systems Analysis and Design, Second Edition

*Also available as a Double Diamond Edition, which is a shortened version of the complete book

SHELLY CASHMAN SERIES—Custom Edition PROGRAM

If you do not find a Shelly Cashman Series traditionally bound textbook to fit your needs, boyd & fraser's unique **Custom Edition** program allows you to choose from a number of options and create a textbook perfectly suited to your course. The customized materials are available in a variety of binding styles, including boyd & fraser's patented **Custom Edition** kit, spiral bound, and notebook bound. Features of the **Custom Edition** program are:

- Textbooks that match the content of your course

- Windows- and DOS-based materials for the latest versions of personal computer applications software

- Shelly Cashman Series quality, with the same full-color materials and Shelly Cashman Series pedagogy found in the traditionally bound books

- Affordable pricing so your students receive the **Custom Edition** at a cost similar to that of traditionally bound books

The table on the right summarizes the available materials. For more information, see your CTCG representative.call 1-800-648-7450

For Shelly Cashman Series information, visit Shelly Cashman online at http://www.bf.com/scseries.html

COMPUTERS	
Computers	Using Computers: A Gateway to Information
	Using Computers: A Gateway to Information, Brief Edition
	Exploring Computers: Record of Discovery
	Introduction to Computers (32-page)
OPERATING SYSTEMS	
Windows	Microsoft Windows 95
	Microsoft Windows 3.1 Introductory Concepts and Techniques
	Microsoft Windows 3.1 Complete Concepts and Techniques
DOS	Introduction to DOS 6 (using DOS prompt)
	Introduction to DOS 5.0 (using DOS shell)
	Introduction to DOS 5.0 or earlier (using DOS prompt)
WINDOWS APPLICATIONS	
Integrated Packages	Microsoft Works 3.0*
	Microsoft Works 3.0—Short Course
	Microsoft Works 2.0
Microsoft Office	Using Microsoft Office (16-page)
	Object Linking and Embedding (OLE) (32-page)
Word Processing	Microsoft Word 6*
	Microsoft Word 2.0
	WordPerfect 6.1*
	WordPerfect 6*
	WordPerfect 5.2
Spreadsheets	Microsoft Excel 5*
	Microsoft Excel 4
	Lotus 1-2-3 Release 5*
	Lotus 1-2-3 Release 4*
	Quattro Pro 6
	Quattro Pro 5
Database Management	Paradox 5
	Paradox 4.5
	Paradox 1.0
	Microsoft Access 2*
	Visual dBASE 5/5.5
Presentation Graphics	Microsoft PowerPoint 4*
DOS APPLICATIONS	
Integrated Package	Microsoft Works 3.0
Word Processing	WordPerfect 6.1
	WordPerfect 6.0
	WordPerfect 5.1 Step-by-Step Function Key Edition
	WordPerfect 5.1 Function Key Edition
	Microsoft Word 5.0
Spreadsheets	Lotus 1-2-3 Release 4
	Lotus 1-2-3 Release 2.4
	Lotus 1-2-3 Release 2.3
	Lotus 1-2-3 Release 2.2
	Lotus 1-2-3 Release 2.01
	Quattro Pro 3.0
	Quattro with 1-2-3 Menus
Database Management	dBASE 5
	dBASE IV Version 1.1
	dBASE III PLUS
	Paradox 4.5
	Paradox 3.5
PROGRAMMING AND NETWORKING	
Programming	Microsoft Visual Basic 3.0 for Windows*
	Microsoft BASIC
	QBasic
Networking	Novell NetWare for Users
Internet	The Internet: Introductory Concepts and Techniques (UNIX)
	Netscape Navigator 2.0
	Netscape Navigator: An Introduction

*Also available as a mini-module

CHAPTER ONE

Introduction to COBOL and Program Development

OBJECTIVES

You will have mastered the material in Chapter 1 when you can:

* Identify the advantages and disadvantages of COBOL

* List the advantages of record input/output

* Name the four divisions of a COBOL program

* Specify the purpose of each COBOL division

* List the steps involved in the programming process

* Describe top-down design and top-down programming

* Name the logic structures used in a structured program

* Identify valid COBOL words

* Describe the format of a line of COBOL source code

INTRODUCTION

COBOL (**CO**mmon **B**usiness **O**riented **L**anguage) was developed in the early 1960s as a result of a joint effort between the U.S. government, businesses, and major universities. The purpose of COBOL is to provide a high-level computer programming language to the business world. COBOL is easy to use and directly addresses the basic needs of information processing. A **high-level language** is one that can be easily transferred from one computer system to another and does not require the programmer to have a working knowledge of a computer's internal components. A **low-level language** is a programming language that requires knowledge of a computer's internal components and cannot be transferred from one computer system to another. COBOL, BASIC, C, FORTRAN, and Pascal are examples of high-level languages. Machine language and assembly language are examples of low-level languages. Table 1-1 describes the nature of a high-level language and a low-level language.

TABLE 1-1 High-level and Low-level Programming Languages

High-level Language:

A programming language in which the program statements are not closely related to the internal characteristics of the computer.

Low-level Language:

A programming language also known as an assembler language that uses symbolic notation to represent machine language instructions and is closely related to the internal architecture of the computer on which it is used.

COBOL programs are designed to handle large amounts of data and produce meaningful information. COBOL programs can literally be found everywhere, in both large and small businesses. COBOL is used on every hardware platform ranging from microcomputers to mainframes, and the need for those conversant in COBOL will remain well into the twenty-first century. Through the sample programs in this book, you will see and understand the usefulness and flexibility of the COBOL language.

This book is designed to be a step-by-step introduction to the COBOL language. It is not designed to be an introduction to computer programming. It is assumed that the reader has had a prior programming class and understands the basic concepts behind planning and coding a computer program. If this is not the case, some supplemental reading may be desirable before moving on to Chapter 2.

Advantages of COBOL

When COBOL was developed, one of the stated objectives of the language was that it be machine independent, meaning that a program written in COBOL should run on a variety of computer systems with little or no change. COBOL was also designed to be "English-like" and to be self-documenting.

The success of COBOL can be credited to two major factors. First, because programming in low-level languages was difficult and error-prone, there was a definite need in the 1960s for a high-level business-oriented language. Second, there was strong pressure from the United States government to establish a common language for business applications. Recognizing the need for such a language, the United States government specified that if a company wanted to sell or lease computers to the government, it had to have COBOL software available unless it could be demonstrated that COBOL was not needed for the particular class of problems to be solved. Because the United States government was the single largest user of computers, manufacturers quickly recognized the value in developing COBOL compilers and related software.

The **COBOL compiler** is a special program supplied by the computer manufacturer that translates the COBOL program into instructions that the computer understands.

After going through a number of revisions, COBOL was officially approved as a United States standard in 1968 by the American National Standards Institute (ANSI). Subsequent revisions of the language led to a 1974 version of American National Standard (ANS) COBOL known as COBOL 74 and to a 1985 ANS COBOL known as COBOL 85. In 1989, enhancements were added to COBOL 85. Another version of ANS COBOL is expected to be released in the near future. This expected new version is currently referred to as COBOL 9x. The programs in this textbook are all compatible with enhanced COBOL 85.

Disadvantages of COBOL

COBOL programs tend to be very wordy. They often require many pages of code to accomplish a task that may take only one or two pages in another language. COBOL also tends to generate object code that is less efficient than object code generated by a low-level language. Remember, the B in COBOL stands for "Business." Scientific applications, process control applications, and operating systems are best handled by other languages.

INFORMATION PROCESSING

All operations that are carried out by a computer require access to data. **Data** consists of numbers and words that are suitable for processing by a computer to produce information. The data is manipulated within the central processing unit (CPU) of a computer under the direction of a computer program stored in the computer's memory. The data is manipulated to produce useful information in the form of screen displays or printed reports. Information produced by the processing of data can be used for whatever functions are required by you or other users of the computer.

The production of information by processing data on a computer is called **information processing** or **electronic data processing**. Data is used in each operation on a computer, including input operations, arithmetic operations, logical operations, output operations, and storage operations. It is important that you understand something about the data that is processed by a computer program.

Stream Input/Output vs. Record Input/Output

In data processing, there are two basic ways for data to flow in and out of a program. In BASIC, C, FORTRAN, and some other languages with which you may already be familiar, data usually comes and goes in continuous streams. This is referred to as **stream input/output** (I/O). With stream I/O, a program typically reads data and assigns it to variables. The variables are manipulated and then printed. COBOL is capable of stream I/O through the use of ACCEPT and DISPLAY statements. The ACCEPT statement is similar to the INPUT statement used in BASIC. The DISPLAY statement is similar to the PRINT statement in BASIC.

It is quicker and more efficient to process data that has been grouped into records. This is called **record I/O** and is the type of processing in which COBOL excels. A **record** is a group of related facts or units of data. Other languages use record I/O, but when it comes to business applications, COBOL is by far the best. In record I/O, a program reads a record and writes a record. With record I/O, the programmer must know in advance the format of the record layout and be aware of the form the data is stored in. The **record layout** is simply the order of data units or data items in the record. A data unit or item within a record is called a **field**. All of the fields within a record are related and pertain to the larger data unit that the record represents. A collection of related records forms a **file**. Figure 1-1 on the next page illustrates the relationship between fields, records, and files. A proper record layout must be developed for every input file used and proper record layouts also must be developed for output reports or output data files that a program will create.

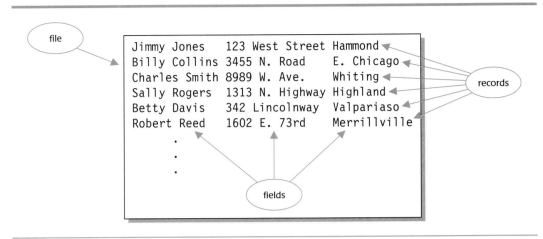

FIGURE 1-1 A file showing the first six records with three fields in each record

Blocking Records

The efficiency of record I/O can be increased further by the use of blocking. **Blocking** refers to the transmitted groups of records from auxiliary storage to the CPU as the program needs them. Once a **block of records** is transferred, the records in the block are supplied to the program as it requests them via READ statements. The block of records is called a **physical record** (Figure 1-2). Each record within a block is called a **logical record**. By using blocks of records stored within CPU buffers, a READ statement does not always cause the physical transfer of a record from auxiliary storage. If this physical transfer were always to occur on a READ statement, most COBOL programs would require a much greater amount of time to execute. By having a block of records in memory, most READ statements in a program do not require a physical transfer of a record because the record is already in the CPU. Hence, the program executes and processes all the records in less time. Modern operating systems handle blocking automatically, and the blocking of records is often transparent to the programmer.

Logical record	Logical record	Logical record	Logical record
record 1	record 2	record 3	record 4

FIGURE 1-2 A block of records with four logical records forming one physical record

DIVISIONS OF A COBOL PROGRAM

All COBOL programs are divided into four divisions. The four divisions are the IDENTI-FICATION DIVISION, ENVIRONMENT DIVISION, DATA DIVISION, and PROCEDURE DIVISION. Each division has its own function in the overall development and execution of the program. The divisions and brief explanations of their purposes follow in the same order in which they must appear within a COBOL program (Figure 1-3).

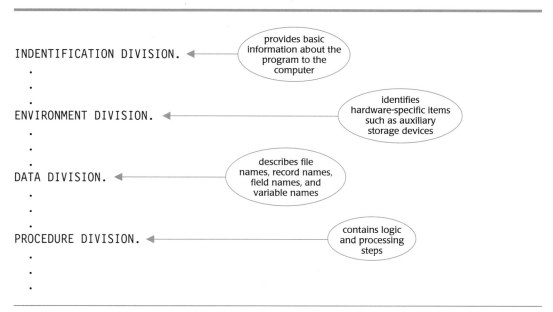

INDENTIFICATION DIVISION. ← *provides basic information about the program to the computer*

ENVIRONMENT DIVISION. ← *identifies hardware-specific items such as auxiliary storage devices*

DATA DIVISION. ← *describes file names, record names, field names, and variable names*

PROCEDURE DIVISION. ← *contains logic and processing steps*

FIGURE 1-3   Four divisions of a COBOL program

IDENTIFICATION DIVISION

The **IDENTIFICATION DIVISION** provides the computer with basic information about the program. As you will see in Chapter 2, there is only one required entry in the IDENTIFICATION DIVISION, but several other entries often are included for the sake of proper documentation.

ENVIRONMENT DIVISION

The **ENVIRONMENT DIVISION** is the most hardware-dependent part of any COBOL program. In taking COBOL source code from one platform and moving it to another, it is the ENVIRONMENT DIVISION that normally requires modifications. It is in this division that the hardware-specific items are listed, such as auxiliary storage devices and/or files. The primary function of the ENVIRONMENT DIVISION is to link the computer's names for files or output devices to the file names you intend to use within your program.

DATA DIVISION

The **DATA DIVISION** is used to more fully describe the nature of input files and output files and to define the record characteristics for each of these files. It also may be used to define variables such as counters and accumulators. It is these file names, record names, and other defined names that you manipulate in the PROCEDURE DIVISION.

PROCEDURE DIVISION

The **PROCEDURE DIVISION** is where the logic and processing steps of the program are included. Every statement within the PROCEDURE DIVISION begins with a COBOL verb. A **COBOL verb** is a command to the computer to execute some action, such as READ a record, COMPUTE the value of an expression, or WRITE a record. Much of the terminology used in the English language is utilized in COBOL. The basic classification of COBOL verbs is presented in Figure 1-4 on the next page. The list is not all-inclusive, but does contain the verbs that will be discussed in this book.

Arithmetic	*Ending*	*Procedure Branching*	*Table Handling*
ADD	STOP	EXIT	SEARCH
COMPUTE		GO TO	SET
DIVIDE	*Inter-Program*	PERFORM	
MULTIPLY	*Communicating*		*Ordering*
SUBTRACT	CALL	*Input-Output*	MERGE
		ACCEPT	RELEASE
Compiler-Directing	*Data Movement*	CLOSE	RETURN
COPY	INITIALIZE	DELETE	SORT
USE	INSPECT	DISPLAY	
	MOVE	OPEN	
Conditional	STRING	READ	
EVALUATE	UNSTRING	REWRITE	
IF		START	
		WRITE	

FIGURE 1-4   Classification of COBOL verbs

As you can see from Figure 1-4, the list of verbs is not that long. It does not take many commands to accomplish a lot in COBOL, and you do not have to rely heavily on documentation within a COBOL program to explain what is going on. If you are careful, neat, and define variable names that are descriptive of the data items being used, the PROCEDURE DIVISION will be easy to understand and easy to modify.

A programmer creates a program by writing source code. **Source code** for the PROCEDURE DIVISION is written in paragraphs. A **paragraph** begins with a **paragraph header** and is broken down into sentences. Each **sentence** is terminated with a period and may contain one or more **statements**. Statements direct the computer to complete an action. Figure 1-5 shows a sample paragraph from a COBOL program. This paragraph moves values from one location within main memory to another, writes a record to a report, increments a counter, and reads the next record.

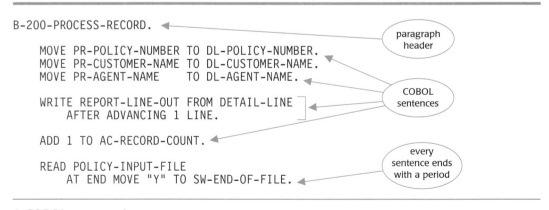

```
B-200-PROCESS-RECORD.

    MOVE PR-POLICY-NUMBER TO DL-POLICY-NUMBER.
    MOVE PR-CUSTOMER-NAME TO DL-CUSTOMER-NAME.
    MOVE PR-AGENT-NAME    TO DL-AGENT-NAME.

    WRITE REPORT-LINE-OUT FROM DETAIL-LINE
        AFTER ADVANCING 1 LINE.

    ADD 1 TO AC-RECORD-COUNT.

    READ POLICY-INPUT-FILE
        AT END MOVE "Y" TO SW-END-OF-FILE.
```

paragraph header

COBOL sentences

every sentence ends with a period

FIGURE 1-5   A COBOL paragraph

STEPS IN THE PROGRAMMING PROCESS

Regardless of the programming language used, computer programs do not just happen. It takes time and effort to come up with solutions. Although computer programs written for business applications can be small, the majority are large and complex. As a result of the complexity of programs written for business, it is important that computer programmers write programs in a systematic, disciplined manner. The steps that follow are typical of the systematic approach that you should use in developing your programs.

Step 1—Understand the Problem

You cannot begin to code a program until you know exactly *what* the program is to do. Talk to the person or persons for whom the program is being developed. Every program has a purpose. Whether it be for a college professor or for a business, establish and maintain channels of communications. Do not be afraid to ask questions.

You must determine what the output from the program is to be. Knowing this, look at what input is available to the program. Determine what mathematical calculations, if any, are to be performed. Overall, obtain a firm grasp of your objectives. Only then can you begin to develop a plan of action.

In summary, before you move on to Step 2, have a complete understanding of the purpose of the program, the output desired, the input available, and the calculations required.

Step 2—Design the Program

Develop the sequence of steps you will use to solve the problem. This does not necessarily involve sitting at the computer. Often, thinking and planning are best accomplished away from the keyboard. Do not hesitate to pick up paper and a pencil to draft your ideas. Flowcharts, hierarchy charts, and/or pseudocode should be used to outline your design.

A **flowchart** is a diagram that pictorially illustrates the steps needed to solve a problem. Table 1-2 on the next page presents the symbols most commonly used in creating flowcharts. Chapter 2 will present a complete flowchart for the program presented in that chapter. A **hierarchy chart** shows the relationship between the paragraphs used in your program and how you have organized your solution. Hierarchy charts will be discussed in detail later in this chapter and in Chapter 2. **Pseudocode** is simply a series of English-like expressions written to describe the actions necessary to solve a problem. Pseudocode is used by many programmers in place of, or along with, diagrams to design program logic.

You need not go into great detail initially, just enough to provide a basic skeleton of the logic. You do not need to design the entire solution. Break your problem into parts, and work on the logic for just one part at a time. Nearly all problems, both in life and in information processing, can be dealt with if divided into manageable parts. This is called the **top-down approach** to problem solving. Before moving to Step 3, you should review your basic design by examining each part as would the computer. If your design does not make sense to you, then you should revise it.

Step 3—Code the Program

Once you know *what* has to be done and *how* you plan to solve the problem, start converting your design into a computer program. If you have divided your problem, as suggested in Step 2, then you should develop your program by writing source code for one paragraph, or **module**, at a time. You do not have to write source code for the entire program before moving on to the next step. As in Step 2, review your logic carefully. Step through the source code as would the computer to see if it works. Reviewing source code in this manner is called **desk checking**.

Source code is entered into a disk file using a program called a **text editor** or simply an **editor**. Many computer systems have language-sensitive editors available. A **language-sensitive editor** is designed to aid you in putting code in the proper columns and to assist in detecting syntax errors as the program is written.

TABLE 1-2   Flowchart Symbols and Their Meanings

Symbol	Name	Meaning
	Process symbol	Represents the process of executing an operation or group of operations that modify the value of fields.
	Input/Output symbol	Represents an I/O operation that makes data available for processing or creates output data
	Flow lines	Connects other symbols and shows the sequence of operations
	Annotation symbol	Represents descriptive information or explanatory notes
	Decision symbol	Represents a decision that determines which logic path to follow
	Terminal symbol	Represents the beginning or end of the logic
	Connector symbol	Represents exit from or entry to another part of the flowchart
	Predefined Process symbol	Represents a named process consisting of one or more operations or steps

Step 4—Test the Program

Submit your source code to the computer for the diagnoses of errors and translation. This is called **compilation**. Compilation is performed by a special program called a **compiler**. As indicated earlier, the COBOL compiler translates a COBOL program into instructions that the computer understands. Compilation of your program will identify syntax errors. **Syntax errors** are exceptions to the rules of the programming language and include missing periods and misspelled names. Correct syntax errors, compile your program again, and when your source code is free of syntax errors, execute your program to test the logic of your solution.

If logic errors exist, fall back to Steps 2 and 3, and then come back to Step 4. The development of your program on a module-by-module basis will require you to repeat the cycle of Steps 1, 2, 3, and 4 many times. As indicated in Steps 2 and 3, you do not have to develop all of your logic at one time, and you do not have to enter all of your source code at one time. Attack problem solving and programming in small, easy-to-manage increments.

Step 5—Document the Program

Documentation of your program can take many forms. External documentation in the form of notes and manuals for programmers who will maintain your program in the future is usually required. Manuals for computer operators who may interact with your program and users who may want to see output from your program need careful attention. Your program may be useless if no one can figure out how to use it, run it, or fix it. External documentation and manuals may be written after the program is complete; however, documentation is also something that you develop along with your solution. Meaningful data names provide self-documentation. Comment lines within your code preceding every block of definitions and logic statements should be inserted in your program as you write it in Step 3.

STRUCTURED PROGRAMMING

Well-written computer programs are developed according to the rules of structured programming. **Structured programming** is a methodology according to which all program logic can be developed using and combining just three basic logic control structures—sequence, selection, and iteration. A **logic control structure** is a way in which statements in a program can be executed. The use of structured programming offers advantages to both the programmer and the programmer's employer. These advantages are summarized in Table 1-3.

TABLE 1-3   Advantages of Structured Programming

1. Programs are neater in appearance and more readable.
2. The reliability and efficiency of programs are improved.
3. Less time is spent debugging, testing, and modifying programs.
4. Programmer productivity is increased.

The logic structures used in structured programs are explained below and are illustrated by flowcharts in Figures 1-6 through 1-10 on pages 1-10 through 1-12.

1. **Sequence structure**—In a sequence structure, one imperative statement is executed after another. An **imperative statement** indicates that some action in the program is to occur. The computer is instructed to complete an action such as READ a record or WRITE a record, then complete another action, and then another, and so on. Figure 1-6 shows a sample flowchart and pseudocode for a sequence structure.

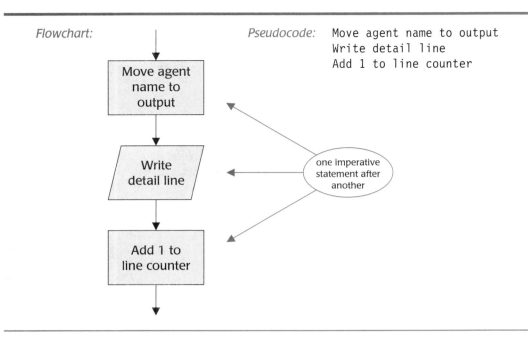

Flowchart:

Pseudocode: Move agent name to output
Write detail line
Add 1 to line counter

FIGURE 1-6 Sequence structure

2. **Selection structure**—A selection structure executes code based on the result of a condition. A **condition**, such as COUNT > 1 (COUNT is greater than 1), can be true or false depending upon the value of the variable COUNT. A selection structure allows for one of two sets of actions to be executed depending on whether a condition is true or false. Figure 1-7 shows a sample flowchart and pseudocode for a selection structure.

A **case structure**, which is an extension of the selection structure, allows for one of several different actions to be executed based on the value of a variable. Figure 1-8 shows a sample flowchart and pseudocode for a case structure.

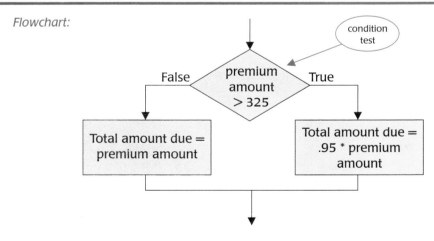

Flowchart:

Pseudocode:
```
If the premium amount > 325
    Total amount due = .95 * premium amount
Else
    Total amount due = premium amount
End-if
```

FIGURE 1-7 Selection structure

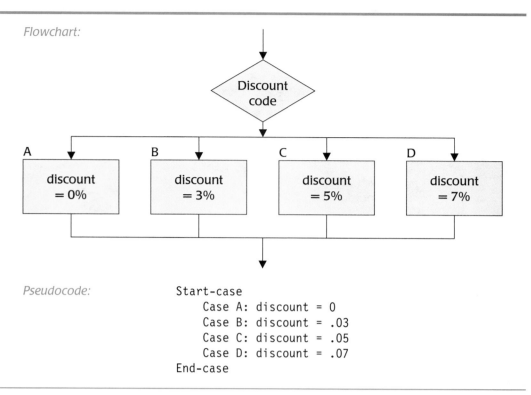

Flowchart:

Pseudocode:

```
Start-case
    Case A: discount = 0
    Case B: discount = .03
    Case C: discount = .05
    Case D: discount = .07
End-case
```

FIGURE 1-8   Case structure

3. **Iteration structure**—Iteration, or **looping,** is another structure fundamental to all computer programming languages. It allows a set of instructions to be executed over and over until some predetermined condition is met. There are two basic iteration structures. The only real difference between the two structures is the point at which a condition test takes place. In the first iteration structure, referred to as the **Do-while structure** (Figure 1-9 on the next page), the testing of the condition takes place before the loop is ever executed. Hence, depending on the results of the test, the computer may never execute any of the code within the loop. If the condition is met, the loop may be terminated before it ever begins.

In the second iteration structure, referred to as the **Do-until structure** (Figure 1-10 on the next page), testing of the condition occurs after the logic in the loop is executed the first time. In a Do-until structure, you are assured the computer will execute the statements within the loop at least once.

In COBOL, the Do-while structure is implemented using a PERFORM-UNTIL. The Do-until structure is implemented by using a PERFORM-WITH TEST AFTER-UNTIL. These structures and associated COBOL statements will be discussed later in the book.

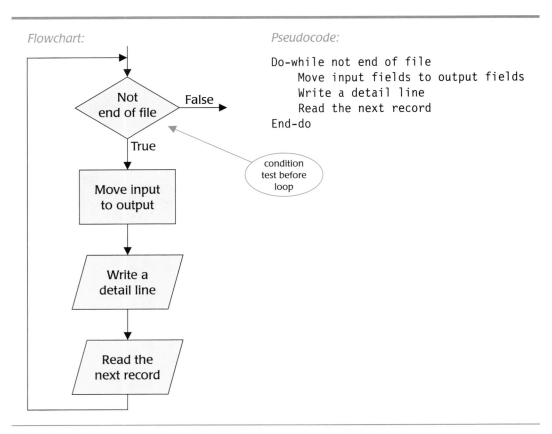

Flowchart:

Pseudocode:

```
Do-while not end of file
    Move input fields to output fields
    Write a detail line
    Read the next record
End-do
```

FIGURE 1-9 Do-while structure

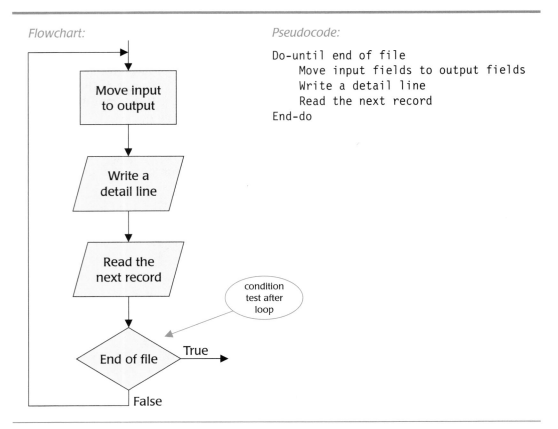

Flowchart:

Pseudocode:

```
Do-until end of file
    Move input fields to output fields
    Write a detail line
    Read the next record
End-do
```

FIGURE 1-10 Do-until structure

TOP-DOWN DESIGN / TOP-DOWN PROGRAMMING

Top-down design and top-down programming are methodologies used to solve large problems. **Top-down design** is a strategy that breaks large, complex problems into smaller, less complex problems. Then, each one of the less complex problems is broken down into even smaller problems. Top-down design can be thought of as a divide-and-conquer strategy. In **top-down programming**, high-level modules are coded as soon as they are designed, generally before the low-level modules have been designed. In the top-down approach, both the design and programming are done beginning with the general and moving to the specific.

The logic in all the programs in this book will be broken down into small, manageable modules, or subroutines. Each **subroutine** will solve a specific part of the overall problem. It is easy to write modular code in COBOL. A subroutine in COBOL forms a paragraph. From a maintenance standpoint, a modular program is easier to understand and modify. Each subroutine should be relatively small, usually no more than one page of source code and should handle just one function of the program. Hence, you should be able to quickly evaluate a program and determine where modifications need to be inserted. The hierarchy chart shown in Figure 1-11 illustrates the top-down organization typical of a COBOL program. Such charts will be formally introduced in Chapter 2.

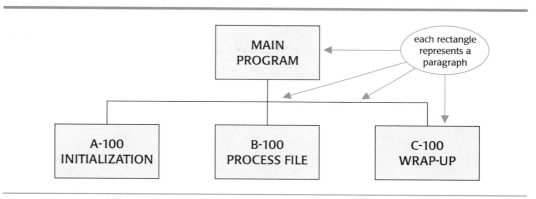

FIGURE 1-11   Hierarchy chart showing top-down organization of a COBOL program

Do not confuse structured programming with top-down programming. They are not the same. Structured programming is a means of coding the logic within the subroutines of a program. Top-down programming allows you to organize the program into manageable subroutines.

COBOL WORDS

COBOL programs are made up of COBOL words. Words, along with punctuation, make up all the entries necessary in a COBOL program. A **COBOL word** may be from 1 to 30 characters long and may contain any combination of alphabetic and numeric characters. No blanks are allowed in COBOL words. The only special character allowed is the hyphen and it must be embedded within the word. A hyphen cannot be at the beginning or end of a word. Typically, you use hyphens to enhance the readability of user-defined words. Many words, including verbs, already have special meanings in COBOL. These are called **reserved words** (Figure 1-12 on the next page). For a complete list of all the COBOL reserved words, see Appendix C. Much of this book is devoted to the description and use of COBOL's reserved words.

Words you create within a program are called **user-defined words** (Figure 1-12). Guidelines will be established in Chapter 2 for the creation of user-defined words that will make it less likely for you to accidentally use a reserved word.

COBOL Words	Description
PROGRAM-ID	Reserved
SELECT	Reserved
OPEN	Reserved
PERFORM	Reserved
INPUT-OUTPUT	Reserved
PREMIUM-INPUT-FILE	User-defined
AC-LINE-COUNT	User-defined
WA-DATE	User-defined
PR-CLIENT-NAME	User-defined
SL-LINE-1	User-defined

FIGURE 1-12 Examples of COBOL words

COBOL CODING FORMAT

A **COBOL program coding sheet** such as the one shown in Figure 1-13 has all the columns and special areas used by COBOL marked off and labeled. Coding sheets, however, have all but disappeared from the information systems scene. Today, you enter a program using a text editor on a computer. The format of each line of COBOL code you will write reflects the following 80-column format.

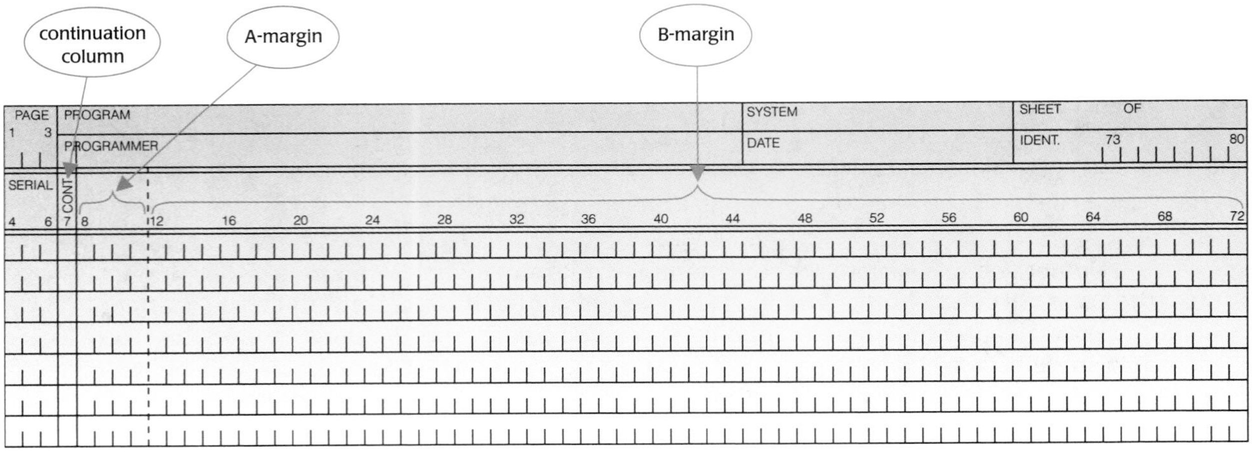

FIGURE 1-13 COBOL coding sheet

Columns 1–6: These columns generally are not used. This area is reserved for sequence numbers that can be used to number the lines of source code.

Column 7: Column 7 is referred to as the **indicator area**. An asterisk (*) in column 7 denotes a comment line in COBOL. **Comment lines** represent documentation and are intended for the programmer's use, not the computer's. A slash (/) in column 7 can be used to force a form-feed in your program listing. A hyphen (–) in this area can be used to indicate the continuance of certain items from one line to another. The asterisk and slash will be utilized extensively in the sample programs presented in this book.

Columns 8–11: This is the **A-margin**, which sometimes is also referred to as the **A-area**. The COBOL compiler expects certain entries to begin within the A-margin. For example, procedure names, section names, and paragraph names must begin in the A-margin. In this book, anything that must begin in the A-margin will begin in column 8, although COBOL allows an A-margin entry to begin in columns 8, 9, 10, or 11.

Columns 12–72: This is the **B-margin**, which sometimes is referred to as the **B-area**. The majority of the statements in a program are placed in this area. You must be careful not to go beyond column 72. The COBOL compiler does not recognize any code beyond column 72.

Columns 73–80: In the past, this area was used for program identification purposes. Today, these positions are usually left blank.

Once written, the program's source code is submitted to the COBOL compiler. If there are no syntax errors, the COBOL compiler generates a machine language or object code version of your program (Figure 1-14). **Machine language** is the only language the computer understands. When a program executes, it is the machine language version of the program that is being utilized by the computer. A computer cannot execute source code. Your instructor should be able to provide you with the information you will need to create, compile, and execute a program on the computer system you are using. Appendix F presents a beginner's guide to Micro Focus Personal COBOL.

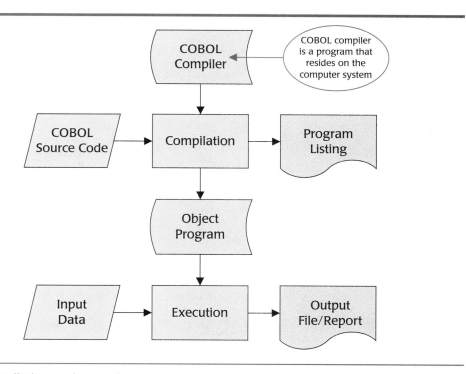

FIGURE 1-14   COBOL compilation and execution

CHAPTER SUMMARY

The following list summarizes this chapter. The summary is designed to help you study and understand the material and concepts presented.

1. **COBOL** is designed to meet the **information processing** needs of business.

2. COBOL is a **high-level language** that can be transported easily from one computer system to another.

3. COBOL excels in the use of **record I/O**.

4. COBOL is English-like and self-documenting.

5. Every COBOL program is composed of four divisions: **IDENTIFICATION**, **ENVIRONMENT**, **DATA**, and **PROCEDURE**.

6. **Flowcharts**, **hierarchy charts**, and/or **pseudocode** should be used to outline your logic.

7. The **top-down** approach to solving problems divides a problem into smaller more manageable problems.

8. **Top-down design** should be used to break a problem down into manageable parts.

9. **Top-down programming** should be used to organize the logic of your COBOL program.

10. **Structured programs** use **sequence**, **selection**, and **iteration** logic structures.

11. A COBOL program is composed of **COBOL words**.

12. Every line of source code in a COBOL program must follow certain format rules.

KEY TERMS

A-area (1-15)
A-margin (1-15)
B-area (1-15)
B-margin (1-15)
blocking (1-4)
block of records (1-4)
case structure (1-10)
COBOL (1-1)
COBOL compiler (1-2)
COBOL program coding sheet (1-14)
COBOL verb (1-5)
COBOL word (1-13)
comment lines (1-14)
compilation (1-8)
compiler (1-8)
condition (1-10)
data (1-3)
DATA DIVISION (1-5)
desk checking (1-7)
Do-until structure (1-11)
Do-while structure (1-11)
editor (1-8)

electronic data processing (1-3)
ENVIRONMENT DIVISION (1-5)
field (1-3)
file (1-3)
flowchart (1-7)
hierarchy chart (1-7)
high-level language (1-1)
IDENTIFICATION DIVISION (1-5)
imperative statement (1-9)
indicator area (1-14)
information processing (1-3)
iteration structure (1-11)
language-sensitive editor (1-8)
logical record (1-4)
logic control structure (1-9)
looping (1-11)
low-level language (1-1)
machine language (1-15)
module (1-7)
paragraph (1-6)
paragraph header (1-6)
physical record (1-4)

PROCEDURE DIVISION (1-5)
pseudocode (1-7)
record (1-3)
record I/O (1-3)
record layout (1-3)
reserved words (1-13)
selection structure (1-10)
sentence (1-6)
sequence structure (1-9)
source code (1-6)

statements (1-6)
stream input/output (1-3)
structured programming (1-9)
subroutine (1-13)
syntax errors (1-8)
text editor (1-8)
top-down approach (1-7)
top-down design (1-13)
top-down programming (1-13)
user-defined words (1-13)

STUDENT ASSIGNMENTS

Student Assignment 1: True/False

Instructions: Circle T if the statement is true or F if the statement is false.

T   F   1. A programmer should develop the logic of a program prior to coding the program.

T   F   2. Syntax errors are the same as logic errors.

T   F   3. The sequence of the divisions must be IDENTIFICATION, ENVIRONMENT, DATA, and PROCEDURE.

T   F   4. Machine language is the only language a computer really understands.

T   F   5. COBOL is high-level language.

T   F   6. COBOL can be used on a wide range of computer platforms.

T   F   7. A compiler is a part of computer hardware.

T   F   8. A compiler is capable of detecting logic errors in source code.

T   F   9. The top-down programming process involves writing the more detailed paragraphs first and the more general ones last.

T   F   10. Top-down programming and structured programming refer to the same thing.

T   F   11. Structured programs eliminate the need for iteration or looping.

T   F   12. A COBOL source program can be executed without translation into machine language.

T   F   13. ANS COBOL is a standardized version of COBOL to which all major computer manufacturers and software suppliers adhere.

T   F   14. A case structure is a special type of iteration structure.

T   F   15. Blocking increases the efficiency of record I/O.

Student Assignment 2: Multiple Choice

Instructions: Circle the correct response.

1. To say that COBOL is machine independent means _____.
   a. COBOL programs do not need a computer to run on
   b. COBOL programs written for one computer system will not work on another system
   c. COBOL programs written on one computer system will, with little change, work on other computer systems
   d. COBOL programs require major modification when taken from one computer system and used on another

2. The B in COBOL stands for _____.
   a. Bob
   b. Basic
   c. Bit or Byte
   d. Business

3. The ENVIRONMENT DIVISION _____.
   a. is the most machine dependent part of a COBOL program
   b. is where input files, output files, and variables are defined
   c. presents the logic that manipulates the defined files and variables
   d. is the first division of every COBOL program

4. In writing a computer program, the programmer should _____.
   a. code a solution and then design the program's logic
   b. understand the problem before designing the program
   c. write the entire program in one setting to insure consistency of the code
   d. keep variable names as short as possible

5. A COBOL word may consist of _____.
   a. letters only
   b. letters and numbers only
   c. letters, numbers, and hyphens only
   d. letters, numbers, and any special character desired

6. All structured programs can be coded using the following logic structures _____.
   a. sequence, selection, and iteration
   b. selection, case, and top-down
   c. iteration, Do-while, and Do-until
   d. ascending, descending, and parallel

7. Top-down design can best be described as a strategy that allows _____.
   a. small problems to be combined into one large problem
   b. large problems to be divided into small, easy-to-manage problems
   c. many problems to be solved at once
   d. many programmers to work on the same problem and create a series of small structured programs

8. The A-margin covers _____ in a line of COBOL code.
   a. columns 7–12
   b. columns 12–72
   c. columns 8–11
   d. columns 7–72

9. The B-margin covers _____ the following columns in a line of COBOL code.
   a. columns 7–12
   b. columns 12–72
   c. columns 8–11
   d. columns 7–72

10. The DATA DIVISION of a COBOL program _____.
    a. contains the coded logic of your program
    b. contains hardware specific references
    c. is used to identify the name of your program
    d. describes files, records, and variables

Student Assignment 3: Drawing a Flowchart

Instructions: Using the symbols presented in Table 1-2 on page 1-8, draw a flowchart to solve the following problem. Assume FIELD-1 and FIELD-2 are numeric fields with values assigned.

   If FIELD-1 is greater than FIELD-2, move FIELD-1 to BIGGER and FIELD-2 to SMALLER.
   If FIELD-2 is greater than FIELD-1, move FIELD-2 to BIGGER and FIELD-1 to SMALLER.
   If FIELD-1 equals FIELD-2, move the value of FIELD-1 to SAME.

Student Assignment 4: Writing Pseudocode

Instructions: Write pseudocode to perform the logic indicated by the flowchart shown in Figure 1-15. Remember, pseudocode is simply a series of English-like statements describing the actions to be taken in solving a problem.

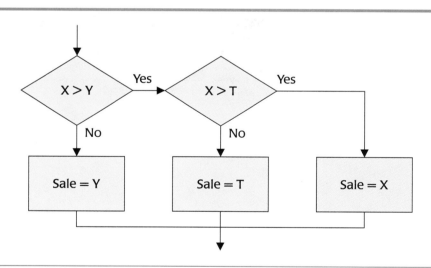

FIGURE 1-15   Flowchart for Student Assignment 4: Writing Pseudocode

Student Assignment 5: Drawing a Flowchart

Instructions: Given three variables (FIELD-X, FIELD-Y, and FIELD-Z) that are all numeric, positive, and no two equal to each other, draw a flowchart that will assign the value of the smallest to the field SMALL.

Student Assignment 6: Writing Pseudocode

Instructions: Write pseudocode to perform the logic indicated by the flowchart shown in Figure 1-16.

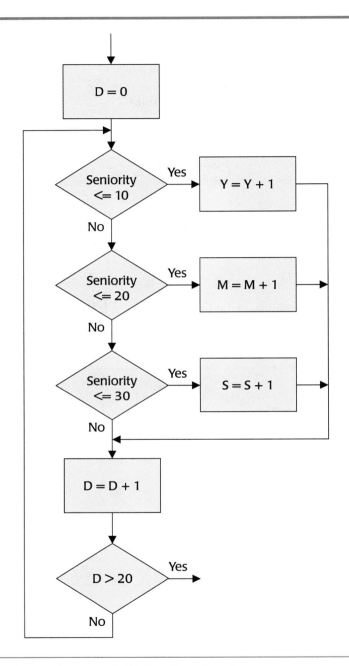

FIGURE 1-16 Flowchart for Student Assignment 6: Writing Pseudocode

Student Assignment 7: Drawing a Flowchart

Instructions: Draw a partial flowchart to calculate the commission paid to a salesperson. Use the variables SALES and COMMISSION. The salesperson receives a 15% commission if his or her sales exceed $20,000. The commission is 12% if sales are less than or equal to $20,000, but greater than $15,000. Sales less than or equal to $15,000 qualify for a commission of 10%.

CHAPTER TWO

A Complete COBOL Program

OBJECTIVES

You will have mastered the material in Chapter 2 when you can:

- Describe the basic organization of the four COBOL divisions
- Describe the purpose of the SELECT and ASSIGN entries
- Describe the use of an FD level entry
- Identify valid level numbers
- Explain the use of a PICTURE clause
- Explain the difference between group and elementary items
- Explain the difference between alphanumeric and numeric fields
- Identify a simple edit pattern with zero suppression
- Describe the purpose of the PERFORM statement
- Describe the function of a PERFORM UNTIL statement
- Understand the function of the ADD statement
- Explain the use of OPEN, CLOSE, READ, and WRITE statements
- Explain the use of the MOVE statement
- Identify the function of a STOP RUN statement

INTRODUCTION

The easiest way to begin learning COBOL is to look at a COBOL program. In doing so, you will be exposed to the organization, syntax, and statements required in every COBOL program. The source code for a complete COBOL program will be presented and discussed. In looking at this source code, you will begin to get a feel for the structure and components of a COBOL program. The sample program will produce a simple report.

AINSWORTH INSURANCE POLICY NUMBER REPORT

To illustrate the basics of processing data and the uses of the COBOL language, the sample program coded in this chapter creates a report listing the policy numbers of people who have purchased insurance from the Ainsworth Insurance Company. The data to be used as program input is stored in the Premium file listed in Appendix A in the back of this book and located on the Student Diskette that accompanies this book. Each record in the Premium file is 80 characters long and contains the customer name, agent name, insurance type, and policy number as well as other data that will not be used in this chapter but will be used in later chapters. The report will contain information found in fields named PR-POLICY-NUMBER, PR-CUSTOMER-NAME, PR-AGENT-NAME, and PR-INSURANCE-TYPE within the program. Each time a record is read from the Premium file, these four fields will be used to produce one line of information in the report. The first six records to be processed are shown in Figure 2-1.

Customer Name (Positions 1-20)	Agent Name (Positions 21-40)	Insurance Type (Positions 41-50)	Policy Number (Positions 51-62)	Unused Data (Positions 63-80)
Allister, Collin	McDonald, Fred	Automobile	AM-1991-9223	
Amfelter, Audrey	McDonald, Fred	Automobile	AM-2199-9229	
Andrews, Robert	Anderson, James	Home	HM-7008-0507	
Antich, Roseanne	McDonald, Fred	Automobile	AM-7211-7261	
Anytime, Seeue	McDonald, Fred	Automobile	AM-7623-1221	
Baker, Bonnie	Jones, William	Renter	RT-4402-3211	

FIGURE 2-1   First six Premium file records

Although there are 72 records in the Premium file, the exact number of records in the file is unimportant. The program presented will execute until all of the records have been processed. The program will read a record, print a line of information, read the next record, and print another line until all records in the Premium file have been processed. The logic remains the same regardless of the number of records in the file.

Designing the Policy Number Report Format

Figure 2-2 shows the basic report format the program is to produce. The report is to have two heading lines, separated by a blank line, and a line of dashes, or hyphens, that print at the top of every page. A page number prints in the upper right-hand corner of each page as part of the first heading line. Detail information begins in position 1 of each line. This information is called the **detail line** for the report. For each customer, the program is to print the policy number, customer name, agent name, and insurance type. As explained earlier, this information is made available to the program from the Premium file.

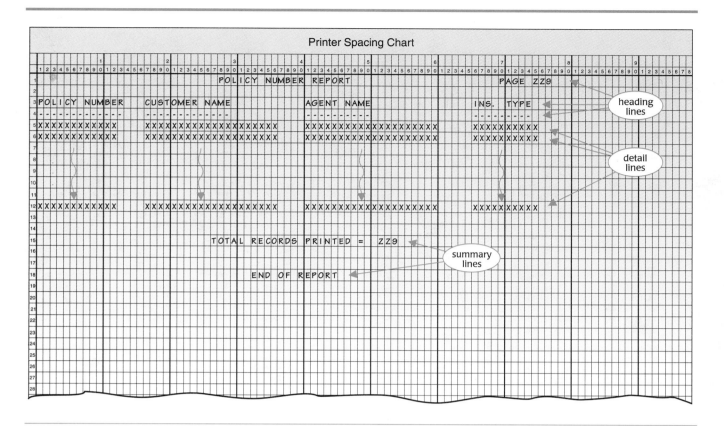

FIGURE 2-2   Report layout on a printer spacing chart

The goal in designing output should be to create a report that is visually attractive and provides all the desired information. The report is based on an 80 character output line. The size of your output line is normally controlled by the type of printer to be used and the width of the paper.

A **printer spacing chart** is often used in designing reports. A printer spacing chart is divided into rows and columns with each being numbered to assist in the accurate coding of the output lines in your program.

In Figure 2-2, notice that the report title, POLICY NUMBER REPORT, begins in print position 28 and the word PAGE begins in position 70. Two lines down, the column headings are printed and a line with hyphens underlines the column headings. Single-spaced detail lines containing customer information then follow. Triple-spaced summary lines indicating the number of customer records printed and designating the end of the report follow the last detail line.

The Output Report

Figure 2-3 on the next page presents the Policy Number Report output by the program to be discussed in this chapter. The report is two pages long and lists 72 records found in the input file. The summary message listing the number of records processed prints at the bottom of the second page along with a message that the report is complete.

```
                    POLICY NUMBER REPORT                 PAGE   1

    POLICY NUMBER   CUSTOMER NAME      AGENT NAME        INS. TYPE
    -------------   -------------      ----------        ---------
    AM-1991-9223    Allister, Collin   McDonald, Fred    Automobile
    AM-2199-9229    Amfelter, Audrey   McDonald, Fred    Automobile
    HM-7008-0507    Andrews, Robert    Anderson, James   Home
    AM-7211-7261    Antich, Roseanne
    AM-7623-1221    Anytime, Seeue
    RT-4402-3211    Baker, Bonnie
    TL-7008-5551    Brannan, Clyde
    HM-1107-2393    Byman, Goodie
    AM-6128-2151    Cannon, Wylde
    HM-5109-4171    Connors, Cinder
    TL-7303-3452    Danners, Sarah
    TL-7007-5691    Duffy, Chester
    AM-7373-1147    Eastling, Edward
    AN-0868-4820    Eman, Sorik
    HM-5555-3234    Estovar, Franko
    RT-1189-8533    Flagg, Wavadee
    AN-4043-6510    Foreman, Otto
    HM-1113-2666    Framptin, Charles
    RT-9083-6762    Franken, Peter
    HM-4441-1662    Franklin, Steven
    AN-1181-6464    Fredricks, Sally
    AN-3453-9834    Garcia, William
    AM-9878-5647    Garfield, Joey
    RT-5421-2221    Glidden, Findda
    AM-7993-4347    Golden, Summer
    AN-4141-1256    Kackel, Henna
    RT-3421-0456    Kracken, Gretchen
    RT-1002-1551    Kramer, Robert
    WL-0221-2422    Kramer, Wally
    AN-4410-0774    Kratchet, Emily
    RT-1122-7326    Krevits, Gloria
    AM-1004-2553    Leach, Raeanne
    RT-5525-0556    Lynch, Agnis
    HM-1144-4426    Machen, Michael
    AN-4551-1102    McColly, Stephen
    AN-3366-2242    McGreger, Karla
    WL-1222-1444    McVickers, Sam
    AN-6566-8802    Michaels, Ramsey
    RT-0944-9251    Motorhead, Ima
    TL-6220-2092    Neierson, Henry
    HM-2112-1255    Nelson, Grace
    HM-4123-6541    Ollenford, Winnie
    AN-4422-2226    Olson, Wally
    TL-5522-2121    Pally, Jane
    TL-6763-0093    Parnelli, Frank
    RT-4421-4091    Partridge, Danny
    HM-5111-4781    Pittman, Betty J.
    RT-9122-8422    Potter, Louise
    RT-3331-3451    Qualizza, Scotter
    HM-4112-2452    Ramsey, Lindsay
    TL-3319-1614    Samson, Delight
```

```
                          POLICY NUMBER REPORT                 PAGE   2

        POLICY NUMBER   CUSTOMER NAME      AGENT NAME         INS. TYPE
        -------------   -------------      ----------         ---------
        RT-6678-5505    Sanders, Kevin     Jones, William     Renter
        AN-5011-0252    Seaweed, Lostin    Anderson, James    Annuity
        AM-3323-3441    Senef, Marcia      McDonald, Fred     Automobile
        AN-0450-9411    Shorts, Jimmy      Benson, Gloria     Annuity
        HM-3308-6647    Skinner, Owen      Benson, Gloria     Home
        HM-8767-8788    Solenfeld, Nancy   Jacobson, Peter    Home
        HM-7878-7065    Solfelt, Wanda     Jones, William     Home
        TL-2762-2728    Solinski, Paula    Jacobson, Peter    Term Life
        HM-2001-7338    Solloday, Tom      Jacobson, Peter    Home
        HM-2322-4488    Sollyfield, Barbara Jacobson, Peter   Home
        RT-4337-7488    Tully, Paula       Jones, William     Renter
        TL-2129-8959    Vlasic, Roberta    McDonald, Fred     Term Life
        RT-0424-0053    Walters, Samuel    Jones, William     Renter
        AN-0993-4104    West, William      Anderson, James    Annuity
        WL-0454-5698    White, Robert      Anderson, James    Whole Life
        AM-3411-1223    Whitman, Walter    Anderson, James    Automobile
        WL-0082-1913    Wilder, Eugene     Jean, Barbara      Whole Life
        RT-9580-0003    Willis, Richard    Anderson, James    Renter
        TL-7682-0903    Winder, Robert     Anderson, James    Term Life
        WL-2721-3904    Winfield, Wally    Anderson, James    Whole Life
        RT-7127-5076    Yackley, Yourto    Jones, William     Renter


                          TOTAL RECORDS PRINTED =    72


                              END OF REPORT
```

FIGURE 2-3   Policy Number Report output by the sample program presented in this chapter

The Premium Input File Record Layout

It is very important that the input record layout in a COBOL program be accurate. The output report can be only as accurate as the input data. The layout of each input record in the Premium file is shown in Figure 2-4. Look at the attribute column in Figure 2-4. The attribute shown for each field is alphanumeric. **Alphanumeric** means that the field may contain any combination of letters, numbers, or special characters. Many of the fields used in a COBOL program will be **alphanumeric fields**.

Field	Position	Length	Attribute
Customer Name	1–20	20	Alphanumeric
Agent Name	21–40	20	Alphanumeric
Insurance Type	41–50	10	Alphanumeric
Policy Number	51–62	12	Alphanumeric
unused positions	63–80	18	Alphanumeric
Total Record Length		80	

FIGURE 2-4   Input record layout

PREPARING PROGRAM LOGIC

Once you know what the output looks like and you know what the input looks like, you can begin to design a program that will create the desired results. Hierarchy charts, pseudo-code, and/or flowcharts can be used in the design process. Regardless of the approach used in designing your program, it must be done carefully and with logic. As discussed in Chapter 1, coding should be done in small steps. Design a little, code a little, and then test a little. The compiler will determine if there are syntax errors, but only you can determine logic errors.

Hierarchy Charts

When there is a need for more than a single module or paragraph in a program, a **hierarchy chart,** or **top-down chart,** can be drawn. A hierarchy chart shows the relationship of the modules in the PROCEDURE DIVISION of a COBOL program and illustrates which modules control other modules. This is the program's top-down organization. A hierarchy chart shows program organization, not program logic. It can be used for both planning and documentation. A hierarchy chart for the Policy Number Report program is shown in Figure 2-5 on the next page.

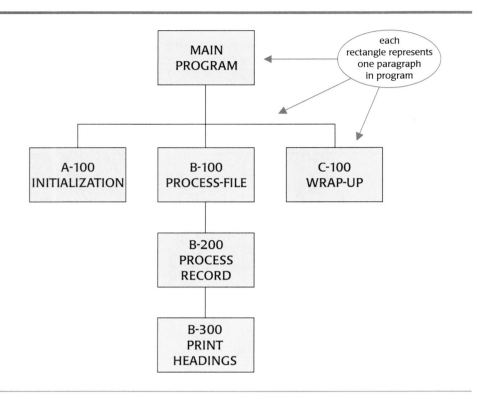

FIGURE 2-5   Hierarchy chart for the Policy Number Report program

Using top-down design techniques discussed in Chapter 1, you can use a hierarchy chart to organize the tasks needed to solve the problem being addressed by your program. Preliminary versions of hierarchy charts might need to be modified once the actual programming begins.

The hierarchy chart in Figure 2-5 shows that a module, or paragraph, named MAIN-PROGRAM transfers control to A-100-INITIALIZATION, B-100-PROCESS-FILE, and C-100-WRAP-UP. A-100-INITIALIZATION and C-100-WRAP-UP do not transfer control to any other paragraphs. B-100-PROCESS-FILE transfers control to B-200-PROCESS-RECORD. Within B-200-PROCESS-RECORD, control is passed to B-300-PRINT-HEADINGS. To design or illustrate the logic of a program, pseudocode or a flowchart can be used.

Pseudocode

Many computer programmers prefer to plan program logic using pseudocode. Pseudocode for the sample program is shown in Figure 2-6. Pseudocode does not have to contain all the minute details of your program, but should be comprehensive enough to use as a guide in writing your code.

```
Initialize counters
Open files
Read a record

Do-while not end of file
     Print headings as needed
     Move input fields to output fields
     Write a detail line
     Read the next record
End-do

Write summary lines
Close files
Terminate program
```

FIGURE 2-6   Pseudocode for the Policy Number Report program

Flowchart

Flowcharts can be used for both planning and documentation. A flowchart that illustrates the logic used in the Policy Number Report program is shown in Figure 2-7 on the next page. Step-by-step, the flowchart shows the logic flow within the program. This logic flow will be discussed in more detail as each paragraph is examined later in this chapter.

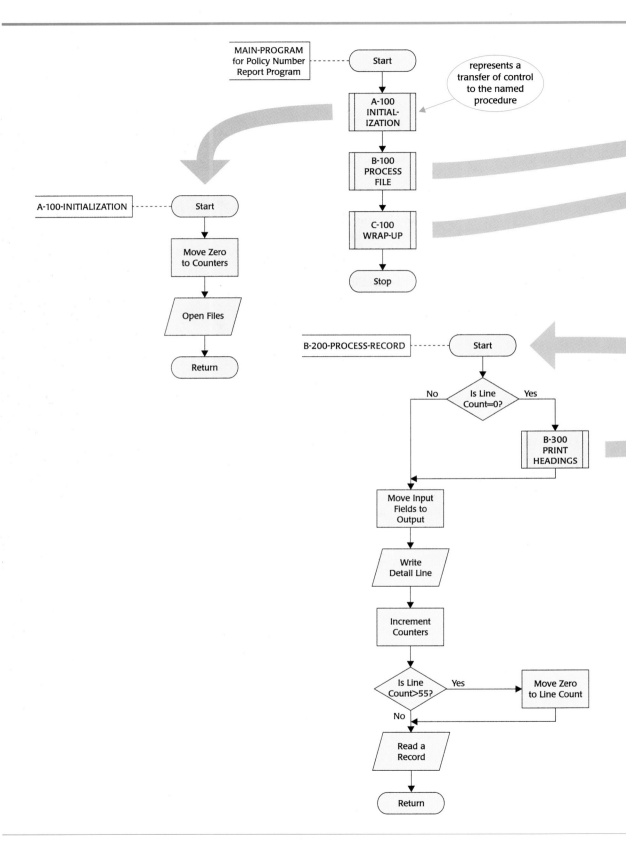

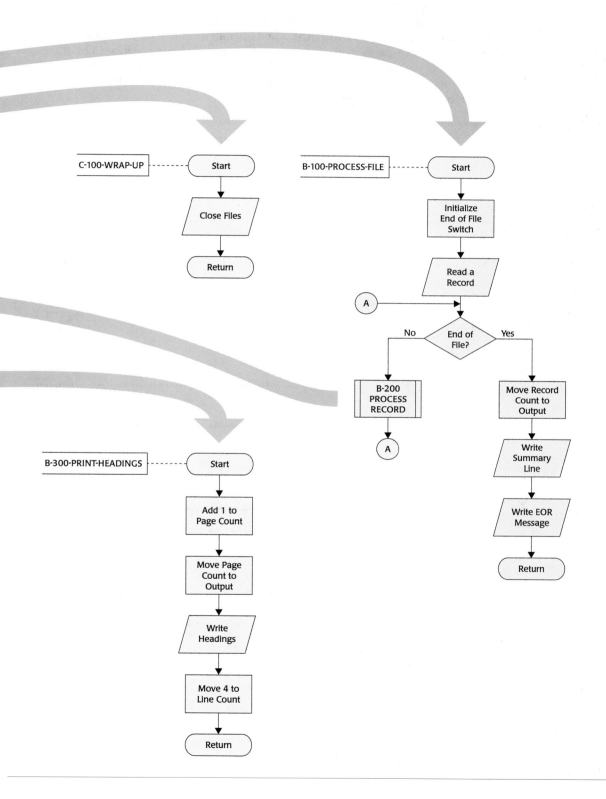

THE SAMPLE PROGRAM

Figure 2-8 shows the source code for the Policy Number Report program. This program is found on the Student Diskette that accompanies this book. COBOL programs are usually much longer than programs developed in BASIC or C because many of the lines are devoted to spacing so that it is easy to read. Comments are generally brief because COBOL is self-documenting. Even if you have never seen a COBOL program before, you can probably understand the program's function by looking at the code. The spacing allows for a neat and orderly presentation of the code.

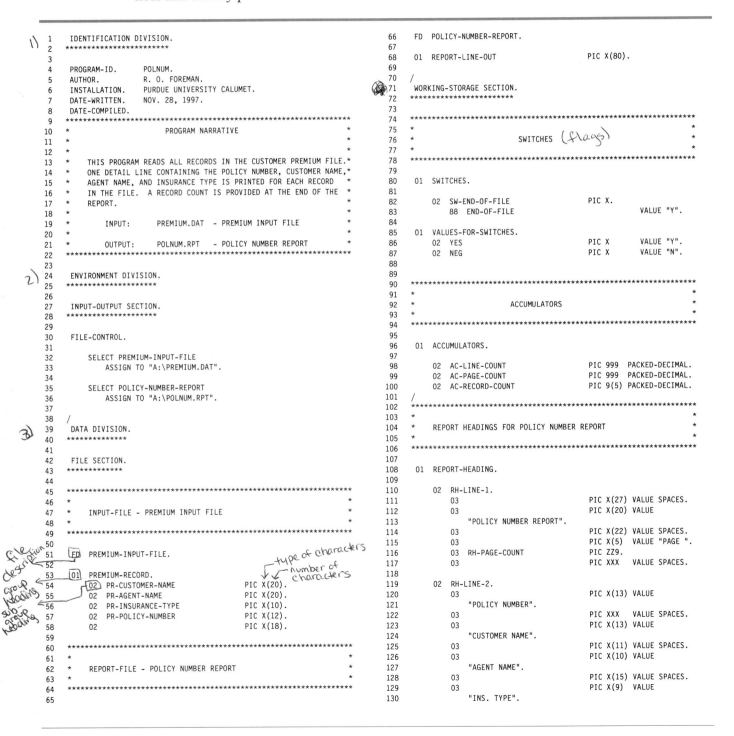

```
  1        IDENTIFICATION DIVISION.
  2        ************************
  3
  4        PROGRAM-ID.      POLNUM.
  5        AUTHOR.          R. O. FOREMAN.
  6        INSTALLATION.    PURDUE UNIVERSITY CALUMET.
  7        DATE-WRITTEN.    NOV. 28, 1997.
  8        DATE-COMPILED.
  9        ****************************************************************
 10        *                    PROGRAM NARRATIVE                        *
 11        *                                                             *
 12        *                                                             *
 13        *    THIS PROGRAM READS ALL RECORDS IN THE CUSTOMER PREMIUM FILE.*
 14        *    ONE DETAIL LINE CONTAINING THE POLICY NUMBER, CUSTOMER NAME,*
 15        *    AGENT NAME, AND INSURANCE TYPE IS PRINTED FOR EACH RECORD *
 16        *    IN THE FILE.  A RECORD COUNT IS PROVIDED AT THE END OF THE *
 17        *    REPORT.                                                   *
 18        *                                                             *
 19        *       INPUT:      PREMIUM.DAT - PREMIUM INPUT FILE          *
 20        *                                                             *
 21        *       OUTPUT:     POLNUM.RPT  - POLICY NUMBER REPORT        *
 22        ****************************************************************
 23
 24        ENVIRONMENT DIVISION.
 25        *********************
 26
 27        INPUT-OUTPUT SECTION.
 28        *********************
 29
 30        FILE-CONTROL.
 31
 32            SELECT PREMIUM-INPUT-FILE
 33                ASSIGN TO "A:\PREMIUM.DAT".
 34
 35            SELECT POLICY-NUMBER-REPORT
 36                ASSIGN TO "A:\POLNUM.RPT".
 37
 38        /
 39        DATA DIVISION.
 40        **************
 41
 42        FILE SECTION.
 43        *************
 44
 45        *********************************************************
 46        *                                                       *
 47        *    INPUT-FILE - PREMIUM INPUT FILE                     *
 48        *                                                       *
 49        *********************************************************
 50
 51        FD  PREMIUM-INPUT-FILE.
 52
 53        01  PREMIUM-RECORD.
 54            02  PR-CUSTOMER-NAME        PIC X(20).
 55            02  PR-AGENT-NAME           PIC X(20).
 56            02  PR-INSURANCE-TYPE       PIC X(10).
 57            02  PR-POLICY-NUMBER        PIC X(12).
 58            02                          PIC X(18).
 59
 60        *********************************************************
 61        *                                                       *
 62        *    REPORT-FILE - POLICY NUMBER REPORT                  *
 63        *                                                       *
 64        *********************************************************
 65

 66        FD  POLICY-NUMBER-REPORT.
 67
 68        01  REPORT-LINE-OUT             PIC X(80).
 69
 70        /
 71        WORKING-STORAGE SECTION.
 72        ***********************
 73
 74        ****************************************************************
 75        *                                                             *
 76        *                    SWITCHES                                 *
 77        *                                                             *
 78        ****************************************************************
 79
 80        01  SWITCHES.
 81
 82            02  SW-END-OF-FILE          PIC X.
 83                88  END-OF-FILE                      VALUE "Y".
 84
 85        01  VALUES-FOR-SWITCHES.
 86            02  YES                     PIC X         VALUE "Y".
 87            02  NEG                     PIC X         VALUE "N".
 88
 89
 90        ****************************************************************
 91        *                                                             *
 92        *                    ACCUMULATORS                             *
 93        *                                                             *
 94        ****************************************************************
 95
 96        01  ACCUMULATORS.
 97
 98            02  AC-LINE-COUNT           PIC 999   PACKED-DECIMAL.
 99            02  AC-PAGE-COUNT           PIC 999   PACKED-DECIMAL.
100            02  AC-RECORD-COUNT         PIC 9(5)  PACKED-DECIMAL.
101        /
102        ****************************************************************
103        *                                                             *
104        *    REPORT HEADINGS FOR POLICY NUMBER REPORT                 *
105        *                                                             *
106        ****************************************************************
107
108        01  REPORT-HEADING.
109
110            02  RH-LINE-1.
111                03                      PIC X(27) VALUE SPACES.
112                03                      PIC X(20) VALUE
113                    "POLICY NUMBER REPORT".
114                03                      PIC X(22) VALUE SPACES.
115                03                      PIC X(5)  VALUE "PAGE ".
116                03  RH-PAGE-COUNT       PIC ZZ9.
117                03                      PIC XXX   VALUE SPACES.
118
119            02  RH-LINE-2.
120                03                      PIC X(13) VALUE
121                    "POLICY NUMBER".
122                03                      PIC XXX   VALUE SPACES.
123                03                      PIC X(13) VALUE
124                    "CUSTOMER NAME".
125                03                      PIC X(11) VALUE SPACES.
126                03                      PIC X(10) VALUE
127                    "AGENT NAME".
128                03                      PIC X(15) VALUE SPACES.
129                03                      PIC X(9)  VALUE
130                    "INS. TYPE".
```

FIGURE 2-8   The complete Policy Number Report program

```
131        03                          PIC X(6)  VALUE SPACES.
132
133     02  RH-LINE-3.
134        03                          PIC X(13) VALUE
135           "-------------".
136        03                          PIC XXX   VALUE SPACES.
137        03                          PIC X(13) VALUE
138           "-------------".
139        03                          PIC X(11) VALUE SPACES.
140        03                          PIC X(10) VALUE
141           "----------".
142        03                          PIC X(15) VALUE SPACES.
143        03                          PIC X(9)  VALUE
144           "---------".
145        03                          PIC X(6)  VALUE SPACES.
146 ******************************************************************
147 *                                                                *
148 *    DETAIL LINE FOR POLICY NUMBER REPORT                        *
149 *                                                                *
150 ******************************************************************
151
152  01  DETAIL-LINE.
153
154     02  DL-POLICY-NUMBER        PIC X(12).
155     02                          PIC X(4)   VALUE SPACES.
156     02  DL-CUSTOMER-NAME        PIC X(20).
157     02                          PIC X(4)   VALUE SPACES.
158     02  DL-AGENT-NAME           PIC X(20).
159     02                          PIC X(5)   VALUE SPACES.
160     02  DL-INSURANCE-TYPE       PIC X(10).
161     02                          PIC X(5)   VALUE SPACES.
162 /
163 ******************************************************************
164 *                                                                *
165 *    SUMMARY LINES FOR POLICY NUMBER REPORT                      *
166 *                                                                *
167 ******************************************************************
168
169  01  SUMMARY-LINES.
170
171     02  SL-LINE-1.
172        03                          PIC X(26) VALUE SPACES.
173        03                          PIC X(24) VALUE
174           "TOTAL RECORDS PRINTED = ".
175        03 SL-RECORD-COUNT          PIC ZZZZ9.
176        03                          PIC X(25) VALUE SPACES.
177
178     02  SL-LINE-2.
179        03                          PIC X(32) VALUE SPACES.
180        03                          PIC X(13) VALUE
181           "END OF REPORT".
182        03                          PIC X(35) VALUE SPACES.
183
184 /
185  PROCEDURE DIVISION.
186  ******************
187 ******************************************************************
188 *                                                                *
189 *  MAIN-PROGRAM - THIS IS THE MAIN ROUTINE OF THIS PROGRAM       *
190 *                                                                *
191 ******************************************************************
192
193  MAIN-PROGRAM.
194
195     PERFORM A-100-INITIALIZATION.
196     PERFORM B-100-PROCESS-FILE.
197     PERFORM C-100-WRAP-UP.
198     STOP RUN.
199
200 ******************************************************************
201 *                                                                *
202 *           THE INITIALIZATION ROUTINE FOLLOWS                   *
203 *                                                                *
204 ******************************************************************
205
206  A-100-INITIALIZATION.
207
208     MOVE ZERO TO AC-PAGE-COUNT
209               AC-LINE-COUNT
210               AC-RECORD-COUNT.
211
212     OPEN INPUT    PREMIUM-INPUT-FILE
213          OUTPUT   POLICY-MUMBER-REPORT.
214
215 /
216 ******************************************************************
217 *                                                                *
218 *         FILE PROCESSING CONTROL ROUTINE                        *
219 *                                                                *
220 ******************************************************************
221
222  B-100-PROCESS-FILE.
223
224     MOVE NEG TO SW-END-OF-FILE.
225     READ PREMIUM-INPUT-FILE
226        AT END MOVE YES TO SW-END-OF-FILE.
227     PERFORM B-200-PROCESS-RECORD
228        UNTIL END-OF-FILE.
229     MOVE AC-RECORD-COUNT TO SL-RECORD-COUNT.
230     WRITE REPORT-LINE-OUT FROM SL-LINE-1
231        AFTER ADVANCING 3 LINES.
232     WRITE REPORT-LINE-OUT FROM SL-LINE-2
233        AFTER ADVANCING 3 LINES.
234 /
235 ******************************************************************
236 *                                                                *
237 *      MOVE INPUT FIELDS TO OUTPUT AREAS AND PRINT               *
238 *                                                                *
239 ******************************************************************
240
241  B-200-PROCESS-RECORD.
242
243     IF AC-LINE-COUNT = 0
244        PERFORM B-300-PRINT-HEADINGS.
245
246     MOVE PR-POLICY-NUMBER   TO DL-POLICY-NUMBER.
247     MOVE PR-CUSTOMER-NAME   TO DL-CUSTOMER-NAME.
248     MOVE PR-AGENT-NAME      TO DL-AGENT-NAME.
249     MOVE PR-INSURANCE-TYPE  TO DL-INSURANCE-TYPE.
250
251     WRITE REPORT-LINE-OUT FROM DETAIL-LINE
252        AFTER ADVANCING 1 LINE.
253     ADD 1 TO AC-LINE-COUNT.
254     ADD 1 TO AC-RECORD-COUNT.
255
256     IF AC-LINE-COUNT > 55
257        MOVE ZERO TO AC-LINE-COUNT.
258
259     READ PREMIUM-INPUT-FILE
260        AT END MOVE YES TO SW-END-OF-FILE.
261
262 ******************************************************************
263 *                                                                *
264 *                 HEADER ROUTINE                                 *
265 *                                                                *
266 ******************************************************************
267
268  B-300-PRINT-HEADINGS.
269
270     ADD 1 TO AC-PAGE-COUNT.
271     MOVE AC-PAGE-COUNT TO RH-PAGE-COUNT.
272     WRITE REPORT-LINE-OUT FROM RH-LINE-1
273        AFTER ADVANCING PAGE.
274     WRITE REPORT-LINE-OUT FROM RH-LINE-2
275        AFTER ADVANCING 2 LINES.
276     WRITE REPORT-LINE-OUT FROM RH-LINE-3
277        AFTER ADVANCING 1 LINES.
278     MOVE 4 TO AC-LINE-COUNT.
279 /
280 ******************************************************************
281 *                                                                *
282 *                 END OF JOB ROUTINE                             *
283 *                                                                *
284 ******************************************************************
285
286  C-100-WRAP-UP.
287
288     CLOSE PREMIUM-INPUT-FILE
289           POLICY-NUMBER-REPORT.
290
291 /
```

The majority of businesses using COBOL have a set of rules, or standards, to follow. These standards are designed to improve programmer productivity and cut down on the time and effort needed to revise existing programs. By imposing a set of standards on its programmers, a **COBOL shop**, as a business using COBOL is called, maintains consistency in its programs and thus makes it easier for programmers to move from one program to another. If all programmers follow the same standards, then all the programs should have a similar style.

The following discussion of the sample program contains a set of development guidelines. Future programs in this book will adhere to these same guidelines, which are offered to assist you in the development of your own programs.

IDENTIFICATION DIVISION

As noted in Chapter 1, every COBOL program begins with an **IDENTIFICATION DIVISION**. The IDENTIFICATION DIVISION for the sample program is reprinted in Figure 2-9. The IDENTIFICATION DIVISION header is the first line of code in the program. Notice that this header ends with a period. In COBOL, all entries are terminated with periods. In some cases, an entry may require several lines. In such cases, the period is not inserted until the multiple-line entry is complete. The IDENTIFICATION DIVISION header in line 1 must begin in the A-margin. For the programs in this book, any entry that must begin in the A-margin will begin in column 8. The asterisks in line 2 under the IDENTIFICATION DIVISION header are a comment line. The first asterisk is in column 7 and just enough asterisks are used to highlight the header, although any number of asterisks could be used. Notice back in Figure 2-8 on pages 2-10 and 2-11 that underlining with asterisks is used for all division headers and section headers in the program. They are not required by COBOL but are included to enhance the readability of the code. Your programs should be as neat and as readable as possible.

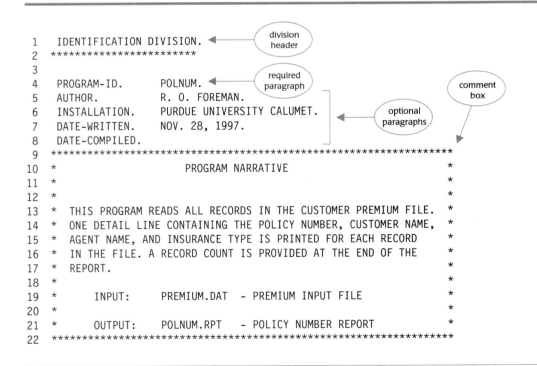

```
 1    IDENTIFICATION DIVISION.          ← division header
 2    ************************
 3
 4    PROGRAM-ID.      POLNUM.          ← required paragraph
 5    AUTHOR.          R. O. FOREMAN.
 6    INSTALLATION.    PURDUE UNIVERSITY CALUMET.    ← optional paragraphs
 7    DATE-WRITTEN.    NOV. 28, 1997.
 8    DATE-COMPILED.
 9    ****************************************************************    ← comment box
10    *                    PROGRAM NARRATIVE                        *
11    *                                                             *
12    *                                                             *
13    *    THIS PROGRAM READS ALL RECORDS IN THE CUSTOMER PREMIUM FILE. *
14    *    ONE DETAIL LINE CONTAINING THE POLICY NUMBER, CUSTOMER NAME, *
15    *    AGENT NAME, AND INSURANCE TYPE IS PRINTED FOR EACH RECORD    *
16    *    IN THE FILE. A RECORD COUNT IS PROVIDED AT THE END OF THE    *
17    *    REPORT.                                                   *
18    *                                                             *
19    *        INPUT:     PREMIUM.DAT   - PREMIUM INPUT FILE         *
20    *                                                             *
21    *        OUTPUT:    POLNUM.RPT    - POLICY NUMBER REPORT       *
22    ****************************************************************
```

FIGURE 2-9   IDENTIFICATION DIVISION

The asterisks underlining the IDENTIFICATION DIVISION header are followed by a blank line (Figure 2-9, line 3). **Blank lines** may be used freely within COBOL programs to improve readability.

The IDENTIFICATION DIVISION is made up of paragraph headers. Each paragraph header, or name, begins in the A-margin (Figure 2-9, lines 4 through 8). In this book, paragraph names always begin in column 8. The entries following the paragraph names must be in the B-margin.

PROGRAM-ID

The only required entry in the IDENTIFICATION DIVISION is the **PROGRAM-ID** paragraph (Figure 2-9, line 4). The program name following PROGRAM-ID may be any valid user-defined COBOL word as described in Chapter 1. This name is used by the computer's operating system to identify the object program created when the program is compiled. In many computer systems, if the PROGRAM-ID entry is longer than eight characters, only the first eight are recognized by the operating system.

AUTHOR, INSTALLATION, DATE-WRITTEN, DATE-COMPILED

The remaining paragraphs in the IDENTIFICATION DIVISION are not required, but are useful for documentation purposes. You may enter whatever you like after **AUTHOR**, **INSTALLATION**, and **DATE-WRITTEN**, unless specific guidelines are provided by your instructor or employer. The entries following these paragraph names are aligned with the PROGRAM-ID entry, though COBOL does not require it. The programmer's name is listed after the AUTHOR paragraph header. The INSTALLATION should include the company name or organization for which the program is being written. DATE-WRITTEN is often the **installation date** of the program, that is, the date it is expected to be ready for production.

The **DATE-COMPILED** paragraph is usually left blank. When this paragraph name is present, most systems automatically insert a date after it every time the program is compiled. A sixth paragraph, **SECURITY**, is not used in the sample program but may be included in the IDENTIFICATION DIVISION. This entry also is treated as a comment.

Comment Box

Lines 9 through 22 in Figure 2-9 contain a series of comments. The comment box begins in column 7 and continues to column 72. Remember that an asterisk in column 7 identifies a comment line and column 72 is the last position available on a line. Thus, the **comment box** serves the added purpose of denoting the last position available for each program line following the comment box. Within the comment box, there is a brief program narrative followed by identification of the input and output files used in the program. Comment lines are ignored by the compiler. Therefore, you may include any words you want within a comment line.

Format Notation

Technical reference manuals developed for COBOL and other languages provide a standard format notation for the various elements of a language. These generalized descriptions are intended to guide the programmer when writing programs. The format notation for the IDENTIFICATION DIVISION is illustrated in Figure 2-10 on the next page. Appendix D contains a complete list of the basic COBOL formats presented in this book.

```
IDENTIFICATION DIVISION.
PROGRAM-ID.  program-name.
[AUTHOR.  [comment-entry] ...]
[INSTALLATION.  [comment-entry] ...]
[DATE-WRITTEN.  [comment-entry] ...]
[DATE-COMPILED.  [comment-entry] ...]
[SECURITY.  [comment-entry] ...]
```

FIGURE 2-10   Basic format of the IDENTIFICATION DIVISION

It is important that you understand this system of notation. The rules for format notations are summarized in the following paragraphs.

1. All words printed entirely in capital letters are reserved words. These words have defined meanings in the COBOL language and are not to be used for any other purpose. In all formats, words written in capital letters and selected for use in a COBOL program must be coded exactly as they appear in the format notation. A complete list of COBOL reserved words is given in Appendix C of this book.

2. All underlined reserved words are required unless the portion of the format containing them is itself optional. These are key words. If any such word is missing or is spelled incorrectly, it is considered a syntax error in the program and will be identified and marked by the compiler. Reserved words that are not underlined may be used or omitted at your option. If they are included, they must be spelled properly.

3. Lowercase words represent information that must be supplied by the programmer.

4. Punctuation, except for commas and semicolons, is required where it is shown. Commas and semicolons are optional. Ellipses (...) indicate that an entry can be repeated.

5. Square brackets ([ ]) are used to indicate that the enclosed item may be used or omitted, depending on the requirements of the particular program.

6. When braces ({ }) enclose a portion of a basic format, one of the options within the braces must be specified or a default value will be used.

7. Options are indicated in a basic format by vertically stacking alternative possibilities, by a series of brackets or braces, or by a combination of both. An option is selected by specifying one of the possibilities from the stack of alternative possibilities or by specifying a combination of possibilities from a series of brackets or braces.

8. Except where noted, entries must be written in the sequence given in the basic formats.

By applying the above rules of format notation to the IDENTIFICATION DIVISION, it can be seen that AUTHOR, INSTALLATION, DATE-WRITTEN, DATE-COMPILED, and SECURITY are optional because they are enclosed in brackets. The division header and the PROGRAM-ID paragraph are the only required entries in the IDENTIFICATION DIVISION.

ENVIRONMENT DIVISION

The second division of a COBOL program is the **ENVIRONMENT DIVISION**. It is the most system-dependent part of a COBOL program. The primary purpose of the ENVIRONMENT DIVISION is to supply the program with actual system names for input and output files and allow these names to be linked to user-defined names. Taking a program developed on a personal computer, minicomputer, or mainframe platform and moving it to another platform usually requires that the ENVIRONMENT DIVISION be altered. Although the basic format of the ENVIRONMENT DIVISION allows for both a **CONFIGURATION SECTION** and **INPUT-OUTPUT SECTION**, the sample program's ENVIRONMENT DIVISION contains only the INPUT-OUTPUT SECTION. The CONFIGURATION SECTION is not always needed, but it is used when a program must access special hardware-related items.

The INPUT-OUTPUT SECTION in the ENVIRONMENT DIVISION (Figure 2-11) assigns names to files that are used for input and output. The **FILE-CONTROL** paragraph contains SELECT entries that assign user-defined names to the system names. **System names** are platform-dependent, and the exact format can vary between computer manufacturers. The system names A:\PREMIUM.DAT and A:\POLNUM.DAT in Figure 2-11 are as they would appear for use on a personal computer.

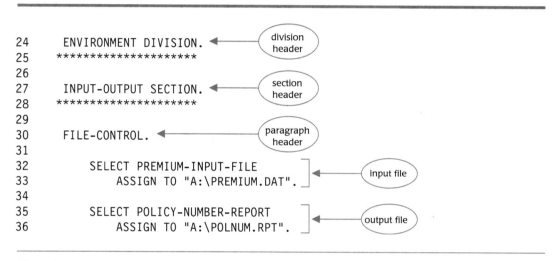

FIGURE 2-11   ENVIRONMENT DIVISION

SELECT Entries

The basic format of the SELECT that will be used for most of the programs in this book is shown in Figure 2-12. Additional entries in the SELECT statement will be discussed later.

```
SELECT file-name
    ASSIGN TO implementor-name-1 [implementor-name-2] ... .
```

FIGURE 2-12   Basic format of a SELECT

The word **SELECT** is used to define a name for each file to be used within the program. A file name can be any user-defined COBOL word. The user-defined names selected here are PREMIUM-INPUT-FILE and POLICY-NUMBER-REPORT. The **ASSIGN** entry is used to assign the user-defined file name to the true system name or device name used for the file. In the general format, **implementor-name** represents system names or device names as they are defined on the computer system.

The system you use may require a different naming convention after the ASSIGN than that used in this book. Your instructor should supply you with the appropriate information. Lines 32 and 33 in Figure 2-11 show the SELECT and ASSIGN for the Premium file used as the input file in the program. Lines 35 and 36 in Figure 2-11 show the SELECT and ASSIGN for the output report file. In both cases, the names in quotes represent files. The file PREMIUM.DAT is to be used as input and, therefore, must be available on the computer system. The A:\ preceding the filename PREMIUM.DAT indicates that the file is on a diskette in the A-drive of the personal computer being used. The other file, POLNUM.RPT, is an output file and will be created by the program on the diskette in the A-drive.

The SELECT entry and its associated ASSIGN are used only to define the name for a file and associate it with the computer's system name for the file. Defining the length and format of the records in the file is done in the DATA DIVISION of the COBOL program.

DATA DIVISION

The **DATA DIVISION** describes the files and data to be processed by the program. The DATA DIVISION is subdivided into the FILE SECTION and WORKING-STORAGE SECTION.

FILE SECTION

The **FILE SECTION** describes the content and organization of the files to be processed. In addition, **record description** entries that describe the individual fields contained in the records of a file are coded. The Policy Number Report program's FILE SECTION appears as shown in Figure 2-13.

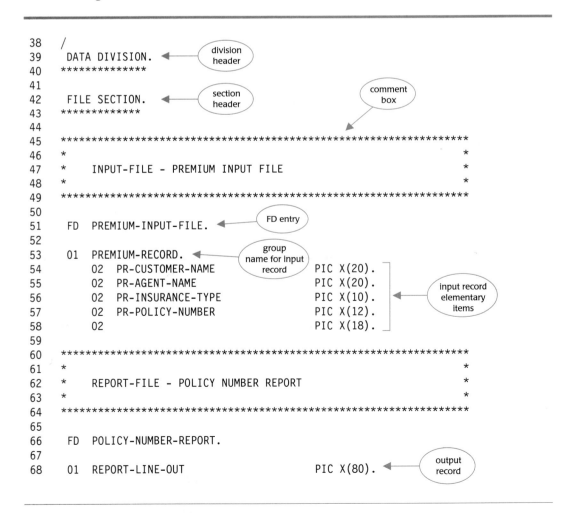

FIGURE 2-13   FILE SECTION of the DATA DIVISION

The slash (/) in the indicator area (column 7) on line 38 is a signal to the COBOL compiler that there should be a page break at this point in the source code listing produced by the compiler. Page breaks should occur on natural boundaries within the source code listing. For example, a page should never break in the middle of a comment box.

The balance of the entries in the FILE SECTION are used to provide a general description of the content and organization of the records contained in the files. The basic format for the FILE SECTION is shown in Figure 2-14.

```
DATA DIVISION.

FILE SECTION.

FD   file-name

[    ; RECORD CONTAINS [integer-1 TO ] integer-2 CHARACTERS ]

[    ; BLOCK CONTAINS [integer-3 TO] integer-4   { RECORDS    } ]
                                                 { CHARACTERS }

[    ; LABEL   { RECORD IS   }   { STANDARD } ]
              { RECORDS ARE  }   { OMITTED  }

[    ; DATA    { RECORD IS   }   data-name-1, [,data-name-2] ... ]
              { RECORDS ARE  }

[record-description-entry] ...
```

FIGURE 2-14   Basic format of the FILE SECTION

The division header, DATA DIVISION, is a required entry. It must appear on a line by itself and be followed by a period and a space. The FILE SECTION is required whenever files are being accessed or created by the program.

The section header FILE SECTION must appear on a separate line below DATA DIVISION. Both DATA DIVISION and FILE SECTION must begin in the A-margin.

FD Level Indicator

FD is an abbreviation for File Description and an **FD level indicator** is used for each file to be processed by the program (lines 51 and 66 in Figure 2-13). Thus, there will be an FD for each SELECT entry in the FILE-CONTROL paragraph of the ENVIRONMENT DIVISION. The name following FD must be the same user-defined name used following SELECT in the FILE-CONTROL paragraph. The FD entry must begin in the A-margin and the file name must begin in the B-margin.

The RECORD CONTAINS, BLOCK CONTAINS, LABEL RECORD, and DATA RECORD clauses shown in the basic format in Figure 2-14 are all optional entries and will not be used in this book. The RECORD CONTAINS entry can be used to document the logical record length for the file being defined. The BLOCK CONTAINS entry can be used to document the size of a block of logical records. The LABEL RECORD entry was required in COBOL 74 and was used to specify the presence or absence of a standard or nonstandard label on files. This task in now performed by the operating system. When required, STANDARD is used in the LABEL RECORD entry for disk files and most tape files. OMITTED applies only to some tape files and to **unit record** input or output devices including scanners, card readers, and printers.

The DATA RECORD entry can be used to specify the name of the record(s) within the file, but it is strictly a form of documentation. When used, the name specified must correspond to the record(s) defined immediately following the FD entry. A period follows the last entry of the FD to terminate the FD. In Figure 2-13, none of the optional FD clauses was used. Therefore, the period is immediately to the right of the file name in each of the two FDs (lines 51 and 66 in Figure 2-13). Table 2-1 summarizes the use of FD entries.

TABLE 2-1   Optional FD Entries

FD Clause	Entry	Use
RECORD CONTAINS	num CHARACTERS	Indicates the number of characters in each record
BLOCK CONTAINS	num RECORDS	Specifies the number of records per block of records
	num CHARACTERS	Specifies the number of characters per block of records
LABEL RECORD(S) IS ARE	STANDARD	Specifies that header labels are used on disk and tape files
	OMITTED	Used for printer files or other unit record devices
DATA RECORD(S) IS ARE	record-name	Identifies logical record name

Be careful when inserting periods in your program. Too many or too few periods can cause both syntax and logic errors in COBOL programs. Avoid punctuation errors by paying strict attention to the format notations and examples given in this book.

Level Numbers

Level numbers are used to show how data items or fields are related to each other. The level number 01 is used to specify an individual record or group of related fields. The basic format for a level number entry is shown in Figure 2-15. Level numbers can range in value from 01 to 49. Special level numbers, 77 and 88, will be introduced later. The **01** and **77 level numbers** must begin in the A-margin. Other level numbers begin in the B-margin.

```
level-number  [ {data-name}  ]    [ {PICTURE}  IS character-string  ]
              [ {FILLER   }  ]    [ {PIC    }                        ]
```

FIGURE 2-15   Basic format of level numbers

Following an FD, names are assigned to be used in conjunction with the records in the files. The 01 entry following each of the FDs defines a logical record name for the file being defined. The 01 entry after the FD for the PREMIUM-INPUT-FILE is PREMIUM-RECORD (line 53 in Figure 2-13). The 01 entry after the FD for the output POLICY-NUMBER-REPORT is REPORT-LINE-OUT. These required entries form a very important part of the program.

Level numbers are used throughout the DATA DIVISION to define names that represent data items manipulated within the program. Level numbers are used to define switches, accumulators, and counters, and to define output record layouts for reports. These items will be discussed later in this chapter. The entry on line 53 in Figure 2-13 on page 2-16, 01 PREMIUM-RECORD, is used to define a name for the PREMIUM-INPUT-FILE record layout. The entry on line 68 in Figure 2-13, 01 REPORT-LINE-OUT, is used to define a name for the POLICY-NUMBER-REPORT record layout. PREMIUM-RECORD is a **group name** because it has no picture clause and is subdivided into subordinate items with other level numbers. REPORT-LINE-OUT is an **elementary item** because it has a picture clause and is not subdivided into other items. Picture clauses are discussed in the next section.

Subordinate data items that constitute a record or group of related fields are grouped in a hierarchy and are identified using the level numbers 02 through 49. All data items defined under an 01 level group name are subordinate to that group name until the next 01 or FD is encountered. The numbers 02 through 48 also may be used to define group names. Level number 49 can never define a group name because it is the maximum level number available for defining items.

In Figure 2-13, the level number 02 is used to identify the fields within the records of the PREMIUM-INPUT-FILE. Four fields are defined under PREMIUM-RECORD. Any number higher than 01 could have been used here. Some programmers prefer to go from 01 to 03 using odd level numbers thereafter. Others go from 01 to 05 using level numbers divisible by five thereafter. It will be the standard in this book to use consecutive level numbers 01, 02, 03, and so on when defining and subdividing group items.

The data names on lines 54 through 57 in Figure 2-13 are all user-defined names and follow the naming rules discussed earlier. The data names defined for fields that are referenced later should be meaningful and describe the actual contents of the field. The names used here, PR-CUSTOMER-NAME, PR-AGENT-NAME, PR-INSURANCE-TYPE, and PR-POLICY-NUMBER, accurately represent the content of each field within the record. Well-chosen names are important, especially when debugging programs, so you can easily identify the purpose of the field. The entry on line 58 has a level number but no name. Such entries are called filler entries, and they will be discussed later in this chapter.

For readability, the 02 level numbers have been indented four spaces from the 01 level number and the data names have been coded two spaces from the level numbers. This adds clarity to the program. The prefix on the data names, PR, is for documentation purposes and comes from the 01 level name PREMIUM-RECORD. Because an 02 item is subordinate to an 01 item, where you see a reference to a PR field, you will know that it is defined under, and is part of, PREMIUM-RECORD. A two- or three-letter prefix will be used on most data names throughout this book for the reasons just mentioned. These two- or three-letter prefixes refer to 01 level group names.

As discussed earlier, subordinate items that are not subdivided are called elementary items. Each of the 02 level entries under the group name PREMIUM-RECORD in Figure 2-13 is an elementary item. Elementary items must contain a picture clause.

Picture Clauses

A **picture clause** specifies a detailed description of an elementary item. This description indicates the number of characters in the data item and the type of data, such as letters only (**alphabetic**); numbers only (**numeric**); or letters, numbers, and special characters (alphanumeric). Only numeric fields can be used in arithmetic operations. The word PICTURE may be used to identify a picture clause, but the abbreviation **PIC** is preferred.

Table 2-2 on the next page presents examples and explanations of picture clauses. In order to define an alphanumeric field, the letter X is used in forming a character string that follows the PIC clause. For alphabetic fields, the letter A is used and for numeric fields, the number 9 is used. A value within parentheses following an A, X, or 9 is a **duplicating factor** and defines the size of the field. The picture clauses PIC XXX and PIC X(3) have the same meaning. As a rule, use what requires the fewest keystrokes. Hence, PIC X(1) is valid, but PIC X should be used. Likewise, PIC XXXXX is valid, but PIC X(5) takes fewer keystrokes. The maximum number of characters allowed in a picture clause is 30. With the use of a duplicating factor, however, you can define entries that are greater than 30 characters. For example, PIC X(68) assigns the corresponding item a size of 68 characters.

TABLE 2-2   Examples of Picture Clauses

Picture Clause	Category	Description
PIC A	Alphabetic	One-character field
PIC AAA		Three-character field
PIC A(6)		Six-character field
PIC X	Alphanumeric	One-character field
PIC XXX		Three-character field
PIX X(6)		Six-character field
PIC 9	Numeric	One-digit number
PIC 999		Three-digit number
PIC 9(6)		Six-digit number

In the record layout for PREMIUM-RECORD, shown in Figure 2-13 on page 2-16, you can see that PR-CUSTOMER-NAME and PR-AGENT-NAME are each 20 character alphanumeric fields. PR-INSURANCE-TYPE is a 10 character alphanumeric field and PR-POLICY-NUMBER is a 12 character alphanumeric field. The four fields along with the 18 unused characters total 80 characters, or bytes, which is the length of each record in the PREMIUM-INPUT-FILE. To define an input record layout in a program, the layout of the records on auxiliary storage must be known. The layouts must agree in character length and field position. A program will produce erroneous results if the layout in the program and the actual format of the records disagree.

Picture clauses can begin anywhere in the B-margin; however, to retain neatness and readability, they should be aligned as shown in Figure 2-13.

The 01 level item REPORT-LINE-OUT under the FD for the POLICY-NUMBER-REPORT (Figure 2-13, line 68) has a picture clause and is, therefore, an elementary item. The output report will have a number of different output lines, such as heading lines, detail lines, and summary lines. Thus, REPORT-LINE-OUT is not subdivided into elementary items as was the case with PREMIUM-RECORD. The layouts for the report lines are defined in the WORKING-STORAGE SECTION of the DATA DIVISION. In Figure 2-13, the 01 level item, REPORT-LINE-OUT, declares each output report line to be 80 characters long. This 01 level name is important, not only because it defines the maximum length of an output line, but also because it will be used later in the PROCEDURE DIVISION in the WRITE statement.

WORKING-STORAGE SECTION

The FILE SECTION of the DATA DIVISION describes the content and organization of the files to be processed within the program. The only fields described in the FILE SECTION are those found in the records of the input and output files. Normally, as in the Policy Number Report program, other fields must be defined. These might not be part of any record layout, but are necessary to accomplish the task of the program. Switches are used in the decision-making logic of a program. **Accumulators**, or counters, are used in arithmetic and contain sums. Output record layouts define the printed formats for the heading lines, detail lines, and summary lines.

Such fields are defined in the **WORKING-STORAGE SECTION** of the DATA DIVISION. The WORKING-STORAGE SECTION of the Policy Number Report program (Figures 2-16, 2-18, and 2-19) has a number of different fields in it and is organized so that related fields are grouped together. This is not required but, again, makes a program easier to read and maintain. The various entries in the WORKING-STORAGE SECTION will now be examined. Each entry in the WORKING-STORAGE SECTION begins with a level number.

SWITCHES

Figure 2-16 shows the beginning of the WORKING-STORAGE SECTION. The slash (/) in column 7 of line 70 forces a page break in the compiler-created listing of the source code so the WORKING-STORAGE SECTION begins on a new page. The title, WORKING-STORAGE SECTION (line 71), must be written on a line by itself, begin in the A-margin, and be followed by a period. The first group of fields defined in the WORKING-STORAGE SECTION are the program switches under the group name SWITCHES (line 80 in Figure 2-16). Only one switch currently exists, yet the group name SWITCHES is used should the need arise to add another switch. Each switch would have a two-letter prefix of SW. A **switch** in a program is either on or off (true or false). The switch, SW-END-OF-FILE, is defined on line 82 as a one character alpha-numeric field (PIC X).

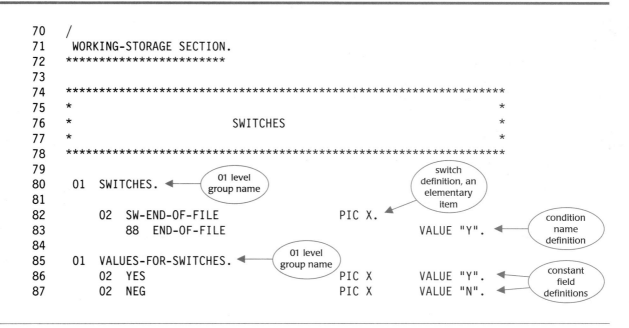

FIGURE 2-16   Switches in WORKING-STORAGE SECTION

The **88 level entry** on line 83, END-OF-FILE, is called a condition name. A **condition name** either is true or false, depending on the contents of the field under which it is defined. The **VALUE clause** in an 88 level entry establishes the value that makes the condition name true. Thus, the condition name END-OF-FILE will be true when the field SW-END-OF-FILE is equal to Y. If SW-END-OF-FILE is equal to another value, the condition name END-OF-FILE is false. An 88 level entry does not reserve storage. An 88 level condition name allows you to base a decision on a name rather than on a condition such as SW-END-OF-FILE = "Y". Condition names will be discussed further in Chapter 3.

The 01 level item VALUES-FOR-SWITCHES (line 85) is used to group together two constant fields, YES and NEG, which are used in conjunction with the switch. A **constant** is a field that will not change value during the execution of the program. If there were more than one switch, the fields YES and NEG would be used with them also. YES and NEG are defined as one-character fields and are assigned values of Y and N, respectively. When a VALUE clause follows a picture clause, the VALUE clause initializes the field to the specified value. The value in the quotation marks is called a **literal**. The basic format for a VALUE clause is shown in Figure 2-17 on the next page.

```
[ VALUE IS literal ]
```

FIGURE 2-17   Basic format of the VALUE clause

The VALUE clause is an optional entry. Often, it is used after picture clauses to assign a value to a field. **Variable fields**, such as SW-END-OF-FILE or the 02 level fields defined under PREMIUM-RECORD in Figure 2-13 on page 2-16, whose values will change during execution, usually are not initialized with a VALUE clause. The literal in the VALUE clause must be of a type consistent with the picture clause. Hence, numeric literals are used to initialize numeric fields and nonnumeric literals in quotation marks are used to initialize alphanumeric fields. Literals must be less than or equal to a field's defined length. As a result of the VALUE clauses used with YES and NEG in Figure 2-16 on the previous page, YES will be a one-character field with a Y in it and NEG will be a one-character field with an N in it when the program begins executing. These values will remain the same, unless some action within the program changes the contents of YES and NEG.

The name NEG is used, rather than NO, in the Policy Number Report program because **NO** is a COBOL reserved word and cannot be a user-defined name in the program.

ACCUMULATORS

The next group of fields defined in the WORKING-STORAGE SECTION in the Policy Number Report program are those used to count lines of output, pages of output, and the number of records processed (Figure 2-18). The 01 level name (line 96) is ACCUMULATORS. Each of the fields at the 02-level has the two letter prefix of AC.

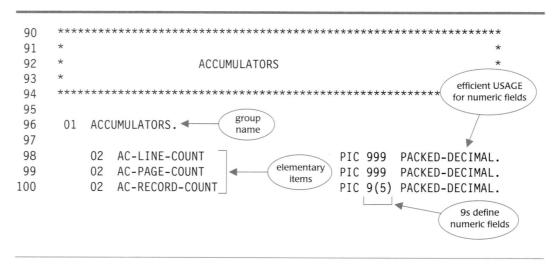

FIGURE 2-18   Accumulators in WORKING-STORAGE

AC-LINE-COUNT, AC-PAGE-COUNT, and AC-RECORD-COUNT are numeric fields. A 9 in a picture clause is used to define a numeric field. The 999 means that AC-LINE-COUNT and AC-PAGE-COUNT can hold up to three digits. The 9(5) for AC-RECORD-COUNT means it can hold up to five digits. PACKED-DECIMAL indicates the field's usage. PACKED-DECIMAL fields efficiently store values that are to be arithmetically manipulated. Usage will be discussed in Chapter 3.

Output Records

The remaining entries in the WORKING-STORAGE SECTION define the format of the output lines written to the report (Figure 2-19). As discussed earlier in Figure 2-13, the 01 level entry under the FD for the POLICY-NUMBER-REPORT defines an 80 character output record called REPORT-LINE-OUT. Each of the output lines defined in Figure 2-19 defines the format of a line that will be written to the POLICY-NUMBER-REPORT file. Each of the lines totals 80 characters.

The 01 level name on line 108, REPORT-HEADING, is a group name. The 02 level items below it are also group names and define the three heading lines used in the POLICY-NUMBER-REPORT. Below the 02 level name on line 110, RH-LINE-1, all of the entries for the first heading line are defined. Below the 02 level name on line 119, RH-LINE-2, all of the entries for the second heading line are defined. Below the 02 level name on line 133, RH-LINE-3, all of the entries for the third heading line are defined. Although it does not matter to COBOL, try to order output record definitions based on their planned sequence of use in the report.

RH-LINE-1 is the first heading line. If a name is not given to a field, the COBOL reserved word FILLER must be used or the field name area must be left blank. The word FILLER and no field name both define a **filler entry**. Only fields that will be referenced later in the program need user-defined names. Lines 111, 112, 114, 115, and 117 below RH-LINE-1 in Figure 2-19 all illustrate filler entries.

```
101    /
102    **************************************************************************
103    *                                                                    *
104    *    REPORT HEADINGS FOR POLICY NUMBER REPORT                         *
105    *                                                                    *
106    **************************************************************************
107
108    01  REPORT-HEADING.
109                                         first
110        02  RH-LINE-1.      ◄────    heading line
111            03                         begins        PIC X(27) VALUE SPACES.
112            03                                       PIC X(20) VALUE
113                "POLICY NUMBER REPORT".
114            03                                       PIC X(22) VALUE SPACES.
115            03                                       PIC X(5)  VALUE "PAGE ".
116            03  RH-PAGE-COUNT                        PIC ZZ9.
117            03                                       PIC X(3)  VALUE SPACES.
118                                         second
119        02  RH-LINE-2.      ◄────    heading line
120            03                         begins        PIC X(13) VALUE
121                "POLICY NUMBER".
122            03                                       PIC X(3)  VALUE SPACES.
123            03                                       PIC X(13) VALUE
124                "CUSTOMER NAME".
125            03                                       PIC X(11) VALUE SPACES.
126            03                                       PIC X(10) VALUE
127                "AGENT NAME".
128            03                                       PIC X(15) VALUE SPACES.
129            03                                       PIC X(9)  VALUE
130                "INS. TYPE".
131            03                                       PIC X(6)  VALUE SPACES.
```

FIGURE 2-19 Output record definitions in WORKING-STORAGE   (continued)

```
132
133        02  RH-LINE-3.              ◄─── third
134            03                           heading line        PIC X(13) VALUE
135                "_____-".              begins
136            03                                               PIC X(3)  VALUE SPACES.
137            03                                               PIC X(13) VALUE
138                "_____-".
139            03                                               PIC X(11) VALUE SPACES.
140            03                                               PIC X(10)  VALUE
141                "_____".
142            03                                               PIC X(15) VALUE SPACES.
143            03                                               PIC X(9)  VALUE
144                "_____-".
145            03                                               PIC X(6)  VALUE SPACES.
146    ***************************************************************************
147    *                                                                         *
148    *     DETAIL LINE FOR POLICY REPORT                                       *
149    *                                                                         *
150    ***************************************************************************
151
152    01  DETAIL-LINE.                ◄─── detail line
153                                         begins
154        02  DL-POLICY-NUMBER               PIC X(12).
155        02                                 PIC X(4)     VALUE SPACES.
156        02  DL-CUSTOMER-NAME               PIC X(20).
157        02                                 PIC X(4)     VALUE SPACES.
158        02  DL-AGENT-NAME                  PIC X(20).
159        02                                 PIC X(5)     VALUE SPACES.
160        02  DL-INSURANCE-TYPE              PIC X(10).
161        02                                 PIC X(5)     VALUE SPACES.
162  /
163    ***************************************************************************
164    *                                                                         *
165    *     SUMMARY LINES FOR POLICY REPORT                                     *
166    *                                                                         *
167    ***************************************************************************
168
169    01  SUMMARY-LINES.
170                                    ◄─── first
171        02  SL-LINE-1.                   summary line
172            03                           begins          PIC X(26)  VALUE SPACES.
173            03                                           PIC X(24)  VALUE
174                "TOTAL RECORDS PRINTED = ".
175            03  SL-RECORD-COUNT                          PIC ZZZZ9.
176            03                                           PIC X(25)  VALUE SPACES.
177                                    ◄─── second
178        02  SL-LINE-2.                   summary line
179            03                           begins          PIC X(32)  VALUE SPACES.
180            03                                           PIC X(13)  VALUE
181                "END OF REPORT".
182            03                                           PIC X(35)  VALUE SPACES.
```

FIGURE 2-19 Output record definitions in WORKING-STORAGE (continued)

The 03 level filler entries below RH-LINE-1 reserve storage locations that are initialized with VALUE clauses. Notice that line 113 does not define a separate item, but is a continuation of line 112. COBOL allows you to freely continue entries on subsequent lines as long as you do not try to break in the middle of a word or literal value. The word SPACES is a reserved word called a **figurative constant**. The figurative constant **SPACES** means the same as a nonnumeric literal with blanks in it such as " ".

Line 116 defines an area for the page number. This is the only field under RH-LINE-1 that is not a filler entry. Before RH-LINE-1 is written to the report, an instruction in the PROCEDURE DIVISION will move the contents of AC-PAGE-COUNT to RH-PAGE-COUNT. The picture ZZ9 is an edit pattern. An **edit pattern** specifies the format to be used when printing a numeric field. The edit pattern ZZ9 calls for the suppression of leading zeros in the two leftmost digit positions. The rightmost digit will print regardless of its value. Hence, if the value of AC-PAGE-COUNT is 001, it would print with two blanks, or spaces, in front of the 1. The value 000 would print as 0, with two blanks, or spaces, in front of the zero. Edit patterns will be discussed in Chapter 3.

RH-LINE-2 on line 119 in Figure 2-19 on page 2-23consists entirely of filler entries and defines column headings for the report. RH-LINE-3 is used to underline the column headings. If you are having trouble visualizing these lines, review Figure 2-2 on page 2-3. The heading lines will be printed at the top of each page in the report.

The definition for DETAIL-LINE begins on line 152 in Figure 2-19. DETAIL-LINE will be written to the report once for every input record that is processed. DETAIL-LINE is subdivided into both filler entries and named fields. The output field names DL-POLICY-NUMBER, DL-CUSTOMER-NAME, DL-AGENT-NAME, and DL-INSURANCE-TYPE correspond to the input fields defined under PREMIUM-RECORD in Figure 2-13 on page 2-16. The field names in DETAIL-LINE are not in the same sequence as in PREMIUM-RECORD. The fields in a detail line often are organized in a sequence different from the input record definition. Notice, however, that the output field sizes are exactly the same as the corresponding input fields. During processing, after the records are read, the program moves the input fields in PREMIUM-RECORD to the output fields in DETAIL-LINE and then writes DETAIL-LINE to the report.

Line 169 of the program defines the group name SUMMARY-LINES, which is subdivided into two different output lines. The program prints these lines when it runs out of input records to process. SL-LINE-1 (line 171) prints a message along with the actual count of records processed. Line 175 defines an output field, SL-RECORD-COUNT, to which the program moves the contents of AC-RECORD-COUNT before the line is written. Notice that SL-RECORD-COUNT defines a five-digit number edit pattern. The five-digit edit pattern corresponds to the size of AC-RECORD-COUNT. Again, the Zs in the edit pattern call for the suppression of leading zeroes. SL-LINE-2 is the last line that the program writes to the report. It contains the message END OF REPORT. All reports should end with such a message.

This marks the end of the WORKING-STORAGE SECTION and also the end of the DATA DIVISION of the program. The PROCEDURE DIVISION will be reviewed next. The PROCEDURE DIVISION contains instructions that instruct the computer how to process the data in the PREMIUM-INPUT-FILE using the fields and record layouts defined in the DATA DIVISION.

PROCEDURE DIVISION

The **PROCEDURE DIVISION** of a COBOL program includes the instructions required to solve a problem. Instructions to read a record, perform computations, make logical decisions, and write a record are expressed in meaningful, English-like statements. These statements employ COBOL verbs to denote actions and to describe procedures. If you planned your logic carefully using pseudocode or flowcharts, you should be able to easily translate your logic into COBOL code. The pseudocode for the Policy Number Report program was presented earlier in this chapter in Figure 2-6 on page 2-7. A flowchart of the logic was presented in Figure 2-7 on pages 2-8 and 2-9.

As indicated in Chapter 1, the PROCEDURE DIVISION is divided into modules called paragraphs. Paragraphs contain one or more sentences. Each sentence is terminated with a period. A paragraph begins with a user-defined paragraph name that must begin in the A-margin. Paragraph names follow the same basic rules as all user-defined COBOL words. As with other names, paragraph names also should be meaningful. Except for the MAIN-PROGRAM paragraph, all of the paragraph names in this book will begin with a letter and a three-digit number. The letter indicates the **flow of logic** within a particular logic stream within the program. Most programs can be divided into three streams of logic, but more can be used when needed. The streams are identified in this book as the A-stream, B-stream, or C-stream. The A-stream is used for initialization purposes to prepare for the processing that is to occur in the B-stream. The B-stream contains the file processing logic. The C-stream is used for program termination, or wrap-up logic.

The three-digit number indicates the paragraph's **hierarchical position** in its stream. The highest level in each stream is the 100 level. The next level in each stream is the 200 level and so on. In general, 100 level paragraphs perform, or transfer control to, 200 level paragraphs. Likewise, 200 level paragraphs perform, or transfer control to, 300 level paragraphs and so on. A-stream paragraphs will perform only other A-stream paragraphs. B-stream paragraphs will perform only other B-stream paragraphs, and so on.

Each paragraph controls some aspect of the program's logic. The sample program contains six paragraphs. All report-producing programs can be organized using a structure similar to that shown in the Policy Number Report program.

MAIN-PROGRAM

The MAIN-PROGRAM paragraph is shown in Figure 2-20. The PROCEDURE DIVISION header (line 185) begins in the A-margin and follows the same format as other division headers. In line 193, the name of the first paragraph in the PROCEDURE DIVISION, MAIN-PROGRAM is defined. This is called MAIN-PROGRAM because it controls the overall flow of the logic.

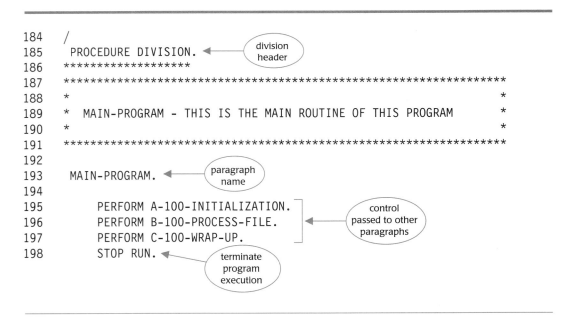

FIGURE 2-20 MAIN-PROGRAM paragraph in the PROCEDURE DIVISION

Program execution begins with the first paragraph in the PROCEDURE DIVISION and execution in a paragraph begins with the first sentence in the paragraph. Each sentence within each paragraph begins with a COBOL verb. Sentences must be in the B-margin. You may use blank lines freely and indent within the B-margin to create easy-to-read code.

MAIN-PROGRAM contains four sentences (lines 195 through 198). The first three sentences use the PERFORM verb to transfer control or branch to other paragraphs. When you **PERFORM** a paragraph, control returns to the sentence following the PERFORM once the performed paragraph ends.

The end of a paragraph is the beginning of the next paragraph or the physical end of your program. The first PERFORM (line 195) transfers control to the paragraph A-100-INITIALIZATION (line 206 in Figure 2-21).

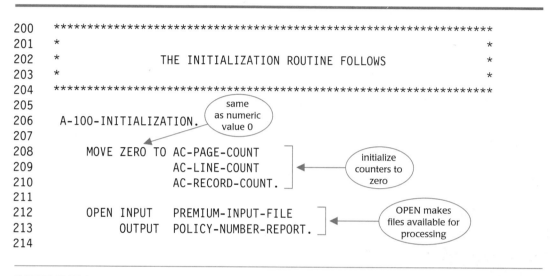

FIGURE 2-21   INITIALIZATION ROUTINE

When control returns from A-100-INITIALIZATION, B-100-PROCESS-FILE is performed (line 196 in Figure 2-20). When control returns from B-100-PROCESS-FILE, C-100-WRAP-UP is performed (line 197). When control returns from C-100-WRAP-UP, the STOP RUN will execute (line 198). **STOP RUN** is the last logical statement in a COBOL program. When STOP RUN executes, the program terminates and control returns to the operating system. Figure 2-22 on the next page illustrates the flow of control for the Policy Number Report program.

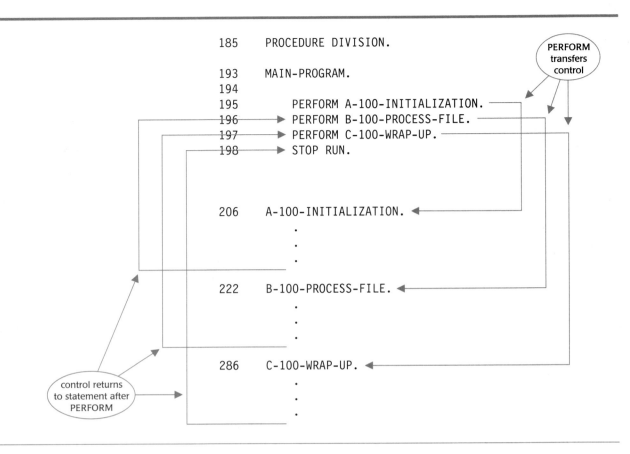

FIGURE 2-22   Flow of control for the Policy Number Report program

Initialization

The paragraph header for `A-100-INITIALIZATION` is on line 206 in Figure 2-21 on the previous page. The first sentence in this paragraph is three-lines long (lines 208, 209, and 210). The `MOVE` statement (line 208, starting in column 12) is used to move data from one location to another. When a computer moves data in a COBOL program, it actually copies the data. Thus, the data resides in two locations in memory immediately after the move. A **MOVE** must have a sending field and at least one receiving field. The `MOVE` in lines 208 through 210 has three receiving fields. The sending field is the figurative constant **ZERO**, which is equal to the number zero (0). `AC-PAGE-COUNT`, `AC-LINE-COUNT`, and `AC-RECORD-COUNT` are the receiving fields and each is being initialized to a value of zero. They are aligned vertically on lines 208, 209, and 210 simply to improve the appearance of the `MOVE` statement. Lines 208 through 210 in Figure 2-21 could have been coded as:

```
MOVE ZERO TO AC-PAGE-COUNT AC-LINE-COUNT AC-RECORD-COUNT.
```

or

```
MOVE ZERO TO AC-PAGE-COUNT, AC-LINE-COUNT, AC-RECORD-COUNT.
```

Commas and semicolons may be used freely in COBOL programs. The compiler treats them as spaces.

Lines 212 and 213 in Figure 2-21 on page 2-27 contain an OPEN statement. The **OPEN** statement is used to make the files to be used in processing available to the program. The OPEN verb tells the operating system on your computer to prepare to read from or write to a file. This OPEN statement covers two lines but could have been coded on a single line. No file may be used unless it is defined in your program in the ENVIRONMENT DIVISION and DATA DIVISION, and no file may be accessed until it is opened.

When you OPEN a file, you must indicate how you are going to use the file. This is called its **open mode**. Most of the files used in this book will be opened either for **INPUT** or **OUTPUT**. Figure 2-23 shows the basic format of the OPEN statement. A file opened for **I-O** will be used for both input and output operations. **EXTEND** is a special way of opening a file for output. When a file is opened for OUTPUT, it is created new as the program executes. In a file that is opened for EXTEND, new data is appended to the end of the file.

```
OPEN   ┌ INPUT    file-name-1 [ file-name-2 ... ] ┐
       │                                          │
       │ OUTPUT   file-name-3 [ file-name-4 ... ] │
       ┤                                          ├
       │ I-0      file-name-5 [ file-name-6 ... ] │
       │                                          │
       └ EXTEND   file-name-7 [ file-name-8 ... ] ┘
```

FIGURE 2-23   Basic format of OPEN statement

The OPEN statement is the last sentence of the A-100-INITIALIZATION paragraph. Control now returns to MAIN-PROGRAM where the statement PERFORM B-100-PROCESS-FILE executes (line 196 in Figure 2-22).

Process File

The paragraph name, B-100-PROCESS-FILE, is on line 222 in Figure 2-24 on the next page. The first sentence in B-100-PROCESS-FILE is a MOVE statement, which moves the value of NEG to SW-END-OF-FILE. The second sentence in this paragraph (lines 225 and 226) is a **READ** statement, which obtains a logical record from the PREMIUM-INPUT-FILE and moves it into PREMIUM-RECORD. This READ statement is referred to as the **priming READ** because it obtains the first record to be processed and is positioned prior to the execution of a loop that processes the file. The **AT END clause** on a READ statement is required for sequential file processing and is executed when there are no more logical records available for processing. The AT END clause moves YES to SW-END-OF-FILE. The AT END clause will execute on the priming READ statement only if the input file is empty. The basic format for a READ statement is shown in Figure 2-25 on the next page.

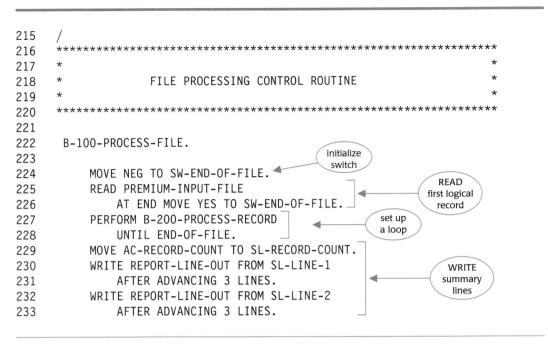

```
215   /
216   ****************************************************************
217   *                                                            *
218   *              FILE PROCESSING CONTROL ROUTINE               *
219   *                                                            *
220   ****************************************************************
221
222    B-100-PROCESS-FILE.
223
224        MOVE NEG TO SW-END-OF-FILE.
225        READ PREMIUM-INPUT-FILE
226            AT END MOVE YES TO SW-END-OF-FILE.
227        PERFORM B-200-PROCESS-RECORD
228            UNTIL END-OF-FILE.
229        MOVE AC-RECORD-COUNT TO SL-RECORD-COUNT.
230        WRITE REPORT-LINE-OUT FROM SL-LINE-1
231            AFTER ADVANCING 3 LINES.
232        WRITE REPORT-LINE-OUT FROM SL-LINE-2
233            AFTER ADVANCING 3 LINES.
```

initialize switch

READ first logical record

set up a loop

WRITE summary lines

FIGURE 2-24 PROCESS-FILE module

```
READ file-name [ INTO    identifier    ]

      [ AT END  imperative-statement-1   ]

      [ NOT AT END imperative-statement-2 ]

      [ END-READ ]
```

FIGURE 2-25 Basic format of a READ statement

The next sentence (lines 227 and 228 in Figure 2-24) is a special form of the PERFORM statement which allows the program to establish a loop that will execute until the condition defined in the **UNTIL clause** is true. Looping continues through the code found in paragraph B-200-PROCESS-RECORD until the given condition is true. The condition, END-OF-FILE, is the condition name assigned by the 88 level entry under the field SW-END-OF-FILE on line 83 in Figure 2-16 on page 2-21. As discussed earlier, a condition name either is true or false. The condition name END-OF-FILE is true when the field SW-END-OF-FILE is equal to Y. Even though the word UNTIL is used, a PERFORM-UNTIL sets up a Do-while logic structure (see Chapter 1, page 1-12. If the condition END-OF-FILE is true after priming READ, then the code in paragraph B-200-PROCESS-RECORD is never executed.

The instructions following the PERFORM UNTIL (lines 229 through 233) will not be executed until the loop has terminated. The MOVE statement on line 229 moves the value of AC-RECORD-COUNT to the output field SL-RECORD-COUNT. The two **WRITE** statements write the two summary lines, SL-LINE-1 and SL-LINE-2 defined in the WORKING-STORAGE SECTION, to the report, POLICY-NUMBER-REPORT. If you look back at the FD entry for POLICY-NUMBER-REPORT in Figure 2-13 on page 2-16, you will see that REPORT-LINE-OUT is the 01 level name defined under the FD. The WRITE statement always writes the 01 level name, which is referred to as the **buffer**. The **FROM** indicates what will be moved into the buffer before it is written to the report. The **AFTER ADVANCING clauses** used in the WRITE statements are for carriage control. The term **carriage control** refers to the spacing in the report. Both AFTER ADVANCING clauses call for the output to be triple-spaced. The basic format of the WRITE statement is shown in Figure 2-26.

```
WRITE record-name   [ FROM  identifier-1        ]

    ⎡ ⎰BEFORE⎱                  ⎰ ⎰identifier-2⎱   ⎡LINE ⎤ ⎱ ⎤
    ⎢ ⎱AFTER ⎰    ADVANCING     ⎱ ⎱integer     ⎰   ⎣LINES⎦ ⎰ ⎥
    ⎢                             ⎰mnemonic-name⎱          ⎥
    ⎣                             ⎱PAGE         ⎰          ⎦
```

FIGURE 2-26 Basic format of a WRITE statement

Process Record

The B-200-PROCESS-RECORD paragraph (Figure 2-27) executes once for every input record processed. The READ on lines 225 and 226 in Figure 2-24 before the PERFORM UNTIL sentence guarantees there will be a record in PREMIUM-RECORD to process. The function of B-200-PROCESS-RECORD is to transfer the data found in PREMIUM-RECORD to DETAIL-LINE and then WRITE the contents of DETAIL-LINE to the report. The first sentence in B-200-PROCESS-RECORD (lines 243 and 244) tests to see if there is a need to WRITE page headings. In this program, a value of zero in AC-LINE-COUNT indicates that headings must be printed before the input record is processed. Recall that a value of zero was moved to AC-LINE-COUNT on line 209 of A-100-INITIALIZATION shown in Figure 2-21 on page 2-27. The **IF** statement is used in COBOL to implement a selection structure and test a condition. You will see there are many ways to code an IF statement. The condition AC-LINE-COUNT = 0 is tested on line 243. If this condition is true, then line 244, PERFORM B-300-PRINT-HEADINGS, executes. If the condition is false, line 244 is skipped and the logic goes on to the next sentence (line 246).

```
234    /
235    *******************************************************************
236    *                                                                 *
237    *          MOVE INPUT FIELDS TO OUTPUT AREAS AND PRINT            *
238    *                                                                 *
239    *******************************************************************
240
241    B-200-PROCESS-RECORD.
242
243        IF AC-LINE-COUNT = 0
244            PERFORM B-300-PRINT-HEADINGS.          ←  time to print headings?
245
246        MOVE PR-POLICY-NUMBER  TO DL-POLICY-NUMBER.
247        MOVE PR-CUSTOMER-NAME  TO DL-CUSTOMER-NAME.   ←  fill in detail line
248        MOVE PR-AGENT-NAME     TO DL-AGENT-NAME.
249        MOVE PR-INSURANCE-TYPE TO DL-INSURANCE-TYPE.
250
```

FIGURE 2-27 PROCESS-RECORD paragraph   *(continued)*

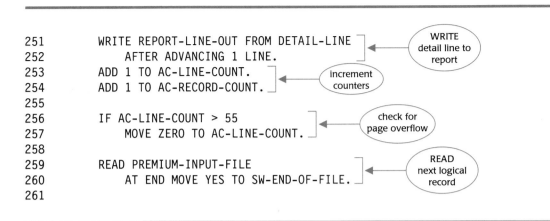

FIGURE 2-27   PROCESS-RECORD paragraph (continued)

Lines 246 through 249 contain MOVE statements that transfer the data found in the input fields defined under PREMIUM-RECORD to the output fields defined under DETAIL-LINE. The WRITE statement on lines 251 and 252 then prints the contents of DETAIL-LINE to the POLICY-NUMBER-REPORT. The AFTER ADVANCING clause will cause the lines to be single-spaced as they are written. The next two sentences use the **ADD** verb to increase the values of both AC-LINE-COUNT and AC-RECORD-COUNT by 1. Lines 256 and 257 contain another IF statement to test whether the report is nearing the end of a page. Once the program has written out 55 lines, it is necessary to reset AC-LINE-COUNT to zero. When the logic loops back to the top of B-200-PROCESS-RECORD, the IF statement there causes the heading paragraph to execute again. The last sentence in B-200-PROCESS-RECORD is another READ statement. This READ is the same as the READ statement discussed in B-100-PROCESS-FILE. This READ obtains the next record, if there is one, for processing.

From here, the program loops back to the PERFORM-UNTIL in B-100-PROCESS-FILE. As long as the condition name END-OF-FILE is false, processing is transferred to B-200-PROCESS-RECORD. Eventually, the program will run out of input records in the PREMIUM-INPUT-FILE. When this occurs, the AT END clause in the READ at the bottom of B-200-PROCESS-RECORD will execute, moving YES to SW-END-OF-FILE. This will make the condition name END-OF-FILE true and terminate the loop.

Heading Routine

Figure 2-28 shows the paragraph that prints the headings for the Policy Number Report program, B-300-PRINT-HEADINGS. B-300-PRINT-HEADINGS is performed from B-200-PROCESS-RECORDS when AC-LINE-COUNT has a value of zero (see lines 243 and 244 in Figure 2-27 on the previous page). The first sentence in B-300-PRINT-HEADINGS adds 1 to AC-PAGE-COUNT (line 270 in Figure 2-28). AC-PAGE-COUNT is then moved (line 271) to the output field RH-PAGE-COUNT. RH-PAGE-COUNT is an edit pattern defined in RH-LINE-1. Lines 272 through 277 contain three WRITE statements that write out the three heading lines, RH-LINE-1, RH-LINE-2, and RH-LINE-3. The first of these WRITE statements (lines 272 and 273) prints the first heading line at the top of a new page. The COBOL reserved word **PAGE** in the AFTER ADVANCING clause forces the line to print on the first line of a page. The MOVE statement on line 278 then sets the value of AC-LINE-COUNT to four, because the three heading lines cover the first four lines of the page.

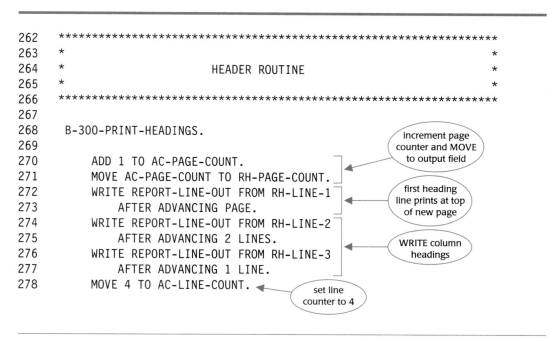

```
262     ****************************************************************
263     *                                                              *
264     *                       HEADER ROUTINE                         *
265     *                                                              *
266     ****************************************************************
267
268     B-300-PRINT-HEADINGS.
269
270         ADD 1 TO AC-PAGE-COUNT.
271         MOVE AC-PAGE-COUNT TO RH-PAGE-COUNT.
272         WRITE REPORT-LINE-OUT FROM RH-LINE-1
273             AFTER ADVANCING PAGE.
274         WRITE REPORT-LINE-OUT FROM RH-LINE-2
275             AFTER ADVANCING 2 LINES.
276         WRITE REPORT-LINE-OUT FROM RH-LINE-3
277             AFTER ADVANCING 1 LINE.
278         MOVE 4 TO AC-LINE-COUNT.
```

increment page counter and MOVE to output field

first heading line prints at top of new page

WRITE column headings

set line counter to 4

FIGURE 2-28   PRINT-HEADINGS paragraph

Wrap-Up

The last paragraph of the program, C-100-WRAP-UP (Figure 2-29), has just one task, which is to **CLOSE** the files that were opened in A-100-INITIALIZATION. The OPEN statement must be coded to explicitly indicate that a file is to be used as INPUT, OUTPUT, I-O, or EXTEND. When the CLOSE statement is coded, it is not necessary to indicate how the file was used. The files to be closed are listed after the CLOSE verb. The CLOSE statement on lines 288 and 289 tells the operating system that the program is finished with PREMIUM-INPUT-FILE and POLICY-NUMBER-REPORT. The files could have been listed side by side on line 288 but were coded vertically aligned for readability. The format of the CLOSE statement is shown in Figure 2-30 on the next page.

```
279  /
280     ****************************************************************
281     *                                                              *
282     *                     END OF JOB ROUTINE                       *
283     *                                                              *
284     ****************************************************************
285
286     C-100-WRAP-UP.
287
288         CLOSE PREMIUM-INPUT-FILE
289               POLICY-NUMBER-REPORT.
```

CLOSE releases control of files

FIGURE 2-29   WRAP-UP paragraph

CLOSE file-name-1 [file-name-2 ...]

FIGURE 2-30 Basic format of a CLOSE statement

Once C-100-WRAP-UP is finished, control returns to MAIN-PROGRAM where the last command of the program, STOP RUN, executes and terminates the program. Once the program is finished, the POLICY-NUMBER-REPORT will be in a file on auxiliary storage. The report can be listed on your computer system's printer by using your system's print command. A listing of the report was presented earlier in this chapter in Figure 2-3 on page 2-4.

CHAPTER SUMMARY

This brings you to the end of the first sample program. Much of the material presented will be covered in more detail later in this book. The goal of this chapter was to give you an overview of a complete COBOL program and to make you comfortable with the basic organization of a COBOL program. There is more to COBOL than what was presented in this chapter. If the sample program and the discussion of its various elements made sense to you, then you are well underway to grasping the COBOL language.

The following list summarizes this chapter. The summary is designed to help you study and understand the material and concepts presented.

1. A **printer spacing chart** is divided into rows and columns and can be used to design reports.

2. **Alphanumeric** fields may contain letters, numbers, or special characters.

3. A **hierarchy chart,** or **top-down chart,** illustrates the relationship between the paragraphs in a program.

4. **Pseudocode** and **flowcharts** can be used to plan the logic of a program.

5. A **COBOL shop** maintains consistency in its programs by imposing a set of standards on its programmers.

6. The only required entry in the **IDENTIFICATION DIVISION** is the **PROGRAM-ID** paragraph. **AUTHOR, INSTALLATION, DATE-WRITTEN,** and **DATE-COMPILED** are optional paragraphs.

7. The **ENVIRONMENT DIVISION** is the most system-dependent part of any COBOL program.

8. A **SELECT** and **ASSIGN** are required for every file to be used in the program.

9. The **DATA DIVISION** describes the files and data to be processed by the program and is divided into the **FILE SECTION** and **WORKING-STORAGE SECTION**.

10. An FD entry is needed in the **FILE SECTION** for every file identified in the **ENVIRONMENT DIVISION** by a **SELECT** entry.

11. The RECORD CONTAINS, LABEL RECORD, and DATA RECORD clauses are all optional in an FD entry.

12. **Level numbers** range from 01 to 49 and are used to show how data items or fields are related to each other.

13. A **picture clause** is used to specify a detailed description of an **elementary item**. A **group item** has no picture clause.

14. The **WORKING-STORAGE SECTION** is used to define switches, counters, accumulators, and output record layouts.

15. The **PROCEDURE DIVISION** contains the instructions required to solve a problem and is subdivided into **paragraphs**.

16. **PERFORM** transfers control from one paragraph to another.

17. **STOP RUN** is the last logical statement of a COBOL program.

18. A **MOVE** copies the contents of one field to another.

19. An **OPEN** statement must be used to make a file available for processing by the program.

20. The **READ** statement retrieves a record from a file that has been opened for **INPUT**.

21. The **WRITE** statement transfers data to a file that has been opened for **OUTPUT**.

22. The **IF** statement is used in COBOL to implement a selection structure.

23. Simple addition can be executed by using the **ADD** statement.

24. The **CLOSE** statement releases control of a file that had been previously opened.

KEY TERMS

01 level numbers (2-18)
77 level numbers (2-18)
88 level entry (2-21)
accumulators (2-20)
ADD (2-32)
AFTER ADVANCING clauses (2-31)
alphabetic (2-19)
alphanumeric (2-5)
alphanumeric fields (2-5)
ASSIGN (2-15)
AT END clause (2-29)
AUTHOR (2-13)
blank lines (2-13)
buffer (2-30)
carriage control (2-31)
CLOSE (2-33)
COBOL shop (2-12)
comment box (2-13)
condition name (2-21)
CONFIGURATION SECTION (2-15)
constant (2-21)
DATA DIVISION (2-16)
DATE-COMPILED (2-13)
DATE-WRITTEN (2-13)
detail line (2-2)
duplicating factor (2-19)
edit pattern (2-25)
elementary item (2-19)
ENVIRONMENT DIVISION (2-14)
EXTEND (2-29)
FD level indicator (2-17)
figurative constant (2-25)
FILE-CONTROL (2-15)
FILE SECTION (2-16)
filler entry (2-23)

FROM (2-30)
flow of logic (2-26)
group name (2-19)
hierarchical position (2-26)
hierarchy chart (2-5)
I-O (2-29)
IDENTIFICATION DIVISION (2-12)
IF (2-31)
implementor name (2-15)
INPUT (2-29)
INPUT-OUTPUT SECTION (2-15)
INSTALLATION (2-13)
installation date (2-13)
level numbers (2-18)
literal (2-21)
MOVE (2-28)
NO (2-22)
numeric (2-19)
OPEN (2-29)
open mode (2-29)
OUTPUT (2-29)
PAGE (2-32)
PERFORM (2-27)
PIC (2-19)
picture clause (2-19)
priming READ (2-29)
printer spacing chart (2-3)
PROCEDURE DIVISION (2-25)
PROGRAM-ID (2-13)
READ (2-29)
record description (2-16)
SECURITY (2-13)
SELECT (2-15)
SPACES (2-25)
STOP RUN (2-27)

STUDENT ASSIGNMENTS

Student Assignment 1: True/False

Instructions: Circle T if the statement is true or F if the statement is false.

T   F   1. Comments may be entered into a source program by placing an asterisk in column 8 of the line containing the comment.

T   F   2. The FILE SECTION is found in the ENVIRONMENT DIVISION.

T   F   3. Each of the four COBOL divisions is composed of sections.

T   F   4. An entry that starts in the A-margin can continue into the B-margin.

T   F   5. Blank lines can be placed anywhere within a COBOL program.

T   F   6. The ENVIRONMENT DIVISION is machine-dependent and generally requires modification when a program is moved to a different computer system.

T   F   7. The PROGRAM-ID is the only mandatory entry within the IDENTIFICATION DIVISION.

T   F   8. SELECT and ASSIGN clauses cannot appear on the same line.

T   F   9. The number of paragraphs contained in the PROCEDURE DIVISION is entirely at the programmer's discretion.

T   F   10. There must be one SELECT statement for each file used.

T   F   11. The CONFIGURATION SECTION is required in all COBOL programs.

T   F   12. Group names require a picture clause in their definition.

T   F   13. Level numbers can range from 01 to 60.

T   F   14. The OPEN statement must be used to make a file available for processing.

T   F   15. The WRITE statement can be used with a file that has an open mode of INPUT.

T   F   16. The PERFORM verb transfers control from one paragraph to another.

T   F   17. User-defined words should be kept as short as possible, usually no more than eight characters long.

T   F   18. A hierarchy chart shows the logic of a program.

T   F   19. A VALUE clause is required on the definition of all elementary items.

T   F   20. Alphanumeric fields can be involved in arithmetic operations.

Student Assignment 2: Multiple Choice

Instructions: Circle the correct response.

1. The ENVIRONMENT DIVISION can consist of the _____ and _____ sections.
   a. CONFIGURATION, INPUT-OUTPUT
   b. INPUT-OUTPUT, FILE
   c. PROGRAM-ID, INPUT-OUTPUT
   d. FILE, WORKING-STORAGE

2. The only required entry in the IDENTIFICATION DIVISION is the _____.
   a. FILE SECTION
   b. INPUT-OUTPUT SECTION
   c. PROGRAM-ID paragraph
   d. AUTHOR paragraph

3. The DATA DIVISION consists of the _____ and _____ sections.
   a. INPUT-OUTPUT, FILE
   b. FILE, WORKING-STORAGE
   c. PROGRAM-ID, FILE
   d. CONFIGURATION, INPUT-OUTPUT

4. A user-defined file name is associated with an actual system file name by a(n) _____.
   a. SELECT and ASSIGN
   b. FD entry
   c. buffer name
   d. OPEN verb

5. All division headers, section headers, and paragraph headers must begin in _____.
   a. column 7
   b. the A-margin
   c. the B-margin
   d. column 1

6. Every COBOL sentence must be terminated by a _____.
   a. space
   b. period
   c. semicolon
   d. verb

7. Uppercase words shown in a programming manual are _____ words.
   a. reserved
   b. required
   c. user-defined
   d. hyphenated

8. The last logical statement of a COBOL program is _____.
   a. EXIT
   b. FINISH-PROGRAM
   c. STOP RUN
   d. END PROGRAM

9. A condition name is defined by _____.
   a. an 01 level entry
   b. an 88 level entry
   c. an elementary item
   d. a reserved word

10. Execution of the logic in a COBOL program begins with _____.
    a. the first paragraph in the IDENTIFICATION DIVISION
    b. the first item defined in the DATA DIVISION
    c. the first statement in the PROCEDURE DIVISION
    d. the program being submitted to the compiler

Student Assignment 3: Coding an IDENTIFICATION DIVISION

Instructions: Code an IDENTIFICATION DIVISION that contains only a PROGRAM-ID paragraph, AUTHOR paragraph, and comments. The program name is to be PAYRPT, and the comments are to indicate that the program does a weekly payroll calculation for workers paid hourly at the ROF Corporation.

Student Assignment 4: Coding a SELECT

Instructions: A file with the system name SALES.DAT is stored on disk. A COBOL program is to reference this file using the name SALES-TRANSACTION-FILE. Code the required SELECT statement.

Student Assignment 5: Coding an FD

Instructions: Code an FD and associated 01 record-layout for STUDENT-FILE given the following information regarding the fields found in each record:

Student ID	7 bytes,	alphanumeric
Student Name	20 bytes,	alphanumeric
Student Address	20 bytes,	alphanumeric
Student Status	2 bytes,	alphanumeric
Student Income	5 bytes,	numeric integer

Student Assignment 6: Coding PERFORM Statements

Instructions: Code a paragraph named B-100-DO-IT that transfers control to B-200-DO-IT-AGAIN, then to B-210-DO-IT-OVER, and finally to B-220-DONE. Control should be transferred to B-210-DO-IT-OVER so the program keeps looping back to B-210-DO-IT-OVER until the condition ALL-RIGHT-NOW is true.

Student Assignment 7: Coding an OPEN and a READ

Instructions: Code an OPEN and a READ for the file named STUDENT-FILE. Move YES to SW-END-OF-FILE in the AT END clause of the READ.

COBOL LABORATORY EXERCISES

Exercise 1: Modified Policy Number Report Program

Purpose: To gain experience in working with COBOL and in formatting output record layouts.

Problem: Open the program PROJ2.CBL on the Student Diskette that accompanies this book and modify it to create a different report. Arrange the fields so the Customer Name prints first on each detail line, followed by the Policy Number, then the Insurance Type, and finally the Agent Name. Title the new report CLIENT INSURANCE REPORT. Do not forget to modify the column headings. Save this program as EX2-1.CBL.

Input Data: Use the Premium file presented in Appendix A as input. This file is named PREMIUM.DAT on the Student Diskette that accompanies this book.

Output Results: The CLIENT INSURANCE REPORT should be output. The report should be based on an 80-column format. List the Customer Name, Policy Number, Insurance Type, and Agent Name on each detail line.

Exercise 2: Customer Record Report

Purpose: To practice designing and coding a COBOL program that produces a report.

Problem: Write a program that produces a Customer Record Report listing the Account Number, Customer Name, Item Purchased, and Credit Limit for each Customer Record on the ABC Department Store Customer file. Supply a report heading with a page number on each page of the report. Double-space detail lines in the report. Also, supply appropriate column headings, a count of the number of records processed, and an End of Report message. Write this program by modifying PROJ2.CBL on the Student Diskette that accompanies this book. Save this program as EX2-2.CBL.

Input Data: Use the Customer File listed in Appendix A as input. This file is named CUSTOMER.DAT on the Student Diskette that accompanies this book. The input record layout follows. The filler fields represent data that is not used in this assignment.

Field Description	Position	Length	Attribute
filler	1–6	6	Alphanumeric
Account Number	7–12	6	Numeric
Customer Name	13–32	20	Alphanumeric
Item Purchased	33–52	20	Alphanumeric
filler	53–65	13	Alphanumeric
Credit Limit	66–70	5	Numeric
filler	71–72	2	Alphanumeric
Record Length		72	

Output Results: Output consists of the Customer Record Report having a format similar to the following:

```
                    CUSTOMER RECORD REPORT              PAGE Z9

    ACCT. NO.   CUSTOMER NAME          ITEM PURCHASED        CR. LIMIT
    ---------   --------------------   --------------------  ---------

     999999     XXXXXXXXXXXXXXXXXXXX   XXXXXXXXXXXXXXXXXXXX    ZZZZ9

     999999     XXXXXXXXXXXXXXXXXXXX   XXXXXXXXXXXXXXXXXXXX    ZZZZ9
       .
       .
       .
                TOTAL NUMBER OF RECORDS LISTED =  ZZ9
                        END OF REPORT
```

Exercise 3: Sales Record Report

Purpose: To practice designing and coding a COBOL program that produces a report.

Problem: Design and code a COBOL program that lists the Customer Name, Auto Make, Purchase Date, and Year of Auto for each record in the EZ Auto Sales Customer file. Supply a report heading with a page number on each page of the report. Double-space detail lines in the report. Also, supply appropriate column headings, a count of the number of records processed, and an End of Report message. Write this program by modifying PROJ2.CBL on the Student Diskette that accompanies this book. Save this program as EX2-3.CBL.

(continued)

Exercise 3 (continued)

Input Data: Use the Sales File listed in Appendix A as input. This file is named CUSTSALE.DAT on the Student Diskette that accompanies this book. The input record layout follows. The filler fields represent data that is not used in this assignment.

Field Description	Position	Length	Attribute
filler	1−13	13	Alphanumeric
Customer Name	14−33	20	Alphanumeric
Purchase Date	34−39	6	Numeric
Auto Make	40−59	20	Alphanumeric
filler	60−66	7	Alphanumeric
Year of Auto	67−70	4	Numeric
filler	71−74	4	Alphanumeric
Record Length		74	

Output Results: A report should be output which lists the fields described above. The report should have a format similar to the following:

```
                      AUTO SALES REPORT                    PAGE Z9

                                             PURCHASE    AUTO
    CUSTOMER NAME         AUTO MAKE          DATE        YEAR
    --------------------  --------------------  --------  -------

    XXXXXXXXXXXXXXXXXXXX  XXXXXXXXXXXXXXXXXXXX  Z9/99/99  9999

    XXXXXXXXXXXXXXXXXXXX  XXXXXXXXXXXXXXXXXXXX  Z9/99/99  9999

    XXXXXXXXXXXXXXXXXXXX  XXXXXXXXXXXXXXXXXXXX  Z9/99/99  9999
        .
        .
        .
              TOTAL NUMBER OF RECORDS LISTED =  ZZ9
                        END OF REPORT
```

CHAPTER THREE

ENVIRONMENT
and DATA DIVISIONS

OBJECTIVES

You will have mastered the material in Chapter 3 when you can:

* Identify the paragraphs in the CONFIGURATION SECTION
* Name the function of the entries in the INPUT-OUTPUT SECTION
* Name the entries found in the FILE SECTION
* Identify valid level numbers
* Specify the purpose of the WORKING-STORAGE SECTION
* Understand the reason for data name qualification
* Identify valid PICTURE clauses
* Identify and explain the use of a numeric edit pattern
* Create a numeric edit pattern
* Create an alphanumeric edit pattern
* Identify an independent data item
* Explain the use of a condition name
* Understand the uses of the REDEFINES clause

INTRODUCTION

The sample program presented in Chapter 2 gave you an overview of the organization of a COBOL program and illustrated how a COBOL program functions. This chapter presents another sample program and reviews the ENVIRONMENT DIVISION and DATA DIVISION.

Some optional entries available for the ENVIRONMENT DIVISION often are used. Your study of COBOL would not be complete if these entries were neglected. Additionally, there are important items yet to be discussed in the DATA DIVISION.

Designing the Premium Amount Report

The sample program presented in this chapter creates the Premium Amount Report for the Ainsworth Insurance Company.

Figure 3-1 illustrates the basic format of this report. Like the Policy Number Report created in Chapter 2, it lists the Policy Number, Customer Number, and Insurance Type for each record in the Premium Input File. Additionally, it lists the contents of two fields not used in Chapter 2, the Premium Amount field and the Payment Status field.

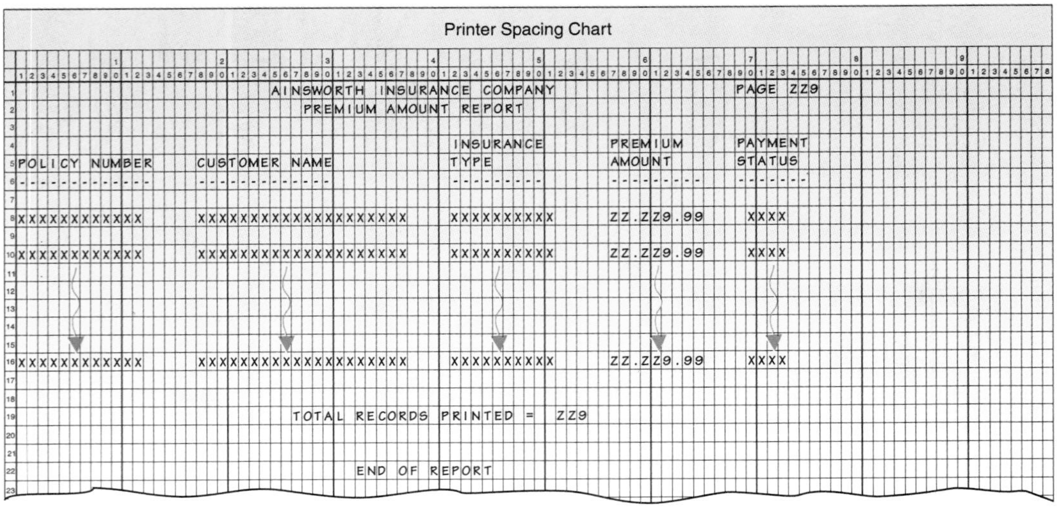

FIGURE 3-1   Premium Amount Report layout

Premium Amount Report

Figure 3-2 shows a partial listing of the report produced by the Premium Amount Report program.

```
                    AINSWORTH INSURANCE COMPANY              PAGE    1
                       PREMIUM AMOUNT REPORT

                               INSURANCE     PREMIUM     PAYMENT
    POLICY NUMBER   CUSTOMER NAME    TYPE     AMOUNT      STATUS
    -------------   -------------    ---------   ---------   -------

    AM-1991-9223    Allister, Collin    Automobile    123.45     P PD

    AM-2199-9229    Amfelter, Audrey    Automobile    456.50     PAID

    HM-7008-0507    Andrews, Robert     Home          560.00     P PD
         .
         .
         .
    TL-7682-0903    Winder, Robert      Term Life     305.50     PAID

    WL-2721-3904    Winfield, Wally     Whole Life    326.00     P PD

    RT-7127-5076    Yackley, Yourto     Renter        240.00     P PD

              TOTAL RECORDS PRINTED = 72

                  END OF REPORT
```

FIGURE 3-2   A partial listing of the Premium Amount Report

Hierarchy Chart

Figure 3-3 presents a hierarchy chart that illustrates the organization of the PROCEDURE DIVISION of the Premium Amount Report program. It is organized exactly like the PROCEDURE DIVISION of the Policy Number Report program presented in Chapter 2. Many report programs can use this same basic organization.

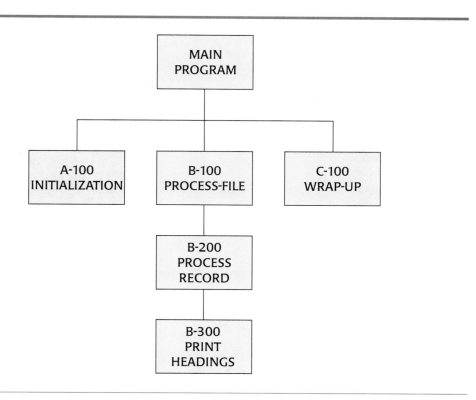

FIGURE 3-3 Hierarchy chart illustrating the organization of the PROCEDURE DIVISION of the Premium Amount Report program

Program Flowchart

Figure 3-4 on the next page presents a flowchart which illustrates the basic logic used in the program. This logic is very similar to the logic used in the program presented in Chapter 2 except that the Payment Status field in each record of the Premium file is tested to determine which message to print in the customer detail line.

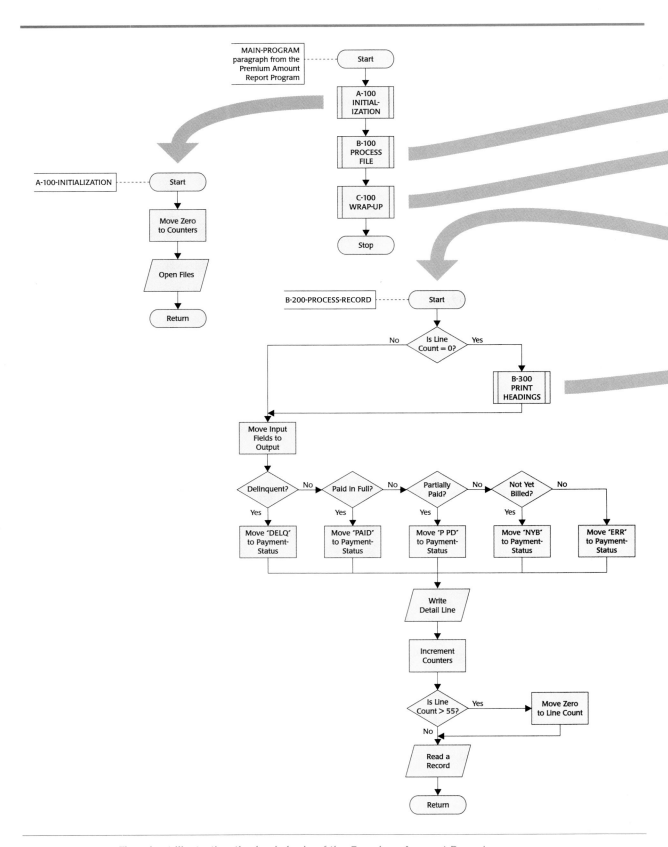

FIGURE 3-4   Flowchart illustrating the basic logic of the Premium Amount Report program

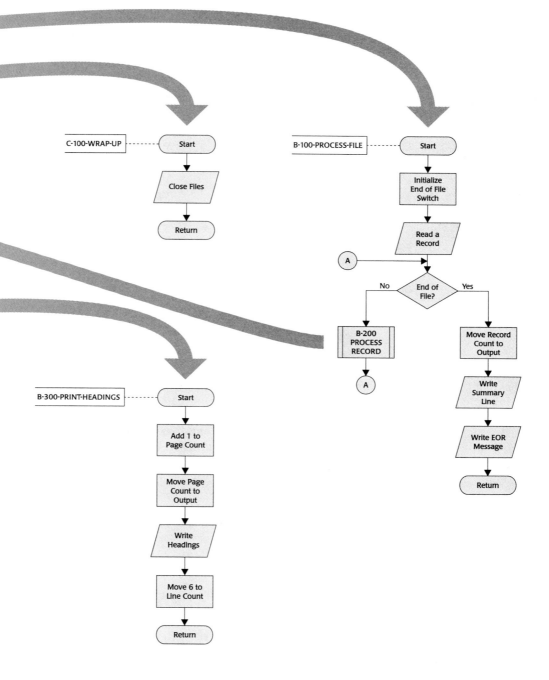

Premium File Record Layout

Figure 3-5 shows the format of the records contained in the Premium file. Notice that as in Chapter 2 the input record layout includes the field for the agent name, but the report here in Chapter 3 does not list an agent name. Not every report requires the use of every field available for processing. The Premium Amount Report program ignores the agent name field.

Field	Position	Length	Attribute
Customer Name	1–20	20	Alphanumeric
Agent Name	21–40	20	Alphanumeric
Insurance Type	41–50	10	Alphanumeric
Policy Number	51–62	12	Alphanumeric
Premium Amount	63–69	7	Numeric, S9(5)V99
Payment Status	70	1	Alphanumeric
unused	71–80	10	Alphanumeric
Total Record Length		80	

FIGURE 3-5   Record layout for the Premium file

The record layout includes two additional fields not used in Chapter 2 and not included in the record layout used there. These fields are the Premium Amount field and the Payment Status field. These two fields were included as part of a filler entry in the Premium file record layout presented in Chapter 2. As indicated earlier, these fields are listed on the Premium Amount report.

The Payment Status field in each customer record contains one of four codes, "D" for delinquent, "F" for paid in full, "P" for partially paid, and "N" for not yet billed. Rather than print the code in the file for each customer, the sample program tests the Payment Status field and prints a corresponding message as follows:

Code	Message Printed
D	DELQ
F	PAID
P	P PD
N	NYB
Other	ERR

Premium Amount Report Program

Figure 3-6 presents the Premium Amount Report program to be discussed in this chapter. This program is found on the Student Diskette that accompanies this book.

```
  1        IDENTIFICATION DIVISION.
  2        ************************
  3
  4        PROGRAM-ID.      PREMAMT.
  5        AUTHOR.          R. O. FOREMAN.
  6        INSTALLATION.    PURDUE UNIVERSITY CALUMET.
  7        DATE-WRITTEN.    NOV. 28, 1997.
  8        DATE-COMPILED.   28-Nov-97.
  9        ****************************************************************
 10      *                       PROGRAM NARRATIVE                       *
 11      *                                                               *
 12      *                                                               *
 13      *    THIS PROGRAM READS ALL RECORDS IN THE CUSTOMER PREMIUM FILE *
 14      *    AND PRINTS POLICY NUMBER, CUSTOMER NAME, INSURANCE TYPE,    *
 15      *    PREMIUM AMOUNT, AND PAYMENT STATUS FOR EACH RECORD IN THE   *
 16      *    FILE.  A RECORD COUNT IS PROVIDED AT THE END OF THE REPORT. *
 17      *                                                               *
 18      *       INPUT:     PREMIUM.DAT - PREMIUM INPUT FILE             *
 19      *                                                               *
 20      *       OUTPUT:    PREMAMT.RPT - PREMIUM AMOUNT REPORT          *
 21      ****************************************************************
 22
 23        ENVIRONMENT DIVISION.
 24        *********************
 25
 26        CONFIGURATION SECTION.
 27        **********************
 28
 29        SOURCE-COMPUTER.  IBM COMPATIBLE.
 30        OBJECT-COMPUTER.  IBM COMPATIBLE.
 31
 32        SPECIAL-NAMES.
 33
 34           C01 IS TOP-OF-PAGE.
 35
 36        INPUT-OUTPUT SECTION.
 37        ********************
 38
 39        FILE-CONTROL.
 40
 41           SELECT PREMIUM-INPUT-FILE
 42              ASSIGN TO "A:\PREMIUM.DAT"
 43              ORGANIZATION IS SEQUENTIAL
 44              ACCESS IS SEQUENTIAL.
 45
 46           SELECT PREMIUM-AMOUNT-REPORT
 47              ASSIGN TO "A:\PREMAMT.RPT"
 48              ORGANIZATION IS SEQUENTIAL
 49              ACCESS IS SEQUENTIAL.
 50
 51      /
 52        DATA DIVISION.
 53        *************
 54
 55        FILE SECTION.
 56        ************
 57
 58        ****************************************************************
 59      *                                                               *
 60      *    INPUT-FILE - PREMIUM INPUT FILE                            *
 61      *                                                               *
 62        ****************************************************************
 63
 64        FD  PREMIUM-INPUT-FILE.
 65
 66        01  PREMIUM-RECORD.
 67            02  PR-CUSTOMER-NAME       PIC X(20).
 68            02  PR-AGENT-NAME          PIC X(20).
 69            02  PR-INSURANCE-TYPE      PIC X(10).
 70            02  PR-POLICY-NUMBER       PIC X(12).
 71            02  PR-PREMIUM-AMOUNT      PIC S9(5)V99.
 72            02  PR-PAYMENT-STATUS      PIC X.
 73                88  DELINQUENT         VALUE "D".
 74                88  PAID-IN-FULL       VALUE "F".
 75                88  PARTIALLY-PAID     VALUE "P".
 76                88  NOT-YET-BILLED     VALUE "N".
 77            02                         PIC X(10).
 78
```

```
 79        ****************************************************************
 80      *                                                               *
 81      *    REPORT-FILE - PREMIUM AMOUNT REPORT                        *
 82      *                                                               *
 83        ****************************************************************
 84
 85        FD  PREMIUM-AMOUNT-REPORT.
 86
 87        01  REPORT-LINE-OUT            PIC X(80).
 88      /
 89        WORKING-STORAGE SECTION.
 90        ***********************
 91
 92        ****************************************************************
 93      *                                                               *
 94      *                    SWITCHES                                   *
 95      *                                                               *
 96        ****************************************************************
 97
 98        01  SWITCHES.
 99
100            02  SW-END-OF-FILE         PIC X.
101                88  END-OF-FILE                      VALUE "Y".
102
103        01  VALUES-FOR-SWITCHES.
104            02  YES                    PIC X      VALUE "Y".
105            02  NEG                    PIC X      VALUE "N".
106
107
108
109        ****************************************************************
110      *                                                               *
111      *                   ACCUMULATORS                                *
112      *                                                               *
113        ****************************************************************
114
115        01  ACCUMULATORS.
116
117            02  AC-LINE-COUNT          PIC 999   PACKED-DECIMAL.
118            02  AC-PAGE-COUNT          PIC 999   PACKED-DECIMAL.
119            02  AC-RECORD-COUNT        PIC 9(5)  PACKED-DECIMAL.
120      /
121        ****************************************************************
122      *                                                               *
123      *    REPORT HEADINGS FOR THE PREMIUM AMOUNT REPORT              *
124      *                                                               *
125        ****************************************************************
126
127        01  REPORT-HEADING.
128
129            02  RH-LINE-1.
130                03                     PIC X(24) VALUE SPACES.
131                03                     PIC X(27) VALUE
132                    "AINSWORTH INSURANCE COMPANY".
133                03                     PIC X(18) VALUE SPACES.
134                03                     PIC X(5)  VALUE "PAGE ".
135                03  RH-PAGE-COUNT      PIC ZZ9.
136                03                     PIC XXX   VALUE SPACES.
137
138            02  RH-LINE-2.
139                03                     PIC X(27) VALUE SPACES.
140                03                     PIC X(21) VALUE
141                    "PREMIUM AMOUNT REPORT".
142                03                     PIC X(32) VALUE SPACES.
143
144            02  RH-LINE-3.
145                03                     PIC X(41) VALUE SPACES.
146                03                     PIC X(9)  VALUE
147                    "INSURANCE".
148                03                     PIC X(6)  VALUE SPACES.
149                03                     PIC X(7)  VALUE
150                    "PREMIUM".
151                03                     PIC X(6)  VALUE SPACES.
152                03                     PIC X(7)  VALUE
153                    "PAYMENT".
154                03                     PIC X(4)  VALUE SPACES.
155
156            02  RH-LINE-4.
```

FIGURE 3-6   Premium Amount Report program

(continued)

```
157        03                        PIC X(13) VALUE                234    MAIN-PROGRAM.
158            "POLICY NUMBER".                                      235
159        03                        PIC X(4)  VALUE SPACES.        236        PERFORM A-100-INITIALIZATION.
160        03                        PIC X(13) VALUE                237        PERFORM B-100-PROCESS-FILE.
161            "CUSTOMER NAME".                                      238        PERFORM C-100-WRAP-UP.
162        03                        PIC X(11) VALUE SPACES.        239        STOP RUN.
163        03                        PIC X(4)  VALUE                240
164            "TYPE".                                               241    ****************************************************************
165        03                        PIC X(11) VALUE SPACES.        242    *                                                              *
166        03                        PIC X(6)  VALUE                243    *          THE INITIALIZATION ROUTINE FOLLOWS                  *
167            "AMOUNT".                                             244    *                                                              *
168        03                        PIC X(7)  VALUE SPACES.        245    ****************************************************************
169        03                        PIC X(6)  VALUE                246
170            "STATUS".                                             247    A-100-INITIALIZATION.
171        03                        PIC X(5)  VALUE SPACES.        248
172                                                                 249        MOVE ZERO TO AC-PAGE-COUNT
173     02  RH-LINE-5.                                              250                    AC-LINE-COUNT
174        03                        PIC X(13) VALUE ALL "-".       251                    AC-RECORD-COUNT.
175        03                        PIC X(4)  VALUE SPACES.        252
176        03                        PIC X(13) VALUE ALL "-".       253        OPEN INPUT   PREMIUM-INPUT-FILE
177        03                        PIC X(11) VALUE SPACES.        254             OUTPUT  PREMIUM-AMOUNT-REPORT.
178        03                        PIC X(9)  VALUE ALL "-".       255
179        03                        PIC X(6)  VALUE SPACES.        256    /
180        03                        PIC X(7)  VALUE ALL "-".       257
181        03                        PIC X(6)  VALUE SPACES.        258    ****************************************************************
182        03                        PIC X(7)  VALUE ALL "-".       259    *                                                              *
183        03                        PIC X(4)  VALUE SPACES.        260    *          FILE PROCESSING CONTROL ROUTINE                     *
184                                                                 261    *                                                              *
185    ****************************************************         262    ****************************************************************
186    *                                               *           263
187    *   DETAIL LINE FOR THE PREMIUM AMOUNT REPORT    *           264    B-100-PROCESS-FILE.
188    *                                               *           265
189    ****************************************************         266        MOVE NEG TO SW-END-OF-FILE.
190                                                                 267        READ PREMIUM-INPUT-FILE
191    01  DETAIL-LINE.                                             268            AT END MOVE YES TO SW-END-OF-FILE.
192                                                                 269        PERFORM B-200-PROCESS-RECORD
193     02  DL-POLICY-NUMBER         PIC X(12).                     270            UNTIL END-OF-FILE.
194     02                           PIC X(5)    VALUE SPACES.      271        MOVE AC-RECORD-COUNT TO SL-RECORD-COUNT.
195     02  DL-CUSTOMER-NAME         PIC X(20).                     272        WRITE REPORT-LINE-OUT FROM SL-LINE-1
196     02                           PIC X(4)    VALUE SPACES.      273            AFTER ADVANCING 3 LINES.
197     02  DL-INSURANCE-TYPE        PIC X(10).                     274        WRITE REPORT-LINE-OUT FROM SL-LINE-2
198     02                           PIC X(5)    VALUE SPACES.      275            AFTER ADVANCING 3 LINES.
199     02  DL-PREMIUM-AMOUNT        PIC ZZ,ZZ9.99BCR.              276
200     02                           PIC XX      VALUE SPACES.      277    /
201     02  DL-PAYMENT-STATUS        PIC X(4).                      278    ****************************************************************
202     02                           PIC X(6)    VALUE SPACES.      279    *                                                              *
203    /                                                           280    *      MOVE INPUT FIELDS TO OUTPUT AREAS AND PRINT             *
204    ****************************************************         281    *                                                              *
205    *                                               *           282    ****************************************************************
206    *   SUMMARY LINES FOR THE PREMIUM AMOUNT REPORT  *           283
207    *                                               *           284    B-200-PROCESS-RECORD.
208    ****************************************************         285
209                                                                286        IF AC-LINE-COUNT = 0
210    01  SUMMARY-LINES.                                          287            PERFORM B-300-PRINT-HEADINGS.
211                                                                288
212     02  SL-LINE-1.                                             289        MOVE PR-POLICY-NUMBER  TO DL-POLICY-NUMBER.
213        03                        PIC X(26) VALUE SPACES.       290        MOVE PR-CUSTOMER-NAME  TO DL-CUSTOMER-NAME.
214        03                        PIC X(24) VALUE               291        MOVE PR-INSURANCE-TYPE TO DL-INSURANCE-TYPE.
215            "TOTAL RECORDS PRINTED = ".                          292        MOVE PR-PREMIUM-AMOUNT TO DL-PREMIUM-AMOUNT.
216        03  SL-RECORD-COUNT       PIC ZZZZ9.                     293
217        03                        PIC X(25) VALUE SPACES.       294        IF DELINQUENT
218                                                                295            MOVE "DELQ" TO DL-PAYMENT-STATUS
219     02  SL-LINE-2.                                             296        ELSE
220        03                        PIC X(32) VALUE SPACES.       297            IF PAID-IN-FULL
221        03                        PIC X(13) VALUE               298                MOVE "PAID" TO DL-PAYMENT-STATUS
222            "END OF REPORT".                                     299            ELSE
223        03                        PIC X(35) VALUE SPACES.       300                IF PARTIALLY-PAID
224    /                                                           301                    MOVE "P PD" TO DL-PAYMENT-STATUS
225    PROCEDURE DIVISION.                                         302                ELSE
226    ******************                                          303                    IF NOT-YET-BILLED
227    ****************************************************         304                        MOVE "NYB" TO DL-PAYMENT-STATUS
228    *                                               *           305                    ELSE
229    *  MAIN-PROGRAM - THIS IS THE MAIN ROUTINE OF THE PREMIUM   306                        MOVE "ERR" TO DL-PAYMENT-STATUS.
230    *              AMOUNT PROGRAM                    *           307
231    *                                               *           308        WRITE REPORT-LINE-OUT FROM DETAIL-LINE
232    ****************************************************         309            AFTER ADVANCING 2 LINES.
233                                                                310        ADD 2 TO AC-LINE-COUNT.
                                                                   311        ADD 1 TO AC-RECORD-COUNT.
```

Handwritten annotation near lines 193-194: "May type 'FILLER' here"

Handwritten annotation near lines 308-309: "double space"

FIGURE 3-6   Premium Amount Report program (continued)

```
312
313         IF AC-LINE-COUNT > 55                                334         WRITE REPORT-LINE-OUT FROM RH-LINE-3
314             MOVE ZERO TO AC-LINE-COUNT.                       335             AFTER ADVANCING 1 LINE.
315                                                               336         WRITE REPORT-LINE-OUT FROM RH-LINE-4
316         READ PREMIUM-INPUT-FILE                               337             AFTER ADVANCING 1 LINE.
317             AT END MOVE YES TO SW-END-OF-FILE.                338         WRITE REPORT-LINE-OUT FROM RH-LINE-5
318                                                               339             AFTER ADVANCING 1 LINE.
319                                                               340         MOVE 6 TO AC-LINE-COUNT.
320     ***************************************************       341     /
321     *                                                 *       342     ***************************************************
322     *                 HEADER ROUTINE                  *       343     *                                                 *
323     *                                                 *       344     *                 END OF JOB ROUTINE               *
324     ***************************************************       345     *                                                 *
325                                                               346     ***************************************************
326     B-300-PRINT-HEADINGS.                                     347
327                                                               348     C-100-WRAP-UP.
328         ADD 1 TO AC-PAGE-COUNT.                               349
329         MOVE AC-PAGE-COUNT TO RH-PAGE-COUNT.                  350         CLOSE PREMIUM-INPUT-FILE
330         WRITE REPORT-LINE-OUT FROM RH-LINE-1                  351               PREMIUM-AMOUNT-REPORT.
331             AFTER ADVANCING TOP-OF-PAGE.                      352
332         WRITE REPORT-LINE-OUT FROM RH-LINE-2                  353     /
333             AFTER ADVANCING 2 LINES.
```

stop run

ENVIRONMENT DIVISION

Figure 3-7 shows the ENVIRONMENT DIVISION from the Policy Number Report program presented in Chapter 2. The ENVIRONMENT DIVISION of that program represents all that is necessary in most COBOL programs. Another section sometimes found in the ENVIRONMENT DIVISION is the CONFIGURATION SECTION.

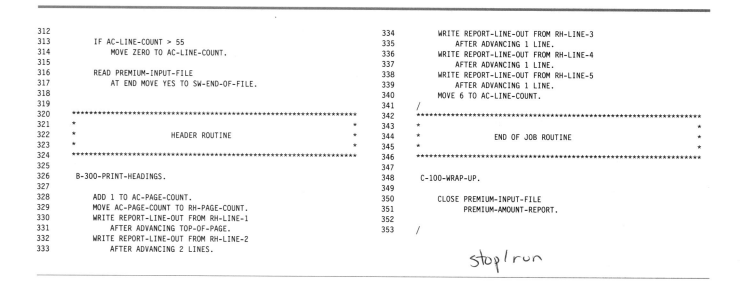

```
24      ENVIRONMENT DIVISION.
25      *********************
26
27      INPUT-OUTPUT SECTION.
28      *********************
29
30      FILE-CONTROL.
31
32          SELECT PREMIUM-INPUT-FILE
33              ASSIGN TO "A:\PREMIUM.DAT".
34
35          SELECT POLICY-NUMBER-REPORT
36              ASSIGN TO "A:\POLNUM.RPT".
```

FIGURE 3-7   ENVIRONMENT DIVISION from the Policy Number Report program in Chapter 2

CONFIGURATION SECTION

The **CONFIGURATION SECTION**, when present, comes before the INPUT-OUTPUT SECTION and is used to identify the computer system on which the program is to be compiled and executed. It also can be used to identify special items used during the execution of the program. Figure 3-8 on the next page shows the ENVIRONMENT DIVISION of the Premium Amount Report program presented in this chapter. Notice the inclusion of a CONFIGURATION SECTION.

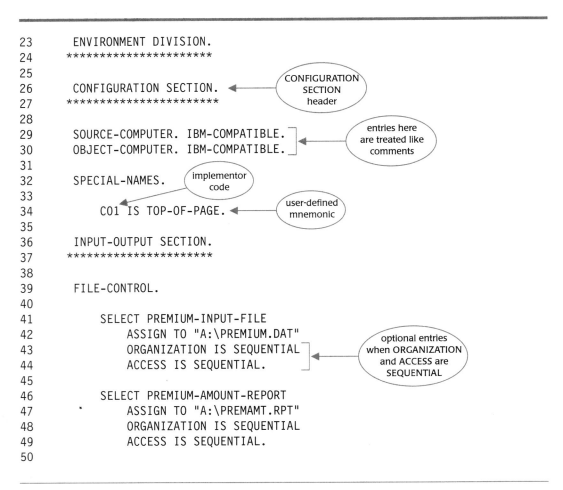

```
23        ENVIRONMENT DIVISION.
24        **********************
25
26        CONFIGURATION SECTION.
27        **********************
28
29        SOURCE-COMPUTER. IBM-COMPATIBLE.
30        OBJECT-COMPUTER. IBM-COMPATIBLE.
31
32        SPECIAL-NAMES.
33
34            C01 IS TOP-OF-PAGE.
35
36        INPUT-OUTPUT SECTION.
37        *********************
38
39        FILE-CONTROL.
40
41            SELECT PREMIUM-INPUT-FILE
42                ASSIGN TO "A:\PREMIUM.DAT"
43                ORGANIZATION IS SEQUENTIAL
44                ACCESS IS SEQUENTIAL.
45
46            SELECT PREMIUM-AMOUNT-REPORT
47         .      ASSIGN TO "A:\PREMAMT.RPT"
48                ORGANIZATION IS SEQUENTIAL
49                ACCESS IS SEQUENTIAL.
50
```

FIGURE 3-8   ENVIRONMENT DIVISION from the Premium Amount Report program

SOURCE-COMPUTER is a paragraph used to identify the computer on which the program is *compiled*. **OBJECT-COMPUTER** is a paragraph used to identify the computer on which the program is *executed*. These two entries always have been optional but, in the past, supplied valuable information to computer programmers and operators. In the early days of COBOL, computers did not have much capacity or speed. Two computers, sometimes from different manufacturers, were often used to speed up the flow of information processing. SOURCE-COMPUTER and OBJECT-COMPUTER entries are treated strictly as comments and have no value except for documentation purposes.

The **SPECIAL-NAMES** paragraph is used to associate a user-defined term with a hardware-specific feature of the computer system. This hardware-specific feature is referred to as the **implementor name** and may be a terminal address on the computer system, a video display feature, or, as in Figure 3-8, a print control feature. These features go beyond the scope of this book, but one of the more commonly used features is presented for illustration purposes.

The code, C01, is the implementor name for skipping to a new page in a report. TOP-OF-PAGE is called a **mnemonic**. TOP-OF-PAGE is defined here as a term that may be used to force a page break. As shown in Chapter 2, the COBOL reserved word PAGE already does this. Given the definition of TOP-OF-PAGE, the WRITE statement that prints the first heading line could use the term TOP-OF-PAGE in place of PAGE. Thus, the first WRITE statement shown in Figure 3-9 performs the same task as the second WRITE statement shown in Figure 3-9.

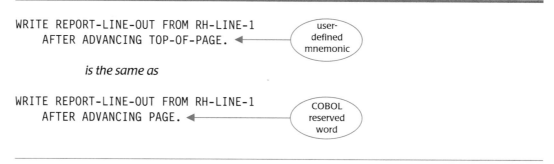

FIGURE 3-9   Two WRITE statements that work the same

INPUT-OUTPUT SECTION

Through the SELECT statements located in the FILE-CONTROL paragraph of the INPUT-OUTPUT SECTION, you are able to associate your user-defined name for a file to the true system name for that file. The SELECT statement for the input file used in the Premium Amount Report program associates the name PREMIUM-INPUT-FILE to the system name for that file, A:\PREMIUM.DAT (Figure 3-10). Notice the addition of two clauses that did not appear in either SELECT used in the Policy Number Report program in Chapter 2. These additional clauses are usually optional; however, there are circumstances where special types of files are used and they are required. These entries are the ORGANIZATION IS clause and the ACCESS IS clause.

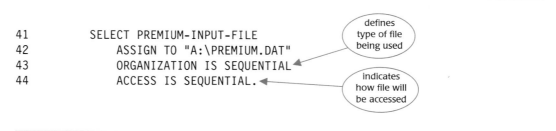

FIGURE 3-10   SELECT statement for the Premium file

The **ORGANIZATION IS clause** specifies the type of file being referenced. ANS COBOL allows for three types of file organization: **SEQUENTIAL**, **INDEXED**, and **RELATIVE**. Indexed and relative files will be discussed later in the book. They are file organizations that may be used when special types of processing are required. ANS COBOL also allows for three methods of accessing files. The **ACCESS IS clause** specifies the method as **SEQUENTIAL**, **RANDOM**, or **DYNAMIC**. RANDOM and DYNAMIC access will be discussed in conjunction with INDEXED and RELATIVE files in Chapter 9.

A SEQUENTIAL file is one in which the records are stored one after the other in the same order they were written to or entered into the file. SEQUENTIAL files may be stored on either disk or tape and the records normally are ordered by a key field. If the ORGANIZATION IS clause is omitted, the default organization is SEQUENTIAL. If the ACCESS IS clause is omitted, the default access is SEQUENTIAL. Hence, when you work with a SEQUENTIAL file, such as the Premium file, you do not need to code ORGANIZATION IS or ACCESS IS. When working with a SEQUENTIAL file, organization and access must be SEQUENTIAL. No other options are available. Table 3-1 on the next page summarizes the entries that can be used in the ACCESS IS clause for each entry that can be used after ORGANIZATION IS.

TABLE 3-1 ACCESS Available for Each ORGANIZATION

If ORGANIZATION is:	Then ACCESS IS can be:
SEQUENTIAL	SEQUENTIAL
INDEXED	SEQUENTIAL
	RANDOM
	DYNAMIC
RELATIVE	SEQUENTIAL
	RANDOM
	DYNAMIC

DATA DIVISION

The FILE SECTION and WORKING-STORAGE SECTION of the DATA DIVISION were presented in Chapter 2. As seen in Chapter 2, a key element of these sections is the use of picture clauses to describe the fields required for processing. Picture clauses are used to define a field's data category. The **data category** of a field refers to how the field may be utilized and manipulated within the program.

Data Categories

Five basic data categories are determined by picture clauses in a COBOL program: alphabetic, alphanumeric, numeric, alphanumeric edited, and numeric edited. An **alphabetic** field is an item that may contain only letters of the alphabet or spaces. The character A is used in a picture clause to define an alphabetic field. Figure 3-11 shows an example of such a definition. WA-ALPHA-FIELD-1 is defined as a three character alphabetic field. Any data other than letters or spaces placed into WA-ALPHA-FIELD-1 results in a run-time error called a data exception. A **data exception** occurs when the data category of a field and the data you are attempting to store in the field disagree.

```
02  WA-ALPHA-FIELD-1          PIC AAA.        3-character
                                              alphabetic
                                              field
```

FIGURE 3-11 An alphabetic field

Alphanumeric fields are defined by using the character X in a picture clause. **Alphanumeric** fields may contain letters, numbers, spaces, and special characters. Because an alphanumeric field may contain any group of characters, it is customary to use them instead of alphabetic fields. Alphabetic fields will not be used in this book. An example of an alphanumeric field, taken from the Premium Amount Report program, is shown in Figure 3-12. SW-END-OF-FILE is defined as a one-character field that can contain any type of data. The program uses the values of the fields YES and NEG with the field SW-END-OF-FILE, but it could contain any value. You can not perform arithmetic operations on alphanumeric fields.

FIGURE 3-12   An alphanumeric field

If it is necessary to perform arithmetic, then you must use **numeric** fields. The character 9 is used to define numeric fields. The Premium Amount Report program has several examples. One of the numeric fields defined is used to keep track of the number of records processed by the program (Figure 3-13). AC-RECORD-COUNT is defined as a five-digit number.

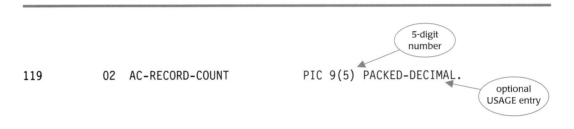

FIGURE 3-13   A numeric field

As discussed in Chapter 2, PACKED-DECIMAL refers to a type of USAGE. The **USAGE** of a field indicates how the field is stored in memory or auxiliary storage. Figure 3-14 shows the various options available for USAGE, and Table 3-2 on the next page summarizes these options. If no USAGE is specified, the default USAGE for a field is DISPLAY. USAGE IS **DISPLAY** generally means that each character or digit in the field requires one byte of storage. Numeric fields are the only items that can have a USAGE other than DISPLAY. **BINARY** provides an efficient way for the computer to work with and manipulate numeric data. Input to and output from a COBOL program occasionally needs to be in BINARY format. **COMP** is short for **COMPUTATIONAL** and was used on many computer systems in the past as a method of identifying fields stored in BINARY format. BINARY, COMP, and COMPUTATIONAL will not be used in this book.

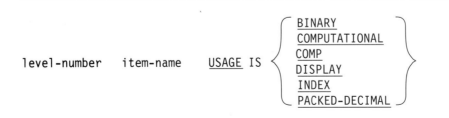

FIGURE 3-14   USAGE clause

PACKED-DECIMAL usage also causes data to be stored in a format that is efficient for the computer's numeric operations. Any field used as an accumulator in this book will be defined with a USAGE of PACKED-DECIMAL. In earlier versions of COBOL, many computer systems utilized a USAGE of COMPUTATIONAL-3, or COMP-3, to represent PACKED-DECIMAL.

TABLE 3-2 Common Types of USAGE

USAGE	Meaning
BINARY	Data stored as a base 2 number
COMPUTATIONAL	System defined, but often the same as BINARY
COMP	Short form of COMPUTATIONAL
DISPLAY	Default usage with data usually stored as one character per byte
INDEX	Special field for holding index values from COBOL tables
PACKED-DECIMAL	Data stored as a base 10 number with two digits per byte

INDEX fields are special fields used to store values used in conjunction with arrays. In COBOL, **arrays** are known as **tables** and they will be discussed later in the book.

Processing numeric data often requires the use of decimal fractions. The use of a V in a numeric picture identifies the **implied decimal position** within the field. No decimal point is actually stored in the field, but whenever numeric processing occurs, the field will be treated as though the decimal point is in the designated position.

Figure 3-15 shows PR-PREMIUM-AMOUNT from the Premium Amount Report program. PR-PREMIUM-AMOUNT is defined as a seven-digit number with five digits before the decimal point and two digits after the decimal point. COBOL guarantees that any arithmetic operation performed on PR-PREMIUM-AMOUNT will properly maintain the decimal value of the field. The S in the picture for PR-PREMIUM-AMOUNT indicates that PR-PREMIUM-AMOUNT is a signed numeric field. A **signed** numeric field is capable of being positive or negative. Without the S, a numeric field is **unsigned** and can never contain a negative value.

71   02 PR-PREMIUM-AMOUNT   PIC S9(5)V99. ← 7-digit number with 2 decimal positions

FIGURE 3-15 Signed numeric field with decimal positions

Figure 3-16 shows examples of other fields with implied decimal positions. WA-NUM-1 is a three-digit number with two digits before the decimal point and one digit after the decimal point. WA-NUM-2 is a two-digit number with one digit before the decimal point and one digit after. WA-NUM-3 is an eight-digit number with five digits before the decimal and three after. Notice the use of the duplicating factor prior to the implied decimal position in WA-NUM-3. WA-NUM-4 is an eight-digit number with four digits before the decimal point and four after. Notice the use of a duplicating factor before and after the implied decimal position in WA-NUM-4. WA-NUM-5 is a three-digit number with all three digits after the decimal point. WA-NUM-4 and WA-NUM-5 are signed numeric fields and can contain negative amounts.

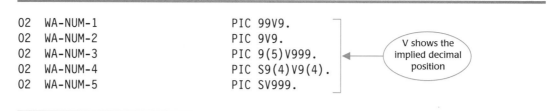

```
02  WA-NUM-1          PIC 99V9.
02  WA-NUM-2          PIC 9V9.
02  WA-NUM-3          PIC 9(5)V999.
02  WA-NUM-4          PIC S9(4)V9(4).
02  WA-NUM-5          PIC SV999.
```

V shows the implied decimal position

FIGURE 3-16 Examples of decimal number fields

If data is to be printed on a business report, it is usually printed in edited format. Editing for numeric fields is accomplished by using special characters to create **numeric edited** fields, also known as **edit patterns,** and then moving numeric fields to them. Edit patterns also can be created for alphanumeric fields. The next section discusses both numeric and alphanumeric editing, but the emphasis is on numeric editing. Edit patterns are defined in output field picture clauses within the DATA DIVISION.

EDIT PATTERNS

Editing numeric output for reports consists of suppressing leading zeros and inserting punctuation to make the output more readable. To edit a field with a dollar sign character or punctuation such as commas and decimal points, the character or punctuation is inserted in the output field's picture clause as it is to appear when the field is printed.

When numeric data is moved to SL-BALANCE-FIELD-1 (Figure 3-17), it is edited according to the format established in the picture clause. SL-BALANCE-FIELD-1 is designed to accommodate a six-digit number that has four digits before the decimal point and two digits after. The **dollar sign** ($) at the beginning of the field, often referred to as a fixed dollar sign, is the first character in the edited results. Table 3-3 shows the results of moving various quantities to SL-BALANCE-FIELD-1. A "v" is used in the data to indicate the decimal position for each value. Not all of the edited results are desirable. When leading zeros exist in the data, SL-BALANCE-FIELD-1 allows them to print. Normally, leading zeros would be suppressed. Also, notice that if there are more digits than are allowed for in the edit pattern, the extra digits are truncated and lost. Edit patterns fill to the left and right from the decimal point. Edit patterns must be large enough to accommodate the data to be edited.

```
02  SL-BALANCE-FIELD-1          PIC $9,999.99.
```

9-character edit pattern

FIGURE 3-17 Numeric edit pattern

TABLE 3-3 Results of Moving Various Quantities to SL-BALANCE-FIELD-1

Data in Memory	SL-BALANCE-FIELD-1	Printed Output
1325v50	$9,999.99	$1,325.50
0406v25	$9,999.99	$0,406.25
0026v50	$9,999.99	$0,026.50
43012v00	$9,999.99	$3,012.00

Zero suppression is the process of replacing leading zeros in a numeric field with spaces or other characters. To zero suppress a field with spaces, the letter Z is placed in the picture clause in each place a zero is to be suppressed. Figure 3-18 shows the definition for DL-PREMIUM-AMOUNT from the Premium Amount Report program. Leading zeros will be suppressed up to the digit just before the decimal point. Zero suppression also is used in the definitions of RH-PAGE-COUNT and SL-RECORD-COUNT (Figure 3-19).

```
199        02  DL-PREMIUM-AMOUNT          PIC ZZ,ZZ9.99BCR.
```
12-character edit pattern with zero suppression

FIGURE 3-18   Definition of DL-PREMIUM-AMOUNT

```
135        02  RH-PAGE-COUNT              PIC ZZ9.

216        02  SL-RECORD-COUNT            PIC ZZZZ9.
```
edit patterns with zero suppression

FIGURE 3-19   RH-PAGE-COUNT and SL-RECORD-COUNT

When a **comma** (,) is placed in a picture clause, the comma will be inserted in the same place as it appears in the picture. If the zero to the left of the comma has been suppressed, then the comma will not be inserted in the position where it appears. Rather, the comma will be replaced by the character that is replacing the zeros in the zero suppression operation, usually a space.

When the letter Z is used in a picture clause, only another Z, a dollar sign, a plus sign, a minus sign, or a comma can precede it. Plus and minus signs are discussed later in this chapter. Table 3-4 shows the definition of and the results of moving quantities to SL-BALANCE-FIELD-2. When the data has no leading zeros, the edited result is the same as for SL-BALANCE-FIELD-1. When the data does have leading zeros, the zeros are replaced with spaces. Notice that when it is not needed, the comma is also suppressed and replaced with a space. Table 3-5 presents more examples of zero suppression. A leading zero is changed to a space if the corresponding position in the picture clause contains a Z. If the corresponding position in the picture clause contains a 9, the zero is printed. After the first significant digit is printed, all following zeros are printed. The **first significant digit** in a numeric field is the first nonzero digit to appear within the number.

TABLE 3-4   Results of Moving Various Quantities to SL-BALANCE-FIELD-2

02 SL-BALANCE-FIELD-2		PIC $Z,ZZZ.99.
Data in Memory	*Edit Pattern*	*Printed Output*
1325v50	$Z,ZZZ.99	$1,325.50
0406v25	$Z,ZZZ.99	$ 406.25
0026v50	$Z,ZZZ.99	$ 26.50
43012v00	$Z,ZZZ.99	$3,012.00

TABLE 3-5   More Examples of Zero Suppression

Data in Memory	Edit Pattern	Printed Output
12595	ZZZ99	12595
00123	ZZZ99	123
00005	ZZZ99	05
00000	ZZZZZ	(all spaces)
00409	ZZZZZ	409

The **asterisk** (*) also can be used for zero suppression. When the corresponding position in the picture clause contains an asterisk, leading zeros are replaced by asterisks. Table 3-6 presents examples. The use of asterisks in zero suppression is usually limited to cases where spaces are not desirable in front of numbers, such as on a payroll check. The dollar sign, comma, and decimal point also may be used in conjunction with asterisks.

TABLE 3-6   Examples of Zero Suppression with Asterisks

Data in Memory	Edit Pattern	Printed Output
12595	***99	12595
00123	***99	**123
00005	***99	***05
00000	***99	***00
00000	*****	*****

When the **decimal point** (.) appears in a picture clause, a decimal point will be inserted at the position occupied by the decimal point in the picture. The data in the field to be moved to the edited picture will be aligned so the implied decimal point, as indicated by the V in the numeric field being edited, corresponds to the actual decimal point. The decimal point can appear in an edit pattern only once. Table 3-7 illustrates the use of the dollar sign, comma, asterisk, and decimal point in edit patterns.

TABLE 3-7   Edit Patterns with Dollar Signs, Commas, Asterisks, and Decimal Points

Data in Memory	Edit Pattern	Printed Output
1259v50	$Z,ZZZ.99	$1,259.50
0000v00	$Z,ZZZ.99	$ .00
0005v50	$*,***.99	$****5.50
0000v05	$*,***.99	$*****.05
1234	$Z,ZZZ.99	$1,234.00

The dollar sign, comma, and decimal point are referred to as **insertion characters**. An insertion character specified in a picture clause will be placed in the corresponding position of the field when data is moved to that field. When insertion characters are used, the picture must be large enough to hold both the data and the insertion character.

In addition to the use of a Z, dollar sign, comma, an asterisk, and a decimal point, COBOL has other characters and options available for edit patterns.

Floating Dollar Signs

The appearance of a single dollar sign symbol ($) in a picture indicates that a dollar sign is to be inserted at the position occupied by the symbol. Several consecutive dollar sign symbols indicate that the data is to be edited with a **floating dollar sign**, which is a dollar sign that prints to the left of and adjacent to the first significant digit. Figure 3-20 illustrates the use of a floating dollar sign in a field named SL-BALANCE-FIELD-3. The field will accommodate a six-digit number that has four digits before the decimal point and two digits after the decimal point. Table 3-8 illustrates the results of using such an edit pattern.

```
02   SL-BALANCE-FIELD-3          PIC $$,$$$.99.
```

edit pattern with floating dollar sign

FIGURE 3-20 Field defined with a floating dollar sign

TABLE 3-8 Edit Patterns with Floating Dollar Signs

Data in Memory	Edit Pattern	Printed Output
1259v50	$$,$$$.99	$1,259.50
0000v00	$$,$$$.99	$.00
0005v50	$$,$$$.99	$5.50
0000v05	$$,$$9.99	$0.05
0012v34	$$,$$9.99	$12.34

Plus Sign

When processing involves the use of signed numeric fields, it is necessary to account for the possibility of negative quantities in the edited output. When a **plus sign** (+) appears at either end of an edit pattern, the sign of the field edited will be indicated in the position where the plus sign appears. If the field is positive, a plus sign (+) will be inserted. If the field is negative, a **minus sign** (−) will be inserted. For purposes of editing, if a field has a value of zero, it is treated as though it is positive.

The plus sign can be a floating plus sign on the left side of an edit pattern. By placing several consecutive plus signs in the leading positions of the edit pattern, a floating plus sign will print either a plus sign or minus sign to the left of and adjacent to the first significant digit to print. Table 3-9 presents examples of edit patterns containing plus signs.

TABLE 3-9 Edit Patterns with Plus Signs

Data in Memory	Edit Pattern	Printed Output
+01259	+ZZ,ZZ9	+ 1,259
-00012	ZZ,ZZ9+	12-
00000	ZZ,ZZ9+	0+
+01259v50	+ZZ,ZZZ.99	+ 1,259.50
-01259v50	ZZ,ZZZ.99+	1,259.50-
+00012v34	+++,+++.99	+12.34

Minus Sign

A minus sign (–) can be used in a manner similar to a plus sign. When a minus sign appears at either end of an edit pattern, the minus sign will be inserted if the field being edited is negative. If the field being edited is positive or zero, a space will be inserted. Thus, a sign appears only if an edited field is negative. As with a floating plus sign, a floating minus sign also can be used. Table 3-10 illustrates the use of a minus sign in edit patterns.

TABLE 3-10   Edit Patterns with Minus Signs

Data in Memory	Edit Pattern	Printed Output
-01259	-ZZ,ZZ9	- 1,259
-00012	ZZ,ZZ9-	12-
+01259v50	-ZZ,ZZZ.99	1,259.50
-01259v50	ZZ,ZZZ.99-	1,259.50-
-00012v34	---,---.99	-12.34

Credit Symbol and Debit Symbol

The **credit symbol**, CR, and **debit symbol**, DB, are used in accounting applications and provide two more ways to indicate the sign of an edited field. When CR appears on the right side of an edit pattern, the CR will be inserted if the field being edited is negative. If the field being edited is positive or zero, two spaces will be inserted. The debit symbol works exactly like the credit symbol. When DB appears on the right side of an edit pattern, the DB will be inserted when the field being edited is negative. Spaces are inserted otherwise. Table 3-11 presents examples of numeric edit patterns using the credit and debit symbols.

TABLE 3-11   Edit Patterns with Credit and Debit Symbols

Data in Memory	Edit Pattern	Printed Output
+01259	ZZ,ZZ9CR	1,259
-00012	ZZ,ZZ9CR	12CR
+01259v50	ZZ,ZZZ.99DB	1,259.50
-01259v50	ZZ,ZZZ.99DB	1,259.50DB
-00012v34	$$,$$$.99CR	$12.34CR
-00012v34	**,***.99DB	****12.34DB

Blank, Zero, and Slash

In all of the previous edit patterns, the fields to be edited had to be numeric. The **blank (B)**, **zero (0)**, and **slash (/)** insertion characters can be used with either numeric or alphanumeric fields. They are the only characters allowed in **alphanumeric edit patterns**. When used, these characters are inserted in the positions in which they appear within edit patterns. The B, 0, and / may appear more than once in an edit pattern and may be combined with each other in an edit pattern. Table 3-12 on the next page illustrates their use in numeric and alphanumeric edit patterns. Whereas numeric edit patterns fill in both directions from the decimal point, alphanumeric edit patterns fill from left to right. Alphanumeric edit patterns are not used in this book.

TABLE 3-12 Edit Patterns with B, 0, and / Insertion Characters

Data in Memory	Edit Pattern	Printed Output
-01259	ZZ,ZZ9BCR	1,259 CR
120497	99/99/99	12/04/97
23452450	990999B99/9	230452 45/0
BLJONES	XBXBXXXX	B L JONES
ABCDEFG	XOXX/XXBXX	AOBC/DE FG

BLANK WHEN ZERO Clause

The **BLANK WHEN ZERO** clause can be used with a numeric edit pattern to cause nothing but spaces to print when the value edited is zero. Figure 3-21 illustrates the use of the BLANK WHEN ZERO clause. Without the BLANK WHEN ZERO clause, zero would print as 0.00 when moved to DL-PREMIUM-AMOUNT. With the BLANK WHEN ZERO clause, only spaces print when a value of zero is moved to DL-PREMIUM-AMOUNT. BLANK WHEN ZERO cannot be used when asterisks are used in an edit pattern for zero suppression.

```
02  DL-PREMIUM-AMOUNT        PIC ZZ,ZZ9.99 BLANK WHEN ZERO.
```

prints all blanks when zero is moved to it

FIGURE 3-21 BLANK WHEN ZERO clause

JUSTIFIED RIGHT Clause

In some applications, it might be desirable to right-justify alphanumeric output data. Normally, an alphanumeric or alphabetic move results in left-justified data. The **JUSTIFIED RIGHT** clause can be used on alphabetic or alphanumeric elementary items. It causes the rightmost character of the sending field to be placed in the rightmost position of the receiving field in a MOVE statement. The moving of characters continues from right to left until the receiving field is filled. Truncation on the left will occur if the sending field is larger than the receiving field. Padding with spaces will occur on the left if the sending field is smaller than the receiving field. Table 3-13 illustrates the use of the JUSTIFIED RIGHT clause. Note the difference in the positioning of customer names when JUSTIFIED RIGHT is used on DL-CUSTOMER-NAME.

TABLE 3-13 Results of Using the JUSTIFIED RIGHT Clause

```
02 DL-CUSTOMER-NAME      PIC X(20).

02 DL-CUSTOMER-NAME      PIC X(20) JUSTIFIED RIGHT.

MOVE PR-CUSTOMER-NAME TO DL-CUSTOMER-NAME.
```

Results in DL-CUSTOMER-NAME without JUSTIFIED RIGHT	Results in DL-CUSTOMER-NAME with JUSTIFIED RIGHT
Allister, Collin	Allister, Collin
Amfelter, Audrey	Amfelter, Audrey
Andrews, Robert	Andrews, Robert
Anytime, Seeue	Anytime, Seeue
Foreman, Otto	Foreman, Otto

Scaling—P Symbol

The **P symbol** is used in a picture clause to indicate scaling positions beyond either end of data in memory for purposes of identifying the true numeric value of a field. Each P in a picture clause represents an implied position and specifies the location of the implied decimal position. A V is not used to imply a decimal position when one or more Ps appear in a picture clause. The P symbol is not used in edit patterns. Its use is restricted to input or internal pictures. Table 3-14 presents examples of scaling. Scaling will not be used in this book.

TABLE 3-14   Examples of Pictures with the Scaling Symbol P

Data in Memory	Picture	Value in Program
123	999PP	12300
12	99P	120
34	PP99	.0034
567	P999	.0567

Each 9 represents a digit in storage. Each P is a scaled position and does not take any storage. Thus, a picture such as PP999 defines a three-digit number; however, this three-digit number will be treated as a five-digit number with all the digits to the right of the implied decimal position for computation purposes. When used, Ps must appear entirely to the right or entirely to the left of 9s in a picture clause.

NAME QUALIFICATION

Following the user-defined name guidelines presented in Chapter 2, every field name should be unique. Although COBOL allows it, it is not wise to define the same name twice. If a user-defined name for a field is used more than once, COBOL requires that each occurrence be subordinate to a higher level name that is unique. In Figure 3-22 on the next page, notice that the two 01 level names TRANSACTION-RECORD and MASTER-RECORD have both group and elementary fields with identical names. For example, both 01 level entries have an EMPLOYEE-NAME group field and a FIRST-NAME elementary field. A reference to one of these fields in your program would result in a syntax error unless the reference was qualified. A **qualified name** involves using the field name along with the COBOL reserved word IN or OF and the group name underneath which the field is defined. Figure 3-23 on the next page shows an example of a COBOL statement using qualified names.

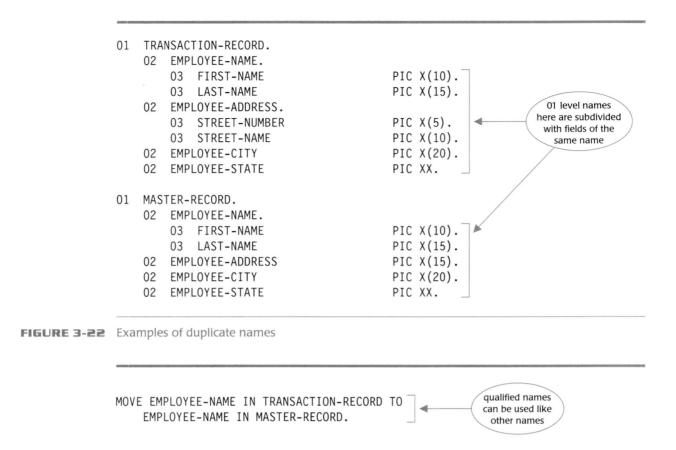

```
01   TRANSACTION-RECORD.
     02  EMPLOYEE-NAME.
         03   FIRST-NAME               PIC X(10).
         03   LAST-NAME                PIC X(15).
     02  EMPLOYEE-ADDRESS.
         03   STREET-NUMBER            PIC X(5).
         03   STREET-NAME              PIC X(10).
     02  EMPLOYEE-CITY                 PIC X(20).
     02  EMPLOYEE-STATE                PIC XX.

01   MASTER-RECORD.
     02  EMPLOYEE-NAME.
         03   FIRST-NAME               PIC X(10).
         03   LAST-NAME                PIC X(15).
     02  EMPLOYEE-ADDRESS              PIC X(15).
     02  EMPLOYEE-CITY                 PIC X(20).
     02  EMPLOYEE-STATE                PIC XX.
```

01 level names here are subdivided with fields of the same name

FIGURE 3-22   Examples of duplicate names

```
MOVE EMPLOYEE-NAME IN TRANSACTION-RECORD TO
     EMPLOYEE-NAME IN MASTER-RECORD.
```

qualified names can be used like other names

FIGURE 3-23   Example using qualified names

The field EMPLOYEE-NAME IN TRANSACTION-RECORD is a qualified name and represents the field to be moved in the given instruction. EMPLOYEE-NAME IN MASTER-RECORD also is a qualified name and is the receiving field in the MOVE. The reserved word OF also may be used to qualify field names. Thus, EMPLOYEE-NAME OF TRANSACTION RECORD means the same as EMPLOYEE-NAME IN TRANSACTION-RECORD. Qualified names will be avoided in this book.

INDEPENDENT ITEMS

The Premium Amount Report program in this chapter and the Policy Number Report program in Chapter 2 use the level numbers 01, 02, 03, and so on to define group and elementary items in the DATA DIVISION. Another method that may be used to define fields is the 77 level number. The use of **77 level numbers** is illustrated in Figure 3-24. The 77 level number must begin in the A-margin and must define an elementary item that has a picture clause.

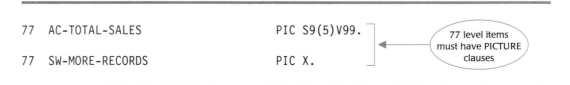

```
77   AC-TOTAL-SALES               PIC S9(5)V99.

77   SW-MORE-RECORDS              PIC X.
```

77 level items must have PICTURE clauses

FIGURE 3-24   Example of 77 level number name definitions

A 77 level number allows a single data item to be defined without it being a member of a group. These items are, therefore, referred to as **independent items**. Although a 77 level number can be used, it is a better programming technique to use 01 level group names in the DATA DIVISION to identify the use of elementary items defined beneath them. This book will not use 77 level numbers.

CONDITION NAMES

Much more useful and meaningful than 77 level number entries are 88 level number entries. These were introduced in Chapter 2 and are used to define **condition names**. Figure 3-25 shows the definition for SW-END-OF-FILE from the Premium Amount Report program. It is the same definition used in the Policy Number Report program in Chapter 2. The 88 level item, END-OF-FILE, is a condition name associated with SW-END-OF-FILE. Condition names are either true or false at any given point during the execution of a program. The VALUE clause on END-OF-FILE indicates that the condition END-OF-FILE will be true when the field SW-END-OF-FILE has a Y in it. Any other value in SW-END-OF-FILE makes the condition END-OF-FILE false. Figure 3-26 shows how this condition name is used in the PROCEDURE DIVISION of the Premium Amount Report program.

```
100      02  SW-END-OF-FILE               PIC X.
101          88  END-OF-FILE                       VALUE "Y".
```
88s reserve no storage

FIGURE 3-25   Definition of SW-END-OF-FILE

Referencing a condition name in a conditional statement within the PROCEDURE DIVISION is equivalent to testing to determine if the value represented by the condition name is stored in the associated field. The statement in Figure 3-26 and the statement in Figure 3-27 are logically the same.

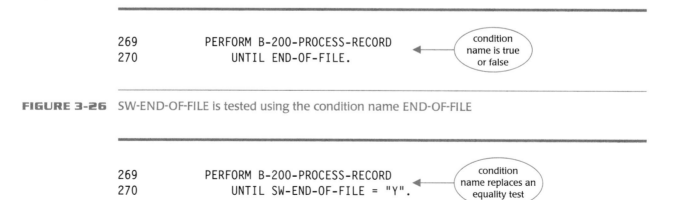

```
269           PERFORM B-200-PROCESS-RECORD
270               UNTIL END-OF-FILE.
```
condition name is true or false

FIGURE 3-26   SW-END-OF-FILE is tested using the condition name END-OF-FILE

```
269           PERFORM B-200-PROCESS-RECORD
270               UNTIL SW-END-OF-FILE = "Y".
```
condition name replaces an equality test

FIGURE 3-27   SW-END-OF-FILE is tested without the condition name

Condition names also are defined under PR-PAYMENT-STATUS in the PREMIUM-RECORD layout (Figure 3-28 on the next page).

```
72        02   PR-PAYMENT-STATUS          PIC X.
73             88   DELINQUENT            VALUE "D".
74             88   PAID-IN-FULL          VALUE "F".
75             88   PARTIALLY-PAID        VALUE "P".
76             88   NOT-YET-BILLED        VALUE "N".
```

multiple
condition names
can be defined

FIGURE 3-28   88 level number entries under PR-PAYMENT-STATUS

Figure 3-29 shows how these condition names are used within the Premium Amount Report program to test the contents of PR-PAYMENT-STATUS. Multiple condition names can be defined under a field, and condition names can be defined to be true for multiple values. In Figure 3-29, if none of the condition names are true the message ERR is moved to the output field DL-PAYMENT-STATUS. Figure 3-30 shows the basic format of an 88 level number entry.

```
294        IF DELINQUENT
295            MOVE "DELQ" TO DL-PAYMENT-STATUS
296        ELSE
297            IF PAID-IN-FULL
298                MOVE "PAID" TO DL-PAYMENT-STATUS
299            ELSE
300                IF PARTIALLY-PAID
301                    MOVE "P PD" TO DL-PAYMENT-STATUS
302                ELSE
303                    IF NOT-YET-BILLED
304                        MOVE "NYB" TO DL-PAYMENT-STATUS
305                    ELSE
306                        MOVE "ERR" TO DL-PAYMENT-STATUS.
```

testing
condition
names

FIGURE 3-29   Use of the 88 level number entries defined under PR-PAYMENT-STATUS

$$88 \text{ condition-name} \begin{Bmatrix} \underline{\text{VALUE}} \text{ IS} \\ \underline{\text{VALUES}} \text{ ARE} \end{Bmatrix} \begin{Bmatrix} \text{literal-1} \begin{bmatrix} \begin{Bmatrix} \underline{\text{THROUGH}} \\ \underline{\text{THRU}} \end{Bmatrix} \text{literal-2} \end{bmatrix} \end{Bmatrix} \ldots$$

FIGURE 3-30   Basic format of an 88 level number entry

Figure 3-31 shows alternative 88 level number entries defined under the field PR-PAYMENT-STATUS. The condition name VALID-STATUS will be true when the field PR-PAYMENT-STATUS has a value of D, F, P, or N. The condition name EXCESSIVE-STATUS will be true when PR-PAYMENT-STATUS has a value of Q through Z.

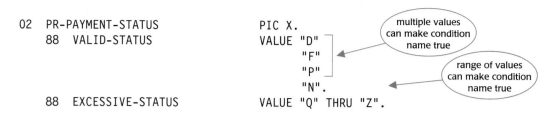

```
02  PR-PAYMENT-STATUS            PIC X.
    88  VALID-STATUS             VALUE "D"
                                       "F"
                                       "P"
                                       "N".
    88  EXCESSIVE-STATUS         VALUE "Q" THRU "Z".
```

FIGURE 3-31   Alternative 88 level number entries for PR-PAYMENT-STATUS

FIGURATIVE CONSTANTS

SPACES and ZEROS were introduced in Chapter 2. These entries are called **figurative constants** because they figuratively represent constant values. **SPACES** represents the nonnumeric literal " ". **ZEROS** represents the numeric value 0. Table 3-15 presents the figurative constants available in COBOL along with their associated values. Singular and plural versions represent identical values and work exactly the same. **Collating sequence** refers to the order in which items are sorted or given priority in comparisons. To say that **HIGH-VALUES** represent the greatest value in a computer's collating sequence simply means that no field will have a value greater than HIGH-VALUES. Likewise, no field can have a value less than **LOW-VALUES**. Typical collating sequences are presented in Figure 3-32.

TABLE 3-15   Figurative Constants

Figurative Constant	Value
ZERO, ZEROS, ZEROES	Numeric constant 0
SPACE, SPACES	Nonnumeric constant " "
HIGH-VALUE, HIGH-VALUES	Highest value in the computer's collating sequence
LOW-VALUE, LOW-VALUES	Lowest value in the computer's collating sequence
QUOTE, QUOTES	One or more occurrences of the character "
ALL literal	One or more occurrences of the character represented by the literal

EBCDIC	ASCII
HIGH-VALUES	HIGH-VALUES
Numbers	Letters
Letters	Numbers
Special characters	Special characters
SPACES	SPACES
LOW-VALUES	LOW-VALUES

EBCDIC	Extended Binary Coded Decimal Interchange Code
ASCII	American Standard Code for Information Interchange

FIGURE 3-32   Commonly used collating sequences (highest to lowest)

Figurative constants may be used following the VALUE clause in the DATA DIVISION of a COBOL program. Examples showing the use of SPACES in the DATA DIVISION were presented in Chapter 2. Figure 3-33 shows RH-LINE-5 from the Premium Amount Report program. The figurative constant SPACES is used following the VALUE clause when a field is to contain nothing but blanks. Notice the use of the figurative constant **ALL** in defining fields used to underline the column headings. The first entry presented, PIC X(13) VALUE ALL "-", is the same as PIC X(13) VALUE "-------------". Thirteen hyphens are needed in the nonnumeric literal following the VALUE clause to define the same entry as a single hyphen preceded by the figurative constant ALL.

```
173    02  RH-LINE-5.                       PIC X(13)  VALUE ALL "-".
174        03                               PIC X(4)   VALUE SPACES.
175        03          13 hyphens           PIC X(13)  VALUE ALL "-".
176        03          created by           PIC X(11)  VALUE SPACES.
177        03          VALUE ALL            PIC X(9)   VALUE ALL "-".
178        03                               PIC X(6)   VALUE SPACES.
179        03                               PIC X(7)   VALUE ALL "-".
180        03                               PIC X(6)   VALUE SPACES.
181        03                               PIC X(7)   VALUE ALL "-".
182        03                               PIC X(4)   VALUE SPACES.
183        03
```

FIGURE 3-33 RH-LINE-5 from the Premium Amount Report program

The figurative constant **QUOTES** represents one or more occurrences of a quotation mark. It cannot be used to replace quotation marks for nonnumeric literals and has limited use.

As seen in both the Policy Number Report program and Premium Amount Report program, figurative constants also may be used in the PROCEDURE DIVISION. Figure 3-34 presents the uses of the figurative constant ZERO from the PROCEDURE DIVISION of the Premium Amount Report program.

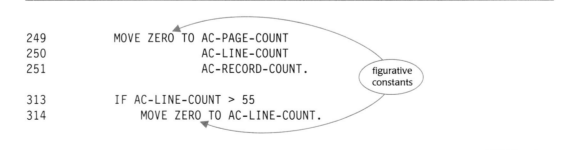

```
249        MOVE ZERO TO AC-PAGE-COUNT
250                      AC-LINE-COUNT
251                      AC-RECORD-COUNT.           figurative
                                                    constants
313        IF AC-LINE-COUNT > 55
314            MOVE ZERO TO AC-LINE-COUNT.
```

FIGURE 3-34 PROCEDURE DIVISION uses of the figurative constant ZERO

REDEFINES CLAUSE

Figure 3-35 presents examples of the REDEFINES clause. The **REDEFINES** clause is used in the DATA DIVISION to provide another name and another picture for an area of storage that already has been defined. Future programs in this book will utilize the REDEFINES clause in a fashion similar to the examples given here. NPR-PREMIUM-AMOUNT in the figure is defined as a seven-digit numeric field. NPR-PREMIUM-AMOUNT-ALPHA represents the same seven positions in the computer's memory but uses an alphanumeric picture. This definition is useful when it is uncertain whether or not a field actually contains numeric data. When data is entered via a terminal or accepted by some other means, mistakes often are made. If nonnumeric characters are present in a numeric field and arithmetic is attempted on that field, the program will terminate. Earlier in this chapter this was referred to as a data exception.

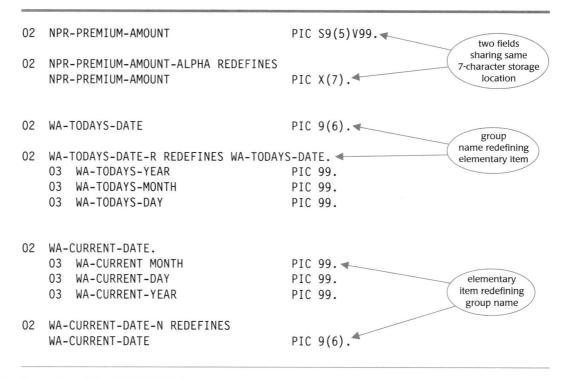

FIGURE 3-35 Examples of the REDEFINES clause

As seen by the other examples, group names may redefine elementary items and elementary items may redefine group names. Table 3-16 on the next page presents the rules governing the use of the REDEFINES clause. Two basic concepts to remember are that the redefining field must have the same level number and must immediately follow the field being redefined.

TABLE 3-16 Rules Governing the REDEFINES Clause

Syntax rules for the REDEFINES clause

1. A redefining field must immediately follow the field being redefined.
2. The level numbers of the redefining field and the field being redefined must be the same.
3. REDEFINES may not be used at the 01 level in the FILE SECTION.
4. The redefining field may not contain an OCCURS clause. (OCCURS will be discussed in a later chapter.)
5. The redefining field must be as long as or shorter than the field being redefined.
6. The field name being redefined may not be qualified.
7. A field name may be redefined more than once.
8. A redefining field may not itself be redefined.

CHAPTER SUMMARY

The Premium Amount Report program in this chapter was used to introduce additional options available for use in the ENVIRONMENT DIVISION and DATA DIVISION of a COBOL program. The following list summarizes this chapter. The summary is designed to help you study and understand the material and concepts presented.

1. The **CONFIGURATION SECTION** of the ENVIRONMENT DIVISION can be used to identify the computer system on which the program is compiled and run.
2. The **SPECIAL-NAMES** paragraph of the CONFIGURATION SECTION can be used to associate user-defined terms with hardware-specific features.
3. **ORGANIZATION IS** and **ACCESS IS** are clauses available in SELECT entries of the INPUT-OUTPUT SECTION, FILE-CONTROL paragraph.
4. ANS COBOL allows for **SEQUENTIAL**, **INDEXED**, and **RELATIVE** file organizations.
5. ANS COBOL allows for **SEQUENTIAL**, **RANDOM**, and **DYNAMIC** access to files.
6. The five basic data categories available in COBOL are **alphabetic**, **alphanumeric**, **numeric**, **alphanumeric edited**, and **numeric edited**.
7. Every elementary field defined within a program has a **USAGE**. The default usage is **DISPLAY**. Only numeric fields may have a USAGE other than DISPLAY.
8. The **implied decimal position** in a decimal number field is indicated by the character V in a picture clause.
9. Edit patterns provide for zero suppression and the insertion of special characters. They are used to improve the appearance of output reports.
10. The **JUSTIFIED RIGHT** clause can be used on alphabetic and alphanumeric elementary items to cause the rightmost characters in a sending field to be placed in the rightmost positions of a receiving field upon the execution of a MOVE statement.
11. The **P symbol** is used in a picture clause to indicate scaling positions.
12. **Data name qualification** is needed only when the same field name is defined more than once.
13. A **77 level number** defines an **independent item**.
14. **Condition names** are defined using 88 level entries and can be used to replace relational tests in a program.
15. **Figurative constants** represent constant values and are commonly used in COBOL programs.
16. The **REDEFINES** clause allows a storage location to have multiple names and pictures.

KEY TERMS
. . . .

77 level numbers (3-22)
ACCESS IS clause (3-11)
ALL (3-26)
alphabetic (3-12)
alphanumeric (3-12)
alphanumeric edit patterns (3-19)
arrays (3-14)
asterisk (3-17)
BINARY (3-13)
blank (B) (3-19)
BLANK WHEN ZERO (3-20)
collating sequence (3-25)
comma (3-16)
COMP (3-13)
COMPUTATIONAL (3-13)
condition names (3-23)
CONFIGURATION SECTION (3-19)
credit symbol (CR) (3-19)
data category (3-12)
data exception (3-12)
debit symbol (DB) (3-19)
decimal point (3-17)
DISPLAY (3-13)
dollar sign (3-15)
DYNAMIC (3-11)
edit patterns (3-15)
figurative constants (3-25)
first significant digit (3-16)
floating dollar sign (3-18)
HIGH-VALUES (3-25)
implementor name (3-10)
implied decimal position (3-14)

independent items (3-23)
INDEX (3-14)
INDEXED (3-11)
insertion characters (3-17)
JUSTIFIED RIGHT (3-20)
LOW-VALUES (3-25)
minus sign (3-18)
mnemonic (3-10)
numeric (3-13)
numeric edited (3-15)
OBJECT-COMPUTER (3-10)
ORGANIZATION IS clause (3-11)
P symbol (3-21)
PACKED-DECIMAL (3-13)
plus sign (3-18)
qualified name (3-21)
QUOTES (3-26)
RANDOM (3-11)
REDEFINES (3-27)
RELATIVE (3-11)
SEQUENTIAL (3-11)
signed (3-14)
slash (/)(3-19)
SOURCE-COMPUTER (3-10)
SPACES (3-25)
SPECIAL-NAMES (3-10)
tables (3-14)
unsigned (3-14)
USAGE (3-13)
zero (0) (3-19)
zero suppression (3-16)
ZEROS (3-25)

STUDENT ASSIGNMENTS
. . . .

Student Assignment 1: True/False

Instructions: Circle T if the statement is true or F if the statement is false.

T   F   1. A numeric field is defined by using 9s in the picture clause.

T   F   2. The character V can be used in the picture of an alphanumeric field.

T   F   3. The SPECIAL-NAMES paragraph is found in the DATA DIVISION.

T   F   4. The OBJECT-COMPUTER paragraph is treated as a comment.

T   F   5. A sequential file can be processed randomly.

T   F   6. 77 and 88 level entries are used for the same types of fields.

T   F   7. There is no difference between an alphabetic field and an alphanumeric field.

(continued)

Student Assignment 1 (continued)

T F 8. The reserved word SPACES is called a figurative constant.

T F 9. A numeric edit pattern can have only one decimal point.

T F 10. Zero suppression is the process of replacing all zeros in a field with blanks.

T F 11. The slash (/), zero (0), and blank (B) are known as insertion characters.

T F 12. SPACE represents just one blank, whereas SPACES represents many blanks.

T F 13. An 88 level condition name is used to speed up the execution of a COBOL program.

T F 14. The character S is used in a picture clause for purposes of scaling.

T F 15. A 77 level item is used to speed up the execution of a COBOL program.

T F 16. It is possible to have a floating minus sign in an edit pattern.

T F 17. The CR symbol and DB symbol work exactly the same in that they only print when a quantity is negative.

T F 18. An asterisk can be used for zero suppression in an edit pattern.

T F 19. The REDEFINES clause is used in the PROCEDURE DIVISION to repeat a COBOL verb.

T F 20. A condition name can be true for multiple values.

Student Assignment 2: Multiple Choice

Instructions: Circle the correct response.

1. Which of the following picture clauses is syntactically incorrect?
   a. PIC X(6)VXX
   b. PIC 999V99
   c. PIC XXXXXX
   d. PIC PPPP9
   e. all of the above

2. Which of the following is not a figurative constant?
   a. SPACES
   b. ZEROES
   c. BLANKS
   d. QUOTES
   e. all of the above

3. An alphanumeric field can contain _____.
   a. letters
   b. numbers
   c. special characters
   d. blanks
   e. all of the above

4. What USAGE is required for alphanumeric fields?
   a. COMPUTATIONAL
   b. DISPLAY
   c. PACKED-DECIMAL
   d. INDEX
   e. none of the above

5. The SPECIAL-NAMES paragraph allows you to associate a user-defined word called a _____ with an implementor feature available on the computer system.
   a. figurative constant
   b. header
   c. data category
   d. mnemonic
   e. none of the above

6. When the same name is defined twice in a program, then a reference in the PROCEDURE DIVISION to that name must be _____.
   a. standardized
   b. qualified
   c. amortized
   d. quantified
   e. none of the above

7. Which of the following can be used to indicate the sign of a numeric field within an edit pattern?
   a. CR
   b. DB
   c. plus sign (+)
   d. minus sign (–)
   e. all of the above

8. Which of the following symbols can be used to indicate scaling within a picture clause?
   a. P
   b. S
   c. 9
   d. X
   e. none of the above

9. When using the REDEFINES clause, the level number of the field being redefined and the level number of the redefining field must _____.
   a. both be 01
   b. be consecutive numbers, such as 02 and 03
   c. be exactly the same
   d. both be 88
   e. none of the above

10. A floating dollar sign cannot be used in conjunction with _____.
    a. an asterisk
    b. commas
    c. a plus or minus sign
    d. the credit symbol (CR)
    e. none of the above

Student Assignment 3: Editing Numeric Fields

Instructions: Indicate the edited result when the given numeric field is moved to the corresponding edit pattern field.

(continued)

Student Assignment 3 (continued)

	Numeric Field	Current Value	Edit Pattern	Edited Result
a.	999V99	12.43	$ZZZ.99	_____
b.	S9(4)V99	1215.50	$$,$$$.99	_____
c.	S9(5)V99	512.25-	ZZ,ZZZ.99CR	_____
d.	S9(5)V99	42.33-	*,***.99	_____

Student Assignment 4: Coding an Edit Pattern

Instructions: Write an edit pattern to cause a seven-digit field with a picture of 9(5)V99 to be printed with a floating dollar sign, a comma, and a decimal point. The field is to be zero suppressed up to the decimal point.

Student Assignment 5: Coding Condition Names

Instructions: Given the one-character alphanumeric field PR-CUSTOMER-FAMILY-STATUS, define the field using a 02 level number and define three condition names for the field. The condition name SINGLE should be true if the field contains an S; MARRIED should be true if the field contains an M; and DIVORCED should be true if the field contains a D.

Student Assignment 6: Coding More Condition Names

Instructions: Given the two-digit numeric field PR-CLIENT-AGE, define the field using a 02 level number and define the following condition names. YOUTH will be true for the range of values 1 to 18. YOUNG-ADULT will be true for the range 19 to 34. MATURE-ADULT will be true for the range 35 to 55. OLDER-ADULT will be true for the range 56 to 99.

Student Assignment 7: Coding a REDEFINES Clause

Instructions: Given the numeric field PR-SALES-AMOUNT with a picture of 9(6)V99, code the definition of the field using a 02 level number and then redefine the field as an alphanumeric field of the same size using the name PR-SALES-AMOUNT-ALPHA.

COBOL LABORATORY EXERCISES

Exercise 1: Modified Premium Amount Report Program

Purpose: To gain experience in COBOL program maintenance and modification.

Problem: Open the file PROJ3.CBL on the Student Diskette that accompanies this book and modify the Premium Amount Report program making the following changes:

1. Eliminate the CONFIGURATION SECTION of the ENVIRONMENT DIVISION and omit the ORGANIZATION IS clause and the ACCESS IS clause in the SELECT statements within the INPUT-OUTPUT SECTION.
2. Print the premium amount for each customer using an edit pattern with a floating dollar sign. Float the dollar sign up to the decimal point.
3. Single-space the detail lines in the report and make any necessary adjustments to the heading routine for starting a new page.
4. When the condition name NOT-YET-BILLED is true, print NOBL instead of NYB.

Save this program as EX3-1.CBL.

Input Data: Use the Premium file presented in Appendix A as input. This file is named PREMIUM.DAT on the Student Diskette that accompanies this book.

Output Results: Output should be a report similar to the example given at the beginning of this chapter but containing the requested modifications.

Exercise 2: Customer Purchases Report

Purpose: To practice the use of edit patterns in the creation of a COBOL program that produces a Customer Purchases Report.

Problem: Write a program that produces a Customer Purchases Report for the ABC Department Store. Print the account number, customer name, balance, purchases, and credit limit on each detail line. Edit the customer balance and purchases using floating dollar signs. Use the credit symbol (CR) at the end of the edit pattern for the balance field. Zero suppress the account number and credit limit fields. Save this program as EX3-2.CBL.

Input Data: Use the Customer file listed in Appendix A as input. This file is named CUSTOMER.DAT on the Student Diskette that accompanies this book. Customer records have the following layout:

Field Description	Position	Length	Attribute
filler	1–6	6	Alphanumeric
Account Number	7–12	6	Numeric
Customer Name	13–32	20	Alphanumeric
filler	33–53	21	Alphanumeric
Balance	54–59	6	Numeric, S9(4)V99
Purchases	60–65	6	Numeric, 9(4)V99
Credit Limit	66–70	5	Numeric, 9(5)
filler	71–72	2	Alphanumeric
Record Length		72	

Output Results: Output consists of the Customer Purchases Report that lists the account number, name, balance, purchases, and credit limit for each customer. Double-space detail lines. Count and print the number of customers processed. The report should have a format similar to the following:

```
                        ABC DEPARTMENT STORE              PAGE Z9
                      CUSTOMER PURCHASES REPORT

   ACCOUNT                                            CREDIT
   NUMBER   CUSTOMER NAME        BALANCE     PURCHASES LIMIT
   -------  --------------------  ----------- --------- --------

   ZZZZZ9   XXXXXXXXXXXXXXXXXXXX  $$,$$$.99CR $$,$$$.99 Z,ZZ9.99

   ZZZZZ9   XXXXXXXXXXXXXXXXXXXX  $$,$$$.99CR $$,$$$.99 Z,ZZ9.99
     .
     .
     .
           TOTAL NUMBER OF RECORDS LISTED = ZZ9

                       END OF REPORT
```

Exercise 3: Customer Sales Report

Purpose: To practice designing and coding a COBOL program and to utilize edit patterns and condition names in the production of a report.

Problem: Design and code a COBOL program that creates a Customer Sales Report for EZ Auto Sales. The report should list the customer's number, name, purchase date, purchase price, and satisfaction rating. Code condition names associated with the satisfaction field and test these condition names in the program. Zero suppress the customer number and insert slashes in the purchase date. Float a dollar sign on the purchase price. Print an appropriate message to correspond to a customer's satisfaction rating. Save this program as EX3-3.CBL.

Input Data: Use the Customer Sales file listed in Appendix A as input. This file is named CUSTSALE.DAT on the Student Diskette that accompanies this book. The record layout for the customer records is as follows:

Field Description	Position	Length	Attribute
filler	1–9	9	Alphanumeric
Customer Number	10–13	4	Numeric
Customer Name	14–33	20	Alphanumeric
Purchase Date	34–39	6	Numeric
filler	40–59	20	Alphanumeric
Purchase Price	60–66	7	Numeric, 9(5)V99
filler	67–73	7	Alphanumeric
Satisfaction Code	74	1	Alphanumeric,
			0 = DISSATISFIED
			1 = UNDECIDED
			2 = SATISFIED
Record Length		74	

Output Results: A report should be output listing the customer's number, name, purchase date, purchase price, and satisfaction rating. Single-space detail lines and provide a count of the number of customers listed at the end of the report. The report should have a format similar to the following:

```
                         EZ AUTO SALES                    PAGE ZZ9
                      CUSTOMER SALES REPORT


CUSTOMER   CUSTOMER                 PURCHASE  PURCHASE    SATISFACTION
NUMBER     NAME                     DATE      PRICE       RATING
--------   --------------------     --------  ----------  -------------
  ZZZ9     XXXXXXXXXXXXXXXXXXXX     Z9/99/99  $$$,$$$.99  XXXXXXXXXXX
  ZZZ9     XXXXXXXXXXXXXXXXXXXX     Z9/99/99  $$$,$$$.99  XXXXXXXXXXX
  ZZZ9     XXXXXXXXXXXXXXXXXXXX     Z9/99/99  $$$,$$$.99  XXXXXXXXXXX
   .
   .
   .

           TOTAL NUMBER OF CUSTOMERS LISTED = ZZ9

                      END OF REPORT
```

CHAPTER FOUR

IF, MOVE, and Data Validation

OBJECTIVES

You will have mastered the material in Chapter 4 when you can:

- Understand and code one-sided decision statements
- Understand and code two-sided decision statements
- Understand and code nested decision statements
- Recognize and understand combined and complex conditions
- Explain the function of the EVALUATE statement
- Explain a MOVE using alphanumeric fields
- Explain a MOVE using numeric fields
- Understand the use of the INITIALIZE statement
- Understand the use of the ACCEPT statement
- Describe the use of reference modification
- Explain the purpose of data validation
- Describe uses of a class test and a sign test
- Describe uses of a range test and a value test

INTRODUCTION

In Chapter 3, you examined the DATA DIVISION of a COBOL program. This chapter covers commands available in the PROCEDURE DIVISION for making decisions and copying the contents of fields from one location to another. The very important process of data validation also will be described. **Data validation** is the process of determining if fields within the records of a file contain acceptable data. The validation process requires the use of conditional statements and special tests available in COBOL. The MOVE statement was introduced in earlier chapters and will be reviewed in more detail within this chapter along with other statements used to copy the contents of one field to another.

The Premium Record Error Report

Figure 4-1 presents a portion of the report output by the sample program presented in this chapter. The report lists errors found in a newly entered version of the Premium Input File. The intended purpose of the report is to supply information that can be used for correcting the contents of the file.

```
11/28/97                              AINSWORTH INSURANCE COMPANY                    PAGE   1
                                      PREMIUM RECORD ERROR REPORT

                                      INSURANCE                       PREMIUM  PAYMENT
CUSTOMER NAME         AGENT NAME      TYPE         POLICY NUMBER       AMOUNT   STATUS   ERROR MESSAGE
------------         ----------      ----         -------------       ------   ------   --------------------

Amfelter, Audrey     McDonald, Fred  Automobile   PM-2199-9229        0045650  F        POLICY CODE INVALID

Andrews, Robert      Anderson, James Home         HM-70P8-0507        0056000  P        CODE #1 NOT NUMERIC

Baker, Bonnie                        Renter       RT-4402-3211        0015000  N        AGENT NAME MISSING

Byman, Goodie        Anderson, James Phone        HM-0007-2393        0245000  N        TYPE NOT VALID
                                                                                        CODE #1 OUT OF RANGE

Connors, Cindy       Jones, William  Home         HM-0009-4171        0085000  N        CODE #1 OUT OF RANGE

                     Anderson, James Automobile   AM-7373-1147        0055000  D        CUST. NAME MISSING

Eman, Sorik          Jean, Barbara   Annuity      AN-0868-0020        0235000  N        CODE #2 OUT OF RANGE

. . .

Vlasic, Roberta      McDonald, Fred  Term Life    TL-0029-9999        0000800  M        CODE #1 OUT OF RANGE
                                                                                        CODE #2 OUT OF RANGE
                                                                                        PREM AMT TOO LOW
                                                                                        PAY STATUS INVALID

Wilder, Eugene       Jean, Barbara   Whole Life   WW-0082-1913        0038000  O        POLICY CODE INVALID
                                                                                        PAY STATUS INVALID

Willis, Richard      Anderson, James Renter       RT-9580-0003        0085000  F        CODE #2 OUT OF RANGE

Winfield, Wally      Anderson, James Whole Life   WL-2721-3904        0032600  P        PREM AMT NOT NUMERIC

          TOTAL ERROR RECORDS PRINTED =    24  OUT OF    72 RECORDS PROCESSED.

                              END OF REPORT
```

FIGURE 4-1   Premium Record Error Report

Hierarchy Chart

A hierarchy chart illustrating the organization of the PROCEDURE DIVISION of the sample program is presented in Figure 4-2. The shading in the upper right-hand corner of the rectangles for B-400-WRITE-REPORT is how this book will indicate that a module is performed by more than one paragraph in a program and appears more than once on a hierarchy chart.

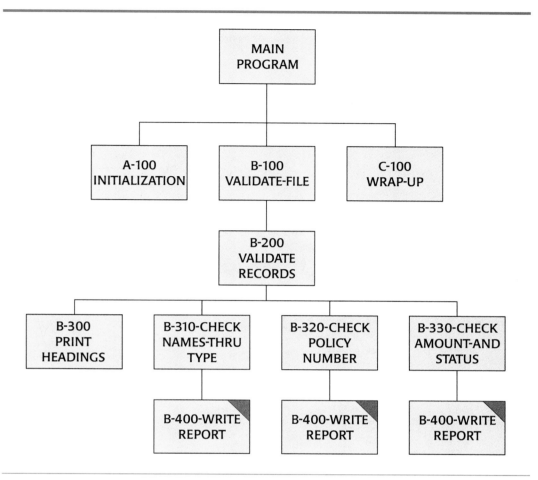

FIGURE 4-2 Hierarchy chart illustrating the organization of the PROCEDURE DIVISION of the Premium File Validation program

Program Flowchart

A partial flowchart illustrating logic used in the sample program is presented in Figure 4-3 on the next page. The logic involves numerous decision statements used in testing the contents of each field of each input record. When an error is discovered, an error message is written to the report. Only records with errors are written to the output report and records with multiple errors will be listed with multiple error messages.

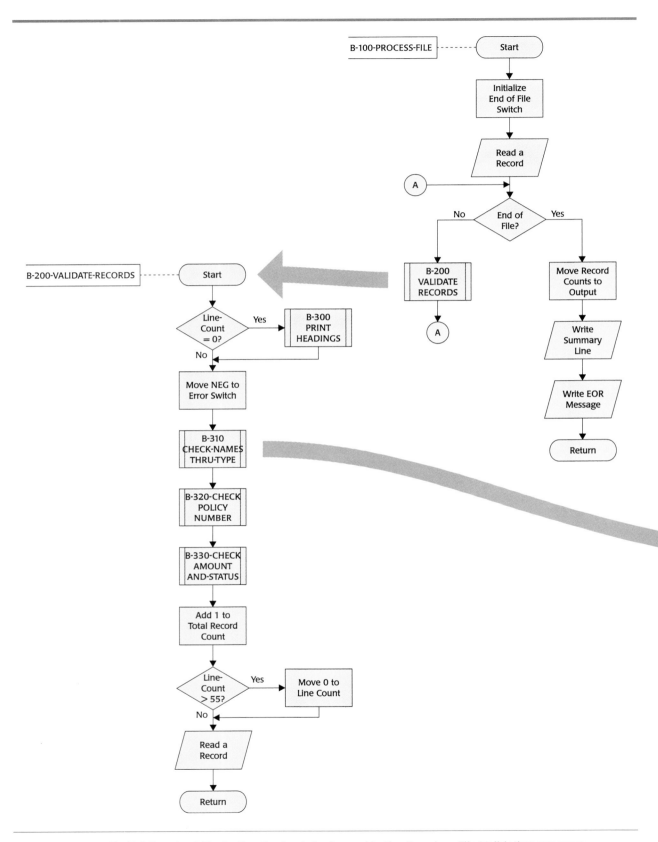

FIGURE 4-3   Partial flowchart illustrating the basic logic used in the Premium File Validation program

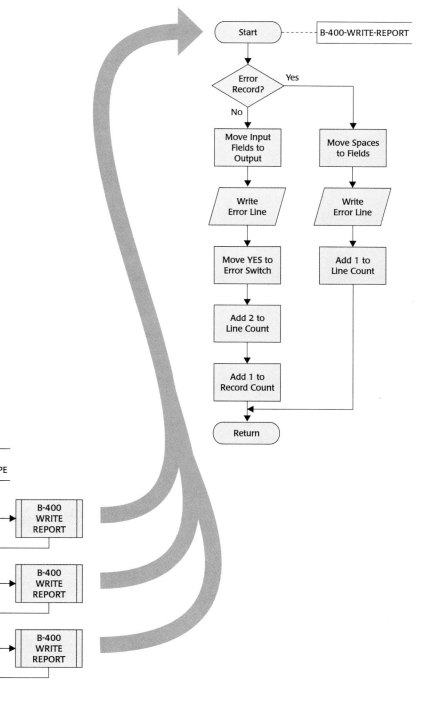

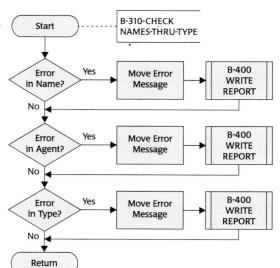

Premium File Record Layout

Figure 4-4 presents the record layout for the newly entered Premium file used as input in the sample program. It has exactly the same fields used in Chapter 3; however, one of the fields, the Premium Amount, is given an alternate name and picture with a REDEFINES clause. Another field, Policy Number, also is redefined in the program to provide access to its individual components. The REDEFINES clause was presented in Chapter 3 and its use in the sample program will be discussed later in this chapter.

Field	Position	Length	Attribute
Customer Name	1–20	20	Alphanumeric
Agent Name	21–40	20	Alphanumeric
Insurance Type	41–50	10	Alphanumeric
Policy Number	51–62	12	Alphanumeric
Premium Amount	63–69	7	Numeric, S9(5)V99
		redefine as	Alphanumeric
Payment Status	70	1	Alphanumeric
unused	71–80	10	Alphanumeric
Total Record Length		80	

FIGURE 4-4 Record layout for the newly entered Premium file

The Premium File Validation Program

Figure 4-5 presents the sample program discussed in this chapter, the Premium File Validation program. This program is found on the Student Diskette that accompanies this book. The program tests fields in a newly created Premium Input File and produces the given report by listing errors found within the fields of the records as they are discovered. The fields are tested, or validated, using conditional statements.

```
1     IDENTIFICATION DIVISION.
2     ***********************
3
4     PROGRAM-ID.     PREMVAL.
5     AUTHOR.         R. O. FOREMAN.
6     INSTALLATION.   PURDUE UNIVERSITY CALUMET.
7     DATE-WRITTEN.   NOV. 28, 1997.
8     DATE-COMPILED.  28-Nov-1997.
9     ****************************************************************
10    *                    PROGRAM NARRATIVE                        *
11    *                                                             *
12    *                                                             *
13    *    THIS PROGRAM READS ALL RECORDS IN A NEWLY ENTERED CUSTOMER *
14    *    PREMIUM FILE AND VALIDATES THE ENTRIES IN EACH FIELD.  AN *
15    *    ERROR REPORT IS CREATED LISTING ALL ERROR RECORDS ALONG  *
16    *    WITH A MESSAGE OR MESSAGES INDICATING THE NATURE OF THE   *
17    *    ERROR OR ERRORS.  A RECORD COUNT INDICATING THE NUMBER OF *
18    *    RECORDS PROCESSED ALONG WITH THE NUMBER OF ERROR RECORDS IS *
19    *    PRINTED AT THE END OF THE REPORT.                         *
20    *                                                             *
21    *       INPUT:    NEWPREM.DAT - NEW PREMIUM FILE              *
22    *                                                             *
23    *       OUTPUT:   PREMERR.RPT - PREMIUM RECORD ERROR REPORT   *
24    ****************************************************************
25
26    ENVIRONMENT DIVISION.
27    ********************

28
29    INPUT-OUTPUT SECTION.
30    *********************
31
32    FILE-CONTROL.
33
34        SELECT NEW-PREMIUM-FILE
35            ASSIGN TO "A:\NEWPREM.DAT".
36
37        SELECT PREMIUM-ERROR-REPORT
38            ASSIGN TO "A:\PREMERR.RPT".
39
40    /
41    DATA DIVISION.
42    **************
43
44    FILE SECTION.
45    *************
46
47    ****************************************************************
48    *                                                             *
49    *    INPUT-FILE - NEWLY ENTERED PREMIUM FILE                  *
50    *                                                             *
51    ****************************************************************
52
53    FD  NEW-PREMIUM-FILE.
54
```

FIGURE 4-5 Premium File Validation program

```
 55    01  NEW-PREMIUM-RECORD.                                        130    01  ACCUMULATORS.
 56        02  NPR-CUSTOMER-NAME           PIC X(20).                 131
 57        02  NPR-AGENT-NAME             PIC X(20).                 132        02  AC-LINE-COUNT             PIC 999  PACKED-DECIMAL.
 58        02  NPR-INSURANCE-TYPE         PIC X(10).                 133        02  AC-PAGE-COUNT             PIC 999  PACKED-DECIMAL.
 59            88  VALID-TYPE             VALUE "Annuity"            134        02  AC-ERROR-RECORD-COUNT     PIC 9(5) PACKED-DECIMAL.
 60                                             "Automobile"         135        02  AC-TOTAL-RECORD-COUNT     PIC 9(5) PACKED-DECIMAL.
 61                                             "Home"               136
 62                                             "Renter"             137
 63                                             "Term Life"          138    ********************************************************************
 64                                             "Whole Life".        139    *                                                                *
 65                                                                  140    *              WORK AREA FIELDS                                  *
 66        02  NPR-POLICY-NUMBER          PIC X(12).                 141    *                                                                *
 67        02  NPR-POLICY-NUMBER-R REDEFINES NPR-POLICY-NUMBER.      142    ********************************************************************
 68            03  NPR-POLICY-CODE        PIC XX.                    143
 69                88  VALID-POLICY-CODE  VALUE "AM"                 144    01  WORK-AREA.
 70                                             "AN"                 145
 71                                             "HM"                 146        02  WA-SYSTEM-DATE.
 72                                             "RT"                 147            03  WA-SYSTEM-YEAR        PIC 99.
 73                                             "TL"                 148            03  WA-SYSTEM-MONTH       PIC 99.
 74                                             "WL".                149            03  WA-SYSTEM-DAY         PIC 99.
 75            03  NPR-HYPHEN-1           PIC X.                     150
 76            03  NPR-CODE-NUMBER-1      PIC X(4).                  151        02  WA-CURRENT-DATE.
 77            03  NPR-HYPHEN-2           PIC X.                     152            03  WA-CURRENT-MONTH      PIC 99.
 78            03  NPR-CODE-NUMBER-2      PIC X(4).                  153            03  WA-CURRENT-DAY        PIC 99.
 79                                                                  154            03  WA-CURRENT-YEAR       PIC 99.
 80        02  NPR-PREMIUM-AMOUNT         PIC S9(5)V99.              155
 81        02  NPR-PREMIUM-AMOUNT-ALPHA REDEFINES                    156        02  WA-CURRENT-DATE-N REDEFINES
 82            NPR-PREMIUM-AMOUNT         PIC X(7).                  157            WA-CURRENT-DATE          PIC 9(6).
 83                                                                  158  /
 84        02  NPR-PAYMENT-STATUS         PIC X.                     159    ********************************************************************
 85            88  VALID-PAYMENT-STATUS   VALUE "D" "F" "P" "N".     160    *                                                                *
 86            88  DELINQUENT             VALUE "D".                 161    *    REPORT HEADINGS FOR PREMIUM RECORD ERROR REPORT             *
 87            88  PAID-IN-FULL           VALUE "F".                 162    *                                                                *
 88            88  PARTIALLY-PAID         VALUE "P".                 163    ********************************************************************
 89            88  NOT-YET-BILLED         VALUE "N".                 164
 90        02                             PIC X(10).                 165    01  REPORT-HEADING.
 91                                                                  166
 92    ********************************************************      167        02  RH-LINE-1.
 93    *                                                      *      168            03  RH-DATE               PIC Z9/99/99.
 94    *    REPORT-FILE - PREMIUM RECORD ERROR REPORT         *      169            03                        PIC X(37) VALUE SPACES.
 95    *                                                      *      170            03                        PIC X(27) VALUE
 96    ********************************************************      171                "AINSWORTH INSURANCE COMPANY".
 97                                                                  172            03                        PIC X(30) VALUE SPACES.
 98    FD  PREMIUM-ERROR-REPORT.                                     173            03                        PIC X(5)  VALUE "PAGE".
 99                                                                  174            03  RH-PAGE-COUNT         PIC ZZ9.
100    01  ERROR-LINE-OUT                 PIC X(132).                175            03                        PIC X(22) VALUE SPACES.
101  /                                                              176
102    WORKING-STORAGE SECTION.                                     177        02  RH-LINE-2.
103    ************************                                     178            03                        PIC X(45) VALUE SPACES.
104                                                                  179            03                        PIC X(27) VALUE
105    ********************************************************      180                "PREMIUM RECORD ERROR REPORT".
106    *                                                      *      181            03                        PIC X(60) VALUE SPACES.
107    *                  SWITCHES                            *      182
108    *                                                      *      183        02  RH-LINE-3.
109    ********************************************************      184            03                        PIC X(48) VALUE SPACES.
110                                                                  185            03                        PIC X(9)  VALUE
111    01  SWITCHES.                                                186                "INSURANCE".
112                                                                  187            03                        PIC X(23) VALUE SPACES.
113        02  SW-END-OF-FILE             PIC X.                     188            03                        PIC X(7)  VALUE
114            88  END-OF-FILE            VALUE "Y".                 189                "PREMIUM".
115        02  SW-ERROR-RECORD            PIC X.                     190            03                        PIC XX    VALUE SPACES.
116            88  ERROR-RECORD           VALUE "Y".                 191            03                        PIC X(7)  VALUE
117                                                                  192                "PAYMENT".
118    01  VALUES-FOR-SWITCHES.                                     193            03                        PIC X(36) VALUE SPACES.
119        02  YES                        PIC X    VALUE "Y".        194
120        02  NEG                        PIC X    VALUE "N".        195        02  RH-LINE-4.
121                                                                  196            03                        PIC X(13) VALUE
122                                                                  197                "CUSTOMER NAME".
123                                                                  198            03                        PIC X(11) VALUE SPACES.
124    ********************************************************      199            03                        PIC X(10) VALUE
125    *                                                      *      200                "AGENT NAME".
126    *                  ACCUMULATORS                        *      201            03                        PIC X(14) VALUE SPACES.
127    *                                                      *      202            03                        PIC X(4)  VALUE
128    ********************************************************      203                "TYPE".
129                                                                  204            03                        PIC X(11) VALUE SPACES.
                                                                     205            03                        PIC X(13) VALUE
```

(continued)

```
206                 "POLICY NUMBER".                          282    /
207          03                     PIC X(4)  VALUE SPACES.    283      PROCEDURE DIVISION.
208          03                     PIC X(6)  VALUE           284      ******************
209                 "AMOUNT".                                 285      ********************************************************************
210          03                     PIC XXX   VALUE SPACES.    286      *                                                                  *
211          03                     PIC X(6)  VALUE           287      *  MAIN-PROGRAM - THIS IS THE MAIN ROUTINE OF THE PREMIUM           *
212                 "STATUS".                                 288      *                 FILE VALIDATION PROGRAM                          *
213          03                     PIC X(4)  VALUE SPACES.    289      *                                                                  *
214          03                     PIC X(33) VALUE           290      ********************************************************************
215                 "ERROR MESSAGE".                          291
216                                                           292      MAIN-PROGRAM.
217       02  RH-LINE-5.                                      293
218          03                     PIC X(13) VALUE ALL "-".   294          PERFORM A-100-INITIALIZATION.
219          03                     PIC X(11) VALUE SPACES.    295          PERFORM B-100-VALIDATE-FILE.
220          03                     PIC X(10) VALUE ALL "-".   296          PERFORM C-100-WRAP-UP.
221          03                     PIC X(14) VALUE SPACES.    297          STOP RUN.
222          03                     PIC X(4)  VALUE ALL "-".   298
223          03                     PIC X(11) VALUE SPACES.    299      ********************************************************************
224          03                     PIC X(13) VALUE ALL "-".   300      *                                                                  *
225          03                     PIC X(4)  VALUE SPACES.    301      *           THE INITIALIZATION ROUTINE FOLLOW                      *
226          03                     PIC X(6)  VALUE ALL "-".   302      *                                                                  *
227          03                     PIC XXX   VALUE SPACES.    303      ********************************************************************
228          03                     PIC X(6)  VALUE ALL "-".   304
229          03                     PIC X(4)  VALUE SPACES.    305      A-100-INITIALIZATION.
230          03                     PIC X(20) VALUE ALL "-".   306
231          03                     PIC X(13) VALUE SPACES.    307          MOVE ZERO TO AC-PAGE-COUNT
232                                                           308                      AC-LINE-COUNT
233      ********************************************************   309                      AC-ERROR-RECORD-COUNT
234      *                                                      *   310                      AC-TOTAL-RECORD-COUNT.
235      *   DETAIL LINE FOR THE PREMIUM RECORD ERROR REPORT    *   311
236      *                                                      *   312          ACCEPT WA-SYSTEM-DATE FROM DATE.
237      ********************************************************   313          MOVE WA-SYSTEM-YEAR    TO WA-CURRENT-YEAR.
238                                                           314          MOVE WA-SYSTEM-MONTH   TO WA-CURRENT-MONTH.
239       01  ERROR-DETAIL-LINE.                              315          MOVE WA-SYSTEM-DAY     TO WA-CURRENT-DAY.
240                                                           316          MOVE WA-CURRENT-DATE-N TO RH-DATE.
241          02  EDL-FIELDS.                                  317
242             03  EDL-CUSTOMER-NAME    PIC X(20).            318          OPEN INPUT   NEW-PREMIUM-FILE
243             03                       PIC X(4)  VALUE SPACES.  319               OUTPUT  PREMIUM-ERROR-REPORT.
244             03  EDL-AGENT-NAME       PIC X(20).            320
245             03                       PIC X(4)  VALUE SPACES.  321    /
246             03  EDL-INSURANCE-TYPE   PIC X(10).            322
247             03                       PIC X(5)  VALUE SPACES.  323      ********************************************************************
248             03  EDL-POLICY-NUMBER    PIC X(12).            324      *                                                                  *
249             03                       PIC X(5)  VALUE SPACES.  325      *            FILE VALIDATION CONTROL ROUTINE                       *
250             03  EDL-PREMIUM-AMOUNT   PIC X(7).             326      *                                                                  *
251             03                       PIC XX    VALUE SPACES.  327      ********************************************************************
252             03  EDL-PAYMENT-STATUS   PIC X(4).             328
253             03                       PIC X(6)  VALUE SPACES.  329      B-100-VALIDATE-FILE.
254          02  EDL-MESSAGE             PIC X(20).            330
255          02                          PIC X(13) VALUE SPACES.  331          MOVE NEG TO SW-END-OF-FILE.
256    /                                                      332          READ NEW-PREMIUM-FILE
257      ********************************************************   333              AT END MOVE YES TO SW-END-OF-FILE.
258      *                                                      *   334          PERFORM B-200-VALIDATE-RECORDS
259      *   SUMMARY LINES FOR THE PREMIUM ERROR REPORT         *   335              UNTIL END-OF-FILE.
260      *                                                      *   336          MOVE AC-ERROR-RECORD-COUNT TO SL-ERROR-COUNT.
261      ********************************************************   337          MOVE AC-TOTAL-RECORD-COUNT TO SL-TOTAL-COUNT.
262                                                           338          WRITE ERROR-LINE-OUT FROM SL-LINE-1
263       01  SUMMARY-LINES.                                  339              AFTER ADVANCING 3 LINES.
264                                                           340          WRITE ERROR-LINE-OUT FROM SL-LINE-2
265          02  SL-LINE-1.                                   341              AFTER ADVANCING 3 LINES.
266             03                       PIC X(20) VALUE SPACES.  342
267             03                       PIC X(30) VALUE        343    /
268                 "TOTAL ERROR RECORDS PRINTED = ".         344      ********************************************************************
269             03  SL-ERROR-COUNT       PIC ZZZZ9.            345      *                                                                  *
270             03                       PIC X(9)  VALUE        346      *            VALIDATE FIELDS AND PRINT ERRORS                      *
271                 "  OUT OF ".                               347      *                                                                  *
272             03  SL-TOTAL-COUNT       PIC ZZZZ9.            348      ********************************************************************
273             03                       PIC X(19) VALUE        349
274                 " RECORDS PROCESSED.".                    350      B-200-VALIDATE-RECORDS.
275             03                       PIC X(44) VALUE SPACES.  351
276                                                           352          IF AC-LINE-COUNT = 0
277          02  SL-LINE-2.                                   353              PERFORM B-300-PRINT-HEADINGS.
278             03                       PIC X(51) VALUE SPACES.  354
279             03                       PIC X(13) VALUE        355          MOVE NEG TO SW-ERROR-RECORD.
280                 "END OF REPORT".                          356
281             03                       PIC X(68) VALUE SPACES.
```

FIGURE 4-5   Premium File Validation program (continued)

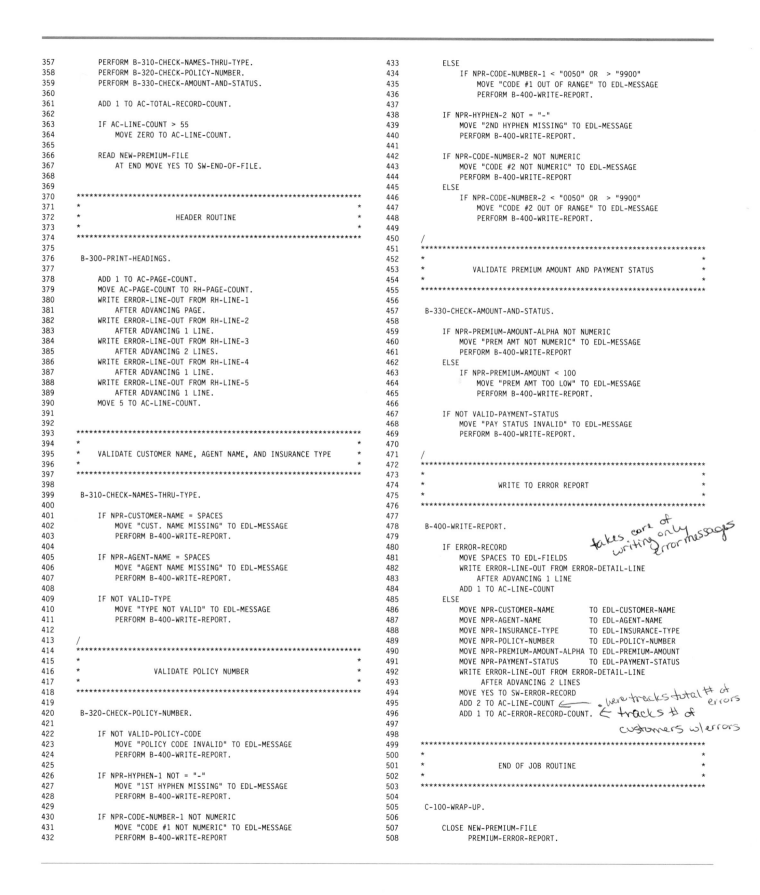

```
357        PERFORM B-310-CHECK-NAMES-THRU-TYPE.
358        PERFORM B-320-CHECK-POLICY-NUMBER.
359        PERFORM B-330-CHECK-AMOUNT-AND-STATUS.
360
361        ADD 1 TO AC-TOTAL-RECORD-COUNT.
362
363        IF AC-LINE-COUNT > 55
364            MOVE ZERO TO AC-LINE-COUNT.
365
366        READ NEW-PREMIUM-FILE
367            AT END MOVE YES TO SW-END-OF-FILE.
368
369
370    *****************************************************************
371    *                                                               *
372    *                     HEADER ROUTINE                            *
373    *                                                               *
374    *****************************************************************
375
376    B-300-PRINT-HEADINGS.
377
378        ADD 1 TO AC-PAGE-COUNT.
379        MOVE AC-PAGE-COUNT TO RH-PAGE-COUNT.
380        WRITE ERROR-LINE-OUT FROM RH-LINE-1
381            AFTER ADVANCING PAGE.
382        WRITE ERROR-LINE-OUT FROM RH-LINE-2
383            AFTER ADVANCING 1 LINE.
384        WRITE ERROR-LINE-OUT FROM RH-LINE-3
385            AFTER ADVANCING 2 LINES.
386        WRITE ERROR-LINE-OUT FROM RH-LINE-4
387            AFTER ADVANCING 1 LINE.
388        WRITE ERROR-LINE-OUT FROM RH-LINE-5
389            AFTER ADVANCING 1 LINE.
390        MOVE 5 TO AC-LINE-COUNT.
391
392
393    *****************************************************************
394    *                                                               *
395    *    VALIDATE CUSTOMER NAME, AGENT NAME, AND INSURANCE TYPE     *
396    *                                                               *
397    *****************************************************************
398
399    B-310-CHECK-NAMES-THRU-TYPE.
400
401        IF NPR-CUSTOMER-NAME = SPACES
402            MOVE "CUST. NAME MISSING" TO EDL-MESSAGE
403            PERFORM B-400-WRITE-REPORT.
404
405        IF NPR-AGENT-NAME = SPACES
406            MOVE "AGENT NAME MISSING" TO EDL-MESSAGE
407            PERFORM B-400-WRITE-REPORT.
408
409        IF NOT VALID-TYPE
410            MOVE "TYPE NOT VALID" TO EDL-MESSAGE
411            PERFORM B-400-WRITE-REPORT.
412
413    /
414    *****************************************************************
415    *                                                               *
416    *                   VALIDATE POLICY NUMBER                      *
417    *                                                               *
418    *****************************************************************
419
420    B-320-CHECK-POLICY-NUMBER.
421
422        IF NOT VALID-POLICY-CODE
423            MOVE "POLICY CODE INVALID" TO EDL-MESSAGE
424            PERFORM B-400-WRITE-REPORT.
425
426        IF NPR-HYPHEN-1 NOT = "-"
427            MOVE "1ST HYPHEN MISSING" TO EDL-MESSAGE
428            PERFORM B-400-WRITE-REPORT.
429
430        IF NPR-CODE-NUMBER-1 NOT NUMERIC
431            MOVE "CODE #1 NOT NUMERIC" TO EDL-MESSAGE
432            PERFORM B-400-WRITE-REPORT
```

```
433        ELSE
434            IF NPR-CODE-NUMBER-1 < "0050" OR > "9900"
435                MOVE "CODE #1 OUT OF RANGE" TO EDL-MESSAGE
436                PERFORM B-400-WRITE-REPORT.
437
438        IF NPR-HYPHEN-2 NOT = "-"
439            MOVE "2ND HYPHEN MISSING" TO EDL-MESSAGE
440            PERFORM B-400-WRITE-REPORT.
441
442        IF NPR-CODE-NUMBER-2 NOT NUMERIC
443            MOVE "CODE #2 NOT NUMERIC" TO EDL-MESSAGE
444            PERFORM B-400-WRITE-REPORT
445        ELSE
446            IF NPR-CODE-NUMBER-2 < "0050" OR > "9900"
447                MOVE "CODE #2 OUT OF RANGE" TO EDL-MESSAGE
448                PERFORM B-400-WRITE-REPORT.
449
450    /
451    *****************************************************************
452    *                                                               *
453    *        VALIDATE PREMIUM AMOUNT AND PAYMENT STATUS            *
454    *                                                               *
455    *****************************************************************
456
457    B-330-CHECK-AMOUNT-AND-STATUS.
458
459        IF NPR-PREMIUM-AMOUNT-ALPHA NOT NUMERIC
460            MOVE "PREM AMT NOT NUMERIC" TO EDL-MESSAGE
461            PERFORM B-400-WRITE-REPORT
462        ELSE
463            IF NPR-PREMIUM-AMOUNT < 100
464                MOVE "PREM AMT TOO LOW" TO EDL-MESSAGE
465                PERFORM B-400-WRITE-REPORT.
466
467        IF NOT VALID-PAYMENT-STATUS
468            MOVE "PAY STATUS INVALID" TO EDL-MESSAGE
469            PERFORM B-400-WRITE-REPORT.
470
471    /
472    *****************************************************************
473    *                                                               *
474    *                    WRITE TO ERROR REPORT                     *
475    *                                                               *
476    *****************************************************************
477
478    B-400-WRITE-REPORT.
479
480        IF ERROR-RECORD
481            MOVE SPACES TO EDL-FIELDS
482            WRITE ERROR-LINE-OUT FROM ERROR-DETAIL-LINE
483                AFTER ADVANCING 1 LINE
484            ADD 1 TO AC-LINE-COUNT
485        ELSE
486            MOVE NPR-CUSTOMER-NAME        TO EDL-CUSTOMER-NAME
487            MOVE NPR-AGENT-NAME           TO EDL-AGENT-NAME
488            MOVE NPR-INSURANCE-TYPE       TO EDL-INSURANCE-TYPE
489            MOVE NPR-POLICY-NUMBER        TO EDL-POLICY-NUMBER
490            MOVE NPR-PREMIUM-AMOUNT-ALPHA TO EDL-PREMIUM-AMOUNT
491            MOVE NPR-PAYMENT-STATUS       TO EDL-PAYMENT-STATUS
492            WRITE ERROR-LINE-OUT FROM ERROR-DETAIL-LINE
493                AFTER ADVANCING 2 LINES
494            MOVE YES TO SW-ERROR-RECORD
495            ADD 2 TO AC-LINE-COUNT
496            ADD 1 TO AC-ERROR-RECORD-COUNT.
497
498
499    *****************************************************************
500    *                                                               *
501    *                    END OF JOB ROUTINE                        *
502    *                                                               *
503    *****************************************************************
504
505    C-100-WRAP-UP.
506
507        CLOSE NEW-PREMIUM-FILE
508            PREMIUM-ERROR-REPORT.
```

(handwritten annotations)
takes care of writing only error messages
here tracks total # of errors
tracks # of customers w/errors

CONDITIONAL EXECUTION

One of the most powerful features of any programming language is the capability to compare the contents of one field with that of another and perform alternative actions based upon the results of the comparison. In Chapter 1 you were introduced to binary and case selection structures (Figure 4-6). The binary selection structure specifies that a condition is to be tested and, if the condition is true, one statement or a series of statements will execute. If the condition is false, a different statement or series of statements will execute. This process is referred to as **IF-THEN-ELSE logic**. Case selection causes one of several alternative actions to occur as a result of a condition test.

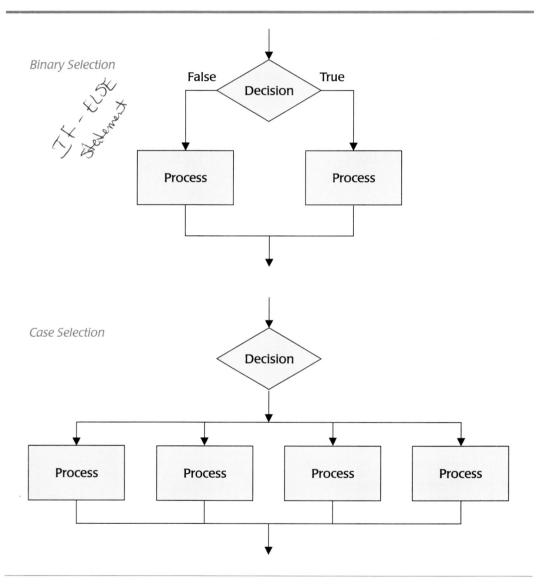

FIGURE 4-6   Basic selection structures

The capability to execute alternative statements based upon conditions that can be tested within the program is most often implemented in COBOL using the IF statement. The **IF** statement compares values of fields and/or literals and directs which statements should be executed based on the results of the comparison. Figure 4-7 shows the basic format of an IF statement.

```
IF condition-1 THEN   ⎰ statement-1 ...  ⎱
                      ⎱ NEXT SENTENCE    ⎰

⎡ ELSE                 ⎰ statement-2 ...  ⎱⎤
⎣                      ⎱ NEXT SENTENCE    ⎰⎦

[ END-IF ]
```

FIGURE 4-7   Basic format of an IF statement

The word **THEN** is optional and is seldom used. **NEXT SENTENCE**, used when no action is to be taken, causes control to be transferred to the next sentence within the program. As shown later in this chapter, the use of the NEXT SENTENCE clause usually can be avoided. **ELSE** is optional and is used to identify the statement or statements that should execute if the condition is false. **END-IF** is used to terminate an IF statement in place of a period or when a period cannot be used.

One-Sided Decisions and Logical Operators

The IF statement can take several forms within a program. The simplest form tests a condition and, if the condition is true, performs some action. No action is taken if the condition is false. This is called a **one-sided decision**, or **one-sided IF** statement, and is illustrated by the flowchart in Figure 4-8.

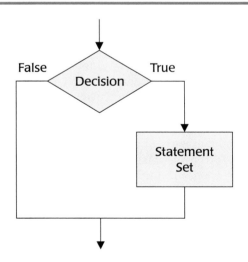

FIGURE 4-8   Flowchart for a one-sided decision

Figure 4-9 on the next page presents an example of a one-sided IF from the Premium File Validation program. The PERFORM on line 353 executes only when the condition IF AC-LINE-COUNT = 0 on line 352 is true.

```
352            IF AC-LINE-COUNT = 0
353                 PERFORM B-300-PRINT-HEADINGS.
```

FIGURE 4-9   One-sided IF statement from the Premium File Validation program

When the condition is false in a one-sided decision, logic flows to the next sentence in the program. An END-IF or a period is used to terminate an IF statement. In situations where the IF is part of some larger sentence and a period cannot be used, the IF must be terminated with an END-IF. Figure 4-10 presents an example of an IF that is part of an in-line PERFORM. The in-line PERFORM is discussed in Chapter 5. A period cannot be used in Figure 4-10 to terminate the IF, therefore, the END-IF is required for proper syntax and execution of the logic. Figure 4-11 presents two equivalent IF statements. In this book, the first example will be the preferred way of coding IF statements. When a period will suffice, a period will be used to terminate an IF. Periods often present problems for beginning COBOL programmers, however, and you may wish to use END-IF for all IF statements in your programs. When END-IF is used, it is customary to have it vertically aligned with its associated IF.

```
PERFORM 10 TIMES
    ADD WA-FIELD-1 TO AC-COUNTER
    IF AC-COUNTER > 100
        MOVE AC-COUNTER TO WA-BIG-FIELD              END-IF
    END-IF  ◄────────────────────────────────     needed here to
    ADD 5 TO WA-FIELD-1                               terminate IF
    MOVE WA-FIELD-1 TO DL-FIELD-OUT
END-PERFORM.
```

FIGURE 4-10   An IF that is part of a larger sentence and must be terminated with an END-IF

It is good practice to code the IF and its related condition on one line and the action or actions to be taken on separate lines, indented four positions under the IF. Any number of actions may be listed under the IF; however, the last one must be terminated with either a period or an END-IF.

The equal sign (=) in Figure 4-11 is called a **relational operator**. It identifies the relation between the two parts of the condition that must be true for the specified action to occur. Table 4-1 lists the relational operators available for a COBOL program. The relational operators may be spelled out, but it is more common to use the symbols. In most cases, the reserved word **NOT** may be used to reverse the meaning of the operator. For the sake of clarity, NOT should be used only when no alternatives are available. For example, NOT < is logically equivalent to >=, therefore, it is good practice to use >= instead of NOT <.

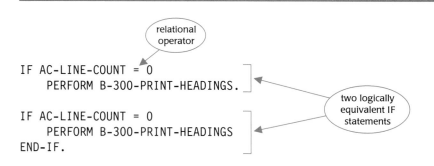

FIGURE 4-11   Use of the END-IF

TABLE 4-1   Relational Operators and Their Meanings

Relational Operator	*Meaning*
IS [NOT] GREATER THAN IS [NOT] >	Greater than; not greater than
IS [NOT] LESS THAN IS [NOT] <	Less than; not less than
IS [NOT] EQUAL TO IS [NOT] =	Equal to; not equal to
IS GREATER THAN OR EQUAL TO IS >=	Greater than or equal to
IS LESS THAN OR EQUAL TO IS <=	Less than or equal to

When both items or fields being compared are numeric, the comparison is based directly on their algebraic values. It is not necessary that the fields have the same number of digits because length differences are ignored, as is USAGE. For example, 09.7000 is considered to be equal to the algebraic value of 00009.70. If no decimal position is indicated in the definition of a numeric field, values in the field represent whole numbers.

For alphanumeric fields, comparison occurs left to right, one character at a time until a difference is found, as determined by your computer's collating sequence, or until it can be determined that the fields are equal. Collating sequences were introduced in Chapter 3. If the fields are not the same size, the shorter field is padded internally with blanks until it is the same length as the longer field.

Figure 4-12 on the next page presents two fields, WA-NAME-1 and WA-NAME-2, and a comparison between them. The fields are the same size and their contents are exactly the same; therefore, the equal condition will be true.

```
02  WA-NAME-1          PIC X(11).          02  WA-NAME-2          PIC X(11).

contents     SIMPSON, H.                   contents     SIMPSON, H.
             -----------                                 -----------

IF WA-NAME-1 = WA-NAME-2
   ADD 1 TO AC-MATCH-COUNT.
```

Comparison begins with the leftmost character and continues to the right.
The condition is true so the ADD instruction will execute.

FIGURE 4-12 Alphanumeric comparison of two fields of equal length and equal content

Figure 4-13 presents WA-NAME-1 and WA-NAME-2 with two names that are similar but not exactly the same. Because the letter V is different from the letter D, the condition will be false and the MOVE will not be executed.

```
02  WA-NAME-1          PIC X(11).          02  WA-NAME-2          PIC X(11).

contents     JOHNSON, V.                   contents     JOHNSON, D.
             -----------                                 -----------

IF WA-NAME-1 = WA-NAME-2
   MOVE WA-NAME-1 TO DL-NAME-OUT.
```

The condition is false so the MOVE will not execute.

FIGURE 4-13 Alphanumeric comparison of two fields of equal length but different content

Figure 4-14 presents two fields of different length. The shorter field is internally padded with spaces before the comparison occurs. The comparison then proceeds left to right. The first padded space is less than the letter E; therefore, the condition is true and the MOVE will execute.

```
02  WA-NAME-3     PIC X(5).          02  WA-NAME-4     PIC X(11).

contents     MITCH                   contents     MITCHELL
             -----                                 -----------

IF WA-NAME-3 < WA-NAME-4
   MOVE WA-NAME-3 TO DL-NAME-OUT.
```

The MITCH is internally padded with blanks to become MITCHbbbbbb.
The condition is true so the MOVE will execute.

FIGURE 4-14 Alphanumeric comparison of two fields of unequal length and different content

It is important to recognize that after execution of an IF statement, the statement following the period, or the END-IF, is executed. In Figure 4-15, after the IF has been executed, the MOVE on line 355 will be executed. It will be executed regardless of the condition found in the IF because it follows the period that terminates the IF. Omitting the period after PERFORM B-300-PRINT-HEADINGS would change the logic. The MOVE then would be considered part of the IF and only would execute if the given condition was true.

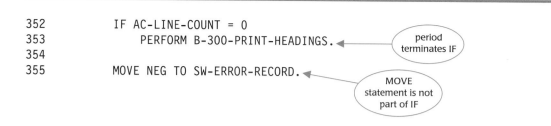

```
352              IF AC-LINE-COUNT = 0
353                   PERFORM B-300-PRINT-HEADINGS.
354
355              MOVE NEG TO SW-ERROR-RECORD.
```

FIGURE 4-15 The statement following the IF executes unconditionally

Two-Sided Decisions

A **two-sided decision**, or **two-sided IF** statement, is illustrated by the flowchart presented for Binary Selection in Figure 4-6 on page 4-10. Such a structure is implemented in COBOL by the use of an ELSE within an IF. Figure 4-16 presents an example of a two-sided decision from the Premium File Validation program. When the condition name ERROR-RECORD is true, the statements on lines 481 through 484 are executed. When the condition name is false, the statements on lines 486 through 496 following the ELSE are executed. The IF statement is terminated with a period.

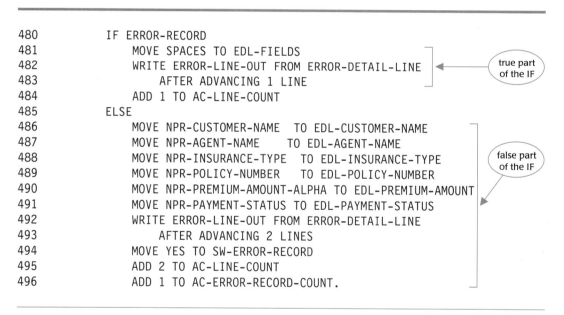

```
480        IF ERROR-RECORD
481            MOVE SPACES TO EDL-FIELDS
482            WRITE ERROR-LINE-OUT FROM ERROR-DETAIL-LINE
483                AFTER ADVANCING 1 LINE
484            ADD 1 TO AC-LINE-COUNT
485        ELSE
486            MOVE NPR-CUSTOMER-NAME   TO EDL-CUSTOMER-NAME
487            MOVE NPR-AGENT-NAME      TO EDL-AGENT-NAME
488            MOVE NPR-INSURANCE-TYPE  TO EDL-INSURANCE-TYPE
489            MOVE NPR-POLICY-NUMBER   TO EDL-POLICY-NUMBER
490            MOVE NPR-PREMIUM-AMOUNT-ALPHA TO EDL-PREMIUM-AMOUNT
491            MOVE NPR-PAYMENT-STATUS TO EDL-PAYMENT-STATUS
492            WRITE ERROR-LINE-OUT FROM ERROR-DETAIL-LINE
493                AFTER ADVANCING 2 LINES
494            MOVE YES TO SW-ERROR-RECORD
495            ADD 2 TO AC-LINE-COUNT
496            ADD 1 TO AC-ERROR-RECORD-COUNT.
```

FIGURE 4-16 Two-sided IF statement

When multiple IFs and ELSEs appear in the same sentence, an ELSE logically relates to the most previous unmatched IF. COBOL does not require that IFs and corresponding ELSEs be aligned but, for the sake of clarity, it is a good idea to align an ELSE with the corresponding IF as shown in Figure 4-16. Notice also that ELSE is on a line by itself. Again, this is not required by COBOL; however, it assists in enhancing readability as well as in deciphering the logic of the statement.

Under no circumstances can the instructions in both the true part and the false part of the IF statement be executed in a single pass through the IF statement. The true part and the false part of the IF statement are separated by the reserved word ELSE.

NESTED IFS

An IF statement may be located in the true part or false part of another IF statement. Such a statement is called a **nested IF**. There is no real limit to the depth of nesting that may occur; however, for the sake of readability and maintenance, it is wise to keep nesting to a minimum. There are several basic formats that nested IFs may assume. Figure 4-17 presents the first such example, a one-sided IF nested within the true part of a one-sided IF. If condition-1 is true, then condition-2 is tested. If condition-2 is true, then statement-set-1 is executed. If condition-1 is false, then condition-2 is never tested and processing continues after the period. If condition-1 is true but condition-2 is false, statement-set-1 will not execute.

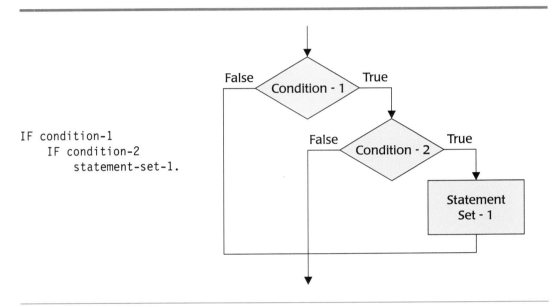

```
IF condition-1
    IF condition-2
        statement-set-1.
```

FIGURE 4-17 One-sided IF nested within a one-sided IF

Figure 4-18 illustrates the logic and COBOL code associated with a two-sided IF nested within the true part of a one-sided IF. If condition-1 is false, condition-2 is never tested and processing continues with the next sentence in the program. If condition-1 is true, then condition-2 is tested. If condition-2 is true, statement-set-1 executes and if condition-2 is false, then statement-set-2 executes.

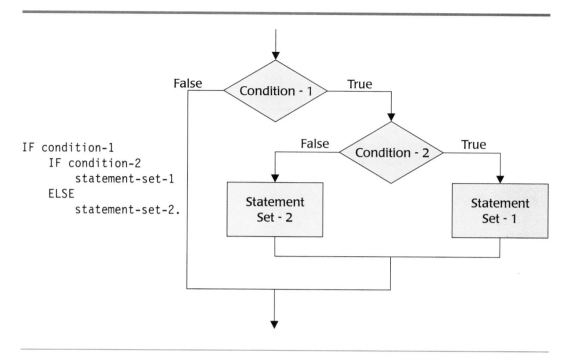

```
IF condition-1
    IF condition-2
        statement-set-1
    ELSE
        statement-set-2.
```

FIGURE 4-18 Two-sided IF nested within a one-sided IF

A two-sided IF nested within the true part of a two-sided IF is shown in Figure 4-19. Only when condition-1 is true will condition-2 be tested. If condition-2 is true, statement-set-1 will be executed. If condition-2 is false, statement-set-2 will be executed. If condition-1 is false, condition-2 is never tested and statement-set-3 is executed.

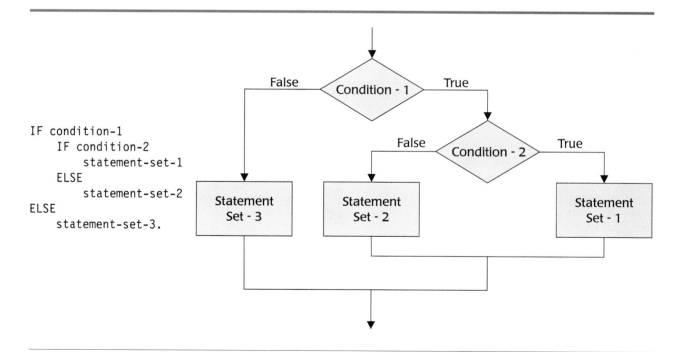

```
IF condition-1
    IF condition-2
        statement-set-1
    ELSE
        statement-set-2
ELSE
    statement-set-3.
```

FIGURE 4-19 Two-sided IF nested within the true part of a two-sided IF

Figure 4-20 illustrates a similar nesting pattern, this time with a two-sided IF nested within the false part of a two-sided IF. If condition-1 is true, statement-set-1 is executed and control passes to the next sentence in the program. If condition-1 is false, then condition-2 is tested. If condition-2 is true, statement-set-2 executes, and if it is false, statement-set-3 executes.

```
IF condition-1
    statement-set-1
ELSE
    IF condition-2
        statement-set-2
    ELSE
        statement-set-3.
```

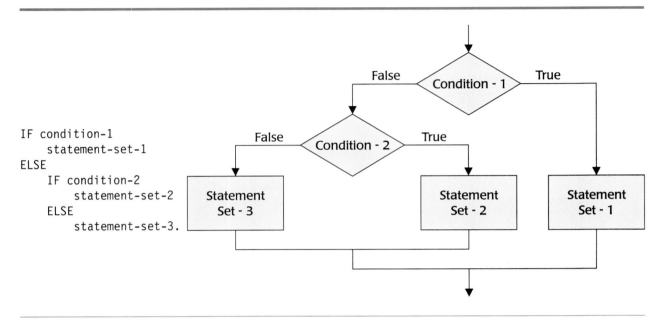

FIGURE 4-20 Two-sided IF nested within the false part of a two-sided IF

A one-sided IF nested within the false part of a two-sided IF is shown in Figure 4-21. The logic is the same as the logic for Figure 4-20, but there is no action to perform if condition-2 is false. Such logic is used in several places in the Premium File Validation program. One such instance is shown in Figure 4-22.

```
IF condition-1
    statement-set-1
ELSE
    IF condition-2
        statement-set-2.
```

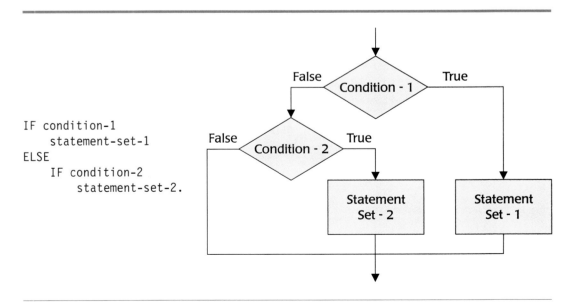

FIGURE 4-21 One-sided IF nested within the false part of a two-sided IF

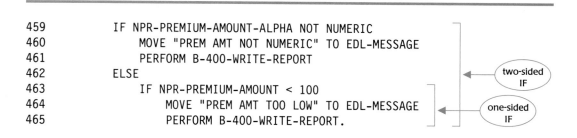

```
459        IF NPR-PREMIUM-AMOUNT-ALPHA NOT NUMERIC
460           MOVE "PREM AMT NOT NUMERIC" TO EDL-MESSAGE
461           PERFORM B-400-WRITE-REPORT
462        ELSE
463           IF NPR-PREMIUM-AMOUNT < 100
464              MOVE "PREM AMT TOO LOW" TO EDL-MESSAGE
465              PERFORM B-400-WRITE-REPORT.
```

FIGURE 4-22 Example from the Premium File Validation program of a one-sided IF nested in the false part of a two-sided IF

A nesting pattern that requires the use of great caution is a one-sided IF nested within the true part of a two-sided IF. Figure 4-23 illustrates such a pattern and points out an erroneous method of coding this logic. As indicated earlier, an ELSE logically relates back to the previous unmatched IF. Hence, an ELSE following the second IF will be logically paired with that IF unless an END-IF or ELSE with NEXT SENTENCE is used in-between. Remember, alignment does not determine logic. Alignment is used simply to improve the readability of the program.

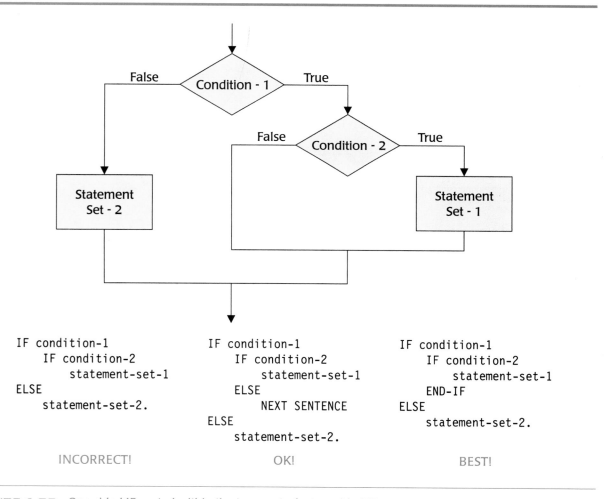

```
IF condition-1              IF condition-1              IF condition-1
   IF condition-2              IF condition-2              IF condition-2
      statement-set-1            statement-set-1            statement-set-1
ELSE                          ELSE                        END-IF
   statement-set-2.              NEXT SENTENCE            ELSE
                              ELSE                           statement-set-2.
                                 statement-set-2.

      INCORRECT!                    OK!                        BEST!
```

FIGURE 4-23 One-sided IF nested within the true part of a two-sided IF

Figure 4-24 illustrates another common nested IF problem, associated with a two-sided IF nested within the true part of another two-sided IF. In this example, statement-set-3 must be executed whether condition-2 is true or false, but not until after either statement-set-1 or statement-set-2 is executed. There is a temptation to simply align statement-set-3 with the IF and ELSE for condition-2. This, however, produces the wrong logic. Aligning statement-set-3 with the IF and ELSE for condition-2 causes statement-set-3 to execute in the false part of condition-2 only. The statement will not execute if condition-2 is true. To produce the desired logic, statement-set-3 either has to be coded twice, once in the true part of condition-2 and once in the false part of condition-2, or it has to be coded after an END-IF that terminates the scope of condition-2.

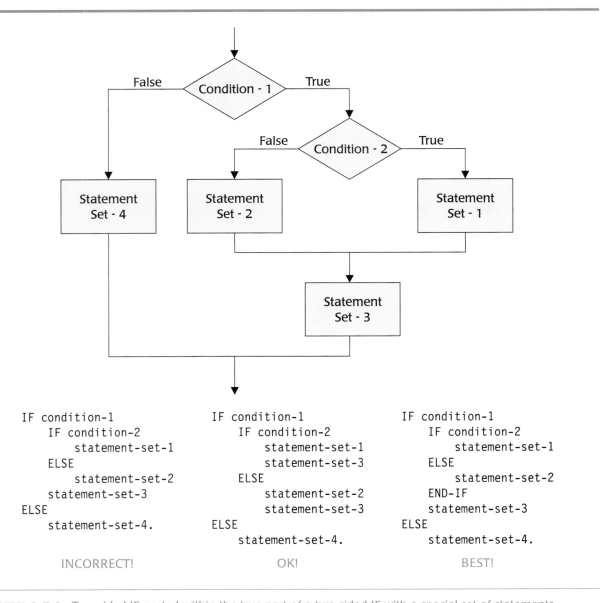

```
IF condition-1                IF condition-1                IF condition-1
    IF condition-2                IF condition-2                IF condition-2
        statement-set-1               statement-set-1               statement-set-1
    ELSE                              statement-set-3           ELSE
        statement-set-2           ELSE                              statement-set-2
    statement-set-3                   statement-set-2           END-IF
ELSE                                  statement-set-3           statement-set-3
    statement-set-4.          ELSE                          ELSE
                                      statement-set-4.              statement-set-4.

        INCORRECT!                       OK!                          BEST!
```

FIGURE 4-24   Two-sided IF nested within the true part of a two-sided IF with a special set of statements to execute

Other combinations are available for nested IFs; however, they simply involve combining the examples given. It is good practice to keep your IFs as short and simple as possible. If a nested IF can be avoided, it is generally a good idea to do so. Also, when nested IFs are used, try to avoid going over three levels deep in the nesting. Nested IFs can be confusing to understand and maintain if they are not developed carefully.

NEXT SENTENCE and CONTINUE

NEXT SENTENCE was introduced in the discussion of the basic format of an IF in Figure 4-7 on page 4-11, and an example of its use is illustrated in Figure 4-23 on page 4-19. With some minor adjustments to the wording of an IF, the use of NEXT SENTENCE generally can be avoided. Figure 4-25 shows an example of the use of NEXT SENTENCE in the false part of a two-sided IF. Such a use is unnecessary and confusing.

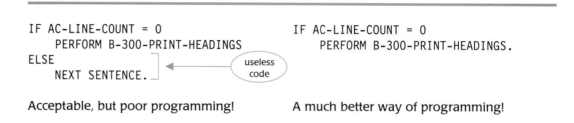

FIGURE 4-25 Using NEXT SENTENCE in the false part of a two-sided IF

Figure 4-26 presents another example and shows that the use of NEXT SENTENCE in the true part of an IF can be avoided with just a slight change in the logic. In this example, NOT is inserted prior to the condition name VALID-TYPE.

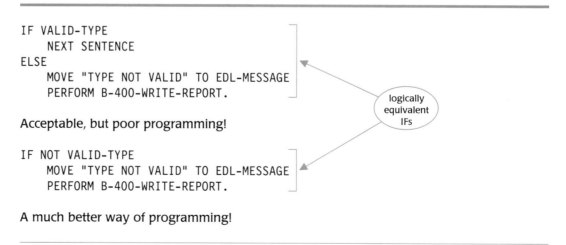

FIGURE 4-26 Using NEXT SENTENCE in the true part of a two-sided IF

The COBOL reserved word **CONTINUE** works much like NEXT SENTENCE and can be used in a fashion similar to NEXT SENTENCE in an IF statement. Be aware of the difference between the two, however. When NEXT SENTENCE is encountered in a conditional statement, control passes to the statement following the next period or to the next sentence in the program. When CONTINUE is encountered in a conditional statement, control passes to the next sentence unless there is an END-IF used. With an END-IF present, control passes to the statement following the END-IF.

Figure 4-27 illustrates the difference between CONTINUE and NEXT SENTENCE. If condition-1 is true and condition-2 is false, control will pass to whatever follows the period. This means that statement-set-2 will not execute if NEXT SENTENCE is encountered. If condition-3 is true and condition-4 is false, control will pass to statement-set-4 because it follows the END-IF. Thus, statement-set-4 will execute whether condition-4 is true or false.

```
IF condition-1                      IF condition-3
    IF condition-2                      IF condition-4
        statement-set-1                     statement-set-3
    ELSE                                ELSE
        NEXT SENTENCE                       CONTINUE
    END-IF                              END-IF
    statement-set-2.                    statement-set-4.
```

If NEXT SENTENCE is encountered   If CONTINUE is encountered,
statement-set-2 doesn't execute.   statement-set-4 executes.

FIGURE 4-27   The difference between NEXT SENTENCE and CONTINUE

As shown in Figure 4-28, these entries could be coded to eliminate the need for either NEXT SENTENCE or CONTINUE. As with NEXT SENTENCE, CONTINUE should be avoided.

```
IF condition-1                      IF condition-3
    IF condition-2                      IF condition-4
        statement-set-1                     statement-set-3
        statement-set-2.                END-IF
                                        statement-set-4.
```

NEXT SENTENCE eliminated   CONTINUE eliminated

FIGURE 4-28   Eliminating NEXT SENTENCE and CONTINUE

Combined and Complex Conditions

A **combined condition** is formed by combining simple conditions using the logical connectors **AND** and **OR**. When AND is used in such a condition, the condition is true only when both of the included conditions are true. If one or both of the included conditions is false, the entire condition is false. When OR is used, the condition is true when one or both of the included conditions is true. The condition is false only when both of the included conditions are false. Table 4-2 presents a truth table that illustrates how AND and OR work in combined conditions.

TABLE 4-2   Truth Tables Illustrating the Use of AND and OR

condition-1 AND condition-2		
condition-1	*condition-2*	*combined condition*
true	true	true
true	false	false
false	true	false
false	false	false

condition-1 OR condition-2		
condition-1	*condition-2*	*combined condition*
true	true	true
true	false	true
false	true	true
false	false	false

Figure 4-29 presents an example of a combined condition. Because OR is used in the given statement, the MOVE and PERFORM will execute if either of the included conditions is true. The MOVE and PERFORM will not execute if both of the included conditions are false.

```
IF NPR-PREMIUM-AMOUNT-ALPHA NOT NUMERIC OR
   NPR-PREMIUM-AMOUNT < 100
      MOVE "PREM AMT NOT VALID" TO EDL-MESSAGE
      PERFORM B-400-WRITE-REPORT.
```

executes if just one of conditions is true

FIGURE 4-29   Combined condition using OR

Two or more combined conditions can be put together to form a **complex condition**. Figure 4-30 presents an example of a complex condition. In the given example, the MOVE statement and PERFORM statement will be executed if either one of the conditions, NPR-PREMIUM-AMOUNT < 100 or NPR-PREMIUM-AMOUNT > 900 is true and the condition NOT VALID-TYPE also is true.

```
IF (NPR-PREMIUM-AMOUNT < 100 OR NPR-PREMIUM-AMOUNT > 900) AND
   NOT VALID-TYPE
      MOVE "BAD AMT AND TYPE" TO EDL-MESSAGE
      PERFORM B-400-WRITE-REPORT.
```

complex condition

FIGURE 4-30   Complex IF statement

Parentheses, in pairs, are sometimes necessary to achieve the desired results in a complex condition. Parentheses are used to create a block of code that is treated as a single condition. This single condition is either true or false. Table 4-3 on the next page presents the order of evaluation used to solve a complex condition. In the sample code presented in Figure 4-30, removing the parentheses would radically modify the logic. As Table 4-3 indicates, AND takes precedence over OR. Thus, in the absence of the parentheses, NPR-PREMIUM-AMOUNT > 900 and NOT VALID-TYPE would be logically combined. The complex condition would then be true if NPR-PREMIUM-AMOUNT < 100 or, instead, both NPR-PREMIUM-AMOUNT > 900 and NOT VALID-TYPE were true.

TABLE 4-3 Order of Evaluation for Complex Conditions

First	If parentheses are used, the contents are evaluated starting with the innermost parentheses
Then	NOT operators, if used, are evaluated
Then	AND operators and their surrounding conditions are evaluated in order from left to right
Finally	OR operators and their surrounding conditions are evaluated in order from left to right

Table 4-4 presents truth tables illustrating the effect the presence and then absence of the parentheses has on the sample complex condition presented in Figure 4-30 on the previous page.

TABLE 4-4 Truth Tables Illustrating the Effect of Parentheses on a Complex Condition

(NPR-PREMIUM-AMOUNT < 100 OR NPR-PREMIUM-AMOUNT > 900) AND NOT VALID-TYPE

NPR-PREMIUM AMOUNT < 100	NPR-PREMIUM AMOUNT > 900	VALID-TYPE	NOT VALID-TYPE	COMPLEX CONDITION
true	true	false	true	true
true	false	false	true	true
false	true	false	true	true
false	false	false	true	false
true	true	true	false	false
true	false	true	false	false
false	true	true	false	false
false	false	true	false	false

NPR-PREMIUM-AMOUNT < 100 OR NPR-PREMIUM-AMOUNT > 900 AND NOT VALID-TYPE

NPR-PREMIUM AMOUNT < 100	NPR-PREMIUM AMOUNT > 900	VALID-TYPE	NOT VALID-TYPE	COMPLEX CONDITION
true	true	false	true	true
true	false	false	true	true
false	true	false	true	true
false	false	false	true	false
true	true	true	false	true
true	false	true	false	true
false	true	true	false	false
false	false	true	false	false

Implied Subjects and Implied Operators

A combined condition may be abbreviated by the use of **implied subjects** and **implied operators**. The **subject** of a condition test is the field being tested. The **operator** is the relational operator used in the comparison. An implied subject may be used only when the subject in both parts of the combined condition is the same. Figure 4-31 presents an example of a combined condition coded first without and then with an implied subject. An implied operator may be used only when both the subject and operator are the same in both parts of the combined condition. Figure 4-32 presents an example that uses both an implied subject and an implied operator.

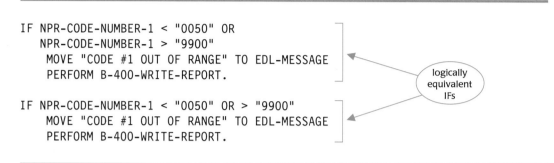

```
IF NPR-CODE-NUMBER-1 < "0050" OR
   NPR-CODE-NUMBER-1 > "9900"
     MOVE "CODE #1 OUT OF RANGE" TO EDL-MESSAGE
     PERFORM B-400-WRITE-REPORT.

IF NPR-CODE-NUMBER-1 < "0050" OR > "9900"
     MOVE "CODE #1 OUT OF RANGE" TO EDL-MESSAGE
     PERFORM B-400-WRITE-REPORT.
```

logically equivalent IFs

FIGURE 4-31   Use of an implied subject, NPR-CODE-NUMBER-1

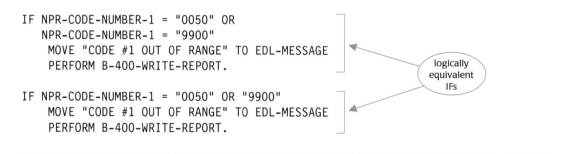

```
IF NPR-CODE-NUMBER-1 = "0050" OR
   NPR-CODE-NUMBER-1 = "9900"
     MOVE "CODE #1 OUT OF RANGE" TO EDL-MESSAGE
     PERFORM B-400-WRITE-REPORT.

IF NPR-CODE-NUMBER-1 = "0050" OR "9900"
     MOVE "CODE #1 OUT OF RANGE" TO EDL-MESSAGE
     PERFORM B-400-WRITE-REPORT.
```

logically equivalent IFs

FIGURE 4-32   Use of an implied subject and implied operator

The use of implied subjects and implied operators is completely optional. Situations exist where their use might be misleading. Use implied subjects and implied operators only in other situations where their use will not impact the clarity of the code.

EVALUATE STATEMENT

The **EVALUATE** statement can be used in place of numerous IF statements when testing a variable for multiple values. It is ideal for handling the case selection structure discussed in Chapter 1. The basic format of an EVALUATE is presented in Figure 4-33 on the next page. Although many options are available, in its simplest form, EVALUATE can be used to replace a series of IFs or a large nested IF.

```
                    ⎧ identifier-1  ⎫            ⎡      ⎧ identifier-2  ⎫ ⎤
                    ⎪ literal-1     ⎪            ⎢      ⎪ literal-2     ⎪ ⎥
      EVALUATE      ⎨ expression-1  ⎬            ⎢ ALSO ⎨ expression-2  ⎬ ⎥
                    ⎪ TRUE          ⎪            ⎢      ⎪ TRUE          ⎪ ⎥
                    ⎩ FALSE         ⎭            ⎣      ⎩ FALSE         ⎭ ⎦


      {{WHEN  ⎧    ANY                                                          ⎫
             ⎪    condition-1                                                  ⎪
             ⎪    TRUE                                                         ⎪
             ⎨    FALSE                                                        ⎬
             ⎪                                                                 ⎪
             ⎪        ⎧ ⎧ identifier-3  ⎫ ⎡ ⎧ THROUGH ⎫ ⎧ identifier-4  ⎫ ⎤ ⎫ ⎪
             ⎩ [NOT ] ⎨ ⎨ literal-3     ⎬ ⎢ ⎨ THRU    ⎬ ⎨ literal-4     ⎬ ⎥ ⎬ ⎭
                      ⎩ ⎩ arithmetic-exp-1 ⎭ ⎣ ⎩       ⎭ ⎩ arithmetic-exp-2 ⎭ ⎦ ⎭


      ⎡        ⎧    ANY                                                          ⎫ ⎤
      ⎢        ⎪    condition-2                                                  ⎪ ⎥
      ⎢        ⎪    TRUE                                                         ⎪ ⎥
      ⎢ ALSO   ⎨    FALSE                                                        ⎬ ⎥
      ⎢        ⎪                                                                 ⎪ ⎥
      ⎢        ⎪        ⎧ ⎧ identifier-5  ⎫ ⎡ ⎧ THROUGH ⎫   identifier-6  ⎤ ⎫ ⎪ ⎥
      ⎣        ⎩ [NOT ] ⎨ ⎨ literal-5     ⎬ ⎢ ⎨ THRU    ⎬   literal-6     ⎥ ⎬ ⎭ ⎦
                        ⎩ ⎩ arithmetic-exp-3 ⎭ ⎣ ⎩       ⎭   arithmetic-exp-4 ⎦ ⎭
                            .
                            .
                            .
          imperative-statement-1 }} ...

      ⎡ WHEN OTHER                          ⎤
      ⎢                                     ⎥
      ⎣     imperative-statement-2          ⎦

      [ END-EVALUATE ]
```

FIGURE 4-33 Basic format of the EVALUATE statement

In Figure 4-34, NPR-PAYMENT-STATUS is being tested for valid entries with appropriate actions occurring for each. The nested IF and EVALUATE represent the same logic. WHEN OTHER in the EVALUATE statement is optional, but is a desirable entry for handling error or unexpected conditions that may occur. By using WHEN OTHER, you are guaranteed that the EVALUATE will take action regardless of what is being tested. As soon as one of the WHEN conditions is true and the statements associated with it have executed, the EVALUATE statement terminates. No more than one set of instructions executes.

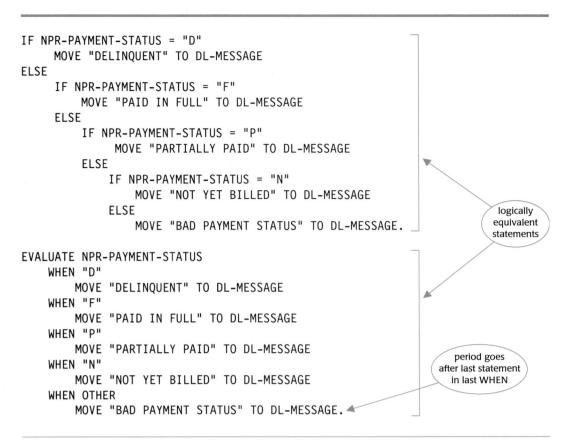

```
IF NPR-PAYMENT-STATUS = "D"
    MOVE "DELINQUENT" TO DL-MESSAGE
ELSE
    IF NPR-PAYMENT-STATUS = "F"
        MOVE "PAID IN FULL" TO DL-MESSAGE
    ELSE
        IF NPR-PAYMENT-STATUS = "P"
            MOVE "PARTIALLY PAID" TO DL-MESSAGE
        ELSE
            IF NPR-PAYMENT-STATUS = "N"
                MOVE "NOT YET BILLED" TO DL-MESSAGE
            ELSE
                MOVE "BAD PAYMENT STATUS" TO DL-MESSAGE.

EVALUATE NPR-PAYMENT-STATUS
    WHEN "D"
        MOVE "DELINQUENT" TO DL-MESSAGE
    WHEN "F"
        MOVE "PAID IN FULL" TO DL-MESSAGE
    WHEN "P"
        MOVE "PARTIALLY PAID" TO DL-MESSAGE
    WHEN "N"
        MOVE "NOT YET BILLED" TO DL-MESSAGE
    WHEN OTHER
        MOVE "BAD PAYMENT STATUS" TO DL-MESSAGE.
```

logically
equivalent
statements

period goes
after last statement
in last WHEN

FIGURE 4-34   Nested IF and equivalent EVALUATE

Figure 4-35 on the next page presents another form of the EVALUATE. This example utilizes the condition names defined under NPR-PAYMENT-STATUS rather than testing for specific values directly. The logic presented in Figures 4-34 and 4-35 is identical. END-EVALUATE need only be used in situations where a period can not be used, in a fashion similar to the use of END-IF.

```
IF DELINQUENT
    MOVE "DELINQUENT" TO DL-MESSAGE
ELSE
    IF PAID-IN-FULL
        MOVE "PAID IN FULL" TO DL-MESSAGE
    ELSE
        IF PARTIALLY-PAID
            MOVE "PARTIALLY PAID" TO DL-MESSAGE
        ELSE
            IF NOT-YET-BILLED
                MOVE "NOT YET BILLED" TO DL-MESSAGE
            ELSE
                MOVE "BAD PAYMENT STATUS" TO DL-MESSAGE.

EVALUATE TRUE
    WHEN DELINQUENT
        MOVE "DELINQUENT" TO DL-MESSAGE
    WHEN PAID-IN-FULL
        MOVE "PAID IN FULL" TO DL-MESSAGE
    WHEN PARTIALLY-PAID
        MOVE "PARTIALLY PAID" TO DL-MESSAGE
    WHEN NOT-YET-BILLED
        MOVE "NOT YET BILLED" TO DL-MESSAGE
    WHEN OTHER
        MOVE "BAD PAYMENT STATUS" TO DL-MESSAGE.
```

logically equivalent statements

FIGURE 4-35   Nested IF and equivalent EVALUATE

MOVE STATEMENT

The **MOVE** statement, used to copy data from one location or field to another, was introduced in Chapter 2. This next section discusses the MOVE in more detail. Figure 4-36 presents the basic format of the MOVE statement. The field, or literal, following the reserved word MOVE is the **sending field**. The field or fields following the reserved word TO make up the **receiving field**. The contents of the sending field are copied to each receiving field. COBOL allows only one sending field, but you can have as many receiving fields as needed. As with comparisons, there are two basic types of MOVEs, an alphanumeric MOVE and a numeric MOVE.

```
MOVE    {field-1}          TO      field-2 [ field-3 ] ...
        {literal}
```

FIGURE 4-36   Basic format of the MOVE statement

Alphanumeric MOVE

An **alphanumeric MOVE** copies data from the sending field to the receiving field, left to right, one character at a time. An alphanumeric MOVE occurs when either the sending field or receiving field or both are defined as alphabetic or alphanumeric type fields. If the fields are the same length, then, as a result of the MOVE, the sending and receiving fields will be identical. If the fields are not the same length, then either padding or truncation occurs, depending on the size of the receiving field.

Figure 4-37 presents the three types of results that may occur in alphanumeric MOVEs. In the first example, WA-FIELD-1 and WA-FIELD-2 are the same size; hence, they end up with identical contents. In the second example, WA-FIELD-1 is smaller than WA-FIELD-2; thus, WA-FIELD-2 is padded with spaces in the rightmost character positions to fill the entire field. In this situation, COBOL insures that extra rightmost positions in the receiving field will be padded with spaces.

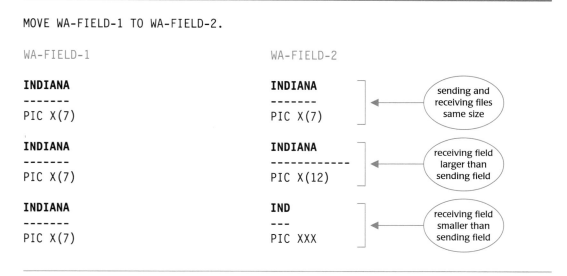

```
MOVE WA-FIELD-1 TO WA-FIELD-2.
```

FIGURE 4-37   Results of alphanumeric MOVEs

In the final example, WA-FIELD-1 is larger than WA-FIELD-2; thus, not all of WA-FIELD-1 will fit into WA-FIELD-2. This will result in rightmost characters being truncated during the MOVE, which would be undesirable in most situations. Close attention must be given to the size of receiving fields used in MOVE statements.

Numeric MOVE

A **numeric MOVE** occurs when both the sending and receiving fields are numeric or when the sending field is numeric and the receiving field is an edit pattern. In a numeric MOVE, the sending and receiving fields are decimally aligned and the receiving field is filled to the left and right of its implied or explicit decimal position. As with an alphanumeric MOVE, the fields do not have to be the same length. In the case of a numeric MOVE, however, padding and/or truncation can occur on the left and/or right, depending on the decimal position. Figure 4-38 illustrates results that may occur when moving numeric fields.

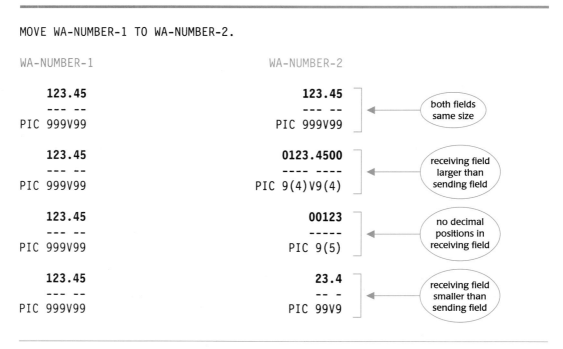

FIGURE 4-38 Results of numeric MOVEs

When the sending and receiving fields are the same size, the fields will have identical contents after the MOVE. When the receiving field is larger than the sending field, either to the left of the decimal position or to the right, padding will occur with zeros. When the receiving field is smaller than the sending field, either to the left or right of the decimal position, truncation of digits will occur.

Figure 4-39 presents examples involving numeric edit patterns as receiving fields. Again, padding and/or truncation is possible, depending on the size of the edit pattern. The implied decimal position of the sending field is aligned with the explicit decimal position of the edit pattern when the MOVE occurs. Editing then takes place as specified by the edit pattern.

MOVE WA-NUMBER-1 TO DL-NUMBER-OUT.

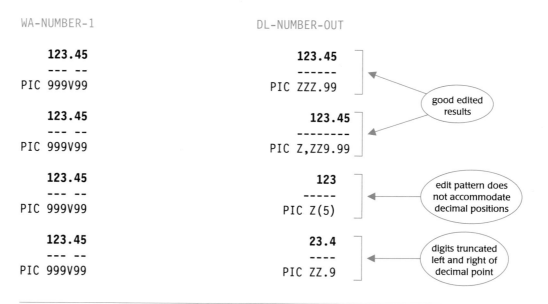

FIGURE 4-39 Results of numeric MOVEs using edit patterns as receiving fields

INITIALIZE STATEMENT

The **INITIALIZE** statement works like a series of MOVE statements in that it causes values to be copied into fields. The INITIALIZE statement is designed to set a field or group of fields to predetermined values. The basic format of the INITIALIZE statement is illustrated in Figure 4-40. The most common use of the INITIALIZE statement is in conjunction with a group name. When used with a group name, the alphanumeric fields under the group name are initialized to spaces while the numeric fields are initialized to zeros.

```
INITIALIZE {field-1 } ...

    [           ┌ ┌ ALPHABETIC        ┐        ┌ field-2  ┐   ]
    |           | | ALPHANUMERIC      |  DATA BY | literal-1 | ...
    | REPLACING ┤ ┤ NUMERIC           ├        └          ┘   |
    |           | | ALPHANUMERIC-EDITED|                       |
    [           └ └ NUMERIC-EDITED    ┘                       ]
```

FIGURE 4-40 Basic format of the INITIALIZE statement

Figure 4-41 on the next page illustrates the use of INITIALIZE on the group name PREMIUM-RECORD. Because it is numeric, PR-PREMIUM-AMOUNT will receive a value of zero. Because all the other fields are alphanumeric, they will receive spaces.

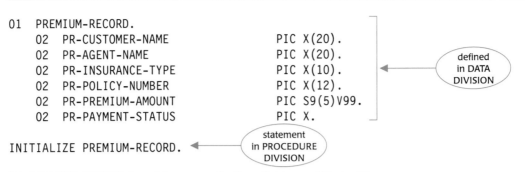

```
01   PREMIUM-RECORD.
     02   PR-CUSTOMER-NAME              PIC X(20).
     02   PR-AGENT-NAME                 PIC X(20).
     02   PR-INSURANCE-TYPE             PIC X(10).
     02   PR-POLICY-NUMBER              PIC X(12).
     02   PR-PREMIUM-AMOUNT             PIC S9(5)V99.
     02   PR-PAYMENT-STATUS             PIC X.

INITIALIZE PREMIUM-RECORD.
```

PR-PREMIUM-AMOUNT is set to zero, all other fields are filled with spaces.

FIGURE 4-41 Sample INITIALIZE statement

With the **REPLACING** option, INITIALIZE can be used to set fields to specific values. When REPLACING is used, only fields of the type specified are affected. Other fields are not initialized. Figure 4-42 presents an example in which the alphanumeric fields under PREMIUM-RECORD are initialized to underscores while PR-PREMIUM-AMOUNT is unchanged. If an elementary item is specified in an INITIALIZE statement, it is initialized to zero if it is numeric and to spaces otherwise.

```
01   PREMIUM-RECORD.
     02   PR-CUSTOMER-NAME              PIC X(20).
     02   PR-AGENT-NAME                 PIC X(20).
     02   PR-INSURANCE-TYPE             PIC X(10).
     02   PR-POLICY-NUMBER              PIC X(12).
     02   PR-PREMIUM-AMOUNT             PIC S9(5)V99.
     02   PR-PAYMENT-STATUS             PIC X.
     02                                 PIC X(10).

INITIALIZE PREMIUM-RECORD REPLACING ALPHANUMERIC BY "_".
```

PR-PREMIUM-AMOUNT is unchanged, all other fields are filled with underscores.

FIGURE 4-42 Sample INITIALIZE REPLACING statement

ACCEPT STATEMENT

The **ACCEPT** statement can be used to move data to a field from an external source such as a computer terminal, or from the computer's operating system. Figure 4-43 shows the two basic formats available for the ACCEPT statement. When Format 1 is used, program execution is halted until a keyboard entry is made by a user. The entered data is then moved into the designated field in a manner similar to an alphanumeric MOVE, left to right, one character at a time. When a mnemonic is used, it must be defined in the SPECIAL-NAMES paragraph within the CONFIGURATION SECTION of the ENVIRONMENT DIVISION. Future programs will utilize Format 1 of the ACCEPT to develop interactive programs that allow for user input. Format 2 uses reserved words to access information from the computer's operating system and place it into specified fields.

Format 1

```
ACCEPT field-1  [ FROM mnemonic-name ]
```

Format 2

```
                         ┌ DATE        ┐
                         │ DAY         │
ACCEPT field-1   FROM   ⟨  DAY-OF-WEEK  ⟩
                         └ TIME        ┘
```

FIGURE 4-43 Two basic formats of the ACCEPT statement

In the Premium File Validation program, the ACCEPT statement is used in A-100-INITIALIZATION to retrieve the current date from the computer system (Figure 4-44). On most computer systems, the current date is available from the operating system as a six-character field in YYMMDD (Year-Month-Day) format. For printing purposes, the date is typically rearranged so it will appear on a report in MMDDYY (Month-Day-Year) format. This also is accomplished in A-100-INITIALIZATION. Using WORK-AREA fields, a series of MOVE statements rearranges the date and then MOVEs the rearranged date to the edited output field, RH-DATE. The field, WA-CURRENT-DATE-N, which redefines WA-CURRENT-DATE, is used in the final MOVE because only an elementary item may be successfully moved to an edit pattern.

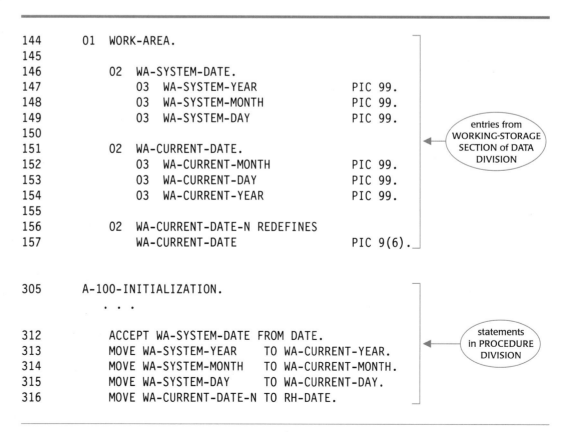

```
144    01  WORK-AREA.
145
146        02  WA-SYSTEM-DATE.
147            03  WA-SYSTEM-YEAR          PIC 99.
148            03  WA-SYSTEM-MONTH         PIC 99.
149            03  WA-SYSTEM-DAY           PIC 99.
150
151        02  WA-CURRENT-DATE.
152            03  WA-CURRENT-MONTH        PIC 99.
153            03  WA-CURRENT-DAY          PIC 99.
154            03  WA-CURRENT-YEAR         PIC 99.
155
156        02  WA-CURRENT-DATE-N REDEFINES
157            WA-CURRENT-DATE             PIC 9(6).


305    A-100-INITIALIZATION.
           . . .

312        ACCEPT WA-SYSTEM-DATE FROM DATE.
313        MOVE WA-SYSTEM-YEAR    TO WA-CURRENT-YEAR.
314        MOVE WA-SYSTEM-MONTH   TO WA-CURRENT-MONTH.
315        MOVE WA-SYSTEM-DAY     TO WA-CURRENT-DAY.
316        MOVE WA-CURRENT-DATE-N TO RH-DATE.
```

entries from WORKING-STORAGE SECTION of DATA DIVISION

statements in PROCEDURE DIVISION

FIGURE 4-44 Retrieving and rearranging the current date in the Premium File Validation program

Table 4-5 summarizes the use of DATE, DAY, TIME, and DAY-OF-WEEK.

TABLE 4-5 ACCEPT Statement Options

Reserved Word	Meaning
DATE	Six-digit date in YYMMDD format
	Example: February 3, 1997 → 970203
DAY	Five-digit date in YYDDD format where DDD is a three-digit number representing the day of the year
	Example: February 3, 1997 → 97034
TIME	Eight-digit number in HHMMSSCC format representing the time of day where: HH is the Hour of the day in 24-hour format MM is the Minutes SS is the Seconds and CC is the Centiseconds
	Example: 1:34 PM → 13340000
DAY-OF-WEEK	One digit representing the week day
	Example: Monday → 1 Tuesday → 2 . . . Sunday → 7

REFERENCE MODIFICATION

A **reference modification** allows you to reference a portion of a field rather than the entire field. Although its use is not restricted to MOVE or IF statements, reference modification often is useful when copying data from one location to another or testing particular parts of a field. Figure 4-45 shows the basic format of a reference modification. Inside parentheses following a field name, the leftmost starting position within the field is defined, followed by a colon, followed by an optional length factor. The starting position may be a literal or an arithmetic expression. In either case, the value must be between one and the number of characters in the field. A colon must follow the starting position. The length, if specified, may be a literal or an arithmetic expression, and its value must neither exceed the length of the field, nor cause a reference to exceed the length of the field. If the length is omitted, the default length is the number of character positions remaining in the field from the starting position.

```
field-name-1 [ ( leftmost-character-position : [length] ) ]
```

FIGURE 4-45 Basic format of a reference modification

Figure 4-46 presents examples illustrating the use of reference modification. Regardless of a field's data category, when a reference modification is used on the field, COBOL treats the referenced data positions alphanumerically. Thus, reference modification cannot be used on a field involved in an arithmetic operation.

```
02  NPR-POLICY-NUMBER                          PIC X(12).

                    RM-7623-1221
                    ------------
```

Action	Result
MOVE NPR-POLICY-NUMBER (1:2) TO DL-ITEM-OUT.	Moves RM to DL-ITEM-OUT.
MOVE "1234" TO NPR-POLICY-NUMBER (4:4).	Changes NPR-POLICY-NUMBER to RM-1234-1221.
IF NPR-POLICY-NUMBER (3:1) NOT = "-" . . .	Tests the third position of NPR-POLICY-NUMBER for a hyphen.
MOVE "4567" TO NPR-POLICY-NUMBER (9:5).	ERROR! Exceeds length of field.

FIGURE 4-46 Use of reference modification

DATA VALIDATION

A frequent use of conditional statements is in the validation of fields contained within the records of a file. **Online applications**, or programs that allow data entry from a terminal or personal computer, validate data as soon as it is entered. **Batch applications**, or programs in which the data is completely entered first and then submitted to the computer, validate data in a large group. The Premium File Validation program presented at the beginning of this chapter is a batch program in which a group of previously entered records is tested to verify that the entries made into the fields of each record are correct, or at least reasonable. As soon as an error is detected in the Premium file, an error message is written to the report.

Data validation can take many different forms and test for many types of entries; however, there are some basic types of tests that can be performed in nearly every application.

Class Test

COBOL allows you to test a field to see if it contains the type of characters required. Such a test is called a **class test**. The two classes of data that may be tested in COBOL are NUMERIC and ALPHABETIC. Figure 4-47 on the next page presents the basic format of a class test. Notice that an equal sign is not used and that the word IS is optional. The **NUMERIC class test** checks each character of a field to see if it contains a digit from 0 to 9. If just one character is not a digit, then the field is not numeric. The **ALPHABETIC class test** checks each character of a field to see if it contains a letter from A to Z or a space. If just one character is not a letter or a space, then the field is not alphabetic.

```
IF field-1 IS [ NOT ]    { NUMERIC   }
                         { ALPHABETIC }

        . . .
```

FIGURE 4-47   NUMERIC and ALPHABETIC class tests

Figure 4-48 illustrates a use of the NUMERIC class test from the Premium File validation program. Note that the test is done on an alphanumeric field, NPR-PREMIUM-AMOUNT-ALPHA, which redefines the numeric field NPR-PREMIUM-AMOUNT. When verifying the presence of numeric data, it is generally wise to perform the NUMERIC class test on an alphanumeric field. A NUMERIC class test on a field with an alphanumeric picture is more thorough than such a test on a field with a numeric picture. Use the name associated with the numeric picture only after you are certain that it contains numeric characters.

```
459        IF NPR-PREMIUM-AMOUNT-ALPHA NOT NUMERIC
460            MOVE "PREM AMT NOT NUMERIC" TO EDL-MESSAGE      ⟵  executes if non-
461            PERFORM B-400-WRITE-REPORT                          digit characters
                                                                   are present
```

FIGURE 4-48   Use of the NUMERIC class test

Sign Test

The COBOL **sign test** is designed to see if signed numeric fields have a value that is **POSITIVE**, **NEGATIVE**, or **ZERO**. Figure 4-49 presents the basic format of a sign test. Note that the word IS is optional and that an equal sign is not used. A sign test is equivalent to performing a relational comparison to zero.

```
IF field-1 IS [ NOT ]    { POSITIVE }
                         { NEGATIVE }
                         { ZERO     }

        . . .
```

FIGURE 4-49   Sign test

Often, special processing must be performed on negative or nonpositive numbers. It is for these circumstances that the sign test is designed. Figure 4-50 presents an example of such a test.

Table 4-6 presents each of the sign tests and its relational test counterpart.

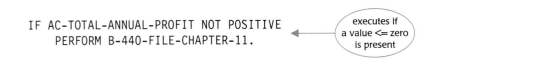

```
IF AC-TOTAL-ANNUAL-PROFIT NOT POSITIVE         executes if
    PERFORM B-440-FILE-CHAPTER-11.      ⟵    a value <= zero
                                              is present
```

FIGURE 4-50   An example of a sign test

TABLE 4-6   Sign Tests and Equivalent Relational Tests

Sign Test	Equivalent Relational Test
IF WA-FIELD-1 POSITIVE	IF WA-FIELD-1 > 0
IF WA-FIELD-1 NEGATIVE	IF WA-FIELD-1 < 0
IF WA-FIELD-1 ZERO	IF WA-FIELD-1 = 0

Value Test

A **value test** is used to ensure that a field has a specific value or one of several allowable values. A value test is performed by comparing the contents of a field against the actual value or values that are allowed or expected in that field. Figure 4-51 presents an example from the Premium File Validation program. In this example, an error message is written to the report if NPR-HYPHEN-1 does not contain a hyphen.

```
426        IF NPR-HYPHEN-1 NOT = "-"
427            MOVE "1ST HYPHEN MISSING" TO EDL-MESSAGE
428            PERFORM B-400-WRITE-REPORT.
```

FIGURE 4-51   Value test

When several values are allowable, a value test can be simplified by using a condition name. Figure 4-52 presents the validation test for NPR-PAYMENT-STATUS and the equivalent test that would be needed if the condition name VALID-PAYMENT-STATUS was not used. As you can see, the condition name greatly simplifies this test. The condition name VALID-PAYMENT-STATUS is defined on line 85 of Figure 4-5 on page 4-7.

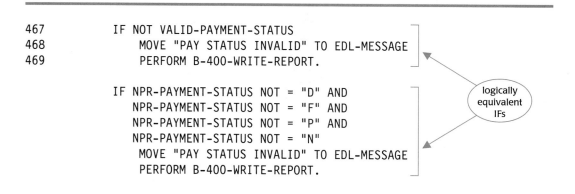

```
467        IF NOT VALID-PAYMENT-STATUS
468            MOVE "PAY STATUS INVALID" TO EDL-MESSAGE
469            PERFORM B-400-WRITE-REPORT.

           IF NPR-PAYMENT-STATUS NOT = "D" AND
              NPR-PAYMENT-STATUS NOT = "F" AND
              NPR-PAYMENT-STATUS NOT = "P" AND
              NPR-PAYMENT-STATUS NOT = "N"
               MOVE "PAY STATUS INVALID" TO EDL-MESSAGE
               PERFORM B-400-WRITE-REPORT.
```

FIGURE 4-52   Two ways to validate NPR-PAYMENT-STATUS

Range Test

A **range test** is similar to a value test; however, in a range test a contiguous series of acceptable values exists. The range test is performed by testing the field against the minimum value, maximum value, or both in the series. Figure 4-53 on the next page presents an example from the Premium File Validation program. Because NPR-CODE-NUMBER-1 is alphanumeric, the comparison is made against nonnumeric literals. The value "0050" is the minimum acceptable value and "9900" is the maximum acceptable value. Any value outside of that range is considered an error.

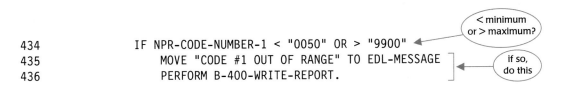

FIGURE 4-53   Range test using a minimum and maximum value

Figure 4-54 presents an example that uses only a minimum value. Any value less than 100 in NPR-PREMIUM-AMOUNT is considered an error and causes a message to be written to the report.

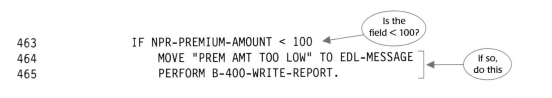

FIGURE 4-54   Range test using just a minimum value

Presence or Absence Test

As the name implies, a **presence or absence test** checks a field to see if there is data other than spaces in the field. This test normally is performed by comparing the field to the figurative constant SPACES. Figure 4-55 presents an example from the Premium File validation program. If there is no data in the field NPR-CUSTOMER-NAME, an error message is written to the report.

FIGURE 4-55   Presence or absence test

CHAPTER SUMMARY

The Premium File Validation program presented in this chapter was used to introduce several important COBOL topics. The following list summarizes this chapter. The summary is designed to help you study and understand the material and concepts presented.

1. Conditional statements allow you to control program execution based on the results of tests using **IF** and **EVALUATE**.

2. **END-IF** is needed only in situations where a period cannot be used.

3. A numeric comparison of two fields is based on the algebraic values of the fields.

4. An alphanumeric comparison of two fields goes from left to right, one character at a time.

5. In an IF statement, ELSE relates back to the previously unmatched IF.

6. The IF statement can be **one-sided**, **two-sided**, or **nested**.

7. To avoid confusion and unnecessary code, **NEXT SENTENCE** and **CONTINUE** should be avoided in IF statements.

8. **Combined conditions** and **complex conditions** are formed by combining simple conditions with the logical connectors **AND** and **OR** along with optional parentheses.

9. A combined condition may be abbreviated by the use of **implied subjects** and **implied operators**.

10. The **EVALUATE** statement can be used in place of numerous IF statements when testing a variable for multiple values.

11. The **MOVE** statement allows the transfer of data from one field to another.

12. The **INITIALIZE** statement is designed to set a field or group of fields to predetermined values.

13. The **ACCEPT** statement can be used to move data to a field from an external source, such as a computer terminal or the computer's operating system.

14. **Reference modification** allows you to process a portion of a field.

15. **Data validation** is the process of checking fields for acceptable contents. Various validation test are available through COBOL such as the **class test**, **sign test**, **value test**, **range test**, and **presence or absence test**.

KEY TERMS

ACCEPT (4-32)
ALPHABETIC class test (4-35)
alphanumeric MOVE (4-29)
AND (4-22)
batch applications (4-35)
class test (4-35)
combined condition (4-22)
complex condition (4-23)
CONTINUE (4-22)
data validation (4-1)
ELSE (4-11)
END-IF (4-11)
EVALUATE (4-25)
IF (4-10)
IF-THEN-ELSE logic (4-10)
implied operators (4-25)
implied subjects (4-25)
INITIALIZE (4-31)
MOVE (4-28)
NEGATIVE sign text (4-36)
nested IF (4-16)
NEXT SENTENCE (4-11)
NOT (4-12)

NUMERIC class test (4-35)
numeric MOVE (4-30)
one-sided decision (4-11)
one-sided IF (4-11)
online applications (4-35)
operator (4-25)
OR (4-22)
POSITIVE sign test (4-36)
presence or absence test (4-38)
range test (4-37)
receiving field (4-28)
reference modification (4-34)
relational operator (4-12)
REPLACING (4-32)
sending field (4-28)
sign test (4-36)
subject (4-25)
THEN (4-11)
two-sided decision (4-15)
two-sided IF (4-15)
value test (4-37)
ZERO sign test (4-36)

STUDENT ASSIGNMENTS

Student Assignment 1: True/False

Instructions: Circle T if the statement is true or F if the statement is false.

T   F   1. NEXT SENTENCE and CONTINUE always work the same.

T   F   2. END-IF is required on all IF statements.

T   F   3. Alphanumeric comparisons occur left to right, one character at a time.

T   F   4. Numeric comparisons occur left to right, one digit at a time.

T   F   5. Only one action may occur in the true part of an IF statement.

T   F   6. The COBOL operator for *not equal to* is < >.

T   F   7. When a shorter field is compared to a longer field in an alphanumeric comparison, the shorter field is internally padded on the right with spaces.

T   F   8. Numeric fields must have the same USAGE and picture in order to be compared.

T   F   9. A two-sided IF can be embedded in the false part of a two-sided IF.

T   F   10. When a longer field is moved to a shorter field in an alphanumeric MOVE, truncation will occur on the right, in the high-order positions.

T   F   11. When moving one numeric field to another numeric field, the numbers will be aligned according to their decimal positions.

T   F   12. COBOL allows a numeric field with no decimal positions to be moved to an edit pattern with an explicit decimal.

T   F   13. In a numeric MOVE, padding and/or truncation may occur on either side of the decimal point.

T   F   14. The INITIALIZE statement may be used only on group items.

T   F   15. Reference modification is always treated alphanumerically.

T   F   16. The ACCEPT statement works like an alphanumeric MOVE in placing data into its receiving field.

T   F   17. The system date on a computer is typically in YYMMDD format.

T   F   18. When validating data, the range test and class test perform the same type of operation.

T   F   19. In a combined or complex IF, AND takes precedence over OR.

T   F   20. When validating data, a sign test may be performed only on signed numeric fields.

Student Assignment 2: Multiple Choice

Instructions: Circle the correct response.

1. Which of the following is a sign test?
    a. IF FIELD-1 NUMERIC ...
    b. IF FIELD-1 POSITIVE ...
    c. IF FIELD-1 = 23 ...
    d. IF FIELD-1 > 0 AND < 10 ...
    e. none of the above

2. In an alphanumeric MOVE, padding and/or truncation must occur _____.
    a. on every MOVE
    b. only on the right, in high-order positions
    c. when fields of the same length are involved
    d. only on the left, in low-order positions
    e. all of the above

3. An alphanumeric field may be compared to _____.
    a. another alphanumeric field
    b. the figurative constant SPACES
    c. the figurative constant ZEROS
    d. a nonnumeric literal
    e. all of the above

4. In a complex IF statement, the order of precedence in evaluating the IF is _____.
    a. parentheses, NOT, AND, OR
    b. parentheses, AND, OR, NOT
    c. AND, parentheses, NOT, OR
    d. AND, OR, NOT, parentheses
    e. none of the above

5. To access a six-digit system date using an ACCEPT statement, you must ACCEPT FROM _____.
    a. TIME
    b. DAY
    c. DATE
    d. DAY-OF-WEEK
    e. none of the above

6. Which reference modification accesses the first four characters of the field WA-LAST-NAME?
    a. WA-LAST-NAME (4:1)
    b. WA-LAST-NAME (1:4)
    c. WA-LAST-NAME (4,1)
    d. WA-LAST-NAME (1,4)
    e. none of the above

7. The EVALUATE statement can be used to _____.
    a. test condition names
    b. replace a nested IF statement
    c. replace a series of IF statements
    d. test a field for specific values
    e. all of the above

(continued)

Student Assignment 2 (continued)

8. The INITIALIZE statement can be used to _____.
   a. place spaces in alphanumeric fields
   b. place zeros in numeric fields
   c. replace a series of MOVE statements
   d. fill a field with a specific character
   e. all of the above

9. The NUMERIC class test validates a field for _____.
   a. letters, numbers, and spaces
   b. letters and numbers
   c. numbers
   d. numbers and spaces
   e. none of the above

10. The ALPHABETIC class test validates a field for _____.
    a. letters, numbers, and spaces
    b. letters and numbers
    c. letters and spaces
    d. letters, spaces, and special characters
    e. none of the above

Student Assignment 3: Coding a Nested IF

Instructions: Code a nested IF statement that causes control to be passed to B-200-FIX-IT if the numeric field AC-ERROR-COUNT is less than 10; control to be passed to B-210-FORGET-IT if AC-ERROR-COUNT is greater than 20; and control to be passed to B-220-PATCH-IT otherwise.

Student Assignment 4: Coding an EVALUATE Statement

Instructions: Write an EVALUATE statement that accomplishes the same task as the following nested IF statement.

```
IF NPR-POLICY-CODE = "AM"
    MOVE "AUTO" TO DL-POLICY
ELSE
    IF NPR-POLICY-CODE = "AN"
        MOVE "ANNUITY" TO DL-POLICY
    ELSE
        IF NPR-POLICY-CODE = "HM"
            MOVE "HOME" TO DL-POLICY
        ELSE
            IF NPR-POLICY-CODE = "RT"
                MOVE "RENTER" TO DL-POLICY
            ELSE
                IF NPR-POLICY-CODE = "TL"
                    MOVE "TERM LIFE" TO DL-POLICY
                ELSE
                    IF NPR-POLICY-CODE = "WL"
                        MOVE "WHOLE LIFE" TO DL-POLICY
                    ELSE
                        MOVE "BAD CODE" TO DL-POLICY.
```

Student Assignment 5: Data Validation

Instructions: Given the following definitions, validate the field to ensure that it is numeric, positive, and has a value less than $4,000. If an error is found, move an appropriate message to the field DL-MESSAGE and transfer control to B-330-WRITE-ERROR.

```
02  ER-SALARY-AMOUNT                PIC S9(6)V99.
02  ER-SALARY-AMOUNT-ALPHA REDEFINES
    ER-SALARY-AMOUNT                PIC X(8).
```

Student Assignment 6: Coding a Readable IF

Instructions: Maintaining its logic, rewrite the following IF so it is readable. Find the value of AC-COUNT for each of the given sets of conditions.

```
IF MALE ADD 3 TO AC-COUNT IF MARRIED IF PROGRAMMER
ADD 2 TO AC-COUNT ELSE ADD 4 TO AC-COUNT ELSE ADD 8 TO AC-COUNT
IF OVER-30 IF EMPLOYED ADD 5 TO AC-COUNT ELSE ADD 3 TO AC-COUNT.
```

	MALE	MARRIED	PROGRAMMER	OVER-30	EMPLOYED
1.	True	False	False	False	True
2.	True	True	True	False	True
3.	True	False	True	True	False
4.	False	True	False	True	False
5.	True	True	False	True	True

Student Assignment 7: ACCEPT the Time

Instructions: Code the necessary work area storage locations and PROCEDURE DIVISION statements to ACCEPT the current time and then move it to the fields defined under HL-TIME-OUT. Using IF statements, the time should be converted from 24-hour clock format to AM/PM format.

```
02  HL-TIME-OUT.
    03  HL-HOUR-OUT          PIC Z9.
    03                       PIC X    VALUE ":".
    03  HL-MINUTES-OUT       PIC 99.
    03  HL-AM-PM             PIC XX.
```

COBOL LABORATORY EXERCISES

Exercise 1: Modified Premium File Validation Program

Purpose: To gain experience in COBOL program maintenance and modification and creating a program that produces two separate reports.

Problem: Open the file PROJ4.CBL on the Student Diskette that accompanies this book, and modify the Premium File Validation program so it still creates the error report but has the following modifications:

1. List the records containing no errors on a second report called the Valid Premium Record Report. The report should have the same format as the Premium Amount Report created by the sample program in Chapter 3.

2. Remove NPR-POLICY-NUMBER-R, which redefines NPR-POLICY-NUMBER under NEW-PREMIUM-RECORD. Using the same validation tests, use reference modification to validate the various parts of NPR-POLICY-NUMBER.

(continued)

Exercise 1 (continued)

3. Print the current time immediately below the current date in the heading lines for the Premium Record Error Report. Print only the hours and minutes, and print the time in AM/PM format.

Save this program as EX4-1.CBL

Input Data: Use the New Premium file presented in Appendix A as input. This file is named NEWPREM.DAT on the Student Diskette that accompanies this book.

Output Results: Output should be an error report similar to the example given at the beginning of this chapter but including the current time in the headings. Also, output is a valid record report with a format similar to the Premium Amount Report created in Chapter 3.

Exercise 2: Customer Purchases Error Report Program

Purpose: To practice the use of data validation in the creation of a COBOL program that produces a Customer Purchases Error Report.

Problem: Write a program that validates Customer Purchases records for the ABC Department Store. Validate using the following criteria:

Account Number — Numeric and not equal to zero
Customer Name — Not equal to spaces
Balance — Numeric
Purchases — Numeric and positive
Credit Limit — Numeric, greater than $499 but less than or equal to $3,000

For each record that contains an error, print the account number, customer name, balance, purchases, credit limit, and a message on each detail line. If a record contains more than one error, print the customer fields only once, but list error messages as needed. Single-space error messages and double-space between records. Print the current date and time in AM/PM format as part of the heading lines. Number each page starting with page 1. At the end of the report, print the total number of error records found as well as the number of error messages printed. Save this program as EX4-2.CBL.

Input Data: Use the New Customer file listed in Appendix A as input. This file is named NEWCUST.DAT on the Student Diskette that accompanies this book. Customer records have the following layout:

Field Description	Position	Length	Attribute
filler	1–6	6	Alphanumeric
Account Number	7–12	6	Alphanumeric
Customer Name	13–32	0	Alphanumeric
filler	33–53	1	Alphanumeric
Balance Amount	54–59	6	Numeric, PIC S9(4)V99 redefine as a PIC X(6)
Purchases Amount	60–65	6	Numeric, PIC 9(4)V99 redefine as a PIC X(6)
Credit Limit	66–70	5	Numeric, PIC 9(5) redefine as a PIC X(5)
filler	71–72	2	Alphanumeric
Record Length		72	

Output Results: Output consists of the Customer Purchases Error Report listing the account number, name, balance, purchases, credit limit, and error message for each customer record found to contain an error. Double-space between records but single-space error messages. Count and print the number of error records processed and the number of error messages listed. The report should have a format similar to the following:

```
Z9/99/99                      ABC DEPARTMENT STORE                 PAGE Z9
Z9:99AM                  CUSTOMER PURCHASES ERROR REPORT

ACCOUNT                                              CREDIT
NUMBER   CUSTOMER NAME          BALANCE   PURCHASES  LIMIT    ERROR MESSAGE
-------  --------------------   -------   ---------  -------  --------------------
XXXXXX   XXXXXXXXXXXXXXXXXXXX   XXXXXX    XXXXXX     XXXXX    XXXXXXXXXXXXXXXXXXXX
XXXXXX   XXXXXXXXXXXXXXXXXXXX   XXXXXX    XXXXXX     XXXXX    XXXXXXXXXXXXXXXXXXXX
                                                             XXXXXXXXXXXXXXXXXXXX
                                                             XXXXXXXXXXXXXXXXXXXX
XXXXXX   XXXXXXXXXXXXXXXXXXXX   XXXXXX    XXXXXX     XXXXX    XXXXXXXXXXXXXXXXXXXX
. . .


TOTAL NUMBER OF RECORDS LISTED =  ZZ9     TOTAL NUMBER OF ERROR MESSAGES PRINTED = ZZ9

                               END OF REPORT
```

Exercise 3: Customer Sales Error Report Program

Purpose: To practice designing and coding a COBOL program that validates newly entered input data and produces a report listing the errors found and a second report listing records with no errors.

Problem: Design and code a COBOL program that validates the fields of a newly entered Customer Sales file for EZ Auto Sales. The program should validate the fields according to the criteria list below:

Customer Number — Numeric and not equal to zero
Customer Name   — Not equal to spaces
Purchase Date   — Numeric and not greater than today's date
                   (assuming today's date is Nov. 28, 1997)
Purchase Price   — Numeric and Positive
Satisfaction Rating — Must contain a 0, 1, or 2

The error report should list the customer's number, name, purchase date, purchase price, satisfaction rating, and an appropriate message for each error found. Include the current date and time in the page headings. Use AM/PM format for the time. The valid record report should list the same fields, edited where appropriate, but no message field. Save this program as EX4-3.CBL.

Input Data: Use the New Customer Sales file listed in Appendix A as input. This file is named NEWSALE.DAT on the Student Diskette that accompanies this book. The record layout for the customer records is as follows:

Field Description	Position	Length	Attribute
filler	1–9	9	Alphanumeric
Customer Number	10–13	4	Alphanumeric
Customer Name	14–33	20	Alphanumeric
Purchase Date	34–39	6	Numeric, PIC 9(6) redefine as PIC X(6)
filler	40–59	20	Alphanumeric
Purchase Price	60–66	7	Numeric, PIC 9(5)V99 redefine as PIC X(7)
filler	67–73	7	Alphanumeric
Satisfaction Code	74	1	Alphanumeric, 0 = DISSATISFIED 1 = UNDECIDED 2 = SATISFIED
Record Length		74	

(continued)

Exercise 3 (continued)

Output Results: An error report should be produced listing the customer's number, name, purchase date, purchase price, satisfaction rating, and an appropriate error message for each error found. Single-space error messages and double-space between records. Provide a count of the number of customers processed and the number of error records found at the end of the report. For records that have no errors, a valid record report should be created that lists the same fields as the error report but no message field. Translate the Satisfaction Code into an appropriate message for the Valid Record Report and double-space the records. Each report should list the current date and time in the headings. The time should be in AM/PM format. The reports should have a format similar to the following:

```
Z9/99/99                      EZ AUTO SALES                     PAGE ZZ9
Z9:99AM                CUSTOMER SALES ERROR RECORD REPORT

CUSTOMER   CUSTOMER              PURCHASE  PURCHASE  SATISFACTION
NUMBER     NAME                  DATE      PRICE     RATING       ERROR MESSAGE
--------   --------------------  --------  --------  ------------ --------------------

  XXXX     XXXXXXXXXXXXXXXXXXXX   XXXXXX    XXXXXXX       X        XXXXXXXXXXXXXXXXXXXX
                                                                  XXXXXXXXXXXXXXXXXXXX

  XXXX     XXXXXXXXXXXXXXXXXXXX   XXXXXX    XXXXXXX       X        XXXXXXXXXXXXXXXXXXXX

  XXXX     XXXXXXXXXXXXXXXXXXXX   XXXXXX    XXXXXXX       X        XXXXXXXXXXXXXXXXXXXX
                                                                  XXXXXXXXXXXXXXXXXXXX
                                                                  XXXXXXXXXXXXXXXXXXXX

  XXXX     XXXXXXXXXXXXXXXXXXXX   XXXXXX    XXXXXXX       X        XXXXXXXXXXXXXXXXXXXX
                                                                  XXXXXXXXXXXXXXXXXXXX
   .
   .
   .

                TOTAL NUMBER OF CUSTOMERS PROCESSED = ZZ9
                TOTAL NUMBER OF ERROR RECORDS FOUND = ZZ9

                              END OF REPORT


Z9/99/99                      EZ AUTO SALES                     PAGE ZZ9
Z9:99AM                CUSTOMER SALES VALID RECORD REPORT

CUSTOMER   CUSTOMER              PURCHASE  PURCHASE  SATISFACTION
NUMBER     NAME                  DATE      PRICE     RATING
--------   --------------------  --------  ----------  ------------
  XXXX     XXXXXXXXXXXXXXXXXXXX   Z9/99/99  $$$,$$$.99  XXXXXXXXXXX

  XXXX     XXXXXXXXXXXXXXXXXXXX   Z9/99/99  $$$,$$$.99  XXXXXXXXXXX

  XXXX     XXXXXXXXXXXXXXXXXXXX   Z9/99/99  $$$,$$$.99  XXXXXXXXXXX
   .
   .
   .

              TOTAL NUMBER OF CUSTOMERS LISTED = ZZ9

                     END OF REPORT
```

CHAPTER FIVE

Arithmetic Statements and Branching

OBJECTIVES

You will have mastered the material in Chapter 5 when you can:

- Recognize and code a valid ADD statement
- Recognize and code a valid SUBTRACT statement
- Identify and code a valid MULTIPLY statement
- Identify and code a valid DIVIDE statement
- Describe and code a valid COMPUTE statement
- Describe the purpose and use of intrinsic functions
- Explain the function of a PERFORM statement
- Define and code a PERFORM UNTIL statement
- Illustrate and code a THRU on a PERFORM statement
- Explain and code a PERFORM TIMES statement
- Explain and code a PERFORM VARYING statement
- Demonstrate and identify uses of the GO TO statement
- Recognize and understand the use of a SECTION
- Identify the use of a CALL statement and a subprogram

INTRODUCTION

Arithmetic operations are essential for most business applications. Previous chapters have touched upon the use of arithmetic in COBOL programs, but this chapter will go into more detail and explain the options available for arithmetic operations. A special set of operators also will be introduced. The PERFORM statement was introduced in earlier chapters as a means of transferring control from one location in a program to another. PERFORM and its variations will be explored in more detail in this chapter along with other methods for transferring control.

The Minimum Payment Report

The sample program presented in this chapter uses arithmetic and other COBOL statements to create a Minimum Payment Report for those customers who have not yet paid their premiums in full (Figure 5-1).

```
DATE: 11/28/97                    AINSWORTH INSURANCE COMPANY                PAGE   1
TIME:  3:18PM                        MINIMUM PAYMENT REPORT

                                 INSURANCE      PREMIUM     PAYMENT    MINIMUM
POLICY NUMBER    CUSTOMER NAME   TYPE           STATUS      AMOUNT     DUE
-------------    -------------   ---------      -------     -------    -------

AM-1991-9223     Allister, Collin      Automobile    P PD       123.45      30.86

HM-7008-0507     Andrews, Robert       Home          P PD       560.00     140.00

AM-7211-7261     Antich, Roseanne      Automobile    P PD       250.50      62.63

RT-4402-3211     Baker, Bonnie         Renter        NYB        150.00      37.50

TL-7008-5551     Brannan, Clyde        Term Life     NYB        550.00     137.50
                 .
                 .
                 .
HM-8767-8788     Solenfeld, Nancy      Home          P PD       980.00     245.00

TL-2762-2728     Solinski, Paula       Term Life     NYB        268.25      67.06

HM-2001-7338     Solloday, Tom         Home          P PD       790.90     197.73

HM-2322-4488     Sollyfield, Barbara   Home          P PD     1,450.50     362.63

RT-4337-7488     Tully, Paula          Renter        P PD       175.00      43.75

TL-2129-8959     Vlasic, Roberta       Term Life     P PD       380.00      95.00

RT-0424-0053     Walters, Samuel       Renter        P PD       220.00      55.00

AN-0993-4104     West, William         Annuity       NYB        400.00     100.00

AM-3411-1223     Whitman, Walter       Automobile    P PD       771.00     192.75

WL-2721-3904     Winfield, Wally       Whole Life    P PD       326.00      81.50

RT-7127-5076     Yackley, Yourto       Renter        P PD       240.00      60.00


                 TOTAL RECORDS PRINTED =      45
                 TOTAL PREMIUMS DUE    = 29,218.50
                 AVERAGE PREMIUM DUE   =    649.30
                 TOTAL MINIMUM DUE     =  7,304.66
                 AVERAGE MINIMUM DUE   =    162.33

                              END OF REPORT
```

FIGURE 5-1   Partial listing of the Minimum Payment Report

The minimum payment due for each customer is 25% of his or her premium payment amount. The program uses addition, multiplication, and division in the creation of the report. Total premium due, average premium due, total minimum due, and average minimum due are calculated and printed at the end of the report.

Hierarchy Chart

A hierarchy chart illustrating the organization of the PROCEDURE DIVISION of the Minimum Payment Report program is presented in Figure 5-2. The organization is very similar to the organization of the programs discussed in Chapters 2 and 3. An extra paragraph exists to accommodate an error routine associated with some of the arithmetic statements used in the program. The function of this error routine will be discussed later in this chapter.

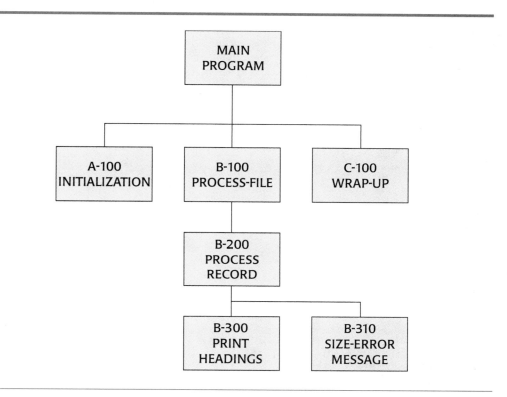

FIGURE 5-2   Hierarchy chart illustrating the organization of the PROCEDURE DIVISION of the Minimum Payment Report program

Program Flowchart

A partial flowchart illustrating the basic logic used in the PROCEDURE DIVISION of the Minimum Payment Report program is shown in Figure 5-3 on the next page. Only those customers who have not fully paid their annual premiums are listed on the report. The COBOL statements that implement this logic are in paragraphs B-100-PROCESS-FILE and B-200-PROCESS-RECORD. This logic will be discussed later in the chapter.

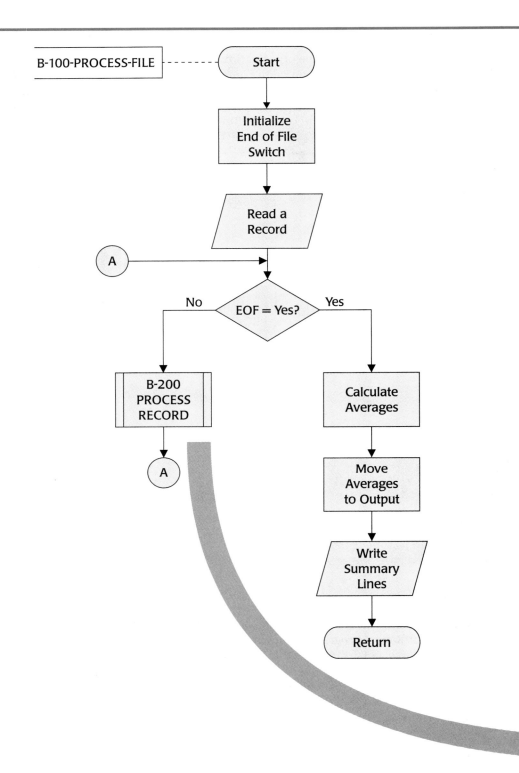

FIGURE 5-3 Flowchart illustrating the basic logic used in B-100-PROCESS-FILE and B-200-PROCESS-RECORD in the Minimum Payment Report program

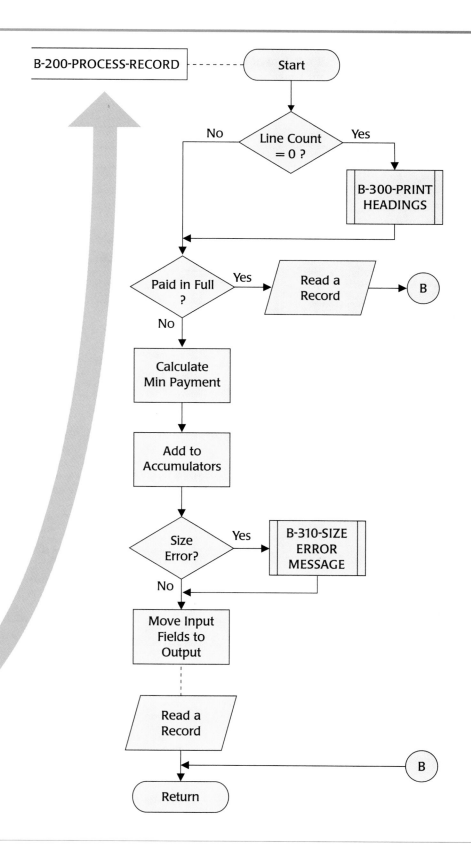

The Minimum Payment Report Program

Figure 5-4 presents the Minimum Payment Report program discussed in this chapter. This program is found on the Student Diskette that accompanies this book.

```
  1    IDENTIFICATION DIVISION.
  2    ***********************
  3
  4    PROGRAM-ID.    MINPREM.
  5    AUTHOR.        R. O. FOREMAN.
  6    INSTALLATION.  PURDUE UNIVERSITY CALUMET.
  7    DATE-WRITTEN.  Nov. 28, 1997.
  8    DATE-COMPILED. 28-Nov-1997.
  9    ************************************************************
 10    *                    PROGRAM NARRATIVE                    *
 11    *                                                         *
 12    *                                                         *
 13    *    THIS PROGRAM READS ALL RECORDS IN THE CUSTOMER PREMIUM FILE *
 14    *    AND CALCULATES THE MINIMUM PAYMENT DUE FROM CUSTOMERS WHO   *
 15    *    HAVE NOT PAID IN FULL.  TOTAL PAYMENTS AND TOTAL MINIMUM    *
 16    *    PAYMENTS ARE ACCUMULATED AND PRINTED AT THE END OF THE      *
 17    *    REPORT.  ONE DETAIL LINE CONTAINING A POLICY NUMBER,        *
 18    *    CUSTOMER NAME, INSURANCE TYPE, PAYMENT STATUS, PREMIUM      *
 19    *    AMOUNT, AND MINIMUM PAYMENT DUE IS PRINTED FOR EACH CUSTOMER*
 20    *    WHO HAS NOT PAID IN FULL.  A RECORD COUNT IS PROVIDED AT    *
 21    *    THE END OF THE REPORT.                                      *
 22    *                                                         *
 23    *       INPUT:     PREMIUM.DAT - PREMIUM INPUT FILE        *
 24    *                                                         *
 25    *       OUTPUT:    MINDUE.RPT  - MINIMUM PAYMENT REPORT    *
 26    ************************************************************
 27
 28    ENVIRONMENT DIVISION.
 29    *********************
 30
 31    INPUT-OUTPUT SECTION.
 32    *********************
 33
 34    FILE-CONTROL.
 35
 36        SELECT PREMIUM-INPUT-FILE
 37            ASSIGN TO "A:\PREMIUM.DAT".
 38
 39        SELECT MINIMUM-DUE-REPORT
 40            ASSIGN TO "A:\MINDUE.RPT".
 41
 42    /
 43    DATA DIVISION.
 44    **************
 45
 46    FILE SECTION.
 47    *************
 48
 49    ************************************************************
 50    *                                                         *
 51    *    INPUT-FILE - PREMIUM INPUT FILE                       *
 52    *                                                         *
 53    ************************************************************
 54
 55    FD  PREMIUM-INPUT-FILE.
 56
 57    01  PREMIUM-RECORD.
 58        02  PR-CUSTOMER-NAME      PIC X(20).
 59        02  PR-AGENT-NAME         PIC X(20).
 60        02  PR-INSURANCE-TYPE     PIC X(10).
 61        02  PR-POLICY-NUMBER      PIC X(12).
 62        02  PR-PREMIUM-AMOUNT     PIC S9(5)V99.
 63        02  PR-PAYMENT-STATUS     PIC X.
 64            88  DELINQUENT        VALUE "D".
 65            88  PAID-IN-FULL      VALUE "F".
 66            88  PARTIALLY-PAID    VALUE "P".
 67            88  NOT-YET-BILLED    VALUE "N".
 68        02                        PIC X(10).
 69
 70    ************************************************************
 71    *                                                         *
 72    *    REPORT-FILE - MINIMUM PAYMENT DUE REPORT              *
 73    *                                                         *
 74    ************************************************************
 75
 76    FD  MINIMUM-DUE-REPORT
 77
 78    01  REPORT-LINE-OUT          PIC X(100).
 79    /
 80    WORKING-STORAGE SECTION.
 81    ***********************
 82
 83    ************************************************************
 84    *                                                         *
 85    *                    SWITCHES                             *
 86    *                                                         *
 87    ************************************************************
 88
 89    01  SWITCHES.
 90
 91        02  SW-END-OF-FILE        PIC X.
 92            88  END-OF-FILE                   VALUE "Y".
 93
 94    01  VALUES-FOR-SWITCHES.
 95        02  YES                  PIC X    VALUE "Y".
 96        02  NEG                  PIC X    VALUE "N".
 97
 98
 99
100    ************************************************************
101    *                                                         *
102    *                    ACCUMULATORS                         *
103    *                                                         *
104    ************************************************************
105
106    01  ACCUMULATORS.
107
108        02  AC-LINE-COUNT        PIC 999      PACKED-DECIMAL.
109        02  AC-PAGE-COUNT        PIC 999      PACKED-DECIMAL.
110        02  AC-RECORD-COUNT      PIC 9(5)     PACKED-DECIMAL.
111        02  AC-TOTAL-PREMIUM     PIC 9(5)V99 PACKED-DECIMAL.
112        02  AC-TOTAL-MINIMUM     PIC 9(5)V99 PACKED-DECIMAL.
113    /
114    ************************************************************
115    *                                                         *
116    *                    WORK AREA FIELDS                     *
117    *                                                         *
118    ************************************************************
119
120    01  WORK-AREA.
121
122        02  WA-SYSTEM-DATE.
123            03  WA-SYSTEM-YEAR       PIC 99.
124            03  WA-SYSTEM-MONTH      PIC 99.
125            03  WA-SYSTEM-DAY        PIC 99.
126
127        02  WA-CURRENT-DATE.
128            03  WA-CURRENT-MONTH     PIC 99.
129            03  WA-CURRENT-DAY       PIC 99.
130            03  WA-CURRENT-YEAR      PIC 99.
131
132        02  WA-CURRENT-DATE-N REDEFINES
133            WA-CURRENT-DATE          PIC 9(6).
134
135        02  WA-SYSTEM-TIME.
136            03  WA-SYSTEM-HOUR       PIC 99.
137            03  WA-SYSTEM-MINUTES    PIC 99.
138            03                       PIC 9(4).
```

FIGURE 5-4   Minimum Payment Report program

```
139
140        02  WA-MINIMUM-PAYMENT           PIC 9(5)V99.
141   /
142   ******************************************************************
143   *                                                                *
144   *    REPORT HEADINGS FOR MINIMUM PAYMENT DUE REPORT              *
145   *                                                                *
146   ******************************************************************
147
148   01  REPORT-HEADING.
149
150        02  RH-LINE-1.
151            03                          PIC X(6)  VALUE "DATE: ".
152            03  RH-DATE                 PIC Z9/99/99.
153            03                          PIC X(26) VALUE SPACES.
154            03                          PIC X(27) VALUE
155                "AINSWORTH INSURANCE COMPANY".
156            03                          PIC X(22) VALUE SPACES.
157            03                          PIC X(5)  VALUE "PAGE ".
158            03  RH-PAGE-COUNT           PIC ZZ9.
159            03                          PIC XXX   VALUE SPACES.
160
161
162        02  RH-LINE-2.
163            03                          PIC X(6)  VALUE "TIME: ".
164            03  RH-HOUR                 PIC Z9.
165            03                          PIC X     VALUE ":".
166            03  RH-MINUTES              PIC 99.
167            03  RH-AM-PM                PIC XX.
168            03                          PIC X(29) VALUE SPACES.
169            03                          PIC X(22) VALUE
170                "MINIMUM PAYMENT REPORT".
171            03                          PIC X(36) VALUE SPACES.
172
173
174        02  RH-LINE-3.
175            03                          PIC X(41) VALUE SPACES.
176            03                          PIC X(9)  VALUE
177                "INSURANCE".
178            03                          PIC X(6)  VALUE SPACES.
179            03                          PIC X(7)  VALUE
180                "PREMIUM".
181            03                          PIC X(6)  VALUE SPACES.
182            03                          PIC X(7)  VALUE
183                "PAYMENT".
184            03                          PIC X(6)  VALUE SPACES.
185            03                          PIC X(7)  VALUE
186                "MINIMUM".
187            03                          PIC X(11) VALUE SPACES.
188   /
189        02  RH-LINE-4.
190            03                          PIC X(13) VALUE
191                "POLICY NUMBER".
192            03                          PIC X(4)  VALUE SPACES.
193            03                          PIC X(13) VALUE
194                "CUSTOMER NAME".
195            03                          PIC X(11) VALUE SPACES.
196            03                          PIC X(4)  VALUE
197                "TYPE".
198            03                          PIC X(11) VALUE SPACES.
199            03                          PIC X(6)  VALUE
200                "STATUS".
201            03                          PIC X(7)  VALUE SPACES.
202            03                          PIC X(6)  VALUE
203                "AMOUNT".
204            03                          PIC X(7)  VALUE SPACES.
205            03                          PIC XXX   VALUE
206                "DUE".
207            03                          PIC X(14) VALUE SPACES.
208
209
210
211        02  RH-LINE-5.
212            03                          PIC X(13) VALUE ALL "-".
213            03                          PIC X(4)  VALUE SPACES.
214            03                          PIC X(13) VALUE ALL "-".
215            03                          PIC X(11) VALUE SPACES.
216            03                          PIC X(9)  VALUE ALL "-".
217            03                          PIC X(6)  VALUE SPACES.
218            03                          PIC X(7)  VALUE ALL "-".
219            03                          PIC X(6)  VALUE SPACES.
220            03                          PIC X(7)  VALUE ALL "-".
221            03                          PIC X(6)  VALUE SPACES.
222            03                          PIC X(7)  VALUE ALL "-".
223            03                          PIC X(11) VALUE SPACES.
224
225
226   ******************************************************************
227   *                                                                *
228   *    DETAIL LINE FOR THE MINIMUM PREMIUM PAYMENT DUE REPORT      *
229   *                                                                *
230   ******************************************************************
231
232   01  DETAIL-LINE.
233
234        02  DL-POLICY-NUMBER            PIC X(12).
235        02                              PIC X(5)   VALUE SPACES.
236        02  DL-CUSTOMER-NAME            PIC X(20).
237        02                              PIC X(4)   VALUE SPACES.
238        02  DL-INSURANCE-TYPE           PIC X(10).
239        02                              PIC X(5)   VALUE SPACES.
240        02  DL-PAYMENT-STATUS           PIC X(4).
241        02                              PIC X(6)   VALUE SPACES.
242        02  DL-PREMIUM-AMOUNT           PIC ZZ,ZZ9.99.
243        02                              PIC X(5)   VALUE SPACES.
244        02  DL-MINIMUM-PAYMENT          PIC ZZ,ZZ9.99.
245        02                              PIC X(11)  VALUE SPACES.
246
247   /
248   ******************************************************************
249   *                                                                *
250   *    SUMMARY LINES FOR THE MINIMUM PAYMENT DUE REPORT            *
251   *                                                                *
252   ******************************************************************
253
254   01  SUMMARY-LINES.
255
256        02  SL-LINE-1.
257            03                          PIC X(26)  VALUE SPACES.
258            03                          PIC X(25)  VALUE
259                "TOTAL RECORDS PRINTED = ".
260            03  SL-RECORD-COUNT         PIC ZZZZ9.
261            03                          PIC X(44)  VALUE SPACES.
262
263        02  SL-LINE-2.
264            03                          PIC X(26)  VALUE SPACES.
265            03                          PIC X(24)  VALUE
266                "TOTAL PREMIUMS DUE    = ".
267            03  SL-TOTAL-PREMIUM        PIC ZZ,ZZ9.99.
268            03                          PIC X(41)  VALUE SPACES.
269
270        02  SL-LINE-3.
271            03                          PIC X(26)  VALUE SPACES.
272            03                          PIC X(24)  VALUE
273                "AVERAGE PREMIUM DUE   = ".
274            03  SL-AVERAGE-PREMIUM      PIC ZZ,ZZ9.99.
275            03                          PIC X(41)  VALUE SPACES.
276
277        02  SL-LINE-4.
278            03                          PIC X(26)  VALUE SPACES.
279            03                          PIC X(24)  VALUE
280                "TOTAL MINIMUM DUE     = ".
281            03  SL-TOTAL-MINIMUM        PIC ZZ,ZZ9.99.
282            03                          PIC X(41)  VALUE SPACES.
283
284        02  SL-LINE-5.
285            03                          PIC X(26)  VALUE SPACES.
286            03                          PIC X(24)  VALUE
287                "AVERAGE MINIMUM DUE   = ".
288            03  SL-AVERAGE-MINIMUM      PIC ZZ,ZZ9.99.
289            03                          PIC X(41)  VALUE SPACES.
290
```

(continued)

```
291        02  SL-LINE-6.                                          366        DIVIDE AC-TOTAL-MINIMUM BY AC-RECORD-COUNT
292            03                      PIC X(32)  VALUE SPACES.    367            GIVING SL-AVERAGE-MINIMUM ROUNDED.
293            03                      PIC X(13)  VALUE            368
294            "END OF REPORT".                                    369        MOVE AC-TOTAL-PREMIUM   TO SL-TOTAL-PREMIUM.
295            03                      PIC X(55)  VALUE SPACES.    370        MOVE AC-TOTAL-MINIMUM   TO SL-TOTAL-MINIMUM.
296    /                                                           371        MOVE AC-RECORD-COUNT    TO SL-RECORD-COUNT.
297    PROCEDURE DIVISION.                                         372
298    ******************                                          373    /
299    ***************************************************************    374    ***************************************************************
300    *                                                     *     375    *                                                     *
301    *  MAIN-PROGRAM - THIS IS THE MAIN ROUTINE OF THE MINIMUM *  376    *         MOVE INPUT FIELDS TO OUTPUT AREAS AND PRINT  *
302    *              PAYMENT DUE REPORT PROGRAM             *     377    *                                                     *
303    *                                                     *     378    ***************************************************************
304    ***************************************************************    379
305                                                                380    B-200-PROCESS-RECORD.
306    MAIN-PROGRAM.                                               381
307                                                                382        IF AC-LINE-COUNT = 0
308        PERFORM A-100-INITIALIZATION.                           383            PERFORM B-300-PRINT-HEADINGS.
309        PERFORM B-100-PROCESS-FILE.                             384
310        PERFORM C-100-WRAP-UP.                                  385        IF PAID-IN-FULL
311        STOP RUN.                                               386            READ PREMIUM-INPUT-FILE
312                                                                387                AT END MOVE YES TO SW-END-OF-FILE
313    ***************************************************************    388            END-READ
314    *                                                     *     389            GO TO B-200-EXIT.
315    *              THE INITIALIZATION ROUTINE FOLLOWS      *     390
316    *                                                     *     391        MULTIPLY 0.25 BY PR-PREMIUM-AMOUNT
317    ***************************************************************    392            GIVING WA-MINIMUM-PAYMENT ROUNDED
318                                                                393                   DL-MINIMUM-PAYMENT ROUNDED.
319    A-100-INITIALIZATION.                                       394
320                                                                395        ADD WA-MINIMUM-PAYMENT TO AC-TOTAL-MINIMUM
321        INITIALIZE ACCUMULATORS.                                396            ON SIZE ERROR PERFORM B-310-SIZE-ERROR-MESSAGE.
322                                                                397        ADD PR-PREMIUM-AMOUNT  TO AC-TOTAL-PREMIUM
323        ACCEPT WA-SYSTEM-DATE FROM DATE.                        398            ON SIZE ERROR PERFORM B-310-SIZE-ERROR-MESSAGE.
324        MOVE WA-SYSTEM-YEAR    TO WA-CURRENT-YEAR.              399
325        MOVE WA-SYSTEM-MONTH   TO WA-CURRENT-MONTH.             400        MOVE PR-POLICY-NUMBER   TO DL-POLICY-NUMBER.
326        MOVE WA-SYSTEM-DAY     TO WA-CURRENT-DAY.               401        MOVE PR-CUSTOMER-NAME   TO DL-CUSTOMER-NAME.
327        MOVE WA-CURRENT-DATE-N TO RH-DATE.                      402        MOVE PR-INSURANCE-TYPE  TO DL-INSURANCE-TYPE.
328                                                                403        MOVE PR-PREMIUM-AMOUNT  TO DL-PREMIUM-AMOUNT.
329        ACCEPT WA-SYSTEM-TIME FROM TIME.                        404
330        IF WA-SYSTEM-HOUR < 12                                  405        EVALUATE TRUE
331            MOVE "AM" TO RH-AM-PM                               406            WHEN DELINQUENT     MOVE "DELQ" TO DL-PAYMENT-STATUS
332            IF WA-SYSTEM-HOUR = 00                              407            WHEN PARTIALLY-PAID MOVE "P PD" TO DL-PAYMENT-STATUS
333                MOVE 12 TO RH-HOUR                              408            WHEN NOT-YET-BILLED MOVE "NYB"  TO DL-PAYMENT-STATUS
334            ELSE                                                409            WHEN OTHER          MOVE "ERR"  TO DL-PAYMENT-STATUS.
335                MOVE WA-SYSTEM-HOUR TO RH-HOUR                  410
336        ELSE                                                    411        WRITE REPORT-LINE-OUT FROM DETAIL-LINE
337            MOVE "PM" TO RH-AM-PM                               412            AFTER ADVANCING 2 LINES.
338            IF WA-SYSTEM-HOUR > 12                              413        ADD 2 TO AC-LINE-COUNT.
339                COMPUTE RH-HOUR = WA-SYSTEM-HOUR - 12           414        ADD 1 TO AC-RECORD-COUNT.
340            ELSE                                                415
341                MOVE 12 TO RH-HOUR.                             416        IF AC-LINE-COUNT > 55
342        MOVE WA-SYSTEM-MINUTES TO RH-MINUTES.                   417            MOVE ZERO TO AC-LINE-COUNT.
343                                                                418
344        OPEN INPUT   PREMIUM-INPUT-FILE                         419        READ PREMIUM-INPUT-FILE
345             OUTPUT  MINIMUM-DUE-REPORT.                        420            AT END MOVE YES TO SW-END-OF-FILE.
346                                                                421
347    /                                                           422
348                                                                423    B-200-EXIT.
349    ***************************************************************    424        EXIT.
350    *                                                     *     425    /
351    *              FILE PROCESSING CONTROL ROUTINE        *     426    ***************************************************************
352    *                                                     *     427    *                                                     *
353    ***************************************************************    428    *                  HEADER ROUTINE                     *
354                                                                429    *                                                     *
355    B-100-PROCESS-FILE.                                         430    ***************************************************************
356                                                                431
357        MOVE NEG TO SW-END-OF-FILE.                             432    B-300-PRINT-HEADINGS.
358        READ PREMIUM-INPUT-FILE                                 433
359            AT END MOVE YES TO SW-END-OF-FILE.                  434        ADD 1 TO AC-PAGE-COUNT.
360                                                                435        MOVE AC-PAGE-COUNT TO RH-PAGE-COUNT.
361        PERFORM B-200-PROCESS-RECORD THRU B-200-EXIT            436        WRITE REPORT-LINE-OUT FROM RH-LINE-1
362            UNTIL END-OF-FILE.                                  437            AFTER ADVANCING PAGE.
363                                                                438        WRITE REPORT-LINE-OUT FROM RH-LINE-2
364        DIVIDE AC-TOTAL-PREMIUM BY AC-RECORD-COUNT              439            AFTER ADVANCING 1 LINE.
365            GIVING SL-AVERAGE-PREMIUM ROUNDED.                  440        WRITE REPORT-LINE-OUT FROM RH-LINE-3
                                                                   441            AFTER ADVANCING 2 LINES.
```

FIGURE 5-4   Minimum Payment Report program (continued)

```
442          WRITE REPORT-LINE-OUT FROM RH-LINE-4
443              AFTER ADVANCING 1 LINE.
444          WRITE REPORT-LINE-OUT FROM RH-LINE-5
445              AFTER ADVANCING 1 LINE.
446          MOVE 5 TO AC-LINE-COUNT.
447
448     ********************************************************************
449     *                                                                  *
450     *                    END OF JOB ROUTINE                            *
451     *                                                                  *
452     ********************************************************************
453
454     B-310-SIZE-ERROR-MESSAGE.
455
456          MOVE "ACCUMULATOR FIELD TOO SMALL!!" TO REPORT-LINE-OUT.
457
458          WRITE REPORT-LINE-OUT
459              AFTER ADVANCING 3 LINES.
460
```

```
461     ********************************************************************
462     *                                                                  *
463     *                    END OF JOB ROUTINE                            *
464     *                                                                  *
465     ********************************************************************
466
467     C-100-WRAP-UP.
468
469          WRITE REPORT-LINE-OUT FROM SL-LINE-1
470              AFTER ADVANCING 3 LINES.
471          WRITE REPORT-LINE-OUT FROM SL-LINE-2
472              AFTER ADVANCING 1 LINE.
473          WRITE REPORT-LINE-OUT FROM SL-LINE-3
474              AFTER ADVANCING 1 LINE.
475          WRITE REPORT-LINE-OUT FROM SL-LINE-4
476              AFTER ADVANCING 1 LINE.
477          WRITE REPORT-LINE-OUT FROM SL-LINE-5
478              AFTER ADVANCING 1 LINE.
479          WRITE REPORT-LINE-OUT FROM SL-LINE-6
480              AFTER ADVANCING 3 LINES.
481          CLOSE PREMIUM-INPUT-FILE
482              MINIMUM-DUE-REPORT.
483
```

ARITHMETIC STATEMENTS

Nearly every program you create will require some form of addition, subtraction, multiplication, and/or division.

In every arithmetic operation, numeric fields, and often numeric literals, are combined to produce some resultant value. This result may be stored in one of the fields involved in the arithmetic or it may be placed in some other field. The results of an arithmetic operation may be positive or negative and may be edited for output to a report.

When using field names within an arithmetic statement, be sure that all fields involved in the arithmetic have been assigned values. Many computer systems initialize numeric fields to zero automatically, but this is not always true. If a field has not been assigned a value in the DATA DIVISION, or if a MOVE, READ, or some arithmetic statement in the PROCEDURE DIVISION has not been executed to place a value in a field, the field might not be initialized. This could cause serious problems in the execution of the program.

ADD Statement

Figure 5-5 on the next page presents two basic formats of the ADD statement. In the first format, the receiving field for the result of the operation is one of the fields involved in the arithmetic. The field following the reserved word TO is involved in the arithmetic and receives the result. In the second format, a separate field that is not involved in the arithmetic receives the result. This separate receiving field follows the word GIVING. In both formats, the receiving field is replaced by the results of the addition operation and the previous contents of the receiving field are lost. In both formats, there may be multiple fields or literals following the word ADD and multiple receiving fields. The word TO is required in Format 1 but is optional in Format 2. Format 1 is generally referred to as the **ADD TO** format of the ADD, while Format 2 is generally known as the **ADD GIVING** format.

Format 1:

```
ADD     {identifier-1}   . . .   TO   {identifier-2 [ ROUNDED ] }  . . .
        {literal-1    }

        [ ON SIZE ERROR    statement-set-1 ]

        [ NOT ON SIZE ERROR  statement-set-2 ]

        [ END-ADD ]
```

Format 2:

```
ADD     {identifier-1}     . . .     TO     {identifier-2}
        {literal-1    }                      {literal-2    }

        GIVING {identifier-3 [ ROUNDED ] } . . .

        [ ON SIZE ERROR    statement-set-1 ]

        [ NOT ON SIZE ERROR  statement-set-2 ]

        [ END-ADD ]
```

FIGURE 5-5   Basic formats of the ADD statement

ADD TO is the simplest and most frequently used format of the ADD statement. Figure 5-6 presents the ADD statements used in the Minimum Payment Report program. They are all examples of ADD TO. Lines 395 through 398 present examples in which fields are added to other fields. Lines 413, 414, and 434 present examples in which numeric literals are added to fields. Figure 5-7 presents other examples of the ADD TO format.

```
395        ADD WA-MINIMUM-PAYMENT TO AC-TOTAL-MINIMUM
396            ON SIZE ERROR PERFORM B-310-SIZE-ERROR-MESSAGE.
397        ADD PR-PREMIUM-AMOUNT  TO AC-TOTAL-PREMIUM
398            ON SIZE ERROR PERFORM B-310-SIZE-ERROR-MESSAGE.

413        ADD 2 TO AC-LINE-COUNT.
414        ADD 1 TO AC-RECORD-COUNT.

434        ADD 1 TO AC-PAGE-COUNT.
```

FIGURE 5-6   ADD statements from the Minimum Payment Report program

```
ADD WA-FIELD-1 WA-FIELD-2 TO AC-FIELD-1.
```

> Adds WA-FIELD-1, WA-FIELD-2, and AC-FIELD-1 together and places the results in AC-FIELD-1.

```
ADD 5 TO AC-FIELD-1
        AC-FIELD-2.
```

> Adds 5 to both AC-FIELD-1 and AC-FIELD-2.

```
ADD 5  WA-FIELD-1 TO AC-FIELD-1
                     AC-FIELD-2.
```

> Adds 5 and WA-FIELD-1 to both AC-FIELD-1 and AC-FIELD-2.

FIGURE 5-7   More examples of the ADD TO statement

When the **ROUNDED** option is used in an arithmetic statement, it causes the results to be rounded to the rightmost digit position available in the receiving field. Without the ROUNDED option, extra digit positions on the right are simply truncated. Figure 5-8 illustrates how ROUNDED works using ADD TO. In the figure, WA-FIELD-1 has two digits to the right of the decimal and WA-FIELD-2 has three digits to the right of the decimal. The receiving field, AC-FIELD-1, has only one digit to the right of the decimal. Thus, the final result can have only one decimal position. In the absence of ROUNDED, the final answer would be truncated to one position to the right of the decimal. With the ROUNDED option present, the final result is rounded to the nearest tenth. ROUNDED works in precisely the same manner for all arithmetic statements.

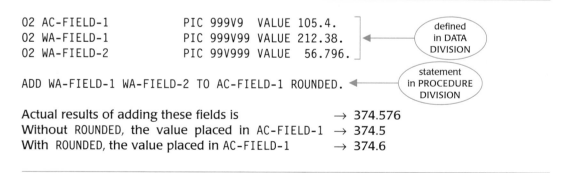

```
02 AC-FIELD-1        PIC 999V9  VALUE 105.4.
02 WA-FIELD-1        PIC 999V99 VALUE 212.38.
02 WA-FIELD-2        PIC 99V999 VALUE  56.796.
```
defined in DATA DIVISION

```
ADD WA-FIELD-1 WA-FIELD-2 TO AC-FIELD-1 ROUNDED.
```
statement in PROCEDURE DIVISION

```
Actual results of adding these fields is            →  374.576
Without ROUNDED, the value placed in AC-FIELD-1  →  374.5
With  ROUNDED, the value placed in AC-FIELD-1    →  374.6
```

FIGURE 5-8   Effects of the ROUNDED option

The **ON SIZE ERROR** option can be used to detect overflow in high-order digit positions. That is, it detects a resultant quantity that is larger than that which can be accommodated by the receiving field. The capability to detect such circumstances can be very important. It is not uncommon for the same COBOL program to be used year after year for the same report. Over a period of time, the number of records processed or the amounts being manipulated can increase to a point where fields need to be enlarged to accommodate the increases. The ON SIZE ERROR option can be used to indicate when such changes are necessary.

Figure 5-9 illustrates the use of ON SIZE ERROR in conjunction with an ADD TO. In the figure, without the ON SIZE ERROR option coded, processing will continue with no indication that an inaccurate amount is in the receiving field. With the ON SIZE ERROR, control passes to an error routine that informs the user of the error. Any action can occur following an ON SIZE ERROR, but it is normal either to display a message on the terminal screen or print out a warning message on a report. ON SIZE ERROR works in precisely the same manner for all arithmetic statements.

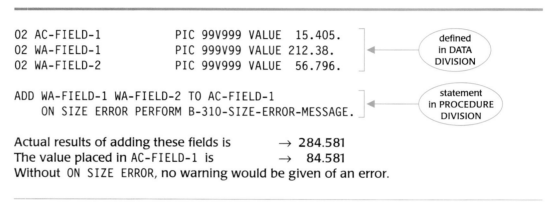

```
02 AC-FIELD-1        PIC 99V999 VALUE  15.405.
02 WA-FIELD-1        PIC 999V99 VALUE 212.38.
02 WA-FIELD-2        PIC 99V999 VALUE  56.796.
```
defined in DATA DIVISION

```
ADD WA-FIELD-1 WA-FIELD-2 TO AC-FIELD-1
    ON SIZE ERROR PERFORM B-310-SIZE-ERROR-MESSAGE.
```
statement in PROCEDURE DIVISION

Actual results of adding these fields is   → 284.581
The value placed in AC-FIELD-1 is   → 84.581
Without ON SIZE ERROR, no warning would be given of an error.

FIGURE 5-9   Use of ON SIZE ERROR

NOT ON SIZE ERROR has limited use. It can be utilized if you wish to perform some special processing when high-order truncation does not occur. NOT ON SIZE ERROR will not be used in this book.

END-ADD is used when an ADD statement is nested within a larger statement and needs to be terminated without the use of a period. This situation arises only when ON SIZE ERROR or NOT ON SIZE ERROR are used in an ADD that is nested within a larger statement or sentence. In such situations, a period would terminate the entire sentence and, therefore, might not be appropriate. Figure 5-10 illustrates the use of an END-ADD in an ADD TO statement. In the figure, if the END-ADD is omitted, the second PERFORM statement will execute only when the ON SIZE ERROR condition is true. All of the arithmetic statements have entries such as the END-ADD available and they all work in the same manner as an END-ADD.

Good

```
IF WA-FIELD-1 < 1
    ADD WA-FIELD-2 TO AC-FIELD-1
        ON SIZE ERROR PERFORM B-310-SIZE-ERROR-MESSAGE
    END-ADD
    PERFORM B-330-SMALL-FIELD-1.
```

END-ADD terminates the ADD statement without terminating the sentence so that PERFORM B-330-SMALL-FIELD-1 can execute when WA-FIELD-1 is less than 1.

Bad

```
IF WA-FIELD-1 < 1
    ADD WA-FIELD-2 TO AC-FIELD-1
        ON SIZE ERROR PERFORM B-310-SIZE-ERROR-MESSAGE
    PERFORM B-330-SMALL-FIELD-1.
```

Without the END-ADD, PERFORM B-330-SMALL-FIELD-1 is considered to be part of the ON SIZE ERROR clause.

FIGURE 5-10   Using END-ADD

Figure 5-11 presents some examples of the ADD GIVING statement. Although it is not used in the Minimum Payment Report program, there are logical situations in which ADD GIVING is required. With this format, fields before the word GIVING are unchanged by the operation. The field or fields named after the word GIVING are strictly receiving fields and are not involved in the arithmetic. Thus, GIVING fields may be either elementary numeric fields or numeric edit pattern fields. The word TO is optional when using the ADD GIVING. If TO is used, it may be coded only once, just before the last field or literal added.

```
ADD WA-FIELD-1 WA-FIELD-2 GIVING AC-FIELD-1.

ADD  5  WA-FIELD-1 GIVING WA-FIELD-2.

ADD WA-FIELD-1 TO 5 GIVING WA-FIELD-2 ROUNDED.

ADD WA-FIELD-1 WA-FIELD-2 WA-FIELD-3 GIVING AC-FIELD-1
    ON SIZE ERROR PERFORM B-310-SIZE-ERROR-MESSAGE.
```

field following GIVING is receiving field

FIGURE 5-11   Examples of the ADD GIVING statement

SUBTRACT **Statement**

As with the ADD statement, there are two basic formats of the SUBTRACT statement (Figure 5-12 on the next page). Format 1 is known as the **SUBTRACT FROM**, while Format 2 is the **SUBTRACT FROM GIVING**. In the SUBTRACT FROM format, one or more fields or literals are subtracted from the field following the word FROM with the difference replacing the FROM field. The FROM field is involved in the arithmetic and is the receiving field for the difference. The previous contents of the FROM field are lost once the SUBTRACT executes.

Format 1:

SUBTRACT   {identifier-1}   . . .   <u>FROM</u> {identifier-2 [<u>ROUNDED</u>] } . . .
{literal-1}

    [ON <u>SIZE</u> <u>ERROR</u>   statement-set-1]

    [<u>NOT</u> ON <u>SIZE</u> <u>ERROR</u>   statement-set-2]

    [<u>END-SUBTRACT</u>]

Format 2:

SUBTRACT   {identifier-1}   . . .   <u>FROM</u> {identifier-2}
{literal-1}   {literal-2}

    <u>GIVING</u> {identifier-3 [<u>ROUNDED</u>] } . . .

    [ON <u>SIZE</u> <u>ERROR</u>   statement-set-1]

    [<u>NOT</u> ON <u>SIZE</u> <u>ERROR</u>   statement-set-2]

    [<u>END-SUBTRACT</u>]

FIGURE 5-12   Basic formats of the SUBTRACT statement

SUBTRACT statements were not used in the Minimum Payment Report program, but Figure 5-13 presents some examples of the SUBTRACT FROM format. In all examples, ROUNDED, ON SIZE ERROR, and NOT ON SIZE ERROR work just as they did with the ADD statement. As with END-ADD, **END-SUBTRACT** need be used only to terminate a SUBTRACT statement when a period cannot be used following ON SIZE ERROR or NOT ON SIZE ERROR.

```
02   AC-FIELD-1                    PIC 999V99   VALUE 312.49.          defined
02   WA-FIELD-1                    PIC 99V9     VALUE  23.8.      ◄───  in DATA
02   WA-FIELD-2                    PIC 999V99   VALUE 102.25.           DIVISION
SUBTRACT WA-FIELD-1 FROM AC-FIELD-1.
```

    Result in AC-FIELD-1 → **288.69**

```
SUBTRACT WA-FIELD-1 WA-FIELD-2 FROM AC-FIELD-1.
```

    Result in AC-FIELD-1 → **186.44**

```
SUBTRACT  7.353  FROM WA-FIELD-2 ROUNDED.
```

    Result in WA-FIELD-2 → **94.90**

```
SUBTRACT WA-FIELD12 FROM AC-FIELD-1
    ON SIZE ERROR PERFORM B-310-SIZE-ERROR-MESSAGE
END-SUBTRACT
```

    Result in AC-FIELD-1 → **210.24** with no size error

FIGURE 5-13   Examples of the SUBTRACT FROM statement; each example is independent of the others

Figure 5-14 presents examples of the SUBTRACT FROM GIVING. In these examples, the receiving field or fields follow the word GIVING and are not involved in the arithmetic. Because they are not involved in the arithmetic, these receiving fields may be either numeric fields or numeric edit pattern fields.

```
02  AC-FIELD-1              PIC 999V99 VALUE 312.49.
02  AC-FIELD-2              PIC 999V9.
02  WA-FIELD-1              PIC 99V9    VALUE 23.8.
02  WA-FIELD-2              PIC 999V99 VALUE 102.25.
```
defined in DATA DIVISION

```
SUBTRACT WA-FIELD-1 FROM WA-FIELD-2 GIVING AC-FIELD-1.
```

   Result in AC-FIELD-1 → 78.45

```
SUBTRACT WA-FIELD-1 WA-FIELD-2 FROM AC-FIELD-1
    GIVING AC-FIELD-2.
```

   Result in AC-FIELD-2 → 186.4

```
SUBTRACT  7.353  FROM WA-FIELD-2 GIVING AC-FIELD-1 ROUNDED.
```

   Result in AC-FIELD-1 → 94.90

```
SUBTRACT WA-FIELD-1  7.358  FROM WA-FIELD-2
    GIVING AC-FIELD-1 ROUNDED
          AC-FIELD-2 ROUNDED.
```

   Result in AC-FIELD-1 → 71.09
   Result in AC-FIELD-2 → 71.1

```
SUBTRACT WA-FIELD-1 FROM AC-FIELD-1 GIVING AC-FIELD-2
    ON SIZE ERROR PERFORM B-310-SIZE-ERROR-MESSAGE
END-SUBTRACT
```

   Result in AC-FIELD-2 → 288.6 with no size error

FIGURE 5-14   Examples of SUBTRACT FROM GIVING statement; each statement is independent of the others

MULTIPLY Statement

The MULTIPLY statement has two basic formats (Figure 5-15 on the next page). Format 1 is the **MULTIPLY BY**, while Format 2 is the **MULTIPLY BY GIVING**. The MULTIPLY BY multiplies a field or literal by the field named after the BY and places the result, or product, in the BY field. Thus, the BY field is involved in the arithmetic and is the receiving field of the operation.

Figure 5-16 on the next page presents some examples of the MULTIPLY BY. ROUNDED, ON SIZE ERROR, and NOT ON SIZE ERROR work exactly as presented earlier in the ADD and SUBTRACT statements. **END-MULTIPLY** works just like END-ADD and END-SUBTRACT and should be used to terminate a MULTIPLY statement only when ON SIZE ERROR or NOT ON SIZE ERROR is used and a period cannot be used to terminate the statement.

Format 1:

```
MULTIPLY   {identifier-1}   BY  {identifier-2 [ ROUNDED ] } . . .
           {literal-1   }

     [ ON SIZE ERROR    statement-set-1 ]

     [ NOT ON SIZE ERROR   statement-set-2 ]

     [ END-MULTIPLY ]
```

Format 2:

```
MULTIPLY   {identifier-1}   BY  {identifier-2}
           {literal-1   }       {literal-2   }

     GIVING {identifier-3 [ ROUNDED ] } . . .

     [ ON SIZE ERROR    statement-set-1 ]

     [ NOT ON SIZE ERROR   statement-set-2 ]

     [ END-MULTIPLY ]
```

FIGURE 5-15 Basic formats of the MULTIPLY statement

```
02  AC-FIELD-1            PIC 9(4)V99 VALUE 312.49.
02  AC-FIELD-2            PIC 999V9   VALUE 8.2.          defined
02  WA-FIELD-1            PIC 99V9    VALUE 23.3.         in DATA
02  WA-FIELD-2            PIC 999V99  VALUE 102.25.       DIVISION

MULTIPLY WA-FIELD-1 BY AC-FIELD-1.
```

Result in AC-FIELD-1 → **7281.01**

```
MULTIPLY 7 BY AC-FIELD-1.
```

Result in AC-FIELD-1 → **2187.43**

```
MULTIPLY WA-FIELD-1 BY AC-FIELD-1 ROUNDED.
```

Result in AC-FIELD-1 → **7281.02**

```
MULTIPLY WA-FIELD-1 BY AC-FIELD-1
                       AC-FIELD-2.
```

Result in AC-FIELD-1 → **7281.01**
Result in AC-FIELD-2 → **191.0**

```
MULTIPLY WA-FIELD-1 BY WA-FIELD-2
    ON SIZE ERROR PERFORM B-310-SIZE-ERROR-MESSAGE
END-MULTIPLY
```

Result in WA-FIELD-2 → **382.42** with a size error!

FIGURE 5-16 Examples of the MULTIPLY BY statement; each example is independent of the others

Notice that the fourth example in Figure 5-16 has two fields listed after the BY. In this statement, two separate multiplication operations will occur and two separate values will be obtained. One of the values will be the product of WA-FIELD-1 and AC-FIELD-1 and will be placed in AC-FIELD-1 after the statement executes. The other value will be the product of WA-FIELD-1 and AC-FIELD-2 and will be placed in AC-FIELD-2 after the statement executes.

MULTIPLY BY GIVING multiplies a field or literal by the field or literal following the word BY and places the product in the field or fields named after the GIVING. Figure 5-17 presents an example of the MULTIPLY BY GIVING from the Minimum Payment Report program. Notice that this statement has two fields listed after the GIVING. After the statement executes, both fields will receive exactly the same ROUNDED value. WA-MINIMUM-PAYMENT, however, is a numeric field that will be used in a subsequent ADD statement, while DL-MINIMUM-PAYMENT is a numeric edit pattern that is defined as part of DETAIL-LINE.

```
62        02   PR-PREMIUM-AMOUNT                    PIC S9(5)V99.
140       02   WA-MINIMUM-PAYMENT                   PIC 9(5)V99.
244       02   DL-MINIMUM-PAYMENT                   PIC ZZ,ZZ9.99.
```

Assume PR-PREMIUM-AMOUNT **has a value of 232.50**

```
391            MULTIPLY 0.25 BY PR-PREMIUM-AMOUNT
392                GIVING WA-MINIMUM-PAYMENT ROUNDED    ◄          two
393                       DL-MINIMUM-PAYMENT ROUNDED.   ◄      receiving
                                                                 fields
```

Result in WA-MINIMUM-PAYMENT → 58.13
Result in DL-MINIMUM-PAYMENT → 58.13

FIGURE 5-17 MULTIPLY BY GIVING statement from the Minimum Payment Report program

DIVIDE Statement

The DIVIDE statement has five different basic formats available. Figure 5-18 on the next page presents these formats. Format 1 is the **DIVIDE INTO** statement. The field or literal following the word DIVIDE is the divisor, while the field following the word INTO is the dividend in the operation. After the statement is executed, the dividend is replaced by the result of the operation, or quotient. More than one dividend may be listed after the INTO, which will result in more than one quotient being obtained.

Format 1:

```
DIVIDE   {identifier-1}       INTO      {identifier-2 [ ROUNDED ] } . . .
         {literal-1   }
         [ ON SIZE ERROR    statement-set-1 ]
         [ NOT ON SIZE ERROR   statement-set-2 ]
         [ END-DIVIDE ]
```

Format 2:

```
DIVIDE   {identifier-1}       INTO      {identifier-2}
         {literal-1   }                 {literal-2   }
         GIVING {identifier-3 [ ROUNDED ] } . . .
         [ ON SIZE ERROR    statement-set-1 ]
         [ NOT ON SIZE ERROR   statement-set-2 ]
         [ END-DIVIDE ]
```

Format 3:

```
DIVIDE   {identifier-1}       BY        {identifier-2}
         {literal-1   }                 {literal-2   }
         GIVING {identifier-3 [ ROUNDED ] } . . .
         [ ON SIZE ERROR    statement-set-1 ]
         [ NOT ON SIZE ERROR   statement-set-2 ]
         [ END-DIVIDE ]
```

Format 4:

```
DIVIDE   {identifier-1}       INTO      {identifier-2}
         {literal-1   }                 {literal-2   }
         GIVING  identifier-3 [ ROUNDED ]   REMAINDER identifier-4
         [ ON SIZE ERROR    statement-set-1 ]
         [ NOT ON SIZE ERROR   statement-set-2 ]
         [ END-DIVIDE ]
```

Format 5:

```
DIVIDE   {identifier-1}       BY        {identifier-2}
         {literal-1   }                 {literal-2   }
         GIVING  identifier-3 [ ROUNDED ]   REMAINDER identifier-4
         [ ON SIZE ERROR    statement-set-1 ]
         [ NOT ON SIZE ERROR   statement-set-2 ]
         [ END-DIVIDE ]
```

FIGURE 5-18   Basic formats of the DIVIDE statement

Format 2, **DIVIDE INTO GIVING**, is similar to Format 1 but has a separate field for the quotient that is listed following the word GIVING. Thus, in this format, the divisor and dividend are unchanged after the statement executes, and both may be literal values. Multiple GIVING fields may be listed, but all will receive the same result.

Format 3, **DIVIDE BY GIVING**, is similar to Format 2; however, the divisor and dividend position are switched. The field or literal following the word DIVIDE is the dividend, and the divisor follows the word BY. This format is used in the Minimum Payment Report program to calculate the average premium due and average minimum payment (Figure 5-19). DIVIDE INTO GIVING could have been used with no effect on the program. The format used is entirely up to the programmer.

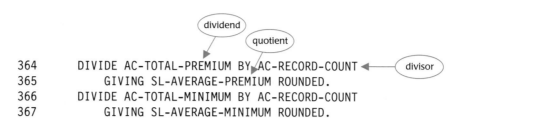

```
364        DIVIDE AC-TOTAL-PREMIUM BY AC-RECORD-COUNT
365            GIVING SL-AVERAGE-PREMIUM ROUNDED.
366        DIVIDE AC-TOTAL-MINIMUM BY AC-RECORD-COUNT
367            GIVING SL-AVERAGE-MINIMUM ROUNDED.
```

FIGURE 5-19   DIVIDE BY GIVING statements from the Minimum Payment Report program

Format 4 and Format 5 are similar to Formats 2 and 3, respectively, with the addition of a **REMAINDER** clause. The REMAINDER clause is most useful when dividing whole numbers. The field name following the word REMAINDER will receive the integer remainder of the DIVIDE operation. Figure 5-20 presents an example of a DIVIDE BY GIVING with a REMAINDER clause. In the sample problem, the quotient value is placed in WA-QUOTIENT and the remainder is placed in WA-REMAINDER.

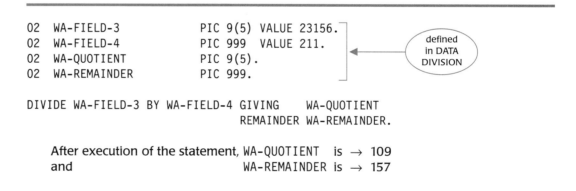

```
02   WA-FIELD-3        PIC 9(5) VALUE 23156.
02   WA-FIELD-4        PIC 999  VALUE 211.
02   WA-QUOTIENT       PIC 9(5).
02   WA-REMAINDER      PIC 999.

DIVIDE WA-FIELD-3 BY WA-FIELD-4 GIVING    WA-QUOTIENT
                                 REMAINDER WA-REMAINDER.
```

After execution of the statement, WA-QUOTIENT is → 109
and   WA-REMAINDER is → 157

FIGURE 5-20   DIVIDE BY GIVING with REMAINDER

In all the DIVIDE statement formats, ROUNDED, ON SIZE ERROR, and NOT ON SIZE ERROR work as described for ADD, SUBTRACT, and MULTIPLY statements. **END-DIVIDE** works just like END-ADD, END-SUBTRACT, and END-MULTIPLY and should be used to terminate a DIVIDE statement only when ON SIZE ERROR or NOT ON SIZE ERROR is used and a period cannot be used to terminate the statement.

COMPUTE Statement

When multiple operations are to be performed on a group of numbers or fields to produce a single answer, it is more efficient to use a single COMPUTE statement. The **COMPUTE** statement allows you to add, subtract, multiply, divide, and use exponents, all in one statement. The basic format of the COMPUTE statement is shown in Figure 5-21 on the next page. The receiving field or fields are listed immediately following the word COMPUTE, to the left of the equal sign. The arithmetic expression to the right of the equal sign may be a single literal or field name, or it may be a combination of many literals and/or field names along with valid mathematical operators.

```
COMPUTE { identifier-1 [ ROUNDED ] } . . . = arithmetic-expression

    [ ON SIZE ERROR    statement-set-1 ]
    [ NOT ON SIZE ERROR  statement-set-2 ]
    [ END-COMPUTE ]
```

FIGURE 5-21   Basic format of the COMPUTE statement

Table 5-1 presents the mathematical operators that may be used with a COMPUTE statement. A mathematical operator must be preceded and followed by a space. Figure 5-22 presents some examples of the COMPUTE statement.

TABLE 5-1   COBOL Mathematical Operators

**	Double asterisk, exponentiation
*	Single asterisk, multiplication
/	Slash, division
+	Plus sign, addition
-	Minus sign, subtraction, or negation

```
02  AC-FIELD-1            PIC 999V99.
02  WA-FIELD-1            PIC 99V9    VALUE 43.3.
02  WA-FIELD-2            PIC 999V99  VALUE 102.25.
02  WA-FIELD-3            PIC 999V9   VALUE 8.2.
```
defined in DATA DIVISION

```
COMPUTE AC-FIELD-1 = 8.
```
field following COMPUTE is receiving field

    Result in AC-FIELD-1 → 8.00

```
COMPUTE AC-FIELD-1 = WA-FIELD-1.
```

    Result in AC-FIELD-1 → 43.30

```
COMPUTE AC-FIELD-1 = WA-FIELD-1 + WA-FIELD-2 * WA-FIELD-3.
```

    Result in AC-FIELD-1 → 881.75

```
COMPUTE AC-FIELD-1 = 2 * WA-FIELD-1 - WA-FIELD-2 / 2 + WA-FIELD-3
    ON SIZE ERROR PERFORM B-310-SIZE-ERROR-MESSAGE
END-COMPUTE
```

    Result in AC-FIELD-1 → 43.67 with no size error

```
COMPUTE AC-FIELD-1 ROUNDED = 4 + WA-FIELD-1 / WA-FIELD-3.
```

    Result in AC-FIELD-1 → 9.28

FIGURE 5-22   Examples of the COMPUTE statement; each example is independent of the others

Parentheses, in pairs, may be used to group operations together either to clarify the actions that are to occur or to override the natural order of operations followed by the COMPUTE statement. Table 5-2 presents this order of operations. Figure 5-23 illustrates the effect of parentheses upon the execution of a COMPUTE statement.

TABLE 5-2   Order of Operations in an Arithmetic Expression

1. Items in parentheses according to the order of operations

2. Negation

3. Exponentiation, from left to right

4. Multiplication and division, from left to right

5. Addition and subtraction, from left to right

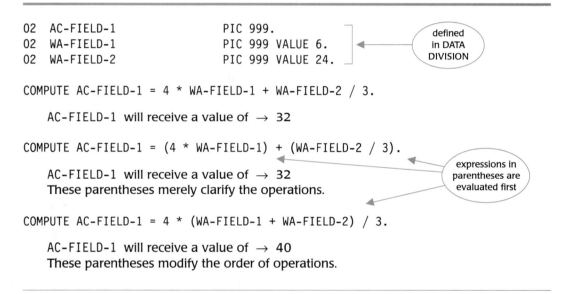

```
02  AC-FIELD-1              PIC 999.
02  WA-FIELD-1              PIC 999 VALUE 6.
02  WA-FIELD-2              PIC 999 VALUE 24.
```

defined in DATA DIVISION

```
COMPUTE AC-FIELD-1 = 4 * WA-FIELD-1 + WA-FIELD-2 / 3.
```

   AC-FIELD-1 will receive a value of → 32

```
COMPUTE AC-FIELD-1 = (4 * WA-FIELD-1) + (WA-FIELD-2 / 3).
```

   AC-FIELD-1 will receive a value of → 32
   These parentheses merely clarify the operations.

expressions in parentheses are evaluated first

```
COMPUTE AC-FIELD-1 = 4 * (WA-FIELD-1 + WA-FIELD-2) / 3.
```

   AC-FIELD-1 will receive a value of → 40
   These parentheses modify the order of operations.

FIGURE 5-23   Effect of parentheses on a COMPUTE statement

For simple arithmetic operations that involve a single operation, use ADD, SUBTRACT, MULTIPLY, or DIVIDE. Use COMPUTE only when the logic involves multiple operations on the same values. Code COMPUTE statements so they are clear and easy to decipher. **END-COMPUTE** works just like END-ADD, END-SUBTRACT, END-MULTIPLY, and END-DIVIDE and should be used to terminate a COMPUTE statement only when ON SIZE ERROR or NOT ON SIZE ERROR is used and a period cannot be used to terminate the statement.

INTRINSIC FUNCTIONS

Relatively new to COBOL is a series of computational items known as intrinsic functions. Some intrinsic functions result in alphanumeric values, but more result in numeric values. An **intrinsic function** is best described as a temporary data item that represents a value computed at the time the function statement is executed in the program. Figure 5-24 presents the basic format of an intrinsic function statement. Each intrinsic function statement requires a list of arguments, enclosed within parentheses, on which the function operates. When multiple arguments are required, the arguments in an argument list can be separated by commas. Arguments are then evaluated individually from left to right. The reference modifier may be specified only for alphanumeric functions. Reference modification was discussed in Chapter 4.

```
FUNCTION function-name [({argument} . . .)] [reference-modifier]
```

FIGURE 5-24 Basic format of an intrinsic function

Intrinsic functions are treated as elementary data items but cannot be used as receiving fields. A numeric intrinsic function can be used anywhere an arithmetic expression can be used. Table 5-3 presents a list of intrinsic function names. Most intrinsic function names are not reserved words and can be used in a program outside of function statements. Figure 5-25 presents selected examples of statements containing intrinsic functions. Later chapters will discuss other intrinsic functions.

TABLE 5-3 Intrinsic Functions

ACOS	LENGTH	ORD-MIN
ANNUITY	LOG	PRESENT-VALUE
ASIN	LOG10	RANDOM
ATAN	LOWER-CASE	RANGE
CHAR	MAX	REM
COS	MEAN	REVERSE
CURRENT-DATE	MEDIAN	SIN
DATE-OF-INTEGER	MIDRANGE	SQRT
DAY-OF-INTEGER	MIN	STANDARD-DEVIATION
FACTORIAL	MOD	SUM
INTEGER	NUMVAL	TAN
INTEGER-OF-DATE	NUMVAL-C	UPPER-CASE
INTEGER-OF-DAY	ORD	VARIANCE
INTEGER-PART	ORD-MAX	WHEN-COMPILED

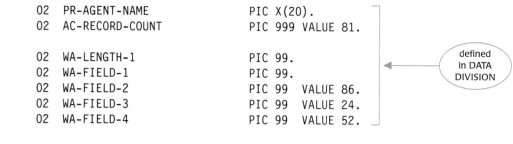

```
02  PR-AGENT-NAME            PIC X(20).
02  AC-RECORD-COUNT          PIC 999 VALUE 81.

02  WA-LENGTH-1              PIC 99.
02  WA-FIELD-1               PIC 99.
02  WA-FIELD-2               PIC 99  VALUE 86.
02  WA-FIELD-3               PIC 99  VALUE 24.
02  WA-FIELD-4               PIC 99  VALUE 52.
```

defined in DATA DIVISION

```
COMPUTE WA-LENGTH-1 = FUNCTION LENGTH (PR-CUSTOMER-NAME).
```

intrinsic functions equate to single value

Assigns the length of the field PR-CUSTOMER-NAME to WA-LENGTH-1 → 20

```
MOVE FUNCTION SQRT (AC-RECORD-COUNT) TO WA-FIELD-1.
```

Moves the value of the square root of AC-RECORD-COUNT to WA-FIELD-1 → 9

```
COMPUTE WA-FIELD-1 =
    FUNCTION MEAN (WA-FIELD-2, WA-FIELD-3, WA-FIELD-4).
```

Assigns the mean or average of WA-FIELD-2, WA-FIELD-3, and WA-FIELD-4 to WA-FIELD-1 → 54

FIGURE 5-25 Examples of intrinsic functions

BRANCHING STATEMENTS

The PERFORM statement was introduced in Chapter 2, and various forms of it have been used in sample programs presented thus far. Virtually every COBOL program is subdivided into paragraphs that are accessed using PERFORM statements. The **PERFORM** statement and its various formats allow you to organize your logic in a top-down fashion and transfer control to a paragraph as needed, returning to the statement following the PERFORM once the logic in the paragraph is complete.

Simple PERFORM

Figure 5-26 presents the basic format of a simple PERFORM. When executed, it transfers control to the first statement in the named paragraph, returning when the end of the paragraph is reached. The end of a paragraph is the beginning of the next paragraph or, in the case of the last paragraph in the program, the physical end of the program. As indicated, control is returned to the statement following the PERFORM.

```
PERFORM paragraph-name  [ { THROUGH } paragraph-name-2 ]
                          { THRU    }
```

FIGURE 5-26 Basic format of a simple PERFORM

Figure 5-27 illustrates the flow of control in a simple PERFORM. Control within the program is passed to A-100-INITIALIZATION and when the end of the paragraph is reached, control returns to the statement following the PERFORM. In this example, that statement is another PERFORM.

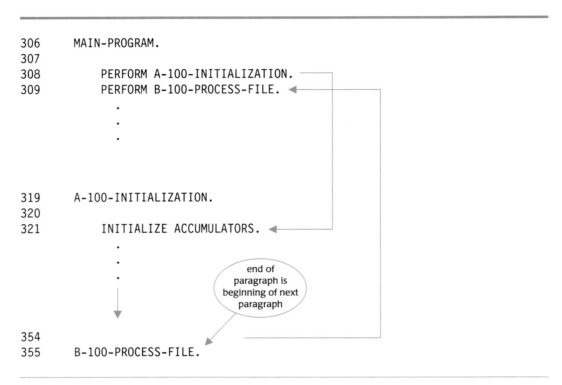

```
306      MAIN-PROGRAM.
307
308          PERFORM A-100-INITIALIZATION.
309          PERFORM B-100-PROCESS-FILE.
                 .
                 .
                 .


319      A-100-INITIALIZATION.
320
321          INITIALIZE ACCUMULATORS.
                 .
                 .
                 .
```

end of paragraph is beginning of next paragraph

```
354
355      B-100-PROCESS-FILE.
```

FIGURE 5-27   Flow of a PERFORM statement

PERFORM UNTIL

The **PERFORM UNTIL** was introduced in earlier chapters and, as you have seen, is a means of establishing a loop. Figure 5-28 presents the basic format of the PERFORM UNTIL. The PERFORM UNTIL is commonly used, as seen in earlier chapters, to continually transfer control to a paragraph until the condition specified after the reserved word UNTIL is true. The Minimum Payment Report program utilizes an option available on all formats of the PERFORM, the THRU option.

```
PERFORM  [ paragraph-name-1  [ { THROUGH }  paragraph-name-2  ] ]
                               {  THRU   }

         [ WITH TEST  { BEFORE } ]
         [            {  AFTER  } ]

         UNTIL  condition-1

         [ statement-set-1    END-PERFORM ]
```

FIGURE 5-28   Basic format of the PERFORM UNTIL

The **THRU**, or **THROUGH**, option allows you to identify a series of consecutive paragraphs to be executed prior to returning to the PERFORM. Figure 5-29 illustrates the use of the THRU option on a simple PERFORM. THRU is often used in conjunction with EXIT paragraphs. An **EXIT paragraph** consists of a paragraph name followed by the reserved word EXIT. An EXIT paragraph is commonly placed at the end of a paragraph and used as a place to branch to when it is necessary to bypass code within a paragraph. The word **EXIT** generates no instructions to the computer.

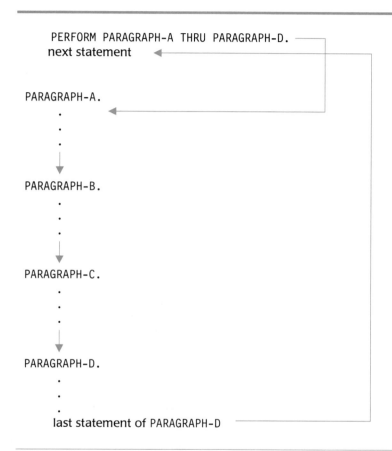

FIGURE 5-29   A simple PERFORM with the THRU option

Figure 5-30 on the next page presents the use of the THRU option and an EXIT paragraph from the Minimum Payment Report program. If a customer owes no money, then he or she is not to be listed on the report. A GO TO is used to branch to the EXIT paragraph and thus bypass logic in B-200-PROCESS-RECORD. The GO TO statement will be discussed later in this chapter. An EXIT paragraph is not illustrated on a hierarchy chart (see Figure 5-2 on page 5-3).

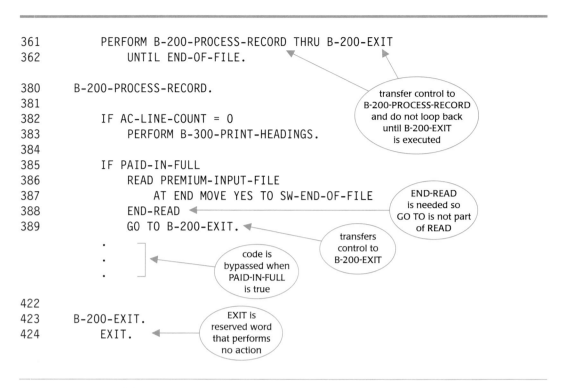

FIGURE 5-30 PERFORM UNTIL with the THRU option and an EXIT paragraph

Chapter 1 discussed two looping structures available in a structured program, the Do-While structure and the Do-Until structure. The difference between the two is the point at which the condition test takes place. In a Do-While structure, the test occurs prior to branching to the named paragraph. Thus, in a Do-While structure the code in the loop will never be executed if the condition is true from the start. In a Do-Until structure, the test occurs after the code in the loop has been executed. Therefore, a Do-Until structure guarantees that the code in the loop is executed at least once.

The PERFORM UNTIL automatically emulates the Do-While structure and tests the condition before the first branch occurs. This may be explicitly indicated by use of the WITH TEST BEFORE option. To emulate the Do-Until structure, WITH TEST AFTER must be explicitly coded within the PERFORM UNTIL. Figure 5-31 presents an example of a PERFORM UNTIL that uses WITH TEST AFTER. In the example, if the condition WA-FIELD-1 > 10 is true from the start, then LOOP-PARAGRAPH still will be executed once because the condition test will not occur until after LOOP-PARAGRAPH has been executed.

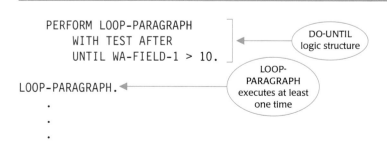

FIGURE 5-31 PERFORM UNTIL using WITH TEST AFTER

In-line PERFORM

The basic format of the PERFORM UNTIL presented in Figure 5-28 on page 5-24 shows that a paragraph name following the word PERFORM is optional. When a paragraph name is omitted, then the statements to be executed are coded in the same paragraph as the PERFORM. Such a structure is called an **in-line PERFORM**. An in-line PERFORM is terminated with an **END-PERFORM**. Figure 5-32 presents an example of an in-line PERFORM. No periods may be used between the PERFORM and END-PERFORM within an in-line PERFORM. Although an in-line PERFORM can be used anywhere a PERFORM can be used, its use normally should be restricted to situations where no more than ten statements are to be executed. Lengthy in-line PERFORM statements can be very difficult to understand and maintain.

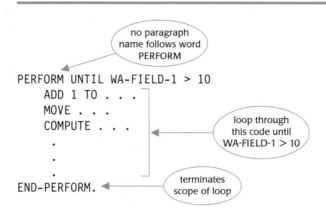

FIGURE 5-32   Example of an in-line PERFORM

PERFORM TIMES

If the exact number of times a loop is to be executed is known or can be computed, the **PERFORM TIMES** can be used. The basic format of PERFORM TIMES is presented in Figure 5-33. It, too, may be coded as an in-line perform.

```
PERFORM  [ paragraph-name-1  [ { THROUGH }  paragraph-name-2 ] ]
                               { THRU    }

         { integer-1    }    TIMES
         { identifier-1 }

         [ statement-set-1   END-PERFORM ]
```

FIGURE 5-33   Basic format of the PERFORM TIMES statement

Figure 5-34 on the next page presents two examples of PERFORM TIMES. In the first example, LOOP-PARAGRAPH will be executed 15 times. Control will then pass to the statement following the PERFORM TIMES. In the second example, LOOP-PARAGRAPH will be executed the number of times specified by the value of WA-FIELD-1. WA-FIELD-1 must be defined as a numeric integer field.

```
PERFORM LOOP-PARAGRAPH 15 TIMES.
next-statement

PERFORM LOOP-PARAGRAPH WA-FIELD-1 TIMES.
next-statement
```

FIGURE 5-34 Examples of the PERFORM TIMES statement

PERFORM VARYING

Occasionally, it is desirable to automatically manipulate the value of a field or fields as a loop executes. The **PERFORM VARYING** statement allows for such manipulation. By using PERFORM VARYING, the value of one or more fields may be increased or decreased until some condition is true. Figure 5-35 presents the basic format of PERFORM VARYING. As with the other formats of the PERFORM, it can be used as an in-line PERFORM, if desired. The field to be manipulated is named immediately after the word VARYING, and multiple fields may be manipulated by using the AFTER option. Although the word VARYING is not used, the AFTER option really means *AFTER VARYING* and may be coded up to six times within a single PERFORM VARYING. The literals or fields following each FROM are used to initialize the VARYING and AFTER fields. The fields or literals following each BY are used to increment each field being varied. These values may be positive or negative.

```
PERFORM   [ paragraph-name-1 [ {THROUGH} paragraph-name-2 ] ]
                               {THRU   }

    [ WITH TEST  {BEFORE} ]
                 {AFTER }

    VARYING  {field-1} FROM  {field-2  } BY {field-3 }
             {index-1}       {index-2  }    {literal-2}
                             {literal-1}

    UNTIL  condition-1

    [ AFTER  {field-4} FROM  {field-5  } BY {field-6 } ]
             {index-3}       {index-4  }    {literal-4}
                             {literal-3}
      UNTIL  condition-2
             .
             .
             .
    [ statement-set-1   END-PERFORM ]
```

FIGURE 5-35 Basic format of the PERFORM VARYING statement

Figure 5-36 presents two examples of PERFORM VARYING statements. In the first example, WA-FIELD-1 will be initialized to 1 before control is passed to LOOP-PARAGRAPH and incremented by 1 upon each return from LOOP-PARAGRAPH. The looping will terminate when WA-FIELD-1 has a value greater than 20. In the second example, WA-FIELD-1 will again be initialized to 1; however, it will not be incremented until WA-FIELD-2 has been initialized to 1 and incremented by 1 each time LOOP-PARAGRAPH is executed and reaches a value greater than 10. Once WA-FIELD-2 reaches a value greater than 10, WA-FIELD-1 will be incremented by 1, WA-FIELD-2 will be reinitialized to 1, and looping will continue until WA-FIELD-2 again reaches a value greater than 10. Looping will not terminate until WA-FIELD-1 reaches a value greater than 20. Table 5-4 summarizes the values of WA-FIELD-1 and WA-FIELD-2 as the looping continues.

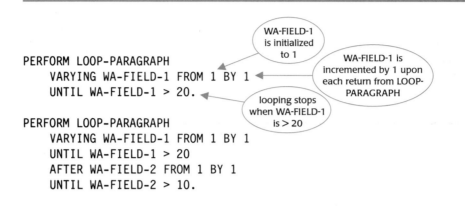

FIGURE 5-36 Examples of PERFORM VARYING

TABLE 5-4   Values of WA-FIELD-1 and WA-FIELD-2 in Execution of a PERFORM VARYING

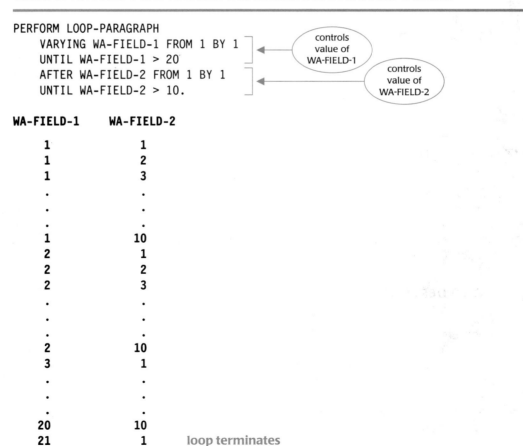

WA-FIELD-1	WA-FIELD-2	
1	1	
1	2	
1	3	
.	.	
.	.	
.	.	
1	10	
2	1	
2	2	
2	3	
.	.	
.	.	
.	.	
2	10	
3	1	
.	.	
.	.	
.	.	
20	10	
21	1	loop terminates

With several AFTER clauses being used, this can be rather confusing. It is recommended that no more than two AFTER clauses be utilized in a PERFORM VARYING. The PERFORM VARYING will be discussed again in Chapter 7 when COBOL arrays are covered.

GO TO

Unlike the PERFORM statement, when a **GO TO** statement is used to transfer the flow of logic to a paragraph, control does not return to the statement following the GO TO. Instead, unless the GO TO is part of some larger PERFORM statement, control passes to the paragraph immediately following the paragraph referenced by the GO TO. Figure 5-37 illustrates how a GO TO statement works. In the figure, unless some statement within PARAGRAPH-1 redirects the logic, once the end of PARAGRAPH-1 is reached, control passes to PARAGRAPH-2. Unless some statement within PARAGRAPH-2 redirects the logic, once the end of PARAGRAPH-2 is reached, control will pass to the next paragraph in the program.

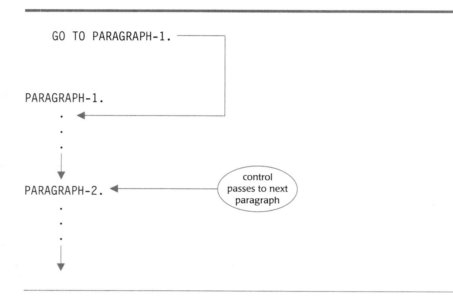

FIGURE 5-37 Execution of a GO TO statement

The use of the GO TO statement should be restricted to situations similar to that presented in the Minimum Payment Report program. GO TO will be used in this book only to bypass statements and branch to an EXIT paragraph that is referenced in a PERFORM THRU statement (see Figure 5-30 on page 5-26). Such restricted use provides tight control over the GO TO statement.

GO TO DEPENDING ON

Because it is a form of a GO TO, the **GO TO DEPENDING ON** statement will not be used in this book. The GO TO DEPENDING ON automatically executes a GO TO to a named paragraph, depending on the value in some specified field. Figure 5-38 presents the basic format of the GO TO DEPENDING ON. When field-1 has a value of 1, control branches to the first paragraph in the list after GO TO. When field-1 has a value of 2, control branches to the second paragraph in the list. If field-1 has a value greater than the number of paragraphs named, no branching occurs. As with the GO TO, the actions of the GO TO DEPENDING ON can be controlled by including the statement in the scope of some larger PERFORM THRU.

```
GO TO paragraph-name-1
      paragraph-name-2
      paragraph-name-3
         .
         .
         .
      DEPENDING ON field-name-1.
```

FIGURE 5-38 Basic format of the GO TO DEPENDING ON statement

SECTIONS

The sample programs used in this book will continue to subdivide the PROCEDURE DIVISION into paragraphs. The PROCEDURE DIVISION, however, can be divided into sections if desired. A SECTION in the PROCEDURE DIVISION is identified just like sections in the ENVIRONMENT DIVISION and DATA DIVISION, by a section name that is followed by the reserved word SECTION. A SECTION in the PROCEDURE DIVISION may be divided into one or more paragraphs. The end of a SECTION is the beginning of the next SECTION. Many early COBOL programs were written using sections. At that time, COBOL had many restrictions that required the use of sections. Most of those restrictions are now gone, and the use of sections within the PROCEDURE DIVISION is no longer required in most situations.

Figure 5-39 illustrates a PERFORM statement in which a SECTION name is used. Execution within the SECTION begins with the first paragraph and continues until the end of the SECTION is reached, unless something within the SECTION redirects the flow of the logic.

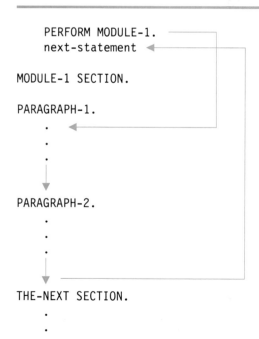

```
      PERFORM MODULE-1.
      next-statement

MODULE-1 SECTION.

PARAGRAPH-1.
   .
   .
   .

PARAGRAPH-2.
   .
   .
   .

THE-NEXT SECTION.
   .
   .
   .
```

FIGURE 5-39 The use of a SECTION in the PROCEDURE DIVISION

SUBPROGRAMS

Another way of breaking down the logic within a COBOL program is through the use of subprograms. A **subprogram** is a COBOL program, written and compiled separately, but linked to the original program through the linkage editor of the operating system (Figure 5-40). A subprogram is accessed using a **CALL** statement and, therefore, the subprogram is usually referred to as the **called program**. The program with the CALL in it is the **calling program**.

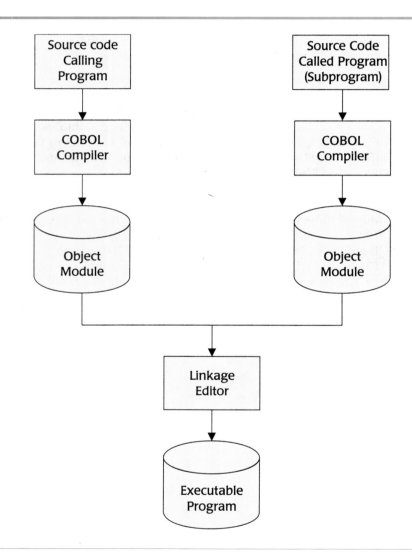

FIGURE 5-40 Linking to a subprogram with the linkage editor

Figure 5-41 presents the basic format of a CALL and Figure 5-42 presents an example of its use. The name following the reserved word CALL must be a nonnumeric literal or a field name that references the name used in the PROGRAM-ID paragraph of the IDENTIFICATION DIVISION of the subprogram. Once the subprogram is complete, control returns to the statement immediately following the CALL. A subprogram is terminated with an **EXIT PROGRAM** statement. Do not use a STOP RUN to terminate a subprogram! STOP RUN will terminate all execution and return control to the operating system.

```
CALL    ┌ field-name-1 ┐
        └ literal-1    ┘

    [ USING  field-name-2  . . . ]
```

FIGURE 5-41   Basic format of a CALL statement

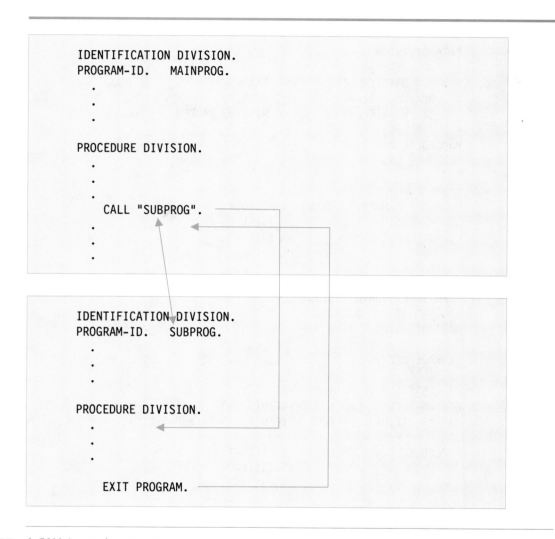

```
        IDENTIFICATION DIVISION.
        PROGRAM-ID.   MAINPROG.
            .
            .
            .


        PROCEDURE DIVISION.
            .
            .
            .
            CALL "SUBPROG".
            .
            .
            .
```

```
        IDENTIFICATION DIVISION.
        PROGRAM-ID.   SUBPROG.
            .
            .
            .

        PROCEDURE DIVISION.
            .
            .
            .


            EXIT PROGRAM.
```

FIGURE 5-42   A CALL to a subprogram

It is often necessary for the calling program to share data with the called program. The **USING** clause in a CALL is used for this purpose. One or more fields may be listed after the word USING. These same fields must be identified in the **LINKAGE SECTION** of the DATA DIVISION in the subprogram. The names used in the LINKAGE SECTION may be different from the names used in the calling program, but the size and usage of each field must match the size and usage defined in the calling program. When USING is coded in the CALL, then USING also must be used in the PROCEDURE DIVISION header of the called program. Also, the sequence of the fields listed after USING in the CALL must match the sequence of the fields listed after USING in the PROCEDURE DIVISION header of the called program. The sequence of the fields after a USING is referred to as the **calling sequence**. Figure 5-43 illustrates the sharing of data between a calling program and a subprogram. Notice that the calling sequence in MAINPROG is the same as the calling sequence in SUBPROG. Any modifications made to the shared fields in the subprogram will be reflected in the calling program once the subprogram ends.

```
IDENTIFICATION DIVISION.
PROGRAM-ID.   MAINPROG.

DATA DIVISION.

    02  WA-FIELD-1        PIC XXX.
    02  WA-FIELD-2        PIC 9(5)V99.
    02  WA-FIELD-3        PIC 9(5)V99 PACKED-DECIMAL.

PROCEDURE DIVISION.
    .
    .
    .
    CALL "SUBPROG" USING WA-FIELD-1
                         WA-FIELD-2
                         WA-FIELD-3.
```

```
IDENTIFICATION DIVISION.
PROGRAM-ID.   SUBPROG.
DATA DIVISION.

LINKAGE SECTION.

01  LS-FIELD-1        PIC XXX.
01  LS-FIELD-2        PIC 9(5)V99.
01  LS-FIELD-3        PIC 9(5)V99 PACKED-DECIMAL.

PROCEDURE DIVISION USING LS-FIELD-1
                         LS-FIELD-2
                         LS-FIELD-3.
    .
    .
    .
    EXIT PROGRAM.
```

FIGURE 5-43   A CALL to a subprogram with a USING

Subprograms often are created for a block of logic that is utilized in many different programs. Generally, the subprogram will be placed in a system library so whenever it is called, it will be available for use to all who need it. Subprograms may themselves CALL other subprograms. No program in this book uses subprograms.

CHAPTER SUMMARY

The following list summarizes this chapter. The summary is designed to help you study and understand the material and concepts presented.

1. Arithmetic operations which combine numeric fields and numeric literals are essential for most business applications.
2. The **ADD** statement has two formats, **ADD TO** and **ADD GIVING**.
3. **ROUNDED** can be used to round an answer to the last position available in the receiving field.
4. **ON SIZE ERROR** is used to detect high-order truncation.
5. The **SUBTRACT** statement has two formats, **SUBTRACT FROM** and **SUBTRACT FROM GIVING**.
6. The **MULTIPLY** statement has two formats, **MULTIPLY BY** and **MULTIPLY BY GIVING**.
7. The DIVIDE statement has five different formats, **DIVIDE INTO**, **DIVIDE INTO GIVING**, **DIVIDE BY GIVING**, **DIVIDE INTO GIVING** with a **REMAINDER**, and **DIVIDE BY GIVING** with a **REMAINDER**.
8. Multiple arithmetic operations on a group of numbers or fields to produce a single answer can be performed more efficiently by using a **COMPUTE** statement.
9. Parentheses, in pairs, can be used within an arithmetic expression to clarify or modify the order of operations.
10. **END-ADD**, **END-SUBTRACT**, **END-MULTIPLY**, **END-DIVIDE**, and **END-COMPUTE** are needed only in situations where a period cannot be used.
11. **Intrinsic functions** are temporary data items that represent values computed at the time function statements are executed.
12. The **PERFORM** statement allows for the structuring of a COBOL program in a top-down fashion.
13. **PERFORM UNTIL** allows for the establishment of Do-While and Do-Until loops.
14. **THRU**, or **THROUGH**, may be used on a PERFORM to allow a series of consecutive paragraphs to be executed.
15. The reserved word **EXIT** causes no action to occur but is used to create an EXIT paragraph that can be used as a place to branch to when there is a need to skip logic in a paragraph.
16. **GO TO** provides another means of branching, but the use of GO TO should be restricted.
17. An **in-line PERFORM** can be used to set up a loop without branching to another paragraph.
18. **PERFORM TIMES** can be used when the exact number of times a loop is to be executed is known or can be computed.
19. **PERFORM VARYING** can be used to manipulate the value of one or more fields as a loop executes.
20. The PROCEDURE DIVISION may be subdivided into sections. The end of a SECTION is the beginning of the next SECTION.
21. A **subprogram** provides another way of subdividing the logic in a COBOL program.
22. The **CALL** statement is used to transfer control to a subprogram and, with the **USING** option, allows the calling program and called program to share data.
23. A **LINKAGE SECTION** must be coded in the DATA DIVISION of a subprogram that is going to share data with a calling program.

KEY TERMS
. . . .

ADD GIVING (5-9)
ADD TO (5-9)
CALL (5-32)
called program (5-32)
calling program (5-32)
calling sequence (5-34)
COMPUTE (5-19)
DIVIDE BY GIVING (5-18)
DIVIDE INTO (5-17)
DIVIDE INTO GIVING (5-18)
END-ADD (5-12)
END-COMPUTE (5-21)
END-DIVIDE (5-19)
END-MULTIPLY (5-15)
END-PERFORM (5-27)
END-SUBTRACT (5-14)
EXIT (5-25)
EXIT paragraph (5-25)
EXIT PROGRAM (5-32)
GO TO (5-30)

GO TO DEPENDING ON (5-30)
in-line PERFORM (5-27)
intrinsic function (5-22)
LINKAGE SECTION (5-33)
MULTIPLY BY (5-15)
MULTIPLY BY GIVING (5-15)
NOT ON SIZE ERROR (5-12)
ON SIZE ERROR (5-12)
PERFORM (5-23)
PERFORM TIMES (5-27)
PERFORM UNTIL (5-24)
PERFORM VARYING (5-28)
REMAINDER (5-19)
ROUNDED (5-11)
subprogram (5-32)
SUBTRACT FROM (5-13)
SUBTRACT FROM GIVING (5-13)
THROUGH (5-25)
THRU (5-25)
USING (5-33)

STUDENT ASSIGNMENTS
. . . .

Student Assignment 1: True/False

Instructions: Circle T if the statement is true or F if the statement is false.

T   F   1. In an ADD TO, the TO field may be an edit pattern.

T   F   2. END-ADD is required on all ADD statements

T   F   3. Alphanumeric fields may be used in arithmetic.

T   F   4. In an ADD TO GIVING, the GIVING field may be an edit pattern.

T   F   5. There is only one format of the SUBTRACT statement.

T   F   6. The MULTIPLY BY GIVING may have more than one receiving field.

T   F   7. DIVIDE BY requires a GIVING.

T   F   8. The answer in a COMPUTE statement may not be ROUNDED.

T   F   9. Parentheses may be used in an arithmetic expression to alter the normal
          order of operations.

T   F   10. The ON SIZE ERROR clause will execute when the rightmost digits are
          truncated.

T   F   11. PERFORM UNTIL cannot be used to create a Do-Until loop.

T   F   12. The THRU option on a PERFORM allows for multiple consecutive paragraphs to
          be executed, one after the other.

T   F   13. GO TO and PERFORM work exactly the same.

T   F   14. A PERFORM VARYING can vary more than one field only when the AFTER
          option is used.

T F 15. An intrinsic function may be used as a receiving field in a MOVE.

T F 16. A SECTION may contain one or more paragraphs.

T F 17. A subprogram must be compiled at the same time as the calling program.

T F 18. A CALL with a USING allows the calling program and called program to share data.

T F 19. An in-line PERFORM does not pass control to another paragraph.

T F 20. END-PERFORM is required to terminate an in-line PERFORM.

Student Assignment 2: Multiple Choice

Instructions: Circle the correct response.

1. Which of the following is *not* a valid arithmetic statement?
    a. ADD 1 TO AC-FIELD-1 GIVING WA-FIELD-2.
    b. SUBTRACT A-FIELD FROM B-FIELD ROUNDED.
    c. DIVIDE A-FIELD BY B-FIELD.
    d. MULTIPLY A-FIELD BY B-FIELD GIVING C-FIELD D-FIELD.
    e. All the above are valid.

2. The ON SIZE ERROR clause will execute when _____ .
    a. there is high-order truncation only
    b. there is low-order truncation only
    c. there is both high-order and low-order truncation
    d. there is either high-order truncation or low-order truncation
    e. none of the above

3. In an arithmetic statement, an edit pattern field may be the receiving field _____ .
    a. only if it is not involved in the arithmetic
    b. in any COBOL arithmetic operation
    c. only when it is listed immediately following the word COMPUTE
    d. as long as there is not high-order truncation possible
    e. all of the above

4. The operators allowed in an arithmetic expression in a COMPUTE statement are _____ .
    a. $\wedge$, +, −, *, and /
    b. **, +, −, *, and /
    c. $\wedge$, +, −, X, and /
    d. **, +, −, >, and <
    e. none of the above

5. The order of operations in a arithmetic expression _____ .
    a. is always modified when parentheses are used
    b. is sometimes modified when parentheses are used
    c. allows multiplication to always occur before division
    d. requires addition to occur before multiplication
    e. none of the above

6. An in-line PERFORM _____ .
    a. must be terminated with an END-PERFORM
    b. can contain any number of statements
    c. is available for every format of the PERFORM
    d. does not transfer control to another paragraph
    e. all of the above

(continued)

Student Assignment 2 (continued)

7. The PERFORM TIMES statement _____.
   a. loops until some condition is true
   b. loops a specified number of times
   c. is used to execute a SECTION only
   d. may not be used to transfer control to another paragraph
   e. all of the above

8. The PERFORM VARYING statement _____.
   a. loops until some condition is true
   b. loops a specified number of times
   c. is used to execute a SECTION only
   d. may not be used to transfer control to another paragraph
   e. none of the above

9. The end of a SECTION _____.
   a. is the last period in the first paragraph
   b. is indicated by an EXIT paragraph
   c. is the beginning of the next SECTION
   d. marks the end of a COBOL program
   e. none of the above

10. A CALL to a subprogram _____.
    a. must identify the subprogram by its PROGRAM-ID
    b. can be included in a subprogram itself
    c. can include options which allow fields to be shared
    d. all of the above
    e. none of the above

Student Assignment 3: Coding an ADD Statement

Instructions: Code an ADD statement that increases the value of AC-ERROR-COUNT by 5 and branches to B-300-BAD-ADD if there is high-order truncation.

Student Assignment 4: Coding a COMPUTE Statement

Instructions: Given the following series of arithmetic statements, code a single COMPUTE statement that accomplishes the same logic.

```
ADD 5 TO A-FIELD.
MULTIPLY 2 BY A-FIELD.
SUBTRACT A-FIELD FROM B-FIELD.
DIVIDE B-FIELD BY 3 GIVING C-FIELD.
```

Student Assignment 5: Coding a PERFORM VARYING Statement

Instructions: Code a PERFORM VARYING statement that transfers control to B-300-DO-IT, initializing WA-COUNT-1 to one and incrementing it by two each time through the loop until WA-COUNT-1 is greater than or equal to 100.

Student Assignment 6: Coding Another COMPUTE Statement

Instructions: Code a COMPUTE statement that adds the value of SR-SALES to SR-YTD-SALES and then divides the result by AC-TOTAL-MONTHS. The final answer should be rounded and placed in the field DL-AVERAGE-SALES.

Student Assignment 7: Coding a CALL to a Subprogram

Instructions: Given the following work area fields, code a CALL to the subprogram MYSUB1 that allows the fields to be shared by the subprogram. Then code the necessary elements of the IDENTIFICATION DIVISION, DATA DIVISION, and PROCEDURE DIVISION of MY-SUB1 so it adds five to each of the shared fields and then transfers control back to the calling program.

```
02  WA-SHARE-1          PIC 999.
02  WA-SHARE-2          PIC 9(5) PACKED-DECIMAL.
02  WA-SHARE-3          PIC 9(5)V99.
```

COBOL LABORATORY EXERCISES

Exercise 1: Modified Minimum Payment Report Program

Purpose: To gain more experience in COBOL program maintenance and modification.

Problem: Open the file PROJ5.CBL on the Student Diskette that accompanies this book and modify the Minimum Payment Report program, making the following modifications:

1. List the records of those customers who have paid in full on a second report called the PAID IN FULL CUSTOMER REPORT. The report should have the same format as the Minimum Payment Report created in this chapter, but the minimum due should be zero and the only summary lines printed should be a record count and a total payment amount.

2. Provide a count of all customers processed in the summary information of the Minimum Payment Report.

3. Increase the minimum due from 25% of the payment amount to 35%.

4. Eliminate the Average Minimum Due from the summary information of the Minimum Payment Report.

Save this program as EX5-1.CBL.

Input Data: Use the Premium file presented in Appendix A as input. This file is named PREMIUM.DAT on the Student Diskette.

Output Results: Output should be a report similar to the example given at the beginning of this chapter but also should include the requested modifications. A report also should be produced listing the customers who have paid in full.

Exercise 2: Customer Purchases Summary Report

Purpose: To practice the use of arithmetic statements and branching statements in the creation of a COBOL program that produces a Customer Purchases Summary Report.

Problem: Write a program that lists Customer Purchase records for the ABC Department Store. For each record, print the account number, customer name, balance, purchases, and minimum payment due. Minimum payment due is 20% of the balance. List only those records with a balance greater than zero. Print the current date and time on every page. Time should be printed in AM/PM format. Number each page starting with page 1. At the end of the report print the total number of records processed, total number of records listed, total balance, average balance, total purchases, average purchase, total minimum payment due, and average minimum payment due. Save this program as EX5-2.CBL.

(continued)

Exercise 2 (continued)

Input Data: Use the Customer file listed in Appendix A as input. This file is named CUSTOMER.DAT on the Student Diskette that accompanies this book. Customer records have the following layout:

Field Description	Position	Length	Attribute
filler	1–6	6	Alphanumeric
Account Number	7–12	6	Alphanumeric
Customer Name	13–32	20	Alphanumeric
filler	33–53	21	Alphanumeric
Balance	54–59	6	Numeric, PIC S9(4)V99
Purchases	60–65	6	Numeric, PIC 9(4)V99
filler	66–72	7	Alphanumeric
Record Length		72	

Output Results: Output consists of the Customer Purchases Summary Report listing the account number, name, balance, purchases, and minimum payment due for each customer. Double-space between records. Count and print the number of records processed, the number of records listed, the total balance, the average balance, the total purchases, the average purchase, the total of minimum payments due, and the average minimum payment due. The report should have a format similar to the following:

```
DATE: Z9/99/99          ABC DEPARTMENT STORE              PAGE Z9
TIME: Z9:99 AM      CUSTOMER PURCHASES SUMMARY REPORT


ACCOUNT                                               MINIMUM
NUMBER   CUSTOMER NAME            BALANCE    PURCHASES  PAYMENT
-------  --------------------     -----------  ---------  -------

XXXXXX   XXXXXXXXXXXXXXXXXXXX     $$,$$$.99CR $$,$$$.99  Z,ZZ9.99

XXXXXX   XXXXXXXXXXXXXXXXXXXX     $$,$$$.99CR $$,$$$.99  Z,ZZ9.99

         .
         .
         .


          RECORDS PROCESSED    =      ZZ9
          RECORDS LISTED       =      ZZ9

          TOTAL BALANCE        =  ZZ,ZZ9.99
          AVERAGE BALANCE      =  ZZ,ZZ9.99

          TOTAL PURCHASES      =  ZZ,ZZ9.99
          AVERAGE PURCHASES    =  ZZ,ZZ9.99

          TOTAL MIN PAYMENT    =  ZZ,ZZ9.99
          AVERAGE MIN PAYMENT  =  ZZ,ZZ9.99


                   END OF REPORT
```

Exercise 3: Satisfied Customer Sales Report

Purpose: To practice coding a COBOL program that uses arithmetic statements and special branching.

Problem: Design and code a COBOL program that processes the records of the Customer Sales file for EZ Auto Sales and creates a Satisfied Customer Sales Report. The report should list the customer's number, name, purchase date, purchase price, and satisfaction rating. Include the current date and time in the page headings. Use AM/PM format for the time. At the end of the report provide summary lines for a record count, total purchases, and average purchase price. Save this program as EX5-3.CBL.

Input Data: Use the Customer Sales file listed in Appendix A as input. This file is named CUSTSALE.DAT on the Student Diskette that accompanies this book. The record layout for the customer records is as follows:

Field Description	Position	Length	Attribute
filler	1–9	9	Alphanumeric
Customer Number	10–13	4	Alphanumeric
Customer Name	14–33	20	Alphanumeric
Purchase Date	34–39	6	Numeric, PIC 9(6)
filler	40–59	20	Alphanumeric
Purchase Price	60–66	7	Numeric, PIC 9(5)V99
filler	67–73	7	Alphanumeric
Satisfaction Code	74	1	Alphanumeric, 0 = DISSATISFIED 1 = UNDECIDED 2 = SATISFIED
Record Length		74	

Output Results: A Satisfied Customer Sales Report should be output listing the customer's number, name, purchase date, purchase price, and satisfaction rating. List satisfied and undecided customers only. Do not list dissatisfied customers on the report. Provide a count of the number of customers listed, total sum of purchases, and average purchase price. Double-space the records on the report and list the current date and time in the headings. The time should be in AM/PM format. The report should have a format similar to the following:

```
DATE: Z9/99/99           EZ AUTO SALES                  PAGE Z9
TIME: Z9:99 AM      SATISFIED CUSTOMER SALES REPORT


CUSTOMER  CUSTOMER                 PURCHASE   PURCHASE  SATISFACTION
NUMBER    NAME                       DATE      PRICE      RATING
--------  --------------------     --------  ---------  ------------

  ZZZ9    XXXXXXXXXXXXXXXXXXXX     Z9/99/99  $$$,$$$.99  XXXXXXXXXX

  ZZZ9    XXXXXXXXXXXXXXXXXXXX     Z9/99/99  $$$,$$$.99  XXXXXXXXXX

  ZZZ9    XXXXXXXXXXXXXXXXXXXX     Z9/99/99  $$$,$$$.99  XXXXXXXXXX

                    .
                    .
                    .


        TOTAL CUSTOMERS LISTED =     ZZ9
        TOTAL PURCHASES        = ZZZ,ZZ9.99
        AVERAGE PURCHASE PRICE = ZZZ,ZZ9.99


                    END OF REPORT
```

CHAPTER SIX

The COBOL SORT Statement and Record Selection Processing

OBJECTIVES

You will have mastered the material in Chapter 6 when you can:

- Identify the purpose of an SD entry
- Code a simple COBOL SORT with USING and GIVING
- Describe the use of INPUT PROCEDURE
- Explain the purpose of the RELEASE statement
- Describe the use of OUTPUT PROCEDURE
- Explain the purpose of the RETURN statement
- Identify the function of a COBOL MERGE
- Understand the logic in record selection programs
- Explain interactive programming using DISPLAY and ACCEPT
- Describe how to create multiple reports in one report file

INTRODUCTION

It is common for records to be listed in a report in an order different from their physical sequence in the input file. Sorting in this manner can be accomplished by using the COBOL SORT statement. The COBOL SORT statement allows records in a file to be rearranged so they are in ascending or descending sequence according to a specified field within the records. The term **ascending sequence** means that items are listed from lowest to highest by the specified field according to the computer's collating sequence. The term **descending sequence** means the items are listed from highest to lowest by the specified field. For a field with alphabetic characters in it, ascending sequence means alphabetical order, from A to Z, while descending sequence means reverse alphabetical order, from Z to A. For a numeric field, ascending sequence means listing items from lowest value to highest value, while descending sequence means listing items from highest value to lowest value. The SORT statement in the Customer Selection Report program presented in this chapter rearranges the records so they print in descending sequence by a numeric field, premium amount.

The programs presented in Chapters 2, 3, and 4 created a detail line for every record processed. These types of reports are called **detail reports**. It is often desirable to produce reports that list just some of the records processed rather than all of them. Such reports are called **extract reports**, or **record selection reports**. In the program discussed in Chapter 5, only those customers with a payment status other than F, PAID-IN-FULL, were printed on the report. In this chapter, the sample program allows the user to determine which records will be printed.

The Customer Selection Report

Figures 6-1, 6-2, and 6-3 present three separate reports created using different selection criteria. Notice in these figures that the records are in descending sequence by premium payment amount. **Selection criteria** describe the field values required in a record for it to be listed on the report. The selection process is accomplished using conditional statements that compare the selection criteria to the actual contents of each record. Many different selection criteria combinations are possible, so many different reports can be produced. The Customer Selection Report program is designed to allow multiple reports to be produced in a single report file.

```
DATE: 11/28/97                          AINSWORTH INSURANCE COMPANY                          PAGE    1
TIME:  9:20AM                             CUSTOMER SELECTION REPORT


CRITERIA:INS. TYPE   = HOME
         PAY STATUS  = F


                                                    INSURANCE    PAYMENT     PAYMENT              SIGNUP
POLICY NUMBER   CUSTOMER NAME    AGENT NAME          TYPE         STATUS      AMOUNT      SEX      DATE
-------------   -------------    ----------          ---------    -------     -------     ---      ------

HM-5555-3234    Estovar, Franko  Benson, Gloria      Home         PAID        1,340.50    M        1993

HM-4441-1662    Franklin, Steven Jean, Barbara       Home         PAID          950.00    M        1991

HM-7878-7065    Solfelt, Wanda   Jones, William      Home         PAID          880.50    F        1994

HM-1113-2666    Framptin, Charles Jean, Barbara      Home         PAID          780.00    M        1990


                     TOTAL CUSTOMERS PRINTED =     4
                         END OF REPORT
```

records in descending sequence by premium payment amount

FIGURE 6-1   Customers with Home Insurance who are fully paid

```
DATE: 11/28/97                     AINSWORTH INSURANCE COMPANY                    PAGE   1
TIME:  9:22AM                       CUSTOMER SELECTION REPORT
CRITERIA:CUST GENDER = F
         SIGNUP DATE = SINCE 1988
```

POLICY NUMBER	CUSTOMER NAME	AGENT NAME	INSURANCE TYPE	PAYMENT STATUS	PAYMENT AMOUNT	SEX	SIGNUP DATE
-------------	-------------	----------	---------	-------	-------	---	------
HM-4123-6541	Ollenford, Winnie	Jean, Barbara	Home	P PD	1,780.00	F	1991
HM-2322-4488	Sollyfield, Barbara	Jacobson, Peter	Home	P PD	1,450.50	F	1992
AM-1004-2553	Leach, Raeanne	Jones, William	Automobile	P PD	1,005.50	F	1991
HM-8767-8788	Solenfeld, Nancy	Jacobson, Peter	Home	P PD	980.00	F	1992
HM-7878-7065	Solfelt, Wanda	Jones, William	Home	PAID	880.50	F	1994
AM-3323-3441	Senef, Marcia	McDonald, Fred	Automobile	PAID	780.80	F	1993
TL-5522-2121	Pally, Jane	Benson, Gloria	Term Life	P PD	460.00	F	1992
AM-2199-9229	Amfelter, Audrey	McDonald, Fred	Automobile	PAID	456.50	F	1996
RT-1122-7326	Krevits, Gloria	McDonald, Fred	Renter	PAID	400.50	F	1993
AN-1181-6464	Fredricks, Sally	Jean, Barbara	Annuity	DELQ	400.00	F	1995
AM-7993-4347	Golden, Summer	Anderson, James	Automobile	PAID	400.00	F	1994
.							
.							
.							
HM-2112-1255	Nelson, Grace	Jones, William	Home	P PD	190.20	F	1996
AN-4141-1256	Kackel, Henna	Benson, Gloria	Annuity	P PD	180.50	F	1995
RT-4337-7488	Tully, Paula	Jones, William	Renter	P PD	175.00	F	1997
RT-3331-3451	Qualizza, Scotter	Jones, William	Renter	P PD	140.50	F	1996
RT-9122-8422	Potter, Louise	McDonald, Fred	Renter	P PD	130.50	F	1997

```
                      TOTAL CUSTOMERS PRINTED =    29
                      END OF REPORT
```

FIGURE 6-2   Partial listing of female customers who have signed up since 1988

```
DATE: 11/28/97                     AINSWORTH INSURANCE COMPANY                    PAGE   1
TIME:  9:25AM                       CUSTOMER SELECTION REPORT
CRITERIA:AGENT NAME  = ANDERSON, JAMES
         PAY STATUS  = F
         SIGNUP DATE = SINCE 1990
```

POLICY NUMBER	CUSTOMER NAME	AGENT NAME	INSURANCE TYPE	PAYMENT STATUS	PAYMENT AMOUNT	SEX	SIGNUP DATE
-------------	-------------	----------	---------	-------	-------	---	------
RT-9580-0003	Willis, Richard	Anderson, James	Renter	PAID	850.00	M	1995
AM-7993-4347	Golden, Summer	Anderson, James	Automobile	PAID	400.00	F	1994
WL-0454-5698	White, Robert	Anderson, James	Whole Life	PAID	360.75	M	1996
TL-7682-0903	Winder, Robert	Anderson, James	Term Life	PAID	305.50	M	1993
AN-4551-1102	McColly, Stephen	Anderson, James	Annuity	PAID	300.00	M	1995
AN-6566-8802	Michaels, Ramsey	Anderson, James	Annuity	PAID	200.30	M	1994

```
                      TOTAL CUSTOMERS PRINTED =     6
                      END OF REPORT
```

FIGURE 6-3   Customers of agent James Anderson who are fully paid and have signed up since 1990

Hierarchy Chart

The Customer Selection Report program is more complex than the programs presented in the first five chapters of this book. To assist you in understanding the program, Figure 6-4 presents a hierarchy chart for the Customer Selection Report program. Recall that a hierarchy chart illustrates the organization of the paragraphs in the PROCEDURE DIVISION. As seen in Chapter 4, the shading in the upper right-hand corner of the rectangles for B-400-PRINT-HEADINGS identifies this paragraph as one that is performed in more than one location, by more than one other paragraph. Although B-500-PRINT-CRITERIA appears more than once on the hierarchy chart, it is not shaded in the upper right-hand corner because it is not performed by more than one other paragraph. It is performed only by B-400-PRINT-HEADINGS.

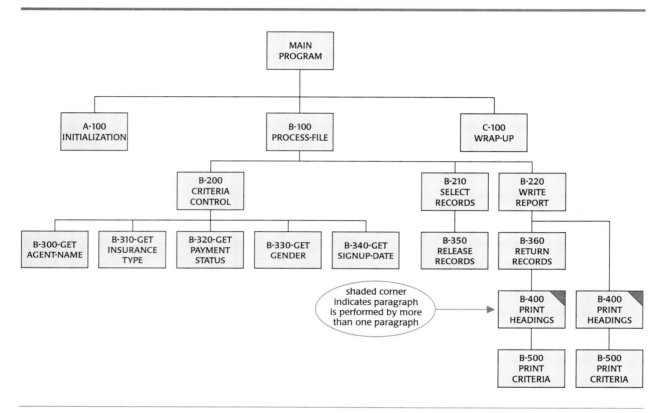

FIGURE 6-4   Hierarchy chart showing the organization of the PROCEDURE DIVISION of the Customer Selection Report program

Program Flowchart

A partial flowchart illustrating record selection logic used in the sample program is presented in Figure 6-5. The contents of each customer record are compared to the contents of the selection criteria entries made by a user. When a mismatch is found, a switch that is used to indicate whether or not a record should be released for further processing is turned off. If the switch is still on after all of the selection criteria entries have been tested, then a customer record is released for further processing. The COBOL statements that implement this logic will be discussed later in the chapter.

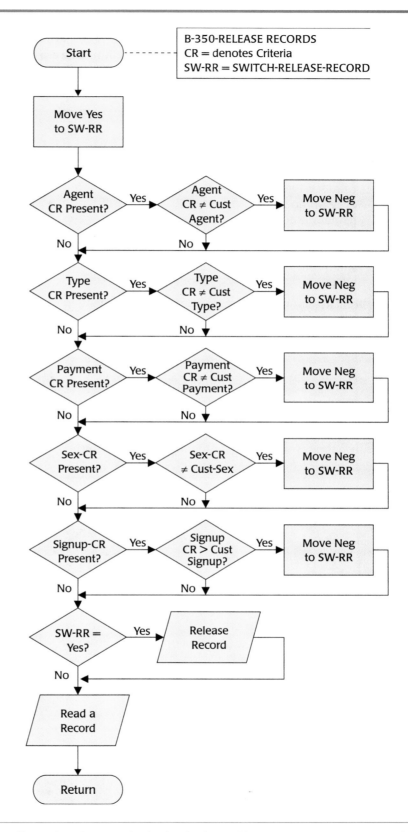

FIGURE 6-5   Partial flowchart illustrating the record selection logic used in B-350-RELEASE-RECORDS in the Customer Selection Report program

Customer Record Layout

Two fields not utilized in previous chapters are now defined in the Customer Record layout (Figure 6-6). The customer's gender and signup date are used in the sample program and listed on the reports. In previous chapters, these fields were included as part of a ten-character filler entry at the end of the record layout.

Field	Position	Length	Attribute
Customer Name	1–20	20	Alphanumeric
Agent Name	21–40	20	Alphanumeric
Insurance Type	41–50	10	Alphanumeric
Policy Number	51–62	12	Alphanumeric
Premium Amount	63–69	7	Numeric, S9(5)V99
Payment Status	70	1	Alphanumeric
Gender	71	1	Alphanumeric
Signup Date	72–75	4	Numeric, 9(4)
unused	75–80	5	Alphanumeric
Total Record Length		80	

FIGURE 6-6   Record layout for the Premium file

The Customer Selection Report Program

Figure 6-7 presents the Customer Selection Report program. This program is found on the Student Diskette that accompanies this book. Through the use of DISPLAY and ACCEPT statements, the program prompts the user for selection criteria and then creates a report which lists those records satisfying the selection criteria.

```
 1  IDENTIFICATION DIVISION.                                          31  FILE-CONTROL.
 2  ************************                                          32
 3                                                                   33      SELECT PREMIUM-INPUT-FILE
 4  PROGRAM-ID.     CUSTSEL.                                         34          ASSIGN TO "A:\PREMIUM.DAT".
 5  AUTHOR.         R. O. FOREMAN.                                   35
 6  INSTALLATION.   PURDUE UNIVERSITY CALUMET.                       36      SELECT CUSTOMER-SELECTION-REPORT
 7  DATE-WRITTEN.   NOV. 28, 1997.                                   37          ASSIGN TO "A:\CUSTSEL.RPT".
 8  DATE-COMPILED.  28-Nov-1997.                                     38
 9  ****************************************************************  39      SELECT SORT-FILE
10  *               PROGRAM NARRATIVE                         *      40          ASSIGN TO "SORTWORK".
11  *                                                         *      41
12  *                                                         *      42 /
13  *    THIS PROGRAM PROMPTS THE USER FOR SELECTION CRITERIA AND *  43  DATA DIVISION.
14  *    PRODUCES A REPORT FOR EACH SET OF CRITERIA ENTERED.    *    44  **************
15  *    CRITERIA ARE VALIDATED AS ENTERED AND A RECORD COUNT IS *  45
16  *    PROVIDED AT THE END OF EACH REPORT.  EACH REPORT LISTS *   46  FILE SECTION.
17  *    CUSTOMERS IN DESCENDING ORDER OF PREMIUM AMOUNT FROM A *   47  **************
18  *    SORTED VERSION OF THE CUSTOMER PREMIUM FILE.          *    48
19  *                                                         *      49  ****************************************************************
20  *       INPUT:    PREMIUM.DAT - PREMIUM INPUT FILE        *      50  *                                                              *
21  *                                                         *      51  *    INPUT-FILE - PREMIUM INPUT FILE                            *
22  *       OUTPUT:   CUSTSEL.RPT - CUSTOMER SELECTION REPORT *      52  *                                                              *
23  ****************************************************************  53  ****************************************************************
24                                                                   54
25  ENVIRONMENT DIVISION.                                            55  FD  PREMIUM-INPUT-FILE.
26  *********************                                            56
27                                                                   57  01  PREMIUM-RECORD.
28  INPUT-OUTPUT SECTION.                                            58      02  PR-CUSTOMER-NAME         PIC X(20).
29  *********************                                            59      02  PR-AGENT-NAME            PIC X(20).
30                                                                   60      02  PR-INSURANCE-TYPE        PIC X(10).
```

FIGURE 6-7   Customer Selection Report program

```
61      02  PR-POLICY-NUMBER            PIC X(12).
62      02  PR-PREMIUM-AMOUNT           PIC S9(5)V99.
63      02  PR-PAYMENT-STATUS           PIC X.
64          88  DELINQUENT              VALUE "D".
65          88  PAID-IN-FULL            VALUE "F".
66          88  PARTIALLY-PAID          VALUE "P".
67          88  NOT-YET-BILLED          VALUE "N".
68      02  PR-SEX                      PIC X.
69          88  MALE                    VALUE "M".
70          88  FEMALE                  VALUE "F".
71      02  PR-SIGNUP-DATE              PIC 9(4).
72      02                              PIC X(5).
73
74  ****************************************************************
75  *                                                              *
76  *      REPORT-FILE - CUSTOMER SELECTION REPORT                 *
77  *                                                              *
78  ****************************************************************
79
80  FD  CUSTOMER-SELECTION-REPORT.
81
82  01  REPORT-LINE-OUT                 PIC X(132).
83
84
85  ****************************************************************
86  *                                                              *
87  *      SORT-FILE - FOR SORTING THE PREMIUM FILE BY PREMIUM AMOUNT  *
88  *                                                              *
89  ****************************************************************
90
91  SD  SORT-FILE.
92
93  01  SORT-RECORD.
94      02                              PIC X(62).
95      02  SR-PREMIUM-AMOUNT           PIC S9(5)V99.
96      02                              PIC X(11).
97  /
98  WORKING-STORAGE SECTION.
99  ************************
100
101 ****************************************************************
102 *                                                              *
103 *                      SWITCHES                                *
104 *                                                              *
105 ****************************************************************
106
107 01  SWITCHES.
108
109     02  SW-VALID-INPUT              PIC X.
110         88  VALID-INPUT                         VALUE "Y".
111
112     02  SW-END-OF-FILE              PIC X.
113         88  END-OF-FILE                         VALUE "Y".
114
115     02  SW-RELEASE-RECORD           PIC X.
116         88  RELEASE-RECORD                      VALUE "Y".
117
118     02  SW-MORE-REPORTS             PIC X.
119         88  NO-MORE-REPORTS                     VALUE "N".
120
121 01  VALUES-FOR-SWITCHES.
122     02  YES                         PIC X     VALUE "Y".
123     02  NEG                         PIC X     VALUE "N".
124
125
126 ****************************************************************
127 *                                                              *
128 *                      ACCUMULATORS                            *
129 *                                                              *
130 ****************************************************************
131
132 01  ACCUMULATORS.
133
134     02  AC-LINE-COUNT               PIC 999    PACKED-DECIMAL.
135     02  AC-PAGE-COUNT               PIC 999    PACKED-DECIMAL.
136     02  AC-RECORD-COUNT             PIC 9(5)   PACKED-DECIMAL.
137 /
138 ****************************************************************
139 *                                                              *
140 *                  WORK AREA FIELDS                            *
141 *                                                              *
142 ****************************************************************
143
144 01  WORK-AREA.
145
146     02  WA-SYSTEM-DATE.
147         03  WA-SYSTEM-YEAR          PIC 99.
148         03  WA-SYSTEM-MONTH         PIC 99.
149         03  WA-SYSTEM-DAY           PIC 99.
150
151     02  WA-CURRENT-DATE.
152         03  WA-CURRENT-MONTH        PIC 99.
153         03  WA-CURRENT-DAY          PIC 99.
154         03  WA-CURRENT-YEAR         PIC 99.
155
156     02  WA-CURRENT-DATE-N REDEFINES
157             WA-CURRENT-DATE         PIC 9(6).
158
159     02  WA-SYSTEM-TIME.
160         03  WA-SYSTEM-HOUR          PIC 99.
161         03  WA-SYSTEM-MINUTES       PIC 99.
162         03                          PIC 9(4).
163
164     02  WA-LINES                    PIC 99.
165
166     02  WA-AGENT                    PIC X(20).
167     02  WA-INSURANCE-TYPE           PIC X(10).
168         88  VALID-INSURANCE-TYPE    VALUE "ANNUITY"
169                                           "AUTOMOBILE"
170                                           "HOME"
171                                           "RENTER"
172                                           "TERM LIFE"
173                                           "WHOLE LIFE".
174     02  WA-PAYMENT-STATUS           PIC X.
175         88  VALID-STATUS            VALUE "D"
176                                           "F"
177                                           "P"
178                                           "N".
179     02  WA-SEX                      PIC X.
180     02  WA-SIGNUP-DATE-ALPHA        PIC X(4).
181     02  WA-SIGNUP-DATE REDEFINES
182             WA-SIGNUP-DATE-ALPHA    PIC 9(4).
183 /
184 ****************************************************************
185 *                                                              *
186 *    REPORT HEADINGS FOR CUSTOMER SELECTION REPORT             *
187 *                                                              *
188 ****************************************************************
189
190 01  REPORT-HEADING.
191
192     02  RH-LINE-1.
193         03                          PIC X(6)  VALUE "DATE: ".
194         03  RH-DATE                 PIC Z9/99/99.
195         03                          PIC X(38) VALUE SPACES.
196         03                          PIC X(27) VALUE
197             "AINSWORTH INSURANCE COMPANY".
198         03                          PIC X(34) VALUE SPACES.
199         03                          PIC X(5)  VALUE "PAGE ".
200         03  RH-PAGE-COUNT           PIC ZZ9.
201         03                          PIC X(11) VALUE SPACES.
202
203     02  RH-LINE-2.
204         03                          PIC X(6)  VALUE "TIME: ".
205         03  RH-HOUR                 PIC Z9.
206         03                          PIC X     VALUE ":".
207         03  RH-MINUTES              PIC 99.
208         03  RH-AM-PM                PIC XX.
209         03                          PIC X(40) VALUE SPACES.
210         03                          PIC X(25) VALUE
211             "CUSTOMER SELECTION REPORT".
```

(continued)

```
212        03                            PIC X(54) VALUE SPACES.
213
214    02  RH-LINE-3.
215        03  RH-CRITERIA-MESSAGE       PIC X(9).
216        03  RH-CRITERIA               PIC X(12).
217        03                            PIC XX     VALUE "= ".
218        03  RH-SELECTION              PIC X(20).
219        03                            PIC X(89) VALUE SPACES.
220
221    02  RH-LINE-4.
222        03                            PIC X(65) VALUE SPACES.
223        03                            PIC X(9)  VALUE
224            "INSURANCE".
225        03                            PIC X(6)  VALUE SPACES.
226        03                            PIC X(7)  VALUE
227            "PREMIUM".
228        03                            PIC X(6)  VALUE SPACES.
229        03                            PIC X(7)  VALUE
230            "PAYMENT".
231        03                            PIC X(13) VALUE SPACES.
232        03                            PIC X(6)  VALUE
233            "SIGNUP".
234        03                            PIC X(13) VALUE SPACES.
235  /
236    02  RH-LINE-5.
237        03                            PIC X(13) VALUE
238            "POLICY NUMBER".
239        03                            PIC X(4)  VALUE SPACES.
240        03                            PIC X(13) VALUE
241            "CUSTOMER NAME".
242        03                            PIC X(11) VALUE SPACES.
243        03                            PIC X(10) VALUE
244            "AGENT NAME".
245        03                            PIC X(14) VALUE SPACES.
246        03                            PIC X(4)  VALUE
247            "TYPE".
248        03                            PIC X(11) VALUE SPACES.
249        03                            PIC X(6)  VALUE
250            "STATUS".
251        03                            PIC X(7)  VALUE SPACES.
252        03                            PIC X(6)  VALUE
253            "AMOUNT".
254        03                            PIC X(5)  VALUE SPACES.
255        03                            PIC XXX   VALUE
256            "SEX".
257        03                            PIC X(6)  VALUE SPACES.
258        03                            PIC X(4)  VALUE
259            "DATE".
260        03                            PIC X(15) VALUE SPACES.
261
262    02  RH-LINE-6.
263        03                            PIC X(13) VALUE ALL "-".
264        03                            PIC X(4)  VALUE SPACES.
265        03                            PIC X(13) VALUE ALL "-".
266        03                            PIC X(11) VALUE SPACES.
267        03                            PIC X(10) VALUE ALL "-".
268        03                            PIC X(14) VALUE SPACES.
269        03                            PIC X(9)  VALUE ALL "-".
270        03                            PIC X(6)  VALUE SPACES.
271        03                            PIC X(7)  VALUE ALL "-".
272        03                            PIC X(6)  VALUE SPACES.
273        03                            PIC X(7)  VALUE ALL "-".
274        03                            PIC X(4)  VALUE SPACES.
275        03                            PIC XXX   VALUE ALL "-".
276        03                            PIC X(6)  VALUE SPACES.
277        03                            PIC X(6)  VALUE ALL "-".
278        03                            PIC X(13) VALUE SPACES.
279  /
280  *****************************************************************
281  *                                                              *
282  *    DETAIL LINE FOR THE SELECTION REPORT                      *
283  *                                                              *
284  *****************************************************************
285
```

```
286  01  DETAIL-LINE.
287
288      02  DL-POLICY-NUMBER              PIC X(12).
289      02                                PIC X(5)   VALUE SPACES.
290      02  DL-CUSTOMER-NAME              PIC X(20).
291      02                                PIC X(4)   VALUE SPACES.
292      02  DL-AGENT-NAME                 PIC X(20).
293      02                                PIC X(4)   VALUE SPACES.
294      02  DL-INSURANCE-TYPE             PIC X(10).
295      02                                PIC X(5)   VALUE SPACES.
296      02  DL-PAYMENT-STATUS             PIC X(4).
297      02                                PIC X(6)   VALUE SPACES.
298      02  DL-PREMIUM-AMOUNT             PIC ZZ,ZZ9.99.
299      02                                PIC X(5)   VALUE SPACES.
300      02  DL-SEX                        PIC X.
301      02                                PIC X(8)   VALUE SPACES.
302      02  DL-SIGNUP-DATE                PIC 9999.
303      02                                PIC X(15)  VALUE SPACES.
304
305  *****************************************************************
306  *                                                              *
307  *    SUMMARY LINES FOR THE SELECTION REPORT                    *
308  *                                                              *
309  *****************************************************************
310
311  01  SUMMARY-LINES.
312
313      02  SL-LINE-1.
314          03                            PIC X(37)  VALUE SPACES.
315          03                            PIC X(27)  VALUE
316              "TOTAL CUSTOMERS PRINTED = ".
317          03  SL-RECORD-COUNT           PIC ZZZZ9.
318          03                            PIC X(63)  VALUE SPACES.
319
320      02  SL-LINE-2.
321          03                            PIC X(44)  VALUE SPACES.
322          03                            PIC X(13)  VALUE
323              "END OF REPORT".
324          03                            PIC X(75)  VALUE SPACES.
325  /
326  PROCEDURE DIVISION.
327  ******************
328  *****************************************************************
329  *                                                              *
330  *   MAIN-PROGRAM - THIS IS THE MAIN ROUTINE OF THE CUSTOMER    *
331  *              SELECTION REPORT PROGRAM                        *
332  *                                                              *
333  *****************************************************************
334
335  MAIN-PROGRAM.
336
337      PERFORM A-100-INITIALIZATION.
338      PERFORM B-100-PROCESS-FILE
339          UNTIL NO-MORE-REPORTS.
340      PERFORM C-100-WRAP-UP.
341      STOP RUN.
342
343  *****************************************************************
344  *                                                              *
345  *            THE INITIALIZATION ROUTINE FOLLOWS                *
346  *                                                              *
347  *****************************************************************
348
349  A-100-INITIALIZATION.
350
351      MOVE YES TO SW-MORE-REPORTS.
352
353      ACCEPT WA-SYSTEM-DATE FROM DATE.
354      MOVE WA-SYSTEM-YEAR    TO WA-CURRENT-YEAR.
355      MOVE WA-SYSTEM-MONTH   TO WA-CURRENT-MONTH.
356      MOVE WA-SYSTEM-DAY     TO WA-CURRENT-DAY.
357      MOVE WA-CURRENT-DATE-N TO RH-DATE.
358
359      OPEN OUTPUT  CUSTOMER-SELECTION-REPORT.
360
```

FIGURE 6-7   Customer Selection Report program (continued)

```
361 /
362 ********************************************************************
363 *                                                                *
364 *               REPORT PROCESSING ROUTINE                        *
365 *                                                                *
366 ********************************************************************
367
368  B-100-PROCESS-FILE.
369
370      PERFORM B-200-CRITERIA-CONTROL.
371
372      SORT SORT-FILE
373          ON DESCENDING KEY SR-PREMIUM-AMOUNT
374          INPUT PROCEDURE B-210-SELECT-RECORDS
375          OUTPUT PROCEDURE B-220-WRITE-REPORT.
376
377      MOVE NEG TO SW-VALID-INPUT.
378      PERFORM UNTIL VALID-INPUT
379          DISPLAY "WOULD YOU LIKE TO CREATE ANOTHER REPORT? Y/N "
380          ACCEPT SW-MORE-REPORTS
381          IF SW-MORE-REPORTS = YES OR NEG
382              MOVE YES TO SW-VALID-INPUT
383          ELSE
384              DISPLAY "ENTER Y FOR YES OR N FOR NO!"
385          END-IF
386      END-PERFORM.
387
388  ********************************************************************
389  *                                                                *
390  *               ACCEPT CRITERIA ROUTINE                          *
391  *                                                                *
392  ********************************************************************
393
394  B-200-CRITERIA-CONTROL.
395
396      PERFORM B-300-GET-AGENT-NAME.
397
398      MOVE NEG TO SW-VALID-INPUT.
399      PERFORM B-310-GET-INSURANCE-TYPE
400          UNTIL VALID-INPUT.
401
402      MOVE NEG TO SW-VALID-INPUT.
403      PERFORM B-320-GET-PAYMENT-STATUS
404          UNTIL VALID-INPUT.
405
406      MOVE NEG TO SW-VALID-INPUT.
407      PERFORM B-330-GET-GENDER
408          UNTIL VALID-INPUT.
409
410      MOVE NEG TO SW-VALID-INPUT.
411      PERFORM B-340-GET-SIGNUP-DATE
412          UNTIL VALID-INPUT.
413 /
414  ********************************************************************
415  *                                                                *
416  *               INPUT RECORD PROCESSING ROUTINE                  *
417  *                                                                *
418  ********************************************************************
419
420  B-210-SELECT-RECORDS.
421
422      OPEN INPUT PREMIUM-INPUT-FILE.
423      MOVE NEG TO SW-END-OF-FILE.
424
425      READ PREMIUM-INPUT-FILE
426          AT END MOVE YES TO SW-END-OF-FILE.
427
428      PERFORM B-350-RELEASE-RECORDS
429          UNTIL END-OF-FILE.
430
431      CLOSE PREMIUM-INPUT-FILE.
432 /
```

```
433  ********************************************************************
434  *                                                                *
435  *               SORT FILE RECORD PROCESSING ROUTINE              *
436  *                                                                *
437  ********************************************************************
438
439  B-220-WRITE-REPORT.
440
441      ACCEPT WA-SYSTEM-TIME FROM TIME.
442      IF WA-SYSTEM-HOUR < 12
443          MOVE "AM" TO RH-AM-PM
444          IF WA-SYSTEM-HOUR = 00
445              MOVE 12 TO RH-HOUR
446          ELSE
447              MOVE WA-SYSTEM-HOUR TO RH-HOUR
448      ELSE
449          MOVE "PM" TO RH-AM-PM
450          IF WA-SYSTEM-HOUR > 12
451              COMPUTE RH-HOUR = WA-SYSTEM-HOUR - 12
452          ELSE
453              MOVE 12 TO RH-HOUR.
454      MOVE WA-SYSTEM-MINUTES TO RH-MINUTES.
455
456      MOVE NEG TO SW-END-OF-FILE.
457      INITIALIZE ACCUMULATORS.
458
459      PERFORM B-400-PRINT-HEADINGS.
460
461      RETURN SORT-FILE INTO PREMIUM-RECORD
462          AT END MOVE YES TO SW-END-OF-FILE.
463
464      PERFORM B-360-RETURN-RECORDS
465          UNTIL END-OF-FILE.
466
467      MOVE AC-RECORD-COUNT   TO SL-RECORD-COUNT.
468      WRITE REPORT-LINE-OUT FROM SL-LINE-1
469          AFTER ADVANCING 3 LINES.
470      WRITE REPORT-LINE-OUT FROM SL-LINE-2
471          AFTER ADVANCING 1 LINE.
472 /
473  ********************************************************************
474  *                                                                *
475  *               ACCEPT AGENT NAME FROM SCREEN                    *
476  *                                                                *
477  ********************************************************************
478
479  B-300-GET-AGENT-NAME.
480
481      DISPLAY "PLEASE ENTER AN AGENT NAME AND HIT RETURN".
482      DISPLAY "JUST HIT RETURN TO BYPASS THIS ENTRY!".
483
484      ACCEPT WA-AGENT.
485      MOVE FUNCTION UPPER-CASE (WA-AGENT) TO WA-AGENT.
486
487 /
488  ********************************************************************
489  *                                                                *
490  *               ACCEPT INSURANCE TYPE FROM SCREEN               *
491  *                                                                *
492  ********************************************************************
493
494  B-310-GET-INSURANCE-TYPE.
495
496      DISPLAY "PLEASE ENTER AN INSURANCE TYPE AND HIT RETURN".
497      DISPLAY "JUST HIT RETURN TO BYPASS THIS ENTRY!".
498      DISPLAY " VALID TYPES = Annuity  Automobile  Home".
499      DISPLAY "               Renter   Term Life    Whole Life".
500      ACCEPT WA-INSURANCE-TYPE.
501
502      MOVE FUNCTION UPPER-CASE (WA-INSURANCE-TYPE) TO
503          WA-INSURANCE-TYPE.
504
505      IF WA-INSURANCE-TYPE = SPACES
506          MOVE YES TO SW-VALID-INPUT
```

(continued)

```
507        ELSE
508            IF VALID-INSURANCE-TYPE
509                MOVE YES TO SW-VALID-INPUT
510            ELSE
511                DISPLAY "INVALID INSURANCE TYPE ENTERED!!".
512
513  ******************************************************************
514  *                                                                *
515  *              ACCEPT PAYMENT STATUS FROM SCREEN                 *
516  *                                                                *
517  ******************************************************************
518
519  B-320-GET-PAYMENT-STATUS.
520
521        DISPLAY "PLEASE ENTER A PAYMENT STATUS AND HIT RETURN".
522        DISPLAY "JUST HIT RETURN TO BYPASS THIS ENTRY!".
523        DISPLAY " VALID STATUS = D-Delinquent      F-Paid in Full".
524        DISPLAY "               P-Partially Paid  N-Not yet Billed".
525        ACCEPT WA-PAYMENT-STATUS.
526
527        MOVE FUNCTION UPPER-CASE (WA-PAYMENT-STATUS) TO
528            WA-PAYMENT-STATUS.
529
530        IF WA-PAYMENT-STATUS = SPACES
531            MOVE YES TO SW-VALID-INPUT
532        ELSE
533            IF VALID-STATUS
534                MOVE YES TO SW-VALID-INPUT
535            ELSE
536                DISPLAY "AN INVALID STATUS HAS BEEN ENTERED!!".
537  /
538  ******************************************************************
539  *                                                                *
540  *              ACCEPT CUSTOMER GENDER FROM SCREEN                *
541  *                                                                *
542  ******************************************************************
543
544  B-330-GET-GENDER.
545
546        DISPLAY "PLEASE ENTER A GENDER AND HIT RETURN".
547        DISPLAY "JUST HIT RETURN TO BYPASS THIS ENTRY!".
548        DISPLAY "M = Male    F = Female ".
549        ACCEPT WA-SEX.
550
551        MOVE FUNCTION UPPER-CASE (WA-SEX) TO WA-SEX.
552
553        IF WA-SEX = SPACES
554            MOVE YES TO SW-VALID-INPUT
555        ELSE
556            IF WA-SEX = "M" OR "F"
557                MOVE YES TO SW-VALID-INPUT
558            ELSE
559                DISPLAY "AN INVALID GENDER HAS BEEN ENTERED!!".
560
561  ******************************************************************
562  *                                                                *
563  *              ACCEPT CUSTOMER SIGNUP YEAR FROM SCREEN           *
564  *                                                                *
565  ******************************************************************
566
567  B-340-GET-SIGNUP-DATE.
568
569        DISPLAY "PLEASE ENTER A 4-DIGIT SIGNUP YEAR AND HIT RETURN".
570        DISPLAY "CUSTOMERS WHO SIGNED UP THE ENTERED YEAR OR LATER".
571        DISPLAY "WILL BE LISTED ON THE REPORT".
572        DISPLAY "JUST HIT RETURN TO BYPASS THIS ENTRY!".
573
574        ACCEPT WA-SIGNUP-DATE-ALPHA.
575
576        IF WA-SIGNUP-DATE-ALPHA = SPACES
577            MOVE YES TO SW-VALID-INPUT
578        ELSE
579            IF WA-SIGNUP-DATE-ALPHA NUMERIC
580                MOVE YES TO SW-VALID-INPUT
```

```
581        ELSE
582            DISPLAY "AN INVALID DATE HAS BEEN ENTERED!!".
583
584  /
585  ******************************************************************
586  *                                                                *
587  *       FIND RECORDS THAT MATCH CRITERIA AND RELEASE TO SORT     *
588  *                                                                *
589  ******************************************************************
590
591  B-350-RELEASE-RECORDS.
592
593        MOVE YES TO SW-RELEASE-RECORD.
594
595        IF WA-AGENT NOT = SPACES
596            IF WA-AGENT NOT = FUNCTION UPPER-CASE (PR-AGENT-NAME)
597                MOVE NEG TO SW-RELEASE-RECORD.
598
599        IF WA-INSURANCE-TYPE NOT = SPACES
600            IF WA-INSURANCE-TYPE NOT =
601                FUNCTION UPPER-CASE (PR-INSURANCE-TYPE)
602                MOVE NEG TO SW-RELEASE-RECORD.
603
604        IF WA-PAYMENT-STATUS NOT = SPACES
605            IF WA-PAYMENT-STATUS NOT = PR-PAYMENT-STATUS
606                MOVE NEG TO SW-RELEASE-RECORD.
607
608        IF WA-SEX NOT = SPACES
609            IF WA-SEX NOT = PR-SEX
610                MOVE NEG TO SW-RELEASE-RECORD.
611
612        IF WA-SIGNUP-DATE-ALPHA NOT = SPACES
613            IF WA-SIGNUP-DATE > PR-SIGNUP-DATE
614                MOVE NEG TO SW-RELEASE-RECORD.
615
616        IF RELEASE-RECORD
617            RELEASE SORT-RECORD FROM PREMIUM-RECORD.
618
619        READ PREMIUM-INPUT-FILE
620            AT END MOVE YES TO SW-END-OF-FILE.
621  /
622  ******************************************************************
623  *                                                                *
624  *              RETURN RECORDS AND WRITE REPORT                   *
625  *                                                                *
626  ******************************************************************
627
628  B-360-RETURN-RECORDS.
629
630        MOVE PR-POLICY-NUMBER  TO DL-POLICY-NUMBER.
631        MOVE PR-CUSTOMER-NAME  TO DL-CUSTOMER-NAME.
632        MOVE PR-AGENT-NAME     TO DL-AGENT-NAME.
633        MOVE PR-INSURANCE-TYPE TO DL-INSURANCE-TYPE.
634        MOVE PR-PREMIUM-AMOUNT TO DL-PREMIUM-AMOUNT.
635
636        EVALUATE TRUE
637            WHEN DELINQUENT     MOVE "DELQ" TO DL-PAYMENT-STATUS
638            WHEN PAID-IN-FULL   MOVE "PAID" TO DL-PAYMENT-STATUS
639            WHEN PARTIALLY-PAID MOVE "P PD" TO DL-PAYMENT-STATUS
640            WHEN NOT-YET-BILLED MOVE "NYB" TO DL-PAYMENT-STATUS
641            WHEN OTHER          MOVE "ERR" TO DL-PAYMENT-STATUS.
642
643        MOVE PR-SEX TO DL-SEX.
644        MOVE PR-SIGNUP-DATE TO DL-SIGNUP-DATE.
645
646        WRITE REPORT-LINE-OUT FROM DETAIL-LINE
647            AFTER ADVANCING 2 LINES.
648
649        ADD 2 TO AC-LINE-COUNT.
650        ADD 1 TO AC-RECORD-COUNT.
651
652        IF AC-LINE-COUNT > 55
653            MOVE ZERO TO AC-LINE-COUNT
654            PERFORM B-400-PRINT-HEADINGS.
655
```

FIGURE 6-7   Customer Selection Report program (continued)

```
656
657        RETURN SORT-FILE INTO PREMIUM-RECORD
658            AT END MOVE YES TO SW-END-OF-FILE.
659 /
660 **********************************************************************
661 *                                                                  *
662 *                      HEADER ROUTINE                              *
663 *                                                                  *
664 **********************************************************************
665
666 B-400-PRINT-HEADINGS.
667
668        ADD 1 TO AC-PAGE-COUNT.
669        MOVE AC-PAGE-COUNT TO RH-PAGE-COUNT.
670        WRITE REPORT-LINE-OUT FROM RH-LINE-1
671            AFTER ADVANCING PAGE.
672        WRITE REPORT-LINE-OUT FROM RH-LINE-2
673            AFTER ADVANCING 1 LINE.
674
675        PERFORM B-500-PRINT-CRITERIA.
676
677        WRITE REPORT-LINE-OUT FROM RH-LINE-4
678            AFTER ADVANCING 2 LINES.
679        WRITE REPORT-LINE-OUT FROM RH-LINE-5
680            AFTER ADVANCING 1 LINE.
681        WRITE REPORT-LINE-OUT FROM RH-LINE-6
682            AFTER ADVANCING 1 LINE.
683        ADD 6 TO AC-LINE-COUNT.
684 /
685 **********************************************************************
686 *                                                                  *
687 *              PRINT REPORT CRITERIA FOR HEADINGS                  *
688 *                                                                  *
689 **********************************************************************
690
691 B-500-PRINT-CRITERIA.
692        MOVE "CRITERIA:" TO RH-CRITERIA-MESSAGE.
693        MOVE 2 TO WA-LINES.
694
695        IF WA-AGENT NOT = SPACES
696            MOVE "AGENT NAME" TO RH-CRITERIA
697            MOVE WA-AGENT TO RH-SELECTION
698            WRITE REPORT-LINE-OUT FROM RH-LINE-3
699                AFTER ADVANCING WA-LINES
700            MOVE SPACES TO RH-CRITERIA-MESSAGE
701            ADD WA-LINES TO AC-LINE-COUNT
702            MOVE 1 TO WA-LINES.
703
704        IF WA-INSURANCE-TYPE NOT = SPACES
705            MOVE "INS. TYPE" TO RH-CRITERIA
706            MOVE WA-INSURANCE-TYPE TO RH-SELECTION
707            WRITE REPORT-LINE-OUT FROM RH-LINE-3
708                AFTER ADVANCING WA-LINES
709            MOVE SPACES TO RH-CRITERIA-MESSAGE
710            ADD WA-LINES TO AC-LINE-COUNT
711            MOVE 1 TO WA-LINES.
712
713        IF WA-PAYMENT-STATUS NOT = SPACES
714            MOVE "PAY STATUS" TO RH-CRITERIA
715            MOVE WA-PAYMENT-STATUS TO RH-SELECTION
716            WRITE REPORT-LINE-OUT FROM RH-LINE-3
717                AFTER ADVANCING WA-LINES
718            MOVE SPACES TO RH-CRITERIA-MESSAGE
719            ADD WA-LINES TO AC-LINE-COUNT
720            MOVE 1 TO WA-LINES.
721
722        IF WA-SEX NOT = SPACES
723            MOVE "CUST GENDER" TO RH-CRITERIA
724            MOVE WA-SEX TO RH-SELECTION
725            WRITE REPORT-LINE-OUT FROM RH-LINE-3
726                AFTER ADVANCING WA-LINES
727            MOVE SPACES TO RH-CRITERIA-MESSAGE
728            ADD WA-LINES TO AC-LINE-COUNT
729            MOVE 1 TO WA-LINES.
730
731        IF WA-SIGNUP-DATE-ALPHA NOT = SPACES
732            MOVE "SIGNUP DATE" TO RH-CRITERIA
733            MOVE "SINCE " TO RH-SELECTION
734            MOVE WA-SIGNUP-DATE-ALPHA TO RH-SELECTION (7:)
735            WRITE REPORT-LINE-OUT FROM RH-LINE-3
736                AFTER ADVANCING WA-LINES
737            ADD WA-LINES TO AC-LINE-COUNT.
738 /
739 **********************************************************************
740 *                                                                  *
741 *                      END OF JOB ROUTINE                          *
742 *                                                                  *
743 **********************************************************************
744
745 C-100-WRAP-UP.
746
747        CLOSE CUSTOMER-SELECTION-REPORT.
748        DISPLAY "REPORT PROCESSING HAS TERMINATED".
749
750 /
```

COBOL SORT STATEMENT

The **SORT** statement is used in the PROCEDURE DIVISION to place records from an input file in a temporary work file where their order will be rearranged. The work file is referred to as the **sort work file**. Once rearranged, the records can be placed back in the original input file, placed in a separate output file, or processed directly from the sort work file. The sort work file must be defined by a SELECT entry in the INPUT-OUTPUT SECTION of the ENVIRONMENT DIVISION. In place of an FD entry in the FILE SECTION of the DATA DIVISION, a sort work file has an SD entry. **SD** stands for **Sort Description**.

Figure 6-8 on the next page presents the SELECT entry and SD for the sort work file used in the Customer Selection Report program. The format of an SD is very similar to that of an FD.

```
25  ENVIRONMENT DIVISION.

28  INPUT-OUTPUT SECTION.

31  FILE-CONTROL.

39      SELECT SORT-FILE
40          ASSIGN TO "SORTWORK".


43  DATA DIVISION.

46  FILE SECTION.

91  SD  SORT-FILE.
92
93  01  SORT-RECORD.
94      02                      PIC X(62).
95      02  SR-PREMIUM-AMOUNT    PIC S9(5)V99.
96      02                      PIC X(11).
```

SD used instead of FD

same number of characters as Input Record

definition of sort key field

FIGURE 6-8   SELECT and SD for the sort work file in the Customer Selection Report program

Figure 6-9 presents the basic format of an SD. All the clauses after the sort-work-file name are optional and will not be used in this book. The record definition entry following the SD is called the **sort record** and must be broken down enough to show the position and size of the sort key field or fields. All other fields can be defined as filler entries. A **sort key field** is a field within the sort record that is used to determine how the records are rearranged. For example, in the white pages of a telephone book, information is in alphabetical order by last name. Thus, last name is a sort key field in the preparation of the telephone book. The total number of characters within the sort record definition must match the number of characters in the records to be sorted.

```
SD  sort-work-file

  ⌈ RECORD  ⌠ CONTAINS  integer-1 CHARACTERS                                      ⌉
  |         | IS VARYING IN SIZE [[FROM integer-2] [TO integer-3] CHARACTERS  |
  |         | [DEPENDING ON field-1 ]                                            |
  ⌊         ⌡ CONTAINS integer-4 TO integer-5 CHARACTERS                        ⌋

  ⌈ DATA   ⌠ RECORD IS   ⌡   {field-2 }. . .  ⌉
  ⌊        ⌡ RECORDS ARE ⌡                       ⌋
```

FIGURE 6-9   Basic format of an SD entry

In the PROCEDURE DIVISION, the sort work file and the sort key field(s) are among the entries named in a SORT statement. Figure 6-10 presents the basic format of a SORT statement. The name of the sort work file must follow the word SORT. This name must be the same as the name used in the SELECT and SD entries. Records can be arranged in either ASCENDING or DESCENDING sequence by the key field or fields specified. When multiple key fields are used, they must be listed most major to most minor. A **major key** takes precedence over a **minor key** in the sorting of the records. For example, in a SORT of the PREMIUM-INPUT-FILE, suppose insurance type was identified as the major key and premium amount was the minor key. The insurance type would be listed first in the SORT statement, and the premium amount would be listed second. Suppose also that ASCENDING was specified for both keys. The records would end up being in alphabetical order by insurance type, but within each insurance type group, the records would be in order from lowest to highest by premium amount. That is, the records are in sequence by premium amount within insurance type.

```
SORT  sort-work-file  { ON { ASCENDING  }   KEY   {sort-key-1} ... } ...
                           { DESCENDING }

          [ WITH DUPLICATES IN ORDER ]

          [ COLLATING SEQUENCE IS special-name-1 ]

          { INPUT PROCEDURE IS procedure-name-1 [ { THROUGH } procedure-name-2 ] }
          {                                     [ { THRU    }                  ] }
          { USING {input-file-name } ...                                         }

          { OUTPUT PROCEDURE IS procedure-name-3 [ { THROUGH } procedure-name-4 ] }
          {                                      [ { THRU    }                  ] }
          { GIVING {output-file-name }...                                         }
```

FIGURE 6-10   Basic format of a SORT statement

When multiple keys are used in a SORT statement, ASCENDING or DESCENDING can be specified for each key. If the sequence is the same for each key, the ON ASCENDING KEY or ON DESCENDING KEY clause need only be coded for the first key. Thus, the SORT statements presented in Figure 6-11 on the next page are equivalent. The entries WITH DUPLICATES and COLLATING SEQUENCE are optional and will not be used in this book. You must use either an INPUT PROCEDURE or the USING phrase in a SORT statement. Also, you must use either an OUTPUT PROCEDURE or the GIVING phrase. INPUT PROCEDURE and/or OUTPUT PROCEDURE are needed when there is special processing to do within a program. Many SORT statements can be coded with just the USING and GIVING phrases. Table 6-1 on the next page summarizes the combinations that can appear within a SORT statement.

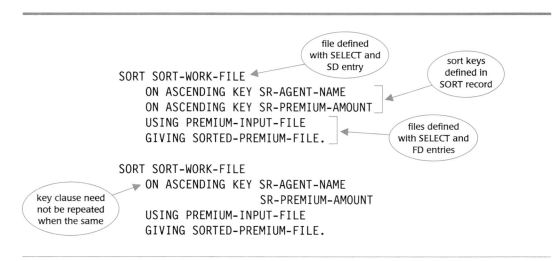

FIGURE 6-11 Equivalent SORT statements using multiple keys sorted in the same sequence

TABLE 6-1 Summary of Available SORT Options

Sort Options Used	Results
USING GIVING	Input file sorted and placed in GIVING file; no special handling
INPUT PROCEDURE GIVING	Special processing of Input file before sorting occurs
USING OUTPUT PROCEDURE	Special processing of the sorted records, but not the Input file
INPUT PROCEDURE OUTPUT PROCEDURE	Special processing of both the Input file and sorted records

Simple SORT

A SORT statement that contains both USING and GIVING phrases is called a **simple SORT**. The **USING** phrase identifies the file to be used as input to the SORT, while the **GIVING** phrase identifies the file to be created as output from the SORT. These files can be the same file. A simple SORT takes all the records contained in the USING file and places them in the sort work file. It then rearranges the records according to the order specified by the KEY entries in the SORT statement. Finally, it places the sorted records in the specified GIVING file.

Assume that the records in the PREMIUM-INPUT-FILE are in an unknown sequence. Figure 6-12 illustrates a simple SORT that uses PREMIUM-INPUT-FILE as input, sorts the records in ASCENDING sequence by customer name, thus putting the records in alphabetical order, and then places the sorted records in SORTED-PREMIUM-FILE. At the time the SORT statement executes, PREMIUM-INPUT-FILE and SORTED-PREMIUM-FILE cannot be open files. All opening and closing of files is handled automatically by the SORT statement in a simple SORT. The SORT will automatically open PREMIUM-INPUT-FILE for input, transfer all of the records to SORT-FILE, close PREMIUM-INPUT-FILE, rearrange the records, open SORTED-PREMIUM-FILE for output, transfer the sorted records to SORTED-PREMIUM-FILE, and then close SORTED-PREMIUM-FILE.

```
ENVIRONMENT DIVISION.
INPUT-OUTPUT SECTION.
FILE-CONTROL.

    SELECT PREMIUM-INPUT-FILE
        ASSIGN TO "A:\PREMIUM.DAT".

    SELECT SORTED-PREMIUM-FILE
        ASSIGN TO "A:\SORTPREM.DAT".

    SELECT SORT-FILE
        ASSIGN TO "SORTWORK".


DATA DIVISION.
FILE SECTION.

FD  PREMIUM-INPUT-FILE.

01  PREMIUM-RECORD.
    02  PR-CUSTOMER-NAME          PIC X(20).
    02     . . .

FD  SORTED-PREMIUM-FILE.

01  SORTED-PREMIUM-RECORD         PIC X(80).


SD  SORT-FILE.

01  SORT-RECORD.
    02  SR-CUSTOMER-NAME          PIC X(20).
    02                            PIC X(60).


PROCEDURE DIVISION.
    .
    .
    .
    SORT SORT-FILE
        ON ASCENDING KEY SR-CUSTOMER-NAME
        USING PREMIUM-INPUT-FILE
        GIVING SORTED-PREMIUM-FILE.
```

FIGURE 6-12 Simple SORT rearranging records in ascending sequence by customer name

Figure 6-13 illustrates how the records would appear in the SORTED-PREMIUM-FILE once the given SORT is finished.

```
Allister, Collin    McDonald, Fred      AutomobileAM-1991-92230012345PM199411
Amfelter, Audrey    McDonald, Fred      AutomobileAM-2199-92290045650FF199606
Andrews, Robert     Anderson, James     Home      HM-7008-05070056000PM199011
Antich, Roseanne    McDonald, Fred      AutomobileAM-7211-72610025050PF199505
Anytime, Seeue      McDonald, Fred      AutomobileAM-7623-12210023400FF199701
Baker, Bonnie       Jones, William      Renter    RT-4402-32110015000NM199302
Brannan, Clyde      Benson, Gloria      Term Life TL-7008-55510055000NM199703
Byman, Goodie       Anderson, James     Home      HM-1107-23930245000NM199604
Cannon, Wylde       Benson, Gloria      AutomobileAM-6128-21510155000NM199705
Connors, Cinder     Jones, William      Home      HM-5109-41710085000NM199607
Danners, Sarah      McDonald, Fred      Term Life TL-7303-34520045000NM199508
Duffy, Chester      Jean, Barbara       Term Life TL-7007-56910045000NM199609
Eastling, Edward    Anderson, James     AutomobileAM-7373-11470055000DM199310
Eman, Sorik         Jean, Barbara       Annuity   AN-0868-48200235000NM199710
          .
          .
          .
Vlasic, Roberta     McDonald, Fred      Term Life TL-2129-89590038000PF199604
Walters, Samuel     Jones, William      Renter    RT-0424-00530022000PF199407
West, William       Anderson, James     Annuity   AN-0993-41040040000NM199507
White, Robert       Anderson, James     Whole LifeWL-0454-56980036075FM199603
Whitman, Walter     Anderson, James     AutomobileAM-3411-12230077100PM199405
Wilder, Eugene      Jean, Barbara       Whole LifeWL-0082-19130038000FM199605
Willis, Richard     Anderson, James     Renter    RT-9580-00030085000FM199504
Winder, Robert      Anderson, James     Term Life TL-7682-09030030550FM199302
Winfield, Wally     Anderson, James     Whole LifeWL-2721-39040032600PM199601
Yackley, Yourto     Jones, William      Renter    RT-7127-50760024000PF199402
```

records sorted by customer name

FIGURE 6-13 Contents of SORTED-PREMIUM-FILE after a SORT in ASCENDING sequence by customer name

Figure 6-14 presents another example of a simple SORT. In this example, two key fields are used. Agent name is the major key field, so it is listed first. Premium amount is the minor key. Once the records are placed into the SORTED-PREMIUM-FILE, they will be in descending sequence by premium amount within agent name.

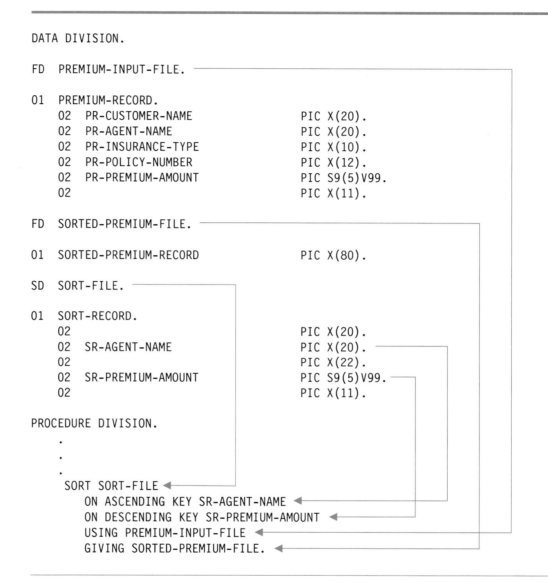

```
DATA DIVISION.

FD   PREMIUM-INPUT-FILE.

01   PREMIUM-RECORD.
     02   PR-CUSTOMER-NAME            PIC X(20).
     02   PR-AGENT-NAME              PIC X(20).
     02   PR-INSURANCE-TYPE          PIC X(10).
     02   PR-POLICY-NUMBER           PIC X(12).
     02   PR-PREMIUM-AMOUNT          PIC S9(5)V99.
     02                              PIC X(11).

FD   SORTED-PREMIUM-FILE.

01   SORTED-PREMIUM-RECORD          PIC X(80).

SD   SORT-FILE.

01   SORT-RECORD.
     02                              PIC X(20).
     02   SR-AGENT-NAME              PIC X(20).
     02                              PIC X(22).
     02   SR-PREMIUM-AMOUNT          PIC S9(5)V99.
     02                              PIC X(11).

PROCEDURE DIVISION.
     .
     .
     .
       SORT SORT-FILE
           ON ASCENDING KEY SR-AGENT-NAME
           ON DESCENDING KEY SR-PREMIUM-AMOUNT
           USING PREMIUM-INPUT-FILE
           GIVING SORTED-PREMIUM-FILE.
```

FIGURE 6-14 Simple SORT rearranging records in DESCENDING sequence by premium amount within ASCENDING sequence by agent name

Figure 6-15 illustrates the results of such a SORT. To process the sorted records, SORTED-PREMIUM-FILE can be opened for INPUT within the program logic after the SORT statement executes, and a READ statement can be used to retrieve the records one at a time.

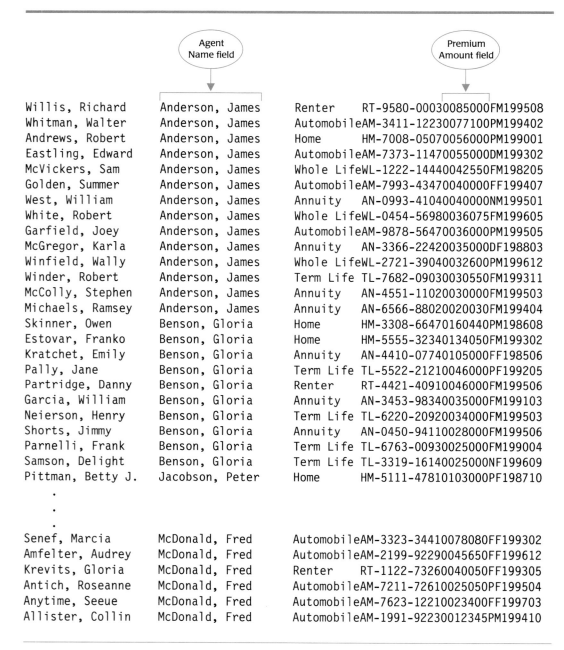

	Agent Name field	Premium Amount field
Willis, Richard	Anderson, James	Renter RT-9580-00030085000FM199508
Whitman, Walter	Anderson, James	AutomobileAM-3411-12230077100PM199402
Andrews, Robert	Anderson, James	Home HM-7008-05070056000PM199001
Eastling, Edward	Anderson, James	AutomobileAM-7373-11470055000DM199302
McVickers, Sam	Anderson, James	Whole LifeWL-1222-14440042550FM198205
Golden, Summer	Anderson, James	AutomobileAM-7993-43470040000FF199407
West, William	Anderson, James	Annuity AN-0993-41040040000NM199501
White, Robert	Anderson, James	Whole LifeWL-0454-56980036075FM199605
Garfield, Joey	Anderson, James	AutomobileAM-9878-56470036000PM199505
McGregor, Karla	Anderson, James	Annuity AN-3366-22420035000DF198803
Winfield, Wally	Anderson, James	Whole LifeWL-2721-39040032600PM199612
Winder, Robert	Anderson, James	Term Life TL-7682-09030030550FM199311
McColly, Stephen	Anderson, James	Annuity AN-4551-11020030000FM199503
Michaels, Ramsey	Anderson, James	Annuity AN-6566-88020020030FM199404
Skinner, Owen	Benson, Gloria	Home HM-3308-66470160440PM198608
Estovar, Franko	Benson, Gloria	Home HM-5555-32340134050FM199302
Kratchet, Emily	Benson, Gloria	Annuity AN-4410-07740105000FF198506
Pally, Jane	Benson, Gloria	Term Life TL-5522-21210046000PF199205
Partridge, Danny	Benson, Gloria	Renter RT-4421-40910046000FM199506
Garcia, William	Benson, Gloria	Annuity AN-3453-98340035000FM199103
Neierson, Henry	Benson, Gloria	Term Life TL-6220-20920034000FM199503
Shorts, Jimmy	Benson, Gloria	Annuity AN-0450-94110028000FM199506
Parnelli, Frank	Benson, Gloria	Term Life TL-6763-00930025000FM199004
Samson, Delight	Benson, Gloria	Term Life TL-3319-16140025000NF199609
Pittman, Betty J.	Jacobson, Peter	Home HM-5111-47810103000PF198710
.		
.		
.		
Senef, Marcia	McDonald, Fred	AutomobileAM-3323-34410078080FF199302
Amfelter, Audrey	McDonald, Fred	AutomobileAM-2199-92290045650FF199612
Krevits, Gloria	McDonald, Fred	Renter RT-1122-73260040050FF199305
Antich, Roseanne	McDonald, Fred	AutomobileAM-7211-72610025050PF199504
Anytime, Seeue	McDonald, Fred	AutomobileAM-7623-12210023400FF199703
Allister, Collin	McDonald, Fred	AutomobileAM-1991-92230012345PM199410

FIGURE 6-15   Contents of SORTED-PREMIUM-FILE after a SORT in DESCENDING sequence by premium amount within ASCENDING sequence by agent name

Input Procedure

Some situations call for the sorting of only certain records from an input file. In such situations, the **INPUT PROCEDURE** option can be used within a SORT statement to transfer control to a paragraph or section that contains the necessary record selection logic. The INPUT PROCEDURE option works just like a PERFORM statement. Figure 6-16 presents the SORT statement from the Customer Selection Report program. Line 374 transfers control to paragraph B-210-SELECT-RECORDS. This paragraph controls the logic used to select those records that will be sorted and eventually reported on. Within B-210-SELECT-RECORDS, PREMIUM-INPUT-FILE is opened for INPUT (see line 422 in Figure 6-7 on page 6-9). When INPUT PROCEDURE is used, the input file will not be opened automatically. It is the programmer's responsibility to open and close all files needed within the INPUT PROCEDURE paragraphs. Only the sort work file will be opened automatically and closed as needed.

```
368 B-100-PROCESS-FILE.
       .
       .
       .
372       SORT SORT-FILE
373           ON DESCENDING KEY SR-PREMIUM-AMOUNT
374           INPUT PROCEDURE B-210-SELECT-RECORDS
375           OUTPUT PROCEDURE B-220-WRITE-REPORT.
```

function like PERFORM statements

FIGURE 6-16   SORT statement from the Customer Selection Report program with an INPUT PROCEDURE and OUTPUT PROCEDURE

Paragraph B-210-SELECT-RECORDS contains a PERFORM UNTIL statement that is used to set up a Do-While loop to the paragraph B-350-RELEASE-RECORDS. The logic within B-350-RELEASE-RECORDS uses values input by the user to filter out those records not required for the report (Figure 6-17 on the next page). The logic used will be discussed later in this chapter. Those records not filtered out will be sent to SORT-FILE so they can be sorted in descending sequence by premium amount, as specified by the SORT statement.

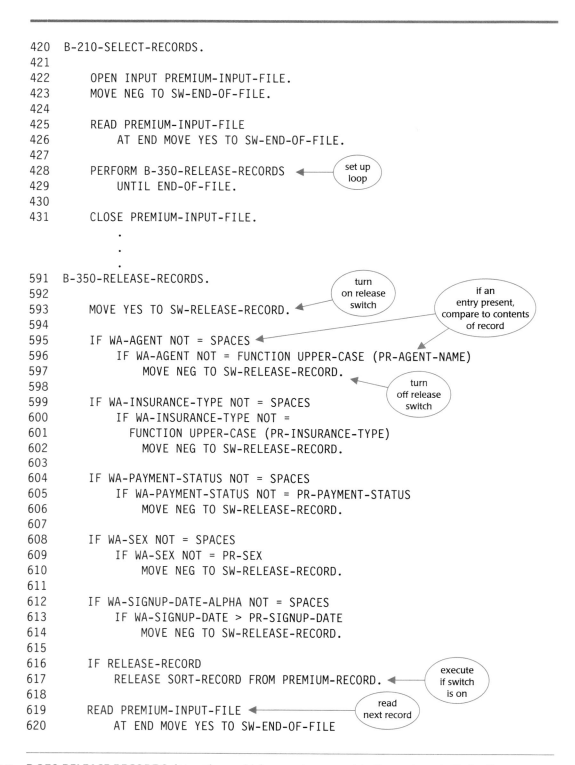

```
420  B-210-SELECT-RECORDS.
421
422      OPEN INPUT PREMIUM-INPUT-FILE.
423      MOVE NEG TO SW-END-OF-FILE.
424
425      READ PREMIUM-INPUT-FILE
426          AT END MOVE YES TO SW-END-OF-FILE.
427
428      PERFORM B-350-RELEASE-RECORDS        ◄──  set up
429          UNTIL END-OF-FILE.                    loop
430
431      CLOSE PREMIUM-INPUT-FILE.
                .
                .
                .
591  B-350-RELEASE-RECORDS.                         turn
592                                                on release
593      MOVE YES TO SW-RELEASE-RECORD.  ◄──        switch          if an
594                                                              entry present,
595      IF WA-AGENT NOT = SPACES  ◄──                         compare to contents
596          IF WA-AGENT NOT = FUNCTION UPPER-CASE (PR-AGENT-NAME)   of record
597              MOVE NEG TO SW-RELEASE-RECORD.  ◄──
598                                                  turn
599      IF WA-INSURANCE-TYPE NOT = SPACES       off release
600          IF WA-INSURANCE-TYPE NOT =            switch
601            FUNCTION UPPER-CASE (PR-INSURANCE-TYPE)
602              MOVE NEG TO SW-RELEASE-RECORD.
603
604      IF WA-PAYMENT-STATUS NOT = SPACES
605          IF WA-PAYMENT-STATUS NOT = PR-PAYMENT-STATUS
606              MOVE NEG TO SW-RELEASE-RECORD.
607
608      IF WA-SEX NOT = SPACES
609          IF WA-SEX NOT = PR-SEX
610              MOVE NEG TO SW-RELEASE-RECORD.
611
612      IF WA-SIGNUP-DATE-ALPHA NOT = SPACES
613          IF WA-SIGNUP-DATE > PR-SIGNUP-DATE
614              MOVE NEG TO SW-RELEASE-RECORD.
615
616      IF RELEASE-RECORD                          execute
617          RELEASE SORT-RECORD FROM PREMIUM-RECORD.  ◄──  if switch
618                                                     is on
619      READ PREMIUM-INPUT-FILE  ◄──        read
620          AT END MOVE YES TO SW-END-OF-FILE  next record
```

FIGURE 6-17 B-350-RELEASE-RECORDS determines which records are sent to the sort work file by the RELEASE statement

The **RELEASE** statement is used in an INPUT PROCEDURE to send records to the sort work file. RELEASE works very much like a WRITE, but can be used only within an INPUT PROCEDURE paragraph and only to transfer records to a sort work file. Figure 6-18 presents the basic format of a RELEASE statement. The name following the reserved word RELEASE must be the 01 level sort record name defined immediately following the SD for the sort work file. If FROM is not used, then the record to be sent to the sort work file must be moved to this record name prior to the execution of the RELEASE. This can be accomplished with a READ INTO or MOVE statement. B-350-RELEASE-RECORD executes until all of the records within PREMIUM-INPUT-FILE have been processed and the AT END clause on line 620 of Figure 6-17 executes moving the contents of the field YES to the field SW-END-OF-FILE. The loop then terminates and control of the logic returns to B-210-SELECT-RECORDS. From there, control returns back to the SORT statement in B-100-PROCESS-FILE. Once the INPUT PROCEDURE is complete, the records released to SORT-FILE are rearranged as specified. Control then passes to the next entry in the SORT statement, which must be either a GIVING clause or, as in the Customer Selection Report program, the OUTPUT PROCEDURE option.

RELEASE sort-record-name   [FROM input-record-layout]

FIGURE 6-18   Basic format of the RELEASE statement

Output Procedure

The **OUTPUT PROCEDURE** option is used when you want to process sorted records directly from the sort work file. That is, instead of creating a separate sorted version of the input file, sorted records can be retrieved directly from the sort work file and a report or other desired output can be created using the records obtained. Such processing eliminates the need for the type of output file required when the GIVING option is used. Thus, the need for a SELECT and FD for a file also is eliminated. As with an INPUT PROCEDURE entry in a SORT, an OUTPUT PROCEDURE entry transfers control just like a PERFORM statement. OUTPUT PROCEDURE does not execute until all of the records are sorted within the sort work file.

The Customer Selection Report program uses the OUTPUT PROCEDURE option to transfer control to B-220-WRITE-REPORT (see Figure 6-16 on page 6-19). B-220-WRITE-REPORT establishes the logic needed to produce an output report (Figure 6-19 on the next page). The logic is very similar to that used in previous programs, but instead of using a READ statement to obtain the first record, on lines 461 and 462, a RETURN statement is used.

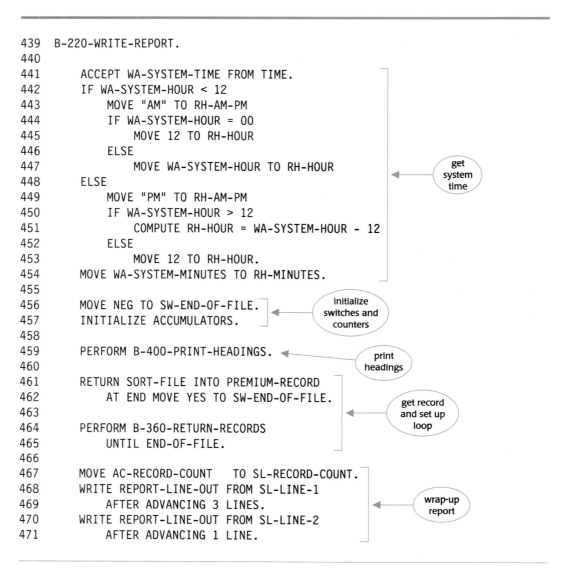

```
439  B-220-WRITE-REPORT.
440
441      ACCEPT WA-SYSTEM-TIME FROM TIME.
442      IF WA-SYSTEM-HOUR < 12
443          MOVE "AM" TO RH-AM-PM
444          IF WA-SYSTEM-HOUR = 00
445              MOVE 12 TO RH-HOUR
446          ELSE
447              MOVE WA-SYSTEM-HOUR TO RH-HOUR
448      ELSE
449          MOVE "PM" TO RH-AM-PM
450          IF WA-SYSTEM-HOUR > 12
451              COMPUTE RH-HOUR = WA-SYSTEM-HOUR - 12
452          ELSE
453              MOVE 12 TO RH-HOUR.
454      MOVE WA-SYSTEM-MINUTES TO RH-MINUTES.
455
456      MOVE NEG TO SW-END-OF-FILE.
457      INITIALIZE ACCUMULATORS.
458
459      PERFORM B-400-PRINT-HEADINGS.
460
461      RETURN SORT-FILE INTO PREMIUM-RECORD
462          AT END MOVE YES TO SW-END-OF-FILE.
463
464      PERFORM B-360-RETURN-RECORDS
465          UNTIL END-OF-FILE.
466
467      MOVE AC-RECORD-COUNT    TO SL-RECORD-COUNT.
468      WRITE REPORT-LINE-OUT FROM SL-LINE-1
469          AFTER ADVANCING 3 LINES.
470      WRITE REPORT-LINE-OUT FROM SL-LINE-2
471          AFTER ADVANCING 1 LINE.
```

Callouts in figure: get system time; initialize switches and counters; print headings; get record and set up loop; wrap-up report

FIGURE 6-19   B-220-WRITE-REPORT paragraph

A **RETURN** statement looks and works just like a READ statement but can be used only as part of an OUTPUT PROCEDURE paragraph and can be used only to obtain records from a sort work file. Figure 6-20 presents the basic format of a RETURN statement.

```
RETURN sort-work-file RECORD  [ INTO record-layout ]

    AT END  statement-set-1

    [ NOT AT END  statement-set-2 ]

    [ END-RETURN ]
```

FIGURE 6-20   Basic format of the RETURN statement

The AT END clause will execute when no more records are available in the sort work file. A second RETURN statement is coded on lines 657 and 658 at the bottom of B-360-RETURN-RECORDS, to obtain the next record for processing before the next pass through the report logic loop (Figure 6-21).

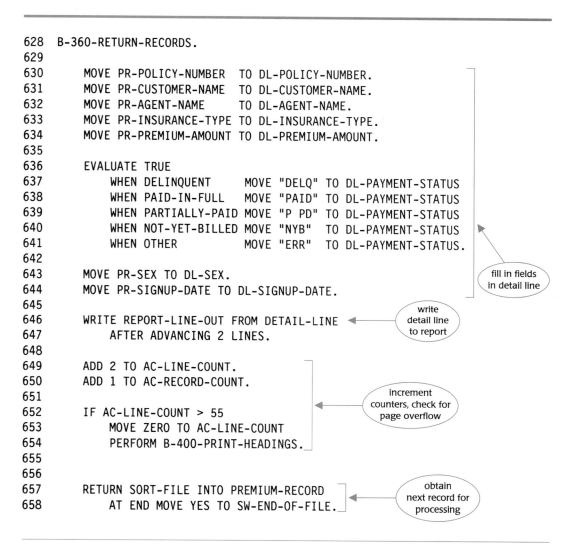

```
628   B-360-RETURN-RECORDS.
629
630       MOVE PR-POLICY-NUMBER  TO DL-POLICY-NUMBER.
631       MOVE PR-CUSTOMER-NAME  TO DL-CUSTOMER-NAME.
632       MOVE PR-AGENT-NAME     TO DL-AGENT-NAME.
633       MOVE PR-INSURANCE-TYPE TO DL-INSURANCE-TYPE.
634       MOVE PR-PREMIUM-AMOUNT TO DL-PREMIUM-AMOUNT.
635
636       EVALUATE TRUE
637           WHEN DELINQUENT     MOVE "DELQ" TO DL-PAYMENT-STATUS
638           WHEN PAID-IN-FULL   MOVE "PAID" TO DL-PAYMENT-STATUS
639           WHEN PARTIALLY-PAID MOVE "P PD" TO DL-PAYMENT-STATUS
640           WHEN NOT-YET-BILLED MOVE "NYB"  TO DL-PAYMENT-STATUS
641           WHEN OTHER          MOVE "ERR"  TO DL-PAYMENT-STATUS.
642
643       MOVE PR-SEX TO DL-SEX.
644       MOVE PR-SIGNUP-DATE TO DL-SIGNUP-DATE.
645
646       WRITE REPORT-LINE-OUT FROM DETAIL-LINE
647           AFTER ADVANCING 2 LINES.
648
649       ADD 2 TO AC-LINE-COUNT.
650       ADD 1 TO AC-RECORD-COUNT.
651
652       IF AC-LINE-COUNT > 55
653           MOVE ZERO TO AC-LINE-COUNT
654           PERFORM B-400-PRINT-HEADINGS.
655
656
657       RETURN SORT-FILE INTO PREMIUM-RECORD
658           AT END MOVE YES TO SW-END-OF-FILE.
```

fill in fields in detail line

write detail line to report

increment counters, check for page overflow

obtain next record for processing

FIGURE 6-21   B-360-RETURN-RECORDS writes a record to the report and executes a RETURN to obtain the next record

When the condition END-OF-FILE is true, the loop terminates and control returns to B-220-WRITE-REPORT. The summary lines are then printed, the OUTPUT PROCEDURE logic terminates, and control passes to the statement following the COBOL SORT. The Customer Selection Report program then asks the user if another report is to be generated.

COBOL MERGE STATEMENT

Often, input data files come from multiple sources such as sales agents, district offices, or regional offices. It is common for this data to be combined and processed together. Figure 6-22 on the next page presents the basic format of a COBOL MERGE statement. A **MERGE** statement is very similar to a SORT statement but allows for the use of multiple input files that can be combined and sorted. The records from the combined files can be placed into one sorted output file or they can be made available to an OUTPUT PROCEDURE. The USING phrase must be used in a MERGE statement because the INPUT PROCEDURE option is not available.

MERGE merge-work-file $\left\{ \text{ON} \left\{ \begin{array}{l} \underline{\text{ASCENDING}} \\ \underline{\text{DESCENDING}} \end{array} \right\} \quad \text{KEY} \quad \{\text{sort-key-1}\} \ldots \right\} \ldots$

[COLLATING SEQUENCE IS special-name-1]

USING input-file-name-1 {input-file-name-2 } ...

$\left\{ \begin{array}{l} \underline{\text{OUTPUT}} \text{ PROCEDURE IS procedure-name-1} \left[\left\{ \begin{array}{l} \underline{\text{THROUGH}} \\ \underline{\text{THRU}} \end{array} \right\} \text{procedure-name-2} \right] \\ \underline{\text{GIVING}} \text{ \{output-file-name \} } \ldots \end{array} \right\}$

FIGURE 6-22 Basic format of the COBOL MERGE statement

As with a sort work file, the **merge work file** must be defined with a SELECT and an SD. The record definition entry following the SD must be subdivided enough to show the position and size of the key field or fields to be used. The key field or fields must be in the same relative position within each record of every input file. If OUTPUT PROCEDURE is used, the RETURN statement is used to obtain records from the merge work file. The COBOL MERGE statement will not be used in any of the programs in this book.

RECORD SELECTION

As indicated at the beginning of the chapter, not every program reports on or processes every record. Often, only certain records are selected for processing. The first step in a record selection report program involves obtaining the selection criteria to be used. This can be done in a batch mode by reading a record from a special file designed to supply selection criteria. The special file must be created before the program executes. In interactive mode, selection criteria can be entered by a user responding to prompts that appear on a computer terminal screen. The latter method is used in the Customer Selection Report program.

The second step in a record selection report program is the selection of those records that are to be listed on the report. Using conditional statements, the fields in each record are compared to the selection criteria until a mismatch is found. If a mismatch is found, the record cannot be printed on the report, regardless of the results of other comparisons. If no mismatch is found, the record can be printed on the report. In the Customer Selection Report program, the report on selected records is created in the OUTPUT PROCEDURE processing, after the selected records are rearranged by the SORT statement. If the records were to be listed in the same order in which they exist in the input file, then the SORT statement would not be needed in the program.

Interactive Dialogue

The selection criteria are obtained by the Customer Selection Report program through an interactive dialogue programmed using DISPLAY and ACCEPT statements. Figure 6-23 presents the PERFORM statement and code for the paragraph B-310-GET-INSURANCE-TYPE, which obtains the selection criterion for the type of insurance. The PERFORM statement on lines

399 and 400 of B-200-CRITERIA-CONTROL, uses the UNTIL option to create a loop that continues to execute until the condition VALID-INPUT is true. VALID-INPUT is true when the field SW-VALID-INPUT contains the letter Y. On line 398, SW-VALID-INPUT is initialized with the letter N just prior to the PERFORM. The DISPLAY statements in B-310-GET-INSURANCE-TYPE are used to present messages to the user, and the ACCEPT statement on line 500 is used to obtain the user's response, which is entered on the terminal. An intrinsic function, UPPER-CASE, is used on lines 502 and 503 to make sure the entry is all uppercase characters, and to simplify validation of the entry. The testing needed for the selection process later in the program also will be simplified. Intrinsic functions were introduced in Chapter 5.

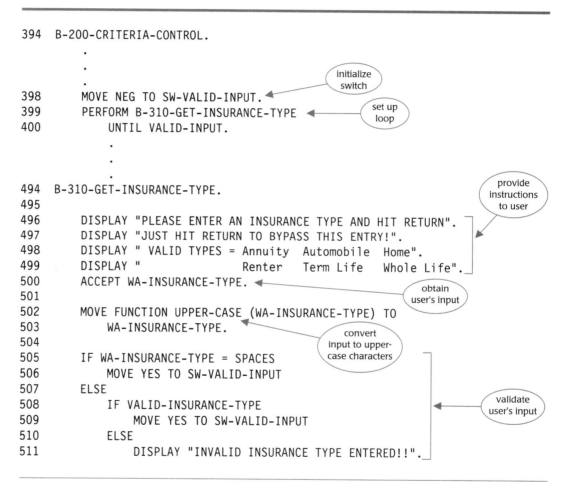

```
394   B-200-CRITERIA-CONTROL.
            .
            .
            .
398       MOVE NEG TO SW-VALID-INPUT.          ◄── initialize switch
399       PERFORM B-310-GET-INSURANCE-TYPE     ◄── set up loop
400          UNTIL VALID-INPUT.
            .
            .
            .
494   B-310-GET-INSURANCE-TYPE.                     provide instructions to user
495
496       DISPLAY "PLEASE ENTER AN INSURANCE TYPE AND HIT RETURN".
497       DISPLAY "JUST HIT RETURN TO BYPASS THIS ENTRY!".
498       DISPLAY " VALID TYPES = Annuity  Automobile   Home".
499       DISPLAY "                      Renter   Term Life   Whole Life".
500       ACCEPT WA-INSURANCE-TYPE.    ◄── obtain user's input
501
502       MOVE FUNCTION UPPER-CASE (WA-INSURANCE-TYPE) TO
503          WA-INSURANCE-TYPE.                convert input to upper-case characters
504
505       IF WA-INSURANCE-TYPE = SPACES
506          MOVE YES TO SW-VALID-INPUT
507       ELSE
508          IF VALID-INSURANCE-TYPE                 validate user's input
509             MOVE YES TO SW-VALID-INPUT
510          ELSE
511             DISPLAY "INVALID INSURANCE TYPE ENTERED!!".
```

FIGURE 6-23 Accepting selection criteria for insurance type

The condition name VALID-INSURANCE-TYPE is defined under the field WA-INSURANCE-TYPE on lines 168 through 173 in Figure 6-7 on page 6-7. If the entry is SPACES or one of the valid types, the letter Y, YES, is moved to SW-VALID-ENTRY making the condition name VALID-ENTRY true and, thus, terminating the loop. Processing then continues in B-200-CRITERIA-CONTROL.

Figure 6-24 on the next page presents the basic format of the **DISPLAY** statement. On most computer systems, the default output device is the user's terminal screen. Thus, the DISPLAY statement can be used to present information to the user and request special input data. If a field name follows the word DISPLAY, the contents of that field are displayed on the screen. If a literal follows the word DISPLAY, the literal is displayed on the screen. A combination of field names and literals can be listed within a DISPLAY statement. The UPON option can be used in conjunction with a name assigned to a remote location or device to cause the displayed items to display somewhere other than the user's terminal screen. Such a name would have to be defined in the SPECIAL-NAMES paragraph in the CONFIGURA-TION SECTION of the ENVIRONMENT DIVISION. The DISPLAY statements on lines 496 through 499 in B-310-GET-INSURANCE-TYPE present messages in the form of nonnumeric literals. These messages tell the user exactly what selection criterion is to be entered at this point in the program.

```
DISPLAY    {field-1  }   ...   [ UPON mnemonic-name-1 ]
           {literal-1 }
```

FIGURE 6-24   Basic format of the DISPLAY statement

The ACCEPT statement was presented in Chapter 4 and, as discussed there, is used to obtain data from a source outside the program. Previous programs used the ACCEPT statement to obtain the current date and time from the computer's operating system. The Customer Selection Report program uses it not only for the date and time, but also to obtain the selection criteria from the user. This format of the ACCEPT suspends the execution of the program and waits for a response. Data must be entered by the user via the terminal keyboard and then the ENTER key or RETURN key must be pressed. The program will then continue execution. The data entered will be moved to the field specified in the ACCEPT statement. The Customer Selection Report program validates this data and will continue to prompt over and over for a response by the user until a valid entry is made. In B-310-GET-INSURANCE-TYPE, the field name WA-INSURANCE-TYPE follows the word ACCEPT (line 500 of Figure 6-23 on the previous page). Thus, the field WA-INSURANCE-TYPE will contain the user's response. If no entry is made and the ENTER key is pressed, ACCEPT causes spaces to be moved to WA-INSURANCE-TYPE. In this program, spaces are considered to be a valid entry. Spaces in a criterion field indicate that the criterion is not to be used in the record selection process. Other than for the agent name, this same basic logic is used to obtain each of the selection criteria. Agent name is not validated due to the variety of entries available.

Selecting a Record

Once the selection criteria are entered, the process of determining which records, if any, satisfy the criteria begins. This process continues until every record in the file has been compared to the selection criteria. Figure 6-5 on page 6-5 presents a flowchart illustrating the record selection logic used in the Customer Selection Report program. Within the program, paragraph B-350-RELEASE-RECORDS (see Figure 6-17 on page 6-20) checks each selection criterion field to determine if an entry is present. If an entry is present, then the contents of the selection criterion field is compared to the appropriate field within PREMIUM-RECORD. When a mismatch is found, the contents of the field NEG, the letter N, is moved to the field SW-RELEASE-RECORD making the condition RELEASE-RECORD false (see lines 115 and 116 in Figure 6-7 on page 6-7). If an entry is not present, or if no mismatch is found, processing continues to the next sentence. The field SW-RELEASE-RECORD is initialized on line 593 of B-350-RELEASE-RECORDS, prior to comparing a record to the selection criteria.

In Figure 6-17, notice further use of the intrinsic function UPPER-CASE on lines 596 and 601 of B-350-RELEASE-RECORDS. It is used here to insure that the characters in the fields PR-AGENT-NAME and PR-INSURANCE-TYPE match the case of the characters in WA-AGENT-NAME and WA-INSURANCE-TYPE.

If a record satisfies all the selection criteria entered, or if all of the selection criteria are equal to spaces, the condition RELEASE-RECORD remains true and the record is accepted for the report by being released to SORT-FILE (see lines 616 and 617 of Figure 6-17). The next record in PREMIUM-INPUT-FILE is then read. Processing continues until the condition END-OF-FILE is true.

Some COBOL programmers prefer to minimize the use of switches in programs. The logic presented in Figure 6-17 can be coded in an alternative manner as illustrated by Figure 6-25. By using the THRU option on the PERFORM, an EXIT paragraph, putting a READ in a separate paragraph, and using GO TO statements to bypass instructions, the switch, SW-RELEASE-RECORD, can be eliminated from the program. The logic presented in Figures 6-17 and 6-25 produce equivalent results. Only the style is different. The style presented in Figure 6-17 is the preferred style in this book when multiple tests or filters are required. The Minimum Payment Report program presented in Chapter 5 used logic similar to that shown in Figure 6-25 to filter out PAID-IN-FULL customers (see lines 385-389 in Figure 5-4 on page 5-8).

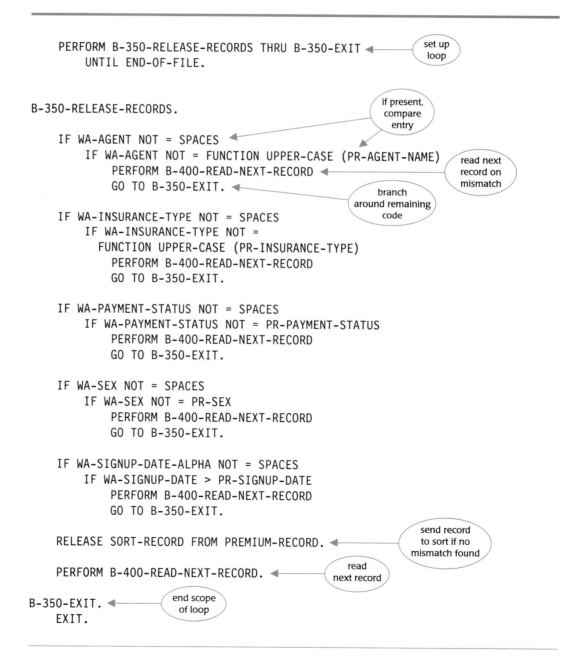

FIGURE 6-25 Alternative code for B-350-RELEASE-RECORDS

Multiple Reports on One Report File

As indicated earlier, once sorted, the records are written to the report in the specified OUTPUT PROCEDURE, B-220-WRITE-REPORT. B-220-WRITE-REPORT sets up the logic needed to loop through B-360-RETURN-RECORDS (see Figure 6-21 on page 6-23) until all of the selected records have been processed. Records are returned from SORT-FILE, fields are moved to DETAIL-LINE, and DETAIL-LINE is written to the report. The report logic used is comparable to the logic used in previous programs with minor modifications. In B-220-WRITE-REPORT, the page headings are forced to print prior to performing B-360-RETURN-RECORDS (see line 459 of Figure 6-19 on page 6-22). This is done to insure that every report, even ones with no selected records, have page headings. Within B-360-RETURN-RECORDS, headings are not printed again until the value of AC-LINE-COUNT exceeds 55 (see line 652 of Figure 6-21).

To produce multiple reports in one report file, CUSTOMER-SELECTION-REPORT, which is opened for OUTPUT in A-100-INITIALIZATION, is not closed until C-100-WRAP-UP is performed. C-100-WRAP-UP is not performed until the condition NO-MORE-REPORTS is true in MAIN-PROGRAM (Figure 6-26).

```
335  MAIN-PROGRAM.
336
337      PERFORM A-100-INITIALIZATION.
338      PERFORM B-100-PROCESS-FILE
339          UNTIL NO-MORE-REPORTS.
340      PERFORM C-100-WRAP-UP.
341      STOP RUN.
```

set up loop that executes until no more reports desired by user

FIGURE 6-26   MAIN-PROGRAM paragraph from the Customer Selection Report program

NO-MORE-REPORTS is true when SW-MORE-REPORTS contains an N (Figure 6-27). In A-100-INITIALIZATION, SW-MORE-REPORTS is initialized to a Y.

```
118      02  SW-MORE-REPORTS              PIC X.
119          88  NO-MORE-REPORTS                       VALUE "N".
```

FIGURE 6-27   Definition of SW-MORE-REPORTS

At the end of paragraph B-100-PROCESS-FILE, a loop created by an in-line PERFORM statement provides the user with an opportunity to enter an N into SW-MORE-REPORTS (Figure 6-28). Until the condition NO-MORE-REPORTS is true, the Customer Selection Report program continues prompting for selection criteria and producing reports based on those criteria. All output goes to the file CUSTOMER-SELECTION-REPORT. Because counter fields and the time are initialized for each set of criteria processed, each report starts with page 1 and has an updated time (see Figure 6-19).

```
368  B-100-PROCESS-FILE.
          .
          .
          .
377      MOVE NEG TO SW-VALID-INPUT.
378      PERFORM UNTIL VALID-INPUT
379          DISPLAY "WOULD YOU LIKE TO CREATE ANOTHER REPORT? Y/N "
380          ACCEPT SW-MORE-REPORTS
381          IF SW-MORE-REPORTS = YES OR NEG
382              MOVE YES TO SW-VALID-INPUT
383          ELSE
384              DISPLAY "ENTER Y FOR YES AND N FOR NO!"
385          END-IF
386      END-PERFORM.
```

FIGURE 6-28 Prompts for more reports in an in-line PERFORM

CHAPTER SUMMARY

The following list summarizes this chapter. The summary is designed to help you study and understand the material and concepts presented.

1. The COBOL **SORT** statement is used in the PROCEDURE DIVISION to rearrange the records of an input file.

2. The sort work file must be defined with a SELECT entry in the ENVIRONMENT DIVISION and an **SD** entry in the DATA DIVISION.

3. A record definition must follow the SD entry and must identify the position and size of the **sort key field** or fields.

4. Records may be sorted in either **ASCENDING** or **DESCENDING** sequence on the sort key field or fields.

5. Sort key fields must be listed most major to most minor in a SORT statement.

6. The **USING** option identifies the input file to the SORT.

7. **INPUT PROCEDURE** works like a PERFORM and can be used in place of the USING option when special processing of records is needed prior to the records being sorted.

8. The **RELEASE** statement works like a WRITE and is used in an INPUT PROCEDURE paragraph to place records in the sort work file.

9. The **GIVING** option identifies the file to be output by the SORT.

10. **OUTPUT PROCEDURE** works like a PERFORM and can be used in place of the GIVING option in a SORT when records are to be retrieved directly from the sort work file.

11. The **RETURN** statement works like a READ and is used in an OUTPUT PROCEDURE paragraph to retrieve records from the sort work file.

12. A **simple SORT** is coded utilizing the USING and GIVING options.

13. The COBOL **MERGE** statement allows multiple input files to be combined and sorted into a single output file.

(continued)

Chapter Summary (continued)

14. **Extract** or **record selection reports** list records based on selection criteria supplied by the user.

15. **DISPLAY** and ACCEPT statements can be used to set up interactive dialogues within COBOL programs.

16. Multiple reports can be listed on a single report file by opening the report file at the beginning of the program and closing it after all reports have been produced.

KEY TERMS
. . . .

ascending sequence (6-1)
descending sequence (6-2)
detail reports (6-2)
DISPLAY (6-25)
extract reports (6-2)
GIVING (6-14)
INPUT PROCEDURE (6-19)
major key (6-13)
MERGE (6-23)
merge work file (6-24)
minor key (6-13)
OUTPUT PROCEDURE (6-21)

record selection reports (6-2)
RELEASE (6-21)
RETURN (6-22)
SD (Sort Description) (6-11)
selection criteria (6-2)
simple SORT (6-14)
SORT (6-11)
Sort Description (SD) (6-11)
sort key field (6-12)
sort record (6-12)
sort work file (6-11)
USING (6-14)

STUDENT ASSIGNMENTS
. . . .

Student Assignment 1: True/False

Instructions: Circle T if the statement is true or F if the statement is false.

T F 1. A record selection report will always create a detail line for every record you READ.

T F 2. The DISPLAY statement can display the contents of a field.

T F 3. The DISPLAY statement can be used to display nonnumeric literals.

T F 4. A sort work file must be defined with SELECT and FD entries.

T F 5. Multiple sort keys can be identified in a SORT statement.

T F 6. The record definition following an SD must show the position and size of all sort key fields.

T F 7. USING and INPUT PROCEDURE can be used in the same SORT statement.

T F 8. GIVING is used to identify an output file.

T F 9. RELEASE can be used only within the scope of an INPUT PROCEDURE.

T F 10. RELEASE works like a READ statement.

T F 11. RETURN works like a READ statement.

T F 12. RETURN can be used only within the scope of an OUTPUT PROCEDURE.

T F 13. A simple SORT is coded using INPUT PROCEDURE with GIVING.

T F 14. In a batch mode, record selection criteria can be obtained through an input file created before the record selection program executes.

T F 15. The ACCEPT statement can be used to obtain user input in an interactive mode.

T F 16. In a SORT statement, multiple keys must be listed from most minor to most major.

T F 17. The name following the word SORT must be a sort work file defined with an SD entry.

T F 18. When the INPUT PROCEDURE option is used, the input file to the sort will automatically be opened and closed by the SORT statement.

T F 19. A MERGE statement allows for multiple input files.

T F 20. The INPUT PROCEDURE option cannot be used in a MERGE statement.

Student Assignment 2: Multiple Choice

Instructions: Circle the correct response.

1. Which of the following best describes a simple SORT?
   a. only one key can be used
   b. USING and GIVING are used
   c. two input files are used
   d. INPUT PROCEDURE and OUTPUT PROCEDURE are used
   e. all of the above describe a simple SORT

2. An INPUT PROCEDURE _____.
   a. is used to process records before they are sorted
   b. uses the RELEASE statement to send records to the sort work file
   c. cannot have a RETURN statement in it
   d. is optional and can be replaced with the USING option
   e. all of the above

3. An OUTPUT PROCEDURE _____.
   a. must use the RETURN statement to retrieve records from the sort work file
   b. cannot be used if the USING option is used in a SORT statement
   c. processes records before they are sorted
   d. must be used if the INPUT PROCEDURE option is used
   e. all the above

4. The RETURN statement _____.
   a. can be used only in an INPUT PROCEDURE
   b. can be used only in an OUTPUT PROCEDURE
   c. can be used in either an INPUT PROCEDURE or OUTPUT PROCEDURE
   d. works in a fashion similar to a WRITE statement
   e. none of the above

5. The RELEASE statement _____.
   a. can be used only in an INPUT PROCEDURE
   b. can be used only in an OUTPUT PROCEDURE
   c. can be used in either an INPUT PROCEDURE or OUTPUT PROCEDURE
   d. works in a fashion similar to a WRITE statement
   e. both a and d

(continued)

Student Assignment 2 (continued)

6. Sort key fields must be _____.
   a. defined in the record definition following the SD
   b. listed from most major to most minor in a SORT
   c. identified in a SORT statement
   d. sequenced in either ASCENDING or DESCENDING order
   e. all of the above

7. The DISPLAY statement can be used to _____.
   a. define fields that have usage of DISPLAY
   b. receive entries entered by the user
   c. stop the execution of a program
   d. show the contents of a field
   e. all of the above

8. A MERGE statement allows for _____.
   a. one input file and multiple output files
   b. multiple input files and one output file
   c. the use of an INPUT PROCEDURE and the RELEASE statement
   d. the use of GIVING and OUTPUT PROCEDURE in the same MERGE statement
   e. none of the above

9. A record selection report program _____.
   a. lists every record processed in the input file
   b. uses selection criteria to determine which records to list
   c. must contain a COBOL SORT
   d. requires that all selection criteria be entered into the program before it is compiled and executed
   e. none of the above

10. An ACCEPT statement _____.
    a. can be used to retrieve input data from a user
    b. has a format that will stop the execution of a program and wait for an entry
    c. will move spaces to a field if no entry is made
    d. all of the above
    e. none of the above

Student Assignment 3: Coding a DISPLAY Statement

Instructions: Code a DISPLAY statement that displays the message, "The Premium Amount for the current record is" followed by the field PR-PREMIUM-AMOUNT-EDITED.

Student Assignment 4: Coding a Simple SORT

Instructions: Given the following definitions, code a simple COBOL SORT statement that rearranges the records in descending order by Customer Identification. Use CUSTOMER-FILE as input and SORTED-CUSTOMER-FILE as output.

```
SD   SORT-FILE.

01   CUSTOMER-SORT-RECORD.
     02   CSR-CUSTOMER-IDENTIFICATION          PIC 9(5).
     02   CSR-LAST-NAME                        PIC X(14).
     02   CSR-FIRST-NAME                       PIC X(12).
     02                                        PIC X(49).
```

Student Assignment 5: Coding Another Simple SORT

Instructions: Using the SD and files named in Student Assignment 4, code a simple COBOL SORT that rearranges the records so that they are in ascending sequence by Last Name within ascending sequence of Customer Identification.

Student Assignment 6: Coding an INPUT PROCEDURE

Instructions: Given the following definitions, code an SD, sort record definition, and COBOL SORT. Use an INPUT PROCEDURE with the GIVING option in the SORT statement. Code all necessary logic for the INPUT PROCEDURE so it selects active customers for processing. Sort the records in ascending sequence by Last Name. Place the sorted records back into SORTED-CUSTOMER-FILE.

```
FD  CUSTOMER-FILE.

01  CUSTOMER-RECORD.
    02  CR-CUSTOMER-IDENTIFICATION        PIC 9(5).
    02  CR-LAST-NAME                      PIC X(14).
    02  CR-FIRST-NAME                     PIC X(12).
    02  CR-CUSTOMER-STATUS                PIC X.
        88  ACTIVE                        VALUE "A".
    02                                    PIC X(48).
```

Student Assignment 7: Coding an INPUT PROCEDURE and an OUTPUT PROCEDURE

Instructions: Given the following definitions, code an SD, sort record, and COBOL SORT. Use both an INPUT PROCEDURE and OUTPUT PROCEDURE in the SORT statement. Code the INPUT PROCEDURE and OUTPUT PROCEDURE paragraphs so customers who are not active are sorted in ascending sequence by Last Name and then have their Last Name, First Name, and Customer Identification displayed on the user's terminal.

```
FD  CUSTOMER-FILE.

01  CUSTOMER-RECORD.
    02  CR-CUSTOMER-IDENTIFICATION        PIC 9(5).
    02  CR-LAST-NAME                      PIC X(14).
    02  CR-FIRST-NAME                     PIC X(12).
    02  CR-CUSTOMER-STATUS                PIC X.
        88  ACTIVE                        VALUE "A".
    02                                    PIC X(48).
```

COBOL LABORATORY EXERCISES

Exercise 1: Modified Customer Selection Report Program

Purpose: To gain experience in COBOL program maintenance and modification.

Problem: Open the file PROJ6.CBL on the Student Diskette that accompanies this book and modify the Customer Selection Report program making the following changes:

(continued)

Exercise 1 (continued)

1. Replace the selection criteria for Insurance Type with an entry that uses the first two characters in the Policy Number field. Validate the criteria as it is entered. Use the following codes:

   AM = Automobile
   AN = Annuity
   HM = Home Insurance
   RT = Renter
   TL = Term Life
   WL = Whole Life

2. Sort the records in ascending sequence by Customer Name.

3. When listing the pertinent criteria as part of the heading routine, use the following entries for the Payment Status instead of the one-character code. Continue to use the code when entering the selection criteria.

   D = Delinquent   P = Partially Paid
   F = Paid in Full   N = Not Yet Billed

4. When no records match the selection criteria, print the message "NO RECORDS MATCH THE SELECTION CRITERIA" on the first line following the column headings.

Save this program as EX6-1.CBL.

Input Data: Use the Premium file presented in Appendix A as input. This file is named PREMIUM.DAT on the Student Diskette that accompanies this book.

Output Results: Output should be a report similar to the examples given at the beginning of the chapter but including the requested modifications. Run the modified program using the following selection criteria:

    Report 1: Agent   = Benson, Gloria
               Sex   = Female

    Report 2: Insurance Type = Automobile
               Payment Status = Paid in Full
               Signup Date   = Since 1994

    Report 3: Insurance Type = Renter
               Sex   = Male
               Signup Date   = Since 1990

    Report 4: Payment Status = Delinquent
               Sex   = Male

Exercise 2: Customer Purchases Selection Report Program

Purpose: To practice the use of the COBOL SORT statement and record selection processing in the creation of a COBOL program that produces a Customer Purchases Selection Report.

Problem: Write a program that lists specific Customer Purchase records for the ABC Department Store. For each report, enter selection criteria via the keyboard, print only those records that satisfy the entered criteria, and list the records in descending sequence by balance. Spaces entered for a selection criterion mean that the criterion is to be ignored.

Use the following selection criteria:

Field	Validation
Date of Purchase	Spaces or a six-character numeric entry in the format of MMDDYY; the month (MM) should be a value in the range of 1 to 12; the day (DD) should be a value in the range of 1 to 31; the year (YY) should be greater than 94. List all records with a Date of Purchase greater than or equal to the entered date. BE CAREFUL!
Account Number	Spaces or a six-character numeric entry in the range of 10000 to 500000. List all records with an Account Number greater than or equal to the one entered.
Item Purchased	No validation required. When not spaces, list purchases of just this item.
Minimum Quantity	Spaces or a one-character numeric entry greater than zero. List all records with a quantity greater than or equal to the one entered.
Maximum Quantity	Spaces or a one-character numeric entry greater than zero. List all records with a quantity less than or equal to the one entered.
Balance	Spaces or a six-character numeric entry treated as PIC 9(4)V99. List all records with a balance greater than or equal to the one entered. BE CAREFUL!

For each record listed, print the date of purchase, account number, customer name, item purchased, quantity purchased, balance, and purchase amount. Print the current date and time on every page. Time should be printed in AM/PM format. Number each page starting each report with page 1. At the end of each report print the total number of records processed, total number of records listed, and total balance.

Input Data: Use the Customer file listed in Appendix A as input. This file is named CUSTOMER.DAT on the Student Diskette that accompanies this book. Customer records have the following layout:

Field Description	Position	Length	Attribute
Date of Purchase	1–6	6	Numeric, PIC 9(6)
Account Number	7–12	6	Alphanumeric
Customer Name	13–32	20	Alphanumeric
Item Purchased	33–52	20	Alphanumeric
Quantity Purchased	53	1	Numeric, PIC 9
Balance	54–59	6	Numeric, PIC S9(4)V99
Purchase Amount	60–65	6	Numeric, PIC 9(4)V99
filler	66–72	7	Alphanumeric
Record Length		72	

(continued)

Exercise 2 (continued)

Use the following specific selection criteria to produce four reports:

Report 1: Purchase Date of 09/01/97;
Minimum Quantity of 3;

Report 2: Account Number of 200001;
Minimum Quantity of 4;
Maximum Quantity of 6;
Balance of $150.00;

Report 3: Purchase Date of 08/26/97;
Item GENERAL LEDGER CARDS;

Report 4: Account Number of 300000;
Balance of $200.00;

Save this program as EX6-2.CBL.

Output Results: Output consists of the Customer Purchases Selection Report listing the date of purchase, account number, customer name, item purchased, quantity purchased, balance, and purchase amount for each customer satisfying the selection criteria entered by the user. Double-space between records. Count and print the number of records processed, the number of records listed, and the total balance. List pertinent selection criteria above the column headings. Do not list selection criteria for which spaces were entered.

The report should have a format similar to the following:

```
DATE: Z9/99/99                    ABC DEPARTMENT STORE                    PAGE Z9
TIME: Z9:99 AM               CUSTOMER PURCHASES SELECTION REPORT


Selection Criteria:  xxxxxxxxxx
                     xxxxxxxxxx

DATE OF   ACCOUNT                                                 PURCHASE
PURCHASE  NUMBER  CUSTOMER NAME         ITEM PURCHASED      QTY  BALANCE     AMOUNT
--------  ------- --------------------  --------------------  ---  ---------   ---------

Z9/99/99  XXXXXX  XXXXXXXXXXXXXXXXXXXX  XXXXXXXXXXXXXXXXXXXX   9   $$,$$$.99-  $$,$$$.99

Z9/99/99  XXXXXX  XXXXXXXXXXXXXXXXXXXX  XXXXXXXXXXXXXXXXXXXX   9   $$,$$$.99-  $$,$$$.99

   .
   .
   .


              RECORDS PROCESSED  =     ZZ9
              RECORDS LISTED     =     ZZ9
              TOTAL BALANCE      =  ZZ,ZZ9.99

                     END OF REPORT
```

Exercise 3: Customer Sales Selection Report Program

Purpose: To practice coding a COBOL program that uses the COBOL SORT and record selection logic.

Problem: Design and code a COBOL program that processes the records of the Customer Sales file for EZ Auto Sales and creates a Customer Sales Selection Report. The report should list the customer's number, name, zip code, purchase date, auto purchased, purchase price, and satisfaction rating. Include the current date and time in the page headings. Use AM/PM format for the time. At the end of the report, provide summary lines for a record count and total purchases. Records should be listed in descending sequence by purchase price.

Process only those records that satisfy selection criteria entered by the user via the keyboard. Spaces entered for a selection criteria mean that criteria is to be ignored. The selection criteria used will be:

Field	Validation
Zip Code	Spaces or a five-character numeric entry greater than 10000 but less than 96000. List all records with a zip code equal to the one entered.
Customer Number	Spaces or a four-character numeric entry. List all records with customer numbers greater than or equal to the number entered.
Purchase Date	Spaces or a six-character numeric date in the form of MMDDYY. The month (MM) should be a value in the range of 1 to 12; the day (DD) should be a value in the range of 1 to 31; the year (YY) should be greater than 94. Process all records with a purchase date greater than or equal to the entered date. BE CAREFUL!
Auto Purchased	No validation. When not spaces, list records with sales of autos of this make.
Purchase Price	Spaces or a seven-character numeric entry in the form of PIC 9(5)V99. List records with purchase prices greater than or equal to the amount entered.
Auto Year	Spaces or a four-digit entry in the range 1901 to 1999. List records with auto years greater than or equal to the entered year.
Satisfaction Code	Spaces or a 0, 1, or 2. List records having the entered satisfaction code.

Save this program as EX6-3.CBL.

Input Data: Use the Customer Sales file listed in Appendix A as input. This file is named CUSTSALE.DAT on the Student Diskette that accompanies this book. The record layout for the customer records is as follows:

Field Description	Position	Length	Attribute
Customer Zip Code	1–5	5	Alphanumeric
Customer Zip + 4	6–9	4	Alphanumeric
Customer Number	10–13	4	Alphanumeric
Customer Name	14–33	20	Alphanumeric
Purchase Date	34–39	6	Numeric, PIC 9(6)
Auto Make	40–59	20	Alphanumeric
Purchase Price	60–66	7	Numeric, PIC 9(5)V99
Year of Auto	67–70	4	Alphanumeric
filler	71–73	3	Alphanumeric
Satisfaction Code	74	1	Alphanumeric, 0 = DISSATISFIED 1 = UNDECIDED 2 = SATISFIED
Record Length		74	

(continued)

Exercise 3 (continued)

Use the following specific selection criteria to produce four reports:

Report 1:	Zip Code of 46410; Purchase Price of $3000.00; Satisfaction Code of 2;
Report 2:	Auto Make of Ford; Auto Year of 1990;
Report 3:	Customer Number of 3050; Purchase Date of 090197; Satisfaction Code of 1;
Report 4:	Purchase Date of 082997; Auto Make of CHEVROLET; Purchase Price of $2000.00; Satisfaction Code of 0;

Output Results: A Customer Sales Selection Report should be output listing the customer's number, name, zip code, purchase date, auto make, purchase price, and satisfaction rating. List record in descending sequence by purchase price. Provide a count of the number of customers listed and total sum of purchases. Double-space the records on the report and list the current date and time in the headings. The time should be in AM/PM format. List pertinent selection criteria prior to the column headings. Do not list nonpertinent selection criteria. The report should have a format similar to the following:

```
DATE: Z9/99/99                   EZ AUTO SALES                        PAGE Z9
TIME: Z9:99 AM              CUSTOMER SALES SELECTION REPORT

SELECTION CRITERIA: XXXXXXXXXX
                    XXXXXXXXXX

CUSTOMER CUSTOMER              ZIP   PURCHASE                    PURCHASE   SATIS.
NUMBER   NAME                  CODE  DATE     AUTO MAKE          PRICE      RATING
-------- -------------------- ----- -------- -------------------- ---------- --------

  XXXX   XXXXXXXXXXXXXXXXXXXX  XXXXX Z9/99/99 XXXXXXXXXXXXXXXXXXXX $$$,$$$.99 XXXXXXXX

  XXXX   XXXXXXXXXXXXXXXXXXXX  XXXXX Z9/99/99 XXXXXXXXXXXXXXXXXXXX $$$,$$$.99 XXXXXXXX

  XXXX   XXXXXXXXXXXXXXXXXXXX  XXXXX Z9/99/99 XXXXXXXXXXXXXXXXXXXX $$$,$$$.99 XXXXXXXX

   .
   .
   .

                    TOTAL CUSTOMERS LISTED =    ZZ9
                    TOTAL PURCHASES        = ZZZ,ZZ9.99

                            END OF REPORT
```

CHAPTER SEVEN

Tables, Table Processing, and Control Breaks

OBJECTIVES

You will have mastered the material in Chapter 7 when you can:

- Define a one-dimensional embedded table

- Define a one-dimensional non-embedded table

- Understand what it means to load a non-embedded table

- Understand the difference between a subscript and an index

- Code a SEARCH statement for a one-dimensional table

- Code a SEARCH ALL statement for a one-dimensional table

- Define multi-dimensional tables

- Understand the logic required for control break processing

INTRODUCTION

The COBOL language provides the capability to process data stored in lists of adjacent data fields with similar characteristics. These lists are known as **arrays** in many programming languages, but in COBOL they are called **tables**. Tables come in many different shapes and sizes. The logic involving the techniques for defining and processing tables is called **table processing**.

In many of the programs presented thus far in this book, the data from records read from input files was formatted in the output areas, one or more calculations or comparisons were made, and a line was printed to a report. As indicated in Chapter 6, such reports are called detail reports. In many business applications, it is necessary to print intermediate information generated from the detail processing, such as totals and/or subtotals. When detail lines are omitted and only totals and subtotals are printed, the report created is said to be a **summary report**. The printing of intermediate information along with detail lines is known as **control break processing** and requires special logic in a COBOL program.

The Agent Subtotal Report

Figure 7-1 presents a partial listing of the Agent Subtotal Report. The report lists all the customers of a specific insurance agent, lists a subtotal premium amount for these customers, and then lists the customers for the next agent. A company total prints at the end of the report after the subtotal for the customers of the last agent. Other elements of the report will be discussed later in this chapter.

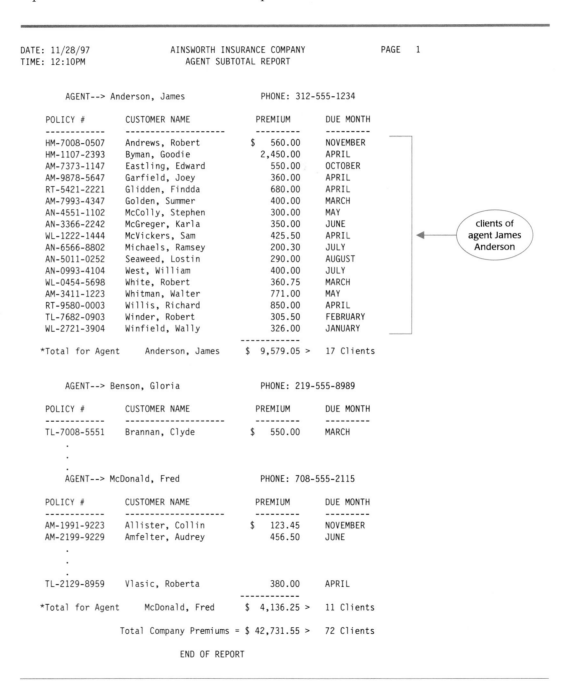

```
DATE: 11/28/97              AINSWORTH INSURANCE COMPANY           PAGE   1
TIME: 12:10PM                  AGENT SUBTOTAL REPORT


     AGENT--> Anderson, James            PHONE: 312-555-1234

     POLICY #        CUSTOMER NAME          PREMIUM      DUE MONTH
     ------------    --------------------   ---------    ---------
     HM-7008-0507    Andrews, Robert        $   560.00   NOVEMBER
     HM-1107-2393    Byman, Goodie            2,450.00   APRIL
     AM-7373-1147    Eastling, Edward           550.00   OCTOBER
     AM-9878-5647    Garfield, Joey             360.00   APRIL
     RT-5421-2221    Glidden, Findda            680.00   APRIL
     AM-7993-4347    Golden, Summer             400.00   MARCH
     AN-4551-1102    McColly, Stephen           300.00   MAY
     AN-3366-2242    McGreger, Karla            350.00   JUNE
     WL-1222-1444    McVickers, Sam             425.50   APRIL
     AN-6566-8802    Michaels, Ramsey           200.30   JULY
     AN-5011-0252    Seaweed, Lostin            290.00   AUGUST
     AN-0993-4104    West, William              400.00   JULY
     WL-0454-5698    White, Robert              360.75   MARCH
     AM-3411-1223    Whitman, Walter            771.00   MAY
     RT-9580-0003    Willis, Richard            850.00   APRIL
     TL-7682-0903    Winder, Robert             305.50   FEBRUARY
     WL-2721-3904    Winfield, Wally            326.00   JANUARY
                                            ------------
     *Total for Agent    Anderson, James   $ 9,579.05 >   17 Clients


        AGENT--> Benson, Gloria          PHONE: 219-555-8989

     POLICY #        CUSTOMER NAME          PREMIUM      DUE MONTH
     ------------    --------------------   ---------    ---------
     TL-7008-5551    Brannan, Clyde         $   550.00   MARCH
        .
        .
        .
        AGENT--> McDonald, Fred           PHONE: 708-555-2115

     POLICY #        CUSTOMER NAME          PREMIUM      DUE MONTH
     ------------    --------------------   ---------    ---------
     AM-1991-9223    Allister, Collin       $   123.45   NOVEMBER
     AM-2199-9229    Amfelter, Audrey           456.50   JUNE
        .
        .
        .
     TL-2129-8959    Vlasic, Roberta            380.00   APRIL
                                            ------------
     *Total for Agent    McDonald, Fred    $ 4,136.25 >   11 Clients

                    Total Company Premiums = $ 42,731.55 >   72 Clients

                         END OF REPORT
```

clients of agent James Anderson

FIGURE 7-1 Partial listing of the Agent Subtotal Report

Hierarchy Chart

The organization of the PROCEDURE DIVISION of the Agent Subtotal Report program is illustrated by the hierarchy chart in Figure 7-2. As discussed in earlier chapters, the rectangles with shaded corners represent paragraphs that are performed in more than one location and in more than one paragraph within the program.

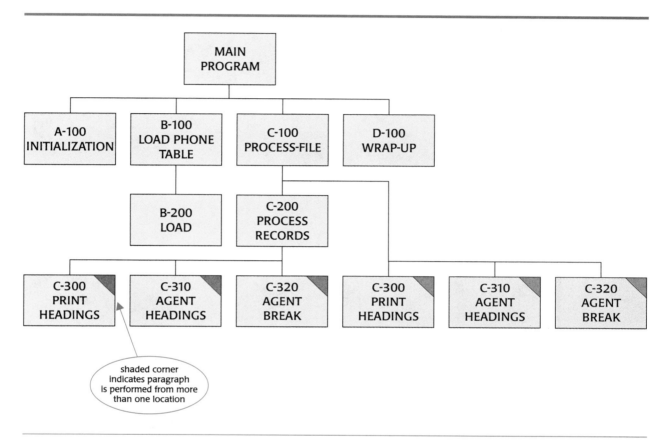

FIGURE 7-2   Hierarchy chart illustrating the organization of the PROCEDURE DIVISION of the Agent Subtotal Report program

Program Flowchart

A flowchart illustrating the control break logic used in the Agent Subtotal Report program is presented in Figure 7-3 on the next page. This logic will be examined later in the chapter. Every control break program utilizes similar logic.

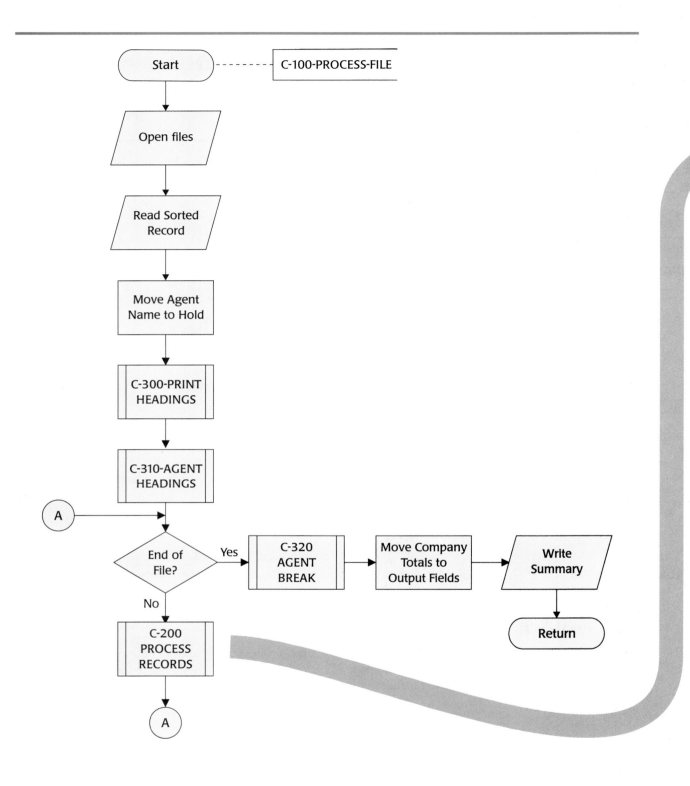

FIGURE 7-3 Flowchart showing the control break logic used in C-100-PROCESS-FILE and C-200-PROCESS-RECORDS in the Agent Subtotal Report program

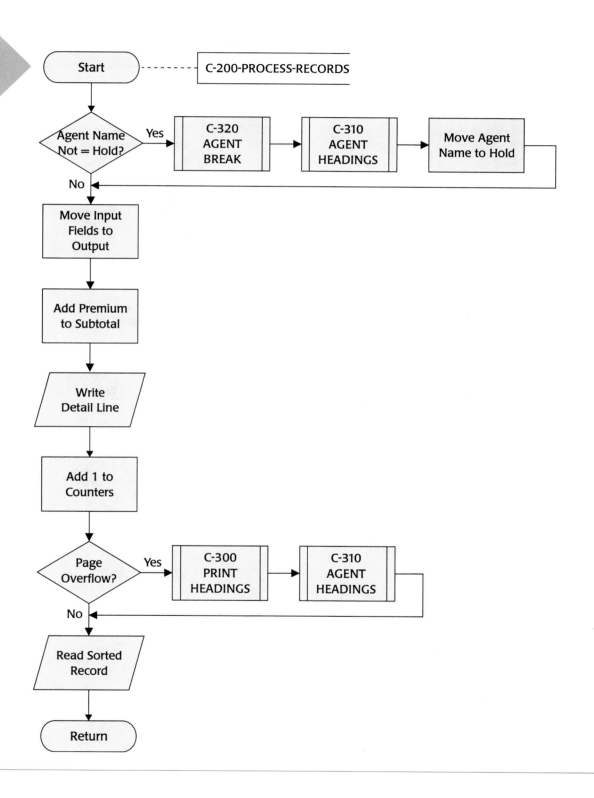

Premium File Record Layout

A field not utilized in the previous chapter is now defined in the record layout for the Premium file (Figure 7-4). The customer's Premium Due Month is used in the sample program where it is translated into a month name that is listed on the report. In the previous chapters, this field was included as part of a filler entry at the end of the record layout.

Field	Position	Length	Attribute
Customer Name	1–20	20	Alphanumeric
Agent Name	21–40	20	Alphanumeric
Insurance Type	41–50	10	Alphanumeric
Policy Number	51–62	12	Alphanumeric
Premium Amount	63–69	7	Numeric
Payment Status	70	1	Alphanumeric
Gender	71	1	Alphanumeric
Signup Date	72–75	4	Numeric
Premium Due Month	76–77	2	Numeric
unused	78–80	3	Alphanumeric
Total Record Length		80	

FIGURE 7-4   Record layout for the Premium file

The Agent Subtotal Report Program

Figure 7-5 presents the Agent Subtotal Report program. This program is found on the Student Diskette that accompanies this book. Within the program, the Premium file is used as input to a simple SORT that arranges the records by agent name and outputs a sorted Premium file. The sorted Premium file is then used as input to the report portion of the program. A COBOL table is used to translate a two-digit number representing the insurance renewal month into a named month. Another COBOL table is used to supply a telephone number for each agent listed.

```
 1  IDENTIFICATION DIVISION.
 2  ************************
 3
 4  PROGRAM-ID.     AGENTSUB.
 5  AUTHOR.         R. O. FOREMAN.
 6  INSTALLATION.   PURDUE UNIVERSITY CALUMET.
 7  DATE-WRITTEN.   NOV. 28, 1997.
 8  DATE-COMPILED.  28-Nov-97.
 9  ********************************************************************
10  *                   PROGRAM NARRATIVE                             *
11  *                                                                 *
12  *                                                                 *
13  *    THIS PROGRAM PRINTS THE ACCOUNT NUMBER, CUSTOMER NAME, AND   *
14  *    PREMIUM AMOUNT FOR EACH CUSTOMER IN SEQUENCE BY AGENT NAME.  *
15  *    A TOTAL PREMIUM AMOUNT IS PRINTED FOR EACH AGENT ALONG WITH  *
16  *    WITH A TOTAL COMPANY PREMIUM AMOUNT AT THE END OF THE        *
17  *    REPORT.  A SIMPLE SORT IS USED TO REARRANGE THE FILE BY      *
18  *    AGENT NAME AND A TABLE IS USED TO SUPPLY THE AGENT TELEPHONE *
19  *    NUMBER FOR THE AGENT HEADING LINE.                           *
20  *                                                                 *
21  *       INPUT:      PREMIUM.DAT - PREMIUM INPUT FILE              *
22  *                                                                 *
23  *       OUTPUT:     AGNTSUB.RPT - AGENT SUBTOTAL REPORT           *
24  ********************************************************************
25
26  ENVIRONMENT DIVISION.
27  *********************
28
29  INPUT-OUTPUT SECTION.
30  *********************
31
32  FILE-CONTROL.
33
34      SELECT PREMIUM-INPUT-FILE
35          ASSIGN TO "A:\PREMIUM.DAT".
36
37      SELECT SORT-FILE
38          ASSIGN TO "SORTWORK".
39
40      SELECT SORTED-PREMIUM-FILE
41          ASSIGN TO "SORTPREM.DAT".
42
43      SELECT AGENT-PHONE-FILE
44          ASSIGN TO "A:\AGENTPHO.DAT".
45
46      SELECT AGENT-SUBTOTAL-REPORT
47          ASSIGN TO "A:\AGENTSUB.RPT".
48
```

FIGURE 7-5   Agent Subtotal Report program

```
 49 /
 50  DATA DIVISION.
 51  **************
 52
 53  FILE SECTION.
 54  **************
 55
 56  **************************************************************
 57  *                                                            *
 58  *      INPUT-FILE - PREMIUM INPUT FILE                       *
 59  *      THE RECORD LAYOUT, PREMIUM-RECORD, IS IN WORKING-STORAGE *
 60  *                                                            *
 61  **************************************************************
 62
 63  FD  PREMIUM-INPUT-FILE.
 64
 65  01  PREMIUM-INPUT-RECORD          PIC X(80).
 66
 67  **************************************************************
 68  *                                                            *
 69  *      SORT-FILE - FOR SORTING THE PREMIUM FILE BY AGENT NAME *
 70  *                                                            *
 71  **************************************************************
 72
 73  SD  SORT-FILE.
 74
 75  01  SORT-RECORD.
 76      02                           PIC X(20).
 77      02  SR-AGENT-NAME            PIC X(20).
 78      02                           PIC X(40).
 79
 80  **************************************************************
 81  *                                                            *
 82  *      SORTED INPUT-FILE - SORTED PREMIUM FILE               *
 83  *                                                            *
 84  **************************************************************
 85
 86  FD  SORTED-PREMIUM-FILE.
 87
 88  01  SORTED-PREMIUM-RECORD         PIC X(80).
 89
 90
 91  **************************************************************
 92  *                                                            *
 93  *      AGENT PHONE NUMBER FILE FOR LOADING NON-EMBEDDED TABLE *
 94  *                                                            *
 95  **************************************************************
 96
 97  FD  AGENT-PHONE-FILE.
 98
 99  01  AGENT-PHONE-RECORD.
100      02  APR-NAME                 PIC X(20).
101      02  APR-NUMBER               PIC X(12).
102
103
104  **************************************************************
105  *                                                            *
106  *      REPORT-FILE - AGENT SUBTOTAL REPORT                   *
107  *                                                            *
108  **************************************************************
109
110  FD  AGENT-SUBTOTAL-REPORT.
111
112  01  REPORT-LINE-OUT              PIC X(80).
113
114
115 /
116  WORKING-STORAGE SECTION.
117  ***********************
118
119  **************************************************************
120  *                                                            *
121  *                    SWITCHES                                *
122  *                                                            *
123  **************************************************************
124
125  01  SWITCHES.
126
127      02  SW-END-OF-FILE           PIC X.
128          88  END-OF-FILE                    VALUE "Y".
129
130  01  VALUES-FOR-SWITCHES.
131      02  YES                      PIC X      VALUE "Y".
132      02  NEG                      PIC X      VALUE "N".
133
134  **************************************************************
135  *                                                            *
136  *                 ACCUMULATORS                               *
137  *                                                            *
138  **************************************************************
139
140  01  ACCUMULATORS.
141
142      02  AC-LINE-COUNT            PIC 999      PACKED-DECIMAL.
143      02  AC-PAGE-COUNT            PIC 999      PACKED-DECIMAL.
144      02  AC-RECORD-COUNT          PIC 9(5)     PACKED-DECIMAL.
145      02  AC-AGENT-RECORD-COUNT    PIC 9(5)     PACKED-DECIMAL.
146      02  AC-PREMIUM-TOTAL         PIC 9(7)V99  PACKED-DECIMAL.
147      02  AC-AGENT-PREMIUM-SUBTOTAL PIC 9(6)V99 PACKED-DECIMAL.
148 /
149  **************************************************************
150  *                                                            *
151  *                 WORK AREA FIELDS                           *
152  *                                                            *
153  **************************************************************
154
155  01  WORK-AREA.
156
157      02  WA-SYSTEM-DATE.
158          03  WA-SYSTEM-YEAR       PIC 99.
159          03  WA-SYSTEM-MONTH      PIC 99.
160          03  WA-SYSTEM-DAY        PIC 99.
161
162      02  WA-CURRENT-DATE.
163          03  WA-CURRENT-MONTH     PIC 99.
164          03  WA-CURRENT-DAY       PIC 99.
165          03  WA-CURRENT-YEAR      PIC 99.
166
167      02  WA-CURRENT-DATE-N REDEFINES
168          WA-CURRENT-DATE          PIC 9(6).
169
170      02  WA-SYSTEM-TIME.
171          03  WA-SYSTEM-HOUR       PIC 99.
172          03  WA-SYSTEM-MINUTES    PIC 99.
173          03                       PIC 9(4).
174
175      02  WA-HOLD-AGENT-NAME       PIC X(20).
176
177 /
178  **************************************************************
179  *                                                            *
180  *            EMBEDDED MONTH NAME TABLE                       *
181  *                                                            *
182  **************************************************************
183
184  01  MONTH-NAME-DATA.
185      02                           PIC X(9) VALUE "JANUARY".
186      02                           PIC X(9) VALUE "FEBRUARY".
187      02                           PIC X(9) VALUE "MARCH".
188      02                           PIC X(9) VALUE "APRIL".
189      02                           PIC X(9) VALUE "MAY".
190      02                           PIC X(9) VALUE "JUNE".
191      02                           PIC X(9) VALUE "JULY".
192      02                           PIC X(9) VALUE "AUGUST".
193      02                           PIC X(9) VALUE "SEPTEMBER".
194      02                           PIC X(9) VALUE "OCTOBER".
195      02                           PIC X(9) VALUE "NOVEMBER".
196      02                           PIC X(9) VALUE "DECEMBER".
197
```

(continued)

```
198  01  MONTH-NAME-TABLE REDEFINES MONTH-NAME-DATA.
199      02  MNT-ENTRY                    OCCURS 12 TIMES.
200          03  MNT-NAME                 PIC X(9).
201
202  *******************************************************************
203  *                                                                 *
204  *              NON-EMBEDDED AGENT PHONE NUMBER TABLE               *
205  *                                                                 *
206  *                                                                 *
207  *******************************************************************
208
209  01  AGENT-PHONE-TABLE.
210      02  APT-ENTRY                    OCCURS 6 TIMES
211                                       INDEXED BY PHONE-INDEX.
212          03  APT-NAME                         PIC X(20).
213          03  APT-NUMBER                       PIC X(12).
214
215 /
216  *******************************************************************
217  *                                                                 *
218  *                 PREMIUM FILE RECORD LAYOUT                       *
219  *                                                                 *
220  *******************************************************************
221
222  01  PREMIUM-RECORD.
223      02  PR-CUSTOMER-NAME         PIC X(20).
224      02  PR-AGENT-NAME            PIC X(20).
225      02  PR-INSURANCE-TYPE        PIC X(10).
226      02  PR-POLICY-NUMBER         PIC X(12).
227      02  PR-PREMIUM-AMOUNT        PIC S9(5)V99.
228      02  PR-PAYMENT-STATUS        PIC X.
229          88  DELINQUENT               VALUE "D".
230          88  PAID-IN-FULL             VALUE "F".
231          88  PARTIALLY-PAID           VALUE "P".
232          88  NOT-YET-BILLED           VALUE "N".
233      02  PR-SEX                   PIC X.
234          88  MALE                     VALUE "M".
235          88  FEMALE                   VALUE "F".
236      02  PR-SIGNUP-DATE           PIC 9(4).
237      02  PR-PREMIUM-DUE-MONTH     PIC 99.
238      02                           PIC XXX.
239 /
240  *******************************************************************
241  *                                                                 *
242  *          REPORT HEADINGS FOR AGENT SUBTOTAL REPORT              *
243  *                                                                 *
244  *******************************************************************
245
246  01  REPORT-HEADING.
247
248      02  RH-LINE-1.
249          03                       PIC X(6)  VALUE "DATE: ".
250          03  RH-DATE              PIC Z9/99/99.
251          03                       PIC X(16) VALUE SPACES.
252          03                       PIC X(27) VALUE
253              "AINSWORTH INSURANCE COMPANY".
254          03                       PIC X(15) VALUE SPACES.
255          03                       PIC X(5)  VALUE "PAGE ".
256          03  RH-PAGE-COUNT        PIC ZZ9.
257
258      02  RH-LINE-2.
259          03                       PIC X(6)  VALUE "TIME: ".
260          03  RH-HOUR              PIC Z9.
261          03                       PIC X     VALUE ":".
262          03  RH-MINUTES           PIC 99.
263          03  RH-AM-PM             PIC XX.
264          03                       PIC X(20) VALUE SPACES.
265          03                       PIC X(21) VALUE
266              "AGENT SUBTOTAL REPORT".
267          03                       PIC X(26) VALUE SPACES.
268
269      02  RH-LINE-3.
270          03                       PIC X(9)  VALUE SPACES.
271          03                       PIC X(9)  VALUE
272              "AGENT--> ".
```

```
273          03  RH-AGENT-NAME        PIC X(20).
274          03                       PIC X(10) VALUE SPACES.
275          03                       PIC X(7)  VALUE "PHONE:".
276          03  RH-AGENT-PHONE       PIC X(12).
277          03                       PIC X(13) VALUE SPACES.
278 /
279      02  RH-LINE-4.
280          03                       PIC X(5)  VALUE SPACES.
281          03                       PIC X(8)  VALUE
282              "POLICY #".
283          03                       PIC X(8)  VALUE SPACES.
284          03                       PIC X(13) VALUE
285              "CUSTOMER NAME".
286          03                       PIC X(13) VALUE SPACES.
287          03                       PIC X(7)  VALUE
288              "PREMIUM".
289          03                       PIC X(7)  VALUE SPACES.
290          03                       PIC X(9)  VALUE
291              "DUE MONTH".
292          03                       PIC X(10) VALUE SPACES.
293
294      02  RH-LINE-5.
295          03                       PIC X(5)  VALUE SPACES.
296          03                       PIC X(12) VALUE ALL "-".
297          03                       PIC X(4)  VALUE SPACES.
298          03                       PIC X(20) VALUE ALL "-".
299          03                       PIC X(6)  VALUE SPACES.
300          03                       PIC X(9)  VALUE ALL "-".
301          03                       PIC X(5)  VALUE SPACES.
302          03                       PIC X(9)  VALUE ALL "-".
303          03                       PIC X(10) VALUE SPACES.
304
305  *******************************************************************
306  *                                                                 *
307  *        DETAIL LINE FOR THE AGENT SUBTOTAL REPORT                *
308  *                                                                 *
309  *******************************************************************
310
311  01  DETAIL-LINE.
312
313      02                           PIC X(5)  VALUE SPACES.
314      02  DL-POLICY-NUMBER         PIC X(12).
315      02                           PIC X(4)  VALUE SPACES.
316      02  DL-CUSTOMER-NAME         PIC X(20).
317      02                           PIC X(5)  VALUE SPACES.
318      02  DL-DOLLAR-SIGN           PIC X.
319      02  DL-PREMIUM-AMOUNT        PIC ZZ,ZZ9.99.
320      02                           PIC X(5)  VALUE SPACES.
321      02  DL-DUE-MONTH             PIC X(9).
322      02                           PIC X(10) VALUE SPACES.
323 /
324  *******************************************************************
325  *                                                                 *
326  *        SUMMARY LINES FOR THE SUBTOTAL REPORT                    *
327  *                                                                 *
328  *******************************************************************
329
330  01  SUMMARY-LINES.
331
332      02  SL-UNDERLINE.
333          03                       PIC X(44) VALUE SPACES.
334          03                       PIC X(12) VALUE ALL "-".
335          03                       PIC X(24) VALUE SPACES.
336
337      02  SL-AGENT-TOTAL.
338          03                       PIC X(4)  VALUE SPACES.
339          03                       PIC X(21) VALUE
340              "*Total for Agent   ".
341          03  SL-AGENT-NAME        PIC X(20).
342          03  SL-AGENT-PREMIUM-TOTAL  PIC $ZZZ,ZZ9.99.
343          03                       PIC XX  VALUE
344              " >".
345          03  SL-AGENT-RECORD-COUNT   PIC ZZZZ9.
346          03                       PIC X(8)  VALUE
347              " Clients".
348          03                       PIC X(9)  VALUE SPACES.
```

FIGURE 7-5   Agent Subtotal Report program (continued)

```
349
350      02  SL-COMPANY-TOTAL.
351          03                          PIC X(20) VALUE SPACES.
352          03                          PIC X(25) VALUE
353              "Total Company Premiums = ".
354          03  SL-COMPANY-PREMIUM-TOTAL  PIC $ZZZ,ZZ9.99.
355          03                          PIC XX    VALUE
356              " >".
357          03  SL-COMPANY-RECORD-COUNT  PIC ZZZZ9.
358          03                          PIC X(8)  VALUE
359              " Clients".
360          03                          PIC X(9)  VALUE SPACES.
361
362      02  SL-END-OF-REPORT.
363          03                          PIC X(32) VALUE SPACES.
364          03                          PIC X(13) VALUE
365              "END OF REPORT".
366          03                          PIC X(35) VALUE SPACES.
367 /
368  PROCEDURE DIVISION.
369  ******************
370  **********************************************************************
371  *                                                                    *
372  *  MAIN-PROGRAM - THIS IS THE MAIN ROUTINE OF THE AGENT SUBTOTAL     *
373  *                  REPORT PROGRAM                                    *
374  *                                                                    *
375  **********************************************************************
376
377  MAIN-PROGRAM.
378
379      PERFORM A-100-INITIALIZATION.
380      PERFORM B-100-LOAD-PHONE-TABLE.
381      PERFORM C-100-PROCESS-FILE.
382      PERFORM D-100-WRAP-UP.
383      STOP RUN.
384
385  **********************************************************************
386  *                                                                    *
387  *               THE INITIALIZATION ROUTINE FOLLOWS                   *
388  *                                                                    *
389  **********************************************************************
390
391  A-100-INITIALIZATION.
392
393      INITIALIZE ACCUMULATORS.
394
395      ACCEPT WA-SYSTEM-DATE FROM DATE.
396      MOVE WA-SYSTEM-YEAR    TO WA-CURRENT-YEAR.
397      MOVE WA-SYSTEM-MONTH   TO WA-CURRENT-MONTH.
398      MOVE WA-SYSTEM-DAY     TO WA-CURRENT-DAY.
399      MOVE WA-CURRENT-DATE-N TO RH-DATE.
400
401      ACCEPT WA-SYSTEM-TIME FROM TIME.
402      EVALUATE TRUE
403          WHEN WA-SYSTEM-HOUR = 00
404              MOVE "AM" TO RH-AM-PM
405              MOVE 12 TO RH-HOUR
406          WHEN WA-SYSTEM-HOUR < 12
407              MOVE "AM" TO RH-AM-PM
408              MOVE WA-SYSTEM-HOUR TO RH-HOUR
409          WHEN WA-SYSTEM-HOUR = 12
410              MOVE "PM" TO RH-AM-PM
411              MOVE WA-SYSTEM-HOUR TO RH-HOUR
412          WHEN WA-SYSTEM-HOUR > 12
413              MOVE "PM" TO RH-AM-PM
414              COMPUTE RH-HOUR = WA-SYSTEM-HOUR - 12.
415      MOVE WA-SYSTEM-MINUTES TO RH-MINUTES.
416
417      SORT SORT-FILE
418          ON ASCENDING KEY SR-AGENT-NAME
419          USING PREMIUM-INPUT-FILE
420          GIVING SORTED-PREMIUM-FILE.
421
422 /
```

```
423  **********************************************************************
424  *                                                                    *
425  *           TABLE LOADING ROUTINE                                    *
426  *                                                                    *
427  **********************************************************************
428
429  B-100-LOAD-PHONE-TABLE.
430
431      OPEN INPUT AGENT-PHONE-FILE.
432
433      READ AGENT-PHONE-FILE
434          AT END MOVE YES TO SW-END-OF-FILE.
435
436      PERFORM B-200-LOAD
437          VARYING PHONE-INDEX FROM 1 BY 1
438          UNTIL END-OF-FILE OR PHONE-INDEX > 6.
439
440      CLOSE AGENT-PHONE-FILE.
441
442  **********************************************************************
443  *                                                                    *
444  *          MOVE PHONE FILE DATA TO PHONE TABLE                       *
445  *                                                                    *
446  **********************************************************************
447
448  B-200-LOAD.
449
450      MOVE APR-NAME TO APT-NAME (PHONE-INDEX).
451      MOVE APR-NUMBER TO APT-NUMBER (PHONE-INDEX).
452
453      READ AGENT-PHONE-FILE
454          AT END MOVE YES TO SW-END-OF-FILE.
455
456 /
457  **********************************************************************
458  *                                                                    *
459  *              REPORT PROCESSING ROUTINE                             *
460  *                                                                    *
461  **********************************************************************
462
463  C-100-PROCESS-FILE.
464
465      OPEN   INPUT    SORTED-PREMIUM-FILE
466             OUTPUT   AGENT-SUBTOTAL-REPORT.
467
468      MOVE NEG TO SW-END-OF-FILE.
469
470      READ SORTED-PREMIUM-FILE INTO PREMIUM-RECORD
471          AT END MOVE YES TO SW-END-OF-FILE.
472
473      MOVE PR-AGENT-NAME TO WA-HOLD-AGENT-NAME.
474      PERFORM C-300-PRINT-HEADINGS.
475      PERFORM C-310-AGENT-HEADINGS.
476
477      PERFORM C-200-PROCESS-RECORDS
478          UNTIL END-OF-FILE.
479
480      PERFORM C-320-AGENT-BREAK.
481      MOVE AC-PREMIUM-TOTAL TO SL-COMPANY-PREMIUM-TOTAL.
482      MOVE AC-RECORD-COUNT TO SL-COMPANY-RECORD-COUNT.
483      WRITE REPORT-LINE-OUT FROM SL-COMPANY-TOTAL
484          AFTER ADVANCING 3 LINES.
485      WRITE REPORT-LINE-OUT FROM SL-END-OF-REPORT
486          AFTER ADVANCING 2 LINES.
487
488
489 /
490  **********************************************************************
491  *                                                                    *
492  *           SORT FILE RECORD PROCESSING ROUTINE                      *
493  *                                                                    *
494  **********************************************************************
495
```

```
496 C-200-PROCESS-RECORDS.
497
498     IF PR-AGENT-NAME NOT = WA-HOLD-AGENT-NAME
499         PERFORM C-320-AGENT-BREAK
500         PERFORM C-310-AGENT-HEADINGS.
501
502     MOVE PR-POLICY-NUMBER  TO DL-POLICY-NUMBER.
503     MOVE PR-CUSTOMER-NAME  TO DL-CUSTOMER-NAME.
504     MOVE PR-PREMIUM-AMOUNT TO DL-PREMIUM-AMOUNT.
505     MOVE MNT-NAME (PR-PREMIUM-DUE-MONTH)
506                   TO DL-DUE-MONTH.
507
508     ADD PR-PREMIUM-AMOUNT TO AC-AGENT-PREMIUM-SUBTOTAL.
509
510     WRITE REPORT-LINE-OUT FROM DETAIL-LINE
511         AFTER ADVANCING 1 LINE.
512
513     ADD 1 TO AC-LINE-COUNT.
514     ADD 1 TO AC-AGENT-RECORD-COUNT.
515     MOVE SPACE TO DL-DOLLAR-SIGN.
516
517     IF AC-LINE-COUNT > 55
518         PERFORM C-300-PRINT-HEADINGS
519         PERFORM C-310-AGENT-HEADINGS.
520
521     READ SORTED-PREMIUM-FILE INTO PREMIUM-RECORD
522         AT END MOVE YES TO SW-END-OF-FILE.
523 /
524 *********************************************************************
525 *                                                                   *
526 *                   PAGE HEADING ROUTINE                            *
527 *                                                                   *
528 *********************************************************************
529
530 C-300-PRINT-HEADINGS.
531
532     ADD 1 TO AC-PAGE-COUNT.
533     MOVE AC-PAGE-COUNT TO RH-PAGE-COUNT.
534     WRITE REPORT-LINE-OUT FROM RH-LINE-1
535         AFTER ADVANCING PAGE.
536     WRITE REPORT-LINE-OUT FROM RH-LINE-2
537         AFTER ADVANCING 1 LINE.
538
539     MOVE 2 TO AC-LINE-COUNT.
540
541 *********************************************************************
542 *                                                                   *
543 *                   AGENT HEADING ROUTINE                           *
544 *                                                                   *
545 *********************************************************************
546
547 C-310-AGENT-HEADINGS.
548
549     MOVE PR-AGENT-NAME TO RH-AGENT-NAME.
550     SET PHONE-INDEX TO 1.
551     SEARCH APT-ENTRY
552         AT END
553             MOVE "NOT FOUND" TO RH-AGENT-PHONE
554         WHEN APT-NAME (PHONE-INDEX) = PR-AGENT-NAME
555             MOVE APT-NUMBER (PHONE-INDEX) TO RH-AGENT-PHONE.
556
557     WRITE REPORT-LINE-OUT FROM RH-LINE-3
558         AFTER ADVANCING 3 LINES.
559     WRITE REPORT-LINE-OUT FROM RH-LINE-4
560         AFTER ADVANCING 2 LINES.
561     WRITE REPORT-LINE-OUT FROM RH-LINE-5
562         AFTER ADVANCING 1 LINE.
563
564     ADD 6 TO AC-LINE-COUNT.
565     MOVE "$" TO DL-DOLLAR-SIGN.
566
567 /
568 *********************************************************************
569 *                                                                   *
570 *               WRITE AGENT CONTROL BREAK TOTAL                     *
571 *                                                                   *
572 *********************************************************************
573
574 C-320-AGENT-BREAK.
575
576     MOVE WA-HOLD-AGENT-NAME TO SL-AGENT-NAME.
577     MOVE AC-AGENT-PREMIUM-SUBTOTAL TO SL-AGENT-PREMIUM-TOTAL.
578     MOVE AC-AGENT-RECORD-COUNT TO SL-AGENT-RECORD-COUNT.
579
580     WRITE REPORT-LINE-OUT FROM SL-UNDERLINE
581         AFTER ADVANCING 1 LINE.
582     WRITE REPORT-LINE-OUT FROM SL-AGENT-TOTAL
583         AFTER ADVANCING 1 LINE.
584
585     ADD AC-AGENT-PREMIUM-SUBTOTAL TO AC-PREMIUM-TOTAL
586         ON SIZE ERROR
587             DISPLAY "COMPANY TOTAL PREMIUM FIELD TOO SMALL!".
588
589     ADD AC-AGENT-RECORD-COUNT TO AC-RECORD-COUNT
590         ON SIZE ERROR
591             DISPLAY "COMPANY RECORD COUNT FIELD TOO SMALL!".
592
593     MOVE PR-AGENT-NAME TO WA-HOLD-AGENT-NAME.
594     MOVE ZERO TO AC-AGENT-PREMIUM-SUBTOTAL
595                  AC-AGENT-RECORD-COUNT.
596
597 *********************************************************************
598 *                                                                   *
599 *                   END OF JOB ROUTINE                              *
600 *                                                                   *
601 *********************************************************************
602
603 D-100-WRAP-UP.
604
605     CLOSE  SORTED-PREMIUM-FILE
606            AGENT-SUBTOTAL-REPORT.
607
608     DISPLAY "THE AGENT SUBTOTAL REPORT PROGRAM HAS TERMINATED".
609
```

FIGURE 7-5 Agent Subtotal Report program (continued)

ONE-DIMENSIONAL EMBEDDED TABLES

A table is a series of related fields with the same attributes stored in consecutive locations in main memory. Data stored in a table can be extracted from the table and processed within the program. The data for a table can be directly coded into the DATA DIVISION of a program or can come from an external source. When the data for a table is coded in the DATA DIVISION of a program, the table is called an **embedded table**. Figure 7-6 presents the data for and definition of the embedded Month Name Table used in the Agent Subtotal Report program.

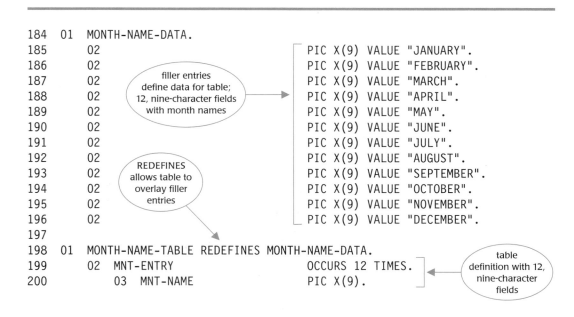

```
184   01   MONTH-NAME-DATA.
185        02                              PIC X(9) VALUE "JANUARY".
186        02                              PIC X(9) VALUE "FEBRUARY".
187        02                              PIC X(9) VALUE "MARCH".
188        02                              PIC X(9) VALUE "APRIL".
189        02                              PIC X(9) VALUE "MAY".
190        02                              PIC X(9) VALUE "JUNE".
191        02                              PIC X(9) VALUE "JULY".
192        02                              PIC X(9) VALUE "AUGUST".
193        02                              PIC X(9) VALUE "SEPTEMBER".
194        02                              PIC X(9) VALUE "OCTOBER".
195        02                              PIC X(9) VALUE "NOVEMBER".
196        02                              PIC X(9) VALUE "DECEMBER".
197
198   01   MONTH-NAME-TABLE REDEFINES MONTH-NAME-DATA.
199        02   MNT-ENTRY                  OCCURS 12 TIMES.
200             03   MNT-NAME              PIC X(9).
```

FIGURE 7-6   Embedded Month Name Table

An embedded table consists of two separate entities. The first entity contains the constant values that are to be stored in the table. Lines 184 through 196 of Figure 7-6 represent an example of this part of an embedded table. The constant values are typically defined as a series of filler entries under a single group name. Each of these entries must be the same size. In Figure 7-6, MONTH-NAME-DATA is the group name used. Each of the twelve filler entries under this group name represents a month of the year. Each filler entry is defined as a nine-character alphanumeric entry. Because there are twelve entries, the group name MONTH-NAME-DATE encompasses a total of nine times twelve characters, or 108 characters.

The names of the individual months cannot be referenced using the filler entries. Therefore, a REDEFINES clause is used to allow the actual table definition to overlay the constant values. The REDEFINES clause and the table definition that follows it make up the second entity of an embedded table. As seen in Chapter 3, the REDEFINES clause allows storage locations that have already been allocated to be given other names and other pictures. Line 198 in Figure 7-6 contains the REDEFINES clause for the sample table. The 01 level entry MONTH-NAME-TABLE redefines the 01 level entry MONTH-NAME-DATA. The table is then defined under MONTH-NAME-TABLE.

OCCURS Clause

A table is defined by using an OCCURS clause. An **OCCURS** clause specifies the number of times a field is repeated. The OCCURS clause can be used with any level number from 02 to 49. It cannot be used on a field defined at the 01 level. In Figure 7-6, the group name MNT-ENTRY is used on line 199 and OCCURS 12 TIMES is specified. MNT-ENTRY is subdivided into one elementary item, MNT-NAME, which is defined with a picture of PIC X(9), the same picture as each filler entry under MONTH-TABLE-DATA. Because MNT-NAME is defined under MNT-ENTRY, MNT-NAME is also repeated twelve times and because of the REDEFINES clause, each of the twelve occurrences of MNT-NAME corresponds to one of the constant values defined under MONTH-NAME-DATA. Table 7-1 on the next page illustrates the relationship between the constant values and the twelve occurrences of MNT-NAME. Each of the twelve occurrences of MNT-NAME is called an **element** within the table.

TABLE 7-1 The Effect of the REDEFINES Clause Combined with the OCCURS Clause

Filler Values		MNT-NAME (Occurrence Number)
JANUARY	$\longrightarrow$	MNT-NAME (1)
FEBRUARY	$\longrightarrow$	MNT-NAME (2)
MARCH	$\longrightarrow$	MNT-NAME (3)
APRIL	$\longrightarrow$	MNT-NAME (4)
MAY	$\longrightarrow$	MNT-NAME (5)
JUNE	$\longrightarrow$	MNT-NAME (6)
JULY	$\longrightarrow$	MNT-NAME (7)
AUGUST	$\longrightarrow$	MNT-NAME (8)
SEPTEMBER	$\longrightarrow$	MNT-NAME (9)
OCTOBER	$\longrightarrow$	MNT-NAME (10)
NOVEMBER	$\longrightarrow$	MNT-NAME (11)
DECEMBER	$\longrightarrow$	MNT-NAME (12)

The two basic formats of the OCCURS clause are presented in Figure 7-7. Format 1 allows a field to be repeated a specific number times. Format 2 allows a field to be repeated a variable number of times based on a value stored in the field identified by field-name-2. Tables with a variable number of repeating fields are discussed later in the chapter. In Format 1 of the OCCURS clause, the number following the word OCCURS identifies the **table limit**. In Format 2, the table limit is defined during processing but cannot exceed the integer following the word TO. No element beyond the table limit can be referenced within a program. The KEY clause and INDEXED BY clause are both optional entries but must be used in certain special situations. These clauses and the situations in which they must be used are also discussed later in this chapter.

Format 1:
```
OCCURS  integer-1 TIMES

        [ { ASCENDING  }      KEY IS  {field-name-1 } ... ] ...
        [ { DESCENDING }                                  ]

        [  INDEXED BY {index-name-1 } ...]
```
Format 2:
```
OCCURS integer-2 TO integer-3  TIMES  DEPENDING ON  field-name-2

        [ { ASCENDING  }      KEY IS  {field-name-3 } ... ] ...
        [ { DESCENDING }                                  ]

        [  INDEXED BY {index-name-2 } ...]
```

FIGURE 7-7 Basic formats of the OCCURS clause

Subscripts

Because the field MNT-NAME occurs twelve times, use of the name MNT-NAME by itself in the program does not identify which of the twelve occurrences is to be referenced. The particular nine-character element to be referenced must be identified through the use of a subscript following the field name. A **subscript** is a numeric value identifying the element within a table that is to be referenced. For example, to reference the first element within the table, which contains the month name JANUARY, the first MOVE statement in Figure 7-8 could be used. To reference the fifth element within the table, which contains the month name MAY, the second MOVE statement in Figure 7-8 could be used. In Figure 7-8, the subscript value of 1 is used to specify that the first element of the table is to be moved to the field DL-DUE-MONTH. The subscript value of 5 is used to specify that the fifth element of the table is to be moved to the field DL-DUE-MONTH.

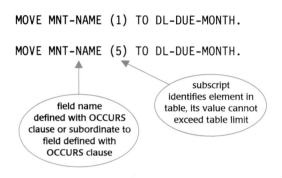

```
MOVE MNT-NAME (1) TO DL-DUE-MONTH.

MOVE MNT-NAME (5) TO DL-DUE-MONTH.
```

field name
defined with OCCURS
clause or subordinate to
field defined with
OCCURS clause

subscript
identifies element in
table, its value cannot
exceed table limit

FIGURE 7-8   Examples of subscript usage

Figure 7-9 presents the basic format of subscript usage.

$$\left\{ \begin{matrix} \text{condition-name-1} \\ \text{field-name-1} \end{matrix} \right\} \quad \left(\left\{ \begin{matrix} \text{integer-1} \\ \text{field-name-1 [+/- integer-2]} \\ \text{index-name-1 [+/- integer-3]} \end{matrix} \right\} \right)$$

FIGURE 7-9   Basic format of subscripts

A subscript value always must be contained within parentheses. Standard COBOL requires a space between the table element name and left parenthesis, but many compilers do not require this space. The right parenthesis must be followed by a space, or a period if it is the end of a sentence. Field names that are subscripted must be defined with an OCCURS clause or be subordinate to a name defined with an OCCURS clause. Therefore, the name MONTH-NAME-TABLE cannot be subscripted, but both MNT-ENTRY and MNT-NAME can be subscripted. In fact, the references MNT-ENTRY (1) and MNT-NAME (1) are equivalent and represent exactly the same element in the table because MNT-NAME is the only elementary item defined under MNT-ENTRY.

Although the literal subscripts used in Figure 7-8 allow the elements within the table to be referenced properly, a more practical method for specifying subscripts is the use of a field name within parentheses. The value in the field acts as the subscript. A MOVE statement that uses a field name as a subscript to access the proper month name from MONTH-NAME-TABLE is illustrated in Figure 7-10 on the next page. PR-PREMIUM-DUE-MONTH is a numeric integer field within PREMIUM-RECORD that contains a value from 1 to 12 for each customer record in the PREMIUM-INPUT-FILE. Any numeric integer field with a value from 1 up to the table limit defined by the OCCURS clause can be used as a subscript to reference a table item.

```
505      MOVE MNT-NAME (PR-PREMIUM-DUE-MONTH)
506                          TO DL-DUE-MONTH.
```

FIGURE 7-10 Using a field name as a subscript in the Agent Subtotal Report program

When using a field name as a subscript within the parentheses, it is permissible to access an element by using the field name followed by a plus or minus sign and an integer value. The value of the field name plus or minus the integer is used to identify an element within the table. The computed value cannot be less than 1 or greater than the table limit. Although permissible, such references can be confusing and, therefore, should generally be avoided. Figure 7-11 presents an example that shows a reference to an element two positions away from the position identified by the subscript, PR-PREMIUM-DUE-MONTH.

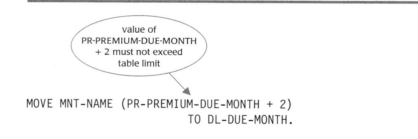

```
MOVE MNT-NAME (PR-PREMIUM-DUE-MONTH + 2)
                    TO DL-DUE-MONTH.
```

FIGURE 7-11 A reference to an element two positions away from the position identified by the value of PR-PREMIUM-DUE-MONTH

Figure 7-12 presents an alternative method of defining the MONTH-NAME-TABLE. Only two filler entries are used in the first entity to define the constant values. The table definition shown in Figure 7-6 on page 7-11 uses twelve nine-character entries to define the 108 characters needed for the constant values. The two filler entries in Figure 7-12 are both fifty-four characters long and, therefore, also define 108 characters. It does not matter how the constant values are defined, as long as the correct number of characters are used and entries are in the proper positions. Both Figure 7-6 and Figure 7-12 use an OCCURS clause on the name MNT-ENTRY; however, in Figure 7-6 this name is a group name, while in Figure 7-12 it is an elementary item.

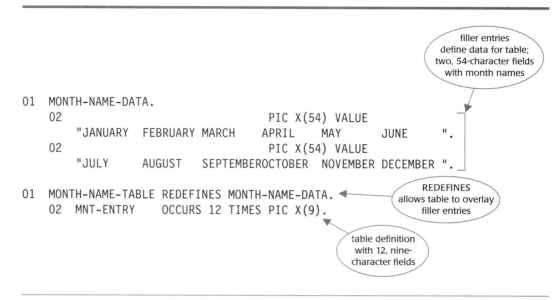

```
01  MONTH-NAME-DATA.
    02                              PIC X(54) VALUE
        "JANUARY   FEBRUARY MARCH     APRIL    MAY      JUNE     ".
    02                              PIC X(54) VALUE
        "JULY     AUGUST   SEPTEMBEROCTOBER  NOVEMBER DECEMBER ".

01  MONTH-NAME-TABLE REDEFINES MONTH-NAME-DATA.
    02  MNT-ENTRY    OCCURS 12 TIMES PIC X(9).
```

filler entries
define data for table;
two, 54-character fields
with month names

REDEFINES
allows table to overlay
filler entries

table definition
with 12, nine-
character fields

FIGURE 7-12   Alternative Month Name Table definition

Although both Figure 7-6 and Figure 7-12 present valid table definitions, Figure 7-6 represents the preferred way of defining tables in this book. The format of the filler entries for the constant values in Figure 7-6 makes it easier to read and modify these entries, if necessary. Also, using the OCCURS clause on a group name allows the group name to be subdivided into any number of elementary elements. Many tables require the use of numerous elementary elements.

ONE-DIMENSIONAL NON-EMBEDDED TABLES

A second table is used in the Agent Subtotal Report program. AGENT-PHONE-TABLE is illustrated in Figure 7-13 on the next page. This table has only one entity, the table definition. No constant values preceding the table definition exist, and a REDEFINES clause is not used. Such a table is known as a **non-embedded table**. The AGENT-PHONE-TABLE is designed to accommodate agent names and their corresponding phone numbers. Prior to accessing data in this table for the report, values must be moved into the storage locations defined by the table. This process, known as **loading** the table, must be done in the PROCEDURE DIVISION. Prior to the table being loaded, no data exists in the table.

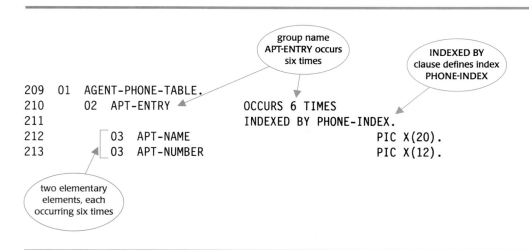

FIGURE 7-13 Agent Phone Table, an example of a non-embedded table

Although most table definitions are more involved, in its simplest form, a non-embedded table might appear as shown in Figure 7-14. This table definition indicates that the two-digit number NT-ITEM is repeated ten times.

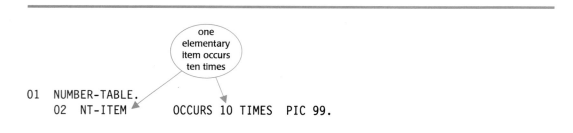

FIGURE 7-14 A simple non-embedded table

The elements of the AGENT-PHONE-TABLE shown in Figure 7-13 cannot be referenced by a field name used as a subscript. Because of the entry on line 211, INDEXED BY PHONE-INDEX, the elements can be referenced only by literal values or the index name PHONE-INDEX. The **INDEXED BY** clause is used to define an index name for a table. When an index name, or simply an index, is defined for a table in a program, its name must be unique and cannot be defined elsewhere in the program.

Indexes vs. Subscripts

An **index** works in a manner similar to a subscript, but there are some major differences between the two. A field used as a subscript can be any elementary numeric integer. The same subscript field can be used with numerous tables. Subscript fields can be modified using MOVE and arithmetic statements. An index can be used only in conjunction with the table in which it is defined. Also, an index name neither can be modified using a MOVE, nor be used in arithmetic. An index can be modified only by using the VARYING option on a PERFORM or by using a SET statement. Table 7-2 summarizes the differences between subscripts and indexes.

TABLE 7-2   The Differences Between Subscripts and Indexes

Subscripts	Indexes
1. Any elementary integer field	1. Must be defined with its table
2. Can be used with numerous tables	2. Can only be used with the table in which it is defined
3. Can be modified with MOVE and arithmetic statements	3. Can only be modified with PERFORM VARYING or SET statement

A **SET** statement is used to modify the contents of an index. Figure 7-15 presents two basic formats of the SET statement. Format 1 is used to set an index to the value of another index, the value of a numeric field, or the value of a literal. It also can be used to set a field to the value of an index. In Format 1, if a field name follows the word SET, then an index name must follow the word TO. Format 2 is used to increment or decrement the value of an index. As with subscripts, under no circumstances should an index be assigned a value less than 1 or greater than the table limit defined by the OCCURS clause. Doing so can result in run-time errors when the program executes.

Format 1:

```
SET   {index-name-1}   ... TO   {index-name-2
      {field-name-1}               field-name-2
                                   integer-1 }
```

Format 2:

```
SET   {index-name-3 } ...   {UP BY  }   {field-name-3}
                            {DOWN BY}   {integer-2   }
```

FIGURE 7-15   Basic formats of the SET statement

Figure 7-16 presents examples of SET statements.

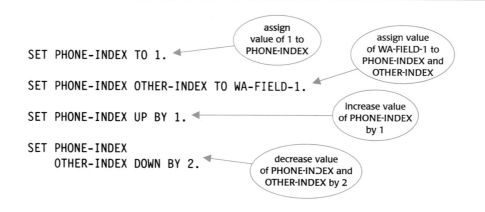

```
SET PHONE-INDEX TO 1.              ← assign value of 1 to PHONE-INDEX

SET PHONE-INDEX OTHER-INDEX TO WA-FIELD-1.   ← assign value of WA-FIELD-1 to PHONE-INDEX and OTHER-INDEX

SET PHONE-INDEX UP BY 1.           ← increase value of PHONE-INDEX by 1

SET PHONE-INDEX
    OTHER-INDEX DOWN BY 2.         ← decrease value of PHONE-INDEX and OTHER-INDEX by 2
```

FIGURE 7-16   Examples of the SET statement

During the execution of a program, a subscript is translated into an address so the proper storage location within the table can be referenced. When an index is defined for a table, the address translation occurs when the program is compiled. Thus, an index provides access more quickly to table elements when the program is executing. The difference among subscripts, indexes, and the way addresses are calculated is transparent to the programmer. Once an index has been set to a specific value, it is used just like a subscript. If necessary, a literal value can be used to reference table elements even when an index is defined.

Loading a Non-Embedded Table

As indicated earlier, a non-embedded table must be loaded in the PROCEDURE DIVISION. Several methods are available to accomplish this task. For example, a series of MOVE statements in the initialization routine of the PROCEDURE DIVISION can be used. The most common method, however, involves obtaining data from a file that is used as input to the program. Non-embedded tables loaded in such a manner are sometimes known as **input-loaded tables**. Figure 7-17 presents the SELECT and FD for the AGENT-PHONE-FILE from the Agent Subtotal Report program. Each record in this file contains two fields, one for the agent name and one for the agent phone number. To use this information in the program, it must be loaded into the AGENT-PHONE-TABLE.

```
43      SELECT AGENT-PHONE-FILE
44          ASSIGN TO "A:\AGENTPHO.DAT".

97  FD  AGENT-PHONE-FILE.
98
99  01  AGENT-PHONE-RECORD.
100     ┌02  APR-NAME                    PIC X(20).
101     └02  APR-NUMBER                  PIC X(12).
```

two fields
in each record:
agent name and
phone number

FIGURE 7-17 SELECT and FD for AGENT-PHONE-FILE

Figure 7-18 presents the code from the Agent Subtotal Report program that accesses the AGENT-PHONE-FILE, and then loads the data from each record into the AGENT-PHONE-TABLE.

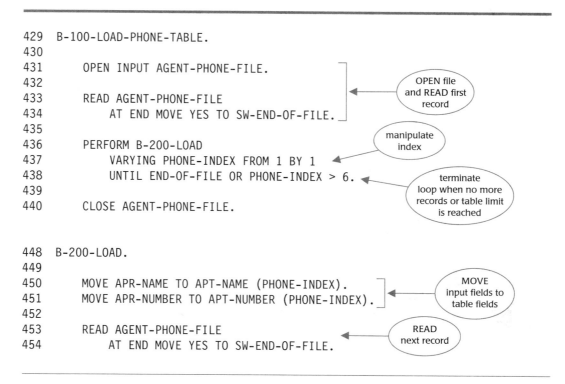

```
429  B-100-LOAD-PHONE-TABLE.
430
431      OPEN INPUT AGENT-PHONE-FILE.
432
433      READ AGENT-PHONE-FILE
434          AT END MOVE YES TO SW-END-OF-FILE.
435
436      PERFORM B-200-LOAD
437          VARYING PHONE-INDEX FROM 1 BY 1
438          UNTIL END-OF-FILE OR PHONE-INDEX > 6.
439
440      CLOSE AGENT-PHONE-FILE.


448  B-200-LOAD.
449
450      MOVE APR-NAME TO APT-NAME (PHONE-INDEX).
451      MOVE APR-NUMBER TO APT-NUMBER (PHONE-INDEX).
452
453      READ AGENT-PHONE-FILE
454          AT END MOVE YES TO SW-END-OF-FILE.
```

Annotations:
- OPEN file and READ first record
- manipulate index
- terminate loop when no more records or table limit is reached
- MOVE input fields to table fields
- READ next record

FIGURE 7-18   Code that loads the AGENT-PHONE-TABLE from AGENT-PHONE-FILE

The logic used to load the table is similar to the logic used in several of the report programs presented earlier in this book. The file, AGENT-PHONE-FILE, is opened for INPUT, the first record is read, and a loop is used to process the records. The VARYING option is used in the PERFORM UNTIL statement to manipulate PHONE-INDEX. An alternative method that uses the SET statement to replace the actions of the VARYING option is shown in Figure 7-19 on the next page. Although both sets of logic are equivalent, use of the VARYING option is more efficient and is the preferred method of manipulating an index under these circumstances.

```
B-100-LOAD-PHONE-TABLE.

    OPEN INPUT AGENT-PHONE-FILE.

    READ AGENT-PHONE-FILE
        AT END MOVE YES TO SW-END-OF-FILE.

    SET PHONE-INDEX TO 1.

    PERFORM B-200-LOAD
        UNTIL END-OF-FILE OR PHONE-INDEX > 6.

    CLOSE AGENT-PHONE-FILE.


B-200-LOAD.

    MOVE APR-NAME TO APT-NAME (PHONE-INDEX).
    MOVE APR-NUMBER TO APT-NUMBER (PHONE-INDEX).

    READ AGENT-PHONE-FILE
        AT END MOVE YES TO SW-END-OF-FILE.

    SET PHONE-INDEX UP BY 1.
```

replaces use of
VARYING option
on PERFORM

FIGURE 7-19 An alternative method of manipulating PHONE-INDEX while loading the AGENT-PHONE-TABLE

For every record processed, data is moved from the input record layout to the table element fields, a process that continues until one of two conditions is true. The looping must terminate when the table limit, as defined by the OCCURS clause, is reached or when no more records are available from the input file. Ideally, both situations will occur simultaneously; however, this cannot always be guaranteed. Therefore, a combined condition such as UNTIL END-OF-FILE OR PHONE-INDEX > 6 is recommended when loading non-embedded tables. Table 7-3 shows the results of loading the AGENT-PHONE-TABLE.

TABLE 7-3   Contents of the AGENT-PHONE-TABLE After It Is Loaded

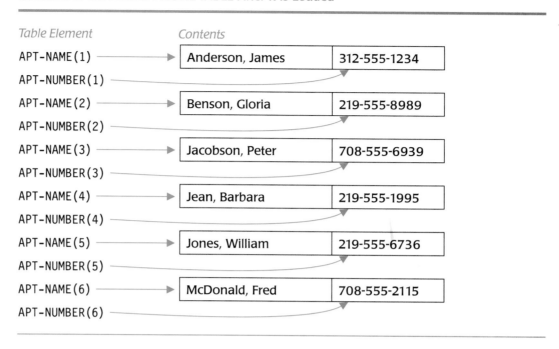

SEARCHING TABLES

When the location of a desired element from a table is unknown, it is necessary to search the table. In the MONTH-NAME-TABLE, the desired element corresponds to the contents of PR-PREMIUM-DUE-MONTH from the PREMIUM-INPUT-FILE. No searching is necessary for the desired element in MONTH-NAME-TABLE. In the AGENT-PHONE-TABLE, the agent name is available from the field PR-AGENT-NAME, but this is an alphanumeric field and does not directly indicate which table element is to be utilized. The only way to find the appropriate element and retrieve the correct phone number is to search the table.

Searching can be accomplished by setting up a loop with a PERFORM UNTIL, but the most efficient method uses the **SEARCH** statement. Only tables that have been defined with an index can be searched using the SEARCH statement. Figure 7-20 on the next page presents the two basic formats of the SEARCH statement. Format 1 is used to perform a **linear search**, which is also known as a **sequential search**. It is typically used to search a table from top to bottom. Format 2 is a **SEARCH ALL** and is generally used to perform a **binary search**. A binary search begins processing in the middle of the table and can find the desired element more quickly than a linear search under certain circumstances. These circumstances will be discussed later in this chapter. The linear search illustrated by Format 1 in Figure 7-20 will be examined first.

Format 1:

```
SEARCH  table-name-1  ┌ VARYING   ⎰ field-name-1 ⎱ ⎤
                      └           ⎱ index-name-1 ⎰ ⎦

        [ AT END  statement-set-1  ]

        ⎰ WHEN  condition-1   ⎰ statement-set-2 ⎱   ⎱ ...
        ⎱                     ⎱ NEXT SENTENCE    ⎰   ⎰

[ END-SEARCH ]
```

Format 2:

```
SEARCH ALL table-name-2  [ AT END statement-set-3 ]

              ⎰ field-name-2  ⎰ IS EQUAL TO ⎱   ⎰ field-name-3 ⎱ ⎱
              ⎰               ⎰ IS =         ⎰   ⎰ literal-1    ⎰ ⎰
     WHEN     ⎱               ⎰              ⎱   ⎱ expression-1 ⎰ ⎰
              ⎰                                                   ⎰
              ⎱ condition-name-1                                  ⎰

    ┌         ⎰ field-name-4  ⎰ IS EQUAL TO ⎱   ⎰ field-name-5 ⎱ ⎱ ⎤
    ⎰         ⎰               ⎰ IS =         ⎰   ⎰ literal-2    ⎰ ⎰ ⎰
    ⎰ AND     ⎱               ⎰              ⎱   ⎱ expression-2}⎰ ⎰ ⎰
    ⎰         ⎰                                                   ⎰ ⎰
    ⎰         ⎱ condition-name-2                                  ⎰ ⎰
    ⎰                                                               ⎰
    ⎰           ⎰ statement-set-4 ⎱                                 ⎰
    └           ⎱ NEXT SENTENCE   ⎰                                 ┘

[ END-SEARCH ]
```

FIGURE 7-20 Basic formats of the SEARCH statement

Linear Search

Before a linear search can be used, the index associated with the table must be set to the number of the element in the table where the search is to begin. If the search is to begin with the first element in the table, which is usually the case, then the index must be set to a value of 1. Figure 7-21 illustrates the logic of a linear search. Starting from the top of a table, comparisons continue until a match is found. Figure 7-22 on page 7-24 presents the SET and SEARCH statements used in the Agent Subtotal Report program to search the AGENT-PHONE-TABLE presented in Figure 7-13 on page 7-16.

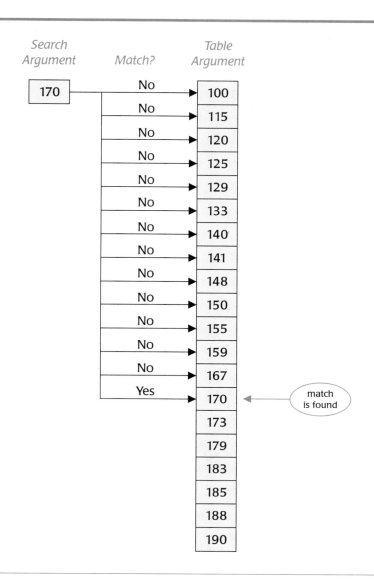

FIGURE 7-21   The logic of a linear search

Line 550 sets the value of PHONE-INDEX to 1, thus ensuring that the searching process begins with the first element in the table. The name following the word SEARCH must be a name defined with an OCCURS clause. In the AGENT-PHONE-TABLE, this is APT-ENTRY. The VARYING clause shown in Format 1 in Figure 7-20 is optional and not used here. It is used when an index from another table or a subscript field is to be manipulated so it ends up pointing to the same element position as the index of the table being searched. VARYING goes beyond the scope of this discussion and will not be used in this book with a SEARCH.

Although optional in a SEARCH statement, the AT END clause is often used. The statement or statements following AT END will execute only if the entire table is searched and no condition within a WHEN clause is found to be true. One WHEN clause is required and other WHEN clauses are optional in a linear search. The condition test following the word WHEN typically compares an element in the table, called the **table argument**, to what is being searched for, called the **search argument**. Any valid COBOL condition test can be specified after WHEN in a linear search. The statement or statements following the condition test will execute only when the condition specified is true.

In the sample program, the condition following the WHEN tests to see if the table argument, APT-AGENT (PHONE-INDEX), is equal to the search argument, PR-AGENT-NAME (line 554 in Figure 7-22). If the fields are equal, then the MOVE statement executes, moving the corresponding phone number, APT-NUMBER (PHONE-INDEX), to the output field RH-AGENT-PHONE (line 555 in Figure 7-22). If the condition is not true, the SEARCH will automatically increment PHONE-INDEX by 1 and compare the next value of APT-AGENT (PHONE-INDEX) to PR-AGENT-NAME. The process continues until the condition after the WHEN is true or the table limit is exceeded by PHONE-INDEX. If the table limit is exceeded, then the MOVE statement on line 553 will execute as part of the AT END.

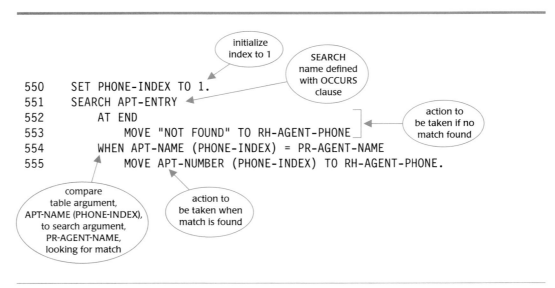

FIGURE 7-22 SET and SEARCH statements for the AGENT-PHONE-TABLE

Binary Search

Instead of searching a table from top to bottom, as a linear search does, a binary search begins its comparisons in the middle of the table, or as close to the middle as possible in the case of an even number of elements. It subsequently continues dividing the table in half in one direction or the other until the condition test following the WHEN is true or it can be determined that the search argument is not in the table.

Figure 7-23 illustrates the logic of a binary search. The first comparison is made at a point near the middle of the table. If the table argument is less than the search argument, the next comparison is made at a point halfway, or approximately halfway, between the middle and end of the table. If the table argument at this point is greater than the search argument, the next comparison is made halfway between the first comparison point and the second comparison point. Comparisons continue until a match is found or the table has been split as much as possible.

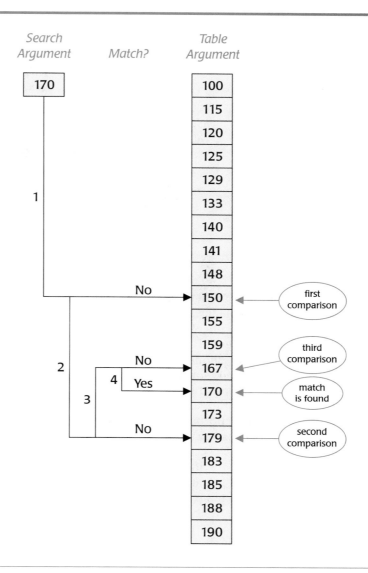

FIGURE 7-23 The logic of a binary search, showing a match on the fourth comparison

Format 2 in Figure 7-20 on page 7-22 presented the basic format of a binary search. It is similar to a linear search with some minor differences. As with the linear search, the table to be searched must be defined with an index. Additionally, the elements of the table must be in either ascending or descending sequence according to a key field defined within the table. This fact must be stated as part of the table definition. Figure 7-7 on page 7-12 shows that ASCENDING KEY and DESCENDING KEY are optional entries in defining a table. These clauses are used to identify the field or fields by which the data in the table is sequenced. A binary search will not work properly unless a table is sequenced by one or more of its elements. Figure 7-24 on the next page presents the AGENT-PHONE-TABLE as it would be defined if a binary search were to be used on it.

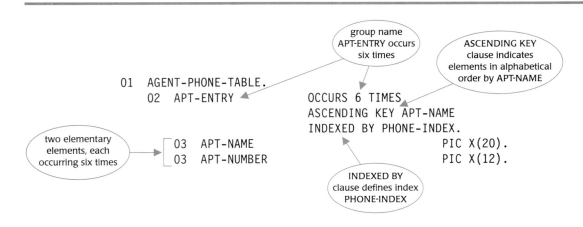

FIGURE 7-24 AGENT-PHONE-TABLE as it would look to accommodate a binary search

The clause ASCENDING KEY APT-NAME has been added to the definition. This clause does not guarantee that the table elements are, in fact, in this sequence. It is the programmers responsibility to ensure that the elements are in the indicated sequence for both embedded and non-embedded tables defined in such a manner. This means that in an embedded table, the filler entries that define the constant values must be entered in the correct sequence. In a non-embedded table, if an input file is used, the input file must be sorted in the proper sequence. If a programmer is unsure of the input file's sequence, a COBOL SORT can be used in the program to sort the input file and thus ensure proper sequence.

A binary search that could be used to search the table presented in Figure 7-24 is shown in Figure 7-25. Because testing begins in the middle of the table, no SET is needed prior to a binary search. SEARCH ALL is used instead of SEARCH. The name following the word ALL must be the name defined with an OCCURS clause. As with a linear search, the AT END clause is optional and will execute only when it can be determined that the element desired does not exist in the table. The condition following the WHEN must be an equality test, or a condition name test, that uses the key field. Only one WHEN is allowed in a binary search; however, combined conditions can be created using AND. The statement or statements following the equality test or condition name will execute when the condition specified is true.

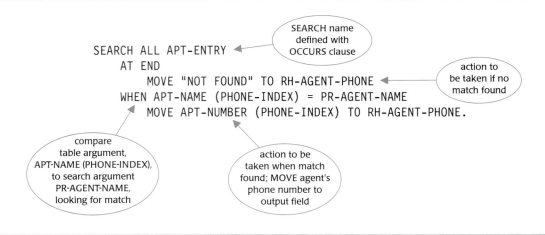

FIGURE 7-25 A binary search for AGENT-PHONE-TABLE

Because a binary search requires more system resources than a linear search, a binary search should be performed only when certain conditions exist. These conditions are summarized in Table 7-4. First, the table should be relatively large. Typically, a table containing thirty or more entries is considered to be a large table. Second, each entry in the table should have the same probability of being selected in the search. If some elements are more likely than others to be selected, then those elements should be placed at the beginning of the table and a linear search should be performed. Finally, the elements must be capable of being sequenced. As indicated earlier, a binary search will not work properly if the elements are not in ASCENDING or DESCENDING sequence by a key field in the table.

TABLE 7-4   Conditions for Use of a Binary Search

1. The table should be large; at least 30 elements

2. Each element should have the same probability of being selected

3. You must be able to sequence the elements

VARIABLE-LENGTH TABLES

Both tables used in the Agent Subtotal Report program are fixed-length tables. A **fixed-length table** is defined with a specific number in the OCCURS clause. Often, when a non-embedded table is loaded from an external source, the exact number of elements to be used cannot be predicted when writing the program. A **variable-length table** allows a table to be defined and the exact number of elements determined at the time the table is loaded. Format 2 in Figure 7-7 on page 7-12 presents the basic format of the OCCURS clause used to define a variable-length table.

The OCCURS clause is used in the table definition to establish a minimum and maximum number of elements allowed. The minimum cannot be less than zero, but no limit is set on the maximum. The field name following the DEPENDING ON clause must be a numeric integer field into which a count of the actual number of elements loaded into the table is placed. This field can be used as the counter during the loading process. This count cannot be less than the minimum number of elements or greater than the maximum number of elements identified by the OCCURS clause. Once a variable length table has been loaded and the number of elements established, it can be accessed or searched just like a fixed-length table.

Figure 7-26 on the next page presents a variable-length example of the AGENT-PHONE-TABLE. It is assumed that there always will be at least one agent in the external file used for loading the table and not more than 100 agents. Loading the table involves logic similar to that presented in Figure 7-18 on page 7-19. The only modifications needed are an ADD statement, to increment AC-AGENT-COUNT by 1 for each record processed, and a higher table limit on the PERFORM VARYING.

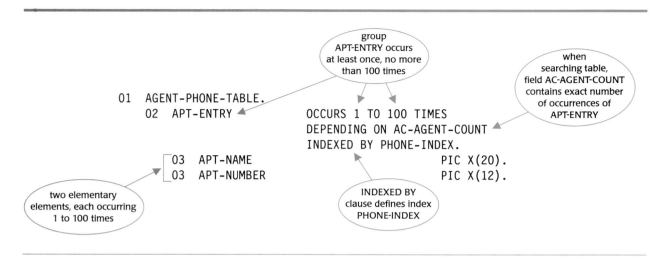

FIGURE 7-26 A variable length AGENT-PHONE-TABLE

Figure 7-27 contains the required modifications and illustrates the logic needed for loading the variable-length table presented in Figure 7-26.

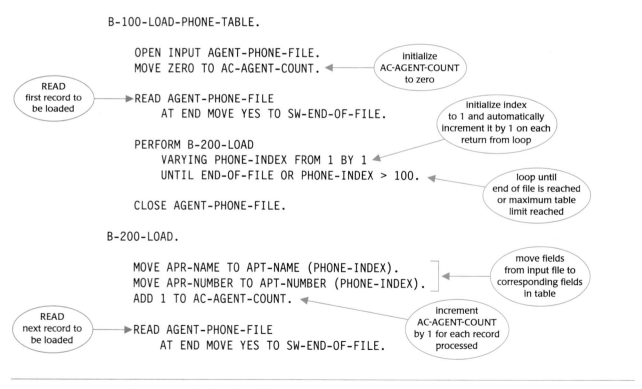

FIGURE 7-27 Loading a variable-length table

MULTI-DIMENSIONAL TABLES

The tables presented so far have been **one-dimensional tables**, which means that each element within the table was identified by a single subscript or index value. It is often necessary within a program to process **multi-dimensional tables**, which are tables that require two or more subscripts or indexes to reference a specific element within the table. Multi-dimensional tables are defined using more than one OCCURS clause.

Figure 7-28 presents data conducive for use with a multi-dimensional table. Suppose each insurance agent has three different phone numbers: a home number, an office number, and a fax number. A one-dimensional table could be used to track this data, but a multi-dimensional table will better organize the data. Using a multi-dimensional table, each agent name can be stored once and have three different numbers associated with it.

Agent Name	Home Phone	Office Phone	Fax Number
Anderson, James	312-555-1234	312-555-4343	312-555-4431
Benson, Gloria	219-555-8989	312-555-1701	219-555-4848
Jacobson, Peter	708-555-6939	312-555-1200	708-555-5764
Jean, Barbara	219-555-1995	312-555-1390	219-555-1675
Jones, William	219-555-6736	312-555-8854	219-555-0991
McDonald, Fred	708-555-2115	312-555-3721	708-555-3323

FIGURE 7-28   Agent names and phone numbers for a multi-dimensional table

Figure 7-29 presents a table definition designed to accommodate the illustrated data. As with one-dimensional tables, multi-dimensional tables may be embedded or non-embedded. If the INDEXED BY clause is omitted, elements are referenced using subscripts.

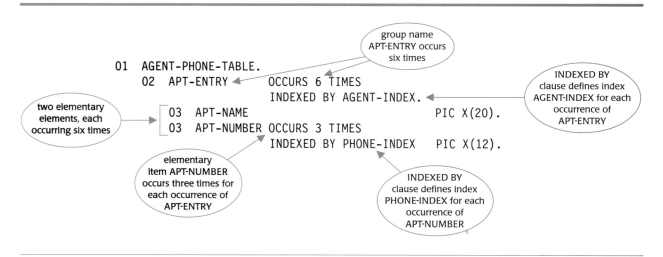

FIGURE 7-29   Multi-dimensional AGENT-PHONE-TABLE

In Figure 7-29 on the previous page, APT-NAME is subordinate to one OCCURS clause, the one on APT-ENTRY, and is referenced using a single index value. APT-NUMBER is defined with an OCCURS clause and is subordinate to the OCCURS clause on APT-ENTRY. Therefore, a reference to APT-NUMBER must be made using two index values. The OCCURS clause can appear up to seven times in a single table definition, each at a different level within the table. Thus, it is possible to have table elements that require the use of seven subscripts or index values. It is recommended that tables be kept as simple as possible and complicated multi-dimensional tables be avoided.

Assuming that the input record from the AGENT-PHONE-FILE contains three phone numbers, Figure 7-30 presents one method for loading the AGENT-PHONE-TABLE presented in Figure 7-29. Notice the use of a subscripted table in the record definition for AGENT-PHONE-RECORD to accommodate the three phone numbers. A literal subscript is used with each occurrence of APR-NUMBER to MOVE the appropriate elements into the table.

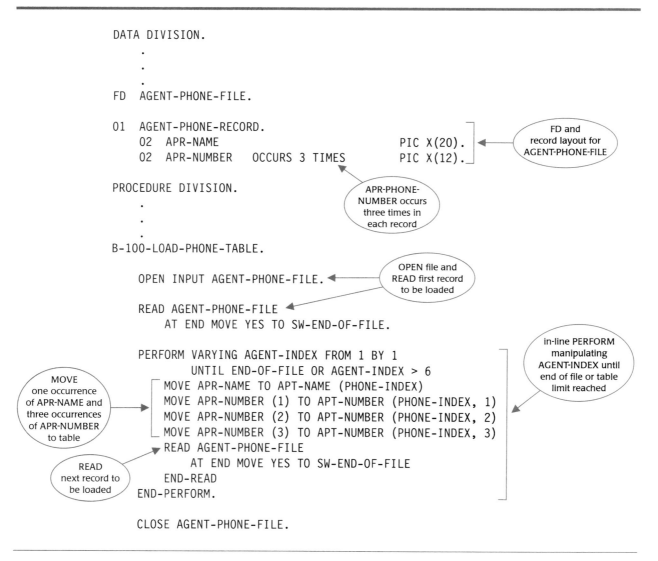

FIGURE 7-30 Loading the multi-dimensional AGENT-PHONE-TABLE

Table 7-5 illustrates references to and values of selected elements once the multi-dimensional AGENT-PHONE-TABLE has been loaded.

TABLE 7-5   References and Values for the Multi-dimensional AGENT-PHONE-TABLE

Reference	Value
APT-NAME (1)	Anderson, James
APT-NUMBER (1,1)	312-555-1234
APT-NUMBER (1,2)	312-555-4343
APT-NUMBER (1,3)	312-555-4431
APT-NAME (2)	Benson, Gloria
APT-NUMBER (2,1)	219-555-8989
APT-NUMBER (2,2)	312-555-1701
APT-NUMBER (2,3)	219-555-4848
.	
.	
.	
APT-NAME (6)	McDonald, Fred
APT-NUMBER (6,1)	708-555-2115
APT-NUMBER (6,2)	312-555-3721
APT-NUMBER (6,3)	708-555-3323

When multiple subscripts or index values are required, it is customary to separate them with commas, although this practice is optional. Multi-dimensional tables can be searched using logic similar to that presented in the examples for one-dimensional tables. When the SEARCH statement is used, the name following the word SEARCH must be a name defined with an OCCURS clause. Only the index name associated with that OCCURS clause will be manipulated by the SEARCH statement. The other indexes must be set to specific values or manipulated by a PERFORM VARYING.

The SEARCH in Figure 7-31 is coded to find the fax number of a specific agent. Assuming that the fax number is always the third element in the second dimension of the table, PHONE-INDEX is set to 3 prior to the SEARCH statement. AGENT-INDEX is set to 1 to ensure that the search begins with the first agent in the table. Because the name APT-ENTRY follows the word SEARCH, only AGENT-INDEX is manipulated by the SEARCH statement. The SEARCH will terminate when the table argument APT-NAME (AGENT-INDEX) matches the search argument PR-AGENT-NAME. At that point, the contents of APT-NUMBER (AGENT-INDEX, PHONE-INDEX) will be moved to the output field RH-AGENT-FAX. If no match is found, a message is moved to RH-AGENT-FAX. A binary search on this table would be coded in a similar fashion.

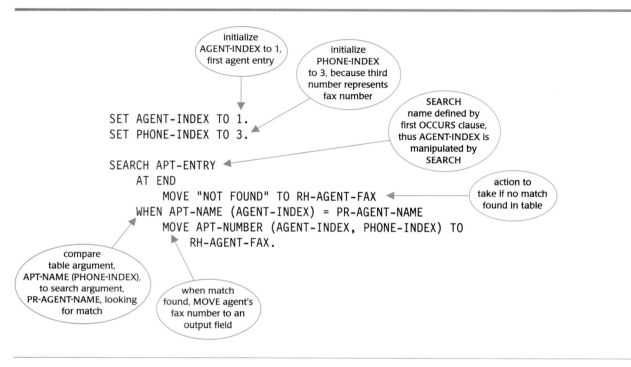

FIGURE 7-31   SET and SEARCH for finding the fax number of an agent in the multi-dimensional AGENT-PHONE-TABLE

Assume that it is necessary to determine if a certain phone number contained in the field WA-PHONE-NUMBER is located in the multi-dimensional table defined in Figure 7-29 on page 7-29. To accomplish this, the entire table must be searched and every phone number in the table must be compared to WA-PHONE-NUMBER. Because the SEARCH statement can manipulate only one index, it will be necessary to embed the SEARCH in a loop that manipulates the other index. Figure 7-32 illustrates logic that can be used in this situation.

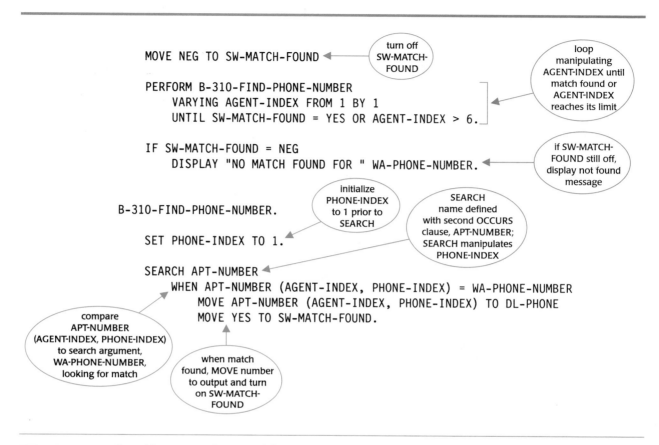

FIGURE 7-32 Searching every element of the AGENT-PHONE-TABLE for a specific phone number in the field WA-PHONE-NUMBER

The loop in Figure 7-32 is executed using a PERFORM VARYING. The PERFORM VARYING manipulates AGENT-INDEX while the SEARCH statement in the paragraph B-310-FIND-PHONE-NUMBER manipulates PHONE-INDEX. The SEARCH statement manipulates PHONE-INDEX because APT-NUMBER is used after the word SEARCH and PHONE-INDEX is defined as the index for APT-NUMBER. Searching will terminate once a match is found or when AGENT-INDEX has reached its limit. In each pass through the loop, PHONE-INDEX is set to 1 so the SEARCH begins with the first phone number listed for each agent.

Because processing must continue to the next value of AGENT-INDEX after all the values of PHONE-INDEX have been exhausted for any one agent, the AT END option is not used in the SEARCH. The phone number is moved to an output field and a switch, SW-MATCH-FOUND, is turned on when a match is found. If no match is found, SW-MATCH-FOUND remains off and a DISPLAY statement executes as a result of the condition test following the PERFORM VARYING statement. Similar processing can be used to search any two-dimensional table.

Multi-dimensional tables with more than two dimensions can be processed in a fashion similar to the examples presented for the two-dimensional AGENT-PHONE-TABLE. The logic presented in the two-dimensional examples must be extended to accommodate each additional subscript or index required by each additional OCCURS clause. Tables of more than two dimensions will not be presented in this book.

CONTROL BREAK PROCESSING

In the Agent Subtotal Report program, logic is designed to detect a change in the field PR-AGENT-NAME and, every time that change occurs, print subtotals. Heading lines for the next agent to be processed also must be printed. As indicated at the beginning of the chapter, such logic is called control break processing. A control break occurs when the value in a given field, called the **control field**, changes from the value found in the previous input record. Multiple control fields are possible. In the sample program, PR-AGENT-NAME is the control field.

A partial listing of the Agent Subtotal Report is presented again in Figure 7-33. Notice that a total customer premium amount is listed for every agent, as well as a grand total for the company at the end of the report. Such processing is possible only if the input file is in sequence by the control field or fields.

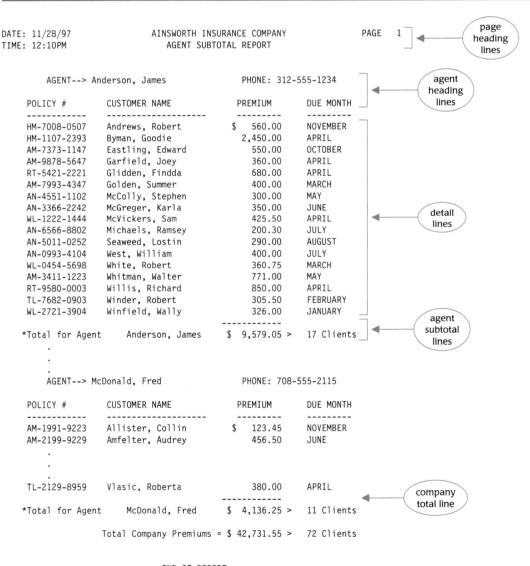

FIGURE 7-33 Partial listing of the Agent Subtotal Report

To ensure that this is true in the Agent Subtotal Report program, a simple COBOL SORT is included in A-100-INITIALIZATION of the sample program (Figure 7-34). This SORT uses the PREMIUM-INPUT-FILE as input and produces the SORTED-PREMIUM-FILE as output. The agent name field is used as the sort key so records in the SORTED-PREMIUM-FILE are in sequence by agent name. The COBOL SORT statement was presented in Chapter 6.

```
391   A-100-INITIALIZATION.
       .
       .
       .
417       SORT SORT-FILE
418          ON ASCENDING KEY SR-AGENT-NAME
419          USING PREMIUM-INPUT-FILE
420          GIVING SORTED-PREMIUM-FILE.
       .
       .
       .
```

FIGURE 7-34 Sorting the PREMIUM-INPUT-FILE by agent name in the Agent Subtotal Report program

Figure 7-35 on the next page presents C-100-PROCESS-FILE, which controls the overall production of the Agent Subtotal Report program and begins the control break processing. SORTED-PREMIUM-FILE is opened for INPUT in C-100-PROCESS-FILE. In programs presented in earlier chapters, the input record layout, PREMIUM-RECORD, was defined under the FD in the FILE SECTION of the DATA DIVISION. In the Agent Subtotal Report program, PREMIUM-RECORD is defined in the WORKING-STORAGE SECTION. To utilize this record layout, the INTO option is used on the READ statement when a record is read from the SORTED-PREMIUM-FILE. A field named WA-HOLD-AGENT-NAME is defined in the WORKING-STORAGE SECTION of the DATA DIVISION and is used to preserve the previous value of PR-AGENT-NAME. To avoid a control break on the very first record processed, WA-HOLD-AGENT-NAME is initialized to the value of PR-AGENT-NAME on line 473 after the first record is read.

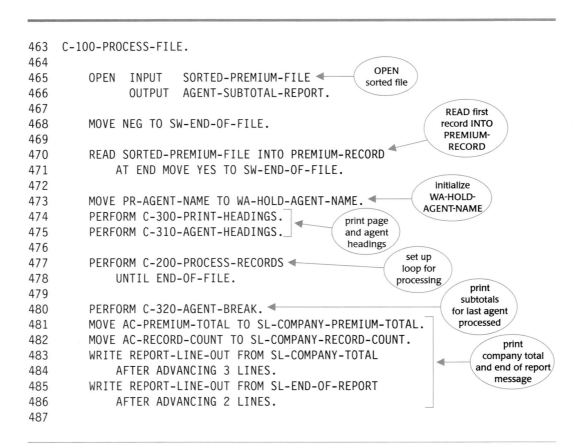

```
463   C-100-PROCESS-FILE.
464
465       OPEN   INPUT   SORTED-PREMIUM-FILE
466              OUTPUT  AGENT-SUBTOTAL-REPORT.
467
468       MOVE NEG TO SW-END-OF-FILE.
469
470       READ SORTED-PREMIUM-FILE INTO PREMIUM-RECORD
471           AT END MOVE YES TO SW-END-OF-FILE.
472
473       MOVE PR-AGENT-NAME TO WA-HOLD-AGENT-NAME.
474       PERFORM C-300-PRINT-HEADINGS.
475       PERFORM C-310-AGENT-HEADINGS.
476
477       PERFORM C-200-PROCESS-RECORDS
478           UNTIL END-OF-FILE.
479
480       PERFORM C-320-AGENT-BREAK.
481       MOVE AC-PREMIUM-TOTAL TO SL-COMPANY-PREMIUM-TOTAL.
482       MOVE AC-RECORD-COUNT TO SL-COMPANY-RECORD-COUNT.
483       WRITE REPORT-LINE-OUT FROM SL-COMPANY-TOTAL
484           AFTER ADVANCING 3 LINES.
485       WRITE REPORT-LINE-OUT FROM SL-END-OF-REPORT
486           AFTER ADVANCING 2 LINES.
487
```

Callouts within the figure:
- OPEN sorted file
- READ first record INTO PREMIUM-RECORD
- initialize WA-HOLD-AGENT-NAME
- print page and agent headings
- set up loop for processing
- print subtotals for last agent processed
- print company total and end of report message

FIGURE 7-35   C-100-PROCESS-FILE control break processing in the Agent Subtotal Report program

The next two statements in Figure 7-35, lines 474 and 475, force the printing of the first page headings and first agent headings for the Agent Subtotal Report. Two separate routines, C-300-HEADINGS and C-310-AGENT-HEADINGS are performed. C-310-AGENT-HEADINGS contains the sequential SEARCH discussed earlier in this chapter and WRITE statements for printing the heading lines associated with each agent (see lines 547 through 565 of Figure 7-5 on page 7-10). Lines 477 and 478 then set up a loop with a PERFORM UNTIL for the paragraph C-200-PROCESS-RECORDS to process all of the records in the SORTED-PREMIUM-FILE. When the loop terminates, subtotals are forced out for the last agent processed, and the report summary lines are printed.

Figure 7-36 presents the code in C-200-PROCESS-RECORDS. The first sentence within this module compares the contents of the control field PR-AGENT-NAME to WA-HOLD-AGENT-NAME. If the fields are the same, processing continues with the printing of the next detail line. If the two fields are not the same, a control break occurs. The control break consists of performing paragraphs that print a subtotal for the agent just completed and the headings for the next agent to be processed.

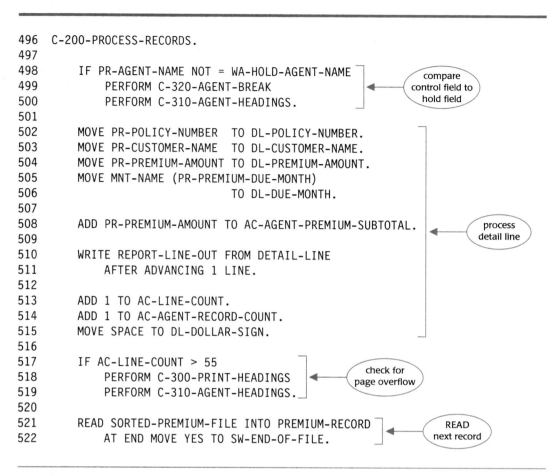

```
496  C-200-PROCESS-RECORDS.
497
498      IF PR-AGENT-NAME NOT = WA-HOLD-AGENT-NAME
499          PERFORM C-320-AGENT-BREAK
500          PERFORM C-310-AGENT-HEADINGS.
501
502      MOVE PR-POLICY-NUMBER  TO DL-POLICY-NUMBER.
503      MOVE PR-CUSTOMER-NAME  TO DL-CUSTOMER-NAME.
504      MOVE PR-PREMIUM-AMOUNT TO DL-PREMIUM-AMOUNT.
505      MOVE MNT-NAME (PR-PREMIUM-DUE-MONTH)
506                            TO DL-DUE-MONTH.
507
508      ADD PR-PREMIUM-AMOUNT TO AC-AGENT-PREMIUM-SUBTOTAL.
509
510      WRITE REPORT-LINE-OUT FROM DETAIL-LINE
511          AFTER ADVANCING 1 LINE.
512
513      ADD 1 TO AC-LINE-COUNT.
514      ADD 1 TO AC-AGENT-RECORD-COUNT.
515      MOVE SPACE TO DL-DOLLAR-SIGN.
516
517      IF AC-LINE-COUNT > 55
518          PERFORM C-300-PRINT-HEADINGS
519          PERFORM C-310-AGENT-HEADINGS.
520
521      READ SORTED-PREMIUM-FILE INTO PREMIUM-RECORD
522          AT END MOVE YES TO SW-END-OF-FILE.
```

compare control field to hold field

process detail line

check for page overflow

READ next record

FIGURE 7-36 C-200-PROCESS-RECORDS control break processing in the Agent Subtotal Report program

Figure 7-37 on the next page presents paragraph C-320-AGENT-BREAK, which writes agent subtotal information to the report. Lines 576 through 583 fill in summary line fields and print them. Once the subtotals have printed, the agent premium accumulator field, AC-AGENT-PREMIUM-SUBTOTAL, is added to the company premium accumulator field, AC-PREMIUM-TOTAL, on lines 585 through 587. The process of adding a subtotal accumulator to the next highest level accumulator during a control break is known as **rolling totals**. Rolling totals here eliminates the need to add a client's premium amount to the company accumulator during detail processing in C-200-PROCESS-RECORDS and thus improves the efficiency of the program. The client counter field for the current agent, AC-AGENT-RECORD-COUNT, is rolled into the client counter for the entire company, AC-RECORD-COUNT, on lines 589 through 591. Notice the use of the ON SIZE ERROR option on lines 586 and 590 of the ADD statements. These will cause a message to display on the user's terminal if high-order truncation occurs. Line 593 saves the new agent name in the hold field, WA-HOLD-AGENT-NAME. The fields AC-AGENT-PREMIUM-SUBTOTAL and AC-AGENT-RECORD-COUNT are initialized to zero on lines 594 and 595 in preparation for processing the clients of the next agent.

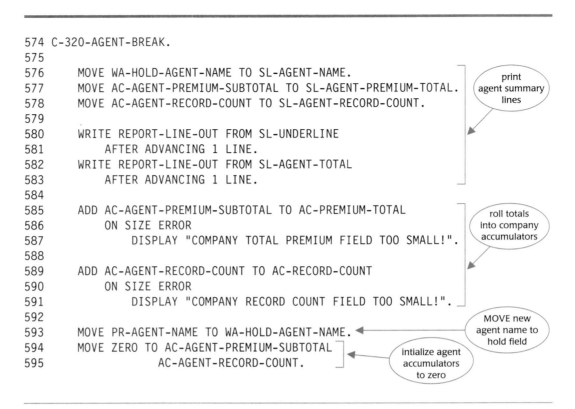

```
574 C-320-AGENT-BREAK.
575
576     MOVE WA-HOLD-AGENT-NAME TO SL-AGENT-NAME.
577     MOVE AC-AGENT-PREMIUM-SUBTOTAL TO SL-AGENT-PREMIUM-TOTAL.
578     MOVE AC-AGENT-RECORD-COUNT TO SL-AGENT-RECORD-COUNT.
579
580     WRITE REPORT-LINE-OUT FROM SL-UNDERLINE
581         AFTER ADVANCING 1 LINE.
582     WRITE REPORT-LINE-OUT FROM SL-AGENT-TOTAL
583         AFTER ADVANCING 1 LINE.
584
585     ADD AC-AGENT-PREMIUM-SUBTOTAL TO AC-PREMIUM-TOTAL
586         ON SIZE ERROR
587             DISPLAY "COMPANY TOTAL PREMIUM FIELD TOO SMALL!".
588
589     ADD AC-AGENT-RECORD-COUNT TO AC-RECORD-COUNT
590         ON SIZE ERROR
591             DISPLAY "COMPANY RECORD COUNT FIELD TOO SMALL!".
592
593     MOVE PR-AGENT-NAME TO WA-HOLD-AGENT-NAME.
594     MOVE ZERO TO AC-AGENT-PREMIUM-SUBTOTAL
595                  AC-AGENT-RECORD-COUNT.
```

print agent summary lines

roll totals into company accumulators

MOVE new agent name to hold field

intialize agent accumulators to zero

FIGURE 7-37 Paragraph C-320-AGENT-BREAK from the Agent Subtotal Report program

Back in Figure 7-36 on the previous page, whether or not a control break occurs, the detail line must be printed and a check made for page overflow. The final action in C-200-PROCESS-RECORDS is to READ the next record. Note than ON SIZE ERROR was not used on any of the ADD statements in C-200-PROCESS-RECORDS. Had ON SIZE ERROR been used it would have been coded in a fashion similar to its use in C-320-AGENT-BREAK.

Multiple-Level Control Breaks

Because only one control field is used in the Agent Subtotal Report program, it is considered to be an example of a **single-level control break**. The use of multiple control fields would allow for **multiple-level control breaks**. Each control field could be used to produce another summary line listing a subtotal amount. When multiple-level control break processing is required, logic is simplified by checking control field values in sequence from most major to most minor. Minor control fields are subordinate to major control fields in the same order as that used to sort the file. A control break on a major control field automatically implies the occurrence of one or more minor level control breaks. Therefore, a change detected in a major control field eliminates the need to test minor level control fields.

For example, suppose a second control break is to occur each time there is a change in insurance type within the customers listed for each agent. It would be necessary for the PREMIUM-INPUT-FILE to be sorted by insurance type within agent name. For the control break processing, agent name would be the major control field and insurance type would be the minor control field. A change in agent name would automatically imply an insurance type control break, so two summary lines would need to be printed. A change in insurance type would not necessarily imply a change in agent name. Figure 7-38 presents an example of how the output report might appear under such circumstances.

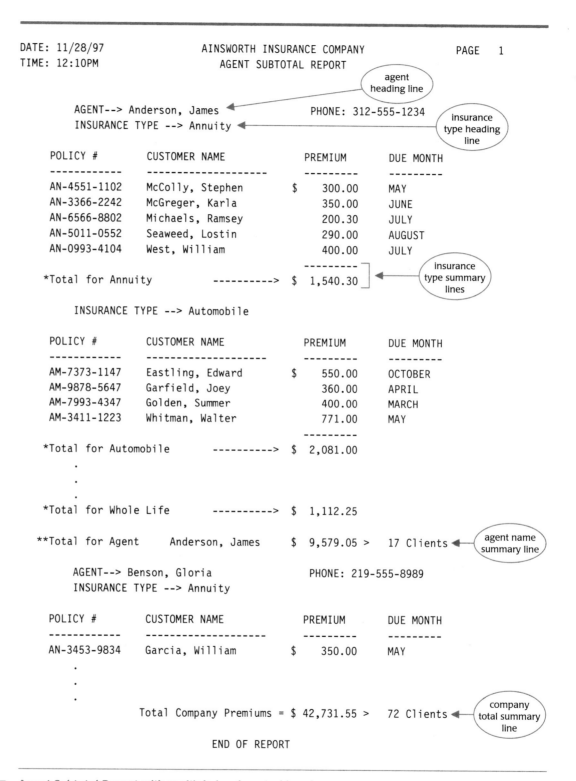

```
DATE: 11/28/97              AINSWORTH INSURANCE COMPANY           PAGE    1
TIME: 12:10PM                   AGENT SUBTOTAL REPORT
                                                        agent
                                                        heading line

        AGENT--> Anderson, James            PHONE: 312-555-1234
        INSURANCE TYPE --> Annuity                            insurance
                                                              type heading
                                                              line

    POLICY #        CUSTOMER NAME          PREMIUM      DUE MONTH
    -----------     --------------------   ---------    ---------
    AN-4551-1102    McColly, Stephen    $    300.00     MAY
    AN-3366-2242    McGreger, Karla          350.00     JUNE
    AN-6566-8802    Michaels, Ramsey         200.30     JULY
    AN-5011-0552    Seaweed, Lostin          290.00     AUGUST
    AN-0993-4104    West, William            400.00     JULY
                                         ---------            insurance
    *Total for Annuity       --------->  $  1,540.30           type summary
                                                               lines

         INSURANCE TYPE --> Automobile

    POLICY #        CUSTOMER NAME          PREMIUM      DUE MONTH
    -----------     --------------------   ---------    ---------
    AM-7373-1147    Eastling, Edward    $    550.00     OCTOBER
    AM-9878-5647    Garfield, Joey           360.00     APRIL
    AM-7993-4347    Golden, Summer           400.00     MARCH
    AM-3411-1223    Whitman, Walter          771.00     MAY
                                         ---------
    *Total for Automobile    --------->  $  2,081.00
              .
              .
              .
    *Total for Whole Life    --------->  $  1,112.25

   **Total for Agent      Anderson, James  $  9,579.05 >   17 Clients       agent name
                                                                            summary line

        AGENT--> Benson, Gloria             PHONE: 219-555-8989
        INSURANCE TYPE --> Annuity

    POLICY #        CUSTOMER NAME          PREMIUM      DUE MONTH
    -----------     --------------------   ---------    ---------
    AN-3453-9834    Garcia, William     $    350.00     MAY
              .
              .
              .
            Total Company Premiums = $ 42,731.55 >   72 Clients      company
                                                                     total summary
                                                                     line
                    END OF REPORT
```

FIGURE 7-38 Agent Subtotal Report with multiple-level control breaks

The flowchart presented in Figure 7-39 illustrates the logic for the multiple-level control break just described.

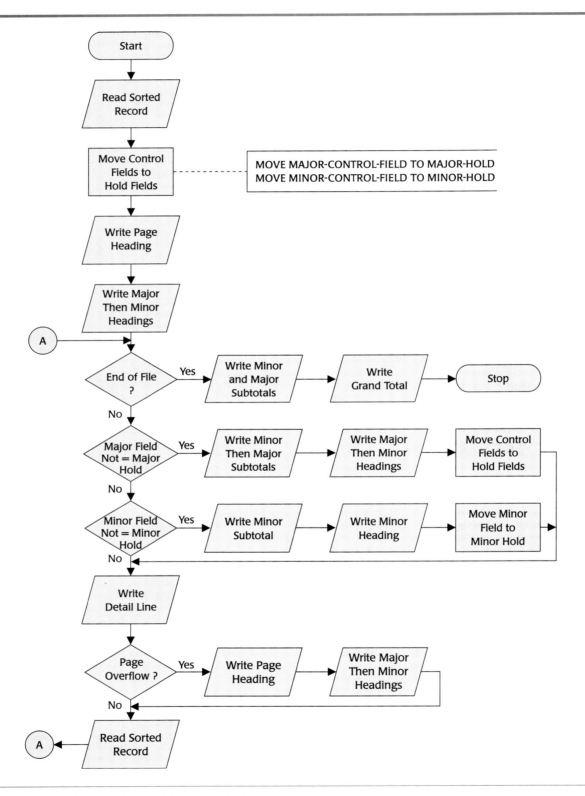

FIGURE 7-39   Multiple-level control break logic

Figures 7-40 and 7-41 on the next page present a partial listing of the COBOL code needed to produce the report illustrated in Figure 7-38 on page 7-39. Each additional control field required for the creation of a report necessitates an additional control field test in the logic.

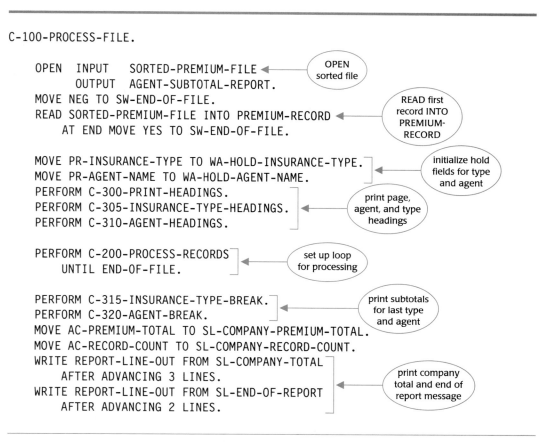

```
C-100-PROCESS-FILE.

    OPEN  INPUT   SORTED-PREMIUM-FILE
          OUTPUT  AGENT-SUBTOTAL-REPORT.
    MOVE NEG TO SW-END-OF-FILE.
    READ SORTED-PREMIUM-FILE INTO PREMIUM-RECORD
        AT END MOVE YES TO SW-END-OF-FILE.

    MOVE PR-INSURANCE-TYPE TO WA-HOLD-INSURANCE-TYPE.
    MOVE PR-AGENT-NAME TO WA-HOLD-AGENT-NAME.
    PERFORM C-300-PRINT-HEADINGS.
    PERFORM C-305-INSURANCE-TYPE-HEADINGS.
    PERFORM C-310-AGENT-HEADINGS.

    PERFORM C-200-PROCESS-RECORDS
        UNTIL END-OF-FILE.

    PERFORM C-315-INSURANCE-TYPE-BREAK.
    PERFORM C-320-AGENT-BREAK.
    MOVE AC-PREMIUM-TOTAL TO SL-COMPANY-PREMIUM-TOTAL.
    MOVE AC-RECORD-COUNT TO SL-COMPANY-RECORD-COUNT.
    WRITE REPORT-LINE-OUT FROM SL-COMPANY-TOTAL
        AFTER ADVANCING 3 LINES.
    WRITE REPORT-LINE-OUT FROM SL-END-OF-REPORT
        AFTER ADVANCING 2 LINES.
```

Callouts:
- OPEN sorted file
- READ first record INTO PREMIUM-RECORD
- initialize hold fields for type and agent
- print page, agent, and type headings
- set up loop for processing
- print subtotals for last type and agent
- print company total and end of report message

FIGURE 7-40   COBOL code for setting up a loop to produce the Agent Subtotal Report with two control fields, PR-INSURANCE-TYPE and PR-AGENT-NAME

```
C-200-PROCESS-RECORDS.

    IF PR-AGENT-NAME NOT = WA-HOLD-AGENT-NAME
        PERFORM C-315-INSURANCE-TYPE-BREAK
        PERFORM C-320-AGENT-BREAK
        PERFORM C-310-AGENT-HEADINGS
        PERFORM C-305-INSURANCE-TYPE-HEADINGS
    ELSE
        IF PR-INSURANCE-TYPE NOT = WA-HOLD-INSURANCE-TYPE
            PERFORM C-315-INSURANCE-TYPE-BREAK
            PERFORM C-305-INSURANCE-TYPE-HEADINGS.


    MOVE PR-POLICY-NUMBER   TO DL-POLICY-NUMBER.
    MOVE PR-CUSTOMER-NAME   TO DL-CUSTOMER-NAME.
    MOVE PR-PREMIUM-AMOUNT  TO DL-PREMIUM-AMOUNT.
    MOVE MNT-NAME (PR-PREMIUM-DUE-MONTH) TO DL-DUE-MONTH.
    ADD PR-PREMIUM-AMOUNT TO AC-INSURANCE-TYPE-SUBTOTAL
                             AC-AGENT-PREMIUM-SUBTOTAL

    WRITE REPORT-LINE-OUT FROM DETAIL-LINE
        AFTER ADVANCING 1 LINE.

    ADD 1 TO AC-LINE-COUNT.
    ADD 1 TO AC-AGENT-RECORD-COUNT.
    MOVE SPACE TO DL-DOLLAR-SIGN.

    IF AC-LINE-COUNT > 55
        PERFORM C-300-PRINT-HEADINGS
        PERFORM C-305-INSURANCE-TYPE-HEADINGS
        PERFORM C-310-AGENT-HEADINGS.

    READ SORTED-PREMIUM-FILE INTO PREMIUM-RECORD
        AT END MOVE YES TO SW-END-OF-FILE.
```

compare control fields to hold fields

process detail line

check for page overflow

READ next record

FIGURE 7-41   COBOL code for producing an Agent Subtotal Report with control breaks on insurance type within agent name

CHAPTER SUMMARY

The following list summarizes this chapter. The summary is designed to help you study and understand the material and concepts presented.

1. A **table** is a series of related fields with the same attributes stored in consecutive locations in main memory.

2. The logic involving the techniques for defining and processing tables is called **table processing**.

3. When the constant data for a table is coded in the program, the table is said to be an **embedded table**.

4. An **OCCURS** clause specifies the number of times a field is repeated.

5. Each occurrence of a field is called an **element** within the table.

6. A **subscript** is a numeric value in parentheses that identifies the element within a table that is to be referenced.

7. No constant values precede the definition of a **non-embedded table**.

8. The process of **loading** a non-embedded table must be done in the PROCEDURE DIVISION.

9. The **INDEXED BY** clause is used to define an index name for a table.

10. An index name can be used only in conjunction with the table in which it is defined. It cannot be modified using a MOVE or be used in arithmetic.

11. An index name can be modified by use of the **SET** statement or a PERFORM VARYING.

12. A **SEARCH** statement performs a **linear search** or **sequential search** and is used to search a table from top to bottom.

13. A **SEARCH ALL** statement performs a **binary search**, which keeps splitting a table in half as it searches.

14. A binary search cannot be used unless a table is sequenced by one or more of its elements and has either an ASCENDING KEY or DESCENDING KEY clause in its definition.

15. A **fixed-length table** is defined with a specific number in the OCCURS clause.

16. A **variable-length table** allows a table definition to be made and the exact number of elements determined at the time the table is loaded.

17. OCCURS DEPENDING ON is used in the definition of a variable-length table to establish a minimum and maximum number of elements allowed.

18. In **one-dimensional tables**, each element within the table is identified by a single subscript or index value.

19. **Multi-dimensional tables** are tables that require two or more subscripts or indexes to reference a specific element within the table and are defined with more than one OCCURS clause.

20. A **control break** occurs when the value of the **control field** changes from the value found in the previous input record.

21. The process of adding a subtotal accumulator to the next highest level accumulator during a control break is known as **rolling totals**.

22. A **single-level control break** involves the use of one control field.

23. A **multiple-level control break** involves the use of two or more control fields.

KEY TERMS

arrays (7-1)
binary search (7-21)
control break processing (7-1)
control field (7-34)
element (7-11)
embedded table (7-10)
fixed-length table (7-27)
index (7-16)
INDEXED BY (7-16)
input-loaded tables (7-18)
linear search (7-21)
loading (7-15)
multi-dimensional tables (7-29)
multiple-level control breaks (7-38)
non-embedded table (7-15)
OCCURS (7-11)

one-dimensional tables (7-29)
rolling totals (7-37)
SEARCH (7-21)
SEARCH ALL (7-21)
search argument (7-23)
sequential search (7-21)
SET (7-17)
single-level control break (7-38)
subscript (7-13)
summary report (7-1)
table argument (7-23)
table limit (7-12)
table processing (7-1)
tables (7-1)
variable-length table (7-27)

STUDENT ASSIGNMENTS

Student Assignment 1: True/False

Instructions: Circle T if the statement is true or F if the statement is false.

T **F** 1. The terms table and array mean the same thing in COBOL.

T **F** 2. An embedded table must be loaded in the PROCEDURE DIVISION before its elements can be accessed.

T **F** 3. The definition of a non-embedded table must be preceded by a REDEFINES clause.

T **F** 4. A subscript field can be any numeric integer item.

T **F** 5. The OCCURS clause allows for the definition of both fixed-length and variable-length tables.

T **F** 6. Literal values cannot be used as subscripts.

T **F** 7. The INDEXED BY clause must be used on tables processed with a SEARCH statement.

T **F** 8. An index can be manipulated with a SET statement and PERFORM VARYING.

T **F** 9. The ASCENDING KEY or DESCENDING KEY clause must be used in the definition of a table processed with a SEARCH ALL.

T **F** 10. The AT END clause is required in both a SEARCH and SEARCH ALL.

T **F** 11. A binary search begins at the top of a table and searches each element, one after the other.

T **F** 12. Multi-dimensional tables are defined by using the OCCURS clause two or more times.

T **F** 13. The OCCURS clause can be used no more than four times in a single table definition.

T **F** 14. The WHEN clause can appear only once in a linear search.

T   F   15. A variable-length table is defined with a minimum and maximum number of occurrences indicated.

T   F   16. In searching a multi-dimensional table, the SEARCH statement can manipulate only the index name defined with the data name following the word SEARCH.

T   F   17. An index name can be used only with elements within the table in which the index is defined.

T   F   18. A control break occurs when the value in the control field changes.

T   F   19. The input file to a control break program must be in sequence by the control field.

T   F   20. Multiple control fields are not allowed in control break processing.

Student Assignment 2: Multiple Choice

Instructions: Circle the correct response.

1. Which of the following tables requires constant values to be defined prior to the table definition?
   a. subscripted
   b. indexed
   c. embedded
   d. non-embedded
   e. none of the above

2. If the OCCURS clause is used more than once in the definition of a table, then the table must be _____.
   a. embedded
   b. non-embedded
   c. indexed
   d. multi-dimensional
   e. none of the above

3. Which term best describes a table that must be loaded before it can be accessed?
   a. subscripted table
   b. indexed table
   c. embedded table
   d. non-embedded table
   e. none of the above

4. The SEARCH statement can be used only on what type of table?
   a. subscripted
   b. indexed
   c. embedded
   d. non-embedded
   e. none of the above

5. A binary search can best be described as _____.
   a. starting at the top of a table and working its way down
   b. starting at the middle of the table and dividing it in half after each comparison
   c. starting at the bottom of a table and dividing it in half after each comparison
   d. something to avoid as much as possible
   e. both a and d

(continued)

Student Assignment 2 (continued)

6. Which of the following statements will increase the value of the index name MY-INDEX by 1?
   a. SET MY-INDEX UP BY 1.
   b. SET MY-INDEX DOWN BY 1.
   c. ADD 1 TO MY-INDEX.
   d. COMPUTE MY-INDEX = MY-INDEX + 1.
   e. all of the above

7. The maximum number of times the OCCURS clause can be used in a table definition is _____.
   a. four
   b. three
   c. seven
   d. one
   e. none of the above

8. A table defined with an INDEXED BY clause and an ASCENDING KEY clause can be searched using _____.
   a. either a linear search or a binary search
   b. only a linear search
   c. only a binary search
   d. a linear search only if it is an embedded table
   e. none of the above

9. A control break occurs when _____.
   a. the previous value of the control field is the same as the current value of the control field
   b. the previous value of the control field is different from the current value of the control field
   c. the subtotal amount reaches a critical level and must be printed to avoid high-order truncation
   d. the next sequential record is accessed and a detail line must be printed
   e. none of the above

10. The number of control fields allowed in control break processing is _____.
   a. limited to three on most computer systems
   b. limited to seven in standard COBOL
   c. unlimited
   d. strictly dependent on the type of computer system used
   e. none of the above

Student Assignment 3: Coding a Non-Embedded Table

Instructions: Code a non-embedded indexed table that will accommodate a three-character job code called WT-JOB-CODE and an associated six-digit wage rate, PIC 9(4)V99, called WT-WAGE-RATE, for fifteen different jobs.

Student Assignment 4: Coding an Embedded Table

Instructions: Write the COBOL code required in the WORKING-STORAGE SECTION of the DATA DIVISION to define an embedded table containing the following list of U.S. presidents:

```
FRANKLIN ROOSEVELT
HARRY TRUMAN
DWIGHT EISENHOWER
JOHN KENNEDY
LYNDON JOHNSON
GERALD FORD
JIMMY CARTER
RONALD REAGAN
GEORGE BUSH
BILL CLINTON
```

Student Assignment 5: Loading a Non-Embedded Table

Instructions: Given the following FD, record definition, and table definition, code the logic needed in the PROCEDURE DIVISION to load the non-embedded table from the given file.

```
FD   PARTS-FILE.

01   PARTS-RECORD.
     02                         PIC XX.
     02   PR-NUMBER             PIC X(12).
     02   PR-NAME               PIC X(20).
     02   PR-QUANTITY           PIC 9(5).

01   PARTS-TABLE.
     02   PT-ITEM OCCURS 50 TIMES
             INDEXED BY PARTS-INDEX.
     03   PT-NUMBER     PIC X(12).
     03   PT-NAME       PIC X(20).
     03   PT-QUANTITY   PIC 9(5).
```

Student Assignment 6: Coding a Sequential SEARCH

Instructions: Using the table defined in Student Assignment 5, use a SEARCH statement to code a sequential search that uses IN-PART-NUMBER as the search argument. When a match is found, move the value of PT-NAME to the field DL-PART-NAME-OUT. If no match is found, move the message "NOT FOUND" to DL-PART-NAME-OUT.

Student Assignment 7: Coding a Binary SEARCH

Instructions: Rewrite the definition of the table given in Student Assignment 5 so a binary search can be performed on the table. Code the table definition as though the elements are in ascending sequence by the field PT-NUMBER. Once you have rewritten the table, code a binary search for the table using the same conditions presented in Student Assignment 6.

COBOL LABORATORY EXERCISES

Exercise 1: Modified Agent Subtotal Report Program

Purpose: To gain experience in COBOL program maintenance and modification and in the use of COBOL tables.

Problem: Open the file PROJ7.CBL on the Student Diskette that accompanies this book and modify the Agent Subtotal Report program making the following changes:

1. In A-100-INITIALIZATION, SORT the records in the PREMIUM-INPUT-FILE so that in SORTED-PREMIUM-FILE they are in sequence by insurance type within agent name.

2. Modify the embedded MONTH-NAME-TABLE and its associated constant data so only the first three letters of each month are used to name a month. Make any necessary changes to DETAIL-LINE to output each three-character month name.

3. Add another field to DETAIL-LINE so that a customer's gender is printed. Print MALE if PR-SEX contains the letter M and print FEMALE if PR-SEX contains the letter F.

4. Modify the control break logic so that a minor control break occurs when a change is made in insurance type and a major control break occurs when a change is made in agent name. In both cases, print subtotals for the premium amount.

Save this program as EX7-1.CBL.

Input Data: Use the Premium file presented in Appendix A as input to the SORT. This file is named PREMIUM.DAT on the Student Diskette that accompanies this book. Use the Agent Phone file as input to load the non-embedded AGENT-PHONE-TABLE. This file is named AGENTPHO.DAT.

Output Results: Output should be a report similar to the sample report presented in Figure 7-38 on page 7-39. Include a company total and an END OF REPORT message.

Exercise 2: Customer Purchases Subtotal Report Program

Purpose: To practice the use of COBOL tables and control break logic in the creation of a COBOL program that produces a Customer Purchases Subtotal Report.

Problem: Write a program that lists purchase records for the ABC Department Store in sequence by sales clerk identification number. Sort the input file in ascending sequence by sales clerk ID, and then use the sorted file as input to the report logic. Each time a change occurs in the sales clerk identification number, print a total for the purchases made by customers of the sales clerk. For each clerk, use data loaded into a non-embedded table to perform a binary search finding the sales clerk identification number and accessing the sales clerk's name.

For each sales date, use an embedded table to translate the month into a three-character abbreviation for that month. Input sales dates are in MMDDYY format and should be printed in DD-MMM-YY format. For example, an input date of 112897 should be printed on the report as 28-NOV-97.

For each purchase record listed, print the date of purchase, account number, customer name, item purchased, and purchase amount. Print the current date and time in the headings on every page. Time should be printed in AM/PM format. Number each page starting each report with page 1. At the end of the report, print the total number of records listed and total purchases. Save this program as EX7-2.CBL.

Input Data: Use the Customer file listed in Appendix A as input to the SORT. This file is named CUSTOMER.DAT on the Student Diskette that accompanies this book. Customer records have the following layout:

Field Description	Position	Length	Attribute
Date of Purchase	1–6	6	Numeric, PIC 9(6)
Account Number	7–12	6	Alphanumeric
Customer Name	13–32	20	Alphanumeric
Item Purchased	33–52	20	Alphanumeric
Quantity Purchased	53	1	Numeric, PIC 9
Balance	54–59	6	Numeric, PIC S9(4)V99
Purchase Amount	60–65	6	Numeric, PIC 9(4)V99
filler	66–70	5	Alphanumeric
Sales Clerk ID	71–72	2	Alphanumeric
Record Length		72	

Use the Clerk Name file listed in Appendix A as input for loading a non-embedded clerk name table. There are 11 records in this file. This file is named CLRKNAME.DAT on the Student Diskette that accompanies this book. Each record of this file has the following layout:

Field Description	Position	Length	Attribute
Sales Clerk ID	1–2	2	Alphanumeric
Sales Clerk Name	3–22	20	Alphanumeric
Record Length		22	

Output Results: Output consists of the Customer Purchases Subtotal Report listing the date of purchase, account number, customer name, item purchased, and purchase amount for each customer. Single-space between records, but double-space after clerk headings and before and after clerk subtotals. Count and print the number of records processed and the total purchases for each clerk as well as a grand total at the end of the report.

The report should have a format similar to the following:

```
DATE: Z9/99/99                  ABC DEPARTMENT STORE                 PAGE Z9
TIME: Z9:99 AM            CUSTOMER PURCHASES SUBTOTAL REPORT

Clerk ID -  XX            Clerk Name -  XXXXXXXXXXXXXXXXXXXX

   DATE OF      ACCOUNT                                             PURCHASE
   PURCHASE     NUMBER    CUSTOMER NAME         ITEM PURCHASED      AMOUNT
   ---------    -------   --------------------  --------------------  ---------
   DD-MMM-YY    XXXXXX    XXXXXXXXXXXXXXXXXXXX  XXXXXXXXXXXXXXXXXXXX  $Z,ZZZ.99
   DD-MMM-YY    XXXXXX    XXXXXXXXXXXXXXXXXXXX  XXXXXXXXXXXXXXXXXXXX   Z,ZZZ.99
      .
      .
      .
   DD-MMM-YY    XXXXXX    XXXXXXXXXXXXXXXXXXXX  XXXXXXXXXXXXXXXXXXXX   Z,ZZZ.99

  *Totals for Clerk  XXXXXXXXXXXXXXXXXXXX - Z9 Customers -  Total Purchases  $ZZ,ZZ9.99

Clerk ID -  XX            Clerk Name -  XXXXXXXXXXXXXXXXXXXX

   DATE OF      ACCOUNT                                             PURCHASE
   PURCHASE     NUMBER    CUSTOMER NAME         ITEM PURCHASED      AMOUNT
   ---------    -------   --------------------  --------------------  ---------
   DD-MMM-YY    XXXXXX    XXXXXXXXXXXXXXXXXXXX  XXXXXXXXXXXXXXXXXXXX  $Z,ZZZ.99
      .
      .
      .
   DD-MMM-YY    XXXXXX    XXXXXXXXXXXXXXXXXXXX  XXXXXXXXXXXXXXXXXXXX   Z,ZZZ.99

  *Totals for Clerk  XXXXXXXXXXXXXXXXXXXX - Z9 Customers -  Total Purchases  $ZZ,ZZ9.99

  **        TOTAL RECORDS PROCESSED   =    ZZ9        TOTAL PURCHASES  = $ZZ,ZZ9.99

                              END OF REPORT
```

Exercise 3: Customer Sales Subtotal Report Program

Purpose: To practice coding a COBOL program that uses COBOL tables and control break processing.

Problem: Design and code a COBOL program that processes the records of the Customer Sales file for EZ Auto Sales and creates a Customer Sales Subtotal Report. The program should list records by auto make, printing the customer's number, name, address, purchase date, purchase price, and satisfaction rating. Include the current date and time in the page headings. Use AM/PM format for the time. Sort records by auto make before producing the report. Each time a change occurs in auto make, print the number of autos listed for that make and the total purchase price. At the end of the report, provide summary lines for a count of all autos sold and total of all purchases.

Customer addresses should be obtained by using a binary search on a non-embedded table that contains the customer numbers and addresses. This table must be loaded before it can be accessed. Obtain the description of each satisfaction rating code by using an embedded table. Perform a sequential search on this table. Save this program as EX7-3.CBL.

Input Data: Use the Customer Sales file listed in Appendix A as input. There are 73 records in this file. This file is named CUSTSALE.DAT on the Student Diskette that accompanies this book. The record layout for the customer records is as follows:

Field Description	Position	Length	Attribute
Customer Zip Code	1–5	5	Alphanumeric
Customer Zip + 4	6–9	4	Alphanumeric
Customer Number	10–13	4	Alphanumeric
Customer Name	14–33	20	Alphanumeric
Purchase Date	34–39	6	Numeric, PIC 9(6)
Auto Make	40–59	20	Alphanumeric
Purchase Price	60–66	7	Numeric, PIC 9(5)V99
Year of Auto	67–70	4	Alphanumeric
filler	71–73	3	Alphanumeric
Satisfaction Code	74	1	Alphanumeric, 0 = DISSATISFIED 1 = UNDECIDED 2 = SATISFIED
Record Length		74	

Use the Customer Address file listed in Appendix A as input for loading the non-embedded customer address table. This file is named CUSTADDR.DAT on the Student Diskette that accompanies this book. The records are already in sequence by customer number. The record layout for the customer records is as follows:

Field Description	Position	Length	Attribute
Customer Number	1–4	4	Alphanumeric
Customer Address	5–24	20	Alphanumeric
Record Length		24	

Output Results: A Customer Sales Subtotal Report should be output listing the customer's number, name, address, purchase date, purchase price, and satisfaction rating. Provide a count of the number of customers listed and total sum of purchases for each auto make as well as a grand total at the end of the report. Single-space detail lines on the report and list the current date and time in the headings. The time should be in AM/PM format. The report should have a format similar to the following:

```
DATE: Z9/99/99                  EZ AUTO SALES                     PAGE Z9
TIME: Z9:99 AM            CUSTOMER SALES SUBTOTAL REPORT


MAKE --> XXXXXXXXXXXXXXXXXXXX
CUSTOMER CUSTOMER               STREET               PURCHASE  PURCHASE   SATIS.
NUMBER   NAME                   ADDRESS              DATE      PRICE      RATING
-------- --------------------   --------------------  --------  ---------  ---------

  XXXX   XXXXXXXXXXXXXXXXXXXX   XXXXXXXXXXXXXXXXXXXX  Z9/99/99  $ZZ,ZZZ.99  XXXXXXXXX
  XXXX   XXXXXXXXXXXXXXXXXXXX   XXXXXXXXXXXXXXXXXXXX  Z9/99/99  $ZZ,ZZZ.99  XXXXXXXXX
  XXXX   XXXXXXXXXXXXXXXXXXXX   XXXXXXXXXXXXXXXXXXXX  Z9/99/99  $ZZ,ZZZ.99  XXXXXXXXX
    .
    .
    .
                                                               ----------
*  TOTAL OF ZZ9 CARS OF MAKE XXXXXXXXXXXXXXXXXXXX SOLD FOR      $ZZZ,ZZZ.99

MAKE --> XXXXXXXXXXXXXXXXXXXX
CUSTOMER CUSTOMER               STREET               PURCHASE  PURCHASE   SATIS.
NUMBER   NAME                   ADDRESS              DATE      PRICE      RATING
-------- --------------------   --------------------  --------  ---------  ---------

  XXXX   XXXXXXXXXXXXXXXXXXXX   XXXXXXXXXXXXXXXXXXXX  Z9/99/99  $ZZ,ZZZ.99  XXXXXXXXX
    .
    .
    .
                                                               ----------
*  TOTAL OF ZZ9 CARS OF MAKE XXXXXXXXXXXXXXXXXXXX SOLD FOR      $ZZZ,ZZZ.99

                        TOTAL CARS SOLD =     ZZ9
                        TOTAL PURCHASES = $ZZZ,ZZ9.99

                             END OF REPORT
```

CHAPTER EIGHT

Data Manipulation and Sequential File Maintenance

OBJECTIVES

You will have mastered the material in Chapter 8 when you can:

- Explain and code an INSPECT TALLYING statement
- Understand and code an INSPECT REPLACING statement
- Describe and code an INSPECT CONVERTING statement
- Understand the function of an UNSTRING statement
- Explain the function of a STRING statement
- Describe how to manipulate data with an intrinsic function
- Identify the function of the COPY command
- Understand the function of a transaction file
- Explain file matching and updating a sequential file
- Understand the function of a REWRITE statement

INTRODUCTION

It is often necessary to manipulate the contents of a field in a manner that allows information about the field to be extracted or the contents of the field to be modified. The COBOL statements examined in this chapter allow for such data manipulation. Often, the data contained within the records of a file must be modified. The process of modifying the records in a file is called **file maintenance**. Chapter 8 examines file maintenance processing for a sequential file.

The sample program presented in this chapter updates the records of the Premium file by adding a dollar amount to the premium amount field and modifying the contents of the agent name field and policy number field. Once the specified fields have been updated, the entire record is written to a new version of the Premium file.

The premium amount field is modified using data supplied by a transaction file. A **transaction file** is a file specifically created to supply data needed during file maintenance processing. A transaction file indicates which records in a file are to be updated and what modifications are to occur.

The Transaction Log Report

Figure 8-1 presents a partial listing of the Transaction Log Report output by the program used in this chapter. The Transaction Log Report indicates the disposition of every transaction processed from the transaction file. Such a report provides an audit trail of the file maintenance activities.

```
DATE: 11/28/97              AINSWORTH INSURANCE COMPANY           PAGE   1
TIME: 12:25PM                  TRANSACTION LOG REPORT


                    TRANSACTION RECORD        DISPOSITION
                    --------------------      --------------------
                    AM-7211 726100000500      HYPHEN(S) MISSING

                    MM-1107-239300000200      POLICY CODE INVALID

                    HM-5109-417W00002200      CODE #2 NOT NUMERIC
                           .
                           .
                           .
                    RT-4QQ1-110200000000      CODE #1 NOT NUMERIC
                                              PREMIUM AMT NOT NUMERIC
                           .
                           .
                           .
                    AM-3411-122300001800      TRANSACTION POSTED

                    AM-6128-215100001200      TRANSACTION POSTED

                    AM-7211-7261              UNMATCHED PREMIUM RECORD

                    AM-7373-114700003000      TRANSACTION POSTED
                           .
                           .
                           .
```

FIGURE 8-1 Partial listing of the Transaction Log Report   *(continued)*

```
          RT-5521-045600000880      UNMATCHED TRANSACTION

          RT-5525-055600000550      TRANSACTION POSTED
                   .
                   .
                   .
          RT-9580-0003              UNMATCHED PREMIUM RECORD

          TL-2129-895900002100      TRANSACTION POSTED

          TL-2762-272800000250      TRANSACTION POSTED

          TL-3319-1614              UNMATCHED PREMIUM RECORD

          TL-5522-212100001000      TRANSACTION POSTED
                   .
                   .
                   .
          TL-7007-569100004500      DUPLICATE TRANSACTION

          TL-7008-555100000800      TRANSACTION POSTED
                   .
                   .
                   .
          WL-2721-390400000600      TRANSACTION POSTED

          Total Bad Transactions          =    7
          Total Posted Transactions       =   67
          Total Unmatched Transactions    =    2
          Total Duplicate Transactions    =    1
          Total Unmatched Premium Records =    5

                    END OF REPORT
```

Figure 8-2 on the next page presents the first five records of the PREMIUM-INPUT-FILE used as input to the sample program and the first five records of the UPDATED-PREMIUM-FILE output by the program. Can you identify the changes made to the specified fields? Some of the changes are made here to simply demonstrate the use of specific COBOL statements.

```
PREMIUM-INPUT-FILE                                          Prem
                      Agent Name              Policy Num   Amt
Leach, Raeanne        Jones, William     Automobile AM-1004-2553 0100550 PF199104
Allister, Collin      McDonald, Fred     Automobile AM-1991-9223 0012345 PM199411
Amfelter, Audrey      McDonald, Fred     Automobile AM-2199-9229 0045650 FF199606
Senef, Marcia         McDonald, Fred     Automobile AM-3323-3441 0078080 FF199307
Whitman, Walter       Anderson, James    Automobile AM-3411-1223 0077100 PM199405
       .
       .
       .


UPDATED-PREMIUM-FILE                                        Prem
                      Agent Name              Policy Num   Amt
Leach, Raeanne        William Jones      Automobile AM*1004*2553 0102050 PF199104
Allister, Collin      Fred McDonald      Automobile AM*1991*9223 0015795 PM199411
Amfelter, Audrey      Fred McDonald      Automobile AM*2199*9229 0052150 FF199606
Senef, Marcia         Fred McDonald      Automobile AM*3323*3441 0078880 FF199307
Whitman, Walter       James Anderson     Automobile AM*3411*1223 0078900 PM199405
       .
       .
       .
```

FIGURE 8-2   The first five records of the PREMIUM-INPUT-FILE and the first five records of the UPDATED-PREMIUM-FILE

Hierarchy Chart

Figure 8-3 presents a hierarchy chart that illustrates the organization of the PROCEDURE DIVISION of the sample program presented in this chapter.

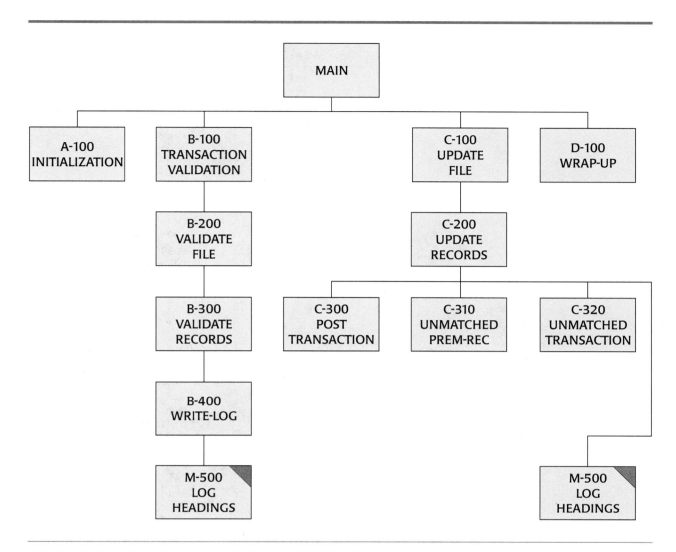

FIGURE 8-3   Hierarchy chart for the Premium File Update program

Program Flowchart

Figure 8-4 on the next page presents a partial flowchart that illustrates the combined file maintenance logic used in paragraphs C-100-UPDATE-FILE, C-200-UPDATE-RECORDS, C-300-POST-TRANSACTION, C-310-UNMATCHED-PREMIUM-RECORD, and C-320-UNMATCHED-TRANSACTION in the sample program presented in this chapter. Other file maintenance considerations will be presented later in the chapter, and the logic for these considerations will be illustrated using other flowcharts.

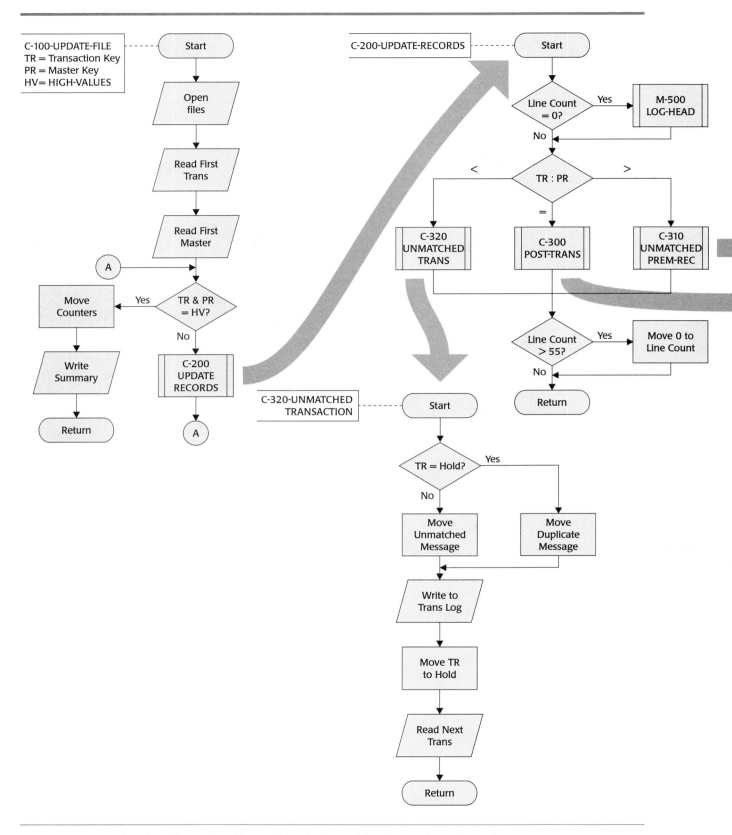

FIGURE 8-4 Flowchart illustrating file matching logic used in the Premium File Update program

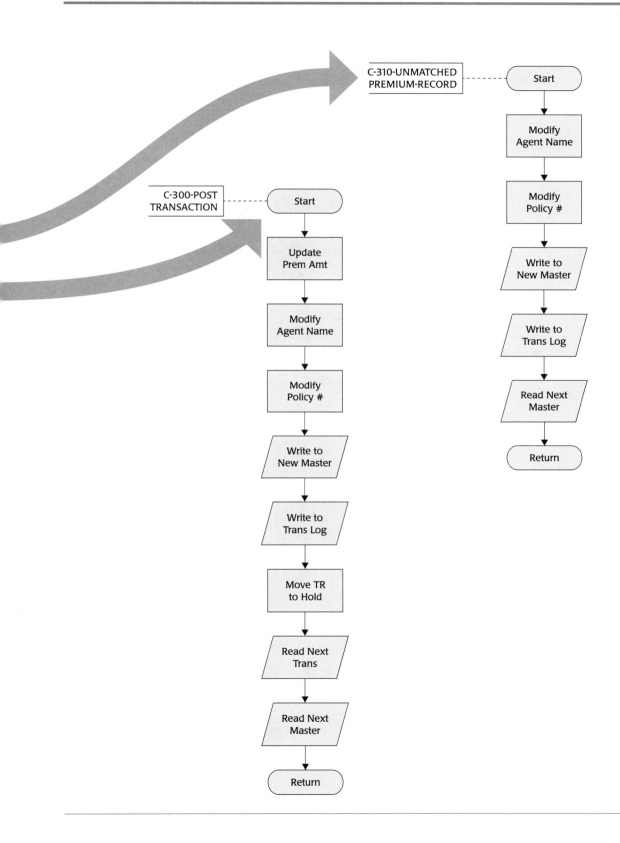

Transaction File Record Layout

The record layout of the Premium file used as input to the sample program in this chapter is exactly the same as the layout used in Chapter 7. Figure 8-5 presents the record layout for the Transaction file, which also is used as input to the sample program in this chapter. The transaction record layout contains just two fields, the policy number and a premium amount. Both fields are redefined for purposes of validation. The validation of these two fields and other processing performed on the transaction file will be discussed later in this chapter.

Field	Position	Length	Attribute
Policy Number	1–12	12	Alphanumeric
	Redefined,	Code	2-characters
	Isolating	Hyphen	1-character
		Code Number	4-characters
		Hyphen	1-character
		Code Number	4-characters
Premium Amount	13–20	8	Numeric, 2 decimal positions
	Redefined		Alphanumeric
Total Record Length		20	

FIGURE 8-5   The transaction record layout

The Premium File Update Program

Figure 8-6 presents the Premium File Update program discussed in this chapter. This program is found on the Student Diskette that accompanies this book. The agent name and policy number fields in the Premium file are modified using COBOL statements designed specifically for rearranging or changing the contents of a field. These statements can be used in any situation where information about the contents of a field is needed or where the contents of a field need to be modified.

```
 1  IDENTIFICATION DIVISION.
 2  ************************
 3
 4  PROGRAM-ID.      PREMUPDT.
 5  AUTHOR.          R. O. FOREMAN.
 6  INSTALLATION.    PURDUE UNIVERSITY CALUMET.
 7  DATE-WRITTEN.    NOV. 28, 1997.
 8  DATE-COMPILED.   28-Nov-1997.
 9  ****************************************************************
10  *                   PROGRAM NARRATIVE                         *
11  *                                                             *
12  *                                                             *
13  *   THIS PROGRAM VALIDATES AND SORTS RECORDS IN A TRANSACTION *
14  *   FILE THAT IS THEN USED TO UPDATE THE PREMIUM AMOUNT IN EACH *
15  *   RECORD OF THE PREMIUM INPUT FILE.  THE PREMIUM INPUT FILE  *
16  *   IS PRE-SEQUENCED BY POLICY NUMBER.  A NEW VERSION OF THE   *
17  *   PREMIUM INPUT FILE IS CREATED.  A TRANSACTION LOG REPORT   *
18  *   IS CREATED LISTING THE DISPOSITION OF EVERY TRANSACTION.   *
19  *   DURING PROCESSING, THE AGENT NAME IS REARRANGED SO THAT THE *
20  *   FIRST NAME IS FIRST IN THE NEW VERSION OF THE PREMIUM FILE. *
21  *                                                             *
22  *      INPUT:      TRANFILE.DAT - TRANSACTION FILE            *
23  *                  SPREMIUM.DAT - SEQUENCED PREMIUM INPUT FILE *
24  *                                                             *
25  *      INPUT/OUTPUT: STRANFL.DAT  - SORTED TRANSACTION FILE   *
26  *                                                             *
27  *      OUTPUT:     UPREMIUM.DAT - UPDATED PREMIUM FILE        *
28  *                  TRANLOG.RPT  - TRANSACTION LOG REPORT      *
29  *                                                             *
30  *      SORT FILE:  SORTWORK    - SORT FILE FOR TRANSACTIONS   *
31  ****************************************************************
32  /
33  ENVIRONMENT DIVISION.
34  ********************
35
36  INPUT-OUTPUT SECTION.
37  ********************
38
39  FILE-CONTROL.
40
41      SELECT TRANSACTION-FILE
42          ASSIGN TO "A:\PREMTRAN.DAT".
43
44      SELECT SORT-FILE
45          ASSIGN TO "SORTWORK".
46
47      SELECT TRANSACTION-LOG-REPORT
48          ASSIGN TO "A:\TRANLOG.RPT".
49
50      SELECT SORTED-TRANSACTION-FILE
51          ASSIGN TO "STRANFL.DAT".
52
53      SELECT PREMIUM-INPUT-FILE
54          ASSIGN TO "A:\SPREMIUM.DAT".
55
56      SELECT UPDATED-PREMIUM-FILE
57          ASSIGN TO "UPREMIUM.DAT".
58
59  /
60  DATA DIVISION.
61  **************
62
63  FILE SECTION.
64  *************
65
66  ****************************************************************
67  *                                                             *
68  *   TRANSACTION FILE - VALIDATED AND SORTED IN THE PROGRAM;   *
69  *   THE LAYOUT, TRANSACTION RECORD, IS IN WORKING-STORAGE     *
70  *                                                             *
71  ****************************************************************
72
73  FD  TRANSACTION-FILE.
74
75  01  TRAN-RECORD              PIC X(20).
76
77  ****************************************************************
78  *                                                             *
79  *   SORT-FILE - FOR SORTING THE TRANSACTION FILE BY POLICY NUMBER *
80  *                                                             *
81  ****************************************************************
82
83  SD  SORT-FILE.
84
85  01  SORT-RECORD.
86      02  SR-POLICY-NUMBER    PIC X(12).
87      02                      PIC X(8).
88
89  ****************************************************************
90  *                                                             *
91  *   TRANSACTION LOG REPORT - A REPORT ON EVERY TRANSACTION    *
92  *                                                             *
93  ****************************************************************
94
95  FD  TRANSACTION-LOG-REPORT.
96
97  01  TRAN-LOG-LINE-OUT        PIC X(80).
98  /
99  ****************************************************************
100 *                                                             *
101 *   SORTED TRANSACTION FILE - CONTAINS SORTED TRANSACTIONS    *
102 *                                                             *
103 ****************************************************************
104
105 FD  SORTED-TRANSACTION-FILE.
106
107 01  SORTED-TRAN-RECORD       PIC X(20).
108
109 ****************************************************************
110 *                                                             *
111 *   INPUT-FILE - SEQUENCED PREMIUM INPUT FILE;               *
112 *   THE RECORD LAYOUT, PREMIUM-RECORD, IS COPIED INTO        *
113 *   WORKING-STORAGE BY A COPY STATEMENT                      *
114 ****************************************************************
115
116 FD  PREMIUM-INPUT-FILE.
117
118 01  PREMIUM-INPUT-RECORD     PIC X(80).
119
120 ****************************************************************
121 *                                                             *
122 *   UPDATED PREMIUM FILE - NEXT GENERATION OF THE PREMIUM FILE *
123 *                                                             *
124 ****************************************************************
125
```

FIGURE 8-6   Premium File Update program   *(continued)*

```
126  FD  UPDATED-PREMIUM-FILE.                            202
127                                                       203  01  TRANSACTION-RECORD.
128  01  UPDATED-PREMIUM-RECORD        PIC X(80).         204      02  TR-POLICY-NUMBER            PIC X(12).
129                                                       205      02  TR-POLICY-NUMBER-R REDEFINES
130  /                                                    206          TR-POLICY-NUMBER.
131  WORKING-STORAGE SECTION.                             207          03  TR-POLICY-CODE         PIC XX.
132  ************************                             208              88  VALID-POLICY-CODE  VALUE "AM"
133                                                       209                                            "AN"
134  *********************************************************  210                                            "HM"
135  *                                            *       211                                            "RT"
136  *                SWITCHES                     *       212                                            "TL"
137  *                                            *       213                                            "WL".
138  *********************************************************  214          03  TR-HYPHEN-1            PIC X.
139                                                       215          03  TR-CODE-NUMBER-1       PIC X(4).
140  01  SWITCHES.                                        216          03  TR-HYPHEN-2            PIC X.
141                                                       217          03  TR-CODE-NUMBER-2       PIC X(4).
142      02  SW-END-OF-FILE            PIC X.             218
143          88  END-OF-FILE                    VALUE "Y". 219      02  TR-PREMIUM-AMOUNT          PIC S9(6)V99.
144                                                       220      02  TR-PREMIUM-AMOUNT-ALPHA REDEFINES
145  01  VALUES-FOR-SWITCHES.                             221          TR-PREMIUM-AMOUNT          PIC X(8).
146      02  YES                      PIC X    VALUE "Y". 222  /
147      02  NEG                      PIC X    VALUE "N". 223  COPY "A:\INSREC.CBL".
148                                                       224L*********************************************************
149  *********************************************************  225L*                                            *
150  *                                            *       226L*            PREMIUM INPUT FILE RECORD LAYOUT         *
151  *              ACCUMULATORS                   *       227L*                                            *
152  *                                            *       228L*********************************************************
153  *********************************************************  229L
154                                                       230L 01  PREMIUM-RECORD.
155  01  ACCUMULATORS.                                    231L     02  PR-CUSTOMER-NAME           PIC X(20).
156                                                       232L     02  PR-AGENT-NAME              PIC X(20).
157      02  AC-LINE-COUNT            PIC 999   PACKED-DECIMAL. 233L     02  PR-INSURANCE-TYPE          PIC X(10).
158      02  AC-PAGE-COUNT            PIC 999   PACKED-DECIMAL. 234L         88  VALID-TYPE             VALUE "Automobile"
159      02  AC-BAD-TRANS-COUNT       PIC 9(5)  PACKED-DECIMAL. 235L                                            "Annuity"
160      02  AC-POSTED-TRANS-COUNT    PIC 9(5)  PACKED-DECIMAL. 236L                                            "Home"
161      02  AC-UNMATCHED-TRANS-COUNT PIC 9(5)  PACKED-DECIMAL. 237L                                            "Renter"
162      02  AC-DUPLICATE-TRANS-COUNT PIC 9(5)  PACKED-DECIMAL. 238L                                            "Term Life"
163      02  AC-UNMATCHED-RECORD-COUNT PIC 9(5) PACKED-DECIMAL. 239L                                            "Whole Life".
164      02  AC-HYPHEN-COUNT          PIC 99    PACKED-DECIMAL. 240L
165  /                                                    241L     02  PR-POLICY-NUMBER           PIC X(12).
166  *********************************************************  242L     02  PR-PREMIUM-AMOUNT          PIC S9(5)V99.
167  *                                            *       243L
168  *              WORK AREA FIELDS               *       244L     02  PR-PAYMENT-STATUS          PIC X.
169  *                                            *       245L         88  DELINQUENT             VALUE "D".
170  *********************************************************  246L         88  PAID-IN-FULL           VALUE "F".
171                                                       247L         88  PARTIALLY-PAID         VALUE "P".
172  01  WORK-AREA.                                       248L         88  NOT-YET-BILLED         VALUE "N".
173                                                       249L
174      02  WA-SYSTEM-DATE.                              250L     02  PR-SEX                     PIC X.
175          03  WA-SYSTEM-YEAR       PIC 99.             251L     02  PR-SIGNUP-YEAR             PIC X(4).
176          03  WA-SYSTEM-MONTH      PIC 99.             252L     02  PR-PREMIUM-DUE-MONTH       PIC 99.
177          03  WA-SYSTEM-DAY        PIC 99.             253L     02                             PIC XXX.
178                                                       254  /
179      02  WA-CURRENT-DATE.                             255  *********************************************************
180          03  WA-CURRENT-MONTH     PIC 99.             256  *                                            *
181          03  WA-CURRENT-DAY       PIC 99.             257  *      REPORT HEADINGS FOR TRANSACTION LOG REPORT    *
182          03  WA-CURRENT-YEAR      PIC 99.             258  *                                            *
183                                                       259  *********************************************************
184      02  WA-CURRENT-DATE-N REDEFINES                  260
185          WA-CURRENT-DATE          PIC 9(6).           261  01  TRANSACTION-REPORT-HEADINGS.
186                                                       262
187      02  WA-SYSTEM-TIME.                              263      02  TRH-LINE-1.
188          03  WA-SYSTEM-HOUR       PIC 99.             264          03                     PIC X(6)  VALUE "DATE: ".
189          03  WA-SYSTEM-MINUTES    PIC 99.             265          03  TRH-DATE           PIC Z9/99/99.
190          03                       PIC 9(4).           266          03                     PIC X(16) VALUE SPACES.
191                                                       267          03                     PIC X(27) VALUE
192      02  WA-ADVANCE-NUMBER        PIC 9.              268              "AINSWORTH INSURANCE COMPANY".
193      02  WA-AGENT-NAME-1          PIC X(12).          269          03                     PIC X(15) VALUE SPACES.
194      02  WA-AGENT-NAME-2          PIC X(12).          270          03                     PIC X(5)  VALUE "PAGE ".
195      02  WA-PREV-POLICY-NUMBER    PIC X(12).          271          03  TRH-PAGE-COUNT     PIC ZZ9.
196  /                                                    272
197  *********************************************************  273      02  TRH-LINE-2.
198  *                                            *       274          03                     PIC X(6)  VALUE "TIME: ".
199  *          TRANSACTION RECORD LAYOUT          *       275          03  TRH-HOUR           PIC Z9.
200  *                                            *       276          03                     PIC X     VALUE ":".
201  *********************************************************  277          03  TRH-MINUTES        PIC 99.
```

FIGURE 8-6   Premium File Update program (continued)

```
278        03  TRH-AM-PM              PIC XX.
279        03                        PIC X(20) VALUE SPACES.
280        03                        PIC X(22) VALUE
281            "TRANSACTION LOG REPORT".
282        03                        PIC X(25) VALUE SPACES.
283
284 /
285    02  TRH-LINE-3.
286        03                        PIC X(18) VALUE SPACES.
287        03                        PIC X(18) VALUE
288            "TRANSACTION RECORD".
289        03                        PIC X(6)  VALUE SPACES.
290        03                        PIC X(11) VALUE
291            "DISPOSITION".
292        03                        PIC X(27) VALUE SPACES.
293
294    02  TRH-LINE-4.
295        03                        PIC X(18) VALUE SPACES.
296        03                        PIC X(20) VALUE ALL "-".
297        03                        PIC X(4)  VALUE SPACES.
298        03                        PIC X(20) VALUE ALL "-".
299        03                        PIC X(18) VALUE SPACES.
300
301 ******************************************************************
302 *                                                                *
303 *            DETAIL LINE FOR THE TRANSACTION LOG                  *
304 *                                                                *
305 ******************************************************************
306
307 01  TRANSACTION-DETAIL-LINE.
308
309    02                            PIC X(18) VALUE SPACES.
310    02  TDL-TRANSACTION-RECORD    PIC X(20).
311    02                            PIC X(4)  VALUE SPACES.
312    02  TDL-MESSAGE               PIC X(25).
313    02                            PIC X(13) VALUE SPACES.
314 /
315 ******************************************************************
316 *                                                                *
317 *        SUMMARY LINES FOR THE TRANSACTION LOG REPORT            *
318 *                                                                *
319 ******************************************************************
320
321 01  TRANSACTION-SUMMARY-LINES.
322
323    02  TSL-BAD-TOTAL.
324        03                        PIC X(18) VALUE SPACES.
325        03                        PIC X(33) VALUE
326            "Total Bad Transactions       =".
327        03  TSL-BAD-TRANS-COUNT   PIC ZZZZ9.
328        03                        PIC X(24) VALUE SPACES.
329
330    02  TSL-POSTED-TOTAL.
331        03                        PIC X(18) VALUE SPACES.
332        03                        PIC X(33) VALUE
333            "Total Posted Transactions    =".
334        03  TSL-POSTED-TRANS-COUNT PIC ZZZZ9.
335        03                        PIC X(24) VALUE SPACES.
336
337    02  TSL-UNMATCHED-TRAN-TOTAL.
338        03                        PIC X(18) VALUE SPACES.
339        03                        PIC X(33) VALUE
340            "Total Unmatched Transactions =".
341        03  TSL-UNMATCHED-TRANS-COUNT PIC ZZZZ9.
342        03                        PIC X(24) VALUE SPACES.
343
344    02  TSL-DUPLICATE-TRAN-TOTAL.
345        03                        PIC X(18) VALUE SPACES.
346        03                        PIC X(33) VALUE
347            "Total Duplicate Transactions =".
348        03  TSL-DUPLICATE-TRANS-COUNT PIC ZZZZ9.
349        03                        PIC X(24) VALUE SPACES.
350
351    02  TSL-UNMATCHED-PREMIUM-RECORDS.
352        03                        PIC X(18) VALUE SPACES.
353        03                        PIC X(33) VALUE
354            "Total Unmatched Premium Records =".
355        03  TSL-UNMATCHED-PREM-RECORDS PIC ZZZZ9.
356        03                        PIC X(24) VALUE SPACES.
357
358    02  TSL-END-OF-REPORT.
359        03                        PIC X(30).
360        03                        PIC X(13) VALUE
361            "END OF REPORT".
362        03                        PIC X(37).
363 /
364 PROCEDURE DIVISION.
365 ******************
366 ******************************************************************
367 *                                                                *
368 *  MAIN-PROGRAM - THIS IS THE MAIN ROUTINE OF THE PREMIUM FILE    *
369 *                 UPDATE PROGRAM                                  *
370 *                                                                *
371 ******************************************************************
372
373 MAIN-PROGRAM.
374
375    PERFORM A-100-INITIALIZATION.
376    PERFORM B-100-TRANSACTION-VALIDATION.
377    PERFORM C-100-UPDATE-FILE.
378    PERFORM D-100-WRAP-UP.
379    STOP RUN.
380
381 ******************************************************************
382 *                                                                *
383 *            THE INITIALIZATION ROUTINE FOLLOWS                   *
384 *                                                                *
385 ******************************************************************
386
387 A-100-INITIALIZATION.
388
389    INITIALIZE ACCUMULATORS.
390
391    ACCEPT WA-SYSTEM-DATE FROM DATE.
392    MOVE WA-SYSTEM-YEAR    TO WA-CURRENT-YEAR.
393    MOVE WA-SYSTEM-MONTH   TO WA-CURRENT-MONTH.
394    MOVE WA-SYSTEM-DAY     TO WA-CURRENT-DAY.
395    MOVE WA-CURRENT-DATE-N TO TRH-DATE.
396
397    ACCEPT WA-SYSTEM-TIME FROM TIME.
398    EVALUATE TRUE
399        WHEN WA-SYSTEM-HOUR = 00
400            MOVE "AM" TO TRH-AM-PM
401            MOVE 12 TO TRH-HOUR
402        WHEN WA-SYSTEM-HOUR < 12
403            MOVE "AM" TO TRH-AM-PM
404            MOVE WA-SYSTEM-HOUR TO TRH-HOUR
405        WHEN WA-SYSTEM-HOUR = 12
406            MOVE "PM" TO TRH-AM-PM
407            MOVE WA-SYSTEM-HOUR TO TRH-HOUR
408        WHEN WA-SYSTEM-HOUR > 12
409            MOVE "PM" TO TRH-AM-PM
410            COMPUTE TRH-HOUR = WA-SYSTEM-HOUR - 12.
411    MOVE WA-SYSTEM-MINUTES TO TRH-MINUTES.
412
413    OPEN OUTPUT TRANSACTION-LOG-REPORT.
414
415 /
416 ******************************************************************
417 *                                                                *
418 *        TRANSACTION VALIDATION - SORT BY POLICY NUMBER           *
419 *                                                                *
420 ******************************************************************
421
422 B-100-TRANSACTION-VALIDATION.
423
424    SORT SORT-FILE
425        ON ASCENDING KEY SR-POLICY-NUMBER
426        INPUT PROCEDURE B-200-VALIDATE-FILE
427        GIVING SORTED-TRANSACTION-FILE.
428
429
```

(continued)

```
430 *******************************************************************
431 *                                                                 *
432 *                   VALIDATE TRANSACTION FILE                     *
433 *                                                                 *
434 *******************************************************************
435
436 B-200-VALIDATE-FILE.
437
438     OPEN INPUT TRANSACTION-FILE.
439
440     READ TRANSACTION-FILE INTO TRANSACTION-RECORD
441         AT END MOVE YES TO SW-END-OF-FILE.
442
443     PERFORM B-300-VALIDATE-RECORDS
444         UNTIL END-OF-FILE.
445
446     CLOSE TRANSACTION-FILE.
447 /
448 *******************************************************************
449 *                                                                 *
450 *               VALIDATE INDIVIDUAL TRANSACTIONS                  *
451 *                                                                 *
452 *******************************************************************
453
454 B-300-VALIDATE-RECORDS.
455
456     MOVE TRANSACTION-RECORD TO TDL-TRANSACTION-RECORD.
457     MOVE 2 TO WA-ADVANCE-NUMBER.
458
459     IF NOT VALID-POLICY-CODE
460         MOVE "POLICY CODE INVALID" TO TDL-MESSAGE
461         PERFORM B-400-WRITE-LOG.
462
463     MOVE ZERO TO AC-HYPHEN-COUNT.
464     INSPECT TR-POLICY-NUMBER
465         TALLYING AC-HYPHEN-COUNT FOR ALL "-".
466
467     IF AC-HYPHEN-COUNT NOT = 2
468         MOVE "HYPHEN(S) MISSING" TO TDL-MESSAGE
469         PERFORM B-400-WRITE-LOG.
470
471     IF TR-CODE-NUMBER-1 NOT NUMERIC
472         MOVE "CODE #1 NOT NUMERIC" TO TDL-MESSAGE
473         PERFORM B-400-WRITE-LOG
474     ELSE
475         IF TR-CODE-NUMBER-1 < "0050" OR > "9900"
476             MOVE "CODE #1 OUT OF RANGE" TO TDL-MESSAGE
477             PERFORM B-400-WRITE-LOG.
478
479     IF TR-CODE-NUMBER-2 NOT NUMERIC
480         MOVE "CODE #2 NOT NUMERIC" TO TDL-MESSAGE
481         PERFORM B-400-WRITE-LOG
482     ELSE
483         IF TR-CODE-NUMBER-2 < "0050" OR > "9900"
484             MOVE "CODE #2 OUT OF RANGE" TO TDL-MESSAGE
485             PERFORM B-400-WRITE-LOG.
486
487     IF TR-PREMIUM-AMOUNT-ALPHA NOT NUMERIC
488         MOVE "PREMIUM AMT NOT NUMERIC" TO TDL-MESSAGE
489         PERFORM B-400-WRITE-LOG.
490
491     IF WA-ADVANCE-NUMBER = 1
492         ADD 1 TO AC-BAD-TRANS-COUNT
493     ELSE
494         RELEASE SORT-RECORD FROM TRANSACTION-RECORD.
495
496     READ TRANSACTION-FILE INTO TRANSACTION-RECORD
497         AT END MOVE YES TO SW-END-OF-FILE.
498 /
499 *******************************************************************
500 *                                                                 *
501 *                   WRITE TO TRANSACTION LOG                      *
502 *                                                                 *
503 *******************************************************************
504
505 B-400-WRITE-LOG.
```

```
506
507     IF AC-LINE-COUNT = 0
508         PERFORM M-500-LOG-HEADINGS.
509
510     WRITE TRAN-LOG-LINE-OUT FROM TRANSACTION-DETAIL-LINE
511         AFTER ADVANCING WA-ADVANCE-NUMBER LINES.
512     ADD WA-ADVANCE-NUMBER TO AC-LINE-COUNT.
513     MOVE SPACES TO TDL-TRANSACTION-RECORD.
514     MOVE 1 TO WA-ADVANCE-NUMBER.
515
516     IF AC-LINE-COUNT > 55
517         MOVE ZERO TO AC-LINE-COUNT.
518 /
519 *******************************************************************
520 *                                                                 *
521 *               PREMIUM FILE UPDATE PROCESSING                   *
522 *                                                                 *
523 *******************************************************************
524
525 C-100-UPDATE-FILE.
526
527     OPEN  INPUT   PREMIUM-INPUT-FILE
528                   SORTED-TRANSACTION-FILE
529           OUTPUT  UPDATED-PREMIUM-FILE.
530
531     READ PREMIUM-INPUT-FILE INTO PREMIUM-RECORD
532         AT END MOVE HIGH-VALUES TO PR-POLICY-NUMBER.
533
534     READ SORTED-TRANSACTION-FILE INTO TRANSACTION-RECORD
535         AT END MOVE HIGH-VALUES TO TR-POLICY-NUMBER.
536
537     PERFORM C-200-UPDATE-RECORDS
538         UNTIL PR-POLICY-NUMBER = HIGH-VALUES AND
539               TR-POLICY-NUMBER = HIGH-VALUES.
540
541     MOVE AC-BAD-TRANS-COUNT TO TSL-BAD-TRANS-COUNT.
542     MOVE AC-POSTED-TRANS-COUNT TO TSL-POSTED-TRANS-COUNT.
543     MOVE AC-UNMATCHED-TRANS-COUNT TO TSL-UNMATCHED-TRANS-COUNT.
544     MOVE AC-DUPLICATE-TRANS-COUNT TO TSL-DUPLICATE-TRANS-COUNT.
545     MOVE AC-UNMATCHED-RECORD-COUNT TO TSL-UNMATCHED-PREM-RECORDS.
546
547     WRITE TRAN-LOG-LINE-OUT FROM TSL-BAD-TOTAL
548         AFTER ADVANCING 3 LINES.
549     WRITE TRAN-LOG-LINE-OUT FROM TSL-POSTED-TOTAL
550         AFTER ADVANCING 1 LINE.
551     WRITE TRAN-LOG-LINE-OUT FROM TSL-UNMATCHED-TRAN-TOTAL
552         AFTER ADVANCING 1 LINE.
553     WRITE TRAN-LOG-LINE-OUT FROM TSL-DUPLICATE-TRAN-TOTAL
554         AFTER ADVANCING 1 LINE.
555     WRITE TRAN-LOG-LINE-OUT FROM TSL-UNMATCHED-PREMIUM-RECORDS
556         AFTER ADVANCING 1 LINE.
557     WRITE TRAN-LOG-LINE-OUT FROM TSL-END-OF-REPORT
558         AFTER ADVANCING 2 LINES.
559 /
560 *******************************************************************
561 *                                                                 *
562 *                   UPDATE RECORD ROUTINE                        *
563 *                                                                 *
564 *******************************************************************
565
566 C-200-UPDATE-RECORDS.
567
568     IF AC-LINE-COUNT = 0
569         PERFORM M-500-LOG-HEADINGS.
570
571     EVALUATE TRUE
572         WHEN TR-POLICY-NUMBER = PR-POLICY-NUMBER
573             PERFORM C-300-POST-TRANSACTION
574         WHEN TR-POLICY-NUMBER > PR-POLICY-NUMBER
575             PERFORM C-310-UNMATCHED-PREMIUM-RECORD
576         WHEN TR-POLICY-NUMBER < PR-POLICY-NUMBER
577             PERFORM C-320-UNMATCHED-TRANSACTION.
578
579     IF AC-LINE-COUNT > 55
580         MOVE ZERO TO AC-LINE-COUNT.
581 /
```

FIGURE 8-6   Premium File Update program (continued)

```
582 *******************************************************************
583 *                                                                 *
584 *                 POSTED TRANSACTION ROUTINE                      *
585 *                                                                 *
586 *******************************************************************
587
588  C-300-POST-TRANSACTION.
589
590      ADD TR-PREMIUM-AMOUNT TO PR-PREMIUM-AMOUNT.
591
592      MOVE SPACES TO WA-AGENT-NAME-1
593                    WA-AGENT-NAME-2.
594
595      UNSTRING PR-AGENT-NAME DELIMITED BY ", " OR ALL SPACES
596          INTO WA-AGENT-NAME-2
597               WA-AGENT-NAME-1.
598
599      MOVE SPACES TO PR-AGENT-NAME.
600      STRING WA-AGENT-NAME-1 DELIMITED BY SPACE
601             " "            DELIMITED BY SIZE
602             WA-AGENT-NAME-2 DELIMITED BY SPACE INTO PR-AGENT-NAME.
603
604      INSPECT PR-POLICY-NUMBER
605          REPLACING ALL "-" BY "*".
606
607      WRITE UPDATED-PREMIUM-RECORD FROM PREMIUM-RECORD.
608      ADD 1 TO AC-POSTED-TRANS-COUNT.
609      MOVE TRANSACTION-RECORD TO TDL-TRANSACTION-RECORD.
610      MOVE "TRANSACTION POSTED" TO TDL-MESSAGE.
611      WRITE TRAN-LOG-LINE-OUT FROM TRANSACTION-DETAIL-LINE
612          AFTER ADVANCING 2 LINES.
613      ADD 2 TO AC-LINE-COUNT.
614      MOVE TR-POLICY-NUMBER TO WA-PREV-POLICY-NUMBER.
615
616      READ PREMIUM-INPUT-FILE INTO PREMIUM-RECORD
617          AT END MOVE HIGH-VALUES TO PR-POLICY-NUMBER.
618
619      READ SORTED-TRANSACTION-FILE INTO TRANSACTION-RECORD
620          AT END MOVE HIGH-VALUES TO TR-POLICY-NUMBER.
621 /
622 *******************************************************************
623 *                                                                 *
624 *              UNMATCHED PREMIUM RECORD ROUTINE                   *
625 *                                                                 *
626 *******************************************************************
627
628  C-310-UNMATCHED-PREMIUM-RECORD.
629
630      MOVE PR-POLICY-NUMBER TO TDL-TRANSACTION-RECORD.
631      MOVE SPACES TO WA-AGENT-NAME-1
632                    WA-AGENT-NAME-2.
633
634      UNSTRING PR-AGENT-NAME DELIMITED BY ", " OR ALL SPACES
635          INTO WA-AGENT-NAME-2
636               WA-AGENT-NAME-1.
637
638      MOVE SPACES TO PR-AGENT-NAME.
639      STRING WA-AGENT-NAME-1 DELIMITED BY SPACE
640             " "            DELIMITED BY SIZE
641             WA-AGENT-NAME-2 DELIMITED BY SPACE INTO PR-AGENT-NAME.
642
643      INSPECT PR-POLICY-NUMBER
644          REPLACING ALL "-" BY "*".
645
646      WRITE UPDATED-PREMIUM-RECORD FROM PREMIUM-RECORD.
647      ADD 1 TO AC-UNMATCHED-RECORD-COUNT.
648      MOVE "UNMATCHED PREMIUM RECORD" TO TDL-MESSAGE.
649      WRITE TRAN-LOG-LINE-OUT FROM TRANSACTION-DETAIL-LINE
650          AFTER ADVANCING 2 LINES.
651      ADD 2 TO AC-LINE-COUNT.
652
653      READ PREMIUM-INPUT-FILE INTO PREMIUM-RECORD
654          AT END MOVE HIGH-VALUES TO PR-POLICY-NUMBER.
655 /
656 *******************************************************************
657 *                                                                 *
658 *                UNMATCHED TRANSACTION ROUTINE                    *
659 *                                                                 *
660 *******************************************************************
661
662  C-320-UNMATCHED-TRANSACTION.
663
664      IF TR-POLICY-NUMBER = WA-PREV-POLICY-NUMBER
665          MOVE "DUPLICATE TRANSACTION" TO TDL-MESSAGE
666          ADD 1 TO AC-DUPLICATE-TRANS-COUNT
667      ELSE
668          MOVE "UNMATCHED TRANSACTION" TO TDL-MESSAGE
669          ADD 1 TO AC-UNMATCHED-TRANS-COUNT.
670
671      MOVE TRANSACTION-RECORD TO TDL-TRANSACTION-RECORD.
672      WRITE TRAN-LOG-LINE-OUT FROM TRANSACTION-DETAIL-LINE
673          AFTER ADVANCING 2 LINES.
674      ADD 2 TO AC-LINE-COUNT.
675
676      MOVE TR-POLICY-NUMBER TO WA-PREV-POLICY-NUMBER.
677      READ SORTED-TRANSACTION-FILE INTO TRANSACTION-RECORD
678          AT END MOVE HIGH-VALUES TO TR-POLICY-NUMBER.
679 /
680 *******************************************************************
681 *                                                                 *
682 *                     END OF JOB ROUTINE                          *
683 *                                                                 *
684 *******************************************************************
685
686  D-100-WRAP-UP.
687
688      CLOSE PREMIUM-INPUT-FILE
689            SORTED-TRANSACTION-FILE
690            TRANSACTION-LOG-REPORT.
691
692      DISPLAY "THE PREMIUM FILE UPDATE PROGRAM HAS TERMINATED".
693
694 *******************************************************************
695 *                                                                 *
696 * TRANSACTION LOG HEADING ROUTINE - PERFORMED IN MULTIPLE STREAMS*
697 *                                                                 *
698 *******************************************************************
699
700  M-500-LOG-HEADINGS.
701
702      ADD 1 TO AC-PAGE-COUNT.
703      MOVE AC-PAGE-COUNT TO TRH-PAGE-COUNT.
704      WRITE TRAN-LOG-LINE-OUT FROM TRH-LINE-1
705          AFTER ADVANCING PAGE.
706      WRITE TRAN-LOG-LINE-OUT FROM TRH-LINE-2
707          AFTER ADVANCING 1 LINE.
708      WRITE TRAN-LOG-LINE-OUT FROM TRH-LINE-3
709          AFTER ADVANCING 2 LINES.
710      WRITE TRAN-LOG-LINE-OUT FROM TRH-LINE-4
711          AFTER ADVANCING 1 LINE.
712
713      MOVE 5 TO AC-LINE-COUNT.
714 /
```

INSPECT STATEMENT

The INSPECT statement is used to examine a field and to either count the number of occurrences of certain characters within the field or to replace certain characters within the field with other characters. INSPECT also can be used both to count and replace at the same time. Four basic formats exist of the INSPECT statement.

Inspect Tallying

Figure 8-7 presents the basic format of the INSPECT TALLYING statement. **INSPECT TALLYING** is used to count the number of occurrences of a certain character or group of characters within a field. Although the basic format might seem confusing, the statement is simple to use. The name referenced by field-1 is the **inspected field** and can be any group or elementary item that has USAGE IS DISPLAY. The USAGE clause was discussed in Chapter 3. The name referenced by field-2 is called the **TALLYING field** and must be an elementary numeric item. The TALLYING field will be used to count the number of times a character or group of characters occurs within the inspected field.

```
INSPECT field-1  TALLYING

    (                    ( CHARACTERS   [ { BEFORE }  INITIAL { field-3   } ] ...         ) )
    (                    (              [ { AFTER  }           { literal-1 }   ]           ) )
    { field-2 FOR        {                                                                 }
    (                    ( { ALL     } { field-4   } [ { BEFORE } INITIAL { field-3   } ] ) )
    (                    ( { LEADING } { literal-2 } [ { AFTER  }         { literal-1 } ] ) )
```

FIGURE 8-7   Basic format of the INSPECT TALLYING statement

When used, the CHARACTERS option counts the number of bytes or positions within the inspected field. BEFORE and AFTER are optional entries that are used to count the number of characters in a field prior to or after the first or INITIAL occurrence of a specific character.

ALL is used to specify that all occurrences of a specific character or group of characters are to be counted. LEADING is used to indicate that occurrences of a specific character at the beginning of the inspected field are to be counted. A LEADING character is represented by one or more occurrences of the same character prior to the occurrence of any other character. LEADING characters always will be at the beginning of the inspected field unless the AFTER option is used. When the AFTER option is used with LEADING, a character must immediately follow the character or string of characters identified with the AFTER option.

Figure 8-8 illustrates the INSPECT TALLYING statement used in the Premium File Update program. It is used in the validation of the transaction record to count the number of hyphens in the field TR-POLICY-NUMBER. In the program, if the count is not equal to 2, then an error message will be listed on the Transaction Log Report. The INSPECT TALLYING statement adds one to the TALLYING field, AC-HYPHEN-COUNT, every time an occurrence of the specified character is encountered. It does not automatically initialize the TALLYING field. Therefore, the MOVE on line 463 in Figure 8-8 is essential to guarantee an accurate count.

Assume TR-POLICY-NUMBER has a value of HM-2341-0268

```
463      MOVE ZERO TO AC-HYPEN-COUNT.
464      INSPECT TR-POLICY-NUMBER
465         TALLYING AC-HYPHEN-COUNT FOR ALL "-".
```
count number of hyphens

After the INSPECT, the result in AC-HYPHEN-COUNT → 2

FIGURE 8-8   The INSPECT TALLYING statement from the Premium File Update program

Figure 8-9 presents other examples of the INSPECT TALLYING statement. In each example, the initial value of AC-COUNT-1 is given before and after the execution of the INSPECT. It is normal to move zero to the TALLYING field prior to the execution of an INSPECT TALLYING statement. If this is not done, as illustrated by the fourth example in Figure 8-9, notice how INSPECT TALLYING simply increases the value in AC-COUNT-1, resulting in an erroneous value.

Assume TR-POLICY-NUMBER has a value of HM-2341-0238 for each INSPECT

Assume AC-COUNT-1 is initialized to zero for all but the fourth example

		AC-COUNT-1	
		Before	*After*
1.	INSPECT TR-POLICY-NUMBER TALLYING AC-COUNT-1 FOR CHARACTERS BEFORE INITIAL "4".	0 *Adds 5*	5
2.	INSPECT TR-POLICY-NUMBER TALLYING AC-COUNT-1 FOR CHARACTERS AFTER INITIAL "4".	0 *Adds 6*	6
3.	INSPECT TR-POLICY-NUMBER TALLYING AC-COUNT-1 FOR ALL "23".	0 *Adds 2*	2
4.	INSPECT TR-POLICY-NUMBER TALLYING AC-COUNT-1 FOR ALL "2" AFTER INITIAL "-".	1 *Adds 2*	3
5.	INSPECT TR-POLICY-NUMBER TALLYING AC-COUNT-1 FOR LEADING "0".	0 *Adds 0*	0
6.	INSPECT TR-POLICY-NUMBER TALLYING AC-COUNT-1 FOR LEADING "2" AFTER INITIAL "-".	0 *Adds 1*	1

FIGURE 8-9   Examples of INSPECT TALLYING statements

Inspect Replacing

Figure 8-10 presents the basic format of the INSPECT REPLACING statement. **INSPECT REPLACING** is used to replace specific characters within a field with other characters. When CHARACTERS is used, every character is replaced by the contents of the field or the literal value specified following the word BY. The BEFORE and AFTER options work as described for the INSPECT TALLYING statement. BEFORE and AFTER cause characters to be replaced in a field prior to or after the occurrence of a specific character.

```
INSPECT field-1  REPLACING

   ⎧  CHARACTERS BY  ⎧field-2  ⎫  ⎡⎧BEFORE⎫ INITIAL ⎧field-3  ⎫⎤        ⎫
   ⎪               ⎩literal-1⎭  ⎣⎩AFTER ⎭         ⎩literal-2⎭⎦ ...    ⎪
   ⎪                                                                   ⎪
   ⎨  ⎧ALL    ⎫ ⎧field-4  ⎫ BY ⎧field-5  ⎫ ⎡⎧BEFORE⎫ INITIAL ⎧field-3  ⎫⎤⎬
   ⎪  ⎨LEADING⎬ ⎩literal-3⎭    ⎩literal-4⎭ ⎣⎩AFTER ⎭         ⎩literal-2⎭⎦⎪
   ⎩  ⎩FIRST  ⎭                                                        ⎭
```

FIGURE 8-10 Basic format of the INSPECT REPLACING statement

ALL is used to identify a specific character or string of characters that is to be replaced. As in the INSPECT TALLYING statement, LEADING characters always will be at the beginning of the inspected field unless the AFTER option is used. When the AFTER option is used with LEADING, a character must immediately follow the character or string of characters identified with the AFTER option in order to be replaced. FIRST is used to specify that the first occurrence of a specific character or string of characters is to be replaced by the value following the word BY.

Figure 8-11 presents one of the INSPECT REPLACING statements used in the Premium File Update program. The hyphens (–) within the policy number field are replaced with asterisks (*) prior to the record being written to the UPDATED-PREMIUM-FILE.

Assume PR-POLICY-NUMBER has a value of HM-2341-0268

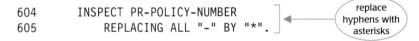

```
604        INSPECT PR-POLICY-NUMBER
605            REPLACING ALL "-" BY "*".
```
replace hyphens with asterisks

After the INSPECT, PR-POLICY-NUMBER contains → HM*2341*0268

FIGURE 8-11 The INSPECT REPLACING statement from the Premium File Update program

Figure 8-12 presents other examples of the INSPECT REPLACING statement. Notice in the fifth example that a string of characters can be replaced by another string of characters. When this is done, both strings must be the same size. Notice in the eighth and ninth examples that multiple replacements can be made.

Assume PR-POLICY-NUMBER has a value of HM-2341-0238

PR-POLICY-NUMBER *after*

```
1.  INSPECT PR-POLICY-NUMBER
        REPLACING CHARACTERS BY "0"        0000041-0238
        BEFORE INITIAL "4".

2.  INSPECT PR-POLICY-NUMBER
        REPLACING CHARACTERS BY "0"        HM-000000000
        AFTER INITIAL "-".

3.  INSPECT PR-POLICY-NUMBER
        REPLACING ALL "2" BY "4".          HM-4341-0438

4.  INSPECT PR-POLICY-NUMBER
        REPLACING ALL "-" BY SPACES.       HM 2341 0238

5.  INSPECT PR-POLICY-NUMBER
        REPLACING ALL "23" BY "00".        HM-0041-0008

6.  INSPECT PR-POLICY-NUMBER
        REPLACING LEADING "2" BY "4"       HM-4341-0238
        AFTER INITIAL "-".

7.  INSPECT PR-POLICY-NUMBER
        REPLACING FIRST "2" BY "4".        HM-4341-0238

8.  INSPECT PR-POLICY-NUMBER
        REPLACING ALL "2" BY "4"           HM*4341* 438
               "0" BY " "
               "-" BY "*".

9.  INSPECT PR-POLICY-NUMBER
        REPLACING ALL "2" BY "4"           HM-4361-0438
               "4" BY "6".
```

FIGURE 8-12   Examples of INSPECT REPLACING statements

When an INSPECT statement executes, it proceeds left to right in the inspected field, one character at a time, TALLYING and/or REPLACING each character position as specified. The same character position will not be tallied or replaced more than once. Thus, in the ninth example, 4s that replaced 2s will not then be replaced by 6s.

Figure 8-13 on the next page presents a third format for the INSPECT statement. This format combines the first two formats and allows TALLYING and REPLACING to be accomplished in one statement.

```
INSPECT field-1

TALLYING
```

```
 (                 (  CHARACTERS   [ (BEFORE) INITIAL (field-3  )] ...      ) )
 (                 (                 (AFTER )         (literal-1)            ) )
{ field-2 FOR     {                                                          }
 (                 ( (ALL    ) (field-4  )[(BEFORE) INITIAL (field-3  )]     ) )
 (                 ( (LEADING) (literal-2) (AFTER )         (literal-1)       ) )
```

```
REPLACING
```

```
 (  CHARACTERS   BY (field-2  )[(BEFORE) INITIAL (field-3  )] ...         )
 (                  (literal-1) (AFTER )         (literal-2)              )
{                                                                         }
 ( (ALL    )                                                             )
 ( (LEADING) (field-4  ) BY (field-5  )[(BEFORE) INITIAL (field-3  )]    )
 ( (FIRST  ) (literal-3)    (literal-4) (AFTER )         (literal-2)     )
```

FIGURE 8-13 Basic format of the INSPECT TALLYING and REPLACING statement

Figure 8-14 illustrates a sample of such an INSPECT statement.

Assume PR-POLICY-NUMBER has a value of HM-2341-0238 and AC-COUNT-1 has a value of zero

```
INSPECT PR-POLICY-NUMBER
    TALLYING AC-COUNT-1 FOR ALL "2"        ◄—— count 2s
    REPLACING ALL "2" BY "0".                   and replace
                                                with 0s
```

After the INSPECT, AC-COUNT-1   → 2
              PR-POLICY-NUMBER → HM-0341-0038

FIGURE 8-14 Example of an INSPECT TALLYING and REPLACING statement

Inspect Converting

Figure 8-15 shows the fourth format of the INSPECT statement. The **INSPECT CONVERTING** statement works in the same manner as an INSPECT REPLACING, but it is easier to code when multiple replacements are to be made. Characters in the inspected field matching those listed in the field or literal preceding the word TO are replaced by the characters in corresponding positions in the field or literal following the word TO. The same character cannot appear more than once in the field or literal preceding the word TO. Also, the field or literal preceding the word TO must be the same size as the field or literal following the word TO. The BEFORE and AFTER options work exactly as described for the other forms of the INSPECT statement.

```
INSPECT field-1 CONVERTING

{field-2 } TO {field-3 } [{BEFORE} INITIAL {field-4  }] ...
{literal-1}    {literal-2}  [{AFTER }         {literal-3}]
```

FIGURE 8-15   Basic format of the INSPECT CONVERTING statement

Figure 8-16 presents an INSPECT REPLACING statement and a logically equivalent INSPECT CONVERTING statement.

Assume PR-POLICY-NUMBER has a value of HM-2341-0238

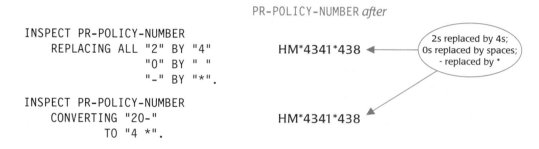

PR-POLICY-NUMBER *after*

```
INSPECT PR-POLICY-NUMBER
    REPLACING ALL "2" BY "4"
                  "0" BY " "          HM*4341*438
                  "-" BY "*".

INSPECT PR-POLICY-NUMBER
    CONVERTING "20-"
             TO "4 *".               HM*4341*438
```

2s replaced by 4s;
0s replaced by spaces;
- replaced by *

FIGURE 8-16   An INSPECT REPLACING statement and logically equivalent INSPECT CONVERTING statement

UNSTRING STATEMENT

The **UNSTRING** statement is designed to distribute or fragment data that is in a single field to one or more other fields. UNSTRING allows a field to be fragmented based on the occurrence of certain characters within the field. Figure 8-17 presents the basic format of the UNSTRING statement.

```
UNSTRING field-1

[DELIMITED BY [ALL] {field-2  } [OR [ALL] {field-3  }] ... ]
                    {literal-1}            {literal-2}

   INTO  { field-4 [DELIMITER IN field-5] [COUNT IN field-6]} ...

[ WITH POINTER field-7 ]

[ TALLYING IN field-8 ]

[ ON OVERFLOW  statement-set-1 ]

[ NOT ON OVERFLOW statement-set-2 ]

[ END-UNSTRING ]
```

FIGURE 8-17   Basic format of the UNSTRING statement

The field to be fragmented, or source field, is named immediately after the word UNSTRING. The source field is not altered by the UNSTRING statement. Fragments of the source field are placed into receiving fields. The fields or literals in the DELIMITED BY clause determine the scope of each fragment and are called **delimiters**. Characters such as commas, periods, and spaces often are used as delimiters. Every time one of the delimiters listed in the DELIMITED BY clause is encountered, a fragment of the source field is placed into a receiving field. The first fragment is placed into the first receiving field listed. The second fragment is placed into the second receiving field listed, and so on. The final fragment within a source field is delimited by the end of the field. The fields following the reserved word INTO are the receiving fields for the fragments of the source field.

Each receiving field can be followed by an optional DELIMITER IN clause. The field or fields following a DELIMITER IN clause are used to capture the character or characters that terminated the fragment placed in the corresponding receiving field. A COUNT IN clause also can follow each receiving field to capture the number of characters from the source field placed into the receiving field. The WITH POINTER clause can be used to indicate the character position in the source field where the fragmenting is to begin and to capture the character position where the fragmenting stops. The TALLYING IN clause is optional and can be used to capture a count of the number of fragments distributed to receiving fields. The ON OVERFLOW clause allows for special processing if the number of fragments from the source field exceeds the number of receiving fields. NOT ON OVERFLOW can be used for special processing, if the number of fragments is less than or equal to the number of receiving fields. END-UNSTRING is needed only when ON OVERFLOW and/or NOT ON OVERFLOW is used, and an UNSTRING statement must be terminated in a situation where a period cannot be used. For example, the UNSTRING might be nested within an IF statement where the use of a period would prematurely terminate the IF. An END-UNSTRING can be coded to terminate the UNSTRING statement without terminating the IF.

Figure 8-18 presents one of the UNSTRING statements used in the Premium File Update program. The agent names in the original file have the last name listed first. A comma and a space separate the last name from the first name and the first name is followed by spaces. The agent name field is being fragmented so the field can be rearranged with the first name first. The first delimiter in the UNSTRING is identified by the two-character, non-numeric literal ", ", while the second delimiter is the entry ALL SPACES. ALL SPACES indicates that consecutive spaces are to be treated as a single delimiter. If the word ALL were omitted, each individual space would be considered a separate delimiter. With the word ALL included, one space or many adjacent spaces are treated the same, as just one delimiter.

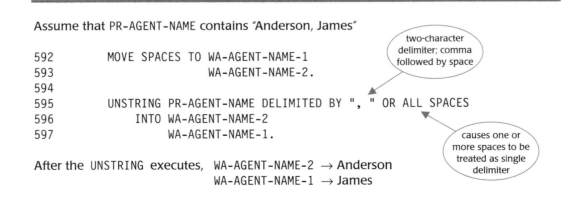

Assume that PR-AGENT-NAME contains "Anderson, James"

```
592        MOVE SPACES TO WA-AGENT-NAME-1
593                       WA-AGENT-NAME-2.
594
595        UNSTRING PR-AGENT-NAME DELIMITED BY ", " OR ALL SPACES
596           INTO WA-AGENT-NAME-2
597              WA-AGENT-NAME-1.
```

two-character delimiter; comma followed by space

causes one or more spaces to be treated as single delimiter

After the UNSTRING executes, WA-AGENT-NAME-2 → Anderson
                              WA-AGENT-NAME-1 → James

FIGURE 8-18 The UNSTRING statement from the Premium File Update program

The UNSTRING statement does not automatically fill rightmost positions in the receiving fields with spaces. Unless the receiving fields are initialized just prior to execution of the UNSTRING statement, some data from previous operations may be left in rightmost positions within the fields. Therefore, the MOVE statement on lines 592 and 593 in Figure 8-18 is very important. Receiving fields always should be initialized to spaces prior to the execution of an UNSTRING statement. Figures 8-19 and 8-20 (on the next page) show other examples of the UNSTRING statement.

Assume that all receiving fields are properly defined and initialized to spaces before each UNSTRING.

1. Assume PR-AGENT-NAME contains Anderson, James T.

    ```
    UNSTRING PR-AGENT-NAME DELIMITED BY ", " OR ALL SPACES
        INTO WA-AGENT-NAME-1
            WA-AGENT-NAME-2
            WA-AGENT-NAME-3
    ```

    After the UNSTRING executes, WA-AGENT-NAME-1 → Anderson
                                            WA-AGENT-NAME-2 → James
                                            WA-AGENT-NAME-3 → T.

2. Assume PR-POLICY-NUMBER contains HM-2045-3434

    ```
    UNSTRING PR-POLICY-NUMBER DELIMITED BY "-"
        INTO WA-NUM-1 DELIMITER IN WA-DEL-1
            WA-NUM-2 DELIMITER IN WA-DEL-2
            WA-NUM-3 DELIMITER IN WA-DEL-3.
    ```

    After the UNSTRING executes, WA-NUM-1 → HM   WA-DEL-1 → -
                                          WA-NUM-2 → 2045   WA-DEL-2 → -
                                          WA-NUM-3 → 3434   WA-DEL-3 →

3. Assume PR-POLICY-NUMBER contains HM*2045-3434

    ```
    UNSTRING PR-POLICY-NUMBER DELIMITED BY "-"
        INTO WA-NUM-1 DELIMITER IN WA-DEL-1
                COUNT IN WA-COUNT-1
            WA-NUM-2 DELIMITER IN WA-DEL-2
                COUNT IN WA-COUNT-2
            WA-NUM-3 DELIMITER IN WA-DEL-3
                COUNT IN WA-COUNT-3.
    ```

    After,   WA-NUM-1 →   HM*2045 WA-DEL-1 → -   WA-COUNT-1 → 7
              WA-NUM-2 →   3434   WA-DEL-2 →   WA-COUNT-2 → 4
              WA-NUM-3 →   WA-DEL-3 →   WA-COUNT-3 → 0

FIGURE 8-19   Examples of the UNSTRING statement

Notice in example number 2 in Figure 8-20, that nothing goes into the second receiving field listed, WA-NUM-2. This is because there are two spaces following HM in PR-POLICY-NUMBER. Because DELIMITED BY SPACES is used in this example instead of DELIMITED BY ALL

SPACES, the two spaces are each recognized as separate delimiters. Nothing exists between them, so nothing is placed in WA-NUM-2. If DELIMITED BY ALL SPACES had been used, then the two spaces would have been treated as a single delimiter and 045 would have been placed in WA-NUM-2 and 3434 in WA-NUM-3.

Assume that all receiving fields are properly defined and initialized to spaces before each UNSTRING.

1. Assume PR-AGENT-NAME contains Anderson, James T.

    ```
    UNSTRING PR-AGENT-NAME DELIMITED BY ALL SPACES
        INTO WA-AGENT-NAME-1
            WA-AGENT-NAME-2
            WA-AGENT-NAME-3
        TALLYING IN WA-TALLY-1.
    ```

    After the UNSTRING executes, WA-AGENT-NAME-1   → Anderson,
                                             WA-AGENT-NAME-2   → James
                                             WA-AGENT-NAME-3   → T.
                                             WA-TALLY-1   → 3

2. Assume PR-POLICY-NUMBER contains HM   045 3434

    ```
    UNSTRING PR-POLICY-NUMBER DELIMITED BY SPACES
        INTO WA-NUM-1 DELIMITER IN WA-DEL-1
            WA-NUM-2 DELIMITER IN WA-DEL-2
            WA-NUM-3 DELIMITER IN WA-DEL-3.
    ```

    all spaces

    After the UNSTRING executes, WA-NUM-1 → HM   WA-DEL-1 →
                                           WA-NUM-2 →   WA-DEL-2 →
                                           WA-NUM-3 → 045   WA-DEL-3 →
                                           Overflow occurs but is not detected

3. Assume PR-POLICY-NUMBER contains HM*2045-3434 and WA-POINTER-1 is initialized to 1.

    ```
    UNSTRING PR-POLICY-NUMBER DELIMITED BY "*" OR "-"
        INTO WA-NUM-1 DELIMITER IN WA-DEL-1
                COUNT IN WA-COUNT-1
            WA-NUM-2 DELIMITER IN WA-DEL-2
                COUNT IN WA-COUNT-2
            WA-NUM-3 DELIMITER IN WA-DEL-3
                COUNT IN WA-COUNT-3
        WITH POINTER WA-POINTER-1.
    ```

    After, WA-NUM-1   → HM   WA-DEL-1 → *   WA-COUNT-1 → 2
                 WA-NUM-2   → 2045   WA-DEL-2 → -   WA-COUNT-2 → 4
                 WA-NUM-3   → 3434   WA-DEL-3 →   WA-COUNT-3 → 4
                 WA-POINTER-1 → 13

FIGURE 8-20   More examples of the UNSTRING statement

UNSTRING can be used very effectively to fragment a field so individual portions or fragments can be isolated. If the fragments are always in the same relative positions within a field, however, UNSTRING is not needed. In such cases it is more efficient to redefine the field using a group name that is subdivided into elementary items or to use reference modification to access the desired fragment. Reference modification was presented in Chapter 4. Figure 8-21 illustrates this point using PR-POLICY-NUMBER. Unlike PR-AGENT-NAME, the fragments of PR-POLICY-NUMBER are always in the same character positions.

Assume PR-POLICY-NUMBER is always in the format of AA-0000-0000

UNSTRING—It works, but is inefficient due to the processing overhead required.

```
UNSTRING PR-POLICY-NUMBER DELIMITED BY "-"
    INTO WA-NUM-1
         WA-NUM-2  ◄─── isolates characters 4 through 7
         WA-NUM-3.
```

REDEFINES—Saves processing time but requires extra DATA DIVISION entries.

```
02  PR-POLICY-NUMBER              PIC X(12).
02  PR-POLICY-NUMBER-R REDEFINES
    PR-POLICY-NUMBER.
    03  PR-POLICY-CODE            PIC XX.
    03  PR-HYPHEN-1               PIC X.
    03  PR-CODE-NUMBER-1          PIC X(4). ◄─── isolates characters 4 through 7
    03  PR-HYPHEN-2               PIC X.
    03  PR-CODE-NUMBER-2          PIC X(4).
```

Reference Modification—Requires no extra processing time or special entries in the DATA DIVISION.

```
MOVE PR-POLICY-NUMBER (4:4) TO WA-NUM-2. ◄─── isolates characters 4 through 7
```

FIGURE 8-21   Multiple ways of isolating characters 4 through 7 of PR-POLICY-NUMBER

Once the fragments of a field have been isolated, it is often desirable to reassemble them in a different sequence. The next section discusses a statement that performs such an operation.

STRING STATEMENT

Data stored in different fields can be concatenated, or joined, into a single field using the **STRING** statement. STRING performs an action opposite of UNSTRING. Figure 8-22 on the next page presents the basic format of the STRING statement. The fields or literals following the word STRING are the source fields. All literals used must be coded as nonnumeric literals. The contents of these fields will be concatenated into the receiving field specified after the word INTO. Delimiters can be specified following a DELIMITED BY clause. These delimiters are used to indicate how much of a source field is to be used in the concatenation process. If no delimiter is specified, the entire source field will be used and is the same as specifying a delimiter of SIZE.

```
STRING  ⎧⎧ field-1  ⎫  ...  DELIMITED BY  ⎧ field-2  ⎫⎫  ...
        ⎨⎩ literal-1⎭              ⎨ literal-2 ⎬⎬
        ⎩                                ⎩ SIZE     ⎭⎭

        INTO  field-3

        [ WITH POINTER field-4 ]

        [ ON OVERFLOW statement-set-1 ]

        [ NOT ON OVERFLOW statement-set-2 ]

        [ END-STRING ]
```

FIGURE 8-22   Basic format of the STRING statement

A WITH POINTER clause can be used to specify a field containing the character position where concatenation is to begin in the receiving field. After the STRING statement executes, the POINTER field will contain the character position of the next available position in the receiving field. ON OVERFLOW can be used for special processing when the receiving field is too small to hold all that is being concatenated. NOT ON OVERFLOW can be used for special processing when there is no overflow. END-STRING is needed only when ON OVERFLOW or NOT ON OVERFLOW is used, and a STRING statement must be terminated in a situation where a period cannot be used.

Figure 8-23 presents one of the STRING statements used in the Premium File Update program. It is used to put an agent's first name and last name together, first name first, in the field PR-AGENT-NAME. UNSTRING is used earlier in the program to isolate the agent's first name and last name into the fields WA-AGENT-NAME-1 and WA-AGENT-NAME-2. The STRING statement concatenates these two fields together and places a space between them. Both WA-AGENT-NAME-1 and WA-AGENT-NAME-2 are delimited by SPACES. This means only that part of each field occurring before the first space is placed into PR-AGENT-NAME. The one-character, nonnumeric literal " " is delimited by SIZE and is used to separate the first name from the last name.

Assume WA-AGENT-NAME-1 contains "James" and that
        WA-AGENT-NAME-2 contains "Anderson"

```
599        MOVE SPACES TO PR-AGENT-NAME.
600        STRING WA-AGENT-NAME-1 DELIMITED BY SPACE
601             " "              DELIMITED BY SIZE
602             WA-AGENT-NAME-2 DELIMITED BY SPACE INTO PR-AGENT-NAME.
```

After the STRING executes, PR-AGENT-NAME → James Anderson

FIGURE 8-23   STRING statement from the Premium File Update program

As with UNSTRING, the receiving field should be initialized prior to the STRING statement's execution to avoid unwanted data in rightmost positions. STRING will not automatically pad rightmost positions with spaces. Therefore, the MOVE on line 599 in Figure 8-23 is very important. Figure 8-24 illustrates more examples of the STRING statement. In the second and third examples, it is important to remember that when WITH POINTER is used, the pointer field must be initialized to 1 for concatenation to begin in the first position of the receiving field. After the STRING statement executes, the pointer field will contain the character position of the next available position within the receiving field. If the receiving field is completely used, the pointer value will be one more than the size of the receiving field. If the pointer field is initialized to zero or to a value greater than the size of the receiving field, no concatenation will occur.

Assume that all receiving fields are properly defined and initialized to spaces before each STRING statement

1. Assume WA-AGENT-NAME-1 contains "James"
    WA-AGENT-NAME-2 contains "T."
    WA-AGENT-NAME-3 contains "Anderson"

```
    STRING WA-AGENT-NAME-1 DELIMITED BY SPACES
           " "             DELIMITED BY SIZE
           WA-AGENT-NAME-2 DELIMITED BY SPACES
           " "             DELIMITED BY SIZE
           WA-AGENT-NAME-3 DELIMITED BY SPACES
        INTO PR-AGENT-NAME.
```

After the STRING executes, PR-AGENT-NAME $\rightarrow$ James T. Anderson

2. Assume WA-NUM-1 contains "HM   045"
    WA-NUM-2 contains "1234   "   WA-POINTER-1 = 1
    WA-NUM-3 contains "3434   "   PR-POLICY-NUMBER = 12 bytes

```
    STRING WA-NUM-1 DELIMITED BY SIZE
           WA-NUM-2 DELIMITED BY SIZE
           WA-NUM-3 DELIMITED BY SIZE
        INTO PR-POLICY-NUMBER
        WITH POINTER WA-POINTER-1.
```

After the STRING executes,   PR-POLICY-NUMBER $\rightarrow$ HM 0451234
overflow occurs, and   WA-POINTER-1 $\rightarrow$ 13

3. Assume WA-NUM-1 contains "HM   045"
    WA-NUM-2 contains "1234   "   WA-POINTER-1 = 1
    WA-NUM-3 contains "3434   "   PR-POLICY-NUMBER = 12 bytes

```
    STRING WA-NUM-1 DELIMITED BY SPACES
           WA-NUM-2 DELIMITED BY SPACES
           WA-NUM-3 DELIMITED BY SPACES
        INTO PR-POLICY-NUMBER
        WITH POINTER WA-POINTER-1.
```

After the STRING executes,   PR-POLICY-NUMBER $\rightarrow$ HM12343434
                             WA-POINTER-1 $\rightarrow$ 11

FIGURE 8-24 Examples of the STRING statement

DATA MANIPULATION WITH INTRINSIC FUNCTIONS

Although most of the intrinsic functions introduced in Chapter 5 return numeric values, a few of them are designed for character manipulation. The function UPPER-CASE was used in earlier programs to assist in data validation and to assist in the comparison of user input against the contents of an input file field. UPPER-CASE converts all the letters in a field or literal to uppercase letters. When used with input from a terminal screen or other source, it allows a program to compare the contents of one field to another regardless of the case used in either field. The fields can be compared as though both contain uppercase letters.

Figure 8-25 presents sample code that compares the contents of one field to another with the help of the function UPPER-CASE. When the case of a field is unknown, the use of a function such as UPPER-CASE allows for a uniform comparison. As indicated in Chapter 5, a function creates a temporary value and does not alter the contents of the original field unless the temporary value is saved by moving it to the original field.

```
Assume  PR-INSURANCE-TYPE  contains  → Whole Life and
        WA-TYPE-INPUT       contains  → whole life

    IF FUNCTION UPPER-CASE (PR-INSURANCE-TYPE) NOT =
       FUNCTION UPPER-CASE (WA-TYPE-INPUT)
         PERFORM B-300-ERROR-ROUTINE.
```

With the use the function UPPER-CASE, the fields are compared as though
        PR-INSURANCE-TYPE contains → WHOLE LIFE and
        WA-TYPE-INPUT   contains → WHOLE LIFE

FIGURE 8-25 Use of the function UPPER-CASE

Figure 8-26 shows sample code using the function **LOWER-CASE**. LOWER-CASE works in a manner identical to UPPER-CASE; however, all letters are converted to lowercase.

```
Assume  PR-INSURANCE-TYPE  contains  → Whole Life    and
        WA-TYPE-INPUT       contains  → WHOLE LIFE

    IF FUNCTION LOWER-CASE (PR-INSURANCE-TYPE) NOT =
       FUNCTION LOWER-CASE (WA-TYPE-INPUT)
         PERFORM B-300-ERROR-ROUTINE.
```

With the use the function LOWER-CASE, the fields are compared as though
        PR-INSURANCE-TYPE contains → whole life and
        WA-TYPE-INPUT   contains → whole life

FIGURE 8-26 Use of the function LOWER-CASE

Figure 8-27 presents a third intrinsic function that manipulates character data. The function **REVERSE** reverses the order of the characters in a field or literal without altering the original field.

Assume `PR-AGENT-NAME` contains → Anderson, James T.

```
MOVE FUNCTION REVERSE (PR-AGENT-NAME) TO WA-AGENT-NAME.
```

After the `MOVE`, `WA-AGENT-NAME` contains → .T semaJ ,nosrednA

FIGURE 8-27   Use of the function REVERSE

COPY COMMAND

Often, an input record layout or a particular block of COBOL code will be required in a number of different programs. To save time and improve programmer efficiency, such record layouts and blocks of code normally are saved as files on the computer system in a special library or directory that is available to all programmers. When a record layout or block of code is needed by a programmer, instead of typing it into the source code, the programmer can include a COPY command to identify the file that is needed.

A **COPY** command causes the COBOL compiler to include code saved in a file as part of the source code prior to checking syntax and translating the source code into machine language. When a program is compiled, the compiler finds the files specified by COPY commands and includes them as part of the program prior to any other actions. A COPY command can appear anywhere in a COBOL program, except as part of another COPY command. Options exist that allow the COPY command to customize and modify the code being copied. These options will not be covered or used within this book but can be found in your computer system's COBOL reference manual.

The input record layout for the PREMIUM-INPUT-FILE used in the Premium File Update program was not included in the original program source code. Instead a COPY command was used in the WORKING-STORAGE SECTION of the DATA DIVISION. Figure 8-28 on the next page shows the COPY command used and the record layout included in the program by the compiler. This record layout can be found on the Student Diskette that accompanies this book. The format of the file name used here may be different from that required on your computer system. Check with your instructor or system manager as to the specific file name format required for use with the COPY command on your computer. You may not need the quotation marks, and you may have to include a specific library or subdirectory name. The "L" after each line number in the record layout is a form of identification used by the compiler to specifically identify the lines of code copied into the program as a result of the COPY command. This form of identification varies from one computer system to another.

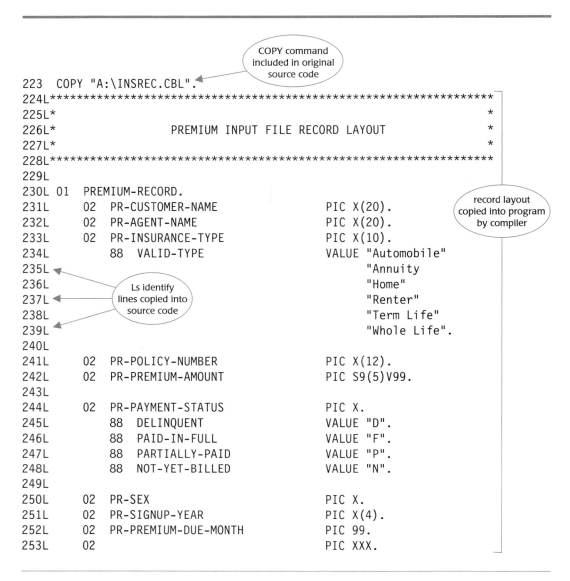

```
223  COPY "A:\INSREC.CBL".
224L***********************************************************
225L*                                                         *
226L*           PREMIUM INPUT FILE RECORD LAYOUT              *
227L*                                                         *
228L***********************************************************
229L
230L 01  PREMIUM-RECORD.
231L     02  PR-CUSTOMER-NAME            PIC X(20).
232L     02  PR-AGENT-NAME               PIC X(20).
233L     02  PR-INSURANCE-TYPE           PIC X(10).
234L         88  VALID-TYPE              VALUE "Automobile"
235L                                           "Annuity
236L                                           "Home"
237L                                           "Renter"
238L                                           "Term Life"
239L                                           "Whole Life".
240L
241L     02  PR-POLICY-NUMBER            PIC X(12).
242L     02  PR-PREMIUM-AMOUNT           PIC S9(5)V99.
243L
244L     02  PR-PAYMENT-STATUS           PIC X.
245L         88  DELINQUENT              VALUE "D".
246L         88  PAID-IN-FULL            VALUE "F".
247L         88  PARTIALLY-PAID          VALUE "P".
248L         88  NOT-YET-BILLED          VALUE "N".
249L
250L     02  PR-SEX                      PIC X.
251L     02  PR-SIGNUP-YEAR              PIC X(4).
252L     02  PR-PREMIUM-DUE-MONTH        PIC 99.
253L     02                              PIC XXX.
```

COPY command included in original source code

record layout copied into program by compiler

Ls identify lines copied into source code

FIGURE 8-28 Use of the COPY command in the Premium File Update program

SEQUENTIAL FILE MAINTENANCE

As indicated at the beginning of this chapter, the process of altering the contents of a file is called file maintenance. File maintenance can involve adding new records to a file, updating existing records in a file, or deleting records from a file. Often, a file maintenance program performs all three tasks. The Premium File Update program merely updates existing records in the PREMIUM-INPUT-FILE by modifying two fields and adding a dollar amount to the PR-PREMIUM-AMOUNT field. A transaction file is used as input to indicate which records are to be modified and how much is to be added to PR-PREMIUM-AMOUNT. Once a record is updated, it is written to a new version of the Premium file called UPDATED-PREMIUM-FILE, and the activity is recorded in a report file. A sequential file is often updated by creating a new version, or generation, of that file. The file to be updated is referred to as the **master file**, and the new version is then called the **new master file**. Figure 8-29 illustrates the flow of data in the updating of a sequential file.

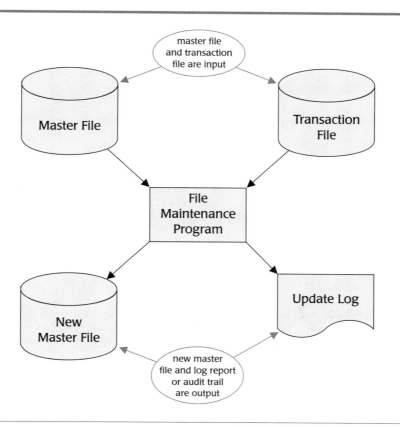

FIGURE 8-29 Data flow in updating a sequential file

Sequential file maintenance is performed by processing the transaction file and master file at the same time. Both files must be sequenced in the same order by a field unique to each record in the master file. This field is known as the key field. The PR-POLICY-NUMBER is used as the key field in PREMIUM-INPUT-FILE and corresponds to the field TR-POLICY-NUMBER in TRANSACTION-FILE. The PREMIUM-INPUT-FILE used in this program is already in sequence by policy number. TRANSACTION-FILE is not pre-sorted and must be rearranged so the transactions are in sequence by policy number. The records in TRANSACTION-FILE also must be validated. That is, both fields in each record of TRANSACTION-FILE must be checked to see that the content is acceptable for use during file maintenance processing.

Transaction File Sorting and Validation

A COBOL SORT with an INPUT PROCEDURE is used in the B-stream of the Premium File Update program to validate and rearrange the transactions. The sorted transactions are placed in SORTED-TRANSACTION-FILE, which then is used as input to the file maintenance. Figure 8-30 presents the SORT statement used in the program.

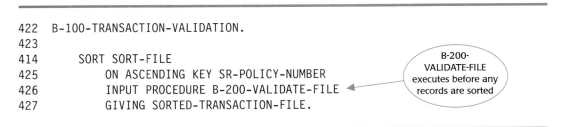

```
422   B-100-TRANSACTION-VALIDATION.
423
414       SORT SORT-FILE
425           ON ASCENDING KEY SR-POLICY-NUMBER
426           INPUT PROCEDURE B-200-VALIDATE-FILE
427           GIVING SORTED-TRANSACTION-FILE.
```

B-200-VALIDATE-FILE executes before any records are sorted

FIGURE 8-30 SORT statement from the Premium File Update program, utilizing INPUT PROCEDURE with GIVING

Figures 8-31, 8-32, and 8-33 (on page 8-32) present the code comprising the INPUT PROCEDURE. The sorting and validating are similar to processing used in earlier programs within this book. As the transaction records are validated, records with errors are written to the report file TRANSACTION-LOG-REPORT. TRANSACTION-LOG-REPORT also will be used to record the actions taken with the sorted transactions used in the file maintenance processing.

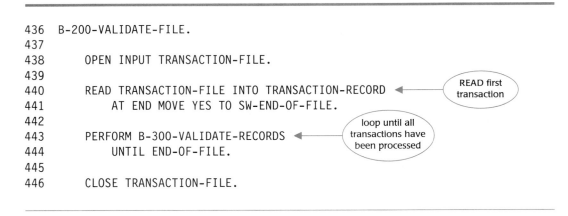

```
436   B-200-VALIDATE-FILE.
437
438       OPEN INPUT TRANSACTION-FILE.
439
440       READ TRANSACTION-FILE INTO TRANSACTION-RECORD
441           AT END MOVE YES TO SW-END-OF-FILE.
442
443       PERFORM B-300-VALIDATE-RECORDS
444           UNTIL END-OF-FILE.
445
446       CLOSE TRANSACTION-FILE.
```

READ first transaction

loop until all transactions have been processed

FIGURE 8-31 Main paragraph for the INPUT PROCEDURE of the Premium File Update program

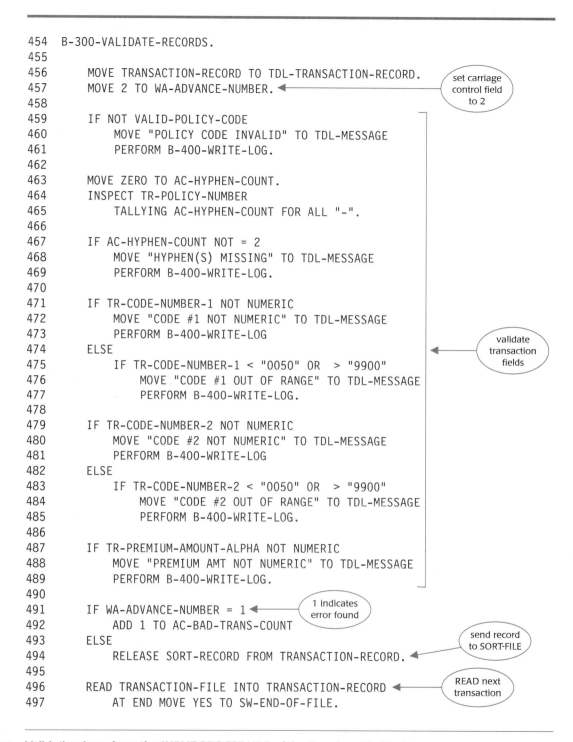

```
454   B-300-VALIDATE-RECORDS.
455
456       MOVE TRANSACTION-RECORD TO TDL-TRANSACTION-RECORD.
457       MOVE 2 TO WA-ADVANCE-NUMBER.          ◄── set carriage
458                                                 control field
459       IF NOT VALID-POLICY-CODE                  to 2
460           MOVE "POLICY CODE INVALID" TO TDL-MESSAGE
461           PERFORM B-400-WRITE-LOG.
462
463       MOVE ZERO TO AC-HYPHEN-COUNT.
464       INSPECT TR-POLICY-NUMBER
465           TALLYING AC-HYPHEN-COUNT FOR ALL "-".
466
467       IF AC-HYPHEN-COUNT NOT = 2
468           MOVE "HYPHEN(S) MISSING" TO TDL-MESSAGE
469           PERFORM B-400-WRITE-LOG.
470
471       IF TR-CODE-NUMBER-1 NOT NUMERIC
472           MOVE "CODE #1 NOT NUMERIC" TO TDL-MESSAGE
473           PERFORM B-400-WRITE-LOG                ◄── validate
474       ELSE                                           transaction
475           IF TR-CODE-NUMBER-1 < "0050" OR  > "9900"   fields
476               MOVE "CODE #1 OUT OF RANGE" TO TDL-MESSAGE
477               PERFORM B-400-WRITE-LOG.
478
479       IF TR-CODE-NUMBER-2 NOT NUMERIC
480           MOVE "CODE #2 NOT NUMERIC" TO TDL-MESSAGE
481           PERFORM B-400-WRITE-LOG
482       ELSE
483           IF TR-CODE-NUMBER-2 < "0050" OR  > "9900"
484               MOVE "CODE #2 OUT OF RANGE" TO TDL-MESSAGE
485               PERFORM B-400-WRITE-LOG.
486
487       IF TR-PREMIUM-AMOUNT-ALPHA NOT NUMERIC
488           MOVE "PREMIUM AMT NOT NUMERIC" TO TDL-MESSAGE
489           PERFORM B-400-WRITE-LOG.
490
491       IF WA-ADVANCE-NUMBER = 1   ◄── 1 indicates
492           ADD 1 TO AC-BAD-TRANS-COUNT   error found
493       ELSE
494           RELEASE SORT-RECORD FROM TRANSACTION-RECORD.  ◄── send record
495                                                             to SORT-FILE
496       READ TRANSACTION-FILE INTO TRANSACTION-RECORD  ◄── READ next
497           AT END MOVE YES TO SW-END-OF-FILE.              transaction
```

FIGURE 8-32   Validation loop from the INPUT PROCEDURE of the Premium File Update program

On lines 510 and 511 in Figure 8-33, the WRITE statement for the TRANSACTION-LOG-REPORT uses a variable name, WA-ADVANCE-NUMBER, to control spacing on the report. Line 457 in Figure 8-32 initializes WA-ADVANCE-NUMBER to 2 for each record processed. Thus, the first time an error is found in a transaction, the error message line output to the report is double-spaced. Line 514 in Figure 8-33 moves 1 to WA-ADVANCE-NUMBER, thus, causing any subsequent error messages for the same transaction to be single-spaced. After a transaction record is validated, WA-ADVANCE-NUMBER contains a value of 1 if one or more errors are found in the transaction. This is used to determine if the transaction should be released to SORT-FILE. The IF statement on lines 491 through 494 in Figure 8-32 on the previous page tests WA-ADVANCE-NUMBER. If its value is 1, the error counter, AC-BAD-TRANS-COUNT, is incremented by one. If WA-ADVANCE-NUMBER is not equal to 1, the current transaction record is released to the sort work file.

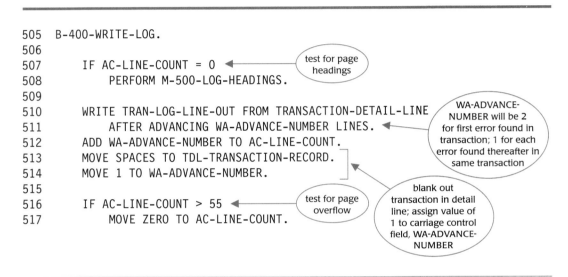

```
505   B-400-WRITE-LOG.
506
507       IF AC-LINE-COUNT = 0              ◄──  test for page
508           PERFORM M-500-LOG-HEADINGS.         headings
509
510       WRITE TRAN-LOG-LINE-OUT FROM TRANSACTION-DETAIL-LINE
511           AFTER ADVANCING WA-ADVANCE-NUMBER LINES.   ◄──  WA-ADVANCE-
512       ADD WA-ADVANCE-NUMBER TO AC-LINE-COUNT.             NUMBER will be 2
513       MOVE SPACES TO TDL-TRANSACTION-RECORD.              for first error found in
514       MOVE 1 TO WA-ADVANCE-NUMBER.                        transaction; 1 for each
515                                                           error found thereafter in
516       IF AC-LINE-COUNT > 55            ◄──  test for page    same transaction
517           MOVE ZERO TO AC-LINE-COUNT.       overflow
```

blank out transaction in detail line; assign value of 1 to carriage control field, WA-ADVANCE-NUMBER

FIGURE 8-33 Paragraph of the INPUT PROCEDURE from the Premium File Update program that writes error records to the Transaction Log Report

When it is necessary to print page headings for the TRANSACTION-LOG-REPORT, control is passed to the paragraph M-500-LOG-HEADINGS (see lines 507 and 508 in Figure 8-33). The letter "M" is used on this paragraph because it is a **multiply performed module**; that is, a paragraph that is performed multiple times from multiple paragraphs. It is performed not only in the B-stream as part of the sort routine, but also in the C-stream during file maintenance processing. Rather than coding two separate heading routines or confusing the logic by have a B module perform a C module or a C module perform a B module, M is used to mark this paragraph as something special. The number 500 is used because the lowest level performing M-500-LOG-HEADINGS is a 400 level module in the B-stream.

Once the transactions have been validated and sorted, the actual file maintenance processing can begin. This is done by opening both the SORTED-TRANSACTION-FILE and PREMIUM-INPUT-FILE for INPUT and then comparing the key fields, TR-POLICY-NUMBER and PR-POLICY-NUMBER. For a record to be updated, TR-POLICY-NUMBER in the transaction being processed must match PR-POLICY-NUMBER in the premium record being processed. Such processing is called file matching.

File Matching

During **file matching**, records are read from a transaction file and a master file and the key fields are compared in an attempt to find matches. In a perfect world, every transaction record would have a match in the master file. Due to typing errors or to the fact that some master records are not to be updated, mismatches do occur. The program logic must be prepared to handle these mismatches. The logic for the Premium File Update program was illustrated earlier in this chapter in Figure 8-4 on pages 8-6 and 8-7.

As a result of comparing the key fields, one of three things is true: (1) the keys are equal; (2) the transaction file key is greater than the master file key; or (3) the transaction file key is less than the master file key. Remember, this processing requires that both files be in the same sequence by the key field.

When the keys are equal, data in the transaction record can be used to update the master file record being processed, and the updated record then can be written to the new master file. A transaction that is actually used to update a master record is said to be posted and is called a **posted transaction**. Once a transaction is posted, assuming there is just one transaction for each master record, the next transaction record and next master file record can be retrieved and the next comparison performed.

When a transaction record key is greater than a master file record key, no transaction corresponding to the current master file record exists. Such a master file record is called an **unmatched master**. The unmatched master often is written to the new master file unmodified. In the sample program this action is noted on the output report, and then the next master file record is retrieved. Noting unmatched records on the output report is typically omitted in most business environments. The comparison process then continues. In the Premium File Update program the agent name and account number fields are modified before the record is written to the new master file, even when no transaction exists for a master record.

When a transaction record key is less than a master file record key, then no master file record corresponds to the current transaction. Such a transaction is called an **unmatched transaction**. In the Premium File Update program, the transaction is merely noted on an output report, and then the next transaction is retrieved. The comparison then executes again.

A special kind of unmatched transaction in the sample program involves the situation where the same transaction is on the transaction file more than once. In the Premium File Update program, only one transaction record per master file record is allowed. The first transaction encountered during processing is used to update a master file record. If another transaction exists with the same key value, it is considered to be a **duplicate transaction**. To distinguish a duplicate transaction from an unmatched transaction, the previous transaction key field value is saved and compared to the current transaction key. When the previous key value is equal to the current key value, the transaction is a duplicate. Otherwise, the transaction is a true unmatched transaction.

Figure 8-34 on the next page presents the code that controls the file matching logic used in the Premium File Update program. Processing continues until all records in both files have been processed. To avoid the unnecessary testing of switches and to utilize consistent logic, the AT END clauses in the READ for the SORTED-TRANSACTION-FILE and the READ for the PREMIUM-INPUT-FILE move the figurative constant HIGH-VALUES to the appropriate key field. Thus, if the end of the SORTED-TRANSACTION-FILE is reached first, logic is forced in the direction of the unmatched masters because HIGH-VALUES is greater than any value possibly contained in PR-POLICY-NUMBER. If the end of the PREMIUM-INPUT-FILE is reached first, logic is forced in the direction of the unmatched transactions, because any value contained in TR-POLICY-NUMBER will be less than HIGH-VALUES. Processing thus continues until both TR-POLICY-NUMBER and PR-POLICY-NUMBER are equal to HIGH-VALUES.

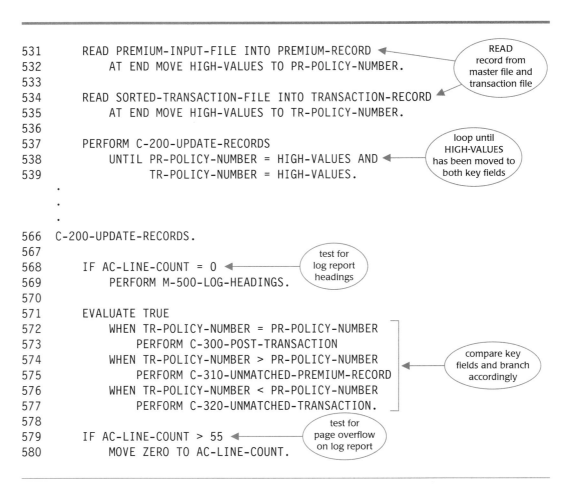

```
531     READ PREMIUM-INPUT-FILE INTO PREMIUM-RECORD
532         AT END MOVE HIGH-VALUES TO PR-POLICY-NUMBER.
533
534     READ SORTED-TRANSACTION-FILE INTO TRANSACTION-RECORD
535         AT END MOVE HIGH-VALUES TO TR-POLICY-NUMBER.
536
537     PERFORM C-200-UPDATE-RECORDS
538         UNTIL PR-POLICY-NUMBER = HIGH-VALUES AND
539               TR-POLICY-NUMBER = HIGH-VALUES.
        .
        .
        .
566  C-200-UPDATE-RECORDS.
567
568     IF AC-LINE-COUNT = 0
569         PERFORM M-500-LOG-HEADINGS.
570
571     EVALUATE TRUE
572         WHEN TR-POLICY-NUMBER = PR-POLICY-NUMBER
573             PERFORM C-300-POST-TRANSACTION
574         WHEN TR-POLICY-NUMBER > PR-POLICY-NUMBER
575             PERFORM C-310-UNMATCHED-PREMIUM-RECORD
576         WHEN TR-POLICY-NUMBER < PR-POLICY-NUMBER
577             PERFORM C-320-UNMATCHED-TRANSACTION.
578
579     IF AC-LINE-COUNT > 55
580         MOVE ZERO TO AC-LINE-COUNT.
```

READ record from master file and transaction file

loop until HIGH-VALUES has been moved to both key fields

test for log report headings

compare key fields and branch accordingly

test for page overflow on log report

FIGURE 8-34 File matching code from the Premium File Update program

Figure 8-35 illustrates the code from the Premium File Update program that processes posted transactions and updates the records before they are written to NEW-PREMIUM-FILE. The premium adjustment amount from the transaction is added to PR-PREMIUM-AMOUNT. The agent name is then reversed and the account number is modified. Notice that the WRITE statement on line 607 does not contain an AFTER ADVANCING clause for line spacing or carriage control. Because records here are being written to a data file and not to a report file, carriage control is not desired. The disposition of all transactions is noted on the TRANSACTION-LOG-REPORT. The transaction record is printed out along with a message that indicates that it has been posted.

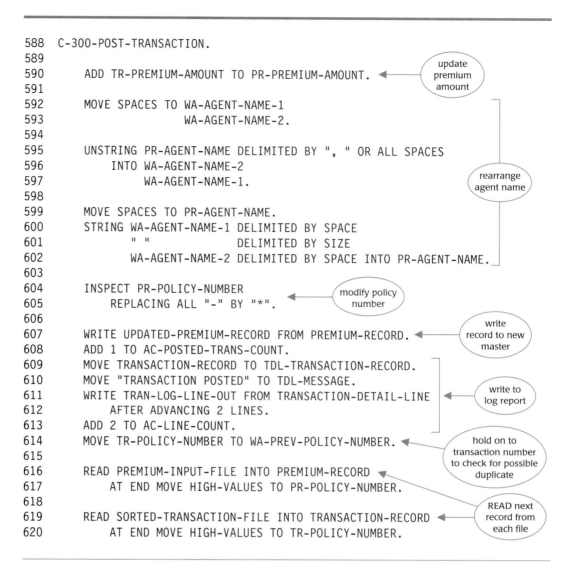

```
588  C-300-POST-TRANSACTION.
589
590      ADD TR-PREMIUM-AMOUNT TO PR-PREMIUM-AMOUNT.          ◄─── update premium amount
591
592      MOVE SPACES TO WA-AGENT-NAME-1
593                    WA-AGENT-NAME-2.
594
595      UNSTRING PR-AGENT-NAME DELIMITED BY ", " OR ALL SPACES
596          INTO WA-AGENT-NAME-2
597               WA-AGENT-NAME-1.                            rearrange agent name
598
599      MOVE SPACES TO PR-AGENT-NAME.
600      STRING WA-AGENT-NAME-1 DELIMITED BY SPACE
601             " "                 DELIMITED BY SIZE
602             WA-AGENT-NAME-2 DELIMITED BY SPACE INTO PR-AGENT-NAME.
603
604      INSPECT PR-POLICY-NUMBER          ◄─── modify policy number
605          REPLACING ALL "-" BY "*".
606
607      WRITE UPDATED-PREMIUM-RECORD FROM PREMIUM-RECORD.    ◄─── write record to new master
608      ADD 1 TO AC-POSTED-TRANS-COUNT.
609      MOVE TRANSACTION-RECORD TO TDL-TRANSACTION-RECORD.
610      MOVE "TRANSACTION POSTED" TO TDL-MESSAGE.
611      WRITE TRAN-LOG-LINE-OUT FROM TRANSACTION-DETAIL-LINE    ◄─── write to log report
612          AFTER ADVANCING 2 LINES.
613      ADD 2 TO AC-LINE-COUNT.
614      MOVE TR-POLICY-NUMBER TO WA-PREV-POLICY-NUMBER.    ◄─── hold on to transaction number to check for possible duplicate
615
616      READ PREMIUM-INPUT-FILE INTO PREMIUM-RECORD
617          AT END MOVE HIGH-VALUES TO PR-POLICY-NUMBER.
618                                                           READ next record from each file
619      READ SORTED-TRANSACTION-FILE INTO TRANSACTION-RECORD    ◄───
620          AT END MOVE HIGH-VALUES TO TR-POLICY-NUMBER.
```

FIGURE 8-35   COBOL code for a posted transaction from the Premium File Update program

Figure 8-36 on the next page lists the code from the Premium File Update program that processes unmatched master records. After modifying the agent name and account number fields, unmatched masters are written to the new master file. The premium amount is unchanged. The account number of the master record is listed on the TRANSACTION-LOG-REPORT along with a message that identifies this entry as an unmatched master.

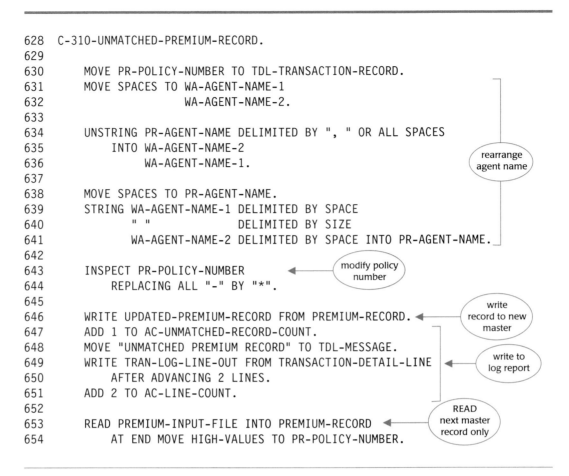

```
628  C-310-UNMATCHED-PREMIUM-RECORD.
629
630     MOVE PR-POLICY-NUMBER TO TDL-TRANSACTION-RECORD.
631     MOVE SPACES TO WA-AGENT-NAME-1
632                    WA-AGENT-NAME-2.
633
634     UNSTRING PR-AGENT-NAME DELIMITED BY ", " OR ALL SPACES
635        INTO WA-AGENT-NAME-2
636            WA-AGENT-NAME-1.
637
638     MOVE SPACES TO PR-AGENT-NAME.
639     STRING WA-AGENT-NAME-1 DELIMITED BY SPACE
640           " "              DELIMITED BY SIZE
641           WA-AGENT-NAME-2 DELIMITED BY SPACE INTO PR-AGENT-NAME.
642
643     INSPECT PR-POLICY-NUMBER
644         REPLACING ALL "-" BY "*".
645
646     WRITE UPDATED-PREMIUM-RECORD FROM PREMIUM-RECORD.
647     ADD 1 TO AC-UNMATCHED-RECORD-COUNT.
648     MOVE "UNMATCHED PREMIUM RECORD" TO TDL-MESSAGE.
649     WRITE TRAN-LOG-LINE-OUT FROM TRANSACTION-DETAIL-LINE
650         AFTER ADVANCING 2 LINES.
651     ADD 2 TO AC-LINE-COUNT.
652
653     READ PREMIUM-INPUT-FILE INTO PREMIUM-RECORD
654         AT END MOVE HIGH-VALUES TO PR-POLICY-NUMBER.
```

rearrange agent name

modify policy number

write record to new master

write to log report

READ next master record only

FIGURE 8-36   COBOL code for an unmatched master record from the Premium File Update program

Figure 8-37 presents the code from the Premium File Update program that processes unmatched transactions. On line 664, TR-POLICY-NUMBER is compared to WA-PREV-POLICY-NUMBER to determine if the transaction is truly unmatched or a duplicate. The disposition of the transaction is noted on the TRANSACTION-LOG-REPORT by listing the transaction record along with the appropriate message.

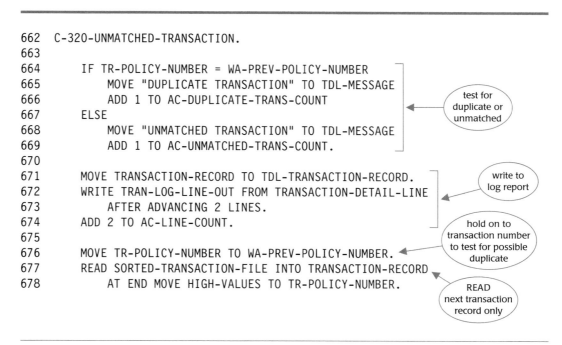

```
662  C-320-UNMATCHED-TRANSACTION.
663
664      IF TR-POLICY-NUMBER = WA-PREV-POLICY-NUMBER
665          MOVE "DUPLICATE TRANSACTION" TO TDL-MESSAGE
666          ADD 1 TO AC-DUPLICATE-TRANS-COUNT
667      ELSE
668          MOVE "UNMATCHED TRANSACTION" TO TDL-MESSAGE
669          ADD 1 TO AC-UNMATCHED-TRANS-COUNT.
670
671      MOVE TRANSACTION-RECORD TO TDL-TRANSACTION-RECORD.
672      WRITE TRAN-LOG-LINE-OUT FROM TRANSACTION-DETAIL-LINE
673          AFTER ADVANCING 2 LINES.
674      ADD 2 TO AC-LINE-COUNT.
675
676      MOVE TR-POLICY-NUMBER TO WA-PREV-POLICY-NUMBER.
677      READ SORTED-TRANSACTION-FILE INTO TRANSACTION-RECORD
678          AT END MOVE HIGH-VALUES TO TR-POLICY-NUMBER.
```

test for duplicate or unmatched

write to log report

hold on to transaction number to test for possible duplicate

READ next transaction record only

FIGURE 8-37 COBOL code for an unmatched transaction from the Premium File Update program

Once all the records in both files have been processed, summary lines for the TRANSACTION-LOG-REPORT are printed, files are closed, and the program terminates. Using commands available from the computer's operating system, the new master file can be renamed and used as the current premium file for all reports and processing until the next generation of the file is created. Consult with your system administrator or check your operating system manual for these commands.

Multiple Updates, Adds, and Deletes

Processing in the Premium File Update program was simplified by allowing only one transaction for each master record and performing the single maintenance task of updating an existing record. Many applications require not only multiple update or change transactions for the same master record but also require the processing of transactions that call for the addition of new records to the file and deletion of existing records.

Because each WRITE to the new master file adds a new record to the file, when multiple updates are allowed to a master record, the master record cannot be written to the new master file until all of the transactions for that master have been processed. This alters the logic used in the Premium File Update program. Figure 8-38 on the next page presents a partial flowchart illustrating a modified version of the file matching logic used in the sample program. Before an updated record is written to the new master file, the next transaction is read and its key field is compared to that of the current master record. If the keys are equal, another update is performed and the next transaction record is read. Only when the key of the next transaction is not equal to the current master record is the master record written to the new master file and the next master record read.

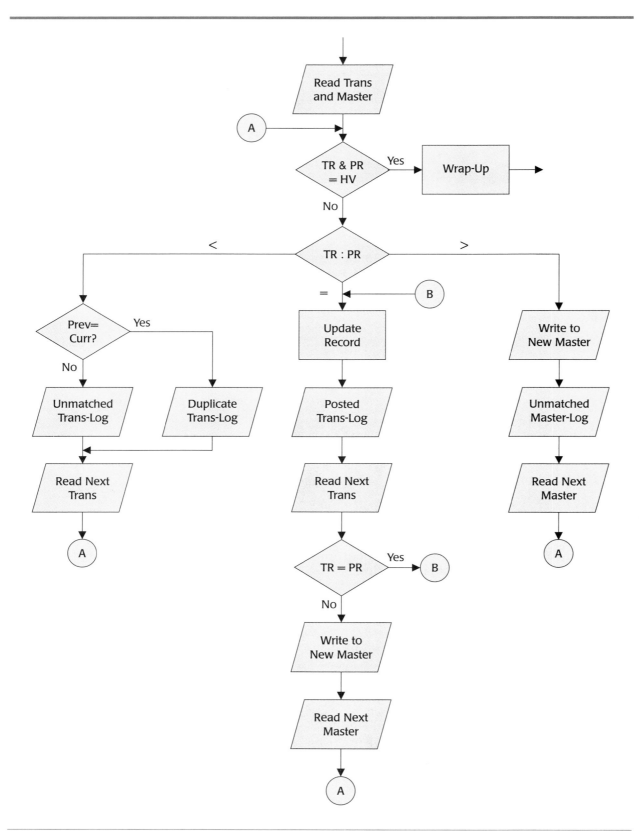

FIGURE 8-38   Partial flowchart of file matching logic allowing multiple updates to the same master record in the Premium File Update program

Sample COBOL code for this logic is presented in Figure 8-39.

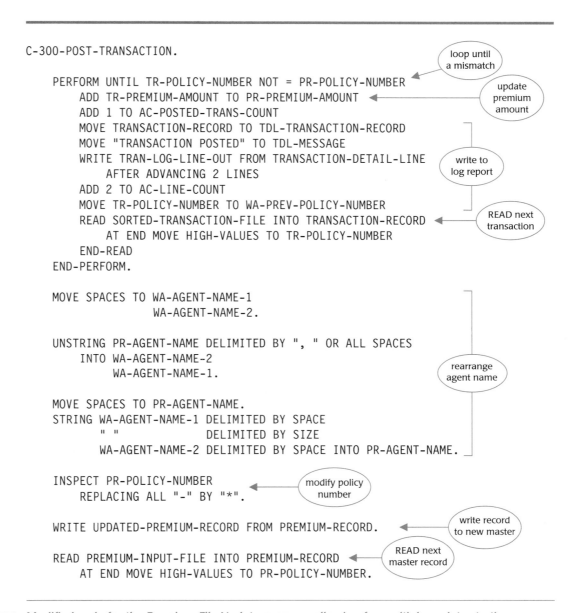

```
C-300-POST-TRANSACTION.

    PERFORM UNTIL TR-POLICY-NUMBER NOT = PR-POLICY-NUMBER
        ADD TR-PREMIUM-AMOUNT TO PR-PREMIUM-AMOUNT
        ADD 1 TO AC-POSTED-TRANS-COUNT
        MOVE TRANSACTION-RECORD TO TDL-TRANSACTION-RECORD
        MOVE "TRANSACTION POSTED" TO TDL-MESSAGE
        WRITE TRAN-LOG-LINE-OUT FROM TRANSACTION-DETAIL-LINE
            AFTER ADVANCING 2 LINES
        ADD 2 TO AC-LINE-COUNT
        MOVE TR-POLICY-NUMBER TO WA-PREV-POLICY-NUMBER
        READ SORTED-TRANSACTION-FILE INTO TRANSACTION-RECORD
            AT END MOVE HIGH-VALUES TO TR-POLICY-NUMBER
        END-READ
    END-PERFORM.

    MOVE SPACES TO WA-AGENT-NAME-1
                   WA-AGENT-NAME-2.

    UNSTRING PR-AGENT-NAME DELIMITED BY ", " OR ALL SPACES
        INTO WA-AGENT-NAME-2
             WA-AGENT-NAME-1.

    MOVE SPACES TO PR-AGENT-NAME.
    STRING WA-AGENT-NAME-1 DELIMITED BY SPACE
           " "                 DELIMITED BY SIZE
           WA-AGENT-NAME-2 DELIMITED BY SPACE INTO PR-AGENT-NAME.

    INSPECT PR-POLICY-NUMBER
        REPLACING ALL "-" BY "*".

    WRITE UPDATED-PREMIUM-RECORD FROM PREMIUM-RECORD.

    READ PREMIUM-INPUT-FILE INTO PREMIUM-RECORD
        AT END MOVE HIGH-VALUES TO PR-POLICY-NUMBER.
```

Callouts: loop until a mismatch; update premium amount; write to log report; READ next transaction; rearrange agent name; modify policy number; write record to new master; READ next master record

FIGURE 8-39   Modified code for the Premium File Update program allowing for multiple updates to the same master record

When transactions that call for the addition of new records, changing of existing records, and deletion of existing records are all contained in the same transaction file, a character is required within each transaction that indicates what activity is to be performed. Figure 8-40 on the next page presents a transaction record layout that could be used for add, change, and delete transactions for the PREMIUM-INPUT-FILE. The transaction record layout contains a code in the first position that indicates for what activity the transaction is to be used. The letter A is used to indicate an add transaction; the letter C is used to indicate a change transaction; and the letter D is used to indicate a delete transaction. The transaction record layout also contains the key field and all the other fields used in the records of the PREMIUM-INPUT-FILE. In the sample program a transaction used to add a record contains an entry in every field. A transaction used to change or update a record contains entries in the code field, the key field, and other entries in just those fields that are to be modified. A delete transaction requires entries in only the code and key fields. This identifies which master record is to be deleted.

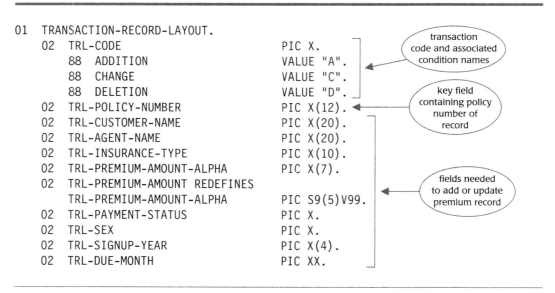

```
01  TRANSACTION-RECORD-LAYOUT.
    02  TRL-CODE                        PIC X.
        88  ADDITION                    VALUE "A".
        88  CHANGE                      VALUE "C".
        88  DELETION                    VALUE "D".
    02  TRL-POLICY-NUMBER               PIC X(12).
    02  TRL-CUSTOMER-NAME               PIC X(20).
    02  TRL-AGENT-NAME                  PIC X(20).
    02  TRL-INSURANCE-TYPE              PIC X(10).
    02  TRL-PREMIUM-AMOUNT-ALPHA        PIC X(7).
    02  TRL-PREMIUM-AMOUNT REDEFINES
        TRL-PREMIUM-AMOUNT-ALPHA        PIC S9(5)V99.
    02  TRL-PAYMENT-STATUS              PIC X.
    02  TRL-SEX                         PIC X.
    02  TRL-SIGNUP-YEAR                 PIC X(4).
    02  TRL-DUE-MONTH                   PIC XX.
```

FIGURE 8-40 Transaction record layout that could be used for addition, update, and deletion transactions for the PREMIUM-INPUT-FILE

Figure 8-41 presents sample add, change, and delete transactions for the PREMIUM-INPUT-FILE.

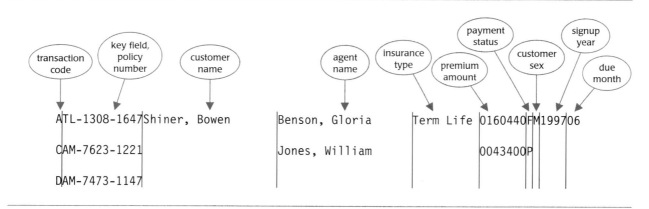

FIGURE 8-41 Sample add, change, and delete transactions for the PREMIUM-INPUT-FILE

When processing a transaction that calls for the addition of a new record, the data in the transaction is used to fill in, or build, a complete new master record. Once a new master record has been built, it can be written to the new master file. If add transactions are all that are to be processed, new records can be added to the end of an existing file by opening the file using EXTEND mode. EXTEND mode was first discussed in Chapter 2 and is a special way of opening a file for output. When a file is open for OUTPUT, the file is newly created. When a file is opened using EXTEND mode, newly written records are appended to the end of the file, following the existing records.

To process a delete transaction, be sure the record identified by the key field in the transaction is not written to the new master file. Thus, a record is deleted simply by leaving it out of the new master file.

The logic used to update a sequential file using three different types of transactions is more complex than the logic presented thus far. Various forms of this logic exist. One popular form, called the **balance line algorithm**, was presented by Barry Dwyer in an article entitled "One More Time - How to Update a Master File" in the *Communications of the ACM*, Volume 24, Number 1, January 1981. The balance line algorithm involves the maintenance of an active key field and an allocation switch. The active key field always contains the smaller value of the current master key and current transaction key. The active key field is used in a comparison to determine the action to be taken and, ultimately, whether the next transaction should be read, the next master record should be read, or both a transaction record and master record should be read.

The allocation switch is used to indicate when a master record is active; that is, to indicate whether or not it exists on the master file. This is used to determine what processing should occur for each of the three types of transactions and also to determine when a master record should be written to the new master file. When the allocation switch is turned on an active master record on the file can be processed. When the allocation switch is turned off no active master remains on the file. If the allocation switch is off, the only transactions that can be processed are add transactions.

Figure 8-42 (on pages 8-42 and 8-43) presents a flowchart that illustrates the logic of the balance line algorithm. Two versions of the master record layout are maintained. One version, old master record, is for the most recently read master record. The other version, new master record, is used for building new records when processing an add transaction or for updating fields when processing a change transaction. Prior to reading the next master record, old master record is moved to new master record. As in the Premium File Update program, the AT END clause in each READ statement used must move HIGH-VALUES to the appropriate key. Processing continues until both keys contain HIGH-VALUES thus causing the active key field to also contain HIGH-VALUES.

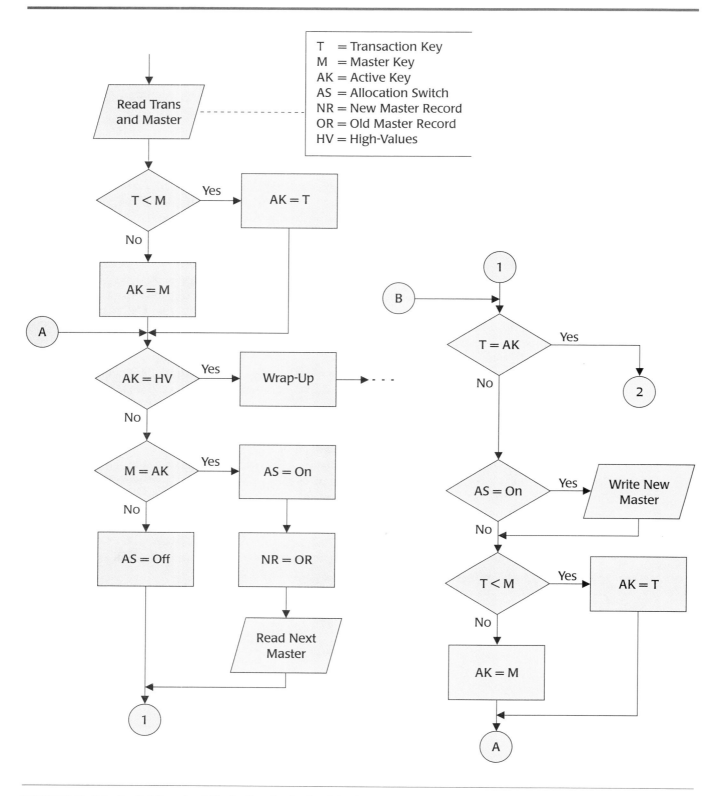

FIGURE 8-42 Partial flowchart illustrating the logic of the balance line algorithm for updating sequential files

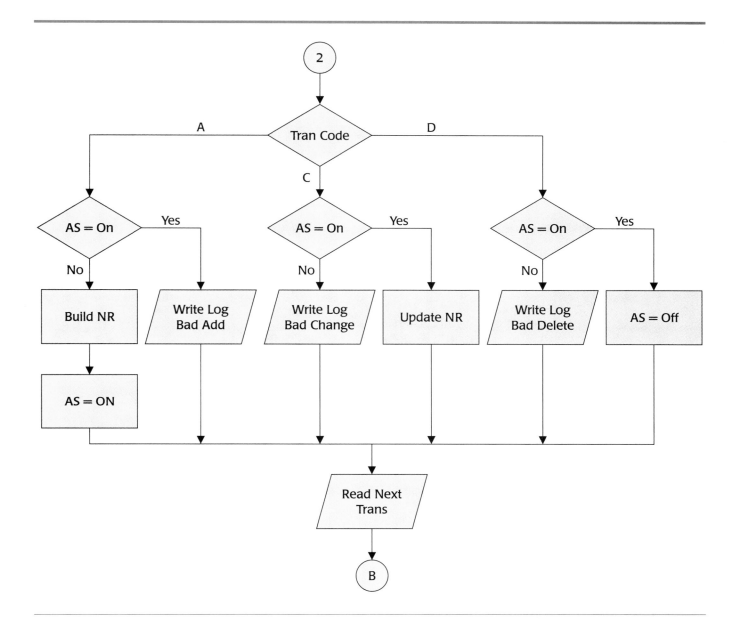

Figures 8-43 (on the next page) and 8-44 (on page 8-45) present a partial listing of COBOL code that implements this logic for the PREMIUM-INPUT-FILE. An EVALUATE statement is used in Figure 8-44 to direct control to the appropriate processing procedure for the current transaction code. SW-ALLOCATION is checked for each transaction code to determine if an active master record exists. No active master is a good condition for an add transaction, code A, but a bad condition for change and delete transactions, codes C and D. A record can be added only when no record on the old master has the specified key value. A record can be changed or deleted only if records with the specified key values exist. No program in this book requires use of the balance line algorithm, but a basic understanding of its logic is important.

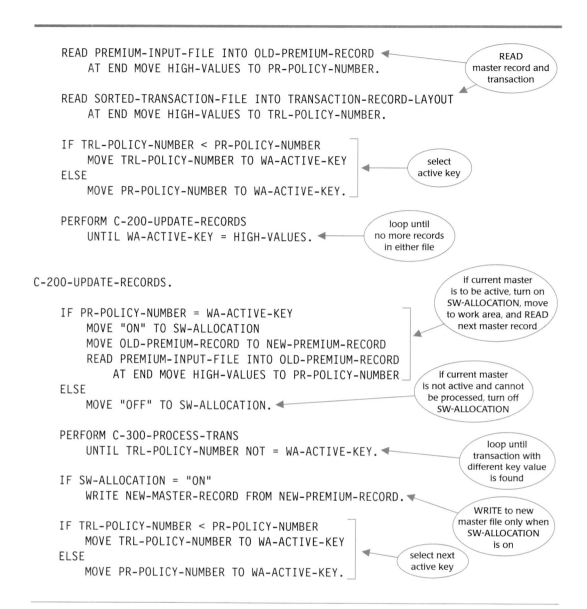

```
READ PREMIUM-INPUT-FILE INTO OLD-PREMIUM-RECORD
    AT END MOVE HIGH-VALUES TO PR-POLICY-NUMBER.

READ SORTED-TRANSACTION-FILE INTO TRANSACTION-RECORD-LAYOUT
    AT END MOVE HIGH-VALUES TO TRL-POLICY-NUMBER.

IF TRL-POLICY-NUMBER < PR-POLICY-NUMBER
    MOVE TRL-POLICY-NUMBER TO WA-ACTIVE-KEY
ELSE
    MOVE PR-POLICY-NUMBER TO WA-ACTIVE-KEY.

PERFORM C-200-UPDATE-RECORDS
    UNTIL WA-ACTIVE-KEY = HIGH-VALUES.


C-200-UPDATE-RECORDS.

    IF PR-POLICY-NUMBER = WA-ACTIVE-KEY
        MOVE "ON" TO SW-ALLOCATION
        MOVE OLD-PREMIUM-RECORD TO NEW-PREMIUM-RECORD
        READ PREMIUM-INPUT-FILE INTO OLD-PREMIUM-RECORD
            AT END MOVE HIGH-VALUES TO PR-POLICY-NUMBER
    ELSE
        MOVE "OFF" TO SW-ALLOCATION.

    PERFORM C-300-PROCESS-TRANS
        UNTIL TRL-POLICY-NUMBER NOT = WA-ACTIVE-KEY.

    IF SW-ALLOCATION = "ON"
        WRITE NEW-MASTER-RECORD FROM NEW-PREMIUM-RECORD.

    IF TRL-POLICY-NUMBER < PR-POLICY-NUMBER
        MOVE TRL-POLICY-NUMBER TO WA-ACTIVE-KEY
    ELSE
        MOVE PR-POLICY-NUMBER TO WA-ACTIVE-KEY.
```

Callouts:
- READ master record and transaction
- select active key
- loop until no more records in either file
- if current master is to be active, turn on SW-ALLOCATION, move to work area, and READ next master record
- if current master is not active and cannot be processed, turn off SW-ALLOCATION
- loop until transaction with different key value is found
- WRITE to new master file only when SW-ALLOCATION is on
- select next active key

FIGURE 8-43   Partial listing of COBOL code that implements the balance line algorithm for updating the PREMIUM-INPUT-FILE

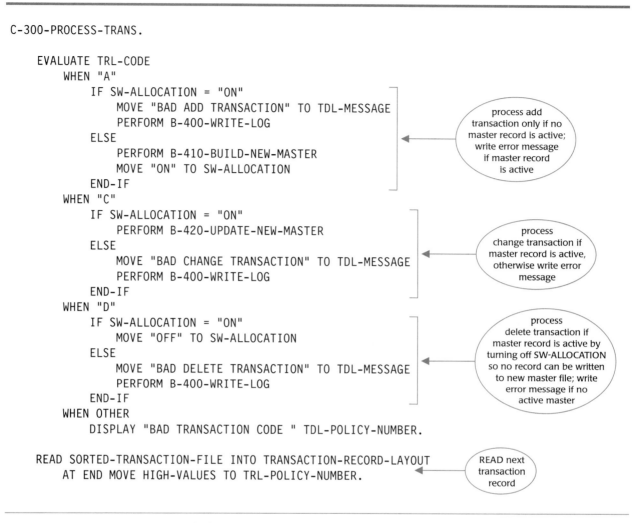

```
C-300-PROCESS-TRANS.

    EVALUATE TRL-CODE
        WHEN "A"
            IF SW-ALLOCATION = "ON"
                MOVE "BAD ADD TRANSACTION" TO TDL-MESSAGE
                PERFORM B-400-WRITE-LOG
            ELSE
                PERFORM B-410-BUILD-NEW-MASTER
                MOVE "ON" TO SW-ALLOCATION
            END-IF
        WHEN "C"
            IF SW-ALLOCATION = "ON"
                PERFORM B-420-UPDATE-NEW-MASTER
            ELSE
                MOVE "BAD CHANGE TRANSACTION" TO TDL-MESSAGE
                PERFORM B-400-WRITE-LOG
            END-IF
        WHEN "D"
            IF SW-ALLOCATION = "ON"
                MOVE "OFF" TO SW-ALLOCATION
            ELSE
                MOVE "BAD DELETE TRANSACTION" TO TDL-MESSAGE
                PERFORM B-400-WRITE-LOG
            END-IF
        WHEN OTHER
            DISPLAY "BAD TRANSACTION CODE " TDL-POLICY-NUMBER.

    READ SORTED-TRANSACTION-FILE INTO TRANSACTION-RECORD-LAYOUT
        AT END MOVE HIGH-VALUES TO TRL-POLICY-NUMBER.
```

process add transaction only if no master record is active; write error message if master record is active

process change transaction if master record is active, otherwise write error message

process delete transaction if master record is active by turning off SW-ALLOCATION so no record can be written to new master file; write error message if no active master

READ next transaction record

FIGURE 8-44   More COBOL code that implements the balance line algorithm for updating the PREMIUM-INPUT-FILE

Updating in Place

When a sequential file is stored on a direct access storage device, it can be **updated in place**. That is, it can be updated without the creation of a new master file. Updated records are placed back into the original master file, in the same location from which they were retrieved. This is accomplished by opening the sequential file using I-0 mode. I-0 mode allows for both input from and output to the file. Input is accomplished by using a READ statement such as those used for the input files in the Premium File Update program. Once a record is modified, output is accomplished by the use of a **REWRITE** statement. Figure 8-45 on the next page presents the basic format of a REWRITE statement for a sequential file. As with a WRITE statement, the record-name following the word REWRITE must be an 01 level name defined under the FD for the file. The FROM option works just as it does for a WRITE statement. END-REWRITE delimits the scope of the REWRITE and is optional.

```
REWRITE record-name [FROM identifier-1 ] [ END-REWRITE ]
```

FIGURE 8-45 Basic format of a REWRITE statement for a sequential file

Figure 8-46 presents the paragraph C-300-POST-TRANSACTION from the Premium File Update program as it might appear if the REWRITE statement were used to place a record back on PREMIUM-INPUT-FILE once it was updated. The record that is rewritten to the file is the last record read from the file. In such a process, new records cannot be added to the file and existing records cannot be deleted. Updating is the only activity that can occur. When a sequential file is opened using I-O mode, the only input/output statements that can be executed are READ and REWRITE. Updates using the REWRITE statement eliminate the need for a third SELECT entry and third FD entry because the old master file and new master file are the same file.

```
C-300-POST-TRANSACTION.

    ADD TR-PREMIUM-AMOUNT TO PR-PREMIUM-AMOUNT.

    MOVE SPACES TO WA-AGENT-NAME-1
                   WA-AGENT-NAME-2.

    UNSTRING PR-AGENT-NAME DELIMITED BY ", " OR ALL SPACES
        INTO WA-AGENT-NAME-2
             WA-AGENT-NAME-1.

    MOVE SPACES TO PR-AGENT-NAME.
    STRING WA-AGENT-NAME-1 DELIMITED BY SPACE
           " "                 DELIMITED BY SIZE
           WA-AGENT-NAME-2 DELIMITED BY SPACE INTO PR-AGENT-NAME.

    INSPECT PR-POLICY-NUMBER
        REPLACING ALL "-" BY "*".

    REWRITE PREMIUM-INPUT-RECORD FROM PREMIUM-RECORD.
    ADD 1 TO AC-POSTED-TRANS-COUNT.
    MOVE TRANSACTION-RECORD TO TDL-TRANSACTION-RECORD.
    MOVE "TRANSACTION POSTED" TO TDL-MESSAGE.
    WRITE TRAN-LOG-LINE-OUT FROM TRANSACTION-DETAIL-LINE
        AFTER ADVANCING 2 LINES.
    ADD 2 TO AC-LINE-COUNT.
    MOVE TR-POLICY-NUMBER TO WA-PREV-POLICY-NUMBER.

    READ PREMIUM-INPUT-FILE INTO PREMIUM-RECORD
        AT END MOVE HIGH-VALUES TO PR-POLICY-NUMBER.

    READ SORTED-TRANSACTION-FILE INTO TRANSACTION-RECORD
        AT END MOVE HIGH-VALUES TO TR-POLICY-NUMBER.
```

update fields in record

REWRITE last read record to original master file

write to log report

hold on to transaction number to check for possible duplicate

READ next records from master and transaction files

FIGURE 8-46 COBOL code for a posted transaction using the REWRITE statement to place an updated record back on the same master file

CHAPTER SUMMARY

The following list summarizes this chapter. The summary is designed to help you study and understand the material and concepts presented.

1. The process of modifying the records in a file is called **file maintenance**.

2. A **transaction file** is a file specifically created to supply data needed during file maintenance processing.

3. **INSPECT TALLYING** is used to count the number of occurrences of a certain character or group of characters within a field.

4. The INSPECT TALLYING adds one to the TALLYING field every time an occurrence of the specified character is encountered and does not automatically initialize the TALLYING field.

5. **INSPECT REPLACING** is used to replace specific characters within a field with other characters.

6. When an INSPECT statement executes, it proceeds left to right in the inspected field one character at a time, TALLYING and/or REPLACING each character position as specified.

7. The **INSPECT CONVERTING** works in the same manner as an INSPECT REPLACING, in that characters in the inspected field corresponding to the characters listed in the field or literal preceding the reserved word TO are replaced by the characters in corresponding positions in the field or literal following the word TO.

8. The **UNSTRING** statement is designed to distribute data in a single field to one or more other fields.

9. The UNSTRING statement does not automatically fill rightmost positions in the receiving fields with spaces, so they must be initialized prior to execution of the statement.

10. The **STRING** statement is the opposite of UNSTRING and concatenates, or joins, data stored in different fields into one field.

11. The receiving field should be initialized prior to the STRING statements execution because STRING will not automatically pad rightmost positions with spaces.

12. The intrinsic function **UPPER-CASE** converts all the letters in a field or literal to upper-case letters.

13. The intrinsic function **LOWER-CASE** converts all the letters in a field or literal to lower-case letters.

14. The intrinsic function **REVERSE** reverses the order of the characters in a field or literal.

15. A **COPY** command causes the COBOL compiler to include specified files as part of the program prior to the program being compiled.

16. One way to update a sequential file is to create a new version, or generation, of that file.

17. During sequential file maintenance, the file to be updated is often referred to as the **master file** and the new version is then called the **new master file**.

18. Both the transaction file and master file must be sequenced in the same order by a key field unique to each record in the master file.

19. A **multiply performed module** is one performed in more than one place and in more than one stream of logic.

(continued)

Chapter Summary (continued)

20. During **file matching**, records are read from both a transaction file and a master file, and the key fields are compared in an attempt to find matches.

21. During sequential file maintenance a transaction can be **posted**, **unmatched**, or a **duplicate**.

22. Add, change, and delete transactions can be processed using logic defined by the **balance line algorithm**.

23. A sequential file can be **updated in place** by using an open mode of I-0 and the **REWRITE** statement.

KEY TERMS
. . . .

balance line algorithm (8-41)
COPY (8-27)
delimiters (8-20)
duplicate transaction (8-33)
file maintenance (8-1)
file matching (8-33)
INSPECT CONVERTING (8-18)
INSPECT REPLACING (8-16)
INSPECT TALLYING (8-14)
inspected field (8-14)
LOWER-CASE (8-26)
master file (8-28)

multiply performed module (8-32)
new master file (8-28)
posted transaction (8-33)
REVERSE (8-27)
REWRITE (8-45)
STRING (8-23)
TALLYING field (8-14)
transaction file (8-2)
unmatched master (8-33)
unmatched transaction (8-33)
UNSTRING (8-19)
updated in place (8-45)

STUDENT ASSIGNMENTS
. . . .

Student Assignment 1: True/False

Instructions: Circle T if the statement is true or F if the statement is false.

T   F   1. A transaction file can be used to indicate which records are to be updated in a file.

T   F   2. File maintenance involves only the deletion of records from a file.

T   F   3. The TALLYING field is initialized to zero automatically in an INSPECT TALLYING statement.

T   F   4. LEADING can be used in an INSPECT TALLYING only if an AFTER INITIAL clause is used.

T   F   5. INSPECT REPLACING executes left to right, one character at a time.

T   F   6. The STRING command can be used to fragment a single field into multiple fields.

T   F   7. Receiving fields should be initialized to spaces just prior to the execution of an UNSTRING statement.

T   F   8. The TALLY IN clause is used in an UNSTRING statement to capture the value of a delimiter.

T   F   9. WITH POINTER is a required entry in a STRING statement.

T F 10. INSPECT CONVERTING can perform the same function as an INSPECT TALLYING statement.

T F 11. The intrinsic function REVERSE can be used to convert uppercase letters to lowercase letters.

T F 12. A COPY command can appear more than once in a COBOL program.

T F 13. The COPY command can appear in only the DATA DIVISION of a COBOL program.

T F 14. File matching logic requires a transaction file and a master file to be in the same sequence by a key field.

T F 15. A multiply performed module is a paragraph performed by more than one paragraph in a program.

T F 16. A posted transaction is the same as an unmatched master record.

T F 17. It is possible to TALLY and REPLACE in a single INSPECT statement.

T F 18. An add transaction cannot be processed if a record with the specified key is already on the master file.

T F 19. File matching processing should be terminated when end of file is reached in the transaction file or master file, whichever occurs first.

T F 20. END-STRING always should be coded with a STRING statement.

Student Assignment 2: Multiple Choice

Instructions: Circle the correct response.

The following INSPECT TALLYING statement is for question 1.

> Assume   WA-NAME contains → John Q. Public

```
INSPECT WA-NAME TALLYING AC-LETTER-COUNT
    FOR CHARACTERS BEFORE INITIAL "P".
```

1. Assuming AC-LETTER-COUNT is initialized to zero, what will its value be after the INSPECT TALLYING executes?
   a. 1
   b. 4
   c. 6
   d. 8
   e. none of the above

The following INSPECT REPLACING statement is for question 2.

> Assume   WA-NAME contains → JJDD1QTSZR12JD

```
INSPECT WA-NAME REPLACING ALL "J" BY "U"
                          "D" BY "3"
                          "T" BY "R".
```

2. What will be the value of WA-NAME after the INSPECT REPLACING executes?
   a. JJDD1QRSZR12U3
   b. UU331QTSZR12JD
   c. UU331QRSZR12U3
   d. UUDD1RRSZR12J3
   e. none of the above

(continued)

Student Assignment 2 (continued)

Use the following UNSTRING statement to answer questions 3 and 4.

Assume   WA-NAME contains → John Q. Public

and all receiving fields have been initialized to spaces.

```
UNSTRING WA-NAME DELIMITED BY "." OR SPACES
     INTO WA-HOLD-1
           WA-HOLD-2
           WA-HOLD-3.
```

3. Which of the following values would be in WA-HOLD-2?
   a. Public
   b. Q
   c. Q.
   d. John
   e. none of the above

4. Which of the following values would be in WA-HOLD-3?
   a. Public
   b. Q
   c. Q.
   d. John
   e. none of the above

Use the following STRING statement to answer question 5.

Assume   WA-HOLD-1 contains → Alfred
          WA-HOLD-2 contains → E.
          WA-HOLD-3 contains → Smith

and all receiving fields have been initialized to spaces.

```
STRING WA-HOLD-1 DELIMITED BY SPACE
       WA-HOLD-2 DELIMITED BY SPACE
       " "       DELIMITED BY SIZE
       WA-HOLD-3 DELIMITED BY SPACE INTO WA-NAME.
```

5. Which of the following values will be in WA-NAME after the STRING executes?
   a. Alfred E. Smith
   b. Alfred Smith
   c. Alfred E Smith
   d. AlfredE. Smith
   e. none of the above

6. The INSPECT CONVERTING statement works like what other statement?
   a. INSPECT REPLACING
   b. INSPECT TALLYING
   c. UNSTRING
   d. FUNCTION LOWER-CASE
   e. none of the above

7. A posted transaction is _____.
   a. a transaction found to be in error
   b. a transaction used to update a master record
   c. a transaction with no matching master record
   d. a transaction with a duplicate following it
   e. none of the above

8. The intrinsic function REVERSE can be used to _____.
   a. change uppercase letters to lowercase letters
   b. change lowercase letters to uppercase letters
   c. change the order of appearance of characters
   d. change a positive value into a negative value
   e. none of the above

9. File matching logic requires _____.
   a. the transaction file and master file to be in the same sequence
   b. the key field in a transaction record to be compared to the key field in a master record
   c. a transaction to be posted when key values are equal
   d. an unmatched master to be written to the new master file
   e. all of the above

10. Overflow will occur on a STRING statement when _____.
    a. the receiving field is initialized to spaces
    b. a POINTER field is initialized to zero
    c. the concatenation of source fields terminates before the receiving field is full
    d. the receiving field cannot hold all that is being placed in it
    e. none of the above

Student Assignment 3: Coding an INSPECT TALLYING

Instructions: Given the following contents for WA-FIELD-1, code an INSPECT TALLYING statement that counts the number or zeros in the field that appear after the first occurrence of the number 2. Use WA-ZERO-COUNT as the TALLYING field. Then list the contents of WA-ZERO-COUNT after the INSPECT executes.

Assume   WA-FIELD-1 contains → 340054293052001

Student Assignment 4: Coding an INSPECT REPLACING

Instructions: Using WA-FIELD-1 with the same contents given in Assignment 3, code an INSPECT REPLACING statement that replaces all zeros with the letter A as long as the zeros occur after the first 2. List the new contents of WA-FIELD-1 as it would appear after the INSPECT statement executes.

Student Assignment 5: Coding an INSPECT CONVERTING

Instructions: Using WA-FIELD-1 with the same contents given in Assignment 3, code an INSPECT CONVERTING statement that replaces all 1s with As, 2s with Bs, and 0s with Zs. List the contents of WA-FIELD-1 as it would appear after the INSPECT statement executes.

Student Assignment 6: Coding an UNSTRING Statement

Instructions: Given the contents below for WA-NAME-1, code an UNSTRING statement that fragments its contents using spaces to determine where each fragment ends. Use WA-PART-1, WA-PART-2, and WA-PART-3 as receiving fields for the operation. List the contents of the receiving fields as they would appear after the execution of the UNSTRING statement. Assume the receiving fields have been initialized to spaces.

Assume   WA-NAME-1 contains → Alfred E. Newman, Jr.

Student Assignment 7: Coding a STRING Statement

Instructions: Given the contents below for WA-PART-1, WA-PART-2, and WA-PART-3, code a STRING statement that takes all of WA-PART-1, that part of WA-PART-2 that occurs before the first space, and that part of WA-PART-3 that occurs before the uppercase letter T, and concatenates these entries into the 20-character field WA-CATCH-IT. Also, include a space in the STRING between each part. List the contents of WA-CATCH-IT as it would appear after the STRING executes. Assume WA-CATCH-IT has been initialized to spaces.

Assume   WA-PART-1 contains → ABC 123   (A seven-byte field)
WA-PART-2 contains → Jeff Blake
WA-PART-3 contains → Samantha Tate

COBOL LABORATORY EXERCISES

Exercise 1: Modified Premium File Update Program

Purpose: To gain experience in COBOL file maintenance programs and to become more familiar with file matching logic.

Problem: Open the file PROJ8.CBL on the Student Diskette that accompanies this book, and modify the Premium File Update program presented in this chapter making the following changes:

1. In the INPUT PROCEDURE, include a validation for TR-PREMIUM-AMOUNT that ensures the amount is not less than $5.00. Transactions with amounts of less than $5.00 are to be considered errors and should not be sorted.

2. Include logic that will rearrange the customer names so they are listed first name first in the new master file.

3. Instead of replacing hyphens with asterisks in PR-POLICY-NUMBER, replace the first hyphen with a space and the second hyphen with a slash (/) before a record is written to the new master file.

4. On the TRANSACTION-LOG-REPORT, include a third column that lists just the last name of the customer processed for all posted transactions and unmatched masters.

Save this program as EX8-1.CBL.

Input Data: Use the Sorted Premium file presented in Appendix A as input to the SORT. This file is named SPREMIUM.DAT on the Student Diskette that accompanies this book. Also use the Transaction file listed in Appendix A as input. This file is named PREMTRAN.DAT on the Student Diskette that accompanies this book.

Output Results: Output should be a report similar to the Transaction Log Report presented in Figure 8-1 on pages 8-2 and 8-3 with the addition of a column for customer last names. Adjust spacing as needed.

Exercise 2: Customer Purchases File Update Program

Purpose: To practice the use of a transaction file and file matching logic in the creation of a COBOL program that updates records on the Customer Purchases file, creating a transaction log report and New Customer Purchases file.

Problem: Write a program that sorts transactions in ascending sequence by account number. Use the sorted transactions to update a master file, the Customer Purchases file, by subtracting a discount amount found on each transaction from the amount of purchases and balance amount in each record on the Customer Purchases file. Write all records, updated or not, to a new master file.

Use an input procedure to validate each transaction before sorting it, making sure the account number is numeric and the discount amount is numeric and less than $50. List the disposition of all transactions on a transaction log report. Also list the account number of all unmatched masters on the transaction log report. Provide summary counts at the end of the transaction log. Save this program as EX8-2.CBL.

Input Data: For the master file, use the Customer file listed in Appendix A. This file is named CUSTOMER.DAT on the Student Diskette that accompanies this book. Customer records are already in sequence by account number and have the following layout:

Field Description	*Position*	*Length*	*Attribute*
Date of Purchase	1–6	6	Numeric, PIC 9(6)
Account Number	7–12	6	Alphanumeric
Customer Name	13–32	20	Alphanumeric
Item Purchased	33–52	20	Alphanumeric
Quantity Purchased	53	1	Numeric, PIC 9
Balance	54–59	6	Numeric, PIC S9(4)V99
Purchase Amount	60–65	6	Numeric, PIC 9(4)V99
filler	66–70	5	Alphanumeric
Sales Clerk ID	71–72	2	Alphanumeric
Record Length		72	

Put this layout in a separate file named CUSTREC.CBL and copy it into your program using a COPY statement.

Use the Customer Discount Transaction file listed in Appendix A as input for updating the Customer Purchases file. This file is named CUSTTRAN.DAT on the Student Diskette that accompanies this book. Transaction records must be sorted and validated as indicated above.

Field Description	*Position*	*Length*	*Attribute*
Account Number	1–6	6	Alphanumeric
Discount Amount	7–12	6	Alphanumeric, PIC X(6) Redefine as Numeric, PIC 9(4)V99
Record Length		12	

Output Results: Output consists of the Customer Purchases Transaction Log listing the disposition of every transaction as well as the account number of unmatched master records. Identify all errors found during validation of the transaction, double-spacing between transactions and single-spacing error messages. List a count of all bad, posted, unmatched, and duplicate transactions. Also provide a count of unmatched master records. A new version of the Customer Purchases file also is output.

(continued)

Exercise 2 (continued)

The transaction log should have a format similar to the following:

```
DATE: Z9/99/99                    ABC DEPARTMENT STORE                    PAGE Z9
TIME: Z9:99 AM                 CUSTOMER PURCHASES TRANSACTION LOG


          TRANSACTION RECORD           MESSAGE
          ------------------           ------------------------


          XXXXXXXXXXX                  XXXXXXXXXXXXXXXXXXXXXXXXX

          XXXXXXXXXXX                  XXXXXXXXXXXXXXXXXXXXXXXXX
             .
             .
             .
          TOTAL BAD TRANSACTIONS       = ZZ9
          TOTAL POSTED TRANSACTIONS    = ZZ9
          TOTAL UNMATCHED TRANSACTIONS = ZZ9
          TOTAL DUPLICATE TRANSACTIONS = ZZ9
          TOTAL UNMATCHED MASTERS      = ZZ9


                       END OF REPORT
```

Exercise 3: Customer Sales Update Program

Purpose: To practice coding a COBOL program that uses a transaction file, master file, and file matching logic to update a sequential input file using the REWRITE statement.

Problem: Design and code a COBOL program that updates the records of the Customer Sales file for EZ Auto Sales and creates a Customer Sales Transaction Report. The program should modify each customer record by updating the auto make, year of auto, purchase date, purchase price, and satisfaction rating of customers on the Customer Sales file. Write updated records back to the Customer Sales file using the REWRITE statement.

Sort transaction records by customer number. Records on the Customer Sales file are already in sequence by customer number. Validate each transaction making sure that:

1. the customer number is numeric

2. the purchase date is numeric and less than or equal to the current date, assuming the current date is greater than or equal to Nov. 28, 1997

3. the purchase price is numeric and greater than 500

4. the auto make is not spaces

5. the auto year is numeric and less than or equal to the current year, assuming the current year is greater than or equal to 1997

6. the satisfaction rating is 0, 1, or 2

Valid transactions should be sorted and placed in a sorted transaction file. Sorted transactions will then be used as input to the file matching logic needed to update the master file. List all transactions on the Customer Sales Transaction Report indicating all errors found, a posted transaction message, an unmatched transaction message, or a duplicate transaction message. Also list the customer number and name for unmatched master records. Save this program as EX8-3.CBL.

Input Data: Use the Customer Sales file listed in Appendix A as the master file. This file is named CUSTSALE.DAT on the Student Diskette that accompanies this book. The record layout for the customer records is as follows:

Field Description	Position	Length	Attribute
Customer Zip Code	1–5	5	Alphanumeric
Customer Zip + 4	6–9	4	Alphanumeric
Customer Number	10–13	4	Alphanumeric
Customer Name	14–33	20	Alphanumeric
Purchase Date	34–39	6	Numeric, PIC 9(6)
Auto Make	40–59	20	Alphanumeric
Purchase Price	60–66	7	Numeric, PIC 9(5)V99
Year of Auto	67–70	4	Alphanumeric
filler	71–73	3	Alphanumeric
Satisfaction Code	74	1	Alphanumeric, 0 = DISSATISFIED 1 = UNDECIDED 2 = SATISFIED
Record Length		74	

Use the Customer Transaction file listed in Appendix A as input to the sort, creating a sorted transaction file to be used as input to the file matching logic. This file is named AUTOTRAN.DAT on the Student Diskette that accompanies this book.

The record layout for the customer sales transaction records is as follows:

Field Description	Position	Length	Attribute
Customer Number	1–4	4	Alphanumeric
Purchase Date	5–10	6	Alphanumeric, PIC X(6) Redefine as Numeric, PIC 9(6)
Auto Make	11–30	20	Alphanumeric
Purchase Price	31–37	7	Alphanumeric, PIC X(7) Redefine as Numeric, PIC 9(5)V99
Year of Auto	38–41	4	Alphanumeric
Satisfaction Code	42	1	Alphanumeric
Record Length		42	

Output Results: A Customer Sales Transaction Report should be output listing the disposition of every transaction as well as the customer number and name of unmatched master records. List a count of all bad, posted, unmatched, and duplicate transactions. Also provide a count of unmatched master records.

To report on the update file, use the updated master file in this exercise as input to the report program created in COBOL Laboratory Exercise 3 in Chapter 7.

(continued)

Exercise 3 (continued)

The Customer Sales Transaction Report should have a format similar to the following:

```
DATE: Z9/99/99                       EZ AUTO SALES                       PAGE Z9
TIME: Z9:99 AM              CUSTOMER SALES TRANSACTION REPORT


    TRANSACTION RECORD                           MESSAGE
    ------------------------------------------   ------------------------
                              .

    XXXXXXXXXXXXXXXXXXXXXXXXXXXXXXXXXXXXXXXXXXXX   XXXXXXXXXXXXXXXXXXXXXXXXXXXX

    XXXXXXXXXXXXXXXXXXXXXXXXXXXXXXXXXXXXXXXXXXXX   XXXXXXXXXXXXXXXXXXXXXXXXXXXX

    XXXXXXXXXXXXXXXXXXXXXXXXXXXXXXXXXXXXXXXXXXXX   XXXXXXXXXXXXXXXXXXXXXXXXXXXX

    XXXX  ---> XXXXXXXXXXXXXXXXXX                  UNMATCHED MASTER RECORD
    .
    .
    .
                TOTAL BAD TRANSACTIONS       =  ZZ9
                TOTAL POSTED TRANSACTIONS    =  ZZ9
                TOTAL UNMATCHED TRANSACTIONS =  ZZ9
                TOTAL DUPLICATE TRANSACTIONS =  ZZ9
                TOTAL UNMATCHED MASTERS      =  ZZ9
                          END OF REPORT
```

CHAPTER NINE

Indexed and Relative Files

OBJECTIVES

You will have mastered the material in Chapter 9 when you can:

- Explain the organization of an indexed file

- Code a WRITE statement that adds a record to an indexed file

- Explain random access and code a random READ statement

- Code a REWRITE statement to update an indexed file record

- Code a DELETE statement to remove an indexed file record

- Code a random READ to access a record using an alternate key

- Understand and code a START statement

- Explain the organization of a relative file

- Code a random READ statement for a relative file

- Code a WRITE statement that adds a record to a relative file

- Code a REWRITE statement to update a relative file record

- Code a DELETE statement to remove a relative file record

INTRODUCTION

All the files used in the sample programs within this book thus far have been sequential files. For that reason, all of the processing done has been sequential. That is, every program presented to this point, processed the data in a file one record after another until the end of the file was reached. Other file organizations are introduced in this chapter along with other means of processing data. Because these other file organizations are widely used, it is very important that you understand how they are utilized and supported in COBOL.

In this chapter, indexed files and relative files are discussed along with random processing of such files. Considerations must be made in the ENVIRONMENT and DATA DIVISIONS to accommodate the use of indexed and relative files. PROCEDURE DIVISION statements are available for the creation, retrieval, modification, and deletion of records stored in indexed and relative files. Indexed file creation and maintenance is presented first, because it represents the more commonly used of these two file organizations.

Two sample programs are presented in this chapter. The first, the Indexed Premium File Creation program, uses a sequential input file to output an indexed version of that same file. A message is printed indicating the number of records processed. The second program, the Indexed Premium File Update program, uses a transaction file to add records to, change records on, and delete records from the indexed version of the Premium file.

The Indexed Premium File Creation Report

Figure 9-1 presents the printed results of the Indexed Premium File Creation program. No headings or page numbers exist. The message indicates the number of records processed.

```
TOTAL NUMBER OF INDEXED RECORDS CREATED =  72

                    END OF REPORT
```

FIGURE 9-1   Report output from the Indexed Premium File Creation program

After an indexed file has been created, it can be processed and reported on in a manner similar to a sequential file. An indexed file also can be easily updated, or modified, using special COBOL statements.

Indexed Premium File Creation Program Hierarchy Chart

Figure 9-2 presents a hierarchy chart that illustrates the organization of the PROCEDURE DIVISION of the Indexed Premium File Creation program. The program has a simple organization when compared to the previous programs presented. The MAIN-PROGRAM paragraph performs the A-100-INITIALIZATION paragraph, the B-100-PROCESS-FILE paragraph, and the C-100-WRAP-UP paragraph. No other paragraphs are involved.

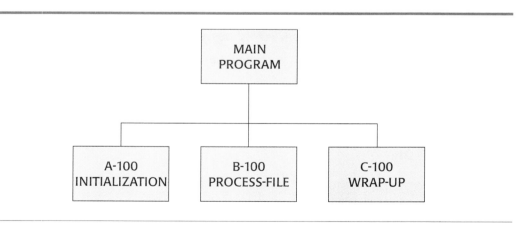

FIGURE 9-2   Hierarchy chart illustrating the organization of the PROCEDURE DIVISION of the Indexed Premium File Creation program

Indexed Premium File Creation Program Flowchart

Figure 9-3 presents a flowchart that illustrates the basic logic used in the Indexed Premium File Creation program. The COBOL statements that implement this logic will be discussed later in this chapter.

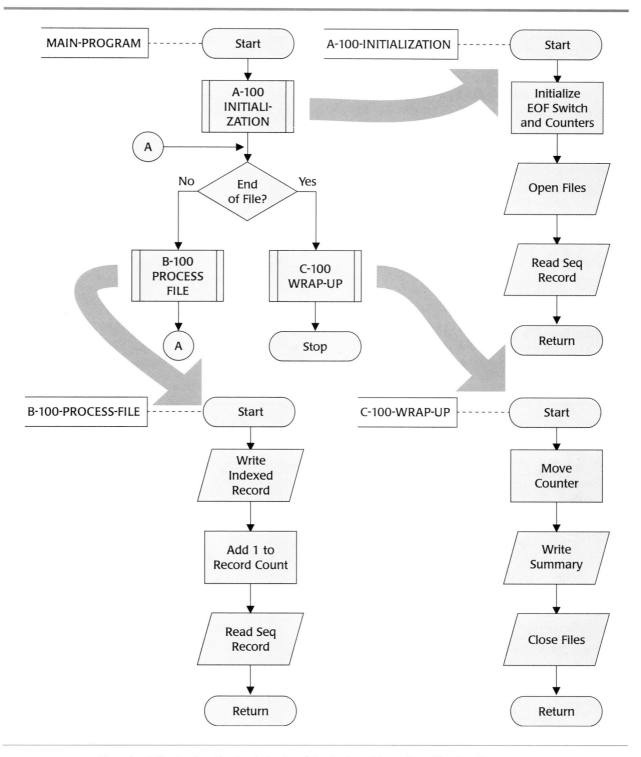

FIGURE 9-3   Flowchart illustrating the basic logic of the Indexed Premium File Creation program

Premium Record Layout

The layout of the records in an indexed file is no different from the record layout used in a sequential file. Figure 9-4 presents the Premium file record layout used in this chapter for both sample programs.

Field	Position	Length	Attribute
Customer Name	1–20	20	Alphanumeric
Agent Name	21–40	20	Alphanumeric
Insurance Type	41–50	10	Alphanumeric
Policy Number	51–62	12	Alphanumeric
Premium Amount	63–69	7	Numeric
Payment Status	70	1	Alphanumeric
Gender	71	1	Alphanumeric
Signup Date	72–75	4	Numeric
Premium Due Month	76–77	2	Numeric
unused	78–80	3	Alphanumeric
Total Record Length		80	

FIGURE 9-4 Record layout for the sequential and indexed Premium files

Indexed Premium File Creation Program

Figure 9-5 presents the Indexed Premium File Creation program. This program is found on the Student Diskette that accompanies this book. The program writes an indexed version of the Premium file from a sequential version of the file used in earlier programs in this book.

```
 1  IDENTIFICATION DIVISION.
 2  ************************
 3
 4  PROGRAM-ID.    BILDINDX.
 5  AUTHOR.        R. O. FOREMAN.
 6  INSTALLATION.  PURDUE UNIVERSITY CALUMET.
 7  DATE-WRITTEN.  NOV. 28,1997.
 8  DATE-COMPILED. 28-Nov-1997.
 9
10  *****************************************************************
11  *                                                              *
12  *                   PROGRAM NARRATIVE                          *
13  *                                                              *
14  *  THIS PROGRAM READS ALL RECORDS IN THE SEQUENTIAL PREMIUM    *
15  *  FILE AND WRITES THEM TO AN INDEXED FILE. A RECORD COUNT AND *
16  *  END OF JOB MESSAGE ARE DISPLAYED AND PRINTED.               *
17  *                                                              *
18  *      INPUT:     SPREMIUM.DAT - PREMIUM INPUT FILE            *
19  *                                                              *
20  *      OUTPUT:    PREMINDX.DAT - INDEXED PREMIUM FILE          *
21  *                              RECORD KEY --> POLICY NUMBER    *
22  *                              ALT. KEY   --> PREM DUE MONTH   *
23  *                                                              *
24  *                 INDXMESS.RPT - INDEXED MESSAGE REPORT FILE   *
25  *                                                              *
26  *****************************************************************
27  /
28  ENVIRONMENT DIVISION.
29  ********************
30
31  INPUT-OUTPUT SECTION.
32  ********************
33
34  FILE-CONTROL.
35
36      SELECT PREMIUM-INPUT-FILE
37          ASSIGN TO "A:\SPREMIUM.DAT".
38
39      SELECT INDEXED-MESSAGE-REPORT
40          ASSIGN TO "A:\INDXMESS.RPT".
41
42      SELECT INDEXED-PREMIUM-FILE
43          ASSIGN TO "A:\PREMINDX.DAT"
44          ORGANIZATION IS INDEXED
45          ACCESS IS SEQUENTIAL
46          RECORD KEY IS IRB-POLICY-NUMBER
47          ALTERNATE RECORD KEY IS IRB-PREMIUM-DUE-MONTH
48              WITH DUPLICATES.
49  /
50  DATA DIVISION.
51  ***************
52
53  FILE SECTION.
54  ***************
```

FIGURE 9-5 Indexed Premium File Creation program

```
55
56  ****************************************************************
57  *                                                            *
58  *      INPUT-FILE - PREMIUM INPUT FILE                       *
59  *                                                            *
60  ****************************************************************
61
62  FD  PREMIUM-INPUT-FILE.
63
64  01  PREMIUM-INPUT-RECORD           PIC X(80).
65
66  ****************************************************************
67  *                                                            *
68  *      REPORT-FILE - INDEXED MESSAGE REPORT                  *
69  *                                                            *
70  ****************************************************************
71
72  FD  INDEXED-MESSAGE-REPORT.
73
74  01  MESSAGE-LINE-OUT               PIC X(80).
75
76  ****************************************************************
77  *                                                            *
78  *      INDEXED-FILE - INDEXED PREMIUM FILE                   *
79  *                                                            *
80  ****************************************************************
81
82  FD  INDEXED-PREMIUM-FILE.
83
84  01  INDEXED-RECORD-BUFFER.
85      02                             PIC X(50).
86      02  IRB-POLICY-NUMBER          PIC X(12).
87      02                             PIC X(13).
88      02  IRB-PREMIUM-DUE-MONTH      PIC XX.
89      02                             PIC XXX.
90  /
91  WORKING-STORAGE SECTION.
92  ***********************
93
94  ****************************************************************
95  *                                                            *
96  *                    SWITCHES                                *
97  *                                                            *
98  ****************************************************************
99
100 01  SWITCHES-WS.
101
102     02  SW-END-OF-FILE             PIC X.
103         88  END-OF-FILE                    VALUE "Y".
104
105
106 01  VALUES-FOR-SWITCHES-WS.
107     02  YES                        PIC X    VALUE "Y".
108     02  NEG                        PIC X    VALUE "N".
109
110 ****************************************************************
111 *                                                            *
112 *                    ACCUMULATORS                            *
113 *                                                            *
114 ****************************************************************
115
116 01  ACCUMULATORS-WS.
117
118     02  AC-RECORD-COUNT            PIC S9(5) PACKED-DECIMAL.
119 /
120 COPY "A:\INSREC.CBL".
121L****************************************************************
122L*                                                            *
123L*              PREMIUM INPUT FILE RECORD LAYOUT              *
124L*                                                            *
125L****************************************************************
126L
127L 01 PREMIUM-RECORD.
128L    02  PR-CUSTOMER-NAME           PIC X(20).
129L    02  PR-AGENT-NAME              PIC X(20).
130L    02  PR-INSURANCE-TYPE          PIC X(10).
131L        88  VALID-TYPE             VALUE "Automobile"
132L                                         "Annuity"
133L                                         "Home"
134L                                         "Renter"
135L                                         "Term Life"
136L                                         "Whole Life".
137L
138L    02  PR-POLICY-NUMBER           PIC X(12).
139L    02  PR-PREMIUM-AMOUNT          PIC S9(5)V99.
140L
141L    02  PR-PAYMENT-STATUS          PIC X.
142L        88  DELINQUENT             VALUE "D".
143L        88  PAID-IN-FULL           VALUE "F".
144L        88  PARTIALLY-PAID         VALUE "P".
145L        88  NOT-YET-BILLED         VALUE "N".
146L
147L    02  PR-SEX                     PIC X.
148L    02  PR-SIGNUP-YEAR             PIC X(4).
149L    02  PR-PREMIUM-DUE-MONTH       PIC 99.
150L    02                             PIC XXX.
151 /
152 ****************************************************************
153 *                                                            *
154 *      SUMMARY LINES FOR INDEXED MESSAGE REPORT             *
155 *                                                            *
156 ****************************************************************
157
158 01  SUMMARY-LINE.
159
160     02  SL-LINE-1.
161         03                         PIC X(14) VALUE SPACES.
162         03                         PIC X(42)
163             VALUE "TOTAL NUMBER OF INDEXED RECORDS CREATED = ".
164         03  SL-RECORD-COUNT        PIC ZZ9.
165         03                         PIC X(21) VALUE SPACES.
166
167     02  SL-LINE-2.
168         03                         PIC X(32) VALUE SPACES.
169         03                         PIC X(13)
170             VALUE "END OF REPORT".
171         03                         PIC X(35) VALUE SPACES.
172 /
173 PROCEDURE DIVISION.
174 ******************
175 ****************************************************************
176 *                                                            *
177 * MAIN-PROGRAM - This is the main routine of this program    *
178 *                                                            *
179 ****************************************************************
180
181 MAIN-PROGRAM.
182     PERFORM A-100-INITIALIZATION.
183     PERFORM B-100-PROCESS-FILE
184         UNTIL END-OF-FILE.
185     PERFORM C-100-WRAP-UP.
186     STOP RUN.
187
188 ****************************************************************
189 *                                                            *
190 * A-100-INITIALIZATION - Housekeeping routine follows        *
191 *                                                            *
192 ****************************************************************
193
194 A-100-INITIALIZATION.
195     MOVE NEG TO SW-END-OF-FILE.
196     MOVE ZERO TO AC-RECORD-COUNT.
197
198     OPEN INPUT PREMIUM-INPUT-FILE
199         OUTPUT INDEXED-PREMIUM-FILE
200                INDEXED-MESSAGE-REPORT.
201
202     READ PREMIUM-INPUT-FILE INTO PREMIUM-RECORD
203         AT END MOVE YES TO SW-END-OF-FILE.
204 /
```

(continued)

```
205 *****************************************************************
206 *                                                               *
207 *   B-100-PROCESS-FILE - File processing control routine        *
208 *                                                               *
209 *****************************************************************
210
211 B-100-PROCESS-FILE.
212
213     WRITE INDEXED-RECORD-BUFFER FROM PREMIUM-RECORD
214         INVALID KEY DISPLAY "PROCESSING SAME RECORD TWICE!!"
215                 DISPLAY "POLICY NUMBER =" PR-POLICY-NUMBER.
216
217     ADD 1 TO AC-RECORD-COUNT.
218
219     READ PREMIUM-INPUT-FILE INTO PREMIUM-RECORD
220         AT END MOVE YES TO SW-END-OF-FILE.
221
222 *****************************************************************
223 *                                                               *
224 *   C-100-WRAP-UP - End of INDEXED PREMIUM FILE creation        *
225 *                                                               *
226 *****************************************************************
```

```
227
228 C-100-WRAP-UP.
229
230     MOVE AC-RECORD-COUNT TO SL-RECORD-COUNT.
231
232     DISPLAY SL-LINE-1.
233     DISPLAY " ".
234     DISPLAY SL-LINE-2.
235
236     WRITE MESSAGE-LINE-OUT FROM SL-LINE-1
237         AFTER ADVANCING PAGE.
238     WRITE MESSAGE-LINE-OUT FROM SL-LINE-2
239         AFTER ADVANCING 2 LINES.
240
241     CLOSE PREMIUM-INPUT-FILE
242           INDEXED-PREMIUM-FILE
243           INDEXED-MESSAGE-REPORT.
244 *****************************************************************
245 *     END OF PROGRAM                                            *
246 *****************************************************************
247 /
```

FIGURE 9-5 Indexed Premium File Creation program (continued)

Indexed Premium File Transaction List Report

Figure 9-6 presents a partial listing of the report produced by the Indexed Premium File Update program, the Transaction List Report. The report shows the records added, records changed, and records deleted from the Indexed Premium file and the disposition of transactions that could not be processed.

```
RUN DATE: 11/28/97                      AINSWORTH INSURANCE COMPANY                           PAGE:   1
RUN TIME: 10:57AM                         TRANSACTION LIST REPORT

TRAN                                        INSURANCE                    PREMIUM   PAY          SIGNUP   PREM
CODE   CUSTOMER NAME      AGENT NAME         TYPE      POLICY NUMBER      AMOUNT    STAT   SEX   YEAR     DUE
----   -------------      ----------         ----      -------------      ------    ----   ---   ----     ---

 A     Baker, Charlie     Benson, Gloria     Renter    RT-7108-5141        350.00    N      M    1994     03

ADuffy, Chester     Jean, Barbara     Term Life TL-7007-56910045000NM199609     ATTEMPTED ADDITION OVER EXISTING RECORD

 A     Framptin, Charles  Jean, Barbara      Renter    RT-1113-2666        780.00    P      M    1994     11
 .
 .
 .
 C     Anytime, Seeue     McDonald, Fred     Automobile AM-7623-1221       234.00    F      F    1997     01
       Anytime, Seeue     Jones, William     Automobile AM-7623-1221       434.00    P      F    1997     01

 C     Danners, Sarah     McDonald, Fred     Term Life  TL-7303-3452       450.00    N      M    1995     08
       Sanders, Sara      McDonald, Fred     Term Life  TL-7303-3452       530.00    P      M    1995     03

 C     Foreman, Otto      Jones, William     Annuity    AN-4043-6510       300.00    F      M    1980     08
       Foreman, Otto      Jean, Barbara      Annuity    AN-4043-6510       210.00    F      M    1981     09


 C          McDonald, Fred           RT-1222-73260055050  199403     ATTEMPTED CHANGE OF NON-EXISTING RECORD

 C     Michaels, Ramsey   Anderson, James    Annuity    AN-6566-8802       200.30    F      M    1994     07
       Michaels, Sammy    McDonald, Fred     Annuity    AN-6566-8802       330.40    D      M    1994     11
 .
 .
 D     Motorhead, Ima     Jones, William     Renter     RT-0944-9251       200.00    P      F    1995     08

 D     Solinski, Paula    Jacobson, Peter    Term Life  TL-2762-2728       268.25    N      F    1993     04

 D                                           HM-2011-7338        ATTEMPTED DELETION OF NON-EXISTING RECORD

 D     Wilder, Eugene     Jean, Barbara      Whole Life WL-0082-1913       380.00    F      M    1996     05

                      THE NUMBER OF RECORDS WITH ERRORS   =    6
                      THE NUMBER OF RECORDS ADDED         =    5
                      THE NUMBER OF RECORDS CHANGED       =   14
                      THE NUMBER OF RECORDS DELETED       =    7

                                      END OF REPORT
```

FIGURE 9-6 Partial listing of the Transaction List Report from the Indexed Premium File Update program

Indexed Premium File Update Program Hierarchy Chart

The organization of the PROCEDURE DIVISION of the Indexed Premium File Update program is illustrated by the hierarchy chart in Figure 9-7. Notice paragraphs exist for the three different file maintenance activities: addition, change, and deletion. Each activity has a separate paragraph performed by B-200-UPDATE-FILE.

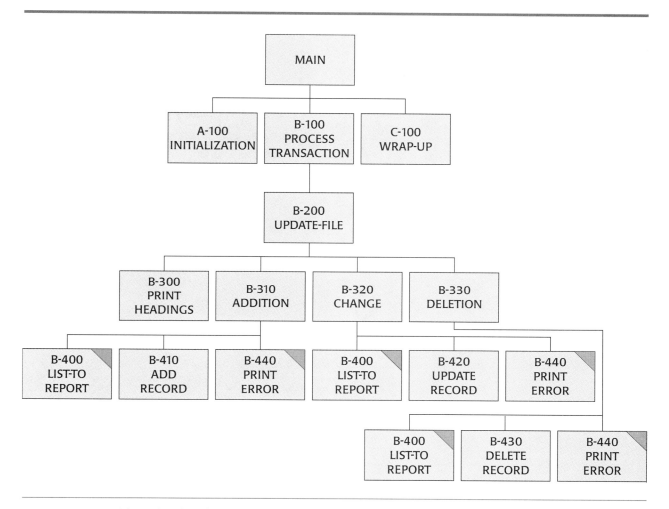

FIGURE 9-7   Hierarchy chart for the Indexed Premium File Update program

Indexed Premium File Update Program Flowchart

The basic logic for the Indexed Premium File Update program is illustrated by the partial flowchart in Figure 9-8 on pages 9-8 and 9-9. The COBOL statements that implement this logic will be discussed later in the chapter.

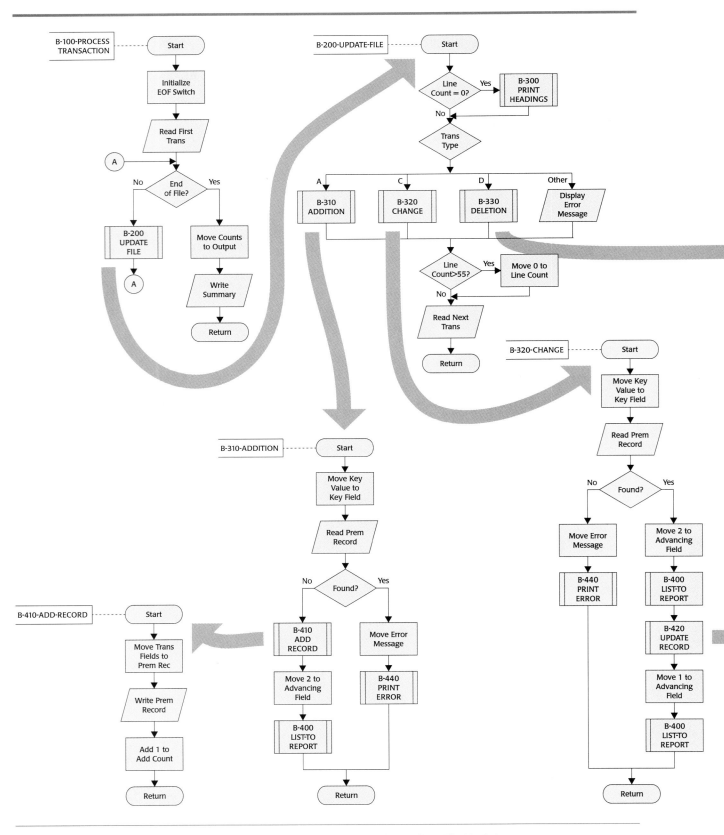

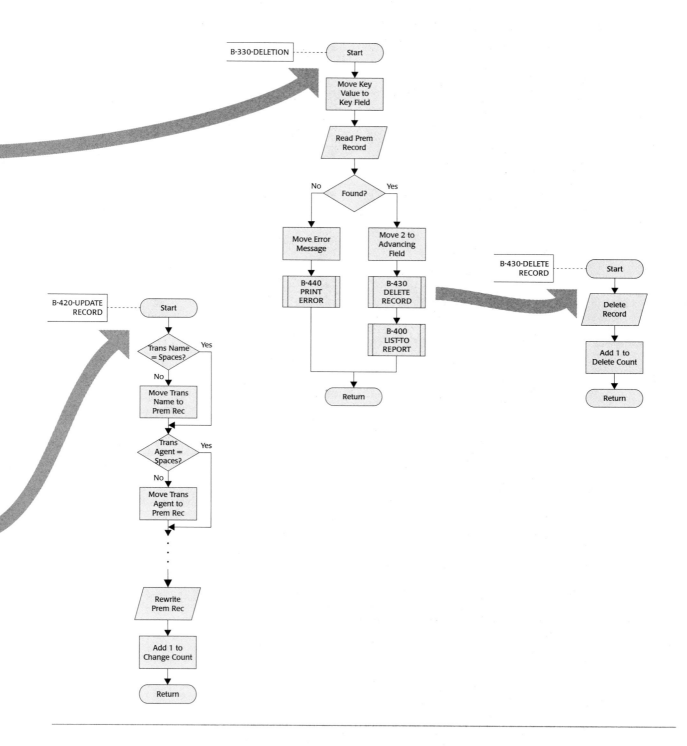

Transaction Record Layout

To indicate which records are to be added, which are to be changed, and which are to be deleted in the indexed version of the Premium file, a transaction file is used as input in the Premium File Update program. Figure 9-9 presents the record format of each transaction. A list of the transactions in the file and the processing of these transactions will be discussed later in this chapter.

Field	Position	Length	Attribute
Transaction Code	1	1	Alphanumeric; A, C, or D
Customer Name	2-21	20	Alphanumeric
Agent Name	22-41	20	Alphanumeric
Insurance Type	42-51	10	Alphanumeric
Policy Number	52-63	12	Alphanumeric
Premium Amount	64-70	7	Numeric when present, 9(5)V99, Spaces otherwise
Payment Status	71	1	Alphanumeric
Customer Gender	72	1	Alphanumeric
Signup Year	73-76	4	Alphanumeric
Due Month	77-78	2	Alphanumeric
Total		78	

FIGURE 9-9 Format of records in the Transaction file used in the Indexed Premium File Update program

Indexed Premium File Update Program

Figure 9-10 presents the Indexed Premium File Update program. This program is found on the Student Diskette that accompanies this book. Using information supplied by the transaction file, the program opens the Indexed Premium file for input and output, I-0, and then adds new records to the file, updates existing records in the file, and deletes existing records from the file. It lists these activities in the output report presented earlier.

```
 1  IDENTIFICATION DIVISION.
 2  ***********************
 3
 4  PROGRAM-ID.     INDXUPDT.
 5  AUTHOR.         R. O. FOREMAN.
 6  INSTALLATION.   PURDUE UNIVERSITY CALUMET.
 7  DATE-WRITTEN.   NOV. 28,1997.
 8  DATE-COMPILED.  28-Nov-1997.
 9
10  ********************************************************************
11  *                                                                 *
12  *                    PROGRAM NARRATIVE                            *
13  *                                                                 *
14  *  THIS PROGRAM PERFORMS INDEXED FILE MAINTENANCE. A TRANSACTION  *
15  *  FILE, PRE-SORTED BY TRANSACTION CODE, IS USED TO UPDATE THE    *
16  *  INDEXED PREMIUM FILE. A NEW RECORD CAN BE ADDED, AN EXISTING   *
17  *  RECORD CAN BE UPDATED, AND AN EXISTING RECORD CAN BE DELETED.  *
18  *                                                                 *
19  *  THE INDEXED PREMIUM FILE IS PROCESSED RANDOMLY WHILE THE       *
20  *  TRANSACTION FILE IS PROCESSED SEQUENTIALLY.                    *
21  *                                                                 *
22  *  A REPORT IS GENERATED SHOWING RECORDS THAT HAVE BEEN           *
23  *  ADDED, UPDATED, AND DELETED. FOR RECORDS THAT HAVE BEEN        *
24  *  UPDATED, THE RECORD IS SHOWN BOTH BEFORE AND AFTER CHANGES.    *
25  *                                                                 *
26  *  TOTALS ARE KEPT ON THE NUMBER OF RECORDS ADDED, THE NUMBER     *
27  *  OF RECORDS CHANGED, THE NUMBER OF RECORDS DELETED, AND         *
28  *  THE NUMBER OF UNPROCESSED TRANSACTION RECORDS.                 *
29  *                                                                 *
30  *  AT THE END OF THE REPORT, THE TOTALS ARE PRINTED ALONG         *
31  *  WITH AN END OF REPORT MESSAGE.                                 *
32  *                                                                 *
33  *      INPUT/OUTPUT: PREMINDX.DAT  - INDEXED PREMIUM FILE         *
34  *                             RECORD KEY - POLICY NUMBER          *
35  *                             ALT KEY    - PREM DUE MONTH         *
36  *                                                                 *
37  *      INPUT:        IDXTRANS.DAT - TRANSACTION FILE              *
38  *                                                                 *
39  *      OUTPUT:       TRANLIST.RPT - TRANSACTION LIST REPORT       *
40  ********************************************************************
41 /
42  ENVIRONMENT DIVISION.
43  ***********************
44
```

FIGURE 9-10 Indexed Premium File Update program

```
45  INPUT-OUTPUT SECTION.
46  ********************
47
48  FILE-CONTROL.
49
50      SELECT INDEXED-PREMIUM-FILE
51          ASSIGN TO "A:\PREMINDX.DAT"
52          ORGANIZATION IS INDEXED
53          ACCESS IS RANDOM
54          RECORD KEY IS IRB-POLICY-NUMBER
55          ALTERNATE RECORD KEY IS IRB-PREMIUM-DUE-MONTH
56              WITH DUPLICATES.
57
58      SELECT TRANSACTION-FILE
59          ASSIGN TO "A:\IDXTRANS.DAT".
60
61      SELECT TRANSACTION-LIST-REPORT
62          ASSIGN TO "A:\TRANLIST.RPT".
63
64  /
65  DATA DIVISION.
66  **************
67  FILE SECTION.
68  **************
69  *********************************************************************
70  *                                                                   *
71  *      INDEXED-PREMIUM-FILE - INDEXED PREMIUM MASTER                 *
72  *                                                                   *
73  *********************************************************************
74
75  FD  INDEXED-PREMIUM-FILE.
76
77  01  INDEX-RECORD-BUFFER.
78      02                          PIC X(50).
79      02  IRB-POLICY-NUMBER       PIC X(12).
80      02                          PIC X(13).
81      02  IRB-PREMIUM-DUE-MONTH   PIC XX.
82      02                          PIC XXX.
83
84  *********************************************************************
85  *                                                                   *
86  *      TRANSACTION-FILE - TRANSACTIONS FOR UPDATING INDEXED FILE     *
87  *                                                                   *
88  *********************************************************************
89
90  FD  TRANSACTION-FILE.
91
92  01  TRANS-RECORD                PIC X(78).
93
94  *********************************************************************
95  *                                                                   *
96  *      REPORT-FILE - TRANSACTION LIST REPORT                        *
97  *                                                                   *
98  *********************************************************************
99
100 FD  TRANSACTION-LIST-REPORT.
101
102 01  REPORT-LINE-OUT             PIC X(132).
103 /
104 WORKING-STORAGE SECTION.
105 ***********************
106 *********************************************************************
107 *                                                                   *
108 *                  SWITCHES                                         *
109 *                                                                   *
110 *********************************************************************
111
112 01  SWITCHES-WS.
113
114     02  SW-END-OF-FILE          PIC X.
115         88  END-OF-FILE                     VALUE "Y".
116
117 01  VALUES-FOR-SWITCHES-WS.
118     02  YES                     PIC X       VALUE "Y".
119     02  NEG                     PIC X       VALUE "N".
120
121 *********************************************************************
122 *                                                                   *
123 *                  ACCUMULATORS                                    *
124 *                                                                   *
125 *********************************************************************
126
127 01  ACCUMULATORS.
128
129     02  AC-LINE-COUNT           PIC S999 PACKED-DECIMAL.
130     02  AC-PAGE-COUNT           PIC S999 PACKED-DECIMAL.
131     02  AC-BAD-RECORD-COUNT     PIC S999 PACKED-DECIMAL.
132     02  AC-ADDED-RECORD-COUNT   PIC S999 PACKED-DECIMAL.
133     02  AC-CHANGED-RECORD-COUNT PIC S999 PACKED-DECIMAL.
134     02  AC-DELETED-RECORD-COUNT PIC S999 PACKED-DECIMAL.
135 /
136 *********************************************************************
137 *                                                                   *
138 *                  WORK AREA                                        *
139 *                                                                   *
140 *********************************************************************
141
142 01  WORK-AREA.
143
144     02  WA-DATE.
145         03  WA-MONTH            PIC 99.
146         03  WA-DAY              PIC 99.
147         03  WA-YEAR             PIC 99.
148
149     02  WA-RUN-DATE
150         REDEFINES WA-DATE       PIC 9(6).
151
152     02  WA-TODAYS-DATE.
153         03  WA-TODAYS-YEAR      PIC 99.
154         03  WA-TODAYS-MONTH     PIC 99.
155         03  WA-TODAYS-DAY       PIC 99.
156
157     02  WA-TODAYS-TIME.
158         03  WA-TODAYS-HOUR      PIC 99.
159         03  WA-TODAYS-MINUTE    PIC 99.
160         03                      PIC X(4).
161
162     02  WA-ADVANCING-FACTOR     PIC 99.
163
164 /
165 COPY "A:\INSREC.CBL".
166L*********************************************************************
167L*                                                                   *
168L*          PREMIUM INPUT FILE RECORD LAYOUT                         *
169L*                                                                   *
170L*********************************************************************
171L
172L 01 PREMIUM-RECORD.
173L    02  PR-CUSTOMER-NAME        PIC X(20).
174L    02  PR-AGENT-NAME           PIC X(10).
175L    02  PR-INSURANCE-TYPE       PIC X(10).
176L        88  VALID-TYPE              VALUE "Automobile"
177L                                          "Annuity"
178L                                          "Home"
179L                                          "Renter"
180L                                          "Term Life"
181L                                          "Whole Life".
182L
183L    02  PR-POLICY-NUMBER        PIC X(12).
184L    02  PR-PREMIUM-AMOUNT       PIC S9(5)V99.
185L
186L    02  PR-PAYMENT-STATUS       PIC X.
187L        88  DELINQUENT              VALUE "D".
188L        88  PAID-IN-FULL           VALUE "F".
189L        88  PARTIALLY-PAID         VALUE "P".
190L        88  NOT-YET-BILLED         VALUE "N".
191L
192L    02  PR-SEX                  PIC X.
193L    02  PR-SIGNUP-YEAR          PIC X(4).
194L    02  PR-PREMIUM-DUE-MONTH    PIC 99.
195L    02                          PIC XXX.
196 /
```

(continued)

```
197  ******************************************************************
198  *                    TRANSACTION RECORD LAYOUT                   *
199  *                                                                *
200  *        CHARACTERISTICS: LAYOUT FOR IDXTRANS.DAT                *
201  *                        FILE LENGTH     - 78 BYTES              *
202  *                        FILE ORGANIZATION -  SEQUENTIAL         *
203  *                                                                *
204  ******************************************************************
205
206  01  TRANSACTION-RECORD.
207      02  TR-CODE                   PIC X.
208          88  ADDITION              VALUE "A".
209          88  CHANGE                VALUE "C".
210          88  DELETION              VALUE "D".
211      02  TR-CUSTOMER-NAME          PIC X(20).
212      02  TR-AGENT-NAME             PIC X(20).
213      02  TR-INSURANCE-TYPE         PIC X(10).
214      02  TR-POLICY-NUMBER          PIC X(12).
215      02  TR-PREMIUM-AMOUNT-ALPHA   PIC X(7).
216      02  TR-PREMIUM-AMOUNT REDEFINES
217          TR-PREMIUM-AMOUNT-ALPHA   PIC S9(5)V99.
218      02  TR-PAYMENT-STATUS         PIC X.
219      02  TR-SEX                    PIC X.
220      02  TR-SIGNUP-YEAR            PIC X(4).
221      02  TR-DUE-MONTH              PIC XX.
222  /
223  ******************************************************************
224  *                                                                *
225  *  REPORT HEADINGS FOR TRANSACTION LIST REPORT                   *
226  *                                                                *
227  ******************************************************************
228
229  01  REPORT-HEADING.
230
231      02  RH-LINE-1.
232          03                        PIC X(10)  VALUE
233              "RUN DATE: ".
234          03  RH-RUN-DATE           PIC Z9/99/99.
235          03                        PIC X(34)  VALUE SPACES.
236          03                        PIC X(27)  VALUE
237              "AINSWORTH INSURANCE COMPANY".
238          03                        PIC X(44)  VALUE SPACES.
239          03                        PIC X(6)   VALUE "PAGE:".
240          03  RH-PAGE-COUNT         PIC ZZ9.
241
242      02  RH-LINE-2.
243          03                        PIC X(10)  VALUE
244              "RUN TIME: ".
245          03  RH-HOUR               PIC Z9.
246          03                        PIC X      VALUE ":".
247          03  RH-MINUTE             PIC 99.
248          03  RH-AM-PM              PIC XX.
249          03                        PIC X(37)  VALUE SPACES.
250          03                        PIC X(23)  VALUE
251              "TRANSACTION LIST REPORT".
252          03                        PIC X(55)  VALUE SPACES.
253
254      02  RH-LINE-3.
255          03                        PIC X(4)   VALUE
256              "TRAN".
257          03                        PIC X(52)  VALUE SPACES.
258          03                        PIC X(9)   VALUE
259              "INSURANCE".
260          03                        PIC X(25)  VALUE SPACES.
261          03                        PIC X(7)   VALUE
262              "PREMIUM".
263          03                        PIC X(4)   VALUE SPACES.
264          03                        PIC XXX    VALUE
265              "PAY".
266          03                        PIC X(11)  VALUE SPACES.
267          03                        PIC X(6)   VALUE
268              "SIGNUP".
269          03                        PIC X(4)   VALUE SPACES.
270          03                        PIC X(4)   VALUE
271              "PREM".
272          03                        PIC XXX    VALUE SPACES.
273  /
274      02  RH-LINE-4.
275          03                        PIC X(4)   VALUE
276              "CODE".
277          03                        PIC X(4)   VALUE SPACES.
278          03                        PIC X(13)  VALUE
279              "CUSTOMER NAME".
280          03                        PIC X(11)  VALUE SPACES.
281          03                        PIC X(10)  VALUE
282              "AGENT NAME".
283          03                        PIC X(14)  VALUE SPACES.
284          03                        PIC X(4)   VALUE
285              "TYPE".
286          03                        PIC X(11)  VALUE SPACES.
287          03                        PIC X(13)  VALUE
288              "POLICY NUMBER".
289          03                        PIC X(7)   VALUE SPACES.
290          03                        PIC X(6)   VALUE
291              "AMOUNT".
292          03                        PIC X(4)   VALUE SPACES.
293          03                        PIC X(4)   VALUE
294              "STAT".
295          03                        PIC X(4)   VALUE SPACES.
296          03                        PIC XXX    VALUE
297              "SEX".
298          03                        PIC XXX    VALUE SPACES.
299          03                        PIC X(4)   VALUE
300              "YEAR".
301          03                        PIC X(6)   VALUE SPACES.
302          03                        PIC XXX    VALUE
303              "DUE".
304          03                        PIC X(4)   VALUE SPACES.
305  /
306      02  RH-LINE-5.
307          03                        PIC X(4)   VALUE ALL "-".
308          03                        PIC X(4)   VALUE SPACES.
309          03                        PIC X(13)  VALUE ALL "-".
310          03                        PIC X(11)  VALUE SPACES.
311          03                        PIC X(10)  VALUE ALL "-".
312          03                        PIC X(14)  VALUE SPACES.
313          03                        PIC X(4)   VALUE ALL "-".
314          03                        PIC X(11)  VALUE SPACES.
315          03                        PIC X(13)  VALUE ALL "-".
316          03                        PIC X(7)   VALUE SPACES.
317          03                        PIC X(6)   VALUE ALL "-".
318          03                        PIC X(4)   VALUE SPACES.
319          03                        PIC X(4)   VALUE ALL "-".
320          03                        PIC X(4)   VALUE SPACES.
321          03                        PIC XXX    VALUE ALL "-".
322          03                        PIC XXX    VALUE SPACES.
323          03                        PIC X(4)   VALUE ALL "-".
324          03                        PIC X(6)   VALUE SPACES.
325          03                        PIC XXX    VALUE ALL "-".
326          03                        PIC X(4)   VALUE SPACES.
327  /
328  ******************************************************************
329  *                                                                *
330  *    DETAIL LINE LAYOUT FOR UNPROCESSED TRANSACTION RECORDS      *
331  *                                                                *
332  ******************************************************************
333
334  01  TRANSACTION-ERROR-LINE.
335      02  TEL-RECORD                PIC X(78).
336      02                            PIC X(4)   VALUE SPACES.
337      02  TEL-MESSAGE               PIC X(41).
338      02                            PIC X(9)   VALUE SPACES.
339
340  ******************************************************************
341  *                                                                *
342  *    DETAIL LINE LAYOUT FOR PROCESSED TRANSACTION RECORDS        *
343  *                                                                *
344  ******************************************************************
345
346  01  DETAIL-LINE.
347      02                            PIC XX     VALUE SPACES.
348      02  DL-CODE                   PIC X.
```

FIGURE 9-10   Indexed Premium File Update program (continued)

```
349     02                          PIC X(5)     VALUE SPACES.
350     02  DL-CUSTOMER-NAME         PIC X(20).
351     02                          PIC X(4)     VALUE SPACES.
352     02  DL-AGENT-NAME            PIC X(20).
353     02                          PIC X(4)     VALUE SPACES.
354     02  DL-INSURANCE-TYPE        PIC X(10).
355     02                          PIC X(5)     VALUE SPACES.
356     02  DL-POLICY-NUMBER         PIC X(12).
357     02                          PIC X(5)     VALUE SPACES.
358     02  DL-PREMIUM-AMOUNT        PIC ZZ,ZZ9.99.
359     02                          PIC X(6)     VALUE SPACES.
360     02  DL-PAYMENT-STATUS        PIC X.
361     02                          PIC X(6)     VALUE SPACES.
362     02  DL-SEX                   PIC X.
363     02                          PIC X(4)     VALUE SPACES.
364     02  DL-SIGNUP-YEAR           PIC X(4).
365     02                          PIC X(7)     VALUE SPACES.
366     02  DL-PREMIUM-DUE-MONTH     PIC X(5).
367     02                          PIC X        VALUE SPACE.
368 /
369 **********************************************************************
370 *                                                                  *
371 *     SUMMARY LINES FOR TRANSACTION LIST REPORT                    *
372 *                                                                  *
373 **********************************************************************
374
375 01  SUMMARY-LINES.
376
377     02  SL-LINE-1.
378         03                      PIC X(46)  VALUE SPACES.
379         03                      PIC X(38)  VALUE
380             "THE NUMBER OF RECORDS WITH ERRORS  = ".
381         03  SL-BAD-RECORD-COUNT  PIC ZZ9.
382         03                      PIC X(45)  VALUE SPACES.
383
384     02  SL-LINE-2.
385         03                      PIC X(46)  VALUE SPACES.
386         03                      PIC X(38)  VALUE
387             "THE NUMBER OF RECORDS ADDED        = ".
388         03  SL-ADDED-RECORD-COUNT  PIC ZZ9.
389         03                      PIC X(45)  VALUE SPACES.
390
391     02  SL-LINE-3.
392         03                      PIC X(46)  VALUE SPACES.
393         03                      PIC X(38)  VALUE
394             "THE NUMBER OF RECORDS CHANGED      = ".
395         03  SL-CHANGED-RECORD-COUNT  PIC ZZ9.
396         03                      PIC X(45)  VALUE SPACES.
397
398     02  SL-LINE-4.
399         03                      PIC X(46)  VALUE SPACES.
400         03                      PIC X(38)  VALUE
401             "THE NUMBER OF RECORDS DELETED      = ".
402         03  SL-DELETED-RECORD-COUNT  PIC ZZ9.
403         03                      PIC X(45)  VALUE SPACES.
404
405     02  SL-EOR-LINE.
406         03                      PIC X(60)  VALUE SPACES.
407         03                      PIC X(13)  VALUE
408             "END OF REPORT".
409         03                      PIC X(59)  VALUE SPACES.
410 /
411 PROCEDURE DIVISION.
412 ******************
413 **********************************************************************
414 *                                                                  *
415 *  MAIN-PROGRAM - This is the main process routine                 *
416 *                                                                  *
417 **********************************************************************
418
419 MAIN-PROGRAM.
420
421     PERFORM A-100-INITIALIZATION.
422     PERFORM B-100-PROCESS-TRANSACTIONS.
423     PERFORM C-100-WRAP-UP.
424     STOP RUN.
```

```
425
426 **********************************************************************
427 *                                                                  *
428 *    A-100-INITIALIZATION - Preprocessing housekeeping routine     *
429 *                                                                  *
430 **********************************************************************
431
432 A-100-INITIALIZATION.
433
434     MOVE NEG TO SW-END-OF-FILE.
435     INITIALIZE ACCUMULATORS.
436
437     ACCEPT WA-TODAYS-DATE FROM DATE.
438     MOVE WA-TODAYS-MONTH TO WA-MONTH.
439     MOVE WA-TODAYS-DAY TO WA-DAY.
440     MOVE WA-TODAYS-YEAR TO WA-YEAR.
441     MOVE WA-RUN-DATE TO RH-RUN-DATE.
442
443     ACCEPT WA-TODAYS-TIME FROM TIME.
444     MOVE WA-TODAYS-MINUTE TO RH-MINUTE.
445     EVALUATE TRUE
446         WHEN WA-TODAYS-HOUR = 0
447             MOVE 12 TO RH-HOUR
448             MOVE "AM" TO RH-AM-PM
449         WHEN WA-TODAYS-HOUR = 12
450             MOVE WA-TODAYS-HOUR TO RH-HOUR
451             MOVE "PM" TO RH-AM-PM
452         WHEN WA-TODAYS-HOUR > 12
453             SUBTRACT 12 FROM WA-TODAYS-HOUR
454             MOVE WA-TODAYS-HOUR TO RH-HOUR
455             MOVE "PM" TO RH-AM-PM
456         WHEN OTHER
457             MOVE WA-TODAYS-HOUR TO RH-HOUR
458             MOVE "AM" TO RH-AM-PM.
459
460     OPEN INPUT   TRANSACTION-FILE
461          OUTPUT  TRANSACTION-LIST-REPORT
462          I-O     INDEXED-PREMIUM-FILE.
463 /
464 **********************************************************************
465 *                                                                  *
466 *  B-100-PROCESS-TRANSACTIONS - Prepare to process transactions    *
467 *                                                                  *
468 **********************************************************************
469
470 B-100-PROCESS-TRANSACTIONS.
471
472     MOVE NEG TO SW-END-OF-FILE.
473     READ TRANSACTION-FILE INTO TRANSACTION-RECORD
474         AT END MOVE YES TO SW-END-OF-FILE.
475
476     PERFORM B-200-UPDATE-FILE
477         UNTIL END-OF-FILE.
478
479     MOVE AC-BAD-RECORD-COUNT TO SL-BAD-RECORD-COUNT.
480     MOVE AC-ADDED-RECORD-COUNT TO SL-ADDED-RECORD-COUNT.
481     MOVE AC-CHANGED-RECORD-COUNT TO SL-CHANGED-RECORD-COUNT.
482     MOVE AC-DELETED-RECORD-COUNT TO SL-DELETED-RECORD-COUNT.
483
484     WRITE REPORT-LINE-OUT FROM SL-LINE-1
485         AFTER ADVANCING 3 LINES.
486     WRITE REPORT-LINE-OUT FROM SL-LINE-2
487         AFTER ADVANCING 1 LINE.
488     WRITE REPORT-LINE-OUT FROM SL-LINE-3
489         AFTER ADVANCING 1 LINE.
490     WRITE REPORT-LINE-OUT FROM SL-LINE-4
491         AFTER ADVANCING 1 LINE.
492     WRITE REPORT-LINE-OUT FROM SL-EOR-LINE
493         AFTER ADVANCING 2 LINES.
494
495 **********************************************************************
496 *                                                                  *
497 *  B-200-UPDATE-FILE - Update Premium file with transactions       *
498 *                                                                  *
499 **********************************************************************
500
```

(continued)

```
501  B-200-UPDATE-FILE.
502
503      IF AC-LINE-COUNT = 0
504          PERFORM B-300-PRINT-HEADINGS.
505
506      EVALUATE TRUE
507          WHEN ADDITION PERFORM B-310-ADDITION
508          WHEN CHANGE   PERFORM B-320-CHANGE
509          WHEN DELETION PERFORM B-330-DELETION
510          WHEN OTHER    DISPLAY "BAD TRANSACTION TYPE".
511
512      IF AC-LINE-COUNT > 55
513          MOVE ZERO TO AC-LINE-COUNT.
514
515      READ TRANSACTION-FILE INTO TRANSACTION-RECORD
516          AT END MOVE YES TO SW-END-OF-FILE.
517  /
518  ******************************************************************
519  *                                                                *
520  *   B-300-PRINT-HEADINGS - Header Routine for List Report        *
521  *                                                                *
522  ******************************************************************
523
524  B-300-PRINT-HEADINGS.
525
526      ADD 1 TO AC-PAGE-COUNT.
527      MOVE AC-PAGE-COUNT TO RH-PAGE-COUNT.
528      WRITE REPORT-LINE-OUT FROM RH-LINE-1
529          AFTER ADVANCING PAGE.
530      WRITE REPORT-LINE-OUT FROM RH-LINE-2
531          AFTER ADVANCING 1 LINE.
532      WRITE REPORT-LINE-OUT FROM RH-LINE-3
533          AFTER ADVANCING 2 LINES.
534      WRITE REPORT-LINE-OUT FROM RH-LINE-4
535          AFTER ADVANCING 1 LINE.
536      WRITE REPORT-LINE-OUT FROM RH-LINE-5
537          AFTER ADVANCING 1 LINE.
538
539      MOVE 7 TO AC-LINE-COUNT.
540
541  ******************************************************************
542  *                                                                *
543  *   B-310-ADDITION - Process Add Transaction                     *
544  *                                                                *
545  ******************************************************************
546
547  B-310-ADDITION.
548
549      MOVE TR-POLICY-NUMBER TO IRB-POLICY-NUMBER.
550      READ INDEXED-PREMIUM-FILE INTO PREMIUM-RECORD
551          INVALID KEY
552              PERFORM B-410-ADD-RECORD
553              MOVE 2 TO WA-ADVANCING-FACTOR
554              PERFORM B-400-LIST-TO-REPORT
555          NOT INVALID KEY
556              MOVE "ATTEMPTED ADDITION OVER EXISTING RECORD" TO
557                  TEL-MESSAGE
558              PERFORM B-440-PRINT-ERROR.
559  /
560  ******************************************************************
561  *                                                                *
562  *   B-320-CHANGE - Process Change Transaction                    *
563  *                                                                *
564  ******************************************************************
565
566  B-320-CHANGE.
567
568      MOVE TR-POLICY-NUMBER TO IRB-POLICY-NUMBER.
569      READ INDEXED-PREMIUM-FILE INTO PREMIUM-RECORD
570          INVALID KEY
571              MOVE "ATTEMPTED CHANGE OF NON-EXISTING RECORD" TO
572                  TEL-MESSAGE
573              PERFORM B-440-PRINT-ERROR
574          NOT INVALID KEY
575              MOVE 2 TO WA-ADVANCING-FACTOR
576              PERFORM B-400-LIST-TO-REPORT
577              PERFORM B-420-UPDATE-RECORD
578              MOVE 1 TO WA-ADVANCING-FACTOR
579              MOVE SPACE TO TR-CODE
580              PERFORM B-400-LIST-TO-REPORT.
581
582  ******************************************************************
583  *                                                                *
584  *   B-330-DELETION - Process Delete Transaction                  *
585  *                                                                *
586  ******************************************************************
587
588  B-330-DELETION.
589
590      MOVE TR-POLICY-NUMBER TO IRB-POLICY-NUMBER.
591      READ INDEXED-PREMIUM-FILE INTO PREMIUM-RECORD
592          INVALID KEY
593              MOVE "ATTEMPTED DELETION OF NON-EXISTING RECORD" TO
594                  TEL-MESSAGE
595              PERFORM B-440-PRINT-ERROR
596          NOT INVALID KEY
597              MOVE 2 TO WA-ADVANCING-FACTOR
598              PERFORM B-430-DELETE-RECORD
599              PERFORM B-400-LIST-TO-REPORT.
600  /
601  ******************************************************************
602  *                                                                *
603  *   B-400-LIST-TO-REPORT - Print Record on List Report           *
604  *                                                                *
605  ******************************************************************
606
607  B-400-LIST-TO-REPORT.
608
609      MOVE TR-CODE           TO DL-CODE.
610      MOVE PR-CUSTOMER-NAME  TO DL-CUSTOMER-NAME.
611      MOVE PR-AGENT-NAME     TO DL-AGENT-NAME.
612      MOVE PR-INSURANCE-TYPE TO DL-INSURANCE-TYPE.
613      MOVE PR-POLICY-NUMBER  TO DL-POLICY-NUMBER.
614      MOVE PR-PREMIUM-AMOUNT TO DL-PREMIUM-AMOUNT.
615      MOVE PR-PAYMENT-STATUS TO DL-PAYMENT-STATUS.
616      MOVE PR-SEX            TO DL-SEX.
617      MOVE PR-SIGNUP-YEAR    TO DL-SIGNUP-YEAR.
618      MOVE PR-PREMIUM-DUE-MONTH TO DL-PREMIUM-DUE-MONTH.
619
620      WRITE REPORT-LINE-OUT FROM DETAIL-LINE
621          AFTER ADVANCING WA-ADVANCING-FACTOR.
622
623      ADD WA-ADVANCING-FACTOR TO AC-LINE-COUNT.
624
625  ******************************************************************
626  *                                                                *
627  *   B-410-ADD-RECORD - Build and Write record                    *
628  *                                                                *
629  ******************************************************************
630
631  B-410-ADD-RECORD.
632
633      MOVE TR-CUSTOMER-NAME  TO PR-CUSTOMER-NAME.
634      MOVE TR-AGENT-NAME     TO PR-AGENT-NAME.
635      MOVE TR-INSURANCE-TYPE TO PR-INSURANCE-TYPE.
636      MOVE TR-POLICY-NUMBER  TO PR-POLICY-NUMBER.
637      MOVE TR-PREMIUM-AMOUNT TO PR-PREMIUM-AMOUNT.
638      MOVE TR-PAYMENT-STATUS TO PR-PAYMENT-STATUS.
639      MOVE TR-SEX            TO PR-SEX.
640      MOVE TR-SIGNUP-YEAR    TO PR-SIGNUP-YEAR.
641      MOVE TR-DUE-MONTH      TO PR-PREMIUM-DUE-MONTH.
642
643      WRITE INDEX-RECORD-BUFFER FROM PREMIUM-RECORD
644          INVALID KEY DISPLAY "WRITE LOGIC ERROR"
645                      STOP RUN.
646
```

FIGURE 9-10   Indexed Premium File Update program (continued)

```
647      ADD 1 TO AC-ADDED-RECORD-COUNT.            686  B-430-DELETE-RECORD.
648 /                                               687
649 *******************************************     688      DELETE INDEXED-PREMIUM-FILE
650 *                                         *     689          INVALID KEY DISPLAY "DELETION LOGIC ERROR"
651 *   B-420-UPDATE-RECORD - Update Premium Record and Rewrite   *   690              STOP RUN.
652 *                                         *     691
653 *******************************************     692      ADD 1 TO AC-DELETED-RECORD-COUNT.
654                                                 693 /
655  B-420-UPDATE-RECORD.                           694 *******************************************
656                                                 695 *                                          *
657      IF TR-CUSTOMER-NAME NOT = SPACES           696 *   B-440-PRINT-ERROR - Print error messages to list report   *
658          MOVE TR-CUSTOMER-NAME TO PR-CUSTOMER-NAME.   697 *                                   *
659      IF TR-AGENT-NAME NOT = SPACES              698 *******************************************
660          MOVE TR-AGENT-NAME TO PR-AGENT-NAME.   699
661      IF TR-INSURANCE-TYPE NOT = SPACES          700  B-440-PRINT-ERROR.
662          MOVE TR-INSURANCE-TYPE TO PR-INSURANCE-TYPE.  701
663      IF TR-PREMIUM-AMOUNT-ALPHA NOT = SPACES    702      MOVE TRANSACTION-RECORD TO TEL-RECORD.
664          MOVE TR-PREMIUM-AMOUNT TO PR-PREMIUM-AMOUNT.  703
665      IF TR-PAYMENT-STATUS NOT = SPACES          704      WRITE REPORT-LINE-OUT FROM TRANSACTION-ERROR-LINE
666          MOVE TR-PAYMENT-STATUS TO PR-PAYMENT-STATUS.  705          AFTER ADVANCING 2 LINES.
667      IF TR-SEX NOT = SPACES                     706
668          MOVE TR-SEX TO PR-SEX.                 707      ADD 2 TO AC-LINE-COUNT.
669      IF TR-SIGNUP-YEAR NOT = SPACES             708      ADD 1 TO AC-BAD-RECORD-COUNT.
670          MOVE TR-SIGNUP-YEAR TO PR-SIGNUP-YEAR. 709
671      IF TR-DUE-MONTH NOT = SPACES               710 *******************************************
672          MOVE TR-DUE-MONTH TO PR-PREMIUM-DUE-MONTH.   711 *                                    *
673                                                 712 *   C-100-WRAP-UP - Termination Routine for Program   *
674      REWRITE INDEX-RECORD-BUFFER FROM PREMIUM-RECORD  713 *                                *
675          INVALID KEY DISPLAY "REWRITE LOGIC ERROR"   714 *******************************************
676                  STOP RUN.                      715
677                                                 716  C-100-WRAP-UP.
678      ADD 1 TO AC-CHANGED-RECORD-COUNT.          717      CLOSE TRANSACTION-LIST-REPORT
679                                                 718              TRANSACTION-FILE
680 *******************************************     719              INDEXED-PREMIUM-FILE.
681 *                                         *     720
682 *   B-430-DELETE-RECORD - Delete Identified Record   *   721 *******************************************
683 *                                         *     722 *   END OF PROGRAM                        *
684 *******************************************     723 *******************************************
685                                                 724 /
```

INDEXED FILES

. . . .

An **indexed file** contains two or more components that work together to provide access to the records in the file. One is the data component, which consists of all the individual records. A second component associated with the file is called an index. An **index** contains the key field values from each record in the file and the disk address where each record is located.

A **key field** is a field common to each record in the file containing a value by which records can be retrieved. In an indexed file, at least one key field must be defined. This key field is referred to as the **primary key**. The primary key must contain a value that is unique to each record. No two records in an indexed file can have the same primary key value. If other key fields are defined, they are known as alternate keys. An **alternate key** field provides a means of accessing records using a field other than the primary key. An additional index component is associated with the file for each alternate key defined. That is, an index is created for the primary key as well as for each alternate key. Alternate key values do not have to be unique, but when duplicate alternate key values are allowed, this fact must be explicitly stated in the program.

Where sequential files can only be processed sequentially, indexed files can be processed both sequentially and randomly. **Random processing,** or **random access,** refers to the capability to retrieve and/or update a record without having to retrieve or process the records that precede it in the file. An indexed file must be created and stored on a **direct access storage device**, or **DASD**, such as a disk drive on a personal computer system or a disk pack on a larger computer system. These types of devices allow for random processing. Devices such as tape drives on a computer system allow for sequential processing only.

Figure 9-11 presents a diagram illustrating the relationship between an indexed file, the index created for the primary key, and the index created for an alternate key. In the given example, the field NUM is the primary key while the field JOB is an alternate key. Records in the file are physically in ascending sequence by NUM, the primary key. The index for NUM contains just two entries, a value for NUM and the disk address of the record with that key value. In the figure, addresses are represented by hexadecimal, base-16 numbers. As indicated earlier, no two records can have the same primary key value in an indexed file. The index for the alternate key field JOB contains each value of JOB along with the primary key value of the record or records with that alternate key value. Alternate key processing will be discussed later in this chapter.

Address	File			Primary Key Index	
	Num	Name	Job	Num	Record Address
01A	001	Jones	Washer	001	01A
02E	002	Smith	Dryer	002	02E
042	004	Watts	Cook	004	042
056	006	Manson	Washer	006	056
06A	007	Watson	Sweeper	007	06A
07E	009	Henry	Waiter	009	07E
092	011	Calvin	Server	011	092
0A6	012	Johns	Sweeper	012	0A6

Alternate Key Index

Job	Primary Key Value
Cook	004
Dryer	002
Server	011
Sweeper	007, 012
Waiter	009
Washer	001, 006

FIGURE 9-11   Sample indexed file with primary key index and alternate key index

CREATING AN INDEXED FILE

Indexed files are commonly created by reading in records from a sequential file and then writing those same records out to an indexed file. The first indication that something other than a sequential file is to be used in a program appears in the SELECT entry within the ENVIRONMENT DIVISION. As discussed in Chapter 3, the ORGANIZATION IS clause is optional when working with a sequential file. When working with a file other than a sequential file, however, the ORGANIZATION IS clause must be coded as part of the SELECT entry and the specific organization indicated.

Figure 9-12 presents the SELECT entry for the Indexed Premium file that is output from the sample program. Line 44 specifically indicates that this is an INDEXED file. The ACCESS IS SEQUENTIAL entry on line 45 indicates that the file will be processed sequentially, one record after another, in this program. Access must be sequential when creating an indexed file.

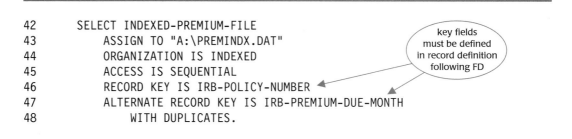

```
42        SELECT INDEXED-PREMIUM-FILE
43            ASSIGN TO "A:\PREMINDX.DAT"
44            ORGANIZATION IS INDEXED
45            ACCESS IS SEQUENTIAL
46            RECORD KEY IS IRB-POLICY-NUMBER
47            ALTERNATE RECORD KEY IS IRB-PREMIUM-DUE-MONTH
48                WITH DUPLICATES.
```

key fields must be defined in record definition following FD

FIGURE 9-12   SELECT entry for the Indexed Premium file

The RECORD KEY IS entry on line 46 in Figure 9-12 identifies the name of the primary key field as it is defined within this program. This key, IRB-POLICY-NUMBER, must be defined within the record definition found immediately after the FD for INDEXED-PREMIUM-FILE. Policy number is used as the primary key for this file because no two customers have the same number.

Lines 47 and 48 in Figure 9-12 define an alternate key field named IRB-PREMIUM-DUE-MONTH for the INDEXED-PREMIUM-FILE. As with the primary key, an alternate key must be defined within the record definition following the FD for the file. The entry on line 48, WITH DUPLICATES, is required if the same alternate key value appears in more than one record. Many customers have the same premium due month, therefore, the WITH DUPLICATES entry is needed in this situation.

Figure 9-13 on the next page presents the FD and associated record definition for the INDEXED-PREMIUM-FILE. The position and size of the primary key field and each alternate key field identified in the SELECT entry must be defined in the record definition. As the indexed file is created, the operating system will use the values contained in these fields to build the required primary key index and each alternate key index. For each record in the Indexed Premium file, the primary key, Policy Number, begins in position 51 and is 12-characters long. The alternate key, Premium Due Month, begins in position 76 and is two-characters long.

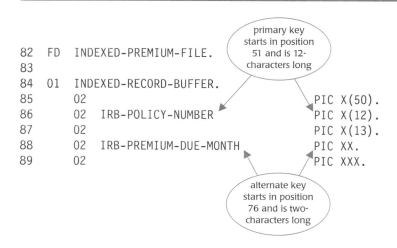

```
82  FD  INDEXED-PREMIUM-FILE.
83
84  01  INDEXED-RECORD-BUFFER.
85      02                            PIC X(50).
86      02  IRB-POLICY-NUMBER         PIC X(12).
87      02                            PIC X(13).
88      02  IRB-PREMIUM-DUE-MONTH     PIC XX.
89      02                            PIC XXX.
```

FIGURE 9-13   FD for the Indexed Premium file

Within the PROCEDURE DIVISION of the Indexed Premium File Creation program presented in Figure 9-5 on page 9-5, a loop is executed to build the INDEXED-PREMIUM-FILE. Each record from the sequential version of the Premium file is read into the record layout PREMIUM-RECORD and then written to INDEXED-PREMIUM-FILE using a WRITE statement. The records in the sequential file must be ordered in ascending sequence by the key field when used to create an indexed file. If you are uncertain of the order of the records, a SORT statement can be used to sequence the records prior to creating the indexed file. In the sample program, the records in the sequential file are already in the proper order, so no SORT statement is necessary.

Figure 9-14 presents paragraph B-100-PROCESS-FILE from the Indexed Premium File Creation program. This paragraph contains the statement that writes the records to INDEXED-PREMIUM-FILE. The first line of the WRITE statement presented, line 213, looks and works like other WRITE statements presented and discussed in this book. Lines 214 and 215 comprise the **INVALID KEY** clause, which is normally required on a WRITE for an indexed file. The statement or statements following an INVALID KEY clause execute when an error occurs during the execution of the WRITE of a record to the indexed file.

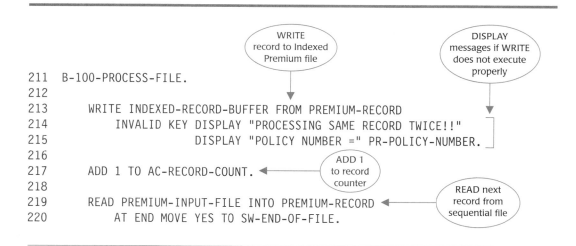

```
211  B-100-PROCESS-FILE.
212
213      WRITE INDEXED-RECORD-BUFFER FROM PREMIUM-RECORD
214          INVALID KEY DISPLAY "PROCESSING SAME RECORD TWICE!!"
215                  DISPLAY "POLICY NUMBER =" PR-POLICY-NUMBER.
216
217      ADD 1 TO AC-RECORD-COUNT.
218
219      READ PREMIUM-INPUT-FILE INTO PREMIUM-RECORD
220          AT END MOVE YES TO SW-END-OF-FILE.
```

FIGURE 9-14   Paragraph B-100-PROCESS-FILE from the Indexed Premium File Creation program

Figure 9-15 presents the basic format of a WRITE statement used to place records in an indexed file. The field name following the word WRITE must be the 01 level name of the record definition following the FD for the indexed file. As in other forms of the WRITE statement, FROM is optional. Although shown as an optional entry, INVALID KEY is required unless replaced by a special error-handling routine in a declarative section. Declarative sections will be presented in Chapter 10. The NOT INVALID KEY clause is optional and can be used to execute one or more statements when the WRITE executes successfully. END-WRITE is optional and must be used to terminate a WRITE when it is nested in a larger statement and a period cannot be used.

```
WRITE  record-name-1    [ FROM record-name-2 ]

    [ INVALID KEY  statement-set-1 ]

    [ NOT INVALID KEY  statement-set-2 ]

[ END-WRITE ]
```

FIGURE 9-15   Basic format of a WRITE statement to an indexed file

Four error conditions can occur during a WRITE to an indexed file and, thus, cause the statement or statements listed after the INVALID KEY clause to execute. Table 9-1 summarizes these conditions. The statement or statements executed as part of an INVALID KEY clause can be any type of nonconditional action. In the sample program, two DISPLAY statements are coded to inform the user that an error has occurred. Some situations may require more involved actions such as passing control to a subroutine that outputs messages, closes files, and stops the program.

TABLE 9-1   Error Conditions that Trigger INVALID KEY in a WRITE to an Indexed File

ACCESS Mode	OPEN Mode	Error
1. SEQUENTIAL	OUTPUT or EXTEND	Primary key value of the record being written is less than or equal to the primary key of the previous record
2. All modes	OUTPUT or I-0	Primary key value of the record being written equals the primary key of a record already on the file
3. All modes	OUTPUT, I-0, or EXTEND	Alternate key value of the record being written equals the alternate key value of a record already on the file and WITH DUPLICATES was not specified
4. All modes	OUTPUT, I-0, or EXTEND	Disk space capacity has been exceeded

In the sample program, once all of the records in the sequential file have been processed and written to the indexed file, summary lines are displayed and printed stating the number of records written, the files are closed, and the program terminates.

RANDOM PROCESSING OF AN INDEXED FILE

The second program presented in this chapter, the Indexed Premium File Update program, uses a transaction file to perform file maintenance activities on the indexed file created by the first program. To improve the readability of the output report, although not necessary, the transaction file has been pre-sorted so all add transactions are processed first, followed by the change transactions, and, finally, the delete transactions.

The first character in each transaction contains a code of A, C, or D, to indicate what type of transaction it is. The contents of the transaction file are presented in Figure 9-16. Notice that add transactions have data in every field. Although only the key field is necessary, every field within PREMIUM-RECORD will be filled in with transaction data when a new record is added to the file. Change transactions contain data only in those fields to be modified. Blank fields on the transaction are ignored. Delete transactions contain only two entries, the transaction code, D, and the policy number of the record to be deleted. Other information is not necessary.

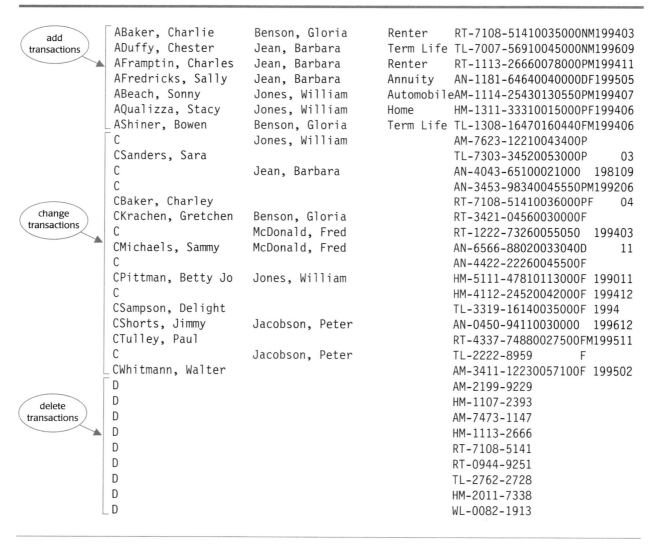

add transactions

```
ABaker, Charlie      Benson, Gloria   Renter     RT-7108-51410035000NM199403
ADuffy, Chester      Jean, Barbara    Term Life  TL-7007-56910045000NM199609
AFramptin, Charles   Jean, Barbara    Renter     RT-1113-26660078000PM199411
AFredricks, Sally    Jean, Barbara    Annuity    AN-1181-64640040000DF199505
ABeach, Sonny        Jones, William   Automobile AM-1114-25430130550PM199407
AQualizza, Stacy     Jones, William   Home       HM-1311-33310015000PF199406
AShiner, Bowen       Benson, Gloria   Term Life  TL-1308-16470160440FM199406
C                    Jones, William              AM-7623-12210043400P
CSanders, Sara                                   TL-7303-34520053000P      03
C                    Jean, Barbara               AN-4043-65100021000   198109
C                                                AN-3453-98340045550PM199206
CBaker, Charley                                  RT-7108-51410036000PF     04
CKrachen, Gretchen   Benson, Gloria              RT-3421-04560030000F
C                    McDonald, Fred              RT-1222-73260055050   199403
CMichaels, Sammy     McDonald, Fred              AN-6566-88020033040D      11
C                                                AN-4422-22260045500F
CPittman, Betty Jo   Jones, William              HM-5111-47810113000F  199011
C                                                HM-4112-24520042000F  199412
CSampson, Delight                                TL-3319-16140035000F  1994
CShorts, Jimmy       Jacobson, Peter             AN-0450-94110030000   199612
CTulley, Paul                                    RT-4337-74880027500FM199511
C                    Jacobson, Peter             TL-2222-8959          F
CWhitmann, Walter                                AM-3411-12230057100F  199502
D                                                AM-2199-9229
D                                                HM-1107-2393
D                                                AM-7473-1147
D                                                HM-1113-2666
D                                                RT-7108-5141
D                                                RT-0944-9251
D                                                TL-2762-2728
D                                                HM-2011-7338
D                                                WL-0082-1913
```

change transactions

delete transactions

FIGURE 9-16 Transactions for the Indexed Premium File Update program

Whether a record is to be added, changed, or deleted, the first step taken in the program for each transaction is to determine if the desired record, as identified by the policy number on the transaction, exists on the file. A record can be added to the file only if it *does not* exist, and a record can be updated or deleted only if it *does* exist. The existence or non-existence of a record is determined by the execution of a random READ.

A **random READ** uses the index associated with an indexed file to locate a specified record in the file. Figure 9-17 presents the SELECT entry for the INDEXED-PREMIUM-FILE from the Indexed Premium File Update program. It is identical to the SELECT entry used in the Indexed Premium File Creation program except for the ACCESS IS entry on line 53. Here, ACCESS IS RANDOM is specified, thus, allowing the use of the random READ. Random processing is allowed only when ACCESS is specified as RANDOM or DYNAMIC. DYNAMIC access allows for both random and sequential processing to be performed on the same file in a program. The Indexed Premium File Update program does not require any sequential processing, therefore DYNAMIC access is not needed.

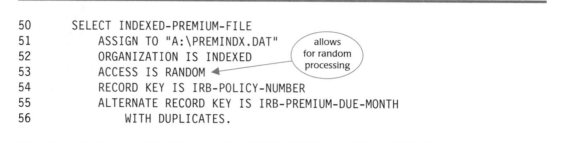

```
50       SELECT INDEXED-PREMIUM-FILE
51           ASSIGN TO "A:\PREMINDX.DAT"         allows
52           ORGANIZATION IS INDEXED            for random
53           ACCESS IS RANDOM  ◄                 processing
54           RECORD KEY IS IRB-POLICY-NUMBER
55           ALTERNATE RECORD KEY IS IRB-PREMIUM-DUE-MONTH
56               WITH DUPLICATES.
```

FIGURE 9-17   SELECT entry from the Indexed Premium File Update program

The basic format of a random READ statement is illustrated in Figure 9-18. The KEY IS phrase is needed only when an alternate key is used for retrieval. Instead of an AT END clause, which is used in a sequential READ, an INVALID KEY clause is coded. The INVALID KEY clause is shown as being optional, but it is a required entry unless a declarative section is coded within the program. As mentioned earlier, declarative sections will be discussed in Chapter 10. The statement or statements following INVALID KEY will execute only if the desired record cannot be located. NOT INVALID KEY is optional and can be used to specify actions to be taken when the desired record is located. As with a sequential READ, END-READ is needed only when the READ cannot be terminated by a period. The desired record is identified by placing a key field value into the record key field just prior to execution of the random READ.

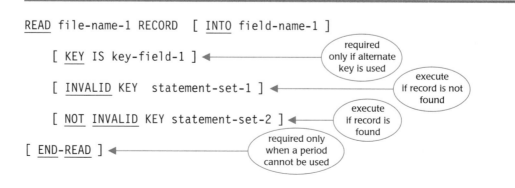

```
READ file-name-1 RECORD  [ INTO field-name-1 ]
                                                 required
     [ KEY IS key-field-1 ] ◄                    only if alternate
                                                 key is used
                                                          execute
     [ INVALID KEY  statement-set-1 ] ◄                  if record is not
                                                          found
                                           execute
     [ NOT INVALID KEY statement-set-2 ] ◄ if record is
                                           found
                            required only
[ END-READ ] ◄              when a period
                            cannot be used
```

FIGURE 9-18   Basic format of a random READ statement

Figure 9-19 presents an example of a random READ from the Indexed Premium File Update program. The policy number from the transaction record, TR-POLICY-NUMBER, is moved to the primary key field IRB-POLICY-NUMBER just before the execution of the random READ. This example is from the logic for adding a record to the file; therefore, the statements following the INVALID KEY clause coordinate the activities needed to build a record and WRITE a record to the INDEXED-PREMIUM-FILE. The statements following NOT INVALID KEY direct logic to an error routine, because it is not possible to add a record to the file if the designated policy number already exists in the file.

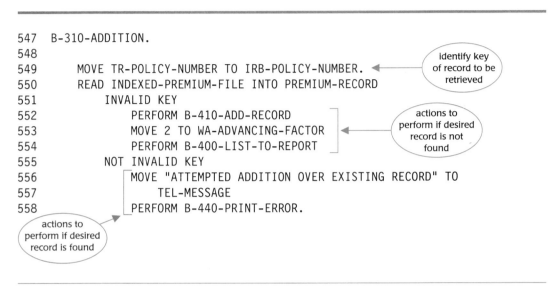

```
547   B-310-ADDITION.
548
549       MOVE TR-POLICY-NUMBER TO IRB-POLICY-NUMBER.
550       READ INDEXED-PREMIUM-FILE INTO PREMIUM-RECORD
551           INVALID KEY
552               PERFORM B-410-ADD-RECORD
553               MOVE 2 TO WA-ADVANCING-FACTOR
554               PERFORM B-400-LIST-TO-REPORT
555           NOT INVALID KEY
556               MOVE "ATTEMPTED ADDITION OVER EXISTING RECORD" TO
557                   TEL-MESSAGE
558               PERFORM B-440-PRINT-ERROR.
```

identify key of record to be retrieved

actions to perform if desired record is not found

actions to perform if desired record is found

FIGURE 9-19 Random READ from the Indexed Premium File Update program for an add transaction

Figure 9-20 presents the random READs from the record change logic and record deletion logic. In these examples, the statements following INVALID KEY direct the logic to print error messages, while the logic following NOT INVALID KEY allows processing of the respective transactions to continue. As indicated earlier, a record can be changed or deleted only if it exists on the file.

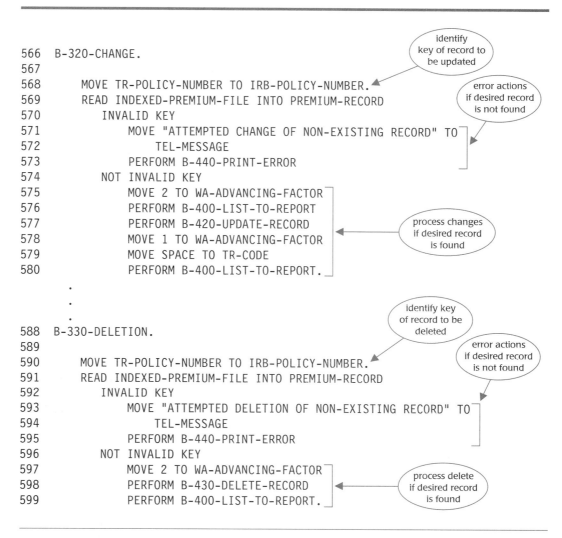

```
566   B-320-CHANGE.
567
568       MOVE TR-POLICY-NUMBER TO IRB-POLICY-NUMBER.
569       READ INDEXED-PREMIUM-FILE INTO PREMIUM-RECORD
570           INVALID KEY
571               MOVE "ATTEMPTED CHANGE OF NON-EXISTING RECORD" TO
572                   TEL-MESSAGE
573               PERFORM B-440-PRINT-ERROR
574           NOT INVALID KEY
575               MOVE 2 TO WA-ADVANCING-FACTOR
576               PERFORM B-400-LIST-TO-REPORT
577               PERFORM B-420-UPDATE-RECORD
578               MOVE 1 TO WA-ADVANCING-FACTOR
579               MOVE SPACE TO TR-CODE
580               PERFORM B-400-LIST-TO-REPORT.

           .
           .
           .
588   B-330-DELETION.
589
590       MOVE TR-POLICY-NUMBER TO IRB-POLICY-NUMBER.
591       READ INDEXED-PREMIUM-FILE INTO PREMIUM-RECORD
592           INVALID KEY
593               MOVE "ATTEMPTED DELETION OF NON-EXISTING RECORD" TO
594                   TEL-MESSAGE
595               PERFORM B-440-PRINT-ERROR
596           NOT INVALID KEY
597               MOVE 2 TO WA-ADVANCING-FACTOR
598               PERFORM B-430-DELETE-RECORD
599               PERFORM B-400-LIST-TO-REPORT.
```

Callout annotations: identify key of record to be updated; error actions if desired record is not found; process changes if desired record is found; identify key of record to be deleted; error actions if desired record is not found; process delete if desired record is found

FIGURE 9-20   Random READs and associated processing from the record change and record deletion logic

INDEXED FILE MAINTENANCE

Once it has been determined, through the use of a random READ, whether or not a specified record exists in the file, processing can continue. In the case of an add transaction, as long as the record does not exist in the INDEXED-PREMIUM-FILE, the record can be added to the file. The process involves building the record from the information supplied by the transaction and then executing a WRITE statement. Figure 9-21 on the next page illustrates the COBOL code used in the Indexed Premium File Update program to add a record to the file. The WRITE statement used works exactly like the WRITE statement presented for the Indexed Premium File Creation program. Because a random READ was used to ensure the record did not exist, the INVALID KEY clause on the WRITE should not execute. If it does, the program has a severe logic problem. When a record is added to an indexed file, all necessary adjustments to the primary key index and any alternate key indexes are automatically made.

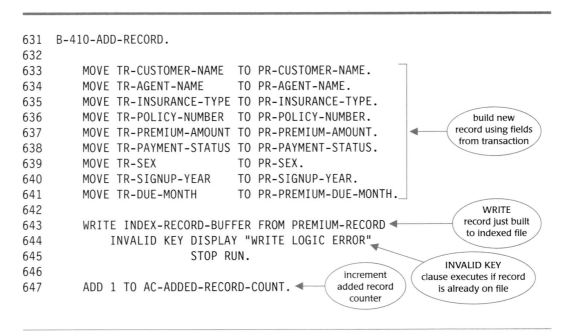

```
631  B-410-ADD-RECORD.
632
633      MOVE TR-CUSTOMER-NAME   TO PR-CUSTOMER-NAME.
634      MOVE TR-AGENT-NAME      TO PR-AGENT-NAME.
635      MOVE TR-INSURANCE-TYPE  TO PR-INSURANCE-TYPE.
636      MOVE TR-POLICY-NUMBER   TO PR-POLICY-NUMBER.
637      MOVE TR-PREMIUM-AMOUNT  TO PR-PREMIUM-AMOUNT.
638      MOVE TR-PAYMENT-STATUS  TO PR-PAYMENT-STATUS.
639      MOVE TR-SEX             TO PR-SEX.
640      MOVE TR-SIGNUP-YEAR     TO PR-SIGNUP-YEAR.
641      MOVE TR-DUE-MONTH       TO PR-PREMIUM-DUE-MONTH.
642
643      WRITE INDEX-RECORD-BUFFER FROM PREMIUM-RECORD
644          INVALID KEY DISPLAY "WRITE LOGIC ERROR"
645                      STOP RUN.
646
647      ADD 1 TO AC-ADDED-RECORD-COUNT.
```

build new
record using fields
from transaction

WRITE
record just built
to indexed file

INVALID KEY
clause executes if record
is already on file

increment
added record
counter

FIGURE 9-21 Logic from the Indexed Premium File Update program that adds a record to the file

Figure 9-22 presents the COBOL code used to update an existing record in the INDEXED-PREMIUM-FILE. Transaction fields are compared to the figurative constant SPACES. Transaction fields not equal to SPACES are used to replace corresponding PREMIUM-RECORD fields. Any field other than the primary key field can be modified. Records in the INDEXED-PREMIUM-FILE are then updated by execution of the REWRITE statement. REWRITE looks and performs very much like a WRITE statement; however, instead of adding a record to the file, **REWRITE** replaces an existing record with an updated version of that record. The record rewritten is the record whose key is in the record key field.

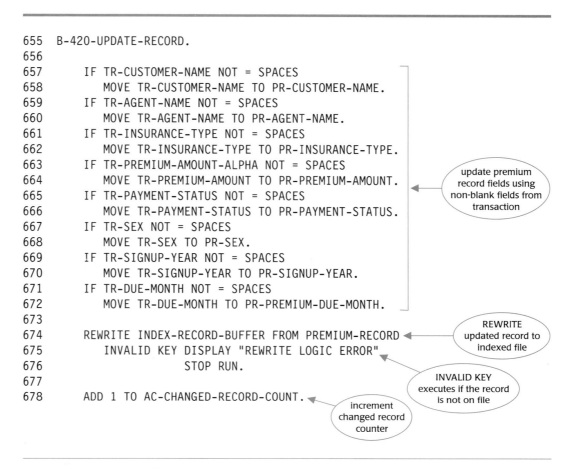

```
655  B-420-UPDATE-RECORD.
656
657      IF TR-CUSTOMER-NAME NOT = SPACES
658          MOVE TR-CUSTOMER-NAME TO PR-CUSTOMER-NAME.
659      IF TR-AGENT-NAME NOT = SPACES
660          MOVE TR-AGENT-NAME TO PR-AGENT-NAME.
661      IF TR-INSURANCE-TYPE NOT = SPACES
662          MOVE TR-INSURANCE-TYPE TO PR-INSURANCE-TYPE.
663      IF TR-PREMIUM-AMOUNT-ALPHA NOT = SPACES
664          MOVE TR-PREMIUM-AMOUNT TO PR-PREMIUM-AMOUNT.
665      IF TR-PAYMENT-STATUS NOT = SPACES
666          MOVE TR-PAYMENT-STATUS TO PR-PAYMENT-STATUS.
667      IF TR-SEX NOT = SPACES
668          MOVE TR-SEX TO PR-SEX.
669      IF TR-SIGNUP-YEAR NOT = SPACES
670          MOVE TR-SIGNUP-YEAR TO PR-SIGNUP-YEAR.
671      IF TR-DUE-MONTH NOT = SPACES
672          MOVE TR-DUE-MONTH TO PR-PREMIUM-DUE-MONTH.
673
674      REWRITE INDEX-RECORD-BUFFER FROM PREMIUM-RECORD
675          INVALID KEY DISPLAY "REWRITE LOGIC ERROR"
676                          STOP RUN.
677
678      ADD 1 TO AC-CHANGED-RECORD-COUNT.
```

update premium record fields using non-blank fields from transaction

REWRITE updated record to indexed file

INVALID KEY executes if the record is not on file

increment changed record counter

FIGURE 9-22 Logic from the Indexed Premium File Update program that changes a record on the file

Figure 9-23 presents the basic format of the REWRITE statement. The statement or statements following the INVALID KEY clause will execute if the record being rewritten does not exist on the file. Because a random READ was performed prior to the execution of the update logic in the Indexed Premium File Update program, the INVALID KEY clause on the REWRITE in Figure 9-22 should never execute. If it does, there is a severe logic problem. NOT INVALID KEY can be used on a REWRITE to perform desired actions when a record is successfully rewritten to a file. END-REWRITE is needed only when a REWRITE cannot be terminated using a period. When a record is updated in an indexed file, any alternate key indexes affected by changes to the record are automatically updated.

```
REWRITE  record-name-1    [ FROM record-name-2 ]

    [ INVALID KEY  statement-set-1 ]

    [ NOT INVALID KEY  statement-set-2 ]

[ END-REWRITE ]
```

FIGURE 9-23 Basic format of a REWRITE statement for an indexed file

Figure 9-24 presents the code used to delete a record from the INDEXED-PREMIUM-FILE. The **DELETE** statement deletes the record whose key is in the record key field.

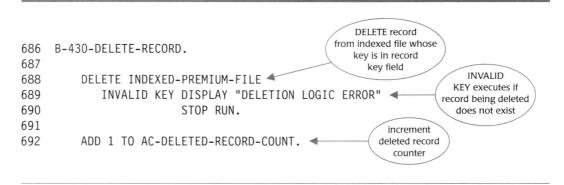

```
686   B-430-DELETE-RECORD.
687
688      DELETE INDEXED-PREMIUM-FILE
689         INVALID KEY DISPLAY "DELETION LOGIC ERROR"
690                    STOP RUN.
691
692      ADD 1 TO AC-DELETED-RECORD-COUNT.
```

DELETE record from indexed file whose key is in record key field

INVALID KEY executes if record being deleted does not exist

increment deleted record counter

FIGURE 9-24 Logic from the Indexed Premium File Update program that deletes a record from the file

Figure 9-25 presents the basic format of the DELETE statement. Notice that the name of the file must follow the word DELETE. The INVALID KEY clause executes only if the record being deleted does not exist on the indexed file. Because a random READ was performed prior to the DELETE to ensure that the desired record existed, the INVALID KEY clause on the DELETE in the sample program should not execute. The statement or statements following the NOT INVALID KEY clause will execute only if the DELETE is successful. END-DELETE is required only if the DELETE must be terminated and a period cannot be used. The primary key index and all alternate key indexes are automatically updated when a record is deleted from an indexed file.

```
DELETE   file-name-1    RECORD

   [ INVALID KEY statement-set-1 ]

   [ NOT INVALID KEY statement-set-2 ]

[ END-DELETE ]
```

FIGURE 9-25 Basic format of a DELETE statement for an indexed file

Alternate Keys and DYNAMIC Access

The retrieval and processing of records in the Indexed Premium File Update program is accomplished strictly through the use of the primary key, Policy Number. Often, it is desirable to retrieve and process records using one or more alternate keys. As indicated earlier in the chapter, an alternate key is a field within each record that can be used much like the primary key to randomly retrieve and process records. Also, unlike the primary key, an alternate key value can exist more than once on the file. Any number of fields within a record can be identified as alternate keys. When an indexed file is created, an index is created for the primary key and each designated alternate key. When the INDEXED-PREMIUM-FILE was created, it was created with an alternate key index for the field IRB-PREMIUM-DUE-MONTH (see Figure 9-12 on page 9-17). This index was created to allow records in the INDEXED-PREMIUM-FILE to be processed, when necessary, by Premium Due Month.

It is often necessary to report on, or process, only certain records in a file; perhaps those with a specific due month. As seen in Chapter 6, a sequential file requires that every record in the file be read and processed with conditional tests used in the program to filter out unwanted records. Such processing can be accomplished more efficiently in an indexed file by the use of the appropriate alternate key field.

Figure 9-26 presents the basic organization of the Premium Due Month alternate key index created for the INDEXED-PREMIUM-FILE. Because duplicates are explicitly allowed, each due month is listed in ascending sequence followed by a list of the primary key values of the records having that specific due month. The primary key values are in ascending sequence for each alternate key index value. Using this index, records can be processed in the file as though they are in sequence by due month. Assume that just those clients with a due month of 02 are to be processed. Using the alternate key index for due month, processing can begin with the first record in the file with a due month of 02 and continue down the list of primary keys in the alternate key index until end of file is reached, or a record with a different due month is encountered.

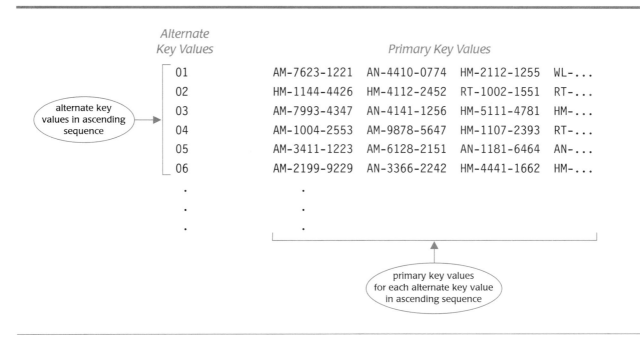

FIGURE 9-26 Partial view of the alternate key index for Premium Due Month in the INDEXED-PREMIUM-FILE

This processing can be accomplished in one of two ways. Both ways require that some sequential processing be done; therefore, ACCESS, as defined in the SELECT entry, cannot be RANDOM. The first method involves the use of a random READ to access the first record in the file with the desired alternate key value and then the use of a sequential READ to access each subsequent record. To perform both random and sequential processing in the same program, ACCESS IS DYNAMIC must be coded in the SELECT for the indexed file. **DYNAMIC access** allows for both random and sequential processing. Figure 9-27 on the next page presents the SELECT entry for the INDEXED-PREMIUM-FILE as it might appear to allow for both random and sequential processing.

```
SELECT INDEXED-PREMIUM-FILE
    ASSIGN TO "A:\PREMINDX.DAT"
    ORGANIZATION IS INDEXED
    ACCESS IS DYNAMIC
    RECORD KEY IS IRB-POLICY-NUMBER
    ALTERNATE RECORD KEY IS IRB-PREMIUM-DUE-MONTH
        WITH DUPLICATES.
```

allow for both random and sequential processing

FIGURE 9-27   SELECT for the INDEXED-PREMIUM-FILE allowing for DYNAMIC access

To perform a random READ using a key other than the primary key, the alternate key field must be explicitly indicated within the READ statement. Figure 9-18 on page 9-21 presented the basic format of a random READ. As discussed earlier in this chapter, the KEY IS phrase is used to randomly retrieve a record based on an alternate key value. Figure 9-28 presents a random READ as it might be coded to retrieve the first record in the INDEXED-PREMIUM-FILE with a due month of 02. As is necessary when using the primary key, a key value must be moved into the record key field prior to the execution of the READ. The INVALID KEY clause executes only if no record in the file has an alternate key value of 02.

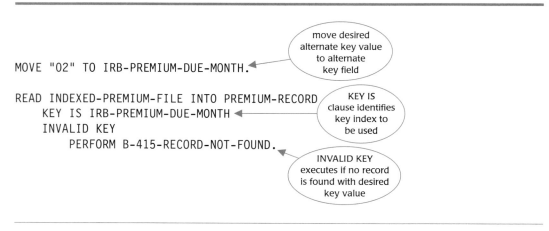

```
MOVE "02" TO IRB-PREMIUM-DUE-MONTH.

READ INDEXED-PREMIUM-FILE INTO PREMIUM-RECORD
    KEY IS IRB-PREMIUM-DUE-MONTH
    INVALID KEY
        PERFORM B-415-RECORD-NOT-FOUND.
```

move desired alternate key value to alternate key field

KEY IS clause identifies key index to be used

INVALID KEY executes if no record is found with desired key value

FIGURE 9-28   A random READ retrieving the first record in the INDEXED-PREMIUM-FILE with a Premium Due Month of 02

To retrieve the next record with a premium due month of 02, a sequential READ must be executed. A sequential READ must include the reserved word NEXT after the name of the file when ACCESS IS DYNAMIC is specified in the SELECT. Figure 9-29 presents a sequential READ as it might appear to retrieve the next available record with a due month of 02. If no additional records with a due month of 02 exist in the file, the first record having the next due month will be retrieved. For each sequential READ executed, processing continues within the alternate key index as long as key values remain for records in the file. The AT END clause executes on the sequential READ only when the end of the file is reached and no more primary key values are available. If only records with a due month of 02 are to be processed, care must be taken to terminate processing when either a record having a due month other than 02 is retrieved or the end of the file is reached.

```
READ INDEXED-PREMIUM-FILE NEXT INTO PREMIUM-RECORD
     AT END MOVE YES TO SW-END-OF-FILE.
```

NEXT
required on a
sequential READ
when ACCESS IS
DYNAMIC

AT END
executes only
when end of file
is reached

FIGURE 9-29   Sequential READ retrieving the next available record when ACCESS IS DYNAMIC is specified

START Statement

A second way of processing records, beginning with the first one having a specific primary key or alternate key value, involves using the START statement. The **START** statement allows for logical positioning within the primary key index or an alternate key index for the purpose of sequentially retrieving records. The START statement does not retrieve a record; it merely positions a logical pointer, often called the **current record pointer**, within an index at the first record that will be retrieved when a sequential READ is executed. The current record pointer is positioned automatically at the first record in a file when that file is opened for INPUT or I-O. The START statement then can be used to position the current record pointer at some record other than the first record in the file, or at the first record available for some alternate key value.

The START statement can be used when ACCESS is specified as either SEQUENTIAL or DYNAMIC. Figure 9-30 presents the basic format of the START statement. The KEY clause is required when accessing records using an alternate key or a partial primary key. A **partial primary key**, or **generic key**, allows for positioning of the current record pointer when just part of a key value is known and used. If the KEY clause is omitted, it is assumed that the primary key is to be used with the IS EQUAL TO condition. The statement or statements following the INVALID KEY clause will execute only if the current record pointer cannot be positioned at any record in the file. When present, the NOT INVALID KEY clause can be used to execute one or more statements after the current record pointer has been successfully positioned to a record. END-START is required only if a period cannot be used to terminate the START statement.

```
                      ┌                                        ┐
                      │         ⎧ EQUAL TO                 ⎫   │
                      │         ⎪ =                        ⎪   │
                      │         ⎪ GREATER THAN             ⎪   │
  START file-name     │ KEY IS  ⎨ >                        ⎬  key-field │
                      │         ⎪ NOT LESS THAN            ⎪   │
                      │         ⎪ NOT <                    ⎪   │
                      │         ⎪ GREATER THAN OR EQUAL TO ⎪   │
                      │         ⎩ >=                       ⎭   │
                      └                                        ┘

        [ INVALID KEY  statement-set-1 ]

        [ NOT INVALID KEY statement-set-2 ]

    [ END-START ]
```

FIGURE 9-30   Basic format of the START statement

Figure 9-31 presents a START statement that can be used to point at the first record in the INDEXED-PREMIUM-FILE that has a Premium Due Month of 02. Just like a random READ, a key value must be moved into the record key field prior to the execution of the statement. Because IRB-PREMIUM-DUE-MONTH is an alternate key field, the KEY = clause must be coded in the START statement. To retrieve the record being pointed to, a sequential READ must be executed. As indicated earlier in this chapter, if access is specified as DYNAMIC, the reserved word NEXT must be coded with the sequential READ. Each time a sequential READ is executed, the current record pointer will be repositioned and left pointing at the next available record until end of the file is reached. The current record pointer can be repositioned by the execution of a random READ, another START statement, or the closing and reopening of the file.

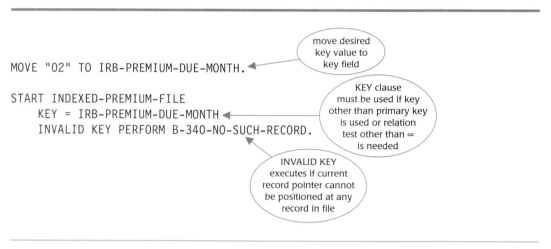

FIGURE 9-31 START statement for positioning the current record pointer at the first record in the INDEXED-PREMIUM-FILE with a due month of 02

RELATIVE FILES

Relative file organization, just as with indexed file organization, allows for both sequential and random processing of records. A **relative file**, however, does not use an index to identify a record's location. A relative file does not use a primary key field, nor does it allow for the use of alternate key fields. The easiest way to visualize the organization of a relative file is as a series of storage locations, each the same size and each being numbered (Figure 9-32). Each storage location, or slot, is either empty or contains a record.

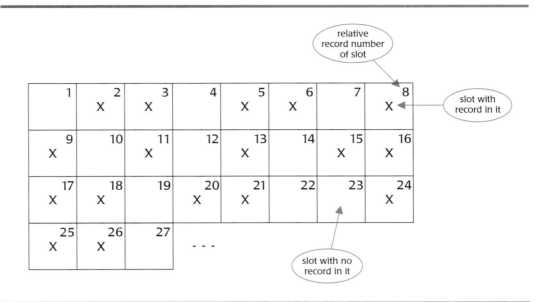

FIGURE 9-32   Organization of a relative file

The location of a record within a relative file is determined by the contents of a relative key field. A **relative key** identifies a records position within the file by using a **relative record number**. A relative record number of 1 identifies the first record in the file, a relative record number of 2 identifies the second record in the file, and so on. The relative key field cannot be contained within the record description entry associated with the FD of the relative file, and it must be an unsigned integer field. Relative key fields are usually defined in the WORKING-STORAGE SECTION of the DATA DIVISION.

The relative record number corresponds to the location of each slot. That is, the eleventh record is the one in slot number 11 and is accessed by a relative key value of 11. The chief advantage of relative file organization is that, because the relative record number instantly identifies the record desired, random retrieval of records occurs more quickly than it does in an indexed file. Among the disadvantages are the fact that records can be randomly retrieved only by their relative record number, and that many of the slots in a relative file are often empty, thus, wasting a lot of disk space on auxiliary storage. Empty slots are automatically skipped when sequential processing is performed.

Figure 9-33 on the next page presents a SELECT entry and FD as they might appear if the Premium file was organized as a relative file. The organization is explicitly indicated as being RELATIVE. ACCESS can be SEQUENTIAL, RANDOM, or DYNAMIC, just as with an indexed file. As indicated earlier, the relative key, WA-RECORD-NUMBER, must be defined in the DATA DIVISION as an unsigned integer having a picture such as PIC 99 or PIC 999. If access is RANDOM or DYNAMIC, a relative record number has to be placed into the relative key field before a record can be randomly retrieved from the file. If directly available, this value could be moved into the relative key field or, if not directly available, it could be computed. The FD for a relative file is the same as that used for sequential files. Figure 9-34 on the next page presents an example of a random read for the relative file identified in Figure 9-33.

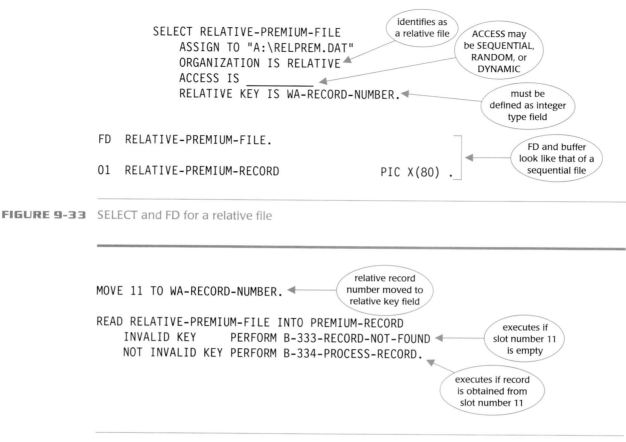

FIGURE 9-33 SELECT and FD for a relative file

FIGURE 9-34 Random READ to obtain the eleventh record in the RELATIVE-PREMIUM-FILE

CREATING AND MAINTAINING RELATIVE FILES

Relative file organization is most efficient when relative record numbers are consecutive and, therefore, leave no empty slots; however, this does not often happen. Usually, the relative record numbers for the records in the file are nonconsecutive, leaving empty storage locations within the file as shown in Figure 9-32 on the previous page. An actual field value can be used as a relative record number, but this is often impractical. Fields that contain data such as Social Security numbers, customer account numbers, and telephone numbers contain too many digits and would require relative files to have storage locations numbering in the billions with a great many empty slots left in the file. It is common for a relative record number to be computed based on the digits in data fields, such as those named above, using a special formula, or **algorithm**. The algorithm will convert the digits found in a data field into a relative record number of reasonable size. Such a conversion is called **hashing**.

Even the most sophisticated hashing algorithm will eventually result in duplicate relative record numbers for two or more records. Such records are called **synonyms**. The slot where a record is supposed to go is referred to as its **home slot**. Only one record can go into a storage location; therefore, when synonyms occur and a record cannot be placed in its home slot, logic must exist to put a record in the next available empty slot, closest to its home slot. Similar logic then must be used to retrieve a record stored somewhere other than its home slot. The development of hashing algorithms and the logic associated with the processing of synonyms goes beyond the scope of this book, but both topics are important when working with relative files.

The statements used to add, update, and delete records in a relative file are identical to those discussed earlier in conjunction with indexed files. Figures 9-35 through 9-38 (on this, and the next, page) present examples of WRITE, REWRITE, DELETE, and START statements that could be used in the processing of the RELATIVE-PREMIUM-FILE presented in earlier examples. The creation of a relative file would closely follow the logic illustrated by the Indexed Premium File Creation program also presented earlier in this chapter in Figure 9-5 on page 9-4. A relative key field would have to be defined and incremented as records are written to the file. Maintenance of a relative file can be accomplished using logic similar to that presented in the Indexed Premium File Update program discussed earlier. Relative files, although not as widely used as indexed files, provide computer professionals with some flexibility in the creation of randomly processed files. Depending on the processing environment and the needs of the organization, relative files can prove to be useful in many situations.

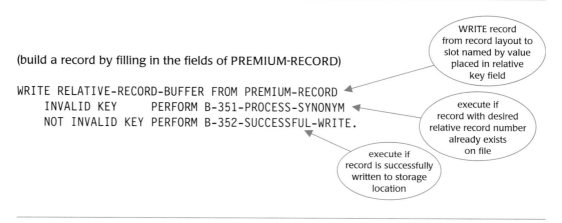

FIGURE 9-35   WRITE statement for a relative file

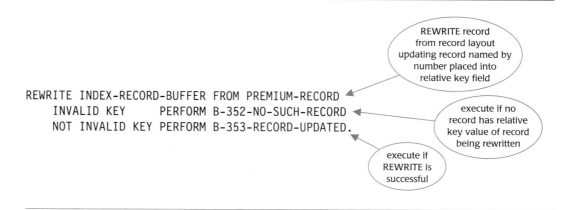

FIGURE 9-36   REWRITE statement for a relative file

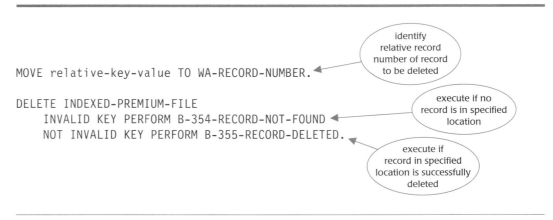

FIGURE 9-37 DELETE statement for a relative file

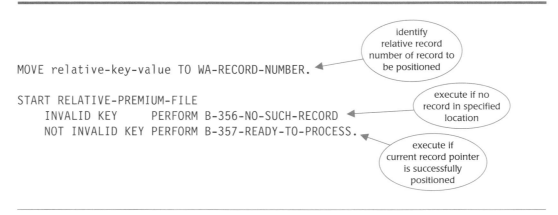

FIGURE 9-38 START statement for a relative file

CHAPTER SUMMARY

The following list summarizes this chapter. The summary is designed to help you study and understand the material and concepts presented.

1. **Indexed files** can be processed both sequentially and randomly.

2. **Random processing** or **random access** refers to the capability to retrieve and/or update a record without having to retrieve or process the records that precede it in the file.

3. An indexed file must be created and stored on a **direct access storage device**, or **DASD**.

4. An **index** contains the values of the key field and the disk address where each record is located.

5. A **key field**, or **primary key**, is a field common to each record and contains a unique value for each record.

6. An **alternate key** field provides a means of accessing records using a field other than the primary key.

7. Indexed files can be created by reading in records from a sequential file and then writing those same records out to an indexed file.

8. Access must be sequential when creating an indexed file.

9. The RECORD KEY IS clause in a SELECT entry identifies the name of the primary key field that must be defined within the record definition after the FD.

10. A **WRITE** statement is used to place records in an indexed file.

11. A **random READ** uses the index associated with an indexed file to locate a specified record in the file.

12. Random processing is allowed only when ACCESS is specified as RANDOM or DYNAMIC.

13. Records in an indexed file can be updated by execution of a **REWRITE** statement.

14. The **DELETE** statement deletes the record whose key is in the record key field.

15. **DYNAMIC access** allows for both random and sequential processing of an indexed file.

16. A sequential READ must include the reserved word NEXT after the name of the file when ACCESS IS DYNAMIC is specified in the SELECT.

17. The **START** statement allows for logical positioning of the current record pointer within the primary key index or an alternate key index for sequential retrieval of records.

18. **Relative file organization** allows for both sequential and random processing of records, but a **relative file** does not use an index to identify a record's location.

19. A **relative key** identifies a record's position within the file by using a **relative record number**.

20. Through a process called **hashing**, it is common for a relative record number to be computed based on the digits in a data field using a special formula, or **algorithm**.

21. Even the most sophisticated hashing algorithm will eventually result in records with duplicate relative record numbers called **synonyms**.

22. The storage location, or slot, where a record is suppose to go is referred to as its **home slot**.

23. The statements used to add, update, and delete records in a relative file are identical to those used in conjunction with indexed files.

KEY TERMS

algorithm (9-32)
alternate key (9-15)
current record pointer (9-29)
DASD (direct access storage device) (9-15)
DELETE (9-26)
direct access storage device (DASD) (9-15)
DYNAMIC access (9-27)
generic key (9-29)
hashing (9-32)
home slot (9-32)
index (9-15)
indexed file (9-15)
INVALID KEY (9-18)

key field (9-15)
partial primary key (9-29)
primary key (9-15)
random access (9-15)
random processing (9-15)
random READ (9-21)
relative file (9-30)
relative file organization (9-30)
relative key (9-31)
relative record number (9-31)
REWRITE (9-24)
START (9-29)
synonyms (9-32)

STUDENT ASSIGNMENTS

Student Assignment 1: True/False

Instructions: Circle T if the statement is true or F if the statement is false.

T   F   1. No two records can have the same primary key value in an indexed file.

T   F   2. No two records can ever have the same alternate key value in an indexed file.

T   F   3. DYNAMIC access allows for both random and sequential processing of records.

T   F   4. WRITE is used to add a record to an indexed file, while REWRITE is used to add a record to a relative file.

T   F   5. For an indexed file, the DELETE statement deletes the record whose key value is in the primary key field.

T   F   6. A random READ for an indexed file retrieves the record whose key value is in a specified key field.

T   F   7. The START statement can be used to position the current record pointer so records can be retrieved sequentially.

T   F   8. For a random READ, statements in the INVALID KEY clause will execute if the desired record is successfully retrieved.

T   F   9. For a REWRITE, statements in the INVALID KEY clause will execute if the record being processed already exists on the file.

T   F   10. Only one alternate key field is allowed for an indexed file.

T   F   11. Indexed and relative files must be stored on a DASD.

T   F   12. The START statement cannot be used in conjunction with an alternate key field.

T   F   13. The reserved word NEXT must be used in a sequential READ statement when access is DYNAMIC.

T   F   14. A relative file contains no index component.

T   F   15. Two records may share the same storage location, or slot, in a relative file.

T   F   16. In a relative file, two records with the same home slot are called synonyms.

T   F   17. For a relative file, the INVALID KEY clause on a WRITE statement will execute if the desired slot already contains a record.

T   F   18. Hashing is a term used to describe the process of calculating a relative record number.

T   F   19. A START statement cannot be used for a relative file.

T   F   20. It is common to have empty slots in a relative file.

Student Assignment 2: Multiple Choice

Instructions: Circle the correct response.

1. For an indexed file, the statements in an INVALID KEY clause on a WRITE statement will execute when _____.
   a. the primary key value already exists on the file
   b. the primary key value does not exist on the file
   c. the primary key value is greater than 1,000
   d. the home slot for the record is empty
   e. none of the above

2. For an indexed file, NOT INVALID KEY for a DELETE statement is _____.
   a. required and executes if the record does not exist
   b. required and executes if the record is deleted
   c. optional and executes if the record does not exist
   d. optional and executes if the record is deleted
   e. none of the above

3. For an indexed file, random processing can occur _____.
   a. only when ACCESS IS DYNAMIC
   b. when ACCESS IS RANDOM or DYNAMIC
   c. only when ACCESS IS RANDOM
   d. when ACCESS IS RANDOM or SEQUENTIAL
   e. none of the above

4. The primary key field for an indexed file must be defined _____.
   a. somewhere in the WORKING-STORAGE SECTION
   b. as the first field in the record under the FD
   c. as an elementary integer field in the record under the FD
   d. with the proper size and location in the record under the FD
   e. none of the above

5. END-WRITE is required on a WRITE statement when _____.
   a. the INVALID KEY clause is used
   b. the NOT INVALID KEY clause is used
   c. a period cannot be used
   d. the record being processed already exists
   e. none of the above

6. In an indexed file, no two records can have the same _____.
   a. alternate key value
   b. primary key value
   c. record format
   d. relative record number
   e. none of the above

7. The records in a relative file _____.
   a. can have the same alternate key values
   b. cannot be processed sequentially
   c. all must be the same size
   d. cannot be processed randomly
   e. none of the above

(continued)

Student Assignment 2 (continued)

8. The relative key field must be _____.
   a. defined somewhere in the WORKING-STORAGE SECTION
   b. defined as the first field in the record under the FD
   c. defined with the proper size and location in the record under the FD
   d. an alphanumeric field defined in DATA DIVISION
   e. none of the above

9. An algorithm is a formula for calculating a relative record number and is often referred to as _____.
   a. file matching
   b. hand wrenching
   c. hashing
   d. differentiation
   e. none of the above

10. Two records in a relative file with the same relative record number are called _____.
   a. twin records
   b. synonyms
   c. INVALID KEY records
   d. home slots
   e. none of the above

Student Assignment 3: Coding a Random READ for an Indexed File

Instructions: Code the necessary COBOL instructions to execute a random READ that will access a record with a primary key value of TR-14 from the indexed file INDEXED-INVENTORY-FILE. Read the record into a layout called INVENTORY-RECORD. If the record is found, perform the procedure B-210-PROCESS-RECORD. If the record is not found, perform the procedure B-220-NO-SUCH-RECORD. The primary key field for INDEXED-INVENTORY-FILE is IR-ITEM-CODE.

Student Assignment 4: Coding for an Indexed File

Instructions: Code a SELECT entry, FD entry, and record description entry for the file INDEXED-INVENTORY-FILE. The system name for the file is INVINDX.DAT. Allow for both sequential and random processing of records. The key field is IR-ITEM-CODE and is a five-character field that starts in the third position of each record. Each record is 90-characters long.

Student Assignment 5: Coding a DELETE Statement

Instructions: Code all necessary COBOL instructions to delete record TS-52 from the INDEXED-INVENTORY-FILE presented in Student Assignment 4. If the deletion is not successful, perform the procedure B-220-NO-SUCH-RECORD.

Student Assignment 6: Coding for a Relative File

Instructions: Code a SELECT entry, FD entry, record description entry, and relative key definition for the file RELATIVE-INVENTORY-FILE. The system name for the file is INVREL.DAT. Allow for just the random processing of records. The relative key field is WA-ITEM-NUMBER and represents a five-digit field. Each record is 90-characters long.

Student Assignment 7: Coding for a Random READ for a Relative File

Instructions: Code all necessary COBOL instruction to retrieve record number 24 from the RELATIVE-INVENTORY-FILE presented in Student Assignment 6. Read the record into the layout INVENTORY-RECORD. If the record is not found, perform the procedure B-220-NO-SUCH-RECORD. If the record is found, perform the procedure B-210-PROCESS-RECORD.

COBOL LABORATORY EXERCISES

Exercise 1: Modified Indexed Premium File Update Program

Purpose: To gain experience in indexed file maintenance programs and to become more familiar with indexed file processing.

Problem: Open the program file PROJ9A.CBL on the Student Diskette that accompanies this book, and create the INDEXED-PREMIUM-FILE that is output by the program. Then open the program file PROJ9B.CBL and modify the Indexed Premium File Update program presented in this chapter making the following changes:

1. Sort the transaction file in descending sequence by transaction code so all delete transactions are processed first, then change transactions, and finally add transactions.

2. Remove the random READ in the add transaction routine from the program and base the processing of error add transactions on the unsuccessful execution of the WRITE statement.

3. For all records processed, rearrange the agent name so it prints on the report first name first but remains last name first on the INDEXED-PREMIUM-FILE.

Save this program as EX9-1.CBL.

Input Data: Use a sorted version of the Premium file presented in Appendix A as input to the program PROJ9A.CBL to create the INDEXED-PREMIUM-FILE. This version is in the file named SPREMIUM.DAT on the Student Diskette that accompanies this book. For the file maintenance program, use the Indexed File Maintenance Transaction file listed in Appendix A as input. This file is named IDXTRANS.DAT on the Student Diskette that accompanies this book.

Output Results: Output should be a report similar to the Transaction List Report presented in Figure 9-6 on page 9-6 with the delete transactions appearing first, add transactions appearing last, and agent names printing first name first.

Exercise 2: Sequential Processing of the Indexed Premium File

Purpose: To gain experience in building and accessing an indexed file and to become more familiar with use of the START statement.

Problem: Open the program file PROJ9A.CBL on the Student Diskette that accompanies this book and create the INDEXED-PREMIUM-FILE that is output by the program. Write a second COBOL program that reports on just those customers whose policy number starts with HM. Use a START statement to position the current record pointer at the first such record in the file, and then process sequentially until the last such record has been reported on. Save this program as EX9-2.CBL.

Input Data: Use a sorted version of the Premium file presented in Appendix A as input to the program PROJ9A.CBL to create the INDEXED-PREMIUM-FILE. This version is in the file named SPREMIUM.DAT on the Student Diskette that accompanies this book. Use the indexed file as input to the second program.

(continued)

Exercise 2 (continued)

Output Results: Output from the second program should consist of a Premium Amount Report that lists a customer's policy number, name, insurance type, premium amount, and payment status. The report headings should include the current date and time. The time should be printed in AM/PM format. The report should be similar to the following:

```
Z9/99/99              AINSWORTH INSURANCE COMPANY            PAGE   1
Z9:99AM                  PREMIUM AMOUNT REPORT

                               INSURANCE    PREMIUM    PAYMENT
POLICY NUMBER    CUSTOMER NAME    TYPE       AMOUNT     STATUS
-------------    -------------  ----------  ---------  -------

HM-XXXX-XXXX     XXXXXXXXXXXXXXXXXXX  XXXXXXXXXX  ZZ,ZZ9.99    X

HM-XXXX-XXXX     XXXXXXXXXXXXXXXXXXX  XXXXXXXXXX  ZZ,ZZ9.99    X
    .
    .
    .
HM-XXXX-XXXX     XXXXXXXXXXXXXXXXXXX  XXXXXXXXXX  ZZ,ZZ9.99    X

             TOTAL RECORDS PRINTED =   ZZ9

             END OF REPORT
```

Exercise 3: Indexed Customer Purchase File Creation and Update

Purpose: To practice the creation of an indexed file and to gain experience in using the statements needed for processing an indexed file. Write a program that uses a sequential input file to create an indexed file. Write a second program to update the indexed file using a transaction file that contains add, change, and delete transactions.

Problem: Write a program that reads in records from a sequential Customer Purchase file and writes them out to an indexed version of the same file. Output a message and record count upon completion of the program. Save this program as EX9-3A.CBL. Write a second program that uses a customer transaction file as input to update the indexed Customer Sales file that was output in the first program. Sort the transaction file in ascending sequence by the transaction code found in the first character of each transaction before updating the indexed file.

   Use add transactions to add new records to the Indexed Customer Purchase file. Use change transactions to update existing records. Change only those fields on a customer record that correspond to non-blank fields on the change transactions. Use delete transactions to identify and delete records on the Indexed Customer Purchase file. List processed records and transactions on a File Maintenance Report file. List transactions that cannot be processed unformatted with an appropriate error message. Provide a count of all add, change, delete, and error transactions at the end of the report. Save this program as EX9-3B.CBL.

Input Data: Use the Customer Purchase file listed in Appendix A as input to the first program. This file is named CUSTOMER.DAT on the Student Diskette that accompanies this book. Customer purchase records are already in sequence by the primary key field, Account Number, and have the following layout:

Field Description	Position	Length	Attribute
Date of Purchase	1–6	6	Numeric, PIC 9(6)
Account Number	7–12	6	Alphanumeric
Customer Name	13–32	20	Alphanumeric
Item Purchased	33–52	20	Alphanumeric
Quantity Purchased	53	1	Numeric, PIC 9
Balance	54–59	6	Numeric, PIC S9(4)V99
Purchase Amount	60–65	6	Numeric, PIC 9(4)V99
filler	66–70	5	Alphanumeric
Sales Clerk ID	71–72	2	Alphanumeric
Record Length		72	

Use the Customer Purchase Transaction file listed in Appendix A as input to the second program for updating the Indexed Customer Purchase file. This file is named CITRANS.DAT on the Student Diskette that accompanies this book. Transaction records must be sorted by the code found in the first character as indicated above.

Field Description	Position	Length	Attribute
Transaction Type	1	1	Alphanumeric, A = Add C = Change D = Delete
Date of Purchase	2–7	6	Alphanumeric Redefine as Numeric, PIC 9(6)
Account Number	8–13	6	Alphanumeric
Customer Name	14–33	20	Alphanumeric
Item Purchased	34–53	20	Alphanumeric
Quantity Purchased	54	1	Alphanumeric Redefine as Numeric, PIC 9
Balance	55–60	6	Alphanumeric Redefine as Numeric, PIC S9(4)V99
Purchase Amount	61–66	6	Alphanumeric Redefine as Numeric, PIC 9(4)V99
Sales Clerk ID	67–69	3	Alphanumeric
Record Length		69	

Output Results: Output consists of an updated Indexed Customer Purchase file and a File Maintenance Report listing all added, changed, and deleted records. Changed records should be listed both as they appeared before the change and as they appear after the change. Also list all unprocessed transactions along with an appropriate error message. Provide a count of all records added, changed, and deleted, as well as a count of all bad transactions.

(continued)

Exercise 3 (continued)

The File Maintenance Report should have a format similar to the following:

```
DATE: Z9/99/99                     ABC DEPARTMENT STORE                      PAGE Z9
TIME: Z9:99 AM             CUSTOMER PURCHASES FILE MAINTENANCE REPORT

TRAN  DATE OF   ACCOUNT                                                    PURCHASE
TYPE  PURCHASE  NUMBER   CUSTOMER NAME        ITEM PURCHASED      BALANCE   AMOUNT
----  --------  -------  --------------------  --------------------  --------  --------

 A    Z9/99/99  XXXXXX   XXXXXXXXXXXXXXXXXXXX XXXXXXXXXXXXXXXXXXXX  Z,ZZZ.99- Z,ZZZ.99

 A    Z9/99/99  XXXXXX   XXXXXXXXXXXXXXXXXXXX XXXXXXXXXXXXXXXXXXXX  Z,ZZZ.99- Z,ZZZ.99
       .
       .
       .
XXXXXXXXXXXXXXXXXXXXXXXXXXXXXXXXXXXXXXXXXXXXXXXXXXXXXXXXXXXX  BAD TRAN MESSAGE

 C    Z9/99/99  XXXXXX   XXXXXXXXXXXXXXXXXXXX XXXXXXXXXXXXXXXXXXXX  Z,ZZZ.99- Z,ZZZ.99
      Z9/99/99  XXXXXX   XXXXXXXXXXXXXXXXXXXX XXXXXXXXXXXXXXXXXXXX  Z,ZZZ.99- Z,ZZZ.99

 C    Z9/99/99  XXXXXX   XXXXXXXXXXXXXXXXXXXX XXXXXXXXXXXXXXXXXXXX  Z,ZZZ.99- Z,ZZZ.99
      Z9/99/99  XXXXXX   XXXXXXXXXXXXXXXXXXXX XXXXXXXXXXXXXXXXXXXX  Z,ZZZ.99- Z,ZZZ.99
       .
       .
       .
 D    Z9/99/99  XXXXXX   XXXXXXXXXXXXXXXXXXXX XXXXXXXXXXXXXXXXXXXX  Z,ZZZ.99- Z,ZZZ.99

 D    Z9/99/99  XXXXXX   XXXXXXXXXXXXXXXXXXXX XXXXXXXXXXXXXXXXXXXX  Z,ZZZ.99- Z,ZZZ.99
       .
       .
       .
                 TOTAL RECORDS ADDED     =  ZZ9
                 TOTAL RECORDS CHANGED   =  ZZ9
                 TOTAL RECORDS DELETED   =  ZZ9
                 TOTAL BAD TRANSACTIONS  =  ZZ9

                            END OF REPORT
```

Exercise 4: Customer Sales Update Program

Purpose: To practice coding a COBOL program that creates an indexed file and a COBOL program that uses a transaction file to update an indexed file.

Problem: Design and code a COBOL program that creates an Indexed Customer Sales file from a sequential version of the same file. Save this program as EX9-4A.CBL. Design and code a second program that adds, updates, and deletes records of the Indexed Customer Sales file and, in the process, generates a Customer Sales File Maintenance Report. Use a transaction file that contains add, change, and delete transactions as input in the second program. Add transactions should be used to add new records to the file. Change transactions should be used to update existing records on the file. Use non-blank fields on the transaction to update corresponding fields on the data record. Delete transactions should be used to delete records from the file.

Bad transactions should be written to a separate Error Transaction Report. Print the entire error transaction, unformatted, with an appropriate error message. Before beginning file maintenance procedures, sort transaction records in ascending sequence by the transaction code that is located in the first by of each transaction. Save this program as EX9-4B.CBL.

Input Data: Use the Customer Sales file listed in Appendix A as input to the first program. This file is named CUSTSALE.DAT on the Student Diskette that accompanies this book. Records on the Customer Sales file are already in sequence by the primary key, Customer Number. The record layout for the customer records is as follows:

Field Description	Position	Length	Attribute
Customer Zip Code	1–5	5	Alphanumeric
Customer Zip + 4	6–9	4	Alphanumeric
Customer Number	10–13	4	Alphanumeric
Customer Name	14–33	20	Alphanumeric
Purchase Date	34–39	6	Numeric, PIC 9(6)
Auto Make	40–59	20	Alphanumeric
Purchase Price	60–66	7	Numeric, PIC 9(5)V99
Year of Auto	67–70	4	Alphanumeric
filler	71–73	3	Alphanumeric
Satisfaction Code	74	1	Alphanumeric, 0 = DISSATISFIED 1 = UNDECIDED 2 = SATISFIED
Record Length		74	

Use the Customer Sales Transaction file listed in Appendix A as input to the SORT, creating a sorted transaction file to be used as input to the file maintenance logic. This file is named AITRANS.DAT on the Student Diskette that accompanies this book.

The record layout for the Customer Sales file transaction records is as follows:

Field Description	Position	Length	Attribute
Transaction Code	1	1	Alphanumeric, A = Add C = Change D = Delete
Zip Code	2–6	5	Alphanumeric
Customer Number	7–10	4	Alphanumeric
Customer Name	11–30	20	Alphanumeric
Purchase Date	31–36	6	Alphanumeric Redefine as Numeric, PIC 9(6)
Auto Make	37–56	20	Alphanumeric
Purchase Price	57–63	7	Alphanumeric Redefine as Numeric, PIC 9(5)V99
Year of Auto	64–67	4	Alphanumeric
Satisfaction Code	68	1	Alphanumeric
Record Length		68	

Output Results: A Customer Sales File Maintenance Report should be output listing every processed record. List records processed by change transactions twice: once as they were before any changes and once as they appear after changes.

(continued)

Exercise 4 (continued)

The Customer Sales File Maintenance Report should have a format similar to the following:

```
DATE: Z9/99/99                      EZ AUTO SALES                          PAGE Z9
TIME: Z9:99 AM           CUSTOMER SALES FILE MAINTENANCE REPORT

     CUST.  CUSTOMER               ZIP    PURCHASE                  PURCHASE   SATIS.
 TR  NUMBER NAME                   CODE   DATE      AUTO MAKE       PRICE      RATING
 --  ------ --------------------   -----  --------  ---------       --------   -------

 A   XXXX   XXXXXXXXXXXXXXXXXX     XXXXX  Z9/99/99  XXXXXXXXXXXXXX  ZZ,ZZZ.99    X

 A   XXXX   XXXXXXXXXXXXXXXXXX     XXXXX  Z9/99/99  XXXXXXXXXXXXXX  ZZ,ZZZ.99    X
        .
        .
        .
 C   XXXX   XXXXXXXXXXXXXXXXXX     XXXXX  Z9/99/99  XXXXXXXXXXXXXX  ZZ,ZZZ.99    X
     XXXX   XXXXXXXXXXXXXXXXXX     XXXXX  Z9/99/99  XXXXXXXXXXXXXX  ZZ,ZZZ.99    X

 C   XXXX   XXXXXXXXXXXXXXXXXX     XXXXX  Z9/99/99  XXXXXXXXXXXXXX  ZZ,ZZZ.99    X
     XXXX   XXXXXXXXXXXXXXXXXX     XXXXX  Z9/99/99  XXXXXXXXXXXXXX  ZZ,ZZZ.99    X
        .
        .
        .
 D   XXXX   XXXXXXXXXXXXXXXXXX     XXXXX  Z9/99/99  XXXXXXXXXXXXXX  ZZ,ZZZ.99    X

                TOTAL RECORDS ADDED     =  ZZ9
                TOTAL RECORDS CHANGED   =  ZZ9
                TOTAL RECORDS DELETED   =  ZZ9
                      END OF REPORT
```

Bad transactions, ones that cannot be processed, should be written to the Error Transaction Report. Use the following mockup as a guide:

```
DATE: Z9/99/99                      EZ AUTO SALES                          PAGE Z9
TIME: Z9:99 AM                  ERROR TRANSACTION REPORT

TRANSACTION RECORD                                            ERROR MESSAGE
-----------------------------------------------------------   -------------------------

XXXXXXXXXXXXXXXXXXXXXXXXXXXXXXXXXXXXXXXXXXXXXXXXXXXXXXXXXXXX   APPROPRIATE ERROR MESSAGE

XXXXXXXXXXXXXXXXXXXXXXXXXXXXXXXXXXXXXXXXXXXXXXXXXXXXXXXXXXXX   APPROPRIATE ERROR MESSAGE

XXXXXXXXXXXXXXXXXXXXXXXXXXXXXXXXXXXXXXXXXXXXXXXXXXXXXXXXXXXX   APPROPRIATE ERROR MESSAGE
        .
        .
        .
              TOTAL NUMBER OF ERROR TRANSACTIONS = ZZ9

                      END OF REPORT
```

Exercise 5: Relative Customer Sales File Processing

Purpose: To practice coding a COBOL program that creates a relative file and a COBOL program that uses a transaction file to update a relative file.

Problem: Design and code a COBOL program that creates a relative Customer Sales file from a sequential version of the same file. Save this program as EX9-5A.CBL. Design and code a second program that adds, updates, and deletes records of the relative Customer Sales file and, in the process, generates a Customer Sales File Maintenance Report. Use a transaction file that contains add, change, and delete transactions as input in the second program. Add transactions should be used to add new records to the file. Change transactions should be used to update existing records on the file. Use non-blank fields on the transaction to update corresponding fields on the data record. Delete transactions should be used to delete records from the file.

Bad transactions should be written to a separate Error Transaction Report. Print the entire error transaction, unformatted, with an appropriate error message. Before beginning file maintenance procedures, sort transaction records in ascending sequence by the transaction code that is located in the first character of each transaction. Save this program as EX9-5B.CBL.

Input Data: Use the Customer Sales file listed in Appendix A as input to the first program. This file is named CUSTSALE.DAT on the Student Diskette that accompanies this book. Records on the Customer Sales file are in sequence by customer number. Develop an algorithm that divides the Customer Number by 2 and adds 1 to compute a three-digit relative record number for each record. The record layout for the customer records is as follows:

Field Description	Position	Length	Attribute
Customer Zip Code	1–5	5	Alphanumeric
Customer Zip + 4	6–9	4	Alphanumeric
Customer Number	10–13	4	Alphanumeric
Customer Name	14–33	20	Alphanumeric
Purchase Date	34–39	6	Numeric, PIC 9(6)
Auto Make	40–59	20	Alphanumeric
Purchase Price	60–66	7	Numeric, PIC 9(5)V99
Year of Auto	67–70	4	Alphanumeric
filler	71–73	3	Alphanumeric
Satisfaction Code	74	1	Alphanumeric, 0 = DISSATISFIED 1 = UNDECIDED 2 = SATISFIED
Record Length		74	

Use the Customer Sales Transaction file listed in Appendix A as input to the SORT, creating a sorted transaction file to be used as input to the file maintenance logic. This file is named AITRANS.DAT on the Student Diskette that accompanies this book.

The record layout for the Customer Sales file transaction records is as follows:

Field Description	Position	Length	Attribute
Transaction Code	1	1	Alphanumeric, A = Add C = Change D = Delete
Zip Code	2–6	5	Alphanumeric
Customer Number	7–10	4	Alphanumeric
Customer Name	11–30	20	Alphanumeric
Purchase Date	31–36	6	Alphanumeric Redefine as Numeric, PIC 9(6)
Auto Make	37–56	20	Alphanumeric
Purchase Price	57–63	7	Alphanumeric Redefine as Numeric, PIC 9(5)V99
Year of Auto	64–67	4	Alphanumeric
Satisfaction Code	68	1	Alphanumeric
Record Length		68	

(continued)

Exercise 5 (continued)

Output Results: A Customer Sales File Maintenance Report should be output listing every processed record. List records processed by change transactions twice: once as they were before any changes and once as they appear after changes.

The Customer Sales File Maintenance Report should have a format similar to the following:

```
DATE: Z9/99/99                      EZ AUTO SALES                         PAGE Z9
TIME: Z9:99 AM            CUSTOMER SALES FILE MAINTENANCE REPORT

     CUST.   CUSTOMER              ZIP    PURCHASE                PURCHASE   SATIS.
TR   NUMBER  NAME                  CODE   DATE      AUTO MAKE     PRICE      RATING
--   ------  --------------------  -----  --------  ---------     --------   -------

A    XXXX    XXXXXXXXXXXXXXXXXXXX   XXXXX  Z9/99/99  XXXXXXXXXXXXXX ZZ,ZZZ.99     X

A    XXXX    XXXXXXXXXXXXXXXXXXXX   XXXXX  Z9/99/99  XXXXXXXXXXXXXX ZZ,ZZZ.99     X
     .
     .
     .
C    XXXX    XXXXXXXXXXXXXXXXXXXX   XXXXX  Z9/99/99  XXXXXXXXXXXXXX ZZ,ZZZ.99     X
     XXXX    XXXXXXXXXXXXXXXXXXXX   XXXXX  Z9/99/99  XXXXXXXXXXXXXX ZZ,ZZZ.99     X

C    XXXX    XXXXXXXXXXXXXXXXXXXX   XXXXX  Z9/99/99  XXXXXXXXXXXXXX ZZ,ZZZ.99     X
     XXXX    XXXXXXXXXXXXXXXXXXXX   XXXXX  Z9/99/99  XXXXXXXXXXXXXX ZZ,ZZZ.99     X
     .
     .
     .
D    XXXX    XXXXXXXXXXXXXXXXXXXX   XXXXX  Z9/99/99  XXXXXXXXXXXXXX ZZ,ZZZ.99     X

                  TOTAL RECORDS ADDED    =  ZZ9
                  TOTAL RECORDS CHANGED  =  ZZ9
                  TOTAL RECORDS DELETED  =  ZZ9
                        END OF REPORT
```

Bad transactions, ones that cannot be processed, should be written to the Error Transaction Report. Use the following mockup as a guide:

```
DATE: Z9/99/99                      EZ AUTO SALES                         PAGE Z9
TIME: Z9:99 AM                  ERROR TRANSACTION REPORT

TRANSACTION RECORD                                          ERROR MESSAGE
-----------------------------------------------------------  -------------------------

XXXXXXXXXXXXXXXXXXXXXXXXXXXXXXXXXXXXXXXXXXXXXXXXXXXXXXXXXXXXX  APPROPRIATE ERROR MESSAGE

XXXXXXXXXXXXXXXXXXXXXXXXXXXXXXXXXXXXXXXXXXXXXXXXXXXXXXXXXXXXX  APPROPRIATE ERROR MESSAGE

XXXXXXXXXXXXXXXXXXXXXXXXXXXXXXXXXXXXXXXXXXXXXXXXXXXXXXXXXXXXX  APPROPRIATE ERROR MESSAGE
     .
     .
     .
                TOTAL NUMBER OF ERROR TRANSACTIONS = ZZ9

                            END OF REPORT
```

CHAPTER TEN

The Report Writer Feature and Declaratives

OBJECTIVES

You will have mastered the material in Chapter 10 when you can:

- Understand the function of the Report Writer feature
- Code an RD entry in a REPORT SECTION
- Name the types of report groups available
- Explain the use of a control field
- Name the options available for defining report group entries
- Identify the options available for line spacing
- Understand the use of the SOURCE option on an output field
- Understand the use of the SUM option on an entry
- Identify and code INITIATE, GENERATE, and TERMINATE statements
- Name the uses of declarative sections

INTRODUCTION

The COBOL **Report Writer feature** provides an alternative method for producing report programs. The Report Writer feature allows for the characteristics of a report to be defined through the use of special entries in the DATA DIVISION and for the creation of a report by the use of just a few statements in the PROCEDURE DIVISION. The sample program presented in this chapter uses the Report Writer feature to produce the Agent Subtotal Report created by conventional means in Chapter 7.

A special COBOL component called a declarative section is utilized in the sample program. A declarative section, or declarative, can be coded to handle special processing outside the normal flow of logic in a program or to capture errors that can occur during processing.

The Agent Subtotal Report

A partial listing of the report created by the sample program, the Agent Subtotal Report, is presented in Figure 10-1 where the various types of output lines are noted. The positioning and use of these output lines is very important to the Report Writer feature.

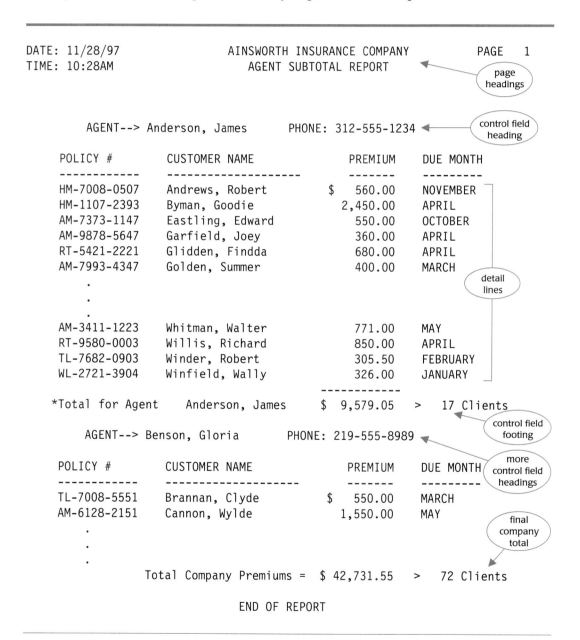

```
DATE: 11/28/97              AINSWORTH INSURANCE COMPANY           PAGE   1
TIME: 10:28AM                  AGENT SUBTOTAL REPORT                          page
                                                                           headings

          AGENT--> Anderson, James      PHONE: 312-555-1234             control field
                                                                           heading

       POLICY #        CUSTOMER NAME              PREMIUM    DUE MONTH
       -----------     --------------------       -------    ---------
       HM-7008-0507    Andrews, Robert         $    560.00   NOVEMBER
       HM-1107-2393    Byman, Goodie              2,450.00   APRIL
       AM-7373-1147    Eastling, Edward             550.00   OCTOBER
       AM-9878-5647    Garfield, Joey               360.00   APRIL
       RT-5421-2221    Glidden, Findda              680.00   APRIL
       AM-7993-4347    Golden, Summer               400.00   MARCH
          .                                                                  detail
          .                                                                  lines
          .
       AM-3411-1223    Whitman, Walter              771.00   MAY
       RT-9580-0003    Willis, Richard              850.00   APRIL
       TL-7682-0903    Winder, Robert               305.50   FEBRUARY
       WL-2721-3904    Winfield, Wally              326.00   JANUARY
                                               -----------
      *Total for Agent     Anderson, James   $  9,579.05   >   17 Clients
                                                                           control field
             AGENT--> Benson, Gloria     PHONE: 219-555-8989                footing

                                                                              more
       POLICY #        CUSTOMER NAME              PREMIUM    DUE MONTH    control field
       -----------     --------------------       -------    ---------      headings
       TL-7008-5551    Brannan, Clyde          $    550.00   MARCH
       AM-6128-2151    Cannon, Wylde              1,550.00   MAY
          .                                                                   final
          .                                                                  company
          .                                                                   total

           Total Company Premiums =  $ 42,731.55   >   72 Clients

                         END OF REPORT
```

FIGURE 10-1 Partial listing of the Agent Subtotal Report

Hierarchy Chart

Figure 10-2 presents a hierarchy chart showing the organization of the PROCEDURE DIVISION for the sample program. Compare this hierarchy chart to the one shown in Figure 7-2 on page 7-3 for the Agent Subtotal Report program. Even with the addition of declaratives, which is a special COBOL component not used in Chapter 7, the PROCEDURE DIVISION of the sample program in this chapter is much easier to write because of the Report Writer feature.

In the hierarchy chart, the declarative section is represented by the box labeled X-100-GET-AGENT-PHONE. Standard COBOL supports three different uses for declaratives. These uses will be discussed, and the declarative example presented in conjunction with the Report Writer feature will be examined.

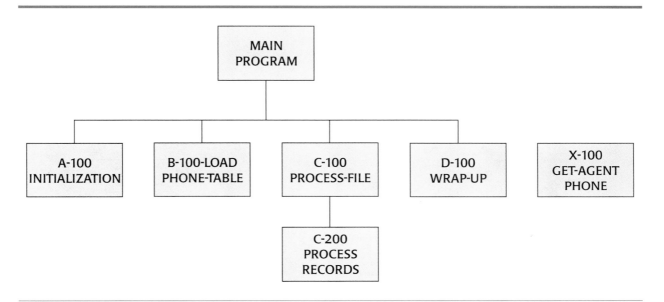

FIGURE 10-2   Hierarchy chart illustrating the organization of the PROCEDURE DIVISION of the Report Writer version of the Agent Subtotal Report program

Program Flowchart

Figure 10-3 on the next page presents a flowchart illustrating the logic used in C-100-PROCESS-FILE and C-200-PROCESS-RECORDS of the sample program. Compare this logic to that illustrated by Figure 7-3 on page 7-4 in Chapter 7. Report Writer's built-in logic eliminates the need for much of the programmer's own logic development. For example, processing logic for page overflow and the detection of control breaks is handled automatically by Report Writer.

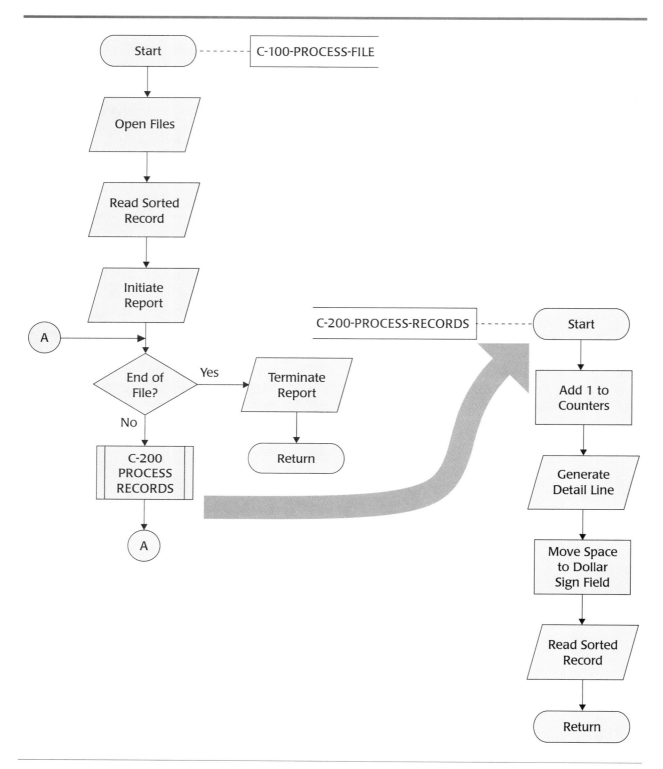

FIGURE 10-3 Flowchart showing the logic used in C-100-PROCESS-FILE and C-200-PROCESS-RECORDS in the sample Report Writer program

Report Writer Version of the Agent Subtotal Report Program

Figure 10-4 presents the sample program discussed in this chapter. This program is found on the Student Diskette that accompanies this book. The Agent Subtotal Report is created by a program that utilizes the Report Writer feature. The sample program uses the same input files used in Chapter 7 and produces the same output. This program will be used to discuss the basic elements necessary for utilization of the Report Writer feature.

```
  1  IDENTIFICATION DIVISION.
  2  ***********************
  3
  4  PROGRAM-ID.     AGENTRW.
  5  AUTHOR.         R. O. FOREMAN.
  6  INSTALLATION.   PURDUE UNIVERSITY CALUMET.
  7  DATE-WRITTEN.   NOV. 28, 1997.
  8  DATE-COMPILED.  28-Nov-1997.
  9  ****************************************************************
 10  *                    PROGRAM NARRATIVE                        *
 11  *                                                             *
 12  *                                                             *
 13  *    THIS PROGRAM PRINTS THE ACCOUNT NUMBER, CUSTOMER NAME, AND *
 14  *    PREMIUM AMOUNT FOR EACH CUSTOMER IN SEQUENCE BY AGENT NAME. *
 15  *    A TOTAL PREMIUM AMOUNT IS PRINTED FOR EACH AGENT ALONG    *
 16  *    WITH A TOTAL COMPANY PREMIUM AMOUNT AT THE END OF THE     *
 17  *    REPORT.  THE REPORT IS CREATED USING THE REPORT WRITER    *
 18  *    FEATURE OF COBOL.                                         *
 19  *                                                             *
 20  *       INPUT:     PREMIUM.DAT  - PREMIUM INPUT FILE           *
 21  *                  AGENTPHO.DAT - AGENT PHONE FILE             *
 22  *                                                             *
 23  *       OUTPUT:    AGENTRW.RPT - AGENT SUBTOTAL REPORT         *
 24  ****************************************************************
 25
 26  ENVIRONMENT DIVISION.
 27  ********************
 28
 29  INPUT-OUTPUT SECTION.
 30  ********************
 31
 32  FILE-CONTROL.
 33
 34      SELECT PREMIUM-INPUT-FILE
 35          ASSIGN TO "A:\PREMIUM.DAT".
 36
 37      SELECT SORT-FILE
 38          ASSIGN TO "SORTWORK".
 39
 40      SELECT SORTED-PREMIUM-FILE
 41          ASSIGN TO "SORTPREM.DAT".
 42
 43      SELECT AGENT-PHONE-FILE
 44          ASSIGN TO "A:\AGENTPHO.DAT".
 45
 46      SELECT AGENT-SUBTOTAL-REPORT
 47          ASSIGN TO "A:\AGENTRW.RPT".
 48
 49  /
 50  DATA DIVISION.
 51  **************
 52
 53  FILE SECTION.
 54  ************
 55
 56  ****************************************************************
 57  *                                                             *
 58  *    INPUT-FILE - PREMIUM INPUT FILE MUST BE SORTED;          *
 59  *    THE RECORD LAYOUT, PREMIUM-RECORD, IS IN WORKING-STORAGE *
 60  *                                                             *
 61  ****************************************************************
 62
 63  FD  PREMIUM-INPUT-FILE.
```

```
 64
 65  01  PREMIUM-INPUT-RECORD          PIC X(80).
 66
 67
 68  ****************************************************************
 69  *                                                             *
 70  *    SORT-FILE - USED TO SORT THE PREMIUM FILE BY AGENT NAME  *
 71  *                                                             *
 72  ****************************************************************
 73
 74  SD  SORT-FILE.
 75
 76  01  SORT-RECORD.
 77      02                           PIC X(20).
 78      02  SR-AGENT-NAME            PIC X(20).
 79      02                           PIC X(40).
 80
 81  ****************************************************************
 82  *                                                             *
 83  *    SORTED INPUT FILE - SORTED VERSION OF THE PREMIUM FILE;  *
 84  *    SORTED BY AGENT NAME                                     *
 85  *                                                             *
 86  ****************************************************************
 87
 88  FD  SORTED-PREMIUM-FILE.
 89
 90  01  SORTED-PREMIUM-RECORD         PIC X(80).
 91
 92  /
 93  ****************************************************************
 94  *                                                             *
 95  *    AGENT PHONE NUMBER FILE FOR LOADING NON-EMBEDDED TABLE   *
 96  *                                                             *
 97  ****************************************************************
 98
 99  FD  AGENT-PHONE-FILE.
100
101  01  AGENT-PHONE-RECORD.
102      02  APR-NAME                 PIC X(20).
103      02  APR-NUMBER               PIC X(12).
104
105  ****************************************************************
106  *                                                             *
107  *    REPORT-FILE - AGENT SUBTOTAL REPORT; USING REPORT WRITER *
108  *                                                             *
109  ****************************************************************
110
111  FD  AGENT-SUBTOTAL-REPORT
112      REPORT IS AGENT-SUBTOTAL.
113  /
114  WORKING-STORAGE SECTION.
115  ***********************
116
117  ****************************************************************
118  *                                                             *
119  *                    SWITCHES                                 *
120  *                                                             *
121  ****************************************************************
122
123  01  SWITCHES.
124
125      02  SW-END-OF-FILE           PIC X.
126          88  END-OF-FILE                  VALUE "Y".
```

FIGURE 10-4 COBOL program using the Report Writer feature   *(continued)*

```
127
128  01  VALUES-FOR-SWITCHES.
129      02  YES                     PIC X       VALUE "Y".
130      02  NEG                     PIC X       VALUE "N".
131
132  ************************************************************
133  *                                                        *
134  *                    ACCUMULATORS                        *
135  *                                                        *
136  ************************************************************
137
138  01  ACCUMULATORS.
139
140      02  AC-RECORD-COUNT         PIC 9(5)    PACKED-DECIMAL.
141      02  AC-AGENT-RECORD-COUNT   PIC 9(5)    PACKED-DECIMAL.
142  /
143  ************************************************************
144  *                                                        *
145  *                  WORK AREA FIELDS                      *
146  *                                                        *
147  ************************************************************
148
149  01  WORK-AREA.
150
151      02  WA-SYSTEM-DATE.
152          03  WA-SYSTEM-YEAR      PIC 99.
153          03  WA-SYSTEM-MONTH     PIC 99.
154          03  WA-SYSTEM-DAY       PIC 99.
155
156      02  WA-CURRENT-DATE.
157          03  WA-CURRENT-MONTH    PIC 99.
158          03  WA-CURRENT-DAY      PIC 99.
159          03  WA-CURRENT-YEAR     PIC 99.
160
161      02  WA-CURRENT-DATE-N REDEFINES
162              WA-CURRENT-DATE     PIC 9(6).
163
164      02  WA-SYSTEM-TIME.
165          03  WA-SYSTEM-HOUR      PIC 99.
166          03  WA-SYSTEM-MINUTES   PIC 99.
167          03                      PIC X(4).
168
169      02  WA-AMPM                 PIC XX.
170      02  WA-AGENT-PHONE          PIC X(12).
171      02  WA-DOLLAR-SIGN          PIC X.
172  /
173  ************************************************************
174  *                                                        *
175  *              EMBEDDED MONTH NAME TABLE                 *
176  *                                                        *
177  ************************************************************
178
179  01  MONTH-NAME-DATA.
180      02                      PIC X(9) VALUE "JANUARY".
181      02                      PIC X(9) VALUE "FEBRUARY".
182      02                      PIC X(9) VALUE "MARCH".
183      02                      PIC X(9) VALUE "APRIL".
184      02                      PIC X(9) VALUE "MAY".
185      02                      PIC X(9) VALUE "JUNE".
186      02                      PIC X(9) VALUE "JULY".
187      02                      PIC X(9) VALUE "AUGUST".
188      02                      PIC X(9) VALUE "SEPTEMBER".
189      02                      PIC X(9) VALUE "OCTOBER".
190      02                      PIC X(9) VALUE "NOVEMBER".
191      02                      PIC X(9) VALUE "DECEMBER".
192
193  01  MONTH-NAME-TABLE REDEFINES MONTH-NAME-DATA.
194      02  MNT-ENTRY               OCCURS 12 TIMES.
195          03  MNT-NAME            PIC X(9).
196
197  ************************************************************
198  *                                                        *
199  *          NON-EMBEDDED AGENT PHONE NUMBER TABLE         *
200  *                                                        *
201  ************************************************************
202
```

```
203  01  AGENT-PHONE-TABLE.
204      02  APT-ENTRY               OCCURS 6 TIMES
205                                  INDEXED BY PHONE-INDEX.
206          03  APT-NAME                        PIC X(20).
207          03  APT-NUMBER                      PIC X(12).
208  /
209  COPY "A:\INSREC.CBL".
210L ************************************************************
211L *                                                        *
212L *          PREMIUM INPUT FILE RECORD LAYOUT              *
213L *                                                        *
214L ************************************************************
215L
216L 01  PREMIUM-RECORD.
217L     02  PR-CUSTOMER-NAME        PIC X(20).
218L     02  PR-AGENT-NAME           PIC X(20).
219L     02  PR-INSURANCE-TYPE       PIC X(10).
220L         88  VALID-TYPE          VALUE "Automobile"
221L                                       "Annuity"
222L                                       "Home"
223L                                       "Renter"
224L                                       "Term Life"
225L                                       "Whole Life".
226L
227L     02  PR-POLICY-NUMBER        PIC X(12).
228L     02  PR-PREMIUM-AMOUNT       PIC S9(5)V99.
229L
230L     02  PR-PAYMENT-STATUS       PIC X.
231L         88  DELINQUENT          VALUE "D".
232L         88  PAID-IN-FULL        VALUE "F".
233L         88  PARTIALLY-PAID      VALUE "P".
234L         88  NOT-YET-BILLED      VALUE "N".
235L
236L     02  PR-SEX                  PIC X.
237L     02  PR-SIGNUP-YEAR          PIC X(4).
238L     02  PR-PREMIUM-DUE-MONTH    PIC 99.
239L     02                          PIC XXX.
240  /
241  REPORT SECTION.
242  ***************
243
244  ************************************************************
245  *                                                        *
246  *   REPORT WRITER RD AND REPORT GROUPS FOLLOW            *
247  *                                                        *
248  ************************************************************
249  RD  AGENT-SUBTOTAL
250      CONTROLS ARE FINAL
251              PR-AGENT-NAME
252
253      PAGE LIMIT      62
254          HEADING     1
255          FIRST DETAIL  7
256          LAST DETAIL  58
257          FOOTING     60.
258
259  ************************************************************
260  *                                                        *
261  *   PAGE HEADING REPORT GROUP FOR THE AGENT SUBTOTAL REPORT  *
262  *                                                        *
263  ************************************************************
264
265  01  TYPE PAGE HEADING.
266
267      02  LINE 1.
268          03          COLUMN 1  PIC X(6)  VALUE "DATE: ".
269          03          COLUMN 7  PIC Z9/99/99 SOURCE
270                                     WA-CURRENT-DATE-N.
271          03          COLUMN 31 PIC X(27) VALUE
272              "AINSWORTH INSURANCE COMPANY".
273          03          COLUMN 73 PIC X(5)  VALUE "PAGE ".
274          03          COLUMN 78 PIC ZZ9   SOURCE PAGE-COUNTER.
275
276      02  LINE 2.
277          03          COLUMN 1  PIC X(6)  VALUE "TIME: ".
278          03          COLUMN 7  PIC Z9 SOURCE WA-SYSTEM-HOUR.
```

FIGURE 10-4 COBOL program using the Report Writer feature (continued)

```
279        03             COLUMN 9    PIC X   VALUE ":".
280        03             COLUMN 10   PIC 99  SOURCE WA-SYSTEM-MINUTES.
281        03             COLUMN 12   PIC XX  SOURCE WA-AMPM.
282        03             COLUMN 34   PIC X(21) VALUE
283                                     "AGENT SUBTOTAL REPORT".
284 /
285 ***************************************************************
286 *                                                             *
287 *    AGENT HEADING REPORT GROUP FOR THE AGENT SUBTOTAL REPORT *
288 *                                                             *
289 ***************************************************************
290
291 01  AGENT-HEADING TYPE CONTROL HEADING PR-AGENT-NAME.
292     02  LINE PLUS 2.
293        03             COLUMN 10   PIC X(9)  VALUE "AGENT--> ".
294        03             COLUMN 19   PIC X(20) SOURCE PR-AGENT-NAME.
295        03             COLUMN 40   PIC X(7)  VALUE "PHONE:".
296        03             COLUMN 47   PIC X(12) SOURCE WA-AGENT-PHONE.
297
298     02  LINE PLUS 2.
299        03             COLUMN 6    PIC X(8)  VALUE "POLICY #".
300        03             COLUMN 22   PIC X(13) VALUE "CUSTOMER NAME".
301        03             COLUMN 49   PIC X(7)  VALUE "PREMIUM".
302        03             COLUMN 60   PIC X(9)  VALUE "DUE MONTH".
303
304     02  LINE PLUS 1.
305        03             COLUMN 6    PIC X(12) VALUE ALL "-".
306        03             COLUMN 22   PIC X(20) VALUE ALL "-".
307        03             COLUMN 49   PIC X(7)  VALUE ALL "-".
308        03             COLUMN 60   PIC X(9)  VALUE ALL "-".
309
310 ***************************************************************
311 *                                                             *
312 *       DETAIL GROUP FOR THE AGENT SUBTOTAL REPORT            *
313 *                                                             *
314 ***************************************************************
315
316 01  DETAIL-LINE TYPE DETAIL.
317
318     02  LINE PLUS 1.
319        03             COLUMN 6    PIC X(12) SOURCE
320                                     PR-POLICY-NUMBER.
321        03             COLUMN 22   PIC X(20) SOURCE
322                                     PR-CUSTOMER-NAME.
323        03             COLUMN 46   PIC X     SOURCE
324                                     WA-DOLLAR-SIGN.
325        03             COLUMN 47   PIC ZZ,ZZ9.99 SOURCE
326                                     PR-PREMIUM-AMOUNT.
327        03             COLUMN 60   PIC X(9)  SOURCE
328                                     MNT-NAME(PR-PREMIUM-DUE-MONTH).
329 /
330 ***************************************************************
331 *                                                             *
332 *     SUMMARY REPORT GROUPS FOR AGENT SUBTOTAL REPORT         *
333 *                                                             *
334 ***************************************************************
335
336 01  TYPE CONTROL FOOTING PR-AGENT-NAME.
337
338     02  LINE PLUS 1.
339        03             COLUMN 45   PIC X(12) VALUE ALL "-".
340
341     02  LINE PLUS 1.
342        03             COLUMN 5    PIC X(18) VALUE
343                                     "*Total for Agent".
344        03             COLUMN 25   PIC X(20) SOURCE PR-AGENT-NAME.
345        03             COLUMN 45   PIC $ZZZ,ZZ9.99 SUM
346                                     PR-PREMIUM-AMOUNT.
347        03             COLUMN 58   PIC XX   VALUE  " >".
348        03             COLUMN 60   PIC ZZZZ9 SOURCE
349                                     AC-AGENT-RECORD-COUNT.
350        03             COLUMN 65   PIC X(8)  VALUE " Clients".
351
352 01  TYPE CONTROL FOOTING FINAL.
353
354     02  LINE PLUS 2.
355        03             COLUMN 19   PIC X(25) VALUE
356                                     "Total Company Premiums = ".
357        03             COLUMN 45   PIC $ZZZ,ZZ9.99 SUM
358                                     PR-PREMIUM-AMOUNT.
359        03             COLUMN 58   PIC XX   VALUE  " >".
360        03             COLUMN 60   PIC ZZZZ9 SOURCE
361                                     AC-RECORD-COUNT.
362        03             COLUMN 65   PIC X(8)  VALUE " Clients".
363
364     02  LINE PLUS 3.
365        03             COLUMN 33   PIC X(13) VALUE
366                                     "END OF REPORT".
367 /
368  PROCEDURE DIVISION.
369  ******************
370 ***************************************************************
371 *                                                             *
372 *      AGENT PHONE NUMBER RETRIEVAL FOR AGENT HEADINGS        *
373 *                                                             *
374 ***************************************************************
375  DECLARATIVES.
376
377  X-100-GET-AGENT-PHONE SECTION.
378      USE BEFORE REPORTING AGENT-HEADING.
379  X-100-AGENT-PHONE.
380
381      SET PHONE-INDEX TO 1.
382      SEARCH APT-ENTRY
383          AT END
384              MOVE "NOT FOUND" TO WA-AGENT-PHONE
385          WHEN PR-AGENT-NAME = APT-NAME (PHONE-INDEX)
386              MOVE APT-NUMBER (PHONE-INDEX) TO WA-AGENT-PHONE.
387
388      MOVE "$" TO WA-DOLLAR-SIGN.
389      MOVE ZERO TO AC-AGENT-RECORD-COUNT.
390
391  END DECLARATIVES.
392
393 ***************************************************************
394 *                                                             *
395 *  MAIN-PROGRAM - THIS IS THE MAIN ROUTINE OF THE AGENT SUBTOTAL *
396 *                 REPORT PROGRAM                              *
397 *                                                             *
398 ***************************************************************
399  MAIN SECTION.
400  MAIN-PROGRAM.
401
402      PERFORM A-100-INITIALIZATION.
403      PERFORM B-100-LOAD-PHONE-TABLE.
404      PERFORM C-100-PROCESS-FILE.
405      PERFORM D-100-WRAP-UP.
406      STOP RUN.
407 /
408 ***************************************************************
409 *                                                             *
410 *          THE INITIALIZATION ROUTINE FOLLOWS                 *
411 *                                                             *
412 ***************************************************************
413
414  A-100-INITIALIZATION.
415
416      INITIALIZE ACCUMULATORS.
417
418      ACCEPT WA-SYSTEM-DATE FROM DATE.
419      MOVE WA-SYSTEM-YEAR    TO WA-CURRENT-YEAR.
420      MOVE WA-SYSTEM-MONTH   TO WA-CURRENT-MONTH.
421      MOVE WA-SYSTEM-DAY     TO WA-CURRENT-DAY.
422
423      ACCEPT WA-SYSTEM-TIME FROM TIME.
424      EVALUATE TRUE
425          WHEN WA-SYSTEM-HOUR = 00
426              MOVE "AM" TO WA-AMPM
427              MOVE 12 TO WA-SYSTEM-HOUR
428          WHEN WA-SYSTEM-HOUR < 12
429              MOVE "AM" TO WA-AMPM
```

(continued)

```
430        WHEN WA-SYSTEM-HOUR = 12
431            MOVE "PM" TO WA-AMPM
432        WHEN WA-SYSTEM-HOUR > 12
433            MOVE "PM" TO WA-AMPM
434            SUBTRACT 12 FROM WA-SYSTEM-HOUR.
435
436    SORT SORT-FILE
437        ON ASCENDING KEY SR-AGENT-NAME
438        USING PREMIUM-INPUT-FILE
439        GIVING SORTED-PREMIUM-FILE.
440 /
441 **********************************************************************
442 *                                                              *
443 *            LOAD PHONE TABLE FROM EXTERNAL FILE               *
444 *                                                              *
445 **********************************************************************
446
447  B-100-LOAD-PHONE-TABLE.
448
449        OPEN INPUT AGENT-PHONE-FILE.
450
451        READ AGENT-PHONE-FILE
452            AT END MOVE YES TO SW-END-OF-FILE.
453
454        PERFORM VARYING PHONE-INDEX FROM 1 BY 1
455                UNTIL END-OF-FILE OR PHONE-INDEX > 6
456
457            MOVE APR-NAME TO APT-NAME (PHONE-INDEX)
458            MOVE APR-NUMBER TO APT-NUMBER (PHONE-INDEX)
459            READ AGENT-PHONE-FILE
460                AT END MOVE YES TO SW-END-OF-FILE
461            END-READ
462        END-PERFORM.
463
464        CLOSE AGENT-PHONE-FILE.
465 /
466 **********************************************************************
467 *                                                              *
468 *              REPORT PROCESSING ROUTINE                       *
469 *                                                              *
470 **********************************************************************
471
472  C-100-PROCESS-FILE.
473
474        MOVE NEG TO SW-END-OF-FILE.
475        OPEN  INPUT    SORTED-PREMIUM-FILE
476              OUTPUT   AGENT-SUBTOTAL-REPORT.
477
478        INITIATE AGENT-SUBTOTAL
479
480        READ SORTED-PREMIUM-FILE INTO PREMIUM-RECORD
481            AT END MOVE YES TO SW-END-OF-FILE.
482
483        PERFORM C-200-PROCESS-RECORDS
484            UNTIL END-OF-FILE.
485
486        TERMINATE AGENT-SUBTOTAL.
487 /
488 **********************************************************************
489 *                                                              *
490 *  PREMIUM RECORD PROCESSING ROUTINE FOR AGENT SUBTOTAL REPORT  *
491 *                                                              *
492 **********************************************************************
493
494  C-200-PROCESS-RECORDS.
495
496        ADD 1 TO AC-AGENT-RECORD-COUNT
497                AC-RECORD-COUNT.
498        GENERATE DETAIL-LINE.
499        MOVE SPACE TO WA-DOLLAR-SIGN.
500
501        READ SORTED-PREMIUM-FILE INTO PREMIUM-RECORD
502            AT END MOVE YES TO SW-END-OF-FILE.
503
504 **********************************************************************
505 *                                                              *
506 *                  END OF JOB ROUTINE                          *
507 *                                                              *
508 **********************************************************************
509
510  D-100-WRAP-UP.
511
512        CLOSE  SORTED-PREMIUM-FILE
513               AGENT-SUBTOTAL-REPORT.
514
515        DISPLAY "THE AGENT SUBTOTAL REPORT PROGRAM HAS TERMINATED".
516 /
```

FIGURE 10-4 COBOL program using the Report Writer feature (continued)

REPORT WRITER FEATURE

To create a report using the Report Writer feature, file and record layout specifications defining what is to be listed on the report must be coded. As with all report files, a SELECT entry must appear in the INPUT-OUTPUT SECTION of the ENVIRONMENT DIVISION and an FD must be coded in the FILE SECTION of the DATA DIVISION. It is in the FD where the first indication appears that the Report Writer feature is to be used (Figure 10-5). A REPORT IS clause or REPORTS ARE clause must be coded as part of the FD. The **REPORT IS** clause is used on line 111 in the sample program to define the name of the specific report to be created by Report Writer. It is possible to produce multiple reports in a Report Writer program, and each report must be identified by a unique name. No record definition is coded following the FD. The WORKING-STORAGE SECTION of the DATA DIVISION contains the same entries used in previous programs except there are no output record definitions.

```
26   ENVIRONMENT DIVISION.
29   INPUT-OUTPUT SECTION.
32   FILE-CONTROL.
         .
         .
         .
46      SELECT AGENT-SUBTOTAL-REPORT          ◄──    SELECT
47          ASSIGN TO "A:\AGENTRW.RPT".                entry
         .
         .
         .
50   DATA DIVISION.
53   FILE SECTION.
         .
         .                                    REPORT IS
         .                                defines report name
110  FD  AGENT-SUBTOTAL-REPORT                 to be used
111      REPORT IS AGENT-SUBTOTAL.  ◄
                                                no record
                                             definition follows
                                                   FD
```

FIGURE 10-5   SELECT and FD for the report file in the sample program

When the Report Writer feature is used, output record definitions must be coded as part of a REPORT SECTION in the DATA DIVISION.

The REPORT SECTION

The **REPORT SECTION** is used to define the characteristics of each page in a report and to define the format of each output line in a report. Each report to be produced begins with a Report Definition, or **RD** entry. Figure 10-6 on the next page presents the basic format of an RD entry, and Figure 10-7 on the next page presents the RD from the sample program. The report name following RD must be the same as the name specified in the REPORT IS clause in the FD for the report file. The optional entry **CONTROL IS** or **CONTROLS ARE** can be used to identify the field or fields that determine at what point control breaks occur. These fields must be listed from most major to most minor. With Report Writer, a control break occurs automatically when the contents of a control field change. As you will recall, in Chapter 7, the logic to detect this change had to be coded into the program. This logic is already built into Report Writer and the programmer only has to identify the control fields. The reserved word **FINAL** is used to indicate the highest level of control and must appear first when it is used. In the sample program, the control fields are FINAL and PR-AGENT-NAME. When the agent name changes, a control break occurs, and when end of file is reached, a control break occurs.

```
RD   report-name

      [{ CONTROL IS  }   {{field-name-1} ...        }]
      [{ CONTROLS ARE }  { FINAL [field-name-1] ... }]


  [PAGE [LIMIT IS  ] integer-1 [LINE ]]
  [     [LIMITS ARE]           [LINES]]

           [ HEADING integer-2 ]
           [ FIRST DETAIL integer-3 ]
           [ LAST DETAIL integer-4 ]
           [ FOOTING integer-5 ]
```

FIGURE 10-6   Basic format of an RD entry

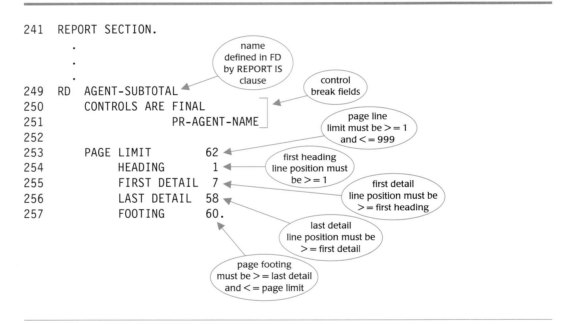

```
241   REPORT SECTION.
      .
      .
      .
249   RD   AGENT-SUBTOTAL
250        CONTROLS ARE FINAL
251                 PR-AGENT-NAME
252
253        PAGE LIMIT      62
254             HEADING     1
255             FIRST DETAIL  7
256             LAST DETAIL  58
257             FOOTING      60.
```

FIGURE 10-7   RD from the sample program

The entries in the **PAGE** clause are used to define the basic format of a page in the report. The **LIMIT IS** or **LIMITS ARE** entry defines the number of lines on each page of the report. In Figure 10-6, integer-1 must be greater than or equal to one and cannot exceed 999. The **HEADING** entry defines the first line on a page where a heading line can print. This value, integer-2 in Figure 10-6, must be greater than or equal to one. **FIRST DETAIL** indicates the line position of the first detail line to be printed on a page. No detail line can print prior to the indicated position, but in some circumstances, can print after the indicated position. This value, integer-3 in Figure 10-6, must be greater than or equal to the value of HEADING integer-2. **LAST DETAIL** specifies that no detail line can print on a page beyond the indicated line number. This value, integer-4 in Figure 10-6, must be greater than or equal to the value of FIRST DETAIL integer-3. **FOOTING** specifies the line number of a page footing, if used. A page footing is used to print a line of output, often with a page number, at the bottom of each page of a report. The value of integer-5 in Figure 10-6, must be greater than or equal to LAST DETAIL integer-4, but must be less than or equal to the LIMIT IS value defined earlier. A period must follow the last entry made in an RD. Once the basic format of a page is established, the individual lines of output can be defined. This definition is accomplished in the REPORT SECTION by the use of entries called report groups.

Report Groups

A **report group** defines one or more related output lines for the report. Table 10-1 summarizes the seven different types of report groups available in Report Writer. The type of group being defined must be explicitly stated at the beginning of each report group. A two-letter abbreviation can be used or the report group type can be spelled out.

TABLE 10-1 Types of Report Groups Available in Report Writer

Type	Function
REPORT HEADING **RH**	Prints once at the beginning of the report
PAGE HEADING **PH**	Prints at the top of each page
CONTROL HEADING **CH**	Prints at the beginning of each new control field group, usually to identify the group
DETAIL **DE**	Prints once for each detail record processed
CONTROL FOOTING **CF**	Prints at the end of a control field group, usually to print summary information
PAGE FOOTING **PF**	Prints at the bottom of each page
REPORT FOOTING **RF**	Prints once at the end of the report

Within each report group, line spacing and the column position of individual fields must be defined. Many different options are available for defining report groups and the fields within report groups. This book concentrates on those options utilized in the sample program. The sample program does not define report groups for REPORT HEADING, PAGE FOOTING, or REPORT FOOTING. Definitions of these groups, however, are similar to those given.

Figure 10-8 on the next page presents the first report group defined in the sample program, the PAGE HEADING report group. Each report group must begin with an 01 level number and the **TYPE**, such as PAGE HEADING in Figure 10-8 on the next page, must be indicated by spelling it out or by using the appropriate two-letter abbreviation. One or more lines of output then can be defined for each report group. Line spacing can be explicitly stated, as shown in Figure 10-8, or it can be relative, as will be illustrated later.

```
265   01   TYPE PAGE HEADING.  ◄─────  report group
266                                    TYPE must be
                                       stated
267        02   LINE 1.
268             03         COLUMN 1    PIC X(6) VALUE "DATE: ".
269             03         COLUMN 7    PIC Z9/99/99 SOURCE
270                                          WA-CURRENT-DATE-N.
271             03         COLUMN 31   PIC X(27) VALUE                PAGE-
272                  "AINSWORTH INSURANCE COMPANY".               COUNTER is a
273             03         COLUMN 73   PIC X(5)  VALUE "PAGE ".     reserved word
274             03         COLUMN 78   PIC ZZ9   SOURCE PAGE-COUNTER.
275
276        02   LINE 2.                                             SOURCE
277             03         COLUMN 1    PIC X(6) VALUE "TIME: ".     replaces a
278             03         COLUMN 7    PIC Z9 SOURCE WA-SYSTEM-HOUR.   MOVE
279             03         COLUMN 9    PIC X   VALUE ":".
280             03         COLUMN 10   PIC 99 SOURCE WA-SYSTEM-MINUTES.
281             03         COLUMN 12   PIC XX SOURCE WA-AMPM.
282             03         COLUMN 34   PIC X(21) VALUE
283                                        "AGENT SUBTOTAL REPORT".
```

FIGURE 10-8 PAGE HEADING report group from the sample program

The sample PAGE HEADING report group has two lines defined within it. The first line prints on line 1 of each page, and the second one prints on line 2. Each line then is subdivided into the individual fields. Notice that filler entries are not used to separate the items on each output line. Only those fields actually containing data that is to be printed are defined.

Each field is positioned by the use of the reserved word **COLUMN** followed by a column number. Each field must have a picture clause to define its data category and size. Because report groups define output records, all data items are either alphanumeric or numeric-edited in the sample program. Following the picture clause, the contents of a field must be defined. This is accomplished two ways in the sample PAGE HEADING report group.

The VALUE clause is used just as it was in earlier programs within this book to explicitly define the contents of a field using a literal value. Also used in Figure 10-8 is the SOURCE clause. The **SOURCE** clause is used to define the input field, or work area field, whose contents are to be moved to the output field being defined. The use of the SOURCE clause within report groups eliminates the need to code MOVE statements in the PROCEDURE DIVISION to fill in output fields. Report Writer automatically moves the contents of the field identified by a SOURCE clause to the corresponding output field when it is time for that output field to print. Thus, SOURCE WA-CURRENT-DATE-N in the first line of the PAGE HEADING report group causes the contents of WA-CURRENT-DATE-N to be moved to this output field before the line prints.

PAGE-COUNTER is a special field, sometimes called a **register**, available in Report Writer for obtaining the page number. PAGE-COUNTER is not defined anywhere within the program but is available automatically when Report Writer is used. Report Writer initializes and increments PAGE-COUNTER as necessary during the execution of the program. Another special field available, but not used in the sample program, is LINE-COUNTER. **LINE-COUNTER** counts lines of output on a page automatically and can be used for testing the current position on a page. As with PAGE-COUNTER, Report Writer will initialize and increment LINE-COUNTER as needed within the program. COBOL will not allow any code in your program to directly modify PAGE-COUNTER or LINE-COUNTER.

Figure 10-9 presents the second report group defined within the sample program, a CONTROL HEADING group. A **CONTROL HEADING** can be defined only for a control field defined in the RD. A name following the 01 level number is optional for all report groups and is coded only if the report group must be referenced by name within the PROCEDURE DIVISION. This CONTROL HEADING must be referenced later in the program in the DECLARATIVE section; therefore, the name AGENT-HEADING has been assigned to the report group. The definition of a CONTROL HEADING must include the name of the control field for which this report group is being defined. Figure 10-9 shows the CONTROL HEADING for PR-AGENT-NAME.

```
291  01  AGENT-HEADING TYPE CONTROL HEADING PR-AGENT-NAME.
292      02  LINE PLUS 2.
293          03          COLUMN 10   PIC X(9)   VALUE "AGENT--> ".
294          03          COLUMN 19   PIC X(20)  SOURCE PR-AGENT-NAME.
295          03          COLUMN 40   PIC X(7)   VALUE "PHONE:".
296          03          COLUMN 47   PIC X(12)  SOURCE WA-AGENT-PHONE.
297
298      02  LINE PLUS 2.
299          03          COLUMN 6    PIC X(8)   VALUE "POLICY #".
300          03          COLUMN 22   PIC X(13)  VALUE "CUSTOMER NAME".
301          03          COLUMN 49   PIC X(7)   VALUE "PREMIUM".
302          03          COLUMN 60   PIC X(9)   VALUE "DUE MONTH".
303
304      02  LINE PLUS 1.
305          03          COLUMN 6    PIC X(12)  VALUE ALL "-".
306          03          COLUMN 22   PIC X(20)  VALUE ALL "-".
307          03          COLUMN 49   PIC X(7)   VALUE ALL "-".
308          03          COLUMN 60   PIC X(9)   VALUE ALL "-".
```

a name is optional on all report groups

FIGURE 10-9   CONTROL HEADING report group from the sample program

Three output lines are defined as part of the CONTROL HEADING for PR-AGENT-NAME. Relative spacing, or carriage control, for the lines is defined using LINE PLUS 2 and LINE PLUS 1 entries. These entries call for double-spacing and single-spacing, respectively from the current page position when these lines are printed. VALUE and SOURCE are used to assign values to the fields defined in the three output lines. The first line of this group identifies the agent name and phone number. The next two lines define column headings.

Figure 10-10 on the next page presents the DETAIL report group for the sample program. The name following the 01 level number, DETAIL-LINE, is necessary because the detail report group is referenced in the PROCEDURE DIVISION. The entry LINE PLUS 1 following the 02 level number is used for carriage control to single-space the report detail lines. All of the fields at the 03 level are assigned values using SOURCE. Although only one is used in the sample program, any number of DETAIL report groups can be defined within the REPORT SECTION. Each, however, must have a unique name following the 01 level number.

```
316  01  DETAIL-LINE TYPE DETAIL.
317
318      02  LINE PLUS 1.
319          03              COLUMN 6    PIC X(12) SOURCE
320                                                PR-POLICY-NUMBER.
321          03              COLUMN 22   PIC X(20) SOURCE
322                                                PR-CUSTOMER-NAME.
323          03              COLUMN 46   PIC X     SOURCE
324                                                WA-DOLLAR-SIGN.
325          03              COLUMN 47   PIC ZZ,ZZ9.99 SOURCE
326                                                PR-PREMIUM-AMOUNT.
327          03              COLUMN 60   PIC X(9)  SOURCE
328                                                MNT-NAME(PR-PREMIUM-DUE-MONTH).
```

this group prints once for every record processed

FIGURE 10-10 DETAIL report group for the sample program

Figure 10-11 presents the CONTROL FOOTING defined for the control field PR-AGENT-NAME. A **CONTROL FOOTING** can be used to print summary information when Report Writer detects a control break. As with a CONTROL HEADING, the control field must be explicitly listed and be declared as a control field in the RD. This CONTROL FOOTING prints two lines. The first line prints dashes to underline the last amount in the column of premium amounts listed for customers of the current agent. The second line prints the agent's name, the total premium amount for the agent's customers, and a count of the number of customers listed for the agent.

```
336  01  TYPE CONTROL FOOTING PR-AGENT-NAME.
337
338      02  LINE PLUS 1.
339          03              COLUMN 45   PIC X(12) VALUE ALL "-".
340
341      02  LINE PLUS 1.
342          03              COLUMN 5    PIC X(18) VALUE
343                                          "*Total for Agent".
344          03              COLUMN 25   PIC X(20) SOURCE PR-AGENT-NAME.
345          03              COLUMN 45   PIC $ZZZ,ZZ9.99 SUM
346                                                PR-PREMIUM-AMOUNT.
347          03              COLUMN 58   PIC XX    VALUE  " >".
348          03              COLUMN 60   PIC ZZZZ9 SOURCE
349                                                AC-AGENT-RECORD-COUNT.
350          03              COLUMN 65   PIC X(8)  VALUE " Clients".
```

this group prints subtotals for each agent

FIGURE 10-11 CONTROL FOOTING for PR-AGENT-NAME in the sample program

The total premium amount is obtained by using the **SUM** clause on line 345, which is used to define an accumulator that will accumulate the values in the specified field automatically. The accumulator will print using the format given by the edit pattern in the picture clause. This accumulator will be reinitialized automatically by Report Writer once its value is printed with the CONTROL FOOTING. The specified field is PR-PREMIUM-AMOUNT. The SUM clause eliminates the need to define an accumulator and the need to execute an

ADD statement in the PROCEDURE DIVISION. The record count for each agent is printed by accessing the value of AC-AGENT-RECORD-COUNT. This field is incremented and reinitialized in the PROCEDURE DIVISION.

Figure 10-12 presents the last report group defined in the sample program. It is another CONTROL FOOTING, this time for the reserved word FINAL, which was specified as a control field in the RD. This report group also prints two lines of output. The first line has a format similar to the output from the CONTROL FOOTING for PR-AGENT-NAME. It prints the grand total of all premium amounts listed and a total customer count. The second line prints the END OF REPORT message. A REPORT FOOTING group could have been used for the END OF REPORT message; however, the spacing is more predictable when used in a CONTROL FOOTING for FINAL. The SUM clause is used to define an accumulator for the grand total. The number of customers processed is obtained by printing the value of the accumulator AC-RECORD-COUNT that is incremented in the program every time a record is processed.

```
352  01   TYPE CONTROL FOOTING FINAL.            this group
353                                               prints company
354       02  LINE PLUS 2.                        totals
355           03          COLUMN 19     PIC X(25) VALUE
356                                      "Total Company Premiums = ".
357           03          COLUMN 45     PIC $ZZZ,ZZ9.99 SUM
358                                                 PR-PREMIUM-AMOUNT.
359           03          COLUMN 58     PIC XX    VALUE " >".
360           03          COLUMN 60     PIC ZZZZ9 SOURCE
361                                                 AC-RECORD-COUNT.
362           03          COLUMN 65     PIC X(8)  VALUE " Clients".
363
364       02  LINE PLUS 3.
365           03          COLUMN 33     PIC X(13) VALUE
366                                                 "END OF REPORT".
```

FIGURE 10-12 CONTROL FOOTING for FINAL in the sample program

After all the required report groups have been defined, logic in the PROCEDURE DIVISION can be coded. Report Writer eliminates the need for many of the statements used in previous report programs; thus, the PROCEDURE DIVISION in a Report Writer program tends to be somewhat shorter than in programs that do not use the Report Writer feature. Because the sample program contains a non-embedded table, the code for loading this table must still be executed. This logic was discussed in Chapter 7.

Next, this chapter examines the elements required to utilize Report Writer in the PROCEDURE DIVISION of the sample program. Although optional, declaratives are often used with Report Writer.

DECLARATIVES

Special processing that falls outside the realm of normal Report Writer logic is sometimes necessary. For example, sometimes a value for a SOURCE field has to be established prior to the printing of a particular report group. In COBOL, **declarative sections**, or simply **declaratives**, are used to handle special processing needs. When used, declarative sections must be defined at the beginning of the PROCEDURE DIVISION, before any other statements, and must begin with the reserved word **DECLARATIVES**. **END DECLARATIVES** must be used to terminate the scope of the declaratives. Figure 10-13 on the next page presents the basic format of a declarative section.

```
PROCEDURE DIVISION.

DECLARATIVES.

section-name-1 SECTION.

    USE statement.

paragraph-name.

    sentence ...

END DECLARATIVES.

section-name-2 SECTION.
```

FIGURE 10-13 Basic format of a declarative section

COBOL sections are coded within the declaratives to handle the desired processing. Although coded at the beginning of the PROCEDURE DIVISION, a declarative section will not execute until the condition specified in a **USE** statement is true. The USE statement must be coded following the section header for each section defined within the declaratives. Because declaratives require the use of COBOL sections, the balance of the program following the END DECLARATIVES delimiter also must be coded in one or more sections. Figure 10-14 presents the three basic formats of the USE statement supported in standard COBOL. Only USE BEFORE REPORTING is covered in detail in this book, but USE FOR DEBUGGING and USE AFTER STANDARD EXCEPTION also are available.

```
                         { cd-name                             }
                         { [ ALL REFERENCES OF ] field-name    }
USE FOR DEBUGGING ON     { file-name                           } ...
                         { procedure-name                      }
                         { ALL PROCEDURES                      }

                                                 { file-name ... }
                                                 { INPUT         }
USE AFTER STANDARD { EXCEPTION } PROCEDURE ON    { OUTPUT        }
                   { ERROR     }                 { I-O           }
                                                 { EXTEND        }

USE BEFORE REPORTING report-group-name
```

FIGURE 10-14 Basic formats of the USE statement

USE FOR DEBUGGING

USE FOR DEBUGGING can be used to identify items that are to be monitored during the execution of the program. Every time a specified item is encountered, actions coded in the declarative section will execute. The items that can be monitored include fields and procedures in the program. When other means are unavailable, USE FOR DEBUGGING can be of great help in debugging a program and in finding logic errors. No program in this book utilizes USE FOR DEBUGGING.

USE AFTER STANDARD EXCEPTION

USE AFTER STANDARD EXCEPTION can be used to replace actions specified in input and output statements by AT END or INVALID KEY clauses. This use of declaratives provides flexibility to the way error conditions related to file input and file output are handled in programs and eliminates the need for AT END and INVALID KEY clauses. No program in this book utilizes declaratives in this fashion.

USE BEFORE REPORTING

USE BEFORE REPORTING can be employed when the Report Writer feature is being utilized. Because Report Writer uses its own built-in logic for page breaks, control breaks, and the printing of summary lines, if something out of the normal flow of Report Writer logic needs to be accomplished, declaratives must be used. In the sample program presented in Figure 10-4 on pages 10-5 to 10-8, an agent's phone number must be found prior to the printing of the CONTROL HEADING for agent name. Because there is no way of knowing when a new CONTROL HEADING will be printed, a declarative section has been coded in the sample program. Figure 10-15 presents this declarative section.

```
368  PROCEDURE DIVISION.
         .
         .
         .
375  DECLARATIVES.
376
377  X-100-GET-AGENT-PHONE SECTION.
378      USE BEFORE REPORTING AGENT-HEADING.        executes just
379  X-100-AGENT-PHONE.                             before control
380                                                  headings are
381      SET PHONE-INDEX TO 1.                       printed
382      SEARCH APT-ENTRY
383          AT END
384              MOVE "NOT FOUND" TO WA-AGENT-PHONE
385          WHEN PR-AGENT-NAME = APT-NAME (PHONE-INDEX)
386              MOVE APT-NUMBER (PHONE-INDEX) TO WA-AGENT-PHONE.
387
388      MOVE "$" TO WA-DOLLAR-SIGN.
389      MOVE ZERO TO AC-AGENT-RECORD-COUNT.
390
391  END DECLARATIVES.
392
393  ****************************************************************
394  *                                                            *
395  *   MAIN-PROGRAM - THIS IS THE MAIN ROUTINE OF THE AGENT SUBTOTAL*
396  *                  REPORT PROGRAM                            *
397  *                                                            *
398  ****************************************************************
399  MAIN SECTION.
400  MAIN-PROGRAM.
```

FIGURE 10-15 Declarative section from the sample program

The reserved word DECLARATIVES on line 375 is the first non-comment entry following the PROCEDURE DIVISION header. The section header, X-100-GET-AGENT-PHONE SECTION on line 377 denotes the beginning of a specific procedure within the declaratives. USE BEFORE REPORTING on line 378 specifies when this procedure is to be performed during execution of the program. The name following USE BEFORE REPORTING must be a name defined with one of the report groups in the REPORT SECTION of the program. In the sample program, AGENT-HEADING is the name associated with the CONTROL HEADING report group for the control field PR-AGENT-NAME. Thus, X-100-GET-AGENT-PHONE SECTION will execute just prior to Report Writer printing the lines defined by that report group.

Each section must be subdivided into one or more paragraphs. Only one paragraph, X-100-AGENT-PHONE on line 379, is used. Within the paragraph X-100-AGENT-PHONE, a linear SEARCH is executed against the agent phone table. Once an agent's name is found in the table, the corresponding phone number is moved to the field WA-AGENT-PHONE, which is used as the SOURCE for an output field in the CONTROL HEADING.

Two MOVE statements also execute as part of the declarative section presented. One moves the dollar sign into the field WA-DOLLAR-SIGN, which is used as a SOURCE field in the DETAIL report group, and the other moves zeros to the customer counter for an individual agent, AC-AGENT-RECORD-COUNT. END DECLARATIVES on line 391 terminates the scope of the declaratives. Once a declarative section has terminated, logic control returns to the normal flow of Report Writer. The section header, MAIN SECTION on line 399, denotes the beginning of the programs main stream of logic. The actual execution of the program begins here.

No set standard exists for naming sections and paragraphs within declaratives. X-100 was chosen in the sample program simply because declaratives offer extra code that can be used when an action outside the normal realm of Report Writer logic must be performed. Depending on the complexity of the desired logic, multiple paragraphs can be coded within a declarative section.

Because no single paragraph necessarily transfers control to declarative sections, when illustrated on a hierarchy chart, they often are drawn in separate boxes, detached from the main hierarchy chart. Figure 10-2 on page 10-3 illustrates this with a drawing of the hierarchy chart for the sample program. The box for X-100-GET-AGENT-PHONE is off to the side and not attached to any branch of the chart.

INITIATE, GENERATE, AND TERMINATE STATEMENTS

The code that actually creates the report illustrated in Figure 10-1 on page 10-2 is in the C-stream of the sample program (Figure 10-16). Files must be opened, input records must be read, and a loop must be created to process all of the records in the file. Because of the SOURCE and SUM clauses used in definition of the report groups in the REPORT SECTION of the DATA DIVISION, all of the MOVE statements and most of the ADD statements have been eliminated. Because of the predefined logic used by Report Writer, it is not necessary to check for headings or page overflow. Testing for control breaks is also unnecessary. Report Writer handles all these functions automatically.

```
472  C-100-PROCESS-FILE.
473
474     MOVE NEG TO SW-END-OF-FILE.
475     OPEN  INPUT    PREMIUM-INPUT-FILE
476           OUTPUT   AGENT-SUBTOTAL-REPORT.
477                                            prepare
478     INITIATE AGENT-SUBTOTAL.  ◄——          counters and
479                                            accumulators
480     READ SORTED-PREMIUM-FILE INTO PREMIUM-RECORD
481        AT END MOVE YES TO SW-END-OF-FILE.
482
483     PERFORM C-200-PROCESS-RECORDS
484        UNTIL END-OF-FILE.
485                                            wrap up
486     TERMINATE AGENT-SUBTOTAL.  ◄——         Report Writer
          .                                    processing
          .
          .
494  C-200-PROCESS-RECORDS.
495
496     ADD 1 TO AC-AGENT-RECORD-COUNT
497              AC-RECORD-COUNT.             cause
498     GENERATE DETAIL-LINE.  ◄——            output lines
499     MOVE SPACE TO WA-DOLLAR-SIGN.         to print
500
501     READ SORTED-PREMIUM-FILE INTO PREMIUM-RECORD
502        AT END MOVE YES TO SW-END-OF-FILE.
```

FIGURE 10-16 Code that creates the report in the sample program

Some special statements must be executed to obtain output from Report Writer. Line 478 in Figure 10-16 contains the INITIATE statement. The **INITIATE** statement causes Report Writer to set all counters and accumulators to zero. This includes the special fields discussed earlier, LINE-COUNTER and PAGE-COUNTER. The name of the report as defined by the REPORT IS clause in the FD must follow the word INITIATE. Proper results cannot be guaranteed unless the INITIATE statement is executed prior to the creation of the report.

Line 498 in Figure 10-16 contains the GENERATE statement. The **GENERATE** statement actually sends output to the report file when using the Report Writer feature. It replaces the need for WRITE statements in the PROCEDURE DIVISION. The name following the word GENERATE normally is the name associated with a DETAIL report group. The named DETAIL report group is printed every time the GENERATE statement is encountered. Additionally, every time page headings, control headings, or control footings are necessary, GENERATE causes them to print automatically. When multiple DETAIL report groups are defined, multiple GENERATE statements can be coded, one for each DETAIL report group.

The report name can be specified following the reserved word GENERATE in place of a DETAIL report group name. When specified, a summary report is created with headings and footings, but no detail report lines.

After processing is complete, a TERMINATE statement is executed to properly conclude the report. Line 486 in Figure 10-16 contains the TERMINATE statement used in the sample program. **TERMINATE** causes all defined control footings to print for the last time and if defined, prints the report footing. The name following the word TERMINATE must be the name of the report as defined in the REPORT IS clause in the FD for the report file.

INITIATE, GENERATE, and TERMINATE do not open and close files or read records from the input file. It is the programmer's responsibility to code such entries and establish a loop to process all records in the file.

ADDITIONAL REPORT WRITER TOPICS

Figures 10-17, 10-18, and 10-19 present the basic formats available in COBOL for defining report groups. Format 1 in Figure 10-17 is used with an 01 level number to define the type of report group. Carriage control can be defined at the 01 level when a single line of output is being defined in a report group. Format 2 in Figure 10-18 can be used to define an item subordinate to an 01 level. This type of an entry is used to establish carriage control for a line of output that is in a report group composed of multiple lines of output. Format 3 in Figure 10-19 is used to define elementary items within a line of output. Several options are presented here that were not used in the sample program. Some of these options can prove to be useful.

Format 1:

```
01  [data-name-1]

      ⎡ LINE NUMBER IS  ⎧ integer-1      [ ON NEXT PAGE ] ⎫ ⎤
      ⎣                 ⎩ PLUS integer-2                   ⎭ ⎦

      ⎡                 ⎧ integer-3      ⎫ ⎤
      ⎢ NEXT GROUP IS  ⎨ PLUS integer-4 ⎬ ⎥
      ⎣                 ⎩ NEXT PAGE      ⎭ ⎦


                        ⎧ ⎧ REPORT HEADING ⎫                             ⎫
                        ⎪ ⎨ RH             ⎬                             ⎪
                        ⎪ ⎩                ⎭                             ⎪
                        ⎪ ⎧ PAGE HEADING ⎫                              ⎪
                        ⎪ ⎨ PH           ⎬                              ⎪
                        ⎪ ⎩              ⎭                              ⎪
                        ⎪ ⎧ CONTROL HEADING ⎫ ⎧ data-name-2 ⎫          ⎪
                        ⎪ ⎨ CH              ⎬ ⎨ FINAL       ⎬          ⎪
     TYPE IS           ⎨ ⎩                 ⎭ ⎩             ⎭          ⎬
                        ⎪ ⎧ DETAIL ⎫                                   ⎪
                        ⎪ ⎨ DE     ⎬                                   ⎪
                        ⎪ ⎩        ⎭                                   ⎪
                        ⎪ ⎧ CONTROL FOOTING ⎫ ⎧ data-name-3 ⎫          ⎪
                        ⎪ ⎨ CF              ⎬ ⎨ FINAL       ⎬          ⎪
                        ⎪ ⎩                 ⎭ ⎩             ⎭          ⎪
                        ⎪ ⎧ PAGE FOOTING ⎫                             ⎪
                        ⎪ ⎨ PF           ⎬                             ⎪
                        ⎪ ⎩              ⎭                             ⎪
                        ⎪ ⎧ REPORT FOOTING ⎫                           ⎪
                        ⎩ ⎨ RF             ⎬                           ⎭
                          ⎩                ⎭

      [ [USAGE IS]  DISPLAY ]  .
```

FIGURE 10-17 Basic format 1 of a report group

Format 2:

```
level-number  [ data-name-1 ]


[ LINE NUMBER IS  { integer-1        [ ON NEXT PAGE ] } ]
                  { PLUS integer-2                     }

  [ [USAGE IS]  DISPLAY ] .
```

FIGURE 10-18 Basic format 2 for lines in a report group

Format 3:

```
level-number  [ data-name-1 ]

{ PICTURE }  IS     string-1
{ PIC     }

  [ [USAGE IS]  DISPLAY ]

  [ [SIGN IS]  { LEADING  }   SEPARATE CHARACTER ]
               { TRAILING }

  [ { JUSTIFIED }   RIGHT ]
    { JUST      }

  [ BLANK WHEN ZERO]

  [ LINE NUMBER IS  { integer-1     [ ON NEXT PAGE ] } ]
                    { PLUS integer-2                 }

  [ COLUMN NUMBER IS   integer-3 ]

  {   SOURCE IS  field-name-1                                      }
  {                                                               }
  {   VALUE IS literal-1                                          }
  {                                                               }
  {   {SUM {field-name-2} ... [UPON {field-name-3} ... ] } ...   }
  {                                                               }
  {   [ RESET ON  { field-name-4 } ]                             }
  {               { FINAL        }                               }

  [ GROUP INDICATE ]
```

FIGURE 10-19 Basic format 3 for fields in a line of output within a report group

In Formats 1 and 2, the LINE NUMBER entry allows for three different options. One of the options, **ON NEXT PAGE**, was not used in the sample program. When ON NEXT PAGE is specified following a line number, a page break will be forced prior to the printing of the report group. Another option that was not used in the sample program is in Format 1, where the NEXT GROUP option is illustrated. The **NEXT GROUP** option can be used in one report group to force the next printing report group to print at a specified interval or even print on the **NEXT PAGE**.

GROUP INDICATE shown in Format 3 is another entry often used with Report Writer. When the **GROUP INDICATE** option is specified on an elementary item in a DETAIL report group, the item will print once after a control break and not print again until the next control break. This entry can be used to improve the appearance of a report when the same value will print in a field for a given group of records. Figure 10-20 illustrates the effect GROUP INDICATE can have on output results. As you can see, with GROUP INDICATE coded for the customer name, the name prints just once for each group of related records. Other options presented in Format 3 deal with editing output results or with the internal storage configuration of data. These options will not be discussed in this chapter.

Without GROUP INDICATE	With GROUP INDICATE

```
Without GROUP INDICATE            With GROUP INDICATE

02  COLUMN 1  PIC X(5) SOURCE     02  COLUMN 1 PIC X(5) SOURCE
    IN-CUST-NAME.                     IN-CUST-NAME GROUP INDICATE.
     .                                 .
     .                                 .
     .                                 .
       PURCHASE REPORT                   PURCHASE REPORT

NAME  ITEM        QTY.  COST      NAME  ITEM        QTY.  COST
-----  ----------  ----  ------   -----  ----------  ----  ------
BETTY BATH ROBE     2    23.50    BETTY BATH ROBE     2    23.50
BETTY TOWELS        3    15.85          TOWELS        3    15.85
BETTY SANDALS       1    12.25          SANDALS       1    12.25
                         ------                            ------
TOTAL                    51.60    TOTAL                    51.60

BRUCE RAZOR KIT     1    18.95    BRUCE RAZOR KIT     1    18.95
BRUCE FL LT BATT    6     6.15          FL LT BATT    6     6.15
BRUCE LIGHTER FL    1     2.19          LIGHTER FL    1     2.19
BRUCE COMPASS       1     7.95          COMPASS       1     7.95
                         ------                            ------
TOTAL                    35.24    TOTAL                    35.24

SALLY UMBRELLA      1    14.50    SALLY UMBRELLA      1    14.50
SALLY SLP BAG       2    34.70          SLP BAG       2    34.70
                         ------                            ------
TOTAL                    49.20    TOTAL                    49.20
     .                                 .
     .                                 .
     .                                 .
```

FIGURE 10-20 The effect of GROUP INDICATE on a field

CHAPTER SUMMARY

The following list summarizes this chapter. The summary is designed to help you study and understand the material and concepts presented.

1. The **Report Writer feature** allows for the characteristics of a report to be defined through the use of special entries in the DATA DIVISION.

2. The **REPORT IS** clause is used in an FD to define the name of the specific report to be created by Report Writer.

3. The **REPORT SECTION** is used to define the characteristics of each page in a report and to define the format of each output line in a report.

4. Each report to be produced begins with a Report Definition or **RD** entry.

5. The optional RD entry **CONTROL IS** or **CONTROLS ARE** can be used to identify the field or fields, most major to most minor, used to trigger control breaks.

6. The reserved word **FINAL** is used to indicate the highest level of control and must appear first when used with CONTROL IS or CONTROLS ARE.

7. The entries in the **PAGE** clause within an RD are used to define the basic format of a page in the report.

8. A **report group** defines one or more related output lines for the report.

9. Within a report group, only those fields containing data to be printed are defined.

10. A name following the 01 level number is optional for all report groups and must be coded only if the report group must be referenced within the PROCEDURE DIVISION.

11. The use of the **SOURCE** clause within report groups eliminates the need to code MOVE statements in the PROCEDURE DIVISION to fill in output fields.

12. **PAGE-COUNTER** is a special field, or **register**, available in Report Writer for accessing the page count.

13. The definition of a **CONTROL HEADING** or **CONTROL FOOTING** must include the name of the control field for which the report group is being defined.

14. The **SUM** clause is used to define an internal accumulator that will accumulate the values in a specified field automatically.

15. The **INITIATE** statement causes Report Writer to set all counters and accumulators to zero.

16. The **GENERATE** statement is what actually causes output lines to print when the Report Writer feature is used.

17. **TERMINATE** causes all defined control footings to print for the last time and if defined, prints the report footing.

18. **Declarative sections**, or **declaratives**, are used to handle special processing needs in COBOL programs.

19. Declarative sections must be defined at the beginning of the PROCEDURE DIVISION, before any other statements, and must begin with the reserved word **DECLARATIVES**.

20. **END DECLARATIVES** must be used to terminate the scope of the declaratives.

21. **USE FOR DEBUGGING** can be used to identify items that are to be monitored during the execution of the program.

(continued)

Chapter Summary (continued)

22. **USE AFTER STANDARD EXCEPTION** can be used to replace actions specified in input and output statements by AT END or INVALID KEY clauses.

23. **USE BEFORE** R**EPORTING** can be employed when an action out of the normal flow of Report Writer logic needs to be accomplished.

24. When **ON NEXT PAGE** is specified following LINE NUMBER, a page break will be forced prior to the printing of the report group.

25. **NEXT GROUP** can be used in one report group to force the next printing report group to print at a specified interval or even print on the **NEXT PAGE**.

26. **GROUP INDICATE** causes an elementary item to print once after a control break and not print again until the next control break.

KEY TERMS

COLUMN (10-12)
CONTROL FOOTING (CF) (10-11, 10-14)
CONTROL HEADING (CH) (10-11, 10-13)
CONTROL IS (10-9)
CONTROLS ARE (10-9)
declaratives (10-15)
declarative sections (10-15)
DECLARATIVES (10-15)
DETAIL (DE) (10-11)
END DECLARATIVES (10-15)
FINAL (10-9)
FIRST DETAIL (10-10)
FOOTING (10-10)
GENERATE (10-19)
GROUP INDICATE (10-22)
HEADING (10-10)
INITIATE (10-19)
LAST DETAIL (10-10)
LIMIT IS (10-10)
LIMITS ARE (10-10)
LINE-COUNTER (10-12)
NEXT GROUP (10-22)

NEXT PAGE (10-22)
ON NEXT PAGE (10-22)
PAGE (10-10)
PAGE-COUNTER (10-12)
PAGE FOOTING (PF) (10-11)
PAGE HEADING (PH) (10-11)
RD (Report Definition) (10-9)
register (10-12)
REPORT FOOTING (RF) (10-11)
report group (10-11)
REPORT HEADING (RH) (10-11)
REPORT IS (10-8)
REPORT SECTION (10-9)
Report Writer feature (10-1)
SOURCE (10-12)
SUM (10-14)
TERMINATE (10-19)
TYPE (10-11)
USE (10-16)
USE AFTER STANDARD EXCEPTION (10-17)
USE BEFORE REPORTING (10-17)
USE FOR DEBUGGING (10-16)

STUDENT ASSIGNMENTS

Student Assignment 1: True/False

Instructions: Circle T if the statement is true or F if the statement is false.

T   F   1. The Report Writer feature generally requires that the PROCEDURE DIVISION contain more instructions than it normally might have if Report Writer was not used.

T   F   2. To use the Report Writer feature, a REPORT SECTION must be coded in the DATA DIVISION.

T   F   3. A REPORT IS or REPORTS ARE clause must be coded in the FD of the report file to use the Report Writer feature.

T F   4. An RD entry is optional in the REPORT SECTION.

T F   5. The PAGE clause is used to identify fields used to trigger control breaks.

T F   6. FINAL is used to indicate the highest level of a control break.

T F   7. Each report group can define exactly one line of output.

T F   8. Filler entries are required within report groups to define spaces between output fields.

T F   9. Every report group must be defined with a name following the 01 level number.

T F   10. The SOURCE clause in a report group replaces the need for a MOVE statement in the PROCEDURE DIVISION.

T F   11. PAGE-COUNTER must be defined as a PIC 9(5) field in the WORKING-STORAGE SECTION of a program using Report Writer.

T F   12. A CONTROL HEADING can be defined only for fields named after a CONTROL IS or CONTROLS ARE clause.

T F   13. A SUM clause in a report group can be used to replace the need for an ADD statement in the PROCEDURE DIVISION.

T F   14. The report name must follow the reserved word INITIATE in the PROCEDURE DIVISION.

T F   15. The report name can follow the reserved word GENERATE in the PROCEDURE DIVISION to create a summary report.

T F   16. A DETAIL report group name must follow the reserved word TERMINATE in the PROCEDURE DIVISION.

T F   17. USE BEFORE REPORTING can be used to define a declarative section to do special processing when using the Report Writer feature.

T F   18. A CONTROL FOOTING prints only when the value in the control field changes or the end of the file is reached.

T F   19. GROUP INDICATE can be used to suppress the printing of a field if its value is the same as the previous value printed.

T F   20. END DECLARATIVES must be coded to terminate the scope of the declaratives.

Student Assignment 2: Multiple Choice

Instructions: Circle the correct response.

1. An RD entry is located in the _____ .
   a. INPUT-OUTPUT SECTION
   b. FILE SECTION
   c. WORKING-STORAGE SECTION
   d. REPORT SECTION
   e. none of the above

2. The CONTROL IS clause is used to define the _____ .
   a. size of each page of output
   b. fields on which control breaks are to occur
   c. size of the accumulator field used with a SUM clause
   d. number of input records to be processed by Report Writer
   e. none of the above

(continued)

Student Assignment 2 (continued)

3. The reserved word FINAL _____ .
   a. is used to specify the highest level of control
   b. is listed first after CONTROL IS or CONTROLS ARE
   c. can be used to define a CONTROL FOOTING
   d. all of the above
   e. none of the above

4. The reserved word COLUMN is used to _____ .
   a. identify the print position of an output field
   b. identify the number of characters in an output field
   c. suppress the printing of a control break field
   d. name the line number on which a line is to print
   e. none of the above

5. A DETAIL report group _____ .
   a. can define any number of output lines
   b. must include a TYPE definition
   c. must have a name associated with it for it to print
   d. all of the above
   e. only a and b

6. Using the SOURCE clause can replace the use of _____ .
   a. a REDEFINES clause
   b. a MOVE statement
   c. an ADD statement
   d. all of the above
   e. none of the above

7. The INITIATE statement causes _____ .
   a. REPORT HEADINGS and the first PAGE HEADINGS to print
   b. all counters and accumulators to be initialized to zero
   c. the control fields to be initialized
   d. the first record to be read
   e. all of the above

8. The GENERATE statement _____ .
   a. causes heading and detail lines to print
   b. causes just one line of output to be printed
   c. must be used in the REPORT SECTION
   d. can appear only once in the PROCEDURE DIVISION
   e. none of the above

9. A declarative section is used in Report Writer to _____ .
   a. detect control breaks for specified fields
   b. define all accumulator fields used in the program
   c. define special logic outside normal Report Writer logic
   d. define logic that will execute after the end of the file has been detected
   e. none of the above

10. The TERMINATE statement _____ .
    a. should execute after the end of the file is reached
    b. causes control and report footings to print
    c. must include the name of the report as defined in the RD
    d. only a and c
    e. all of the above

Student Assignment 3: Coding a CONTROL HEADING Report Group

Instructions: Given the 10-byte control field ER-JOB-TYPE, code a CONTROL HEADING report group named JOB-HEADING that prints the message shown below. The message should print two lines beneath the last line that printed, it should begin in position 15, and the whole entry should be underlined with hyphens:

```
HEADING FOR JOB TYPE -->  XXXXXXXXXX
------------------------------------
```

Student Assignment 4: Coding a PAGE HEADING Report Group

Instructions: Code a PAGE HEADING report group that prints the following heading lines for a report. Assume the date is in a 6-digit field named WA-TODAYS-DATE. Be sure to include page numbers.

```
DATE: Z9/99/99     AINSWORTH INSURANCE COMPANY          PAGE ZZ9
                      AGENT SALARY REPORT
```

Student Assignment 5: Coding a DETAIL Report Group

Instructions: Given the following input record fields, code a DETAIL report group that prints the given fields in the specified positions. Detail lines should be single-spaced.

Field	Picture	Print Position
ER-EMPLOYEE-NAME	PIC X(20)	2
ER-JOB-TYPE	PIC X(10)	24
ER-SALARY	PIC 9(5)V99	36
ER-ANNIVERSARY-DATE	PIC 9(6) (mmddyy)	48

Student Assignment 6: Coding a CONTROL FOOTING Report Group

Instructions: Code a CONTROL FOOTING report group for the control field ER-JOB-TYPE that prints the total salary for the records printed by the DETAIL report group created in Student Assignment 5. Double-space before printing the report group. The count is in the field AC-EMPLOYEE-JOB-COUNT. The output should be similar to the following:

```
*COUNT AND SALARY FOR JOB TYPE XXXXXXXXXX - ZZ9 - $ZZ,ZZ9.99
```

Student Assignment 7: Coding a Declarative Section

Instructions: Code a complete declarative section that moves zero to the field AC-EMPLOYEE-JOB-COUNT just prior to the printing of the CONTROL HEADING report group created in Student Assignment 3. If necessary, go back to Assignment 3 and add a name to the report group.

COBOL LABORATORY EXERCISES

Exercise 1: Modified Agent Subtotal Report Program

Purpose: To gain experience in COBOL program maintenance and modification and in the use of the COBOL Report Writer feature.

Problem: Open the file PROJ10.CBL on the Student Diskette that accompanies this book and modify the Agent Subtotal Report program making the following changes:

1. In A-100-INITIALIZATION, sort the records in the PREMIUM-INPUT-FILE so that in SORTED-PREMIUM-FILE, they are in sequence by insurance type within agent name. Use the sorted file as input to the report.

2. Modify the embedded MONTH-NAME-TABLE and its associated constant data so only the first three letters of each month are used to name a month. Make any necessary changes to the DETAIL report group to output each three-character month name.

3. Add another field to the DETAIL report group so a customer's gender is printed. Print MALE if PR-SEX contains the letter M and print FEMALE if PR-SEX contains the letter F.

4. Modify the control break logic so a minor control break occurs when there is a change in insurance type and a major control break occurs when there is a change in agent name. In both cases, print appropriate headings and footings.

Save this program as EX10-1.CBL.

Input Data: Use the Premium file presented in Appendix A as input to the SORT. This file is named PREMIUM.DAT on the Student Diskette that accompanies this book. Use the Agent Phone file as input to load the non-embedded AGENT-PHONE-TABLE. This file is named AGENTPHO.DAT on the Student Diskette that accompanies this book.

Output Results: Output should be a report similar to the sample report presented in Figure 10-21. Include a company total with a final CONTROL FOOTING and an END OF REPORT message.

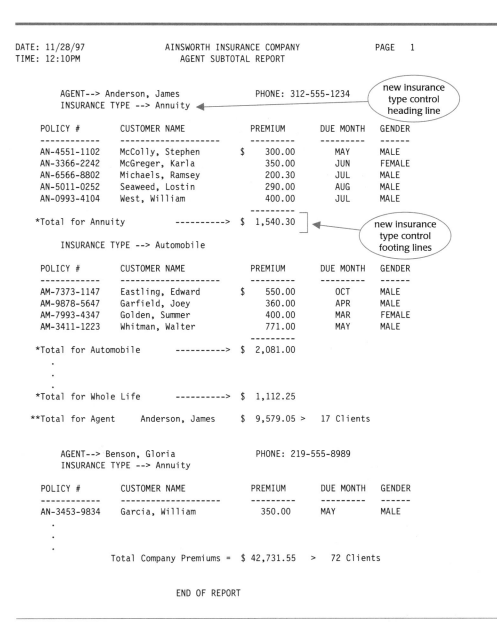

```
DATE: 11/28/97            AINSWORTH INSURANCE COMPANY         PAGE   1
TIME: 12:10PM                AGENT SUBTOTAL REPORT


        AGENT--> Anderson, James           PHONE: 312-555-1234
        INSURANCE TYPE --> Annuity

     POLICY #        CUSTOMER NAME          PREMIUM      DUE MONTH    GENDER
     -----------     --------------------   ---------    ---------    ------
     AN-4551-1102    McColly, Stephen     $   300.00      MAY         MALE
     AN-3366-2242    McGreger, Karla          350.00      JUN         FEMALE
     AN-6566-8802    Michaels, Ramsey         200.30      JUL         MALE
     AN-5011-0252    Seaweed, Lostin          290.00      AUG         MALE
     AN-0993-4104    West, William            400.00      JUL         MALE
                                          ---------
     *Total for Annuity      ----------> $ 1,540.30

        INSURANCE TYPE --> Automobile

     POLICY #        CUSTOMER NAME          PREMIUM      DUE MONTH    GENDER
     -----------     --------------------   ---------    ---------    ------
     AM-7373-1147    Eastling, Edward     $   550.00      OCT         MALE
     AM-9878-5647    Garfield, Joey           360.00      APR         MALE
     AM-7993-4347    Golden, Summer           400.00      MAR         FEMALE
     AM-3411-1223    Whitman, Walter          771.00      MAY         MALE
                                          ---------
     *Total for Automobile   ----------> $ 2,081.00
             .
             .
             .
     *Total for Whole Life   ----------> $ 1,112.25

    **Total for Agent     Anderson, James   $ 9,579.05 >   17 Clients


        AGENT--> Benson, Gloria            PHONE: 219-555-8989
        INSURANCE TYPE --> Annuity

     POLICY #        CUSTOMER NAME          PREMIUM      DUE MONTH    GENDER
     -----------     --------------------   ---------    ---------    ------
     AN-3453-9834    Garcia, William          350.00      MAY         MALE
             .
             .
             .
           Total Company Premiums = $ 42,731.55  >   72 Clients


                          END OF REPORT
```

new insurance type control heading line

new insurance type control footing lines

FIGURE 10-21 Agent Subtotal Report with multiple-level control breaks

Exercise 2: Customer Purchases Subtotal Report Program

Purpose: To practice the use of COBOL tables and Report Writer logic in the creation of a COBOL program that produces a Customer Purchases Subtotal Report. If already coded, use the program created in Laboratory Exercise 2 in Chapter 7 as a basis for this program.

Problem: Using the Report Writer feature of COBOL, write a program that lists Purchase records for the ABC Department Store in sequence by sales clerk identification number. Sort the input file in ascending sequence by sales clerk identification (ID) number and then use the sorted file as input to the report logic. Each time there is a change in the sales clerk ID number, print a total for the purchases made by customers of the sales clerk. For each clerk, use data loaded into a non-embedded table to perform a binary search finding the sales clerk ID number and accessing the sales clerk's name.

(continued)

Exercise 2 (continued)

For each sales date, use an embedded table to translate the month into a three-character abbreviation for that month. Input sales dates are in MMDDYY format and should be printed in DD-MMM-YY format. For example, an input date of 112897 should be printed on the report as 28-NOV-97.

For each purchase record listed, print the date of purchase, account number, customer name, item purchased, and purchase amount. Print the current date and time in the heading on every page. Time should be printed in AM/PM format. Number each page, starting the report with page 1. At the end of report, print the total number of records listed and total purchases. Save this program as EX10-2.CBL.

Input Data: Use the Customer file listed in Appendix A as input to the SORT. This file is named CUSTOMER.DAT on the Student Diskette that accompanies this book. Customer records have the following layout:

Field Description	Position	Length	Attribute
Date of Purchase	1–6	6	Numeric, PIC 9(6)
Account Number	7–12	6	Alphanumeric
Customer Name	13–32	20	Alphanumeric
Item Purchased	33–52	20	Alphanumeric
Quantity Purchased	53	1	Numeric, PIC 9
Balance	54–59	6	Numeric, PIC S9(4)V99
Purchase Amount	60–65	6	Numeric, PIC 9(4)V99
filler	66–70	5	Alphanumeric
Sales Clerk ID	71–72	2	Alphanumeric
Record Length		72	

Use the Clerk Name file listed in Appendix A as input for loading a non-embedded clerk name table. This file is named CLRKNAME.DAT on the Student Diskette that accompanies this book. Each record of this file has the following layout:

Field Description	Position	Length	Attribute
Sales Clerk ID	1–2	2	Alphanumeric
Sales Clerk Name	3–22	20	Alphanumeric
Record Length		22	

Output Results: Output consists of the Customer Purchases Subtotal Report listing the date of purchase, account number, customer name, item purchased, and purchase amount for each customer. Single-space between records, but double-space after clerk headings and before and after clerk subtotals. Count and print the number of records processed and the total purchases for each clerk as well as grand total at the end of the report.

The report should have a format similar to the following:

```
DATE: Z9/99/99                    ABC DEPARTMENT STORE                    PAGE Z9
TIME: Z9:99 AM                CUSTOMER PURCHASES SUBTOTAL REPORT

Clerk ID - XX           Clerk Name -  XXXXXXXXXXXXXXXXXXX

  DATE OF       ACCOUNT                                              PURCHASE
  PURCHASE      NUMBER    CUSTOMER NAME          ITEM PURCHASED       AMOUNT
  ---------     -------   --------------------   --------------------  ---------
  DD-MMM-YY     XXXXXX    XXXXXXXXXXXXXXXXXXXX   XXXXXXXXXXXXXXXXXXXX  $Z,ZZZ.99
  DD-MMM-YY     XXXXXX    XXXXXXXXXXXXXXXXXXXX   XXXXXXXXXXXXXXXXXXXX   Z,ZZZ.99
     .
     .
     .
  DD-MMM-YY     XXXXXX    XXXXXXXXXXXXXXXXXXXX   XXXXXXXXXXXXXXXXXXXX   Z,ZZZ.99

  *Totals for Clerk  XXXXXXXXXXXXXXXXXXX - Z9 Customers -  Total Purchases $ZZ,ZZ9.99

Clerk ID - XX           Clerk Name -  XXXXXXXXXXXXXXXXXXX

  DATE OF       ACCOUNT                                              PURCHASE
  PURCHASE      NUMBER    CUSTOMER NAME          ITEM PURCHASED       AMOUNT
  ---------     -------   --------------------   --------------------  ---------
  DD-MMM-YY     XXXXXX    XXXXXXXXXXXXXXXXXXXX   XXXXXXXXXXXXXXXXXXXX  $Z,ZZZ.99
     .
     .
     .
  DD-MMM-YY     XXXXXX    XXXXXXXXXXXXXXXXXXXX   XXXXXXXXXXXXXXXXXXXX   Z,ZZZ.99

  *Totals for Clerk  XXXXXXXXXXXXXXXXXXX - Z9 Customers -  Total Purchases $ZZ,ZZ9.99

**          TOTAL RECORDS PROCESSED   =   ZZ9          TOTAL PURCHASES  = $ZZ,ZZ9.99

                              END OF REPORT
```

Exercise 3: Customer Sales Subtotal Report Program

Purpose: To practice coding a COBOL program that uses the Report Writer feature. If already coded, use the program created in Laboratory Exercise 3 in Chapter 7 as a basis for this program.

Problem: Design and code a COBOL program using Report Writer that processes the records of the Customer Sales file for EZ Auto Sales and creates a Customer Sales Subtotal Report. The program should list records by auto make, printing the customer's number, name, address, purchase date, purchase price, and satisfaction rating. Include the current date and time in the page headings. Use AM/PM format for the time. Sort records by auto make before producing the report. Each time there is a change in auto make, print the number of autos listed for that make and the total purchase price. At the end of the report, provide summary lines for a count of all autos sold and total of all purchases.

Customer addresses should be obtained by using a binary search on a non-embedded table that contains the customer numbers and addresses. This table must be loaded before it can be accessed. Obtain the description of each satisfaction rating code by using an embedded table. Perform a sequential search on this table. Save this program as EX10-3.CBL.

(continued)

Exercise 3 (continued)

Input Data: Use the Customer Sales file listed in Appendix A as input. This file is named CUSTSALE.DAT on the Student Diskette that accompanies this book. The record layout for the customer records is as follows:

Field Description	Position	Length	Attribute
Customer Zip Code	1–5	5	Alphanumeric
Customer Zip + 4	6–9	4	Alphanumeric
Customer Number	10–13	4	Alphanumeric
Customer Name	14–33	20	Alphanumeric
Purchase Date	34–39	6	Numeric, PIC 9(6)
Auto Make	40–59	20	Alphanumeric
Purchase Price	60–66	7	Numeric, PIC 9(5)V99
Year of Auto	67–70	4	Alphanumeric
filler	71–73	3	Alphanumeric
Satisfaction Code	74	1	Alphanumeric, 0 = DISSATISFIED 1 = UNDECIDED 2 = SATISFIED
Record Length		74	

Use the Customer Address file listed in Appendix A as input for loading the non-embedded customer address table. This file is named CUSTADDR.DAT on the Student Diskette that accompanies this book. The records are already in sequence by customer number. The record layout for the customer records is as follows:

Field Description	Position	Length	Attribute
Customer Number	1–4	4	Alphanumeric
Customer Address	5–24	20	Alphanumeric
Record Length		24	

Output Results: A Customer Sales Subtotal Report should be output listing the customer's number, name, address, purchase date, purchase price, and satisfaction rating. Provide a count of the number of customers listed and total sum of purchases for each auto make as well as a grand total at the end of the report. Single-space detail lines on the report, and list the current date and time in the heading. The time should be in AM/PM format. The report should have a format similar to the following:

```
DATE: Z9/99/99                    EZ AUTO SALES                   PAGE Z9
TIME: Z9:99 AM              CUSTOMER SALES SUBTOTAL REPORT

MAKE --> XXXXXXXXXXXXXXXXXXXX
CUSTOMER CUSTOMER             STREET                PURCHASE  PURCHASE   SATIS.
NUMBER   NAME                 ADDRESS               DATE      PRICE      RATING
-------- --------------------  --------------------  --------  ---------  ---------

   XXXX  XXXXXXXXXXXXXXXXXXXX  XXXXXXXXXXXXXXXXXXXX  Z9/99/99  $ZZ,ZZZ.99  XXXXXXXXX
   XXXX  XXXXXXXXXXXXXXXXXXXX  XXXXXXXXXXXXXXXXXXXX  Z9/99/99  $ZZ,ZZZ.99  XXXXXXXXX
   XXXX  XXXXXXXXXXXXXXXXXXXX  XXXXXXXXXXXXXXXXXXXX  Z9/99/99  $ZZ,ZZZ.99  XXXXXXXXX
            . . .
                                                               ----------
*  TOTAL OF ZZ9 CARS OF MAKE XXXXXXXXXXXXXXXXXXXX SOLD FOR      $ZZZ,ZZZ.99

MAKE --> XXXXXXXXXXXXXXXXXXXX
CUSTOMER CUSTOMER             STREET                PURCHASE  PURCHASE   SATIS.
NUMBER   NAME                 ADDRESS               DATE      PRICE      RATING
-------- --------------------  --------------------  --------  ---------  ---------

   XXXX  XXXXXXXXXXXXXXXXXXXX  XXXXXXXXXXXXXXXXXXXX  Z9/99/99  $ZZ,ZZZ.99  XXXXXXXXX
            . . .

                                                               ----------
*  TOTAL OF ZZ9 CARS OF MAKE XXXXXXXXXXXXXXXXXXXX SOLD FOR      $ZZZ,ZZZ.99

                        TOTAL CARS SOLD =     ZZ9
                        TOTAL PURCHASES = $ZZZ,ZZ9.99

                            END OF REPORT
```

Laboratory Assignment Test Data

This appendix lists the data found in the files used as input to the sample programs and programming assignments contained in this book. These files also can be found on the Student Diskette that accompanies this book.

Test Data Set 1: PREMIUM.DAT

This data is used in COBOL Laboratory Exercise 1 in Chapters 2, 3, 5, 6, 7, and 10.

```
         1         2         3         4         5         6         7
1234567890123456789012345678901234567890123456789012345678901234567890123456789

Allister, Collin    McDonald, Fred      AutomobileAM-1991-92230012345PM199411
Amfelter, Audrey    McDonald, Fred      AutomobileAM-2199-92290045650FF199606
Andrews, Robert     Anderson, James     Home      HM-7008-05070056000PM199011
Antich, Roseanne    McDonald, Fred      AutomobileAM-7211-72610025050PF199505
Anytime, Seeue      McDonald, Fred      AutomobileAM-7623-12210023400FF199701
Baker, Bonnie       Jones, William      Renter    RT-4402-32110015000NM199302
Brannan, Clyde      Benson, Gloria      Term Life TL-7008-55510055000NM199703
Byman, Goodie       Anderson, James     Home      HM-1107-23930245000NM199604
Cannon, Wylde       Benson, Gloria      AutomobileAM-6128-21510155000NM199705
Connors, Cindy      Jones, William      Home      HM-5109-41710085000NM199607
Danners, Sarah      McDonald, Fred      Term Life TL-7303-34520045000NM199508
Duffy, Chester      Jean, Barbara       Term Life TL-7007-56910045000NM199609
Eastling, Edward    Anderson, James     AutomobileAM-7373-11470055000DM199310
Eman, Sorik         Jean, Barbara       Annuity   AN-0868-48200235000NM199710
Estovar, Franko     Benson, Gloria      Home      HM-5555-32340134050FM199309
Flagg, Wavadee      Benson, Gloria      Renter    RT-1189-85330088000NM199609
Foreman, Otto       Jones, William      Annuity   AN-4043-65100030000FM198008
Framptin, Charles   Jean, Barbara       Home      HM-1113-26660078000FM199008
Franken, Peter      Jean, Barbara       Renter    RT-9083-67620030725FM199207
Franklin, Steven    Benson, Gloria      Home      HM-4441-16620095000FM199106
Fredricks, Sally    Jean, Barbara       Annuity   AN-1181-64640040000DF199505
Garcia, William     Benson, Gloria      Annuity   AN-3453-98340035000FM199105
Garfield, Joey      Anderson, James     AutomobileAM-9878-56470036000PM199504
Glidden, Findda     Anderson, James     Renter    RT-5421-22210068000NM199504
Golden, Summer      Anderson, James     AutomobileAM-7993-43470040000FF199403
Kackel, Henna       Benson, Gloria      Annuity   AN-4141-12560018050PF199503
Kracken, Gretchen   Jones, William      Renter    RT-3421-04560028080PF199603
Kramer, Robert      Jones, William      Renter    RT-1002-15510038025FM199302
Kramer, Wally       Jones, William      Whole LifeWL-0221-24220020020FM199001
Kratchet, Emily     Benson, Gloria      Annuity   AN-4410-07740105000FF198501
Krevits, Gloria     McDonald, Fred      Renter    RT-1122-73260040050FF199302
```

```
          1         2         3         4         5         6         7
12345678901234567890123456789012345678901234567890123456789012345678901234567890123456789

Leach, Raeanne      Jones, William    AutomobileAM-1004-25530100550PF199104
Lynch, Agnis        Jean, Barbara     Renter    RT-5525-05560023050PF199603
Machen, Michael     Jones, William    Home      HM-1144-44260156000NM199202
McColly, Stephen    Anderson, James   Annuity   AN-4551-11020030000FM199505
McGreger, Karla     Anderson, James   Annuity   AN-3366-22420035000DF198806
McVickers, Sam      Anderson, James   Whole LifeWL-1222-14440042550FM198204
Michaels, Ramsey    Anderson, James   Annuity   AN-6566-88020020030FM199407
Motorhead, Ima      Jones, William    Renter    RT-0944-92510020000PF199508
Neierson, Henry     Benson, Gloria    Term Life TL-6220-20920034000FM199509
Nelson, Grace       Jones, William    Home      HM-2112-12550019020PF199601
Ollenford, Winnie   Jean, Barbara     Home      HM-4123-65410178000PF199110
Olson, Wally        McDonald, Fred    Annuity   AN-4422-22260055000PF199611
Pally, Jane         Benson, Gloria    Term Life TL-5522-21210046000PF199212
Parnelli, Frank     Benson, Gloria    Term Life TL-6763-00930025000FM199012
Partridge, Danny    Benson, Gloria    Renter    RT-4421-40910046000FM199511
Pittman, Betty J.   Jacobson, Peter   Home      HM-5111-47810103000PF198703
Potter, Louise      McDonald, Fred    Renter    RT-9122-84220013050PF199705
Qualizza, Scotter   Jones, William    Renter    RT-3331-34510014050PF199606
Ramsey, Lindsay     McDonald, Fred    Home      HM-4112-24520038000PF199702
Samson, Delight     Benson, Gloria    Term Life TL-3319-16140025000NF199604
Sanders, Kevin      Jones, William    Renter    RT-6678-55050055050FM199409
Seaweed, Lostin     Anderson, James   Annuity   AN-5011-02520029000PF199608
Senef, Marcia       McDonald, Fred    AutomobileAM-3323-34410078080FF199307
Shorts, Jimmy       Benson, Gloria    Annuity   AN-0450-94110028000FM199507
Skinner, Owen       Benson, Gloria    Home      HM-3308-66470160440PM198605
Solenfeld, Nancy    Jacobson, Peter   Home      HM-8767-87880098000PF199206
Solfelt, Wanda      Jones, William    Home      HM-7878-70650088050FF199403
Solinski, Paula     Jacobson, Peter   Term Life TL-2762-27280026825NF199304
Solloday, Tom       Jacobson, Peter   Home      HM-2001-73380079090PM199507
Sollyfield, Barbara Jacobson, Peter   Home      HM-2322-44880145050PF199209
Tully, Paula        Jones, William    Renter    RT-4337-74880017500PF199703
Vlasic, Roberta     McDonald, Fred    Term Life TL-2129-89590038000PF199604
Walters, Samuel     Jones, William    Renter    RT-0424-00530022000PF199407
West, William       Anderson, James   Annuity   AN-0993-41040040000NM199507
White, Robert       Anderson, James   Whole LifeWL-0454-56980036075FM199603
Whitman, Walter     Anderson, James   AutomobileAM-3411-12230077100PM199405
Wilder, Eugene      Jean, Barbara     Whole LifeWL-0082-19130038000FM199605
Willis, Richard     Anderson, James   Renter    RT-9580-00030085000FM199504
Winder, Robert      Anderson, James   Term Life TL-7682-09030030550FM199302
Winfield, Wally     Anderson, James   Whole LifeWL-2721-39040032600PM199601
Yackley, Yourto     Jones, William    Renter    RT-7127-50760024000PF199402


TOTAL RECORDS = 72
```

Test Data Set 2: CUSTOMER.DAT

This data is used in COBOL Laboratory Exercise 2 in Chapters 2, 3, 5, 6, 7, 8, and 10, and in Exercise 3 in Chapter 9.

```
          1         2         3         4         5         6         7
1234567890123456789012345678901234567890123456789012345678901234567890123456789012

083097100101ALBERT, PETER A.     SVGA MONITOR        10120210330890150001
082597100103ALLENSON, SHEILA M.  OAK DESK            20238680874300150003
090197100105ANDERSON, ALENE T.   SWIVEL DESK CHAIR   40137830535900150005
082697100107BILLINGS, BARBARA    EXECUTIVE DESK CHAIR20038500174500150006
082697100110CANNON, FREDDY B.B.  PLASTIC FLOOR MAT   10000000040600150011
082997100113CHAPMAN, CHARLES M.  METAL COAT RACK     20140000160000200002
082797100125CLAFFLIN, WALTER E.  5 DRAWER CABINET    30125000230850210003
082797100127COMPANA, ESTER       PRINTER TABLE       10115500100000150006
082897100141COOPER, BART B.      CORRUGATED ORGANIZER10000000030890100004
082897100153CRAIG, BOBO B.       5" MESSAGE PADS     20010000024300150005
082897100166DOGGINS, CARL        DELUXE LABEL MAKER  10090000150000150004
082997100169DOWNING, M. JR.      OAK TABLE           30155500395500200001
082797100180DRIFT, ELWOOD G.     #14 RUBBER BANDS    20000000004600250006
082997100193ERIKSON, LEAF E.     SHIPPING TAPE       20009400009400300006
082897100225FREELAND, ROBERT A.  560M HARD DRIVE     20100000387900150004
082697100247FRONT, EDDIE         CONST. ADHESIVE     30080500114500150009
```

```
         1         2         3         4         5         6         7
1234567890123456789012345678901234567890123456789012345678901234567890012

083097100301GARCIA, JOSE I.       RUBBER STATIC MAT  30040000067000100011
090297100313HATFIELD, BRADLEY     DELUXE DESK PAD    50045000084500150003
083097100345HELLER, HELEN H.      3-HOLE PUNCH       20047600085900150006
083097100357HENDRIX, JAMES D.     FLOOR LAMP         10000000071500150005
090197100360ISLANDER, JENNEY      LEATHER ATTACHE CASE30200000240000100011
090197100383LADA, LAWRENCE        STANDARD STAPLES   50009500009500150002
090397100385LADD, WALTER          CORDLESS WALL CLOCK 30102200145200150003
090197100397LAMB, FREDRICK E.     NO. 1 PRINT RIBBON  50091500111500150005
090297100440LEELAND, WESLEY       CORRUGATED ORGANIZER10000000030890200004
090297100453LOFTIS, DOUGLAS L.    RECYCLING BIN      40110000190000250006
090297100461MILLER, SUSAN S.      METAL STORAGE CLOSET10078800104500150004
090397100469MUDGLEY, BRENDA       WORK ROOM TABLE    30125500210000150003
090397100480NICKELS, KATHY        6' BOOK SHELF      20050000120600150006
090197100493NOWAKOWSKI, WILLIAM   3-1/2" DISK HOLDER  40000000024400150002
090397100535PATTERSON, PATRICK    28.8 FAX MODEM     20040000140000150001
090397100547PETERSON, ROBERT A.   MARKER BOARD       30092250092500150009
082697100551POTTER, WINFRED I.    LARGE BINDERS      40010250030250150001
090497100563PUCKETT, CHARLIE M.   OAK DESK           20238680874300150003
090497100605PYLE, G. ALFRED       SWIVEL DESK CHAIR  20100500305000100005
082597100617RASKIN, RUTH ANN      EXECUTIVE DESK CHAIR10009500124000150006
090497100710RAYMOND, RONALD       RUBBER FLOOR MAT   80230000230000150011
090197100713REYNOLDS, LARRY       STAINLESS COAT RACK 30235000350000150002
090497100735RICHMOND, RICHARD     2 DRAWER CABINET   40100000260950150003
090497100787ROAMES, RICHARD       CD HEADSET         10095500955000100006
090597100811SANDERSON, PAULETTE   GENERAL LEDGER CARDS20005000006020100004
090597100843SINGER, ALEXIS E.     4" MESSAGE PADS    40015000004300150005
090597100886SUMMERS, SUSAN        STANDARD LABELS    40075500090500150004
090597100909SWEET, VIRGIL         6' OAK TABLE       20100500255500150001
090497100940SWIFT, RANDOLPH       GENERAL LEDGER CARDS10000000002400150004
090397100993TANDY, SANDI          RED SHIPPING TAPE  60010450012450150006
090297200025TERRY, LARRY M.       720M HARD DRIVE    20530000650000150004
090197200047THOMPSON, RODNEY      GENERAL LEDGER CARDS40180000234600200009
083097200111TONEY, ANTHONY A.     RUBBER STATIC MAT  60120000130000150011
083097200123TOYOTA, SEMINEW       75 WATT DESK LAMP  30105000140500150003
082697200245TYLANDI, SHONI        STANDARD OAK DESK  50450000065000150006
082797200357UPLAND, JILL O.       FLOOR LAMP         20095000131500100005
090197200360UZUBELL, RINGA        INSULATED BRIEF CASE10110000160000150011
082597200383VANBUREN, WINSTON     STANDARD STAPLES   20003500004500150002
090297200485VANWINKLE, RALPH      CORDLESS WALL CLOCK 50312500395500200003
090297200557VONRYAN, ERICK        NO. 7 PRINT RIBBON  70140500172500150005
082997200646VYLASTIC, JAYLAND     CORRUGATED ORGANIZER10020000030950150004
090597200753WALLACE, MICHAEL      RECYCLING BIN      60220000380000150006
090197200871WALTON, JOHN B.       GENERAL LEDGER CARDS30160800154500150004
082597300069WILLIAMS, RONDA       METAL WORK TABLE   30225000310000150003
082797300281WYMAN, JANE           4' BOOK SHELF      40250000320000150006
082897300333YULANE, WANDA         3-1/2" DISK HOLDER 20060000014400200002
090397300415ZIPPO, ARTHUR         14.4 FAX MODEM     10070000120000150001
090497300444ZOONEY, WILLIAM       DESK SET W/CLOCK   30450000030000150009

TOTAL RECORDS = 64
```

Test Data Set 3: CUSTSALE.DAT

This data is used in COBOL Laboratory Exercise 3 in Chapters 2, 3, 5, 6, 7, 8, and 10, and in Exercises 4 and 5 in Chapter 9.

```
         1         2         3         4         5         6         7
12345678901234567890123456789012345678901234567890123456789012345678901234

4641012341001ALBERT, CARL T.       082597FORD          02550001991    2
4630712011003ANDREWS, ROBERT       082697CHEVROLET     07000001958    0
4642323111008ANZIO, RAFELINO       090197CHEVROLET     04560501978    0
4642401211010ASHLEY, WILLIAM B.    090297PIERCE-ARROW  12400001932    2
4637531101015ATKINSON, MARK        082797STUDEBAKER    00500001958    1
4640512911025AVERY, ALFRED A.      082997HUDSON        02300001954    1
4630112341031BEZZMEK, JENNIFER     082797FORD          04550001995    2
4630312011033BLAKE, DONALD         082997FORD          07220501989    1
4641323111041BLONDELL, BONNIE      090497CHEVROLET     03560501988    0
4640401211045BONADIO, JAMES        090397PIERCE-ARROW  11500001935    2
```

```
        1         2         3         4         5         6         7
12345678901234567890123456789012345678901234567890123456789012345678901234

4630731101055BUCKO, ONIEDA        082897STUDEBAKER         02450001964   1
4641012911056BYMANN, FREDRICK     082997FORD               03300001994   1
4634212341061CALBERT, RONALD      090597FORD               03550001993   2
4630712111063CHELSEA, MARTHA S.   083097DODGE BROS.        03500001935   0
4641023111067CLAFLIN, WAYNE R.    090197CHEVROLET          04560501990   0
4641001211070COLE, CHARLES C.     090297PIERCE-ARROW       10500001929   2
4630531111075COLEMAN, THOMAS      082797STUDEBAKER         01670501961   1
4641012211076COLWELL, RICHARD L.  082997HUDSON             04300001940   1
4641412311080COOPER, JOHNATHAN    090597FORD               12560001996   2
4630712012002COREY, SARAH D.      082797CHEVROLET          06500501994   0
4642123112004CRACKLIN, GOODMAN    090197CHEVROLET          14560501996   0
4632301212011CRAWFORD, TIMOTHY    090197PIERCE-ARROW       10400001931   2
4631531102012CURRIE, RAYMOND      082897STUDEBAKER         01500251956   1
4642512912024CYBORG, IZORE M.     090597HUDSON             01300001949   1
4641012342031DALTON, DAVID P.     082597FORD               02340001990   2
4630712012043DAVIES, RALPH O.     082697CHEVROLET          03330001989   0
4642323112048DENNICK, DONNA       090197CHEVROLET          06560251997   0
4642401212050DERBIN, DEANNA       090297PIERCE-ARROW       16400251937   2
4637531102065DONNEHUE, PHILLIP    090497STUDEBAKER         00540001966   1
4640512912085DOPPLER, RADAR O.    083097HUDSON             03110001951   1
4631012342091DUNLOP, RITA         082597FORD               14500451996   2
4630312013003DYKES, CYNTHIA       082697FORD               04100501987   1
4641323113011EATON, ESTER B.      090197CHEVROLET          13560501996   0
4640401213015EFFLEY, BAILY        090297PIERCE-ARROW       14460451933   2
4630731103025EGGERTON, AMANDA     082997STUDEBAKER         03350001965   1
4641012913026EPPLEY, DAVID        082897FORD               04140001995   1
4634212343031ERKLE, ROSA          090397FORD               03550201993   2
4630712113043FARNSWORTH, WESLEY   090597DODGE BROS.        11500001996   0
4641023113047FLANNERY, JAMES      090197CHEVROLET          04500501992   0
4641001213050FOREMAN, OTTO J.     090297PIERCE-ARROW       09400001927   2
4630531113055FOWLER, KATHLEEN     082797STUDEBAKER         02670501964   1
4641012213056FURNACE, DAVID       082997HUDSON             05300001948   1
4641412313061GALLAGHER, CLARENCE  090497FORD               10060001992   2
4630712013062GENNERRO, TONY S.    083097CHEVROLET          03200501989   0
4642123113066GOEBEL, NANCY K.     090297CHEVROLET          06430501990   0
4632301213072GUNTHER, FREDERICK   090397PIERCE-ARROW       12600001930   2
4631531103080HAINES, MARSHALL     082997STUDEBAKER         02500251959   1
4642512913094HANCOCK, JONATHON    090397HUDSON             03300001953   1
4642323113098HARTNETT, ROBERTO    090597CHEVROLET          03260401988   0
4642401214005HENNING, SONIA       090597PIERCE-ARROW       13050001928   2
4637531104009HORNSBY, ROGERS      082597STUDEBAKER         01675001962   1
4640512914012HYATT, JANET F.      083097HUDSON             01550001951   1
4630112344021IDZIOR, RAYMOND      090197FORD               14600001996   2
4630312014022JENNINGS, WILLIAM    082697FORD               06120401992   1
4641023114024JOHNSON, JACK        090397CHEVROLET          02560501985   0
4640401214032KULKA, ROBERT C.     090497PIERCE-ARROW       09700001934   2
4630731104035KURTZ, DONALD        083097STUDEBAKER         03450001966   1
4641012914038LEVANDOWSKI, JILL    082897DODGE BROS.        04300001988   1
4634212344044METZ, ARNOLD E.      090197FORD               13230001996   2
4630712114046NORRIS, CHARLES S.   090597CHEVROLET          08440001992   0
4641023114047NOWAKOWSKI, ALFRED   090197DODGE BROS.        06560501994   1
4641001214053O'BOYLE, NIEL        090397PIERCE-ARROW       15500001938   2
4630531114056O'BRIAN, PATRICK     083097STUDEBAKER         03470501962   1
4641012214059PATTERSON, LENNI R.  082997HUDSON             02500001946   1
4641412314061PERRY, SHAMUS        090597FORD               08950001994   2
4630712014066REED, ROBERT B.      082797CHEVROLET          07400501996   0
4642123114067RODRIGUEZ, ALONZO    090597DODGE BROS.        10500501995   0
4632301214073SANCHEZ, HENRY       090197PIERCE-ARROW       08300001925   2
4631531104081SWARTZ, HECTOR       082897STUDEBAKER         00750251954   1
4630112344084TORREZ, MARTIN       082797FORD               05650001994   2
4630312014090TUTTLE, MARK         082997FORD               07100501996   1
4641323114094WARNER, JACK         090497CHEVROLET          08560501996   0
4640401214115YACKLEY, YOURTO      090497PIERCE-ARROW       10000001930   2
```

TOTAL RECORDS = 73

Test Data Set 4: NEWPREM.DAT

This data is used in COBOL Laboratory Exercise 1 in Chapter 4.

```
         1         2         3         4         5         6         7
1234567890123456789012345678901234567890123456789012345678901234567890123456789
Allister, Collin   McDonald, Fred      AutomobileAM-1991-92230012345PM199411
Amfelter, Audrey   McDonald, Fred      AutomobilePM-2199-92290045650FF199606
Andrews, Robert    Anderson, James     Home      HM-70P8-05070056000PM199011
Antich, Roseanne   McDonald, Fred      AutomobileAM-7211-72610025050PF199405
Anytime, Seeue     McDonald, Fred      AutomobileAM-7623-12210023400FF199501
Baker, Bonnie                          Renter    RT-4402-32110015000NM199702
Brannan, Clyde     Benson, Gloria      Term Life TL-7008-55510055000NM199303
Byman, Goodie      Anderson, James     Phone     HM-0007-23930245000NM199704
Cannon, Wylde      Benson, Gloria      AutomobileAN-6128-21510155000NM199605
Connors, Cindy     Jones, William      Home      HM-0009-41710085000NM199707
Danners, Sarah     McDonald, Fred      Term Life TL-7303-34520045000NM199608
Duffy, Chester     Jean, Barbara       Term Life TL-7007-56910045000NM199609
                   Anderson, James     AutomobileAM-7373-11470055000DM199510
Eman, Sorik        Jean, Barbara       Annuity   AN-0868-00200235000NM199610
Estovar, Franko    Benson, Gloria      Home      HM-5555-32340134050FM199309
Flagg, Wavadee     Benson, Gloria      Renter    RT-1189-85330000800NM199709
Foreman, Otto      Jones, William      Annuity   AN-4043-6510003J000FM198308
Framptin, Charles  Jean, Barbara       Homely    HM-1113-26660078000SS199008
Franken, Peter     Jean, Barbara       Renter    RT-9083-67620030725FM199207
Franklin, Steven   Benson, Gloria      Home      HM-4441-16620095000FM199100
Fredricks, Sally                       Annuity   AN-1181-64640000000DN199505
Garcia, William    Benson, Gloria      Annuity   AN-3453-98340035000FM199105
Garfield, Joey     Anderson, James     AutomobileAM-9878-56470036000PM1995
Glidden, Findda    Anderson, James     Renter    RT-5421-22210068000NM199504
Golden, Summer     Anderson, James     AutomobileRT-7993-43470040000FF199403
Kackel, Henna      Benson, Gloria      Annuity   AN-4141-12560018050PF199503
Kracken, Gretchen  Jones, William      Renter    RT-3421-04560028080PF199603
Kramer, Robert     Jones, William      Renter    RT-0002-00000038025FM199302
Kramer, Wally      Jones, William      Whole LifeWL-0221-24220020020FM199001
Kratchet, Emily    Benson, Gloria      Annuity   AN-4410-07740105000FF1985A1
Krevits, Gloria    McDonald, Fred      Renter    RR-1122-73260040050FF199302
Leach, Raeanne     Jones, William      AutomobileAM-1004-25530100550PF199104
Lynch, Agnis       Jean, Barbara       Renter    RT-5525-05560023050PF199603
Machen, Michael    Jones, William      Home      HM-1144-44260156000NM199202
McColly, Stephen   Anderson, James     Annuity   AN-4551-11020030000FM199505
McGreger, Karla    Anderson, James     Annuity   AN-3366-22420035000DF198806
McVickers, Sam     Anderson, James     Whole LifeWL-1222-14440042550FM198204
                   Anderson, James               AN-6566-88020020030FM199407
Motorhead, Ima     Jones, William      Renter    RT-0944-92510020000PF199508
Neierson, Henry    Benson, Gloria      Term Life TL-6220-20920034000FM199509
Nelson, Grace      Jones, William      Home      HM-2112-12550019020PF199601
Ollenford, Winnie  Jean, Barbara       Home      HM-4123-65410178000PF199110
Olson, Wally       McDonald, Fred      Annuity   AN-4422-22260055000PF199611
Pally, Jane        Benson, Gloria      Term Life TL-5522-21210000000VF199212
Parnelli, Frank    Benson, Gloria      Term Life TL-6763-00930025000FM199012
Partridge, Danny   Benson, Gloria      Renter    RT-4421-40910046000FM199511
Pittman, Betty J.  Jacobson, Peter     Home      HM-5111-47810103000PF198703
Potter, Louise     McDonald, Fred      Renter    RT-9122-84220013050PF199705
Qualizza, Scotter  Jones, William      Blender   RT-3331-34510014050PB199606
Ramsey, Lindsay    McDonald, Fred      Home      HM-4112-24Q2003800PPF199702
Samson, Delight    Benson, Gloria      Term Life TL-3319-16140025000NF199604
Sanders, Kevin     Jones, William      Renter    RT-6678-55050055050FM199409
Seaweed, Lostin    Anderson, James     Annuity   AM-0011-02520000290AF199608
Senef, Marcia      McDonald, Fred      AutomobileAM-3323-34410078080FG199307
Shorts, Jimmy      Benson, Gloria      Annuity   AN-0450-94110028000FM199507
Skinner, Owen      Benson, Gloria      Home      HM-3308-66470160440PM198605
Solenfeld, Nancy   Jacobson, Peter     Home      HM-8767-87880098000PF199206
Solfelt, Wanda                         Home      HN-UU98 706500AA050VG199803
Solinski, Paula    Jacobson, Peter     Term Life TL-2762-27280026825NF199604
Solloday, Tom      Jacobson, Peter     Home      HM-2001-73380079090PM199407
Sollyfield, Babara Jacobson, Peter     Home      HM-2322-44880145050PF199509
Tully, Paula       Jones, William      Renter    RT-4337-74880017500PF199603
Vlasic, Roberta    McDonald, Fred      Term Life TL-0029-99990000800MN199W04
Walters, Samuel    Jones, William      Renter    RT-0424-00530022000PF199507
West, William      Anderson, James     Annuity   AN-0993-41040040000NM199607
White, Robert      Anderson, James     Whole LifeWL-0454-56980036075FM199403
```

```
          1         2         3         4         5         6         7
1234567890123456789012345678901234567890123456789012345678901234567890123456789

Whitman, Walter    Anderson, James   AutomobileAM-3411-12230077100PM199605
Wilder, Eugene     Jean, Barbara     Whole LifeWW-0082-191300380000M199505
Willis, Richard    Anderson, James   Renter    RT-9580-00030085000FM199404
Winder, Robert     Anderson, James   Term Life TL-7682-09030030550FM199302
Winfield, Wally    Anderson, James   Whole LifeWL-2721-39040032600PM199601
Yackley, Yourto    Jones, William    Renter    RT-7127-50760024000PF199402


TOTAL RECORDS = 72
```

Test Data Set 5: NEWCUST.DAT

This data is used in COBOL Laboratory Exercise 2 in Chapter 4.

```
          1         2         3         4         5         6         7
123456789012345678901234567890123456789012345678901234567890123456789012

083097100101ALBERT, PETER A.     SVGA MONITOR        10120210330890150001
082597100103ALLENSON, SHEILA M.  OAK DESK            20238680874300150003
090197100105ANDERSON, ALENE T.   SWIVEL DESK CHAIR   40137830535500150005
082697100107BILLINGS, BARBARA    EXECUTIVE DESK CHAIR20038500174500050006
082697A00110CANNON, FREDDY B.B.  PLASTIC FLOOR MAT   10000000040600150011
082997100113CHAPMAN, CHARLES M.  METAL COAT RACK     20140000160000200002
082797100125CLAFFLIN, WALTER E.  5 DRAWER CABINET    30125000230850210003
082797100127COMPANA, ESTER       PRINTER TABLE       10115500100000150006
082897100141COOPER, BART B.      CORRUGATED ORGANIZER10000000030890100004
0828971  153CRAIG, BOBO B.       5" MESSAGE PADS     20010000024300150005
082897100166DOGGINS, CARL        DELUXE LABEL MAKER  10090000150000150004
082997100169DOWNING, M. JR.      OAK TABLE           30155500395500200001
082797100180DRIFT, ELWOOD G.     #14 RUBBER BANDS    20000000004600250006
082997100193ERIKSON, LEAF E.     SHIPPING TAPE       20009400009400300006
08289710K225                     560M HARD DRIVE     20Z000003879Z0150004
082697100247FRONT, EDDIE         CONST. ADHESIVE     30080500114500150009
083097100301GARCIA, JOSE I.      RUBBER STATIC MAT   30040000000000100011
090297100313HATFIELD, BRADLEY    DELUXE DESK PAD     50045000084500150003
083097100345HELLER, HELEN H.     3-HOLE PUNCH        20047600000000550006
083097100357HENDRIX, JAMES D.    FLOOR LAMP          10000000071500000005
090197100360ISLANDER, JENNEY     LEATHER ATTACHE CASE302000002400001S0011
090197100383LADA, LAWRENCE       STANDARD STAPLES    50009500009500150002
090397100385LADD, WALTER         CORDLESS WALL CLOCK 30102200145200150003
090197100397LAMB, FREDRICK E.    NO. 1 PRINT RIBBON  50091500111500150005
090297100440LEELAND, WESLEY      CORRUGATED ORGANIZER10000000030890200004
090297100453LOFTIS, DOUGLAS L.   RECYCLING BIN       40110000190000250006
090297100461MILLER, SUSAN S.     METAL STORAGE CLOSET10078800104500150004
090397100469MUDGLEY, BRENDA      WORK ROOM TABLE     30125500210000150003
090397100480NICKELS, KATHY       6' BOOK SHELF       200500001SS600150006
090197100493NOWAKOWSKI, WILLIAM  3-1/2" DISK HOLDER  40000000024400150002
090397100535PATTERSON, PATRICK   28.8 FAX MODEM      20040000140000150001
090397100547PETERSON, ROBERT A.  MARKER BOARD        30092250092500150009
082697100551POTTER, WINFRED I.   LARGE BINDERS       40010250030250150001
0904971005 3PUCKETT, CHARLIE M.  OAK DESK            20238680 74300150003
090497100605PYLE, G. ALFRED      SWIVEL DESK CHAIR   20100500305000100005
082597100617RASKIN, RUTH ANN     EXECUTIVE DESK CHAIR10009500012400015000
090497100710RAYMOND, RONALD      RUBBER FLOOR MAT    80230000230000008011
090197100713REYNOLDS, LARRY      STAINLESS COAT RACK 30235000350000150002
090497100735RICHMOND, RICHARD    2 DRAWER CABINET    40100000260950150003
090497000000ROAMES, RICHARD      CD HEADSET          10095500955000100006
090597100811SANDERSON, PAULETTE  GENERAL LEDGER CARDS20005000006020100004
090597100843SINGER, ALEXIS E.    4" MESSAGE PADS     40015000004300150005
090597100886                     STANDARD LABELS     40075V00090500090004
090597100909SWEET, VIRGIL        6' OAK TABLE        20100500255500150001
090497100940SWIFT, RANDOLPH      GENERAL LEDGER CARDS10000000002400150006
090397100993TANDY, SANDI         RED SHIPPING TAPE   600X0450012450150006
090297200025TERRY, LARRY M.      720M HARD DRIVE     20530000650000150004
090197200047THOMPSON, RODNEY     GENERAL LEDGER CARDS40180000234600200009
083097200111TONEY, ANTHONY A.    RUBBER STATIC MAT   60120000130000150011
083097200123TOYOTA, SEMINEW      75 WATT DESK LAMP   30105000140500150003
082697200245                     STANDARD OAK DESK   50G50000065000150006
082797200357UPLAND, JILL O.      FLOOR LAMP          20095000131500100005
090197200360UZUBELL, RINGA       INSULATED BRIEF CASE10110000160000450011
```

```
          1         2         3         4         5         6         7
1234567890123456789012345678901234567890123456789012345678901234567890123456789012

082597000383VANBUREN, WINSTON    STANDARD STAPLES    20003500004500150002
090297200485VANWINKLE, RALPH     CORDLESS WALL CLOCK 50312500000000000003
090297200557VONRYAN, ERICK       NO. 7 PRINT RIBBON  70140500172500150005
082997200646VYLASTIC, JAYLAND    CORRUGATED ORGANIZER100200000309501A0004
0905972[[753WALLACE, MICHAEL     RECYCLING BIN       60220000380000150006
090197200871WALTON, JOHN B.      GENERAL LEDGER CARDS30160800154500350004
082597300069WILLIAMS, RONDA      METAL WORK TABLE    30225000310000150003
082797300281WYMAN, JANE          4' BOOK SHELF       40250000320000150006
082897300333YULANE, WANDA        3-1/2" DISK HOLDER  20060000014400200002
090397300415ZIPPO, ARTHUR        14.4 FAX MODEM      10070000120000150001
090497300444ZOONEY, WILLIAM      DESK SET W/CLOCK    30450000030000150009

TOTAL RECORDS = 64
```

Test Data Set 6: NEWSALE.DAT

This data is used in COBOL Laboratory Exercise 3 in Chapter 4.

```
          1         2         3         4         5         6         7
1234567890123456789012345678901234567890123456789012345678901234567890123456789901234

4641012341001ALBERT, CARL T.      082597FORD          02550001991  2
4630712011003ANDREWS, ROBERT      082697CHEVROLET     07000001958
4642323140000ANZIO, RAFELINO      090197CHEVROLET     04560501978  A
4642401211010ASHLEY, WILLIAM B.   090297PIERCE-ARROW  12400001932  2
4637531101015ATKINSON, MARK       082797STUDEBAKER    00500001958  1
4640512911025AVERY, ALFRED A.     082997HUDSON        02300001954  1
4630112341031BEZZMEK, JENNIFER    082797FORD          04550001995  2
4630312011033BLAKE, DONALD        002997FORD          00000001989  1
4641323111041BLONDELL, BONNIE     090497CHEVROLET     03560501988  0
4640401211045                     090397PIERCE-ARROW  11500001935  4
46307311010AABUCKO, ONIEDA        082897STUDEBAKER    02450001964  1
4641012911056BYMANN, FREDRICK     082997FORD          03300001994  1
4634212341061CALBERT, RONALD      090597FORD          03550001993  2
4630712111063CHELSEA, MARTHA S.   083097DODGE BROS.   03500001935  0
4641023111067CLAFLIN, WAYNE R.    090197CHEVROLET     04560501990  0
4641001211070COLE, CHARLES C.     090299PIERCE-ARROW  10500001929  2
4630531111075COLEMAN, THOMAS      082797STUDEBAKER    01670501961  1
4641012211076COLWELL, RICHARD L.  082997HUDSON        043000]1940  1
4641412311080COOPER, JOHNATHAN    090597FORD          12560001996  3
4630712012002COREY, SARAH D.      082797CHEVROLET     06500501994  0
4642123112004CRACKLIN, GOODMAN    090197CHEVROLET     14560501996  0
463230121Z011CRAWFORD, TIMOTHY    090197PIERCE-ARROW  10400001931  2
4631531102012CURRIE, RAYMOND      082897STUDEBAKER    01500251956  1
4642512912024CYBORG, IZORE M.     090597HUDSON        01300001949  1
4641012342031DALTON, DAVID P.     082597FORD          02340001990  2
4630712012043DAVIES, RALPH O.     082697CHEVROLET     03330001989  0
4642323112048DENNICK, DONNA       090197CHEVROLET     06560251995  0
4642401212050DERBIN, DEANNA       A90297PIERCE-ARROW  16400251937  2
4637531102065DONNEHUE, PHILLIP    090497STUDEBAKER    00540001966  1
4640512912085DOPPLER, RADAR O.    083097HUDSON        03110001951  1
4631012342091DUNLOP, RITA         082597FORD          1ZZ00451996  2
4630312013003DYKES, CYNTHIA       082697FORD          04100501987  1
4641323113011EATON, ESTER B.      090197CHEVROLET     13560501996  0
4640401213015EFFLEY, BAILY        090297PIERCE-ARROW  14460451933  2
4630731103025EGGERTON, AMANDA     082997STUDEBAKER    03350001965  1
4641012913026EPPLEY, DAVID        122897FORD          04140001995  1
4634212343031ERKLE, ROSA          090397FORD          03550201993  2
4630712113043FARNSWORTH, WESLEY   090597DODGE BROS.   11500001996  0
4641023113047FLANNERY, JAMES      090197CHEVROLET     04500501992  0
4641001213050FOREMAN, OTTO J.     090297PIERCE-ARROW  09400001927  2
4630531113055FOWLER, KATHLEEN     082797STUDEBAKER    02670501964  1
4641012213056FURNACE, DAVID       082997HUDSON        05300001948  1
4641412313061GALLAGHER, CLARENCE  090497FORD          10060001992  2
46307120130 GENNERRO, TONY S.     083097CHEVROLET     03200501989  0
4642123113066GOEBEL, NANCY K.     090297CHEVROLET     06430501990  0
4632301213072GUNTHER, FREDERICK   090397PIERCE-ARROW  12600001930  2
4631531103080HAINES, MARSHALL     082997STUDEBAKER    02500251959  1
4642512913094HANCOCK, JONATHON    090397HUDSON        03300001953  1
```

```
         1         2         3         4         5         6         7
1234567890123456789012345678901234567890123456789012345678901234567890123

4642323113098HARTNETT, ROBERTO    090597CHEVROLET       03260401988  0
4642401214005HENNING, SONIA       090597PIERCE-ARROW    13050001928  2
4637531104009HORNSBY, ROGERS      082597STUDEBAKER      01675001962  1
4640512914012                     083098HUDSON          01550 1951   Q
4630112344021IDZIOR, RAYMOND      090197FORD            14600001996  2
4630312014022JENNINGS, WILLIAM    082697FORD             120401992   1
4641023114024JOHNSON, JACK        090397CHEVROLET       02560501985  0
4640401214032KULKA, ROBERT C.     090497PIERCE-ARROW    09700001934  2
4630731104035KURTZ, DONALD        083000STUDEBAKER      03450001966  1
4641012914038LEVANDOWSKI, JILL    082897DODGE BROS.     00000001988  1
4634212344044METZ, ARNOLD E.      090197FORD            13230001996
4630712114046NORRIS, CHARLES S.   090597CHEVROLET       08440001992  0
4641023114047NOWAKOWSKI, ALFRED   090197DODGE BROS.     06560501994  1
46410012140530'BOYLE, NIEL        090397PIERCE-ARROW    15500001938  2
46305311140560'BRIAN, PATRICK     083097STUDEBAKER      03470501962  1
4641012214059PATTERSON, LENNI R.  082997HUDSON          02500001946  1
4641412314061PERRY, SHAMUS        090597FORD            08950001994  2
4630712014066REED, ROBERT B.      082797CHEVROLET       07400501996  0
4642123114067RODRIGUEZ, ALONZO    0905  DODGE BROS.     10500501995  0
4632301214073SANCHEZ, HENRY       090197PIERCE-ARROW    08300001925  2
4631531104081SWARTZ, HECTOR       082897STUDEBAKER      00750251954  1
4630112344084TORREZ, MARTIN       082797FORD            05650001994  2
4630312014090TUTTLE, MARK         082997FORD            07100501996  1
4641323114094WARNER, JACK         090497CHEVROLET       08560501996  0
4640401214115YACKLEY, YOURTO      090497PIERCE-ARROW    10000001930  2

TOTAL RECORDS = 73
```

Test Data Set 7: AGENTPHO.DAT

This data is used in COBOL Laboratory Exercise 1 in Chapters 7 and 10.

```
         1         2         3
123456789012345678901234567890012

Anderson, James    312-555-1234
Benson, Gloria     219-555-8989
Jacobson, Peter    708-555-6939
Jean, Barbara      219-555-1995
Jones, William     219-555-6736
McDonald, Fred     708-555-2115

TOTAL RECORDS = 6
```

Test Data Set 8: CLRKNAME.DAT

This data is used in COBOL Laboratory Exercise 2 in Chapters 7 and 10.

```
         1         2
1234567890123456789012

01ROGER CARTER
02SAM STONE
03SUSAN ANTON
04ANNA SANCHEZ
05ROY KELSEY
06BETTY MEYERSON
07RICHARD SAMPSON
08KARLA KAZMIRE
09JOHN ADAMS
10CONNIE YOUNG
11RODNEY ALLEN

TOTAL RECORDS = 11
```

Test Data Set 9: CUSTADDR.DAT

This data is used in COBOL Laboratory Exercise 3 in Chapters 7 and 10.

```
         1         2                              1         2
12345678901234567890123 4                   123456789012345678901234

1001123 EAST STREET                         304750 W. EAST STREET
100310202 WEST 73RD                         3050999 RIGHTWAY ROAD
10083495 WELMONT ROAD                       30557808 STURDY ROAD
10104502 ASHLEY DRIVE                       3056404 EASY STREET
1015123 NORTH 109TH ST.                     30614521 MANARD ROAD
102545 W. GRAND BLVD.                       306298 W. LINCOLN HWY.
1031239 COLORADO ST.                        3066444 KENNEDY AVE.
1033925 LINCOLN HIGHWAY                     3072707 JOLIET ROAD
10411011 BELVIEW DR.                        30801912 MADISON AVE.
104523W. 123 NORTH                          30943101 CHECKER ST.
10554705 AINSWORTH RD.                      309856 E. 89TH AVE.
1056349 W. 73RD AVE.                        4005606 MONUMENT CIRCLE
10612021 CRESTWOOD DR.                      40091792 WHITLEY AVE.
10631823 N. ADAMS                           401298 BAKER STREET
10674575 HIGHLAND PKWY.                     4021109 WASHINGTON ST.
1070879 MISSISSIPPI ST.                     4022774 N. JEFFERSON
10751903 THOMAS DR.                         40247645 HOWARD AVE.
1076542 OAKLAND CIRCLE                      40328811 CLOVERLEAF
10807021 CONGRESS PKWY.                     4035505 HICKEY STREET
20021756 CONKEY ROAD                        403852123 ROOSEVELT RD.
2004876 JOE MARTIN RD.                      40441414 VIRGINIA ST.
20112122 HOWARD ST.                         40462529 W. 86TH AVE.
201245 N. ASHLAND AVE.                      40471991 KING BLVD.
2024456 LAKESHORE DR.                       40534002 WHEELING ROAD
20316621 183RD AVE.                         40564013 CHESTERFIELD
20439809 MORRIS DR.                         40591020 BUTTERFIELD RD.
20485505 GREENE ST.                         4061515 BEVERLY STREET
2050401 TAFT ST.                            4066455 ENTERPRISE WAY
2065725 HARRISON AVE.                       406791 W. 114TH NORTH
20851212 BUCKLEY ROAD                       40738181 CHESTNUT LANE
20918008 W. 93RD AVE.                       408120021 MARTIN ROAD
30039420 STATE RD. 49                       4084391 MONROE, APT. 12
30115520 E. PAYTON ST.                      4090905 APPLE ORCHARD
30152200 BEATTY ST.                         409411223 SUNSET DRIVE
302512123 HIGHWAY 6                         41151185 PINTO STEET
3026659 WISCONSIN ST.
30312850 ROSEMONT ROAD                      TOTAL RECORDS = 73
3043840 DIRT ROAD
```

Test Data Set 10: PREMTRAN.DAT

This data is used in COBOL Laboratory Exercise 1 in Chapter 8.

```
         1         2                              1         2
12345678901234567890                        12345678901234567890

AM-1991-922300003450                        RT-9083-676200000550
AM-2199-922900006500                        HM-4441-166200001000
HM-7008-050700001050                        AN-1181-646400002200
AM-7211 726100000500                        AN-3453-983400000200
AM-7623-122100002000                        AM-9878-564700000350
RT-4402-321100006200                        RT-5421-222100010000
TL-7008-555100000800                        AM-7993-434700000000
MM-1107-239300000200                        AN-4141-125600000590
AM-6128-215100001200                        RT-3421-045600000880
HM-5109-417W00002200                        RT-5521-045600000880
TL-7303-345200000050                        RT-1002-155100001250
TL-7007-569100004500                        WL-0221-242200002250
TL-7007-569100004500                        AN-4410-077400000500
AM-7373-114700003000                        RT-1122-732600000500
AN-0868-482000000650                        AM-1004-255300001500
HM-5555-323400000540                        RT-5525-055600000550
RT-1189-853300004000                        HM-1144-442600000600
AN-4043-651000005000                        AN-4551-1102000W0000
HM-1113-266600000700                        AN-4551-110200004000
```

```
        1         2                          1         2
12345678901234567890              12345678901234567890

AN-3366-224200000300              HM-3308-664700004400
WL-1222-144400001530              HM-8767-878800000500
AN-6566-880200001300              HM-7878-706500001500
RT-0944-925100000000              TL-2762-272800000250
TL-6220-209200000250              HM-2001-733800000900
HM-2112-125500002200              HM-2322-448800000590
HM-4123-654100001100              RT-4337-748800005400
AN-4422-222600000800              TL-2129-895900002100
TL-5522-212100001000              RT-0424-005300001100
TL-6763-009300000900              AN-0993-410400000400
RT-4421-409100003000              WL-0454-569800000750
HM-5111-478100004000              AM-3411-122300001800
RT-9122-842200001500              WL-0082-191300001350
RT-3331-345100000500              RT-9580-000300000210
HM-4112-245200008000              TL-7682-090300000500
TL-3319-16140000012E              WL-2721-390400000600
RT-6678-550500000500              RT-7127-507600002100
AN-5011-025200003200              AN-4441-110200000300
AM-3323-344100000800              RT-4QQ1-110200000000
AN-0450-941100001800
                                  TOTAL RECORDS = 77
```

Test Data Set 11: CUSTTRAN.DAT

This data is used in COBOL Laboratory Exercise 2 in Chapter 8.

```
       1                                1
123456789012                     123456789012

100107000550                     200485000230
100110000210                     200557002000
100110000125                     200646001100
100125003000                     200753000490
100127000050                     200871000000
100141002100                     300069000030
100563000875                     100153001500
100605000350                     100166001000
100617000445                     100169000800
100710000310                     100180006000
100713000400                     100190001200
100735001000                     300099000830
100787001400                     300281001250
100811003100                     300333000950
100843000250                     300333001150
100886001140                     300415000750
100909000S00                     300444000550
1  940000 00                     100225000950
100993000000                     100345000450
200025000700                     100355000650
200047001200                     100357002500
200111004010                     100360004010
200111003010                     100383000530
200123000780                     100385001400
200245000800                     100397002000
100227000950                     100440001100
10024700ZZ00                     100453001300
100301000210                     100461000300
1003T3000330                     100469001200
100101000100                     100480005500
100103001000                     100493000800
100105001200                     100535001100
200357001200                     100547000900
200360001010                     100551000700
200383001100
                                 TOTAL RECORDS = 69
```

Test Data Set 12: AUTOTRAN.DAT

This data is used in COBOL Laboratory Exercise 3 in Chapter 8.

```
         1         2         3         4
1234567890123456789012345678901234567890012

2065111297STUDEBAKER        010800019651
2085110997HUDSON            040000019551
2091100597FORD              089000019942
3003092997FORD              070000019941
3011102297CHEVROLET         110000019970
3015112197PIERCE-ARROW      120000019272
3025091997STUDEBAKER        062000019661
3026112597STUDEBAKER        043000019961
3031111397PIERCE-ARROW      130000019332
3043102597DODGE BROS.       090000019950
3047102197CHEVROLET         050000019940
3050110597PIERCE-ARROW      105000019312
3055091797AUBURN            130000019291
3056110997HUDSON            070000019571
3061102297FORD              110000019960
1067103197PIERCE-ARROW      150000019360
1070111297PIERCE-ARROW      120000019310
1075112297HUDSON            100000019571
1076112097HUDSON            030005019470
1080102397FORD              090500019952
1001082797FORD              035500019952
1003082897FORD              072000019640
1008100297HUDSON            050005019932
1010110197PIERCE-ARROW      105000019350
1015110297STUDEBAKER        005500019591
1020110297STUDEBAKER        005500019591
4061111797FORD              075000019952
4NN6102797CHEVROLET         044005019940
4066110797CHEVROLET         080005019960
4051101597DODGE BROS.       095005019944
4067112597DODGE BROS.       110000019960
4073102697PIERCE-ARROW      098000019292
4081112797STUDEBAKER        040000019641
4084110797FORD              0LL5000199L2
4084110797FORD              050000019940
4090100997FORD              082000019951
4094101497CHEVROLET         035000019930
4115102397PIERCE-ARROW      120000019320
1025092197STUDEBAKER        028800019551
1031090997FORD              025500019960
1033090397HUDSON            120000019562
1041091497CHEVROLET         034000019860
1045101497FORD              100000019852
1055112897STUDEBAKER        035000019661
II56102197FORD              000500019951
1056102197FORD              043000019951
1061101597DODGE BROS.       130000019962
1063092797DODGE BROS.       080000019950
2002090797FORD              115000019960
2004111397CHEVROLET         085000019970
2011102197PIERCE-ARROW      120000019320
2012102097PIERCE-ARROW      115002519342
2024101597HUDSON            033000019531
2031111297FORD              120000019962
2043111697STUDEBAKER        130000019660
2048102197CHEVROLET         110000019960
2050101297PIERCE-ARROW      140000019342
3062101097CHEVROLET         045000019950
3066092297AUBURN            140900019330
3072102497PIERCE-ARROW      146000019322
3080112197STUDEBAKER        060000019631
3094101397HUDSON            050000019571
3094101397HUDSON            040000019571
3098111497HUDSON            042000019520
4005102597PIERCE-ARROW      120000019262
4009112097AUBURN            110000019341
```

```
            1         2         3         4
   12345678901234567890123456789012345678012

   4012101297HUDSON          045000019551
   4021111197FORD            087000019950
   4022101797FORD            068000019931
   4024110197                0M5000019950
   4032102897PIERCE-ARROW    120000019352
   4035003097STUDEBAKER      040000019651
   4038100897DODGE BROS.     036000019891
   4044110997STUDEBAKER      100000019662
   4047111297DODGE BROS.     030000019891
   4049102197DODGE BROS.     060000019951
   4053092397PIERCE-ARROW    130000019370
   4056092897STUDEBAKER      050000019631
   4059102097AUBURN          100000019351

   TOTAL RECORDS = 79
```

Test Data Set 13: IDXTRANS.DAT

This data is used in COBOL Laboratory Exercise 1 in Chapter 9.

```
            1         2         3         4         5         6         7
   1234567890123456789012345678901234567890123456789012345678901234567890112345678

   ABaker, Charlie     Benson, Gloria    Renter    RT-7108-51410035000NM199403
   ADuffy, Chester     Jean, Barbara     Term Life TL-7007-56910045000NM199609
   AFramptin, Charles  Jean, Barbara     Renter    RT-1113-26660078000PM199411
   AFredricks, Sally   Jean, Barbara     Annuity   AN-1181-64640040000DF199505
   ABeach, Sonny       Jones, William    AutomobileAM-1114-25430130550PM199407
   AQualizza, Stacy    Jones, William    Home      HM-1311-33310015000PF199406
   AShiner, Bowen      Benson, Gloria    Term Life TL-1308-16470160440FM199406
   C                   Jones, William              AM-7623-12210043400P
   CSanders, Sara                                  TL-7303-34520053000P      03
   C                   Jean, Barbara               AN-4043-65100021000   198109
   C                                               AN-3453-98340045550PM199206
   CBaker, Charley                                 RT-7108-51410036000PF     04
   CKrachen, Gretchen  Benson, Gloria              RT-3421-04560030000F
   C                   McDonald, Fred              RT-1222-73260055050   199403
   CMichaels, Sammy    McDonald, Fred              AN-6566-88020033040D      11
   C                                               AN-4422-22260045500F
   CPittman, Betty Jo  Jones, William              HM-5111-47810113000F 199011
   C                                               HM-4112-24520042000F 199412
   CSampson, Delight                               TL-3319-16140035000F 1994
   CShorts, Jimmy      Jacobson, Peter             AN-0450-94110030000   199612
   CTulley, Paul                                   RT-4337-74880027500FM199511
   C                   Jacobson, Peter             TL-2222-8959        F
   CWhitmann, Walter                               AM-3411-12230057100F 199502
   D                                               AM-2199-9229
   D                                               HM-1107-2393
   D                                               AM-7473-1147
   D                                               HM-1113-2666
   D                                               RT-7108-5141
   D                                               RT-0944-9251
   D                                               TL-2762-2728
   D                                               HM-2011-7338
   D                                               WL-0082-1913

   TOTAL RECORDS = 32
```

Test Data Set 14: CITRANS.DAT

This data is used in COBOL Laboratory Exercise 3 in Chapter 9.

```
          1         2         3         4         5         6
123456789012345678901234567890123456789012345678901234567890123456789012345678

A092697100104ALLEN, BETTY      CHAIR AND DESK     101900002900003
A101197100106ASHTON, CHARLES   NIGHT STAND/DESK   201000003500004
C082997100107                   DELUXE PEN/PENCIL  1003850005050
C      100110CANNON, FREDRICK                                  10
D      100113
D      100153
A102897100168DOMINICK, MABLE    HARD WOOD CABINET  202500003500003
A100997100169DOWNING, M. JR.    MOUNTING BRACKETS  200400005000001
C100797100180                   #2 PENCILS         400100000210004
C100897100313HATFIELD, BRAD E.                     3
C100397100345                   DELUXE PAPER CUTTER 1006760010590
C100597100347                   TRACK LIGHTS       200500000715004
D      100360
D      100463
A092397100470MYRAN, MICHAEL     CONFERENCE TABLE   203055004100005
A092597100482NICKELS, KATHY     EXECUTIVE DESK SET 100420005206001
C092197100493                   PORT-A-CART        300800000160002
C      100551POTTER, FRED                          009000
C091497100563                   OAK DESK CHAIR     2       085430
C      100710RANDOLF, RANDY                        6
D      100713
D      100755
C100597100886                                                  11
A101597100919SVETINOFF, W. E.   8' OAK TABLE       100920001150001
A101697100930SWIFTON, ANNE      STEEL DESK CHAIR   200500001000007
C101797200123TOYOTA, LIKENEW                       2
C      200245                   DELUXE OAK DESK
D      200357
D      200380
C091597200753                   RECYCLING CONTAINER            11
A091197200871WALLACE, JOHNATHON LARGE DESK CHAIR   100900001050003
C      300281                   6' BOOK SHELF      4       035000
D      300333
C102397300415                   28.8 FAX MODEM     201000002200011
C110197300444ZOOMEY, WILLIAM                       035000

TOTAL RECORDS = 35
```

Test Data Set 15: AITRANS.DAT

This data is used in COBOL Laboratory Exercises 4 and 5 in Chapter 9.

```
         1         2         3         4         5         6
12345678901234567890123456789012345678901234567890123456789012345678

A464121012AMBROSE, SAMUEL    110697FORD             045500019932
A464011014AMMIGO, DON A.     101797STUDEBAKER       025000019621
C464101025                   AUBURN                 12300001934
C     1031BEZZMEK, JENNY      082897
C     1055                                           02300001963
D     1056
D     1061
A463101064CHESTER, AUTHUR    092197HUDSON           032000019550
C464121076                   090497                 04500001941
C     1080                   091597                        1995
D     2001
D     2004
A463202012CUSSINS, CYNTHIA   092197FORD             094000019942
A464212048DENNICK, DONNA A.  091197CHEVROLET        065000019950
C     2050DERBIN, DEANNA A.  091297                         0
C463152065                   HUDSON                        2
C     2085                   090197FORD             031100019952
D     2091
D     3002
D     3015
A463123023EFFLEY, BAILY      091597AUBURN           110500019352
C     3026                   100697                 0430000
C     3031ERKLE, ROSA B.                                    0
C     3043                   100597                 1050000    2
D     3047
A463213067GEORGE, JEFF E.    092297CHEVROLET        055000019940
C463203072                   092397                 12000001931
C     3081HAINES, MARSHA     092997
D     3094
A464234005HENSWORTH, JOHN    092597FORD             095000019312
C     4022                   092297PIERCE-ARROW     081204019320
D     4033
A463204039LEZZONO, GETSKI    090397DODGE BROS.      050000019900
C     4044                   101197                 10230001995
D     4046
D     4048
A464204068RODNEY, KYSONE     100597STUDEBAKER       065000019662
C464104073SANCHEZ, HENRY J.                         08500001926
C     4081                   090597                         2
D     4084
C464234094WARNER, JOHN                              0686000
D     4115

TOTAL RECORDS = 42
```

Test Data Set 16: SPREMIUM.DAT

This data is used in COBOL Laboratory Exercise 1 in Chapter 8 and in Exercises 1 and 2 in Chapter 9.

```
         1         2         3         4         5         6         7
1234567890123456789012345678901234567890123456789012345678901234567890123456789

Leach, Raeanne      Jones, William    AutomobileAM-1004-25530100550PF199104
Allister, Collin    McDonald, Fred    AutomobileAM-1991-92230012345PM199411
Amfelter, Audrey    McDonald, Fred    AutomobileAM-2199-92290045650FF199606
Senef, Marcia       McDonald, Fred    AutomobileAM-3323-34410078080FF199307
Whitman, Walter     Anderson, James   AutomobileAM-3411-12230077100PM199405
Cannon, Wylde       Benson, Gloria    AutomobileAM-6128-21510155000NM199705
Antich, Roseanne    McDonald, Fred    AutomobileAM-7211-72610025050PF199505
Eastling, Edward    Anderson, James   AutomobileAM-7373-11470055000DM199310
Anytime, Seeue      McDonald, Fred    AutomobileAM-7623-12210023400FF199701
Golden, Summer      Anderson, James   AutomobileAM-7993-43470040000FF199403
Garfield, Joey      Anderson, James   AutomobileAM-9878-56470036000PM199504
Shorts, Jimmy       Benson, Gloria    Annuity   AN-0450-94110028000FM199507
Eman, Sorik         Jean, Barbara     Annuity   AN-0868-48200235000NM199710
West, William       Anderson, James   Annuity   AN-0993-41040040000NM199507
Fredricks, Sally    Jean, Barbara     Annuity   AN-1181-64640040000DF199505
McGreger, Karla     Anderson, James   Annuity   AN-3366-22420035000DF198806
Garcia, William     Benson, Gloria    Annuity   AN-3453-98340035000FM199105
Foreman, Otto       Jones, William    Annuity   AN-4043-65100030000FM198008
Kackel, Henna       Benson, Gloria    Annuity   AN-4141-12560018050PF199503
Kratchet, Emily     Benson, Gloria    Annuity   AN-4410-07740105000FF198501
Olson, Wally        McDonald, Fred    Annuity   AN-4422-22260055000PF199611
McColly, Stephen    Anderson, James   Annuity   AN-4551-11020030000FM199505
Seaweed, Lostin     Anderson, James   Annuity   AN-5011-02520029000PF199608
Michaels, Ramsey    Anderson, James   Annuity   AN-6566-88020020030FM199407
Byman, Goodie       Anderson, James   Home      HM-1107-23930245000NM199604
Framptin, Charles   Jean, Barbara     Home      HM-1113-26660078000FM199008
Machen, Michael     Jones, William    Home      HM-1144-44260156000NM199202
Solloday, Tom       Jacobson, Peter   Home      HM-2001-73380079090PM199507
Nelson, Grace       Jones, William    Home      HM-2112-12550019020PF199601
Sollyfield, Barbara Jacobson, Peter   Home      HM-2322-44880145050PF199209
Skinner, Owen       Benson, Gloria    Home      HM-3308-66470160440PM198605
Ramsey, Lindsay     McDonald, Fred    Home      HM-4112-24520038000PF199702
Ollenford, Winnie   Jean, Barbara     Home      HM-4123-65410178000PF199110
Franklin, Steven    Benson, Gloria    Home      HM-4441-16620095000FM199106
Connors, Cinder     Jones, William    Home      HM-5109-41710085000NM199607
Pittman, Betty J.   Jacobson, Peter   Home      HM-5111-47810103000PF198703
Estovar, Franko     Benson, Gloria    Home      HM-5555-32340134050FM199309
Andrews, Robert     Anderson, James   Home      HM-7008-05070056000PM199011
Solfelt, Wanda      Jones, William    Home      HM-7878-70650088050FF199403
Solenfeld, Nancy    Jacobson, Peter   Home      HM-8767-87880098000PF199206
Walters, Samuel     Jones, William    Renter    RT-0424-00530022000PF199407
Motorhead, Ima      Jones, William    Renter    RT-0944-92510020000PF199508
Kramer, Robert      Jones, William    Renter    RT-1002-15510038025FM199302
Krevits, Gloria     McDonald, Fred    Renter    RT-1122-73260040050FF199302
Flagg, Wavadee      Benson, Gloria    Renter    RT-1189-85330088000NM199609
Qualizza, Scotter   Jones, William    Renter    RT-3331-34510014050PF199606
Kracken, Gretchen   Jones, William    Renter    RT-3421-04560028080PF199603
Tully, Paula        Jones, William    Renter    RT-4337-74880017500PF199703
Baker, Bonnie       Jones, William    Renter    RT-4402-32110015000NM199302
Partridge, Danny    Benson, Gloria    Renter    RT-4421-40910046000FM199511
Glidden, Findda     Anderson, James   Renter    RT-5421-22210068000NM199504
Lynch, Agnis        Jean, Barbara     Renter    RT-5525-05560023050PF199603
Sanders, Kevin      Jones, William    Renter    RT-6678-55050055050FM199409
Yackley, Yourto     Jones, William    Renter    RT-7127-50760024000PF199402
Franken, Peter      Jean, Barbara     Renter    RT-9083-67620030725FM199207
Potter, Louise      McDonald, Fred    Renter    RT-9122-84220013050PF199705
Willis, Richard     Anderson, James   Renter    RT-9580-00030085000FM199504
Vlasic, Roberta     McDonald, Fred    Term Life TL-2129-89590038000PF199604
Solinski, Paula     Jacobson, Peter   Term Life TL-2762-27280026825NF199304
Samson, Delight     Benson, Gloria    Term Life TL-3319-16140025000NF199604
Pally, Jane         Benson, Gloria    Term Life TL-5522-21210046000PF199212
Neierson, Henry     Benson, Gloria    Term Life TL-6220-20920034000FM199509
Parnelli, Frank     Benson, Gloria    Term Life TL-6763-00930025000FM199012
Duffy, Chester      Jean, Barbara     Term Life TL-7007-56910045000NM199609
Brannan, Clyde      Benson, Gloria    Term Life TL-7008-55510055000NM199703
```

```
          1         2         3         4         5         6         7
1234567890123456789012345678901234567890123456789012345678901234567890123456789

Danners, Sarah      McDonald, Fred      Term Life TL-7303-34520045000NM199508
Winder, Robert      Anderson, James     Term Life TL-7682-09030030550FM199302
Wilder, Eugene      Jean, Barbara       Whole LifeWL-0082-19130038000FM199605
Kramer, Wally       Jones, William      Whole LifeWL-0221-24220020020FM199001
White, Robert       Anderson, James     Whole LifeWL-0454-56980036075FM199603
McVickers, Sam      Anderson, James     Whole LifeWL-1222-14440042550FM198204
Winfield, Wally     Anderson, James     Whole LifeWL-2721-39040032600PM199601

TOTAL RECORDS = 72
```

Answers to
Student Assignments

CHAPTER 1

Student Assignment 1: True/False

1. T	6. T	11. F
2. F	7. F	12. F
3. T	8. F	13. T
4. F	9. F	14. F
5. T	10. F	15. T

Student Assignment 2: Multiple Choice

1. c	6. a
2. d	7. b
3. a	8. c
4. b	9. b
5. c	10. d

Student Assignment 3 (answers may vary)

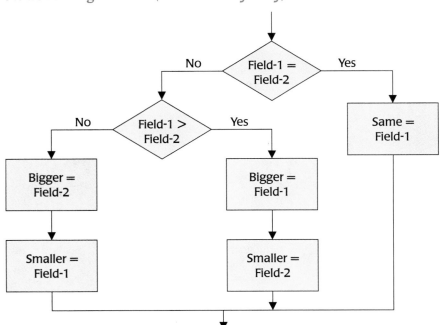

Student Assignment 4 (answers may vary)

```
if X > Y then
    if X > T then
        SALE = X
    else
        SALE = T
else
    SALE = Y
end-if
```

Student Assignment 5 (answers may vary)

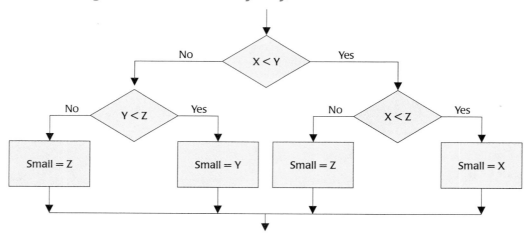

Student Assignment 6 (answers may vary)

```
let D = 0
do-until D > 20
    if Seniority <= 10 then add 1 to Y
    else-if Seniority <= 20 then add 1 to M
    else-if Seniority <= 30 then add 1 to S ;
    add 1 to D
end-do
```

Student Assignment 7 (answers may vary)

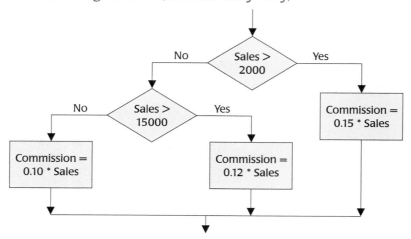

CHAPTER 2

Student Assignment 1: True/False

1. F	6. T	11. F	16. T
2. F	7. T	12. F	17. F
3. F	8. F	13. F	18. F
4. T	9. T	14. T	19. F
5. T	10. T	15. F	20. F

Student Assignment 2: Multiple Choice

1. a	6. b
2. c	7. a
3. b	8. c
4. a	9. b
5. b	10. c

Student Assignment 3

```
 IDENTIFICATION DIVISION.
 PROGRAM-ID.  PAYRPT.
 AUTHOR.      Your Name.
 **********************************************************************
 *                     PROGRAM NARRATIVE                              *
 *                                                                    *
 *    THIS PROGRAM PRODUCES THE WEEKLY PAYROLL CALCULATIONS           *
 *    FOR HOURLY PAID EMPLOYEES OF THE ROF CORPORATION.               *
 *                                                                    *
 **********************************************************************
```

Student Assignment 4

```
SELECT SALES-TRANSACTION-FILE
    ASSIGN TO "SALES.DAT".
```

Student Assignment 5 (answers may vary)

```
FD  STUDENT-FILE.

01  STUDENT-RECORD.
    02  SR-STUDENT-ID          PIC X(7).
    02  SR-STUDENT-NAME        PIC X(20).
    02  SR-STUDENT-ADDRESS     PIC X(20).
    02  SR-STUDENT-STATUS      PIC XX.
    02  SR-STUDENT-INCOME      PIC 9(5).
```

Student Assignment 6

```
B-100-DO-IT.

    PERFORM B-200-DO-IT-AGAIN.
    PERFORM B-210-DO-IT-OVER
        UNTIL ALL-RIGHT-NOW.
    PERFORM B-220-DONE.
```

Student Assignment 7

```
OPEN INPUT STUDENT-FILE.

READ STUDENT-FILE
    AT END MOVE "Y" TO SW-END-OF-FILE.
```

CHAPTER 3

Student Assignment 1: True/False

1. T	6. F	11. T	16. T
2. F	7. F	12. F	17. T
3. F	8. T	13. F	18. T
4. T	9. T	14. F	19. F
5. F	10. F	15. F	20. T

Student Assignment 2: Multiple Choice

1. a	6. b
2. c	7. e
3. e	8. a
4. b	9. c
5. d	10. a

Student Assignment 3

a. $ 12.43   b. $1,215.50   c.   512.25CR   d. ***42.33
   -------   ---------   -----------   --------

Student Assignment 4

PIC $$$,$$$.99.

Student Assignment 5

```
02   PR-CUSTOMER-FAMILY-STATUS          PIC X.
     88   SINGLE                        VALUE "S".
     88   MARRIED                       VALUE "M".
     88   DIVORCED                      VALUE "D".
```

Student Assignment 6

```
02   PR-CLIENT-AGE                      PIC 99.
     88   YOUTH                         VALUE  1 THRU 18.
     88   YOUNG-ADULT                   VALUE 19 THRU 34.
     88   MATURE-ADULT                  VALUE 35 THRU 55.
     88   OLDER-ADULT                   VALUE 56 THRU 99.
```

Student Assignment 7

```
02   PR-SALES-AMOUNT                    PIC 9(6)V99.
02   PR-SALES-AMOUNT-ALPHA  REDEFINES
     PR-SALES-AMOUNT                    PIC X(8).
```

CHAPTER 4

Student Assignment 1: True/False

1. F	6. F	11. T	16. T
2. F	7. T	12. T	17. T
3. T	8. F	13. T	18. F
4. F	9. T	14. F	19. T
5. F	10. T	15. T	20. T

Student Assignment 2: Multiple Choice

1. b	6. b
2. b	7. e
3. e	8. e
4. a	9. c
5. c	10. c

Student Assignment 3

```
IF AC-ERROR-COUNT < 10
    PERFORM B-200-FIX-IT
ELSE
    IF AC-ERROR-COUNT > 20
        PERFORM B-210-FORGET-IT
    ELSE
        PERFORM B-220-PATCH-IT.
```

Student Assignment 4

```
EVALUATE NPR-POLICY-CODE
    WHEN "AM"  MOVE "AUTO"       TO DL-POLICY
    WHEN "AN"  MOVE "ANNUITY"    TO DL-POLICY
    WHEN "HM"  MOVE "HOME"       TO DL-POLICY
    WHEN "RT"  MOVE "RENTER"     TO DL-POLICY
    WHEN "TL"  MOVE "TERM LIFE"  TO DL-POLICY
    WHEN "WL"  MOVE "WHOLE LIFE" TO DL-POLICY
    WHEN OTHER MOVE "BAD CODE"   TO DL-POLICY.
```

Student Assignment 5

```
IF ER-SALARY-AMOUNT-ALPHA NOT NUMERIC
    MOVE "SALARY NOT NUMERIC" TO DL-MESSAGE
    PERFORM B-330-WRITE-ERROR
ELSE
    IF ER-SALARY-AMOUNT NOT POSITIVE
        MOVE "SALARY NOT POSITIVE" TO DL-MESSAGE
        PERFORM B-330-WRITE-ERROR
    ELSE
        IF ER-SALARY-AMOUNT >= 4000
            MOVE "SALARY TOO LARGE" TO DL-MESSAGE
            PERFORM B-330-WRITE-ERROR.
```

Student Assignment 6

```
IF MALE
    ADD 3 TO AC-COUNT
    IF MARRIED
        IF PROGRAMMER
            ADD 2 TO AC-COUNT
        ELSE
            ADD 4 TO AC-COUNT
    ELSE
        ADD 8 TO AC-COUNT
        IF OVER-30
            IF EMPLOYED
                ADD 5 TO AC-COUNT
            ELSE
                ADD 3 TO AC-COUNT.
```

1. 11   2. 5   3. 14   4. 0   5. 7

Student Assignment 7 (answers may vary)

```
02  WA-CURRENT-TIME.
    03  WA-CURRENT-HOUR      PIC 99.
    03  WA-CURRENT-MINUTE    PIC 99.
    03                       PIC 9(4).


ACCEPT WA-CURRENT-DATE FROM DATE.
MOVE WA-CURRENT-MINUTE TO HL-MINUTES-OUT.
IF WA-CURRENT-HOUR = 0
    MOVE 12 TO HL-HOUR-OUT
    MOVE "AM" TO HL-AM-PM
ELSE
    IF WA-CURRENT-HOUR < 12
        MOVE WA-CURRENT-HOUR TO HL-HOUR-OUT
        MOVE "AM" TO HL-AM-PM
    ELSE
        IF WA-CURRENT-HOUR = 12
            MOVE WA-CURRENT-HOUR TO HL-HOUR-OUT
            MOVE "PM" TO HL-AM-PM
        ELSE
            SUBTRACT 12 FROM WA-CURRENT-HOUR
                GIVING HL-HOUR-OUT
            MOVE "PM" TO HL-AM-PM.
```

CHAPTER 5

Student Assignment 1: True/False

1. F	6. T	11. F	16. T
2. F	7. T	12. T	17. F
3. F	8. F	13. F	18. T
4. T	9. T	14. T	19. T
5. F	10. F	15. F	20. T

Student Assignment 2: Multiple Choice

1. c	6. e
2. a	7. b
3. a	8. a
4. b	9. c
5. b	10. d

Student Assignment 3

```
ADD 5 TO AC-ERROR-COUNT
    ON SIZE ERROR PERFORM B-300-BAD-ADD.
```

Student Assignment 4

```
COMPUTE C-FIELD = (B-FIELD - (2 * (5 + A-FIELD))) / 3
```

Student Assignment 5

```
PERFORM B-300-DO-IT
    VARYING WA-COUNT-1 FROM 1 BY 2
    UNTIL WA-COUNT-1 >= 100.
```

Student Assignment 6

```
COMPUTE DL-AVERAGE-SALES ROUNDED =
    (SR-SALES + SR-YTD-SALES) / AC-TOTAL-MONTHS.
```

Student Assignment 7

```
        CALL "MYSUB1" USING WA-SHARE-1
                            WA-SHARE-2
                            WA-SHARE-3.


IDENTIFICATION DIVISION.
PROGRAM-ID.  MYSUB1.
    .
    .
    .
DATA DIVISION.
LINKAGE SECTION.

01   SHARED-FIELDS.
     02   SF-SHARE-1              PIC 999.
     02   SF-SHARE-2              PIC 9(5) PACKED-DECIMAL.
     02   SF-SHARE-3              PIC 9(5)V99.

PROCEDURE DIVISION USING SF-SHARE-1
                         SF-SHARE-2
                         SF-SHARE-3.


MAIN-PARAGRAPH.
     ADD 5 TO SF-SHARE-1
              SF-SHARE-2
              SF-SHARE-3.

     EXIT PROGRAM.
```

CHAPTER 6

Student Assignment 1: True/False

1. F	6. T	11. T	16. F
2. T	7. F	12. T	17. T
3. T	8. T	13. F	18. F
4. F	9. T	14. T	19. T
5. T	10. F	15. T	20. T

Student Assignment 2: Multiple Choice

1. b	6. e
2. e	7. d
3. a	8. b
4. b	9. b
5. e	10. d

Student Assignment 3

```
DISPLAY "The Premium Amount for the current record is "
    PR-PREMIUM-AMOUNT-EDITED.
```

Student Assignment 4

```
SORT SORT-FILE
    ON DESCENDING KEY CSR-CUSTOMER-IDENTIFICATION
    USING  CUSTOMER-FILE
    GIVING SORTED-CUSTOMER-FILE.
```

Student Assignment 5

```
SORT SORT-FILE
    ON ASCENDING KEY CSR-CUSTOMER-IDENTIFICATION
                     CSR-LAST-NAME
    USING   CUSTOMER-FILE
    GIVING SORTED-CUSTOMER-FILE.
```

Student Assignment 6 (answers may vary)

```
SD  SORT-WORK-FILE.

01  CUSTOMER-SORT-RECORD.
    02                                PIC X(5).
    02   CSR-LAST-NAME                PIC X(14).
    02                                PIC X(61).


    SORT SORT-WORK-FILE
        ON ASCENDING KEY CSR-LAST-NAME
        INPUT PROCEDURE B-200-INPUT
        GIVING SORTED-CUSTOMER-FILE.


B-200-INPUT.
    OPEN INPUT CUSTOMER-FILE.
    MOVE NEG TO SW-END-OF-FILE.
    READ CUSTOMER-FILE
        AT END MOVE YES TO SW-END-OF-FILE.
    PERFORM UNTIL END-OF-FILE
        IF ACTIVE
            RELEASE CUSTOMER-SORT-RECORD FROM CUSTOMER-RECORD
        END-IF
        READ CUSTOMER-FILE
            AT END MOVE YES TO SW-END-OF-FILE
        END-READ
    END-PERFORM.
    CLOSE CUSTOMER-FILE.
```

Student Assignment 7 (answers may vary)

```
SD  SORT-WORK-FILE.

01  CUSTOMER-SORT-RECORD.
    02                                PIC X(5).
    02   CSR-LAST-NAME                PIC X(14).
    02                                PIC X(61).


    SORT SORT-WORK-FILE
        ON ASCENDING KEY CSR-LAST-NAME
        INPUT PROCEDURE B-200-INPUT
        OUTPUT PROCEDURE B-210-OUTPUT.
```

```
B-200-INPUT.
    OPEN INPUT CUSTOMER-FILE.
    MOVE NEG TO SW-END-OF-FILE.
    READ CUSTOMER-FILE
        AT END MOVE YES TO SW-END-OF-FILE.
    PERFORM UNTIL END-OF-FILE
        IF NOT ACTIVE
            RELEASE CUSTOMER-SORT-RECORD FROM CUSTOMER-RECORD
        END-IF
        READ CUSTOMER-FILE
            AT END MOVE YES TO SW-END-OF-FILE
        END-READ
    END-PERFORM.
    CLOSE CUSTOMER-FILE.


B-210-OUTPUT.
    MOVE NEG TO SW-END-OF-FILE.
    RETURN SORT-WORK-FILE INTO CUSTOMER-RECORD
        AT END MOVE YES TO SW-END-OF-FILE.
    PERFORM UNTIL END-OF-FILE
        DISPLAY CR-LAST-NAME
        DISPLAY CR-FIRST-NAME
        DISPLAY CR-CUSTOMER-IDENTIFICATION
        RETURN SORT-WORK-FILE INTO CUSTOMER-RECORD
            AT END MOVE YES TO SW-END-OF-FILE
        END-RETURN
    END-PERFORM.
```

CHAPTER 7

. . . .

Student Assignment 1: True/False

1. T	6. F	11. F	16. T
2. F	7. T	12. T	17. T
3. F	8. T	13. F	18. T
4. T	9. T	14. F	19. T
5. T	10. F	15. T	20. F

Student Assignment 2: Multiple Choice

1. c	6. a
2. d	7. c
3. d	8. a
4. b	9. b
5. b	10. c

Student Assignment 3 (answers may vary)

```
01 WAGE-TABLE.
    02  WT-ENTRY OCCURS 15 TIMES
                INDEXED BY WAGE-INDEX.
        03  WT-JOB-CODE          PIC XXX.
        03  WT-WAGE-RATE         PIC 9(4)V99.
```

Student Assignment 4 (answers may vary)

```
01   PRESIDENT-NAME-DATA.
     02            PIC X(18) VALUE "FRANKLIN ROOSEVELT".
     02            PIC X(18) VALUE "HARRY TRUMAN".
     02            PIC X(18) VALUE "DWIGHT EISENHOWER".
     02            PIC X(18) VALUE "JOHN KENNEDY".
     02            PIC X(18) VALUE "LYNDON JOHNSON".
     02            PIC X(18) VALUE "GERALD FORD".
     02            PIC X(18) VALUE "JIMMY CARTER".
     02            PIC X(18) VALUE "RONALD REAGAN".
     02            PIC X(18) VALUE "GEORGE BUSH".
     02            PIC X(18) VALUE "BILL CLINTON".

01   PRESIDENT-TABLE REDEFINES PRESIDENT-NAME-DATA.
     02  PT-NAME OCCURS 10 TIMES
               PIC X(18).
```

Student Assignment 5 (answers may vary)

```
B-100-LOAD-PARTS-TABLE.
    MOVE NEG TO SW-END-OF-FILE.
    OPEN INPUT PARTS-FILE.
    READ PARTS-FILE
        AT END MOVE YES TO SW-END-OF-FILE.
    PERFORM B-200-MOVE-PARTS-DATA
        VARYING PARTS-INDEX FROM 1 BY 1
        UNTIL END-OF-FILE OR PARTS-INDEX > 50.
    CLOSE PARTS-FILE.

B-200-MOVE-PARTS-DATA.
    MOVE PR-NUMBER TO PT-NUMBER (PARTS-INDEX).
    MOVE PR-NAME TO PT-NAME (PARTS-INDEX).
    MOVE PR-QUANTITY TO PT-QUANTITY (PARTS-INDEX).
    READ PARTS-FILE
        AT END MOVE YES TO SW-END-OF-FILE.
```

Student Assignment 6 (answers may vary)

```
SET PARTS-INDEX TO 1.
SEARCH PT-ITEM
    AT END MOVE "NOT FOUND" TO DL-PART-NAME-OUT
    WHEN PT-NUMBER (PARTS-INDEX) = IN-PART-NUMBER
        MOVE PT-NAME (PARTS-INDEX) TO DL-PART-NAME-OUT.
```

Student Assignment 7 (answers may vary)

```
01   PARTS-TABLE.
     02  PT-ITEM OCCURS 50 TIMES
               ASCENDING KEY PT-NUMBER
               INDEXED BY PARTS-INDEX.
         03  PT-NUMBER     PIC X(12).
         03  PT-NAME       PIC X(20).
         03  PT-QUANTITY   PIC 9(5).
```

```
SEARCH ALL PT-ITEM
    AT END MOVE "NOT FOUND" TO DL-PART-NAME-OUT
    WHEN PT-NUMBER (PARTS-INDEX) = IN-PART-NUMBER
        MOVE PT-NAME (PARTS-INDEX) TO DL-PART-NAME-OUT.
```

CHAPTER 8
. . . .

Student Assignment 1: True/False

1. T	6. F	11. F	16. F
2. F	7. T	12. T	17. T
3. F	8. F	13. F	18. T
4. F	9. F	14. T	19. F
5. T	10. F	15. T	20. F

Student Assignment 2: Multiple Choice

1. d	6. a
2. c	7. b
3. b	8. c
4. e	9. e
5. d	10. d

Student Assignment 3

```
INSPECT WA-FIELD-1 TALLYING WA-ZERO-COUNT
    FOR ALL "0" AFTER INITIAL "2".
```

WA-ZERO-COUNT --> 3

Student Assignment 4

```
INSPECT WA-FIELD-1
    REPLACING ALL "0" BY "A" AFTER INITIAL "2".
```

WA-FIELD-1 --> 340054293A52AA1

Student Assignment 5

```
INSPECT WA-FIELD-1 CONVERTING "120"
                        TO "ABZ".
```

WA-FIELD-1 --> 34ZZ54B93Z5BZZA

Student Assignment 6

```
UNSTRING WA-NAME-1 DELIMITED BY ALL " "
    INTO WA-PART-1
        WA-PART-2
        WA-PART-3.
```

WA-PART-1 --> ALFRED   WA-PART-2 --> E.   WA-PART-3 --> NEWMAN,

Student Assignment 7

```
STRING WA-PART-1 DELIMITED BY SIZE
       " "        DELIMITED BY SIZE
       WA-PART-2 DELIMITED BY SPACE
       " "        DELIMITED BY SIZE
       WA-PART-3 DELIMITED BY "T"
    INTO WA-CATCH-IT.
```

WA-CATCH-IT --> ABC 123 JEFF Samanth

CHAPTER 9

Student Assignment 1: True/False

1. T	6. T	11. T	16. T
2. F	7. T	12. F	17. T
3. T	8. F	13. T	18. T
4. F	9. F	14. T	19. F
5. T	10. F	15. F	20. T

Student Assignment 2: Multiple Choice

1. a	6. b
2. d	7. c
3. b	8. a
4. d	9. c
5. c	10. b

Student Assignment 3

```
MOVE "TR-14" TO IR-ITEM-CODE.
READ INDEXED-INVENTORY-FILE INTO INVENTORY-RECORD
    INVALID KEY PERFORM B-220-NO-SUCH-RECORD
    NOT INVALID KEY PERFORM B-210-PROCESS-RECORD.
```

Student Assignment 4

```
    SELECT INDEXED-INVENTORY-FILE
        ASSIGN TO "INVINDX.DAT"
        ORGANIZATION IS INDEXED
        ACCESS IS DYNAMIC
        RECORD KEY IS IR-ITEM-CODE.


FD  INDEXED-INVENTORY-FILE.
01  INDEXED-RECORD.
    02                      PIC XX.
    02  IR-ITEM-CODE        PIC X(5).
    02                      PIC X(83).
```

Student Assignment 5

```
MOVE "TS-52" TO IR-ITEM-CODE.
DELETE INDEXED-INVENTORY-FILE
    INVALID KEY PERFORM B-220-NO-SUCH-RECORD.
```

Student Assignment 6

```
ENVIRONMENT DIVISION.
INPUT-OUTPUT SECTION.
FILE-CONTROL.

    SELECT RELATIVE-INVENTORY-FILE
        ASSIGN TO "INVREL.DAT"
        ORGANIZATION IS RELATIVE
        ACCESS IS RANDOM
        RELATIVE KEY IS WA-ITEM-NUMBER.

DATA DIVISION.
FILE SECTION.

FD  RELATIVE-INVENTORY-FILE.
01  RELATIVE-RECORD        PIC X(90).
```

```
WORKING-STORAGE SECTION.

    02  WA-ITEM-NUMBER        PIC 9(5).
```

Student Assignment 7

```
MOVE 24 TO WA-ITEM-NUMBER.
READ RELATIVE-INVENTORY-FILE INTO INVENTORY-RECORD
    INVALID KEY PERFORM B-220-NO-SUCH-RECORD
    NOT INVALID KEY PERFORM B-210-PROCESS-RECORD.
```

CHAPTER 10
. . . .

Student Assignment 1: True/False

1. F	6. T	11. F	16. F
2. T	7. F	12. T	17. T
3. T	8. F	13. T	18. T
4. F	9. F	14. T	19. T
5. F	10. T	15. T	20. T

Student Assignment 2: Multiple Choice

1. d	6. b
2. b	7. b
3. d	8. a
4. a	9. c
5. d	10. e

Student Assignment 3 (answers may vary)

```
01  JOB-HEADING TYPE CONTROL HEADING ER-JOB-TYPE.
    02  LINE PLUS 2.
        03              COLUMN 15  PIC X(26) VALUE
            "HEADING FOR JOB TYPE -->  ".
        03              COLUMN 41  PIC X(10) SOURCE ER-JOB-TYPE.

    02  LINE PLUS 1.
        03              COLUMN 15  PIC X(36) VALUE ALL "-".
```

Student Assignment 4

```
01  TYPE PAGE HEADING.

    02  LINE 1.
        03              COLUMN 1   PIC X(6)  VALUE "DATE: ".
        03              COLUMN 7   PIC Z9/99/99 SOURCE
                                            WA-TODAYS-DATE.
        03              COLUMN 21  PIC X(27) VALUE
            "AINSWORTH INSURANCE COMPANY".
        03              COLUMN 58  PIC X(5)  VALUE "PAGE ".
        03              COLUMN 63  PIC ZZ9   SOURCE PAGE-COUNTER.

    02  LINE 2.
        03              COLUMN 25  PIC X(19) VALUE
            "AGENT SALARY REPORT".
```

Student Assignment 5 (answers may vary)

```
01  DETAIL-LINE-OUT TYPE DETAIL.
    02  LINE PLUS 1.
        03      COLUMN 2  PIC X(20) SOURCE ER-EMPLOYEE-NAME.
        03      COLUMN 24 PIC X(10) SOURCE ER-JOB-TYPE.
        03      COLUMN 36 PIC ZZ,ZZZ.99 SOURCE ER-SALARY.
        03      COLUMN 48 PIC Z9/99/99 SOURCE ER-ANNIVERSARY-DATE.
```

Student Assignment 6

```
01  TYPE CONTROL FOOTING ER-JOB-TYPE.
    02  LINE PLUS 2.
        03      COLUMN 1  PIC X(31) VALUE
            "*COUNT AND SALARY FOR JOB TYPE ".
        03      COLUMN 32 PIC X(10) SOURCE ER-JOB-TYPE.
        03      COLUMN 43 PIC X     VALUE "-".
        03      COLUMN 45 PIC ZZ9   SOURCE AC-EMPLOYEE-JOB-COUNT.
        03      COLUMN 49 PIC X     VALUE "-".
        03      COLUMN 51 PIC $ZZ,ZZ9.99 SUM ER-SALARY.
```

Student Assignment 7

```
DECLARATIVES.

X-100-ZERO-OUT-JOB-COUNT SECTION.
    USE BEFORE REPORTING JOB-HEADING.
X-100-ZERO-JOB.

    MOVE ZERO TO AC-EMPLOYEE-JOB-COUNT.

END DECLARATIVES.
```

COBOL
Reserved Words

(Included in COBOL Reference Guide)

ACCEPT
ACCESS
ADD
ADVANCING
AFTER
ALL
ALPHABET
ALPHABETIC
ALPHABETIC-LOWER
ALPHABETIC-UPPER
ALPHANUMERIC
ALPHANUMERIC-EDITED
ALSO
ALTER
ALTERNATE
AND
ANY
ARE
AREA
AREAS
ASCENDING
ASSIGN
AT
AUTHOR

BEFORE
BINARY
BLANK

BLOCK
BOTTOM
BY

CALL
CANCEL
CD
CF
CH
CHARACTER
CHARACTERS
CLASS
CLOCK-UNITS
CLOSE
COBOL
CODE
CODE-SET
COLLATING
COLUMN
COMMA
COMMON
COMMUNICATION
COMP
COMPUTATIONAL
COMPUTE
CONFIGURATION
CONTAINS
CONTENT

CONTINUE
CONTROL
CONTROLS
CONVERTING
COPY
CORR
CORRESPONDING
COUNT
CURRENCY

DATA
DATE
DATE-COMPILED
DATE-WRITTEN
DAY
DAY-OF-WEEK
DE
DEBUG-CONTENTS
DEBUG-ITEM
DEBUG-LINE
DEBUG-NAME
DEBUG-SUB-1
DEBUG-SUB-2
DEBUG-SUB-3
DEBUGGING
DECIMAL-POINT
DECLARATIVES
DELETE

DELIMITED
DELIMITER
DEPENDING
DESCENDING
DESTINATION
DETAIL
DISABLE
DISPLAY
DIVIDE
DIVISION
DOWN
DUPLICATES
DYNAMIC

EGI
ELSE
EMI
ENABLE
END-ADD
END-CALL
END-COMPUTE
END-DELETE
END-DIVIDE
END-EVALUATE
END-IF
END-MULTIPLY
END-OF-PAGE
END-PERFORM
END-READ
END-RECEIVE
END-RETURN
END-REWRITE
END-SEARCH
END-START
END-STRING
END-SUBTRACT
END-UNSTRING
END-WRITE
ENTER
ENVIRONMENT
EOP
EQUAL
ERROR
ESI
EVALUATE
EVERY
EXCEPTION
EXIT
EXTEND
EXTERNAL

FALSE
FILE

FILE-CONTROL
FILLER
FIRST
FOOTING
FOR
FROM

GENERATE
GIVING
GLOBAL
GREATER
GROUP

HEADING
HIGH-VALUE
HIGH-VALUES

I-O
I-O-CONTROL
IDENTIFICATION
INDEX
INDEXED
INDICATE
INITIAL
INITIALIZATION
INITIATE
INPUT
INPUT-OUTPUT
INSPECT
INSTALLATION
INTO
INVALID

JUST
JUSTIFIED

KEY

LABEL
LAST
LEADING
LEFT
LENGTH
LESS
LIMIT
LIMITS
LINAGE
LINAGE-COUNTER
LINE
LINE-COUNTER

LINES
LINKAGE
LOCK
LOW-VALUE
LOW-VALUES

MEMORY
MERGE
MESSAGE
MODE
MODULES
MOVE
MULTIPLE
MULTIPLY

NATIVE
NEGATIVE
NEXT
NOT
NUMBER
NUMERIC
NUMERIC-EDITED

OBJECT-COMPUTER
OCCURS
OMITTED
OPEN
OPTIONAL
ORDER
ORGANIZATION
OTHER
OVERFLOW

PACKED-DECIMAL
PADDING
PAGE
PAGE-COUNTER
PERFORM
PF
PH
PIC
PICTURE
PLUS
POINTER
POSITION
POSITIVE
PRINTING
PROCEDURE
PROCEDURES

PROCEED	SECTION	THEN
PROGRAM	SECURITY	THROUGH
PROGRAM-ID	SEGMENT	THRU
PURGE	SEGMENT-LIMIT	TIME
	SELECT	TIMES
QUEUE	SEND	TO
QUOTE	SENTENCE	TOP
QUOTES	SEPARATE	TRAILING
	SEQUENCE	TRUE
RANDOM	SEQUENTIAL	TYPE
RD	SET	
READ	SIGN	UNIT
RECEIVE	SIZE	UNSTRING
RECORD	SORT	UNTIL
RECORDS	SORT-MERGE	UP
REDEFINES	SOURCE	UPON
REEL	SOURCE-COMPUTER	USAGE
REFERENCE	SPACE	USE
REFERENCES	SPACES	USING
RELATIVE	SPECIAL-NAMES	
RELEASE	STANDARD	VALUE
REMAINDER	STANDARD-1	VALUES
REMOVAL	STANDARD-2	VARYING
RENAMES	START	
REPLACE	STATUS	WHEN
REPLACING	STOP	WITH
REPORT	STRING	WORDS
REPORTING	SUB-QUEUE-1	WORKING-STORAGE
REPORTS	SUB-QUEUE-2	WRITE
RERUN	SUB-QUEUE-3	
RESERVE	SUBTRACT	ZERO
RESET	SUM	ZEROES
RETURN	SUPPRESS	ZEROS
REVERSED	SYMBOLIC	
REWIND	SYNC	+
REWRITE	SYNCHRONIZED	−
RF		*
RH	TABLE	/
RIGHT	TALLYING	**
ROUNDED	TAPE	>
RUN	TERMINAL	<
	TERMINATE	>=
SAME	TEST	<=
SD	TEXT	=
SEARCH	THAN	

[FOREMAN page C-4 blank/blind folio]

COBOL Basic Formats

(Included in COBOL Reference Guide)

Basic formats presented within this book are listed below. PROCEDURE DIVISION statements are in alphabetical order.

BASIC FORMAT OF THE IDENTIFICATION DIVISION

```
IDENTIFICATION DIVISION.
PROGRAM-ID.       program-name.
[AUTHOR.          [comment-entry] ...]
[INSTALLATION.    [comment-entry] ...]
[DATE-WRITTEN.    [comment-entry] ...]
[DATE-COMPILED.   [comment-entry] ...]
[SECURITY.        [comment-entry] ...]
```

BASIC FORMAT OF THE ENVIRONMENT DIVISION

```
ENVIRONMENT DIVISION.    ( The entire division is optional )

 CONFIGURATION SECTION.

 SOURCE-COMPUTER. [source-computer-name]
 OBJECT-COMPUTER. [object-computer-name]
 SPECIAL-NAMES. [implementor-code IS mnemonic-name .]

INPUT-OUTPUT SECTION.

FILE-CONTROL.
```

```
SELECT file-name
     ASSIGN TO implementor-name-1 [,implementor-name-2] ...
[[ ORGANIZATION IS ] SEQUENTIAL ]
[ ACCESS MODE IS SEQUENTIAL ]
[ FILE STATUS IS data-name ] .

SELECT file-name
     ASSIGN TO implementor-name-1 [,implementor-name-2] ...
[ ORGANIZATION IS ] INDEXED


    ⎡ ACCESS MODE IS ⎧ SEQUENTIAL ⎫ ⎤
    ⎢                ⎨ RANDOM     ⎬ ⎥
    ⎣                ⎩ DYNAMIC    ⎭ ⎦


    RECORD KEY IS key-field-name

[ ALTERNATE RECORD KEY IS alt-key-field [WITH DUPLICATES]] ...

[ FILE STATUS IS data-name ].

SELECT file-name
     ASSIGN TO implementor-name-1 [,implementor-name-2] ...

[ ORGANIZATION IS ] RELATIVE

    ⎡ ACCESS MODE IS ⎧ SEQUENTIAL [RELATIVE KEY IS rel-key] ⎫ ⎤
    ⎢                ⎨ ⎧ RANDOM  ⎫                          ⎬ ⎥
    ⎣                ⎩ ⎩ DYNAMIC ⎭ RELATIVE KEY IS rel-key  ⎭ ⎦

[ FILE STATUS IS data-name ].
```

BASIC FORMAT OF THE DATA DIVISION

```
DATA DIVISION.        (The entire division is optional)

FILE SECTION.

FD file-name

[    RECORD CONTAINS [integer-1 TO ] integer-2 CHARACTERS ]

⎡    BLOCK CONTAINS [integer-3 TO ] integer-4  ⎧ RECORDS    ⎫ ⎤
⎣                                              ⎩ CHARACTERS ⎭ ⎦

⎡    LABEL ⎧ RECORD IS   ⎫ ⎧ STANDARD ⎫ ⎤
⎣         ⎩ RECORDS ARE  ⎭ ⎩ OMITTED  ⎭ ⎦

⎡    DATA  ⎧ RECORD IS   ⎫ data-name-1, [,data-name-2] ...  ⎤
⎣         ⎩ RECORDS ARE  ⎭                                  ⎦

[record-description-entry] ...
```

<u>SD</u> sort-work-file

```
[ RECORD  ⎧ CONTAINS  integer-1 CHARACTERS                                     ⎫ ]
[         ⎨ IS VARYING IN SIZE [FROM integer-2] [TO integer-3] CHARACTERS      ⎬ ]
[         ⎪     [DEPENDING ON field-1 ]                                        ⎪ ]
[         ⎩ CONTAINS integer-4 TO integer-5 CHARACTERS                         ⎭ ]
```

```
[ DATA  ⎧ RECORD IS  ⎫ {field-2 } ... ]
[       ⎨ RECORDS ARE ⎬                ]
```

<u>WORKING-STORAGE</u> <u>SECTION</u>.

```
level-number [ ⎧ data-name ⎫ ]   [ REDEFINES data-name-2 ]
[              ⎩ FILLER    ⎭ ]
```

```
                    [ ⎧ PICTURE ⎫  IS character-string ]
                    [ ⎨ PIC     ⎬                       ]
```

```
                [                ⎧ BINARY        ⎫           ]
                [                ⎪ COMPUTATIONAL ⎪           ]
                [                ⎪ COMP          ⎪           ]
                [    USAGE IS    ⎨ DISPLAY       ⎬           ]
                [                ⎪ INDEX         ⎪           ]
                [                ⎩ PACKED-DECIMAL ⎭          ]
```

```
[ OCCURS integer-1 TIMES                                       ]
[                                                              ]
[     [ ⎧ ASCENDING  ⎫   KEY IS { field-name-1 } ... ] ...     ]
[     [ ⎩ DESCENDING ⎭                               ]         ]
[                                                              ]
[     [ INDEXED BY { index-name-1 } ...]                       ]
```

```
[ OCCURS integer-2 TO integer-3 TIMES DEPENDING ON field-name-2 ]
[                                                               ]
[     [ ⎧ ASCENDING  ⎫   KEY IS { field-name-3 } ... ] ...      ]
[     [ ⎩ DESCENDING ⎭                               ]          ]
[                                                               ]
[     [ INDEXED BY { index-name-2 } ... ]                       ]
```

```
[ ⎧ JUSTIFIED ⎫ RIGHT ]
[ ⎩ JUST      ⎭       ]
```

[BLANK WHEN ZERO]

[VALUE IS literal]

```
[ 88 condition-name ⎧ VALUE IS   ⎫ ⎧ literal-1 [ ⎧ THROUGH ⎫ literal-2 ] ⎫ ... ]
[                   ⎩ VALUES ARE ⎭ ⎩           [ ⎩ THRU    ⎭           ] ⎭      ]
```

REPORT SECTION.

RD report-name

```
[ { CONTROL IS   }   { {field-name-1} ...            } ]
  { CONTROLS ARE }   { FINAL [field-name-1]...       }

[ PAGE [ LIMIT IS  ] integer-1 [ LINE  ]                ]
  ───── [ LIMITS ARE]            [ LINES ]

         [ HEADING integer-2 ]
         [ FIRST DETAIL integer-3 ]
         [ LAST DETAIL integer-4 ]
         [ FOOTING integer-5 ]                          ] .
```

Format 1:

01 [data-name-1]

```
[ LINE NUMBER IS { integer-1   [ ON NEXT PAGE ] } ]
                 { PLUS integer-2                }

[ NEXT GROUP IS { integer-3       } ]
                { PLUS integer-4   }
                { NEXT PAGE        }
```

```
              ( { REPORT HEADING }                      )
              ( { RH            }                       )
              (                                         )
              ( { PAGE HEADING  }                       )
              ( { PH           }                        )
              (                                         )
              ( { CONTROL HEADING } { data-name-2 }     )
              ( { CH             } { FINAL       }      )
              (                                         )
   TYPE IS    ( { DETAIL }                              )
              ( { DE     }                              )
              (                                         )
              ( { CONTROL FOOTING } { data-name-3 }     )
              ( { CF             } { FINAL       }      )
              (                                         )
              ( { PAGE FOOTING }                        )
              ( { PF          }                         )
              (                                         )
              ( { REPORT FOOTING }                      )
              ( { RF            }                       )
```

[[USAGE IS] DISPLAY] .

Format 2:

```
level-number  [ data-name-1 ]
```

$$\left[\underline{\text{LINE}} \text{ NUMBER IS } \left\{ \begin{array}{l} \text{integer-1} \quad [\text{ ON } \underline{\text{NEXT}} \ \underline{\text{PAGE}} \ ] \\ \underline{\text{PLUS}} \text{ integer-2} \end{array} \right\} \right]$$

```
[ [USAGE IS] DISPLAY ] .
```

Format 3:

```
level-number  [ data-name-1 ]
```

$$\left\{ \begin{array}{l} \underline{\text{PICTURE}} \\ \underline{\text{PIC}} \end{array} \right\} \text{ IS } \quad \text{string-1}$$

```
[ [USAGE IS] DISPLAY ]
```

$$\left[[\underline{\text{SIGN}} \text{ IS}] \quad \left\{ \begin{array}{l} \underline{\text{LEADING}} \\ \underline{\text{TRAILING}} \end{array} \right\} \quad \underline{\text{SEPARATE}} \text{ CHARACTER} \right]$$

$$\left[\left\{ \begin{array}{l} \underline{\text{JUSTIFIED}} \\ \underline{\text{JUST}} \end{array} \right\} \quad \text{RIGHT} \right]$$

```
[ BLANK WHEN ZERO]
```

$$\left[\underline{\text{LINE}} \text{ NUMBER IS } \left\{ \begin{array}{l} \text{integer-1} \quad [\text{ ON } \underline{\text{NEXT}} \ \underline{\text{PAGE}} \ ] \\ \underline{\text{PLUS}} \text{ integer-2} \end{array} \right\} \right]$$

```
[ COLUMN NUMBER IS  integer-3 ]
```

$$\left\{ \begin{array}{l} \underline{\text{SOURCE}} \text{ IS } \text{ field-name-1} \\[1em] \underline{\text{VALUE}} \text{ IS literal-1} \\[1em] \{\underline{\text{SUM}} \ \{\text{field-name-2}\} \ ... \ [\underline{\text{UPON}} \ \{\text{field-name-3}\} \ ... \ ] \ \} \ ... \\ \qquad \left[\underline{\text{RESET}} \text{ ON } \left\{ \begin{array}{l} \text{field-name-4} \\ \text{FINAL} \end{array} \right\} \right] \end{array} \right\}$$

```
[ GROUP INDICATE ] .
```

BASIC FORMATS OF THE PROCEDURE DIVISION

```
PROCEDURE DIVISION
     [ USING  identifier ... ] .

DECLARATIVES.

section-name SECTION.
                         ┌ cd-name                           ┐
                         │ [ ALL REFERENCES OF ] field-name  │
USE FOR DEBUGGING ON  ⟨  │ file-name                         │  ...
                         │ procedure-name                    │
                         └ ALL PROCEDURES                    ┘

                                                              ┌ file-name ... ┐
USE AFTER STANDARD ⟨EXCEPTION⟩ PROCEDURE ON  ⟨  INPUT        │
                   ⟨ERROR    ⟩                                │ OUTPUT         │
                                                              │ I-O            │
                                                              └ EXTEND         ┘

USE BEFORE REPORTING report-group-name

paragraph-name.
        .
        .
        .

END DECLARATIVES.

[ section-name SECTION. ]

paragraph-name.
```

ACCEPT

```
ACCEPT field-1  [ FROM mnemonic-name ]


                            ┌ DATE        ┐
                            │ DAY         │
ACCEPT field-1  FROM     ⟨  │ DAY-OF-WEEK │  ⟩
                            │ TIME        │
                            └             ┘
```

ADD

```
ADD  ⟨field-name-1⟩       TO   { field-name-2 [ ROUNDED ] }...
     ⟨literal-1   ⟩

        [ ON SIZE ERROR    statement-set-1   ]
        [ NOT ON SIZE ERROR  statement-set-2 ]

[ END-ADD ]

ADD  ⟨field-name-1⟩    ...     TO  ⟨field-name-2⟩
     ⟨literal-1   ⟩                ⟨literal-2   ⟩

        GIVING { field-name-3  [ ROUNDED ] } ...
        [ ON SIZE ERROR    statement-set-1   ]
        [ NOT ON SIZE ERROR  statement-set-2 ]

[ END-ADD ]
```

CALL

```
CALL   {field-name-1 }
       {literal-1    }

       [ USING  field-name-2 ... ]
```

Class Test

```
field-name-1 IS   [ NOT ]   {NUMERIC   }
                            {ALPHABETIC}
```

CLOSE

```
CLOSE   filename-1  [ filename-2  ... ]
```

COMPUTE

```
COMPUTE { field-name-1 [ ROUNDED ] } ... = arithmetic-expression
        [ ON SIZE ERROR      statement-set-1 ]
        [ NOT ON SIZE ERROR  statement-set-2 ]
[ END-COMPUTE ]
```

DELETE

```
DELETE  file-name-1   RECORD

        [ INVALID KEY statement-set-1 ]
        [ NOT INVALID KEY statement-set-2 ]

[ END-DELETE ]
```

DISPLAY

```
DISPLAY {field-1  }        [ UPON mnemonic-name-1 ] [ WITH NO ADVANCING ]
        {literal-1}
```

DIVIDE

```
DIVIDE  {field-name-1}   INTO  { field-name-2 [ ROUNDED ] } ...
        {literal-1   }
        [ ON SIZE ERROR      statement-set-1 ]
        [ NOT ON SIZE ERROR  statement-set-2 ]
[ END-DIVIDE ]

DIVIDE  {field-name-1}      INTO    {field-name-2}
        {literal-1   }              {literal-2   }
        GIVING { field-name-3 [ ROUNDED ] } ...
        [ ON SIZE ERROR      statement-set-1 ]
        [ NOT ON SIZE ERROR  statement-set-2 ]
[ END-DIVIDE ]
```

```
    DIVIDE   ⎰ field-name-1 ⎱          BY      ⎰ field-name-2 ⎱
             ⎱ literal-1    ⎰                  ⎱ literal-2    ⎰
             GIVING { field-name-3 [ ROUNDED ] } ...
             [ ON SIZE ERROR    statement-set-1 ]
             [ NOT ON SIZE ERROR  statement-set-2 ]
[ END-DIVIDE ]

    DIVIDE   ⎰ field-name-1 ⎱          INTO    ⎰ field-name-2 ⎱
             ⎱ literal-1    ⎰                  ⎱ literal-2    ⎰
             GIVING   field-name-3 [ ROUNDED ]  REMAINDER field-name-4
             [ ON SIZE ERROR    statement-set-1 ]
             [ NOT ON SIZE ERROR  statement-set-2 ]
[ END-DIVIDE ]

    DIVIDE   ⎰ field-name-1 ⎱          BY      ⎰ field-name-2 ⎱
             ⎱ literal-1    ⎰                  ⎱ literal-2    ⎰
             GIVING   field-name-3 [ ROUNDED ]  REMAINDER field-name-4
             [ ON SIZE ERROR    statement-set-1    ]
             [ NOT ON SIZE ERROR  statement-set-2 ]
[ END-DIVIDE ]
```

EVALUATE

```
                  ⎧ field-name-1 ⎫           ⎡      ⎧ field-name-2 ⎫ ⎤
                  ⎪ literal-1    ⎪           ⎢      ⎪ literal-2    ⎪ ⎥
    EVALUATE      ⎨ expression-1 ⎬           ⎢ ALSO ⎨ expression-2 ⎬ ⎥ ...
                  ⎪ TRUE         ⎪           ⎢      ⎪ TRUE         ⎪ ⎥
                  ⎩ FALSE        ⎭           ⎣      ⎩ FALSE        ⎭ ⎦

    {{ WHEN  ⎧  ANY                                                        ⎫
             ⎪  condition-1                                                ⎪
             ⎪  TRUE                                                       ⎪
             ⎨  FALSE                                                      ⎬
             ⎪          ⎧ field-name-3 ⎫ ⎡ ⎧ THROUGH ⎫ ⎧ field-name-4 ⎫ ⎤ ⎪
             ⎪  [NOT ] ⎨ literal-3     ⎬ ⎢ ⎨ THRU    ⎬ ⎨ literal-4     ⎬ ⎥ ⎪
             ⎩          ⎩ arithmetic-exp-1 ⎭ ⎣ ⎩         ⎭ ⎩ arithmetic-exp-2 ⎭ ⎦ ⎭

    ⎡ ALSO  ⎧  ANY                                                        ⎫ ⎤
    ⎢       ⎪  condition-2                                                ⎪ ⎥
    ⎢       ⎪  TRUE                                                       ⎪ ⎥
    ⎢       ⎨  FALSE                                                      ⎬ ⎥ ...
    ⎢       ⎪          ⎧ field-name-5 ⎫ ⎡ ⎧ THROUGH ⎫ ⎧ field-name-6 ⎫ ⎤ ⎪ ⎥
    ⎢       ⎪  [NOT ] ⎨ literal-5     ⎬ ⎢ ⎨ THRU    ⎬ ⎨ literal-6     ⎬ ⎥ ⎪ ⎥
    ⎣       ⎩          ⎩ arithmetic-exp-3 ⎭ ⎣ ⎩         ⎭ ⎩ arithmetic-exp-4 ⎭ ⎦ ⎭ ⎦

             statement-set-1 }} ...

    ⎡ WHEN OTHER                        ⎤
    ⎢                                   ⎥
    ⎣     statement-set-2               ⎦

[ END-EVALUATE ]
```

EXIT PROGRAM

        EXIT PROGRAM

GENERATE

        GENERATE $\begin{Bmatrix} \text{data-name} \\ \text{report-name} \end{Bmatrix}$

GO TO

        GO TO paragraph-1.

GO TO DEPENDING ON

        GO TO paragraph-name-1
            paragraph-name-2
            paragraph-name-3
               .
               .
               .
          DEPENDING ON field-name-1 .

IF

        IF condition-1 THEN $\begin{Bmatrix} \text{statement-1 ...} \\ \text{NEXT SENTENCE} \end{Bmatrix}$

        $\left[\text{ELSE} \qquad\qquad \begin{Bmatrix} \text{statement-2 ...} \\ \text{NEXT SENTENCE} \end{Bmatrix}\right]$

        [END-IF]

INITIALIZE

        INITIALIZE { field-1 } ...

        $\left[\text{REPLACING} \left\{\begin{Bmatrix} \text{ALPHABETIC} \\ \text{ALPHANUMERIC} \\ \text{NUMERIC} \\ \text{ALPHANUMERIC-EDITED} \\ \text{NUMERIC-EDITED} \end{Bmatrix}\right\} \text{DATA BY} \begin{Bmatrix} \text{field-2} \\ \text{literal-1} \end{Bmatrix} ...\right]$

INITIATE

        INITIATE { report-name } ...

INSPECT

INSPECT field-1 TALLYING

```
⎧                  ⎧ CHARACTERS  [⎧⎧BEFORE⎫ INITIAL ⎧field-3 ⎫]...      ⎫
⎨ field-2  FOR ⎨             [⎨⎩AFTER ⎭         ⎩literal-1⎭]          ⎬
⎩                  ⎩ ⎧ALL    ⎫⎧field-4 ⎫⎡⎧BEFORE⎫ INITIAL ⎧field-3 ⎫⎤  ⎭
                       ⎩LEADING⎭⎩literal-2⎭⎣⎩AFTER ⎭         ⎩literal-1⎭⎦
```

INSPECT field-1 REPLACING

```
⎧ CHARACTERS  BY ⎧field-2 ⎫ [⎧⎧BEFORE⎫ INITIAL ⎧field-3 ⎫]...       ⎫
⎪                  ⎩literal-1⎭  [⎨⎩AFTER ⎭         ⎩literal-2⎭]          ⎪
⎨ ⎧ALL    ⎫ ⎧field-4 ⎫ BY ⎧field-5 ⎫⎡⎧BEFORE⎫INITIAL ⎧field-3 ⎫⎤  ⎬
⎪ ⎨LEADING⎬ ⎩literal-3⎭    ⎩literal-4⎭⎣⎩AFTER ⎭        ⎩literal-2⎭⎦  ⎪
⎩ ⎩FIRST  ⎭                                                          ⎭
```

INSPECT field-1

TALLYING

```
⎧                  ⎧ CHARACTERS  [⎧⎧BEFORE⎫ INITIAL ⎧field-3 ⎫]...      ⎫
⎨ field-2  FOR ⎨             [⎨⎩AFTER ⎭         ⎩literal-1⎭]          ⎬
⎩                  ⎩ ⎧ALL    ⎫⎧field-4 ⎫⎡⎧BEFORE⎫ INITIAL ⎧field-3 ⎫⎤  ⎭
                       ⎩LEADING⎭⎩literal-2⎭⎣⎩AFTER ⎭         ⎩literal-1⎭⎦
```

REPLACING

```
⎧ CHARACTERS  BY ⎧field-2 ⎫ [⎧⎧BEFORE⎫ INITIAL ⎧field-3 ⎫]...       ⎫
⎪                  ⎩literal-1⎭  [⎨⎩AFTER ⎭         ⎩literal-2⎭]          ⎪
⎨ ⎧ALL    ⎫ ⎧field-4 ⎫ BY ⎧field-5 ⎫⎡⎧BEFORE⎫INITIAL ⎧field-3 ⎫⎤  ⎬
⎪ ⎨LEADING⎬ ⎩literal-3⎭    ⎩literal-4⎭⎣⎩AFTER ⎭        ⎩literal-2⎭⎦  ⎪
⎩ ⎩FIRST  ⎭                                                          ⎭
```

INSPECT field-1 CONVERTING

```
⎧field-2 ⎫ TO ⎧field-3 ⎫ ⎡⎧BEFORE⎫ INITIAL ⎧field-4 ⎫⎤...
⎩literal-1⎭    ⎩literal-2⎭ ⎣⎩AFTER ⎭         ⎩literal-3⎭⎦
```

Intrinsic Function

FUNCTION function-name [({argument} ...)] [reference-modifier]

MERGE

MERGE merge-work-file $\left\{ \text{ON} \left\{ \begin{array}{l} \underline{\text{ASCENDING}} \\ \underline{\text{DESCENDING}} \end{array} \right\} \text{KEY} \quad \{\text{sort-key-1}\} \ldots \right\} \ldots$

[COLLATING <u>SEQUENCE</u> IS special-name-1]
<u>USING</u> input-file-name-1 { input-file-name-2 } ...

$\left\{ \begin{array}{l} \underline{\text{OUTPUT}} \ \underline{\text{PROCEDURE}} \ \text{IS procedure-name-1} \ \left[\left\{ \begin{array}{l} \underline{\text{THROUGH}} \\ \underline{\text{THRU}} \end{array} \right\} \text{procedure-name-2} \right] \\ \underline{\text{GIVING}} \ \{ \text{output-file-name} \} \ \ldots \end{array} \right\}$

MOVE

MOVE $\left\{ \begin{array}{l} \text{field-1} \\ \text{literal} \end{array} \right\}$ <u>TO</u>   field-2 [field-3] ...

MULTIPLY

<u>MULTIPLY</u> $\left\{ \begin{array}{l} \text{field-name-1} \\ \text{literal-1} \end{array} \right\}$ <u>BY</u> { field-name-2 [<u>ROUNDED</u>] } ...

[ON <u>SIZE</u> <u>ERROR</u>   statement-set-1]
[<u>NOT</u> ON <u>SIZE</u> <u>ERROR</u>   statement-set-2]

[<u>END-MULTIPLY</u>]

<u>MULTIPLY</u> $\left\{ \begin{array}{l} \text{field-name-1} \\ \text{literal-1} \end{array} \right\}$ <u>BY</u> $\left\{ \begin{array}{l} \text{field-name-2} \\ \text{literal-2} \end{array} \right\}$

<u>GIVING</u> { field-name-3 [<u>ROUNDED</u>] } ...

[ON <u>SIZE</u> <u>ERROR</u>   statement-set-1]
[<u>NOT</u> ON <u>SIZE</u> <u>ERROR</u>   statement-set-2]

[<u>END-MULTIPLY</u>]

OPEN

<u>OPEN</u> $\left\{ \begin{array}{ll} \underline{\text{INPUT}} & \text{file-name-1 [file-name-2 } \ldots \text{]} \\ \underline{\text{OUTPUT}} & \text{file-name-3 [file-name-4 } \ldots \text{]} \\ \underline{\text{I-O}} & \text{file-name-5 [file-name-6 } \ldots \text{]} \\ \underline{\text{EXTEND}} & \text{file-name-7 [file-name-8 } \ldots \text{]} \end{array} \right\}$

PERFORM

<u>PERFORM</u> paragraph-name $\left[\left\{ \begin{array}{l} \underline{\text{THROUGH}} \\ \underline{\text{THRU}} \end{array} \right\} \text{paragraph-name-2} \right]$

PERFORM TIMES

PERFORM [paragraph-name-1 [$\left\{ \begin{array}{l} \underline{THROUGH} \\ \underline{THRU} \end{array} \right\}$ paragraph-name-2]]

$\left\{ \begin{array}{l} integer-1 \\ field-name-1 \end{array} \right\}$ $\underline{TIMES}$

[statement-set-1 $\underline{END-PERFORM}$]

PERFORM UNTIL

PERFORM [paragraph-name-1 [$\left\{ \begin{array}{l} \underline{THROUGH} \\ \underline{THRU} \end{array} \right\}$ paragraph-name-2]]

[WITH $\underline{TEST}$ $\left\{ \begin{array}{l} \underline{BEFORE} \\ \underline{AFTER} \end{array} \right\}$]

$\underline{UNTIL}$ condition-1

[statement-set-1 $\underline{END-PERFORM}$]

PERFORM VARYING UNTIL

PERFORM [paragraph-name-1 [$\left\{ \begin{array}{l} \underline{THROUGH} \\ \underline{THRU} \end{array} \right\}$ paragraph-name-2]]

[WITH $\underline{TEST}$ $\left\{ \begin{array}{l} \underline{BEFORE} \\ \underline{AFTER} \end{array} \right\}$]

$\underline{VARYING}$ $\left\{ \begin{array}{l} field-1 \\ index-1 \end{array} \right\}$ $\underline{FROM}$ $\left\{ \begin{array}{l} field-2 \\ index-2 \\ literal-1 \end{array} \right\}$ $\underline{BY}$ $\left\{ \begin{array}{l} field-3 \\ literal-2 \end{array} \right\}$

$\underline{UNTIL}$ condition-1

$\left[\begin{array}{l} \underline{AFTER} \left\{ \begin{array}{l} field-4 \\ index-3 \end{array} \right\} \underline{FROM} \left\{ \begin{array}{l} field-5 \\ index-4 \\ literal-3 \end{array} \right\} \underline{BY} \left\{ \begin{array}{l} field-6 \\ literal-4 \end{array} \right\} \\ \underline{UNTIL} \quad condition-2 \\ \qquad \cdot \\ \qquad \cdot \\ \qquad \cdot \end{array} \right]$

[statement-set-1 $\underline{END-PERFORM}$]

READ

$\underline{READ}$ file-name-1 [$\underline{NEXT}$] RECORD [$\underline{INTO}$ record-layout-1]

[AT $\underline{END}$ statement-set-1]
[$\underline{NOT}$ AT $\underline{END}$ statement-set-2]

[$\underline{END-READ}$]

```
READ file-name-1 RECORD  [ INTO record-layout-1 ]

    [ KEY IS key-field-1 ]
    [ INVALID KEY  statement-set-1 ]
    [ NOT INVALID KEY statement-set-2 ]

[ END-READ ]
```

Reference Modification

```
field-name-1 [ ( leftmost-character-position : [length] ) ]
```

RELEASE

```
RELEASE sort-record-name  [ FROM input-record-layout ]
```

RETURN

```
RETURN sort-work-file RECORD  [ INTO record-layout-1 ]

    AT END  statement-set-1
  [ NOT AT END  statement-set-2 ]

[ END-RETURN ]
```

REWRITE

```
REWRITE  record-name-1   [ FROM record-name-2 ]

    [ INVALID KEY  statement-set-1 ]
    [ NOT INVALID KEY  statement-set-2 ]

[ END-REWRITE ]
```

SEARCH

```
SEARCH  table-name-1  [ VARYING { field-name-1 } ]
                                 { index-name-1 }

    [ AT END statement-set-1 ]

    { WHEN condition-1 { statement-set-2 } } ...
    {                  { NEXT SENTENCE   } }

[ END-SEARCH ]
```

```
SEARCH ALL table-name-1  [ AT END statement-set-1 ]

        ⎧ field-name-1 ⎧ IS EQUAL TO ⎫  ⎧ field-name-2 ⎫ ⎫
        ⎪              ⎨ IS =        ⎬  ⎨ literal-1     ⎬ ⎪
  WHEN  ⎨              ⎩             ⎭  ⎩ expression-1  ⎭ ⎬
        ⎪                                                ⎪
        ⎩ condition-name-1                               ⎭

    ⎡        ⎧ field-name-3 ⎧ IS EQUAL TO ⎫  ⎧ field-name-4 ⎫ ⎫ ⎤
    ⎢        ⎪              ⎨ IS =        ⎬  ⎨ literal-2     ⎬ ⎪ ⎥
    ⎢  AND   ⎨              ⎩             ⎭  ⎩ expression-2  ⎭ ⎬ ⎥ ...
    ⎢        ⎪                                                ⎪ ⎥
    ⎣        ⎩ condition-name-2                               ⎭ ⎦

              ⎧ statement-set-2 ⎫
              ⎨ NEXT SENTENCE   ⎬
              ⎩                 ⎭

  [ END-SEARCH ]
```

SET

```
  SET  ⎧ index-name-1 ⎫  ...  TO  ⎧ index-name-2 ⎫
       ⎨ field-name-1 ⎬          ⎨ field-name-2  ⎬
       ⎩              ⎭          ⎩ integer-1      ⎭

  SET  { index-name-1 } ...  ⎧ UP BY   ⎫   ⎧ field-name-1 ⎫
                             ⎨ DOWN BY ⎬   ⎨ integer-1     ⎬
                             ⎩         ⎭   ⎩               ⎭
```

Sign Test

```
  field-name-1 IS  [ NOT ]  ⎧ POSITIVE ⎫
                            ⎨ NEGATIVE ⎬
                            ⎩ ZERO     ⎭
```

SORT

```
SORT sort-work-file  ⎧ ON ⎧ ASCENDING  ⎫  KEY {sort-key-1} ... ⎫ ...
                     ⎩    ⎨ DESCENDING ⎬                        ⎭
                          ⎩            ⎭

    [ WITH DUPLICATES IN ORDER ]
    [ COLLATING SEQUENCE IS special-name-1 ]

    ⎧ INPUT PROCEDURE IS procedure-1    ⎡ ⎧ THROUGH ⎫ procedure-2 ⎤ ⎫
    ⎨                                   ⎢ ⎨ THRU    ⎬             ⎥ ⎬
    ⎩ USING { input-file-name } ...     ⎣ ⎩         ⎭             ⎦ ⎭

    ⎧ OUTPUT PROCEDURE IS procedure-3   ⎡ ⎧ THROUGH ⎫ procedure-4 ⎤ ⎫
    ⎨                                   ⎢ ⎨ THRU    ⎬             ⎥ ⎬
    ⎩ GIVING { output-file-name } ...   ⎣ ⎩         ⎭             ⎦ ⎭
```

START

$$
\underline{\text{START}}\ \text{file-name}\ \left[\ \underline{\text{KEY}}\ \text{IS}\ \left\{\begin{array}{l}\underline{\text{EQUAL}}\ \text{TO} \\ = \\ \underline{\text{GREATER}}\ \text{THAN} \\ > \\ \underline{\text{NOT}}\ \underline{\text{LESS}}\ \text{THAN} \\ \underline{\text{NOT}}\ < \\ \underline{\text{GREATER}}\ \text{THAN}\ \underline{\text{OR}}\ \underline{\text{EQUAL}}\ \text{TO} \\ >= \end{array}\right\}\ \text{key-field}\ \right]
$$

```
        [ INVALID KEY statement-set-1    ]
        [ NOT INVALID KEY statement-set-2 ]

    [ END-START ]
```

STOP

$$
\underline{\text{STOP}}\ \left\{\begin{array}{l}\underline{\text{RUN}} \\ \text{literal-1}\end{array}\right\}
$$

STRING

$$
\underline{\text{STRING}}\ \left\{\ \left\{\begin{array}{l}\text{field-1} \\ \text{literal-1}\end{array}\right\}\ ...\ \underline{\text{DELIMITED}}\ \text{BY}\ \left\{\begin{array}{l}\text{field-2} \\ \text{literal-2} \\ \underline{\text{SIZE}}\end{array}\right\}\ \right\}\ ...
$$

```
        INTO  field-3

        [ WITH POINTER field-4 ]
        [ ON OVERFLOW statement-set-1 ]
        [ NOT ON OVERFLOW statement-set-2 ]

    [ END-STRING ]
```

SUBTRACT

$$
\underline{\text{SUBTRACT}}\ \left\{\begin{array}{l}\text{field-name-1} \\ \text{literal-1}\end{array}\right\}\ ...\ \underline{\text{FROM}}\ \{\ \text{field-name-2}\ [\ \underline{\text{ROUNDED}}\ ]\ \}...
$$

```
        [ ON SIZE ERROR    statement-set-1 ]
        [ NOT ON SIZE ERROR  statement-set-2 ]

    [ END-SUBTRACT ]
```

$$
\underline{\text{SUBTRACT}}\ \left\{\begin{array}{l}\text{field-name-1} \\ \text{literal-1}\end{array}\right\}\ ...\ \underline{\text{FROM}}\ \left\{\begin{array}{l}\text{field-name-2} \\ \text{literal-2}\end{array}\right\}
$$

```
            GIVING { field-name-3 [ ROUNDED ] } ...

            [ ON SIZE ERROR    statement-set-1 ]
            [ NOT ON SIZE ERROR  statement-set-2 ]

        [ END-SUBTRACT ]
```

TERMINATE

TERMINATE { report-name } ...

UNSTRING

UNSTRING field-1

$$\left[\underline{\text{DELIMITED}} \text{ BY } [\underline{\text{ALL}}] \begin{Bmatrix} \text{field-2} \\ \text{literal-1} \end{Bmatrix} \left[\underline{\text{OR}} \ [\underline{\text{ALL}}] \begin{Bmatrix} \text{field-3} \\ \text{literal-2} \end{Bmatrix} \right] \ \dots \right]$$

INTO { field-4 [DELIMITER IN field-5] [COUNT IN field-6]}...

[WITH POINTER field-7]
[TALLYING IN field-8]
[ON OVERFLOW statement-set-1]
[NOT ON OVERFLOW statement-set-2]

[END-UNSTRING]

USE

$$\underline{\text{USE}} \text{ FOR } \underline{\text{DEBUGGING}} \text{ ON } \begin{Bmatrix} \text{cd-name} \\ [\underline{\text{ALL}} \text{ REFERENCES OF }] \text{ field-name} \\ \text{file-name} \\ \text{procedure-name} \\ \text{ALL } \underline{\text{PROCEDURES}} \end{Bmatrix} \ \dots$$

$$\underline{\text{USE}} \ \underline{\text{AFTER}} \text{ STANDARD} \begin{Bmatrix} \underline{\text{EXCEPTION}} \\ \underline{\text{ERROR}} \end{Bmatrix} \underline{\text{PROCEDURE}} \text{ ON } \begin{Bmatrix} \text{file-name} \ \dots \\ \underline{\text{INPUT}} \\ \underline{\text{OUTPUT}} \\ \underline{\text{I-O}} \\ \underline{\text{EXTEND}} \end{Bmatrix}$$

USE BEFORE REPORTING report-group-name

WRITE

WRITE record-name-1 [FROM record-name-2   ]

$$\left[\begin{Bmatrix} \underline{\text{BEFORE}} \\ \underline{\text{AFTER}} \end{Bmatrix} \text{ ADVANCING } \begin{Bmatrix} \begin{Bmatrix} \text{field-name-1} \\ \text{integer} \end{Bmatrix} \begin{bmatrix} \text{LINE} \\ \text{LINES} \end{bmatrix} \\ \begin{Bmatrix} \text{mnemonic-name} \\ \underline{\text{PAGE}} \end{Bmatrix} \end{Bmatrix} \right]$$

WRITE record-name-1   [FROM record-name-2]

[INVALID KEY statement-set-1]
[NOT INVALID KEY statement-set-2]

[END-WRITE]

APPENDIX E

Variable-Length Records

All of the files processed in this book contain fixed-length records. That is, in each file, each record contains the same number of characters. It is common to process sequential and indexed files in which the size of the records varies. Such records are referred to as **variable-length records**. Although optional, it is common to code a RECORD clause in the FD of a file containing variable-length records. The RECORD clause format for fixed-length records was presented in Chapter 2. Figure E-1 presents the formats available for defining variable-length records.

```
FD   file-name

     RECORD CONTAINS integer-1 TO integer-2 CHARACTERS

FD   file-name

     RECORD IS VARYING IN SIZE
        [[ FROM integer-1 ]  [TO integer-2] CHARACTERS ]
        [ DEPENDING ON field-name-1 ]
```

FIGURE E-1   FD entry RECORD clause format options for defining variable-length records

The first format, RECORD CONTAINS, allows for the minimum and maximum lengths of the records to be defined. Any attempt to perform an input or output operation, such as a READ or WRITE, with a record whose size is less than the specified minimum or greater than the specified maximum, will result in a run-time error. When the second format, RECORD IS VARYING, is used, minimum and maximum values are optional. If coded, then the rules are the same as those stated for RECORD CONTAINS. If the DEPENDING ON clause is coded in this format, then the record size must be moved to the field named by the DEPENDING ON clause before the execution of a WRITE, REWRITE, or RELEASE statement. If a READ or RETURN statement is executed, then the size of the record obtained will be placed automatically into the field named by the DEPENDING ON clause. If the RECORD clause is omitted in an FD, then record size is determined completely by the record definition following the FD. Two primary means are available for defining such variable-length records.

REPEATING GROUPS

For the Premium file applications discussed in Chapters 1 through 10, assume it is necessary to maintain a history of the payments made by each customer in each customer's record. Because some customers have been insured longer than others, these customers will have more payment history information than the others. It is inefficient to waste computer resources by reserving the same amount of space for each customer record. Each customer record should contain some basic information along with individual entries for each payment made. Figure E-2 illustrates this concept.

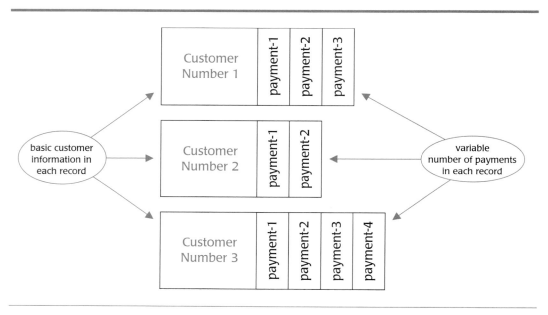

FIGURE E-2   Variable-length customer payment history records

Figure E-2 illustrates records with variable numbers of repeating groups. Each record has a fixed-length portion followed by a variable-length portion. A **repeating group** is a block of data that can appear multiple times in a record. In some cases, the block might not appear at all. The 01 level record definition following the FD is coded containing an OCCURS clause that uses the DEPENDING ON option to define a variable-length table as part of the record definition. Variable-length tables were presented in Chapter 7.

The field named following the DEPENDING ON option in the table definition must be in the fixed-length portion of the record and must be an integer-type field. Figure E-3 presents the basic FD and record format typically used for defining variable-length records with repeating groups. Figure E-4 presents an example that allows payment history information to be maintained for the Premium file applications used in this book. If necessary, the variable-length table could be defined with an index and either the ASCENDING KEY or DESCENDING KEY clause could be coded. Great care must be taken when creating such a file. For each record, it is extremely important that the field named by the DEPENDING ON clause have an accurate count of the repeating groups in that record. Errors will occur during file processing otherwise.

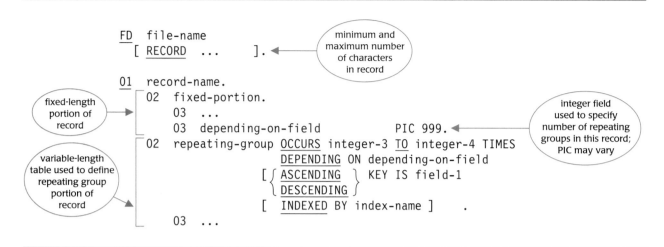

```
FD  file-name
    [ RECORD  ...     ].

01  record-name.
    02  fixed-portion.
        03  ...
        03  depending-on-field         PIC 999.
    02  repeating-group OCCURS integer-3 TO integer-4 TIMES
                        DEPENDING ON depending-on-field
                        [ { ASCENDING  } KEY IS field-1
                          { DESCENDING }
                        [ INDEXED BY index-name ]     .
        03  ...
```

minimum and maximum number of characters in record

fixed-length portion of record

variable-length table used to define repeating group portion of record

integer field used to specify number of repeating groups in this record; PIC may vary

FIGURE E-3   Basic FD and record formats for using variable-length records with repeating groups

```
FD  PREMIUM-INPUT-FILE
    RECORD CONTAINS 82 TO 418 CHARACTERS.

01  PREMIUM-RECORD.
    02  PR-BASIC-DATA.
        03  PR-CUSTOMER-NAME         PIC X(20).
        03  PR-AGENT-NAME            PIC X(20).
        03  PR-INSURANCE-TYPE        PIC X(10).
        03  PR-POLICY-NUMBER         PIC X(12).
        03                           PIC X(18).
        03  PR-HISTORY-COUNT         PIC 99.
    02  PR-PAYMENT-HISTORY OCCURS 0 TO 24 TIMES
                        DEPENDING ON PR-HISTORY-COUNT.
        03  PR-PAYMENT-DATE          PIC 9(6).
        03  PR-PAYMENT               PIC 9(5)V99.
        03  PR-PAYMENT-METHOD        PIC X.
            88  CASH                 VALUE "1".
            88  CHECK                VALUE "2".
```

FIGURE E-4   Variable-length premium record definition allowing for payment history data

MULTIPLE FIXED-LENGTH RECORDS

A second method available for defining and creating a file that contains variable-length records involves defining multiple 01 level entries following the FD. Each 01 level entry can be defined with a different record length. Figure E-5 on the next page illustrates a definition for the PREMIUM-INPUT-FILE. Record layouts for such records can be defined in the WORKING-STORAGE SECTION.

```
FD   PREMIUM-INPUT-FILE.

01   BASIC-PREMIUM-RECORD                PIC X(82).

01   ONE-PAYMENT-RECORD                  PIC X(96).

01   TWO-PAYMENT-RECORD                  PIC X(110).
```

FIGURE E-5   Variable-length premium record definition using multiple 01 level entries

Figure E-6 presents three WRITE statements that can be used to write records out to the PREMIUM-INPUT-FILE. To write a record containing 82 characters to the file, the name BASIC-PREMIUM-RECORD would follow the word WRITE. To write a record containing 96 characters, the name ONE-PAYMENT-RECORD would follow the word WRITE. To write a record containing 110 characters to the file, the name TWO-PAYMENT-RECORD would follow the word WRITE. Any number of 01 level definitions can be defined following the FD. All of the 01 level definitions share the same area of storage, just as though the REDEFINES clauses were used. Remember, however, that COBOL does not allow the REDEFINES clause to be used at the 01 level in the FILE SECTION of the DATA DIVISION. The amount of storage allocated is determined by the largest record defined.

```
WRITE BASIC-PREMIUM-RECORD FROM record-layout-1.

WRITE ONE-PAYMENT-RECORD FROM record-layout-2.

WRITE TWO-PAYMENT-RECORD FROM record-layout-3.
```

FIGURE E-6   Three WRITE statements that write records of different lengths

Other means of defining variable-length records exist; however, the methods presented in this book are the more commonly used. Over the years, as computer resources such as disk space and memory have become more and more economical, the trend has moved away from variable-length records and toward the less complex processing of fixed-length records.

APPENDIX **F**

A Beginner's Guide to Micro Focus Personal COBOL

Micro Focus, a leading company in COBOL technology, has an inexpensive **Personal COBOL** compiler available for students. The Personal COBOL compiler is designed to run on IBM PC or compatible systems using MS-DOS version 3.3 or later. It requires 640K of main memory and at least 8 megabytes of free space on a hard drive. Personal COBOL can be valuable to students who find working on their own computers more convenient and more comfortable than working in a computer laboratory.

Personal COBOL comes with a simple setup program that installs the necessary software on the computer's hard disk drive. Once installed, the command PCOBOL starts Personal COBOL from the DOS prompt. The initial screen contains copyright information (Figure F-1).

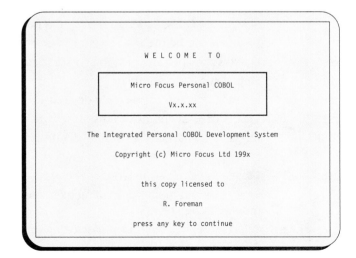

FIGURE F-1   Personal COBOL copyright screen

After pressing any key, Personal COBOL displays the Edit window with the main menu at the bottom (Figure F-2). Most of the menu items are self-explanatory and identify editing actions associated with the function keys on your keyboard.

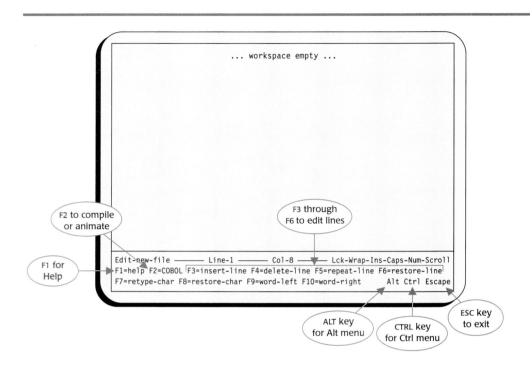

FIGURE F-2   Personal COBOL Edit window and the main menu

Table F-1 summarizes key functions available while the main menu is active. From the main menu, the ESC key is used to exit Personal COBOL.

TABLE F-1   Key Functions Available while the Main Menu Is Active

F1=help	Provides help for the Main menu
F2=COBOL	Selects the COBOL menu for program functions
F3=insert-line	Inserts a line before the current cursor position
F4=delete-line	Deletes the line on which the cursor is currently positioned
F5=repeat-line	Duplicates the current line
F6=restore-line	Inserts the line most recently deleted
F7=retype-char	Inserts the last character erased
F8=restore-char	Inserts the character most recently deleted
F9=word-left	Moves the cursor one word to the left
F10=word-right	Moves the cursor one word to the right
ALT	Selects the Alt menu for loading files, saving files, and manipulating lines
CTRL	Selects the Ctrl menu for fast scrolling and text find
ESC	Exits from the current view, if more than one file is open, or, if only one file is open, exits the Editor
ALT+Q	Exits the Editor regardless of the number of open files

Besides the main menu, two other Edit menus are available. One is accessed by pressing the CTRL key and the other is accessed by pressing the ALT key. The CTRL key or ALT key must be held down while accessing the corresponding menu until a menu option is selected. The **Ctrl menu** provides a search facility; enables you to select block operations; lets you clear the screen and alter the margins; allows you to draw screens and automate wordwrap; and provides commands for fast scrolling through a file (Figure F-3).

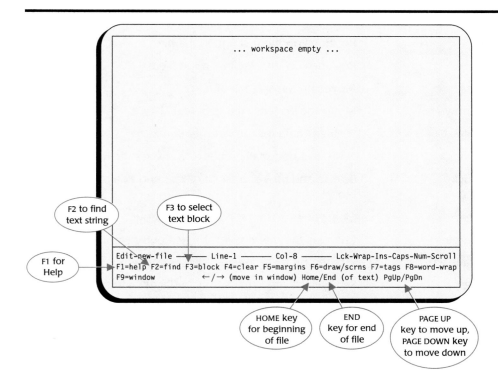

FIGURE F-3   Personal COBOL Edit window and the Ctrl menu

Table F-2 summarizes the functions of the keys while the Ctrl menu is active.

TABLE F-2 Key Functions Available while the Ctrl Menu Is Active

CTRL +

←	Moves window text up
→	Moves window text down
HOME	Positions on the first line in the file
END	Positions on the last line in the file
PAGE UP	Moves up ten screens of text
PAGE DOWN	Moves down ten screens of text
F1=help	Provides help for the Ctrl menu
F2=find	Finds and optionally replaces a string of text
F3=block	Selects and moves a block of text and edits the text within the block
F4=clear	Clears all text from the current window
F5=margins	Changes the margins for the text entry within the Editor
F6=draw/scrns	Screen and text handling utilities submenu
F7=tags	Sets, selects, and clears tagged (flagged) text lines
F8=word-wrap	Selects wordwrap at margin limit
F9=window	Enters the window control submenu for window creation, sizing, and movement on the screen

The **Alt menu** enables you to load and edit files referred to by COPY statements; load, save, and print program files; and manipulate text within files (Figure F-4). Table F-3 summarizes the functions of the keys while in the Alt menu.

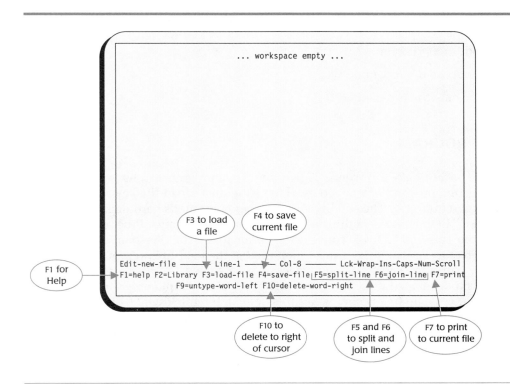

FIGURE F-4   Personal COBOL Edit window and the Alt menu

TABLE F-3   Key Functions Available while the Alt Menu Is Active

ALT +	
F1=help	Provides help for the Alt menu
F2=Library	Edits a COPY of a file; you must place the cursor on a COPY or CALL statement before using
F3=load-file	Loads an existing file into the Editor
F4=save-file	Copies the current edited file to disk
F5=split-line	Splits the current line at the cursor position
F6=join-line	Joins the next line onto the end of the current line
F7=print	Prints the current file
F9=untype-word-left	Untypes the word to the left of the cursor
F10=delete-word-right	Deletes the word to the right of the cursor; if the cursor is at the start of a line, then spaces before the first words are deleted

The three primary tasks to concentrate on while using Personal COBOL are:

1. Edit the program
2. Compile the program
3. Execute the program

EDIT THE PROGRAM

At the beginning of a Personal COBOL session, a program can be typed in immediately or an existing program can be retrieved by using the F3 load-file key, which is found on the Alt menu (ALT+F3). The subdirectory on your computer's hard disk drive containing Personal COBOL is the default directory for loading programs. Program files can be copied into the Personal COBOL subdirectory prior to starting Personal COBOL or a different subdirectory or disk drive can be identified at the load-file prompt. Figure F-5 shows the Policy Number Report program loaded into Personal COBOL. This program is the report program developed in Chapter 2 of this book. This sample program can be found on the Student Diskette that accompanies this book in the file PROJ2.CBL. Once editing is complete, the program can be saved by using the F4 save-file key in the Alt menu. After using ALT+F4, if the file name is correct, press ENTER. If the file name is incorrect, fix it and then press ENTER to save the file.

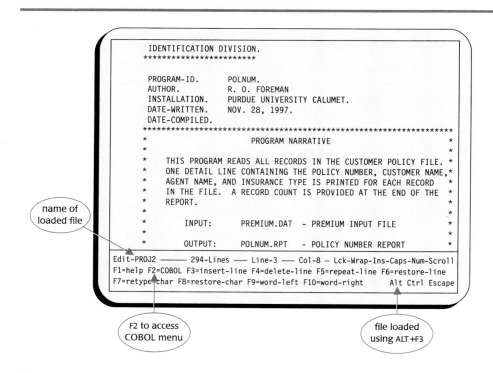

FIGURE F-5 Personal COBOL Edit window with loaded program and the main menu

COMPILE THE PROGRAM

Once a program is saved, it can be compiled, or **checked**, by using the F2 key on the main menu to activate the COBOL menu. Figure F-6 shows the COBOL menu that provides access to COBOL program functions such as checking for and locating syntax errors.

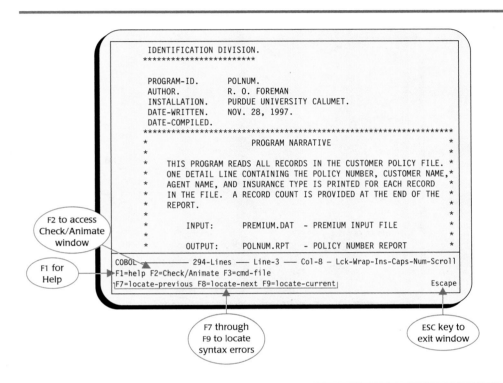

FIGURE F-6   COBOL window

Table F-4 summarizes the use of the function keys in the COBOL menu. If necessary, a program can be edited while in the COBOL menu; however, ESC must be used to return to the Edit window and ALT+F4 must be used to save changes before the program is checked.

TABLE F-4   Key Functions Available while the COBOL Menu Is Active

F1=help	Provides help for the COBOL menu
F2=Check/Animate	Enters the Checker menu to start checking or begin animating a program
F3=cmd-file	Enters the Command File menu that provides the capability to load the Checker error message file and for positioning on the first program error
F7=locate-previous	Positions to the previous program error
F8=locate-next	Positions to the next program error
F9=locate-current	Repositions to the current program error
ESC	Returns to the main menu

To check a program, press the F2 key while in the COBOL menu. This will activate the Check/Animate menu (Figure F-7). Make sure the word *check* is just to the left of the file name at the bottom of the screen. If the word *check* does not appear to the left of the file name, press the F2 key until it does. Pressing the ENTER key will then begin the checking and compiling of a program.

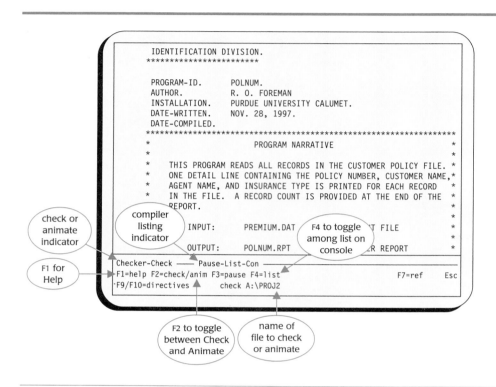

FIGURE F-7   Check/Animate window ready to check the Policy Number Report program

If a syntax error is encountered, Personal COBOL stops so the error can be seen, but it cannot be corrected at this point (Figure F-8). In response to the prompt to continue checking, type Y for Yes to continue checking, type N for No to terminate checking, or type Z for Zoom to continue checking without stopping at subsequent errors. Typing Y for Yes or Z for Zoom is the recommended action at this point.

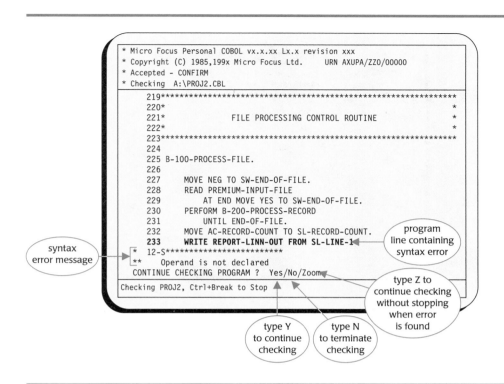

FIGURE F-8   Syntax error found during check

Once checking is complete, if a program has syntax errors, Personal COBOL returns to edit mode and the main menu. The first syntax error will be highlighted and an error message will display at the bottom of the screen (Figure F-9 on the next page). The error can be corrected at this point. To find the next syntax error, press F2 to return to the COBOL menu, and then press the F8 key to execute the locate-next command (see Figure F-6 on page F-7). The next error will appear highlighted with a message at the bottom of the screen. If a printed listing of the program with the errors noted is desired, the F4 list key can be used while in the Check/Animate menu (see Figure F-7). The F4 key will scroll through four options; List-Con, which lists the program on the screen; Print, which sends a listing of the program to the printer; List File, which creates a listing of the file on the disk; and No-list, which produces no checker listing.

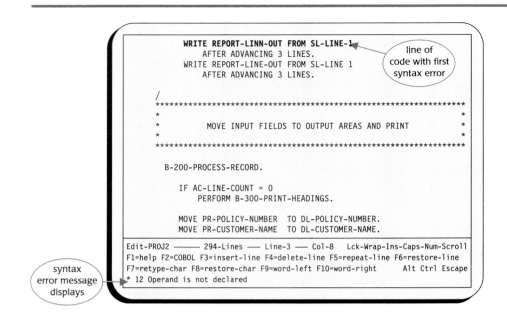

FIGURE F-9   Edit window with main menu active and first syntax error highlighted

Once all errors have been located and fixed, return to the Alt menu (see Figure F-4 on page F-5), save the program, and from the main menu, press F2 to return to the COBOL menu. From the COBOL menu, check the program again. Checking and editing must continue until all syntax errors have been eliminated. Once all syntax errors are eliminated, the Personal COBOL checker will return to the main menu without displaying any error messages. The program then is ready to be executed.

EXECUTE THE PROGRAM

Execution of a program is accomplished by Personal COBOL in animation mode. **Animation mode** provides the capability to execute a program, line by line, on the screen. To animate a program, press F2 while in the COBOL menu and make sure the word *animate* appears next to the file name at the bottom of the screen. If the word *animate* does not appear, press the F2 key until it does, and then press the ENTER key to begin animation.

The Animate menu allows the execution of a program to be controlled (Figure F-10). Table F-5 summarizes commands available while in animation. Some options change the way the program is shown or movement of the cursor around the screen or program. Other options change the order or speed of execution. Variables can be displayed and altered while the program is executing, or execution can be performed quickly without displaying the source code. One very useful feature available from this menu is the capability to create breakpoints. A **breakpoint** is a location within the program, either a paragraph name or line of code, at which animation stops until the Go command is given again. Press B to access the Breakpoint menu.

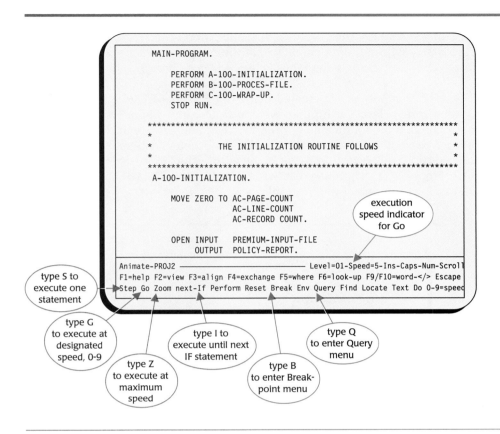

FIGURE F-10   Animate window and menu

TABLE F-5   Special Animation Commands

Step	Executes one instruction
Go	Executes slowly
Zoom	Executes at full speed
next-If	Executes until next IF
Perform	Sets executed perform level
Reset	Resets execution position
Break	Sets/unsets breakpoints
Env	Sets execution environment
Query	Examines data-item
Find	Finds next occurrence
Locate	Locates declaration of item
Text	Sets screen separator
Do	Executes typed COBOL syntax
0–9=Speed	Sets default Go speed

Once a program has finished, output files created will be in the default subdirectory on your computer's hard disk drive or in the location indicated in the ASSIGN portion of the SELECT entry within the program. To exit the Animate menu, simply press the ESC key to return to the main menu, where the cycle of editing, checking, and animating can begin again.

Files used as input can be created using the Personal COBOL Editor or they can be downloaded from a larger computer system. If an input file is created by a text editor, Personal COBOL may not be able to properly read and process it due to carriage returns or line feeds used at the end of each record. This problem can be overcome by including the clause ORGANIZATION IS LINE SEQUENTIAL within the SELECT entry for the input file as shown in Figure F-11. The entry ORGANIZATION IS LINE SEQUENTIAL will allow Personal COBOL to treat each line of the input file as a separate record.

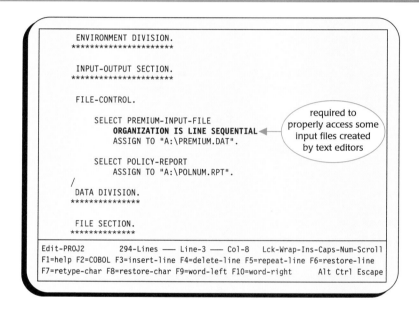

FIGURE F-11 Edit window showing the ORGANIZATION IS LINE SEQUENTIAL clause included in the SELECT for the input file

When necessary, drive indicators and subdirectory paths can be used as part of your file name in the ASSIGN portion of a SELECT entry. A **drive indicator** consists of a letter, identifying the drive on your computer to be used, followed by a colon. For example, if the input file is located on a diskette in drive A of your computer system, the input file name must be prefixed by A:. If the output file is to be created on drive A of your computer, then the output file name also must be prefixed with the drive indicator A:. Figure F-12 calls attention to the drive indicator of A: used on both the input file and output file in the Policy Number Report program. All of the programs presented in this book use drive indicators on the input and output files.

```
        ENVIRONMENT DIVISION.
        **********************

        INPUT-OUTPUT SECTION.
        *********************

        FILE-CONTROL.

            SELECT PREMIUM-INPUT-FILE
                ORGANIZATION IS LINE SEQUENTIAL        A: is the
                ASSIGN TO "A:\PREMIUM.DAT".            drive indicator

            SELECT POLICY-REPORT
                ASSIGN TO "A:\POLNUM.RPT".
        /
        DATA DIVISION.
        ***************

        FILE SECTION.
        **************

Edit-PROJ2      294-Lines ──── Line-3 ──── Col-8   Lck-Wrap-Ins-Caps-Num-Scroll
F1=help F2=COBOL F3=insert-line F4=delete-line F5=repeat-line F6=restore-line
F7=retype-char F8=restore-char F9=word-left F10=word-right     Alt Ctrl Escape
```

FIGURE F-12   Edit window showing the drive A indicator used in the ASSIGN portion of the SELECT for the input file and output file

As shown by Figure F-13, subdirectory paths also can be specified when needed as part of the ASSIGN entry file name. A **subdirectory path** identifies the subdirectory containing an input file or the subdirectory in which an output file is to be placed. A **subdirectory** is a portion of a diskette or hard disk drive reserved for special groups of files. Figure F-13 shows that the input file is on a diskette in drive A in a subdirectory named DATA. The output file is to be created on drive A in a subdirectory named REPORTS. When using Personal COBOL, close attention must be paid to the use of proper drive indicators and subdirectory paths.

```
        ENVIRONMENT DIVISION.
        **********************

        INPUT-OUTPUT SECTION.
        *********************

        FILE-CONTROL.

            SELECT PREMIUM-INPUT-FILE                  \DATA and
                ORGANIZATION IS LINE SEQUENTIAL        \REPORTS are
                ASSIGN TO "A:\DATA\PREMIUM.DAT".        subdirectory
                                                       paths
            SELECT POLICY-REPORT
                ASSIGN TO "A:\REPORTS\POLNUM.RPT".
        /
        DATA DIVISION.
        ***************

        FILE SECTION.
        **************

Edit-PROJ2      294-Lines ──── Line-3 ──── Col-8   Lck-Wrap-Ins-Caps-Num-Scroll
F1=help F2=COBOL F3=insert-line F4=delete-line F5=repeat-line F6=restore-line
F7=retype-char F8=restore-char F9=word-left F10=word-right     Alt Ctrl Escape
```

FIGURE F-13   Edit window showing the drive A indicator and subdirectory paths used in the ASSIGN portion of the SELECT for the input file and output file

A Beginner's Guide to Micro Focus Workbench

Micro Focus Workbench allows computer programmers to develop and test mainframe applications in a personal computer environment. This type of development frees resources on the mainframe computer system for production applications. Also, because the programmer can control his or her own environment on a personal computer, development generally can progress more rapidly. Micro Focus GUI (graphical user interface) Workbench is designed to work in UNIX, OS/2, or Microsoft Windows environments. It is a sophisticated package, and its many capabilities cannot be fully presented in this brief appendix. Therefore, this appendix is designed to introduce the basic features available for editing, compiling, and executing a COBOL program.

Figure G-1 on the next page shows the Program Manager window in Microsoft Windows with the Micro Focus COBOL 3.2 Graphical System group icon highlighted. In a GUI environment, commands and programs can be accessed with a mouse. To open the Micro Focus COBOL group, point to and double-click its icon. The term **double-click** means quickly press and release the left mouse button twice in rapid succession. The term **click** means press and release the left mouse button once.

Figure G-2 on the next page shows the COBOL 3.2 Graphical System group window containing the Workbench and On-line Reference program-item icons. To open the Workbench group, double-click the Workbench program-item icon.

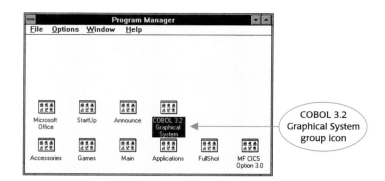

FIGURE G-1 Program Manager window with Micro Focus COBOL group icon highlighted

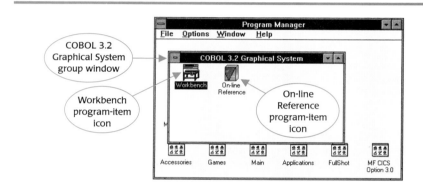

FIGURE G-2 COBOL 3.2 Graphical System group window

Figure G-3 presents the open Micro Focus Workbench v3.2.20 desktop. Many tools are available; however, the **Edit+Animate** tool provides the access needed to edit, compile, and execute a program.

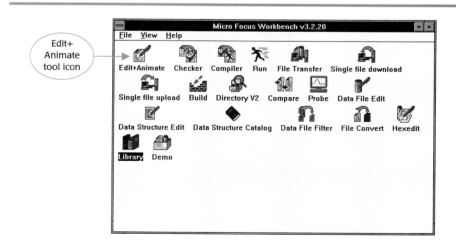

FIGURE G-3 Open Micro Focus Workbench v3.2.20 window

EDITING A PROGRAM

When you double-click the Edit+Animate tool icon, Workbench opens the Edit+Animate options dialog box for entering the name of a program (Figure G-4). If the exact location of the program file is not known, the Find file button can be used to search for the program. Workbench compiler options can be modified if necessary by clicking the Compiler Directives button; however, the default options generally can be utilized.

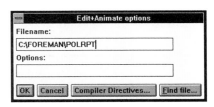

FIGURE G-4   Edit+Animate options dialog box

Once you have entered the program name, click the OK button and Workbench will display the Animator Version 2 window (Figure G-5). Using the menu commands, the toolbar, the vertical scroll bar, the arrow keys, the PAGE UP key, and the PAGE DOWN key, a program can be entered and modified. To save the program on a diskette, use the Save command on the File menu or simply click the Save File button on the toolbar. Once saved, the program must be compiled before it can be tested.

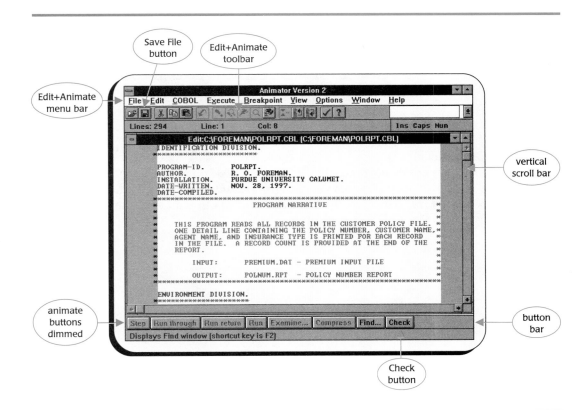

FIGURE G-5   Animator Version 2 window with the program POLRPT loaded

COMPILING A PROGRAM

From the Animator Version 2 window shown in Figure G-5 on the previous page, the Check button at the bottom of the screen can be used to begin finding syntax errors and compiling a program. Animate options, used for executing a program, are not available and appear dimmed on the button bar at the bottom of the screen until the program has been successfully compiled. If a syntax error is found, a Checking dialog box displays describing the error (Figure G-6). This dialog box allows one of three options or access to the Help file. Choose **Zoom** to continue checking the program without stopping when other syntax errors are found. Choose **Yes** to continue checking and to stop when the next error is found. Choose **No** to terminate syntax checking.

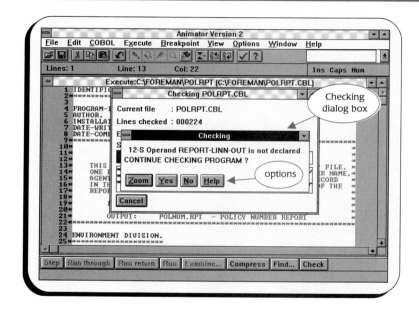

FIGURE G-6   Syntax error found during check of POLRPT

Once checking is complete, Workbench returns to the Animator Version 2 window. If syntax errors are discovered, they are highlighted on the screen (Figure G-7). The **Compress** button on the button bar can be used to show only those lines of code that have been marked as errors. Errors can be corrected at this point and then the program can be saved again.

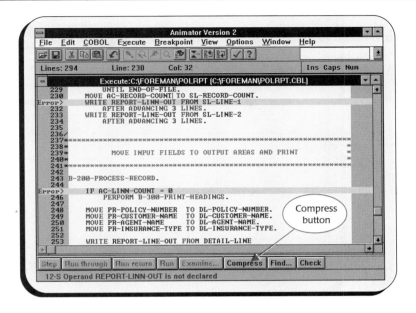

FIGURE G-7   Animator Version 2 window with syntax errors highlighted

If no errors are found, Workbench returns to the Animator Version 2 window with the animate buttons now active on the button bar at the bottom of the screen (Figure G-8 on the next page).

EXECUTING A PROGRAM

Once a program is free of syntax errors, it can be executed from the Animator Version 2 window using the animate buttons shown in Figure G-8. The **Step** button allows execution of the program one instruction at a time, thus enabling you to view the flow of the logic. The **Run through** button is used to complete execution of a single paragraph. The highlight must be positioned on the PERFORM statement that executes the paragraph before clicking the Run through button. The program will stop once control returns from the paragraph. The **Run** button can be used to execute the program from start to finish without stopping until the end of the program is reached, or until a breakpoint is encountered. A **breakpoint** is a location within the program at which you have instructed Workbench to stop. Breakpoints can be defined by using the Set command on the Breakpoint menu. The **Examine** button can be used to display the contents of a field during execution of the program.

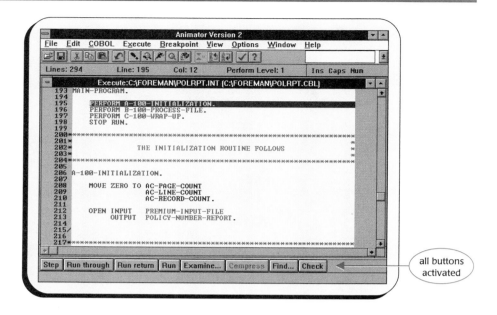

FIGURE G-8   Animate buttons activated for execution of program

If the program terminates abnormally, a Run Time Error dialog box will display describing the error (Figure G-9). After clicking the OK button, the Animator Version 2 window will redisplay with the location of the error highlighted.

FIGURE G-9   Run Time Error dialog box

When the program finishes normally, Workbench displays a message indicating that STOP RUN has been reached (Figure G-10).

FIGURE G-10   Program completion message indicating successful completion after execution

Clicking the OK button will cause Workbench to return to the Animator Version 2 window (Figure G-11). If the program's logic needs to be modified, the cycle of editing, compiling, and executing can begin again.

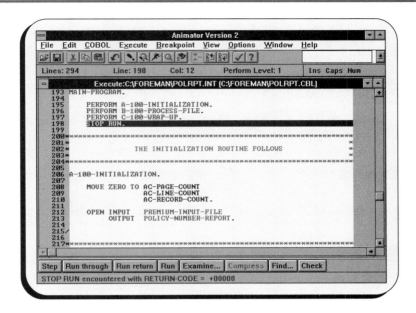

FIGURE G-11   Animator Version 2 window after successful execution of the program

Data files used as input to a program can be created using the Data File Edit tool available in the Micro Focus Workbench v3.2.20 window (see Figure G-3 on page G-2). Files also can be created using other text editors or they can be downloaded from a larger computer system. If an input file is created by a text editor, Micro Focus Workbench may not be able to properly read and process it due to carriage returns or line feeds used at the end of each record. This problem can be overcome by including the clause ORGANIZATION IS LINE SEQUENTIAL within the SELECT entry for the input file. The entry ORGANIZATION IS LINE SEQUENTIAL will allow Micro Focus Workbench to treat each line of the input file as a separate record. Drive indicators and/or subdirectory paths also may need to be included with file names.

This discussion was meant to be a starting point for utilizing Workbench. As illustrated earlier in Figure G-3, Workbench capabilities far exceed the features covered in this brief discussion. With a little experimentation and use of the online Help file, you should have no difficulty in mastering most of the other available functions.

Index